# A Bibliography
of American Autobiographies

# A BIBLIOGRAPHY OF
# AMERICAN
# AUTOBIOGRAPHIES

*compiled by*
**LOUIS KAPLAN**

*in association with*
**James Tyler Cook**
Clinton E. Colby, Jr.
Daniel C. Haskell

THE UNIVERSITY OF WISCONSIN PRESS
*Madison, 1962*

Published by

THE UNIVERSITY OF WISCONSIN PRESS
430 Sterling Court, Madison 6, Wisconsin

Copyright © 1961 by the Regents of the
University of Wisconsin

Second printing 1962

Printed in the United States of America by
Cushing-Malloy, Inc., Ann Arbor, Michigan

Library of Congress Catalog Card Number 61-5499

Z
1224
K3

# Introduction

## I. WORKS EXCLUDED

To prevent this bibliography from growing so large that no press could afford to publish it, several classes of materials were excluded. These are:

A. Most episodic accounts, such as those relating to Indian captivities, military imprisonments, "overland" narratives, and escapes from slavery.

B. Certain works in which the autobiographical element is insignificant, as is frequently true of stories of travel, exploration, sporting adventures, reminiscences of persons and of places, and of military history.

C. Also excluded were autobiographies in books of genealogy, manuscript autobiographies, those appearing in newspapers or periodicals (unless independently reprinted), and those found in works of "collected" biography. Journals, diaries and collections of letters were not included.

D. Works known to be spurious.

E. Works commonly recognized as fictional even when the factual element is strong.

F. Works published after 1945.

## II. WORKS INCLUDED

With regard to authors born in the United States who lived abroad, the decision was made to include their autobiographies. Also included were authors born outside the United States who lived in this country for an appreciable period.

A large number of autobiographies have been ghost written, and on many an amanuensis was employed. These types have been included in this compilation.

I have sought within the means at my command to list every autobiography falling within the limits described in the preceding paragraphs. Despite the inevitable omissions, here for the first time American autobiographies have been caught up in a comprehensive net.

## III. EXPLANATION OF ENTRIES

Each entry normally contains these elements: name of the author, date of birth of the author; title; edition; place of publication; publisher; date of publication; pagination; name of library in which a copy can be found; and annotation.

A. Edition. No attempt was made to list more than a single edition, the one cited being the edition that could conveniently be found for description.

B. Publishers. No attempt was made to give the publishers exactly as found on the title pages of books. For reasons of economy, these usually have been cited in abbreviated form.

C. Pagination. No effort was made to cite preliminary pages of books. Whenever the autobiography does not comprise the whole of a book, the specific pages of autobiography have been indicated.

D. Location of Copies in Libraries. For each book there is shown the library in which the book was described. Naturally, some of these books are widely owned, and readers will find little difficulty in locating copies. Perhaps one-fourth, however, are quite scarce and not easy to find.

Preceding the main list, the reader will find a guide to the abbreviations used to indicate the libraries in which these books can be found.

E. Annotations. Each annotation contains the following ingredients: the occupation of the author; and the states in which he lived.

IV. SUBJECT INDEX

See the comments preceding the subject index.

# Acknowledgments

I began to compile this bibliography in 1946.

My first move was to consult a large number of existing bibliographies, such as Streeter on Michigan, Work on the Negro, Publishers' Weekly, Evans, Sabin, and the Dictionary of American Biography.

In 1949, I spent five months in the states west of the Mississippi during which time I visited those libraries owning outstanding collections of Americana. This trip was made possible by the Committee on the Study of American Civilization (Rockefeller Foundation), and by the Research Committee of the Graduate School of the University of Wisconsin.

Before leaving for the West I had learned that Mr. Daniel C. Haskell had conceived the idea of a bibliography of American autobiographies owned by the New York Public Library, where he was then employed. Mr. Haskell, fortunately, agreed to join me in my efforts. Perhaps 15-per cent of the entries in this bibliography were subsequently supplied by him.

Upon my return from the West, Mr. Haskell, my wife Esther, and I fought our way through the printed author catalog of the Library of Congress.

At this point I should mention the start that had been made at the Library of Congress on a selective bibliography of American autobiographies. The fruits of this work were in 1947 made available to me, and I am happy to acknowledge this assistance.

Between 1953 and 1956, I looked longingly towards libraries in the East but failed in my efforts to enlist further support from foundations. Then one happy day my good friend Cecil Byrd of Indiana advised me to appeal to Stanley Pargellis of the Newberry Library. This led to a grant of funds by the trustees of that library. With these funds Clinton Colby and then James T. Cook were employed to inspect several thousand books at the Library of Congress, and the American Antiquarian Society. Upon Cook's return from the East, the Research Committee of the Graduate School of the University of Wisconsin granted him a stipend enabling him to compile the subject index to this work.

I am indebted to many others. Several persons sent titles of books, and aided in describing them. These were Claude E. Spencer (Disciples of Christ Historical Society), Charles C. Ware (Christian Churches of North Carolina), Miss Valborg E. Bestul (Luther Theological Seminary, St. Paul), Edward Fortney (Drew University), Mrs. James Sterling and F. Clever Bald (Michigan Historical Collections), Miss Isabel Mayhew (University of Washington), Miss Mary Ogilvie (Swarthmore College), Niels H. Sonne (General Theological Seminary), Robert Dolliver (Methodist Historical Society), Lewis O. Hartman (New England Conference Methodist Historical Society), Miss Evalois St. John (Seventh Day Baptist Historical Society), Mrs. Sara Steele Hettinger (Juniata College), and Nelson P. Springer (Goshen College).

While in the West I met a number of book collectors, the memory of whose hospitality still warms the heart. These were David Duniway (Salem, Oregon), Robert A. Griffen (Reno, Nevada), Alexander Leggat (Butte, Montana), and George Babbitt, Junior, (Flagstaff, Arizona).

Several hundred volumes, at my request were inspected and described in various libraries. I could not possibly list all these, but I do wish to acknowledge my debt to some more specifically. These were the Huntington Library, University of

Kentucky (especially Miss Norma Cass), Newberry Library, New York Public Library, Library of Congress, University of North Carolina (especially Olan V. Cook), University of Texas, Western Reserve Historical Society, Boston Public Library, Yale University, and the National War College Library.

I wish also to thank Mr. Lloyd W. Griffin, my Humanities Reference Librarian, who helped with a number of knotty problems. And to my good friend William Matthews, of U.C.L.A., who turned out two while I was struggling with this one, many thanks for the numerous titles thrown my way.

Louis Kaplan

Madison, Wisconsin
May, 1960

# Guide to Symbols

## Used for Names of Libraries

| | | | |
|---|---|---|---|
| ArLH | Arkansas History Commission | G | Georgia State Library |
| ArU | University of Arkansas | GEU | Emory University |
| AU | University of Alabama | IaCrM | Iowa Masonic Library, Cedar Rapids |
| BM | British Museum, London | | |
| C | California State Library | IaDL | Luther College, Decorah, Iowa |
| CBB | Baptist Divinity School, Berkeley | IaDm | Des Moines Public Library |
| | | IaGG | Grinnell College |
| CBCh | Church Divinity School of the Pacific, Berkeley | Ia-HA | Iowa State Department of History and Archives, Des Moines |
| CBPac | Pacific School of Religion, Berkeley | IaHi | State Historical Society of Iowa, Iowa City |
| CBSK | Starr King School for the Ministry, Berkeley | IaMpI | Iowa Wesleyan College, Mt. Pleasant |
| CHi | California Historical Society | ICHi | Chicago Historical Society |
| CL | Los Angeles Public Library | ICMILC | Midwest Inter-Library Center, Chicago |
| CLSM | Southwest Museum, Los Angeles | ICN | Newberry Library, Chicago |
| CLSU | University of Southern California, Los Angeles | ICU | University of Chicago |
| | | IdB | Boise (Idaho) Public Library |
| CLU | University of California, Los Angeles | IdIf | Idaho Falls Public Library |
| | | IdP | Pocatello (Idaho) Public Library |
| CLU-C | William Andrews Clark Memorial Library, Los Angeles | IdU | University of Idaho |
| | | IEN | Northwestern University |
| Co | Colorado State Library | IHi | Illinois State Historical Society |
| CoD | Denver Public Library | In | Indiana State Library |
| CoHi | State Historical Society of Colorado | InGo | Goshen College, Goshen, Indiana |
| CoU | University of Colorado | InU | Indiana University |
| CSfSP | Society of California Pioneers, San Francisco | IU | University of Illinois |
| | | IU-M | Medical Sciences Library, University of Illinois |
| CSmH | Huntington Library, San Marino | KHi | Kansas State Historical Society |
| CtHT | Hartford Seminary Foundation | KKc | Kansas City, Kansas, Public Library |
| CtMW | Wesleyan University, Middletown | | |
| | | KU | University of Kansas |
| CtY | Yale University | KyBC | Berea College |
| CU | University of California, Berkeley | KyBgW | Western Kentucky State College |
| | | KyLo | Louisville Public Library |
| CU-B | Bancroft Library, University of California, Berkeley | KyLoF | Filson Club, Louisville |
| | | KyLoS | Southern Baptist Theological Seminary, Louisville |
| DAFM | National Library of Medicine | | |
| DI | U.S. Department of the Interior | KyMidF | Female Orphan School, Midway, Kentucky |
| DLC | Library of Congress | | |
| DNW | United States National War College Library | KyRE | Eastern Kentucky State College, Richmond |
| DSI | Smithsonian Institution Library | KyU | University of Kentucky |

# GUIDE TO SYMBOLS

| | | | |
|---|---|---|---|
| LND | Dillard, New Orleans | MoU | University of Missouri |
| LNHT | Howard-Tilton Memorial Library of Tulane University | MPiB | Berkshire Athenaeum, Pittsfield Massachusetts |
| LNX | Xavier College, New Orleans | MtBu | Butte Public Library |
| LU | Louisiana State University | MtHi | Historical Society of Montana |
| MB | Boston Public Library | MtU | Montana State University |
| MBAt | Boston Athenaeum | MWA | American Antiquarian Society, Worcester |
| MBNew | New England Methodist Historical Society | MWC | Clark University, Worcester |
| MBUn | Unitarian Association, Boston | N | New York State Library, Albany |
| MdBE | Enoch Pratt Library, Baltimore | NbHi | Nebraska State Historical Society |
| MdBP | Peabody Institute, Baltimore | NBLiHi | Long Island Historical Society |
| MeWaC | Colby College | NbLU | Union College, Lincoln, Nebraska |
| MH | Harvard | NbO | Omaha Public Library |
| MH-BA | Graduate School of Business Administration, Harvard | NbOC | Creighton University, Omaha |
| | | NbU | University of Nebraska |
| MHi | Massachusetts Historical Society, Boston | NBuG | Grosvenor Library, Buffalo |
| | | Nc | North Carolina State Library, Raleigh |
| MH-L | Harvard Law School | | |
| MiD-B | Burton Historical Collection, Detroit Public Library | NcD | Duke University |
| | | NcGW | Woman's College of the University of North Carolina |
| MiU | University of Michigan | | |
| MiU-C | Clements Library, University of Michigan | NcU | University of North Carolina |
| | | NcWAtC | Atlantic Christian College, Wilson, North Carolina |
| MiU-H | Michigan Historical Collection, University of Michigan | | |
| | | Nh | New Hampshire State Library, Concord |
| MMeT | Tufts College, Medford | | |
| MnHi | Minnesota Historical Society | NhD | Dartmouth College |
| MnM | Minneapolis Public Library | NHi | New York Historical Society |
| MnMAu | Augsberg College and Theological Seminary, Minneapolis | NjMD | Drew University, Madison, New Jersey |
| MnNS | St. Olaf College, Northfield, Minnesota | NjP | Princeton University |
| | | NjR | Rutgers University |
| MnS | St. Paul Public Library | NmU | University of New Mexico |
| MnSC | Concordia College, St. Paul | NN | New York Public Library |
| MnSL | Luther Theological Seminary, St. Paul | NNC | Columbia University |
| | | NNG | General Theological Seminary of the Protestant Episcopal Church, New York |
| MnU | University of Minnesota | | |
| MoCanC | Culver-Stockton College, Canton, Missouri | | |
| | | NNNAM | New York Academy of Medicine |
| MoCanD | Historical Society of the Disciples of Christ, Canton, Missouri | NNQ | Queensborough Public Library, Jamaica, New York |
| | | NNUT | Union Theological Seminary, New York |
| MoHi | Missouri State Historical Society | | |
| | | NRCR | Colgate-Rochester Divinity School |
| MoK | Kansas City, Missouri, Public Library | | |
| | | NRCR-S | Samuel Colgate Baptist Historical Collection, Colgate-Rochester Divinity School |
| MoKU | University of Kansas City, Kansas City, Missouri | | |
| MoS | St. Louis Public Library | NSmB | Smithtown (New York) Public Library |
| MoSC | Concordia Seminary, St. Louis | | |
| MoSC-H | Concordia Historical Institute, St. Louis | NUt | Utica Public Library |
| | | Nv | Nevada State Library |
| MoSHi | Missouri Historical Society, St. Louis | NvHi | Nevada Historical Society |
| | | OC | Public Library of Cincinnati |
| MoSM | Mercantile Library Association, St. Louis | OCl | Cleveland (Ohio) Public Library |
| | | OClWHi | Western Reserve Historical Society, Cleveland |
| MoSU | St. Louis University | | |
| MoSW | Washington University, St. Louis | OCX | Xavier University, Cincinnati |

| Symbol | Institution |
|---|---|
| ODW | Ohio Wesleyan University, Delaware |
| OkHi | Oklahoma Historical Society |
| OkOk | Oklahoma City Public Library |
| OkU | University of Oklahoma |
| OO | Oberlin College |
| Or | Oregon Stage Library |
| OrEuN | Northwest Christian College, Eugene, Oregon |
| OrHi | Oregon Historical Society |
| OrMcL | Linfield College, McMinnville, Oregon |
| OrNeGF | George Fox College, Newberg, Oregon |
| OrP | Library Association of Portland, Oregon |
| OrPU | University of Portland, (Oregon) |
| OrSaW | Willamette University, Salem, Oregon |
| OrU | University of Oregon |
| OU | Ohio State University |
| PCA | American Baptist Historical Society, Chester, Pennsylvania |
| PCC | Crozer Theological Seminary, Chester, Pennsylvania |
| PHC | Haverford College |
| PHi | Historical Society of Pennsylvania |
| PHuJ | Juniata College, Huntingdon, Pennsylvania |
| PP | Free Library of Pennsylvania |
| PPLT | Lutheran Theological Seminary, Krauth Library, Philadelphia |
| PPP | Divinity School of the Prot. Epis. Church, Philadelphia |
| PPPrHi | Presbyterian Historical Society, Philadelphia |
| PSC | Swarthmore College |
| PSew | Sewickley (Pa.) Public Library |
| PU | University of Pennsylvania |
| PV | Villanova College |
| RPB | Brown University |
| RPJCB | John Carter Brown Library, Providence |
| ScU | University of South Carolina |
| SdHi | Historical Society of South Dakota |
| SdSifA | Augustana College, Sioux Falls, South Dakota |
| SdU | University of South Dakota |
| TNF | Fisk University, Nashville |
| Tx | Texas State Library and Historical Commission |
| TxAbH | Hardin-Simmons University |
| TxBea | Tyrrell Public Library Beaumont |
| TxBel | Belton (Texas) Public Library |
| TxDaM | Southern Methodist University |
| TxGR | Rosenberg Public Library, Galveston |
| TxH | Houston Public Library |
| TxU | University of Texas |
| TxWB | Baylor University |
| UHi | Utah Historical Society |
| USlC | Church Historian's Office, Church of the Latter Day Saints |
| USlGS | Genealogical Society Library, Salt Lake City |
| UU | University of Utah |
| Vi | Virginia State Library |
| ViHaI | Hampton (Va.) Institute |
| ViLxW | Washington and Lee University |
| ViU | University of Virginia |
| WA | Washington State Library, Olympia |
| WaPS | State College of Washington, Pullman |
| WaS | Seattle Public Library |
| WaSp | Spokane Public Library |
| WaTC | College of Puget Sound, Tacoma |
| WaU | University of Washington, Seattle |
| WHi | State Historical Society of Wisconsin |
| WU | University of Wisconsin |
| Wv-Ar | West Virginia Department of Archives and History |
| WyHi | Wyoming Historical Society |
| WyU | University of Wyoming |

# Contents

INTRODUCTION, v
ACKNOWLEDGMENTS, vii
GUIDE TO SYMBOLS USED FOR NAMES OF LIBRARIES, ix
AUTHOR ENTRIES, 3
A NOTE ON THE SUBJECT INDEX, 326
SUBJECT INDEX, 327

# A Bibliography
of American Autobiographies

# Author Entries

A–No. 1 (pseud.). See Livingston, Leon Ray.

A., B.C. My life as a dissociated [1] personality...with an introduction by Morton Prince, M.D. Boston: R. G. Badger, 1909. 47 p. DLC. Written by the patient after her recovery.

Aakus, Eivind P., b. 1854. Minne [2] ...Kristiansand: Johanssen & Tangens, 1932. 112 p. MnHi. Minnesota violinist.

Abbot, Willis John, 1863–1934. [3] Watching the world go by. Boston: Little,Brown, 1934. 358 p. WU. Reporter in Chicago and N.Y.

Abbott, Augustus. A boy pioneer [4] ...No imprint. 128 p. C. Story of youth in California about 1850.

Abbott, Carlisle Stewart, b. 1828. [5] Recollections of a California pioneer. N.Y.: Neale, 1917. 235 p. WHi. Railroad promoter, politician, California "forty-niner".

Abbott, Edward Charles, b. 1860. [6] We pointed them north; recollections of a cow-puncher. N.Y.: Farrar & Rinehart, 1939. 270 p. WHi. Montana.

Abbott, Eleanor Hallowell, b. 1872. [7] Being little in Cambridge...N.Y.: D. Appleton-Century, 1936. 280 p. WU. In the days of Lowell.

Abbott, Mrs. Eloise Mills. Person- [8] al sketches and recollections. Boston: Abel Tompkins, 1861. 359 p. WHi. Bookseller and teacher.

Abbott, Emma, b. 1850. The life [9] and professional career of Emma Abbott. By Sadie E. Martin. Minneapolis: L. Kimball printing co., 1891. 192 p. MWA. Chicago born opera singer. A significant portion of this book is autobiographical.

Abbott, L.A., b. 1813. Seven wives [10] and seven prisons. N.Y.: Pub. for author, 1870. 205 p. DLC. Matrimonial troubles in New York.

Abbott, Lyman, 1835–1922. [11] Reminiscences...Boston & N.Y.: Houghton Mifflin, 1915. 509 p. WHi. Congregational clergyman and writer on religious subjects (New York City). Editor of Outlook.

Abbott, Othman A., b. 1842. Recol- [12] lections of a pioneer lawyer. Lincoln: Nebraska state historical society, 1929. 176 p. NbO. Lawyer, lt. gov. Nebraska. Union army soldier.

Abdullah, Achmed, 1881–1945. The [13] cat had nine lives...N.Y.: Farrar & Rinehart, 1933. 312 p. NN. Crimean born novelist who spent a number of years in this country.

Abernathy, John R., b. 1876."Catch [14] 'em alive Jack;" the life and adventures of an American pioneer. N.Y.: Association press, 1936. 224 p. NN. A reissue, with variations, of his, In camp with Theodore Roosevelt, 1933. Cowboy in Texas and Oklahoma. Wolf hunter, U.S. marshal in Oklahoma, and oil operator.

Abernathy, John R., b. 1876. A [15] son of the frontier. Croton-on-Hudson: News press, 1935. 57 p. NN. In Texas and Oklahoma.

Abrey, Daniel, b. 1841. Reminis- [16] cences...Corunna, Mich.: Sheardy, 1903. 195 p. NN. A lumberman in Michigan discusses his experiences during 1861–1901.

Abt, Isaac Arthur, b. 1867...Baby [17] doctor. N.Y.: McGraw-Hill, 1944. 310 p. DLC. In Chicago.

Acheson, Edward Goodrich, 1856– [18] 1931. A pathfinder: discovery, invention and industry; how the world came to have aquadag and oildag;

also, carborundum, artificial graphite and other valuable products of the electric furnace... N.Y.: The Press scrapbook,1910. 143 p. NN. In effect an autobiography of Dr. Acheson, with brief account of his discoveries and business career.

Ackley, Mrs. Mary E., b. 1842. [19] Crossing the plains...Memories of girlhood days in California's golden age. San Francisco: 1928. 68 p. Priv. pr., DLC. Story of married life in pioneer California.

Adair, Bethenia Angelina (Owens), [20] 1840-1926. Dr. Owens-Adair; some of her life experiences. Portland, Oreg.: Mann & Beach, printers, 1906? 537 p. WHi. Autobiography, p. 7-114. Pioneer woman physician in Oregon.

Adair, Ward William, b. 1870. The [21] road to New York. N.Y.: Association press, 1936. 278 p. WHi. YMCA workers with railroad men.

Adamic, Louis, b. 1899. Laughing [22] in the jungle; the autobiography of an immigrant in America. N.Y.: Harper & brothers, 1932. 335 p. NN. Came to America from Yugoslavia in 1913 at age of fourteen. Early experiences here, life in the army and later in California. Active in labor movement. For his earlier life in Europe see, Cradle of Life (1936).

Adams, Alfred P., b. 1887. A review...Detroit: N.D. 29 p. CoD. Laborer in Pa., Mich. Coal miner in W. Va. Real estate dealer, insurance salesman in Michigan. [23]

Adams, Charles Francis, 1835- [24] 1915. Charles Francis Adams, an autobiography. Boston & N.Y.: Houghton Mifflin, 1916. 224 p. WHi. Historian, railroad executive, educator, expert; civic leader. New England.

Adams, Charles Francis, b. 1857. [25] Forty years a fool. Sonora, Texàs: The Author, 1914? 100 p. DLC. Manager of wild west shows, salesman. Texas and California.

Adams, Dorothy. We stood alone. [27] N.Y.: Longmans,Green,1941. 284 p. DLC. American in Poland, 1925-39.

Adams, Eliashib, 1733-1855. A [28] successful life...Bangor: Printed by Benjamin A. Burr, 1871. 109, 23 p. WHi. The religious aspects of the life of a businessman in Maine.

Adams, Elizabeth Laura. Dark [29] symphony. N.Y.: Sheed & Ward, 1942. 194 p. NN. The account of a colored girl's childhood in California and her struggles against prejudice.

Adams, Francis Colburn. Story of [30] a trooper with much of interest concerning the campaign on the Peninsula...N.Y.: Dick & Fitzgerald, 1865. 616 p. DNW. In the Union army.

Adams, Hannah, 1755-1831. A [31] memoir of Miss Hannah Adams, written by herself. Boston: Gray & Bowen, 1832. 110 p. WHi. New England historian.

Adams, Henry, 1838-1918. The [32] education of Henry Adams. Boston & N.Y.: Houghton Mifflin, 1918. 519 p. WHi. Historian, social and political commentator.

Adams, Isaac, b. 1872. Darkness [33] and daybreak. Personal experiences, manners, customs...in Persia. Grand Rapids: Dickinson, 1898. 229 p. DLC. American experiences of a Persian-born student who returned to his country as a Baptist preacher.

Adams, Israel, b. 1776. A narrative of the life, travels and adventures of Capt. Israel Adams... Utica: Printed by D. Bennett, 1847. 36 p. NN. A New York man tells of his life as a sailor, and of his experiences in the War of 1812. [34]

Adams, James Capen, b. 1807. [35] The adventures of James Capen Adams, mountaineer and Grizzly bear hunter, of California. By Theodore H. Hittell. San Francisco: Towne & Bacon, 1860. 378 p. CSmH. Dictated by Adams. See also the next item.

Adams, James Capen, b. 1807. The [36] Life of J.C.Adams...N.Y.: Printed by Wynkoop, Hallenbeck & Thomas. 1860. 53 p. CSmH. Hunter in the Rocky Mountains.

Adams, John. Life of "Reformation" John Adams, an Episcopal elder of the Methodist Episcopal Church...Boston: Rand, 1853. 2 vols. Nh. In New England. [37]

Adams, John, 1735-1826. The [38] works of John Adams...Boston: C.C. Little & James Brown,

1850-56. 10 vols. Auto., vol. 2, p. 503-517; vol. 3, p. 3-88. WHi. This account closes with 1776, and stresses his accomplishments in the Congress.

Adams, John Quincy, b. 1845. Narrative...Harrisburg: Sieg, printer, 1872. 64 p. MH. Slave in Virginia; free laborer in Pa. [39]

Adams, John Quincy, 1849-1940. An old boy remembers. Boston: Ruth Hill, 1935. 125 p. NN. The writer, a Presbyterian minister, devotes the greater portion of his book to his early life in western New York state and to his schooling including his years at the University of Rochester and the Auburn Theological Seminary. [40]

Adams, Juliette (Graves), b. 1858. Chapters from a musical life. A short autobiographical narrative, by Mrs. Crosby Adams. Chicago: C. Adams 1903. 138 p. DLC. Music teacher in New York and Chicago. [41]

Adams, Mary Still, b. 1839. Autobiography...Los Angeles: Buckingham bros., printers, 1893. 288 p. CLSU. Kansas schoolteacher marries clergyman and devotes self to work with fallen women. [42]

Adams, Nelson, b. 1831. The Elijah Adams family of Hubbardston, Mass., and a retrospect of activities in seven cities and seven decades; an autobiography. Springfield, Mass.: Published by the author, 1910. 236 p. NN. The writer was active in the livestock byproducts industry for many years in New England and New York. [43]

Addams, Jane, 1860-1935. Twenty years at Hull House. N.Y.: Macmillan, 1910. 462 p. WU. Social reformer in Chicago. See also the next entry. [44]

Addams, Jane, 1860-1935. The second twenty years at Hull House. N.Y.: Macmillan, 1930. 413 p. WU. [45]

Adger, John Bailey, 1810-1899. My life and times, 1810-1899. Richmond, Va.: The Presbyterian Committee of publications, 1899. 681 p. NN. Presbyterian minister. Early life, missionary labors in Armenia and among Negroes of Charleston, S.C., active in Southern Presbyterian Church in theological and scientific controversies. [46]

Adkins, Ettie Aurelia. One Texas old maid. Dallas: W. T. Tardy, 1938. 285 p. TxH. Dietitian. [47]

Adler, Cyrus, b. 1863. I have considered the days. Phila.: Jewish publication society of America, 1941. 429 p. WHi. Archeologist at Smithsonian. President of Dropsie College (theology) in Phila. [48]

Adler, Felix, 1851-1933. An ethical philosophy of life...N.Y.: D. Appleton, 1913. 380 p. WU. A spiritual autobiography by a Jew who deserted Judaism. [49]

Adolph, Paul Ernest, b. 1901. Surgery speaks to China. Philadelphia: China inland mission, 1945. 195 p. DLC. A missionary surgeon in China during the thirties and forties. [50]

Agle, William C., b. 1859. In the footsteps of Pizarro...Seattle: Homer M. Hill Co., 1903. 365 p. DLC. The adventures of a mining engineer in the gold mines of South America. [51]

Agnew, (Mrs.) Anna. From under the cloud. Cinc.: 1886. 196 p. DLC. Experiences in a hospital for the mentally ill. [52]

Ainslie, Peter. Some experiments in living. N.Y.: Association press, 1933. 190 p. MoCanD. By a clergyman of the Disciples of Christ. [53]

Ainslie, Peter. Working with God ...St. Louis: Christian board of education, 1917. 383 p. MoCanD. In Baltimore, by a clergyman of the Disciples of Christ. [54]

Ainsworth, Danforth Hurlbut, 1828-1904. Recollections of a civil engineer; experiences in New York, Iowa, Nebraska, Dakota, Illinois, Missouri, Minnesota and Colorado. Newton, Iowa: 1893. 177 p. NN. Railroad construction work. [55]

Ajax. See Cox, W.D.

Ake, Jeff, b. 1845. They die but once...by James B. O'Neil. N.Y.: Knight, 1935. 228 p. DLC. Texas cowboy and rancher; sheriff in New Mexico and Arizona. An account based on conversations with the biographee. [56]

Akeley, Carl Ethan, 1864-1926. In brightest Africa. Garden City, N.Y.: Doubleday, Page, 1923. 267 p. [57]

WHi. By a naturalist.

Albee, Fred Houdlett, b. 1876. A [58] surgeon's fight to rebuild men. N.Y.: E.P.Dutton, 1943. 349 p. DLC. Physician.

Albee, John, 1833-1915. Confes- [59] sions of boyhood. Boston: Badger, 1910. 267 p. DLC. In Massachusetts.

Albertson, Garrett Vinton. King- [60] dom stories. Boston: Ruth Hill, 1935. 240 p. DLC. Presbyterian clergyman in Florida, Oklahoma and Illinois.

Alby, Mrs. Ann Eliza (Dow), b. [61] 1790. Life, adventures. No imprint. 24 p. MiD-B. A prostitute who later married a deacon.

Alcott, Amos Bronson, 1799-1888. [62] New Connecticut. An autobiographical poem. Boston: Priv. pr., 1881. 158 p. WU. Boyhood on a farm in Connecticut, followed by experiences as itinerant peddler in New England and Virginia.

Alcott, William Andrus, 1798-1859. [63] Confessions of a school master. Andover: Gould, Newman & Saxton, 1839. 316 p. NN. Experiences as a country school teacher in Connecticut. The writer was a cousin of Bronson Alcott.

Alcott, William Andrus, 1798-1859. [64] Forty years in the wilderness of pills and powders...Boston: John P. Jewett, 1859. 384 p. WU. By a pioneer physician in New England.

Alda, Frances...Men, women and [65] tenors...Boston: Houghton Mifflin. 1937. 307 p. DLC. Opera singer.

Alden, Isabella (Macdonald),1841- [66] 1930. Memories of yesterdays. Philadelphia: J. B. Lippincott company. 1931. 302 p. WU. A story of literary life.

Alden, John, 1806-1894. The story [67] of a Pilgrim family...with autobiography...Boston: J.H.Earle, 1889. 429 p. Auto., p. 23-147. WHi. Baptist clergyman and teacher in New England.

Alden, Timothy, 1771-1839. An [68] account of sundry missions performed among the Senecas and Munsees...N.Y.: Pr. by J. Seymour, 1827. 180 p. WHi. Missionary experiences among the Indians in New York.

Alderson, Nannie (Tiffany),b.1860. [69] A bride goes west. N.Y.: Farrar & Rinehart, 1942. 273 p. NN. Pioneer life in early Montana.

Aldredge, J.D., b. 1883. The ro- [70] mance of growing a boy in Texas. ...Jacksonville, Texas: 1923. 288 p. TxU. The youth of a Baptist clergyman.

Aldrich, Lillian (Woodman), [71] d. 1927. Crowding memories. Boston: Houghton Mifflin, 1920. 295 p. WU. By the wife of Thomas Bailey Aldrich.

Aldridge, Reginald, Life on a [72] ranch; ranch notes in Kansas, Colorado, the Indian territory, and northern Texas. N.Y.: D. Appleton & company, 1884. 227 p. WHi. As described by the title.

Alexander, John Brevard, b. 1834. [73] Reminiscences of the past sixty years. Charlotte: Ray printing co., 1908. DLC. By a southern physician.

Alexander, Robert, b. 1863. [74] Memories of the World War, 1917-1918. N.Y.: Macmillan, 1931. 309 p. DLC. The author served in the Service of Supply as Inspector General.

Alexander, Tony. Experiences of [75] a trapper and hunter from youth to old age. Portland, Oreg.: 1924. 119 p. Auto., p. 1-83. DLC. In the southern states, Arkansas, Oklahoma and California.

Alexson, Jacob. The triumph of [76] personal thought; and how I became a mason. Washington: Randsell, 1941. 92 p. DLC. A Jewish photographer in Chicago and St. Louis who suffered from delusions of persecution.

Alford, Thomas Wildcat, b. 1860. [77] Civilization...Norman: Univ. of Okla. press, 1936. 203 p. WHi. A Shawnee Indian tells of his boyhood days and of his work for the Indian Service.

Algeo, Mrs. Sara (MacCormack). [78] The story of a sub-pioneer. Providence: Snow & Farnham, 1925. 318 p. WHi. Rhode Island suffragist.

Allan, Allan Alexander, d. 1941. [79] Gold, men and dogs. N.Y. & London: G. P. Putnam's sons, 1931. 337 p. WHi. Mining in the Klondike.

Allan, Mrs. Elizabeth Randolph [80] (Preston), b. 1848. A march past. Richmond: The Dietz press, 1938.

274 p. WHi. Social life in Virginia during the Civil War and after.

Alldredge, Eugene Perry. [81] Cowboys and coyotes. Nashville: 1945. 184 p. NmU. Outdoor life in New Mexico, where he went for his health.

Allen, Elizabeth. Sketches of [82] Green Mountain life, with an autobiography of the author. Lowell, Mass.: Nathaniel L. Dayton, 1846. 160 p. Auto., p. 7–17. DLC. A Vermont girlhood described by a song composer.

Allen, Errol V. Incidents of home- [83] stead days in North Central Kansas. No imprint. 20 p. KHi. The period covered is 1871–81.

Allen, Frank Gibbs, 1836–1887. [84] Autobiography. Cinc.: Guide pr. & pub. co., 1887. 259 p. DLC. Baptist clergyman in various southern states and especially in Kentucky.

Allen, George, 1792–1883. [85] Reminiscences of the Rev. George Allen of Worcester. Worcester, Mass.: Putnam & Davis, 1883. 127 p. NN. Congregational minister serving mostly in Massachusetts.

Allen, Hervey, b. 1889. Toward [86] the flame, by Hervey Allen. N.Y.: George H. Doran co., 1926. 250 p. WHi. Experiences in the first World War.

Allen, J. Sidna. Memoirs... [87] Madison, N.C.: Alwith pub. co., 1929. 142 p. NcU. Virginia merchant.

Allen, James, 1809–1837. [88] Narrative of the life of James Allen, alias George Walton, alias Jonas Pierce, alias James H. York, alias Burley Grove the highwayman. Being his death-bed confession, to the warden of the Massachusetts State Prison. Boston: Harrington & co., 1837. 32 p. NN. As described by the title.

Allen, James Lane, 1849–1925. [89] A Kentucky cardinal and aftermath. New ed. Revised by Hugh Thomson. N.Y.: Macmillan, 1900. p. XI–XXXII. CSmH. An author tells of his youth on a farm in Kentucky.

Allen, Jirah Isham, b. 1839. [90] ...Montana pioneer...1839 to 1929. Rutland, Vt.: Tuttle pub. co., N.d. 162 p. WaS. Government scout, guide, hunter and Indian fighter in Montana and Dakota during the years 1862–78.

Allen, Joel Asaph, 1838–1921. [91] Autobiographical notes and a bibliography of the scientific publications of Joel Asaph Allen. N.Y.: American museum of natural history, 1916. 215 p. Auto., p. 1–46. NN. Ornithologist and mammalogist connected with the Museum of Comparative Zoology at Harvard and later with the American Museum of Natural History.

Allen, John J., b. 1843. Uncle John [92] Allen's rambles in the Rockies ...Hermitage, Tenn.: For the author, 1917. 94 p. DLC. Hunter, trapper and miner in California and the mountain states.

Allen, John Taylor, b. 1848. Early [93] pioneer days in Texas. Dallas: Wilkinson, 1918. 267 p. TxAbH. The author was a farmer and cattle rancher.

Allen, Richard, 1760–1831. The [94] life, experience, and gospel labors...Phila.: A.M.E. book co., 1887. 69 p. LND. Negro Methodist clergyman in Philadelphia.

Allen, Stanton P. Down in Dixie; [95] life in a cavalry regiment in the War days, from the Wilderness to Appomattox. Boston: D. Lothrop co., 1892. 494 p. DLC. As described by the title.

Allen, Stanton P., A summer revival [96] and what brought it about. N.Y.: Hunt & Eaton. 1894. 200 p. MWA. How he became a Methodist clergyman.

Allen, William Alonzo, b. 1848. [97] Adventures with Indians and game, or twenty years in the Rocky Mountains. Chicago: A. W. Bowen, 1903. 302 p. WHi. By a hunter and Indian fighter.

Allen, William M. Five years [98] in the West...Nashville: Southern Methodist pub. house, 1884. 211 p. DLC. Methodist clergyman.

Allen, William R., b. 1871. The [99] Chequemegon...N.Y.: William Frederick, 1949. 205 p. MtHi. Miner and politician in Montana.

Alley, Norman. I witness. N.Y.: [100] Wilfred Funk, 1941. 370 p. DLC. Newspaper and newsreel photographer.

Allison, Young Ewing, 1853-1932. [101] "Unfinished autobiography." (In his, Selected works...Louisville: John P. Morton, 1935) p. 62-83. DLC. Kentucky publisher and journalist.

Allman, Norwood Francis, b. 1893.[102] Shanghai lawyer. N.Y.: McGraw-Hill, 1943. 283 p. NN. The author spent 26 years in China as an American consul, member of the International Mixed Court and as a practicing lawyer.

Allsopp, Frederick William. [103] Little adventures in newspaperdom. Little Rock: Arkansas writer pub. co., 1922. 239 p. DLC. In Arkansas.

Allsopp, Frederick William. [104] Twenty years in a newspaper office...Little Rock: Central printing co., 1907. 266 p. WHi. In Arkansas.

Allyn, George W. When Blue [105] Earth county was young. Madison Lake, Minn.: 1919. 40 p. MnHi. Minnesota homesteader and lumber dealer.

Allyn, Gurdon L., b. 1799. [106] The old sailor's story...Norwich, Conn.: Printed by Gordon Wilcox, 1879. 111 p. CSmH. A merchantman tells of his New England boyhood.

A'Lord, George. See Lord, George A.

Altgelt, Emma (Murck). [107] Beobachtungen und Errinnerungen. Neu-Braunfels, Texas: Druck der Neu-Braunfelfer Zeitung, 1930. 80 p. Tx. By the wife of a Texas farmer. The period covered is 1850-1905.

Alverson, Mrs. Rosana Margaret [108] (Kroh) Blake, b. 1836. Sixty years of California song. Oakland: M.B. Alverson, 1913, 275 p. DLC. By a concert singer and music teacher.

Ameringer, Oscar, 1870-1943. [109] If you don't weaken. N.Y.: Henry Holt & co., 1940. 476 p. NN. Came to this country at sixteen. Painter and musician in his early days; later Socialist and labor leader and journalist.

Ames, Charles Gordon, 1828-1912.[110] A spiritual autobiography. Boston: Houghton Mifflin, 1913. 228 p. WHi. Baptist and Unitarian clergyman in New England and Minn.

Ames, John Quincy. On the [111] wings of tomorrow...Nappanee: E.V. pub. house, 1939. 307 p. DLC. A varied career in civil service, education and social work in Chicago.

Ames, Levi, 1752-1773. The last [112] words and dying speech... Worcester: Seth Clapp, 1836. 8 p. WHi. By a thief in Massachusetts.

Ames, Nathaniel, d. 1835. A [113] mariner's sketches...Providence: Cory, Marshall & Hammond, 1830. 312 p. DLC. See next item.

Ames, Nathaniel, d. 1835. Nauti- [114] cal reminiscences. By the author of A mariner's sketches. Providence: William Marshall, 1832. 216 p. Auto., p. 5-132. DLC. A Rhode Island merchant sailor who also served in the U.S. Navy.

Ammen, Daniel, 1820-1898. The [115] old navy and the new by Rear-Admiral Daniel Ammen. Philadelphia: J.B. Lippincott, 1891. 553 p. NN. Life in the old navy under sail before the Civil War, largely cruises in various parts of the world; Civil War experiences; activities in connection with the Nicaragua canal route.

Amory, Charles Bean, b. 1841. [116] A brief record of the army life ...Boston: Priv. pr., 1903. 43 p. DLC. Officer in the Union Army.

Amos, Mary Jane (Davies), b. [117] 1872. "Blessed are the pure in heart"...By Mary S. Collins, pseud. Boston: Meador, 1940. 122 p. DLC. A Pennsylvania mystic relates her religious experiences.

Anderson, Abraham Archibald. [118] Experiences and impressions. N.Y.: Macmillan, 1933. 245 p. WHi. Painter, and ranch owner in Wyoming.

Anderson, Andrew. Autobiography.[119] Olympia: Washington Recorder, 1916. 19 p. WaTC. Methodist clergyman in early Pacific Northwest.

Anderson, Charles V. Twenty- [120] three years in Cincinnati... Salt Lake City: N.d. 48 p. UU. A businessman tells of his activities on behalf of the Mormons.

Anderson, Ephraim M., Memoirs: [121] historical and personal, including the campaigns of the First Missouri

Confederate brigade. St. Louis: Times pr. co., 1868. 436 p. DLC. As described by the title.

Anderson, Garland. From news- [122] boy and bellhop to playwright. No imprint, 1925? 30 p. CU-B. By a Negro playwright.

Anderson, Idella Alderman. [123] When you and I were young. Holton, Kan.: The Recorder press, 1927. 41 p. KHi. Youth on a farm in Kansas.

Anderson, Mrs. Isabel Weld [124] (Perkins), b. 1876. Zigzagging. Boston & N.Y.: Houghton Mifflin co., 1918. 269 p. DLC. Canteen worker in France during the first World War.

Anderson, John Wesley, b. 1855. [125] From the plains to the pulpit. Goose Creek, Texas: J.W. Anderson & sons, 1907, 315 p. WHi. By a Baptist clergyman.

Anderson, Joshua, b. 1817. [126] Autobiography. No imprint. 4 p. MoHi. Farmer in Missouri and Kansas.

Anderson, Margaret C. My thirty [127] years' war; an autobiography. N.Y.: Covici, Friede, 1930. 274 p. NN. Chicago journalist, and editor of the Little Review.

Anderson, Mary. See Navarro, Mary (Anderson) De.

Anderson, Mrs. Mary Jane Hill, [128] 1827-1924. Autobiography. Minneapolis: Priv. pr., 1934. 39 p. DLC. Life on a farm in Minnesota.

Anderson, Mrs. Mary Mabbette. [129] Lights and shadows of the life in Canaan. Columbia, S.C.: J.M. Pike, 1906. 92 p. ScU. A lay mission worker in South Carolina.

Anderson, Micajah, b. 1803. [130] The life of Micajah Anderson, of Edgecombe County. By himself. Tarboro, N.C.: From Wm. A. Hearne's printing & publishing house, 1870. 47 p. NcU. North Carolina farmer.

Anderson, Rasmus B., b. 1846. [131] Life story...2d ed., rev. Madison: Priv. pr., 1917. 671 p. WHi. Wisconsin professor who also served as U.S. Minister to Denmark.

Anderson, Mrs. Rebecca Anne [132] (Warwick), b. 1840. Autobiography ...Seattle: 1932. 26 p. WaS. The wife of an Ohio merchant tells of her lay church work in Ohio and of her life on a farm in Kansas, and of her childhood in Virginia.

Anderson, Robert, b. 1819. [133] The life of Rev. Robert Anderson. Macon: Priv. pr., 1892. 151 p. WHi. Negro (Methodist) clergyman in Georgia.

Anderson, Robert, b. 1843. From [134] slavery to affluence; memoirs of Robert Anderson, ex-slave. Hemingford, Neb.: The Hemingford Ledger, 1927. 59 p. NN. Born in Kentucky, served in a Negro regiment during the Civil War, and farmed in Nebraska.

Anderson, Robert A. Fighting [135] the Mill Creeks. Chico, Calif.: Priv. pr., 1909. CSmH. In the northern Sierras.

Anderson, William J., b. 1811. [136] Life and narrative of William J. Anderson, twenty-four years a slave...Chicago: Daily Tribune, 1857. 81 p. MH. As described by the title.

Andrews, Andrew Jackson, [137] b. 1842. A sketch of his boyhood days...and his experience as a soldier...Richmond, Va.: Hermitage press, 1905. 163 p. DLC. Confederate soldier whose youth was spent in Virginia.

Andrews, Christopher Columbus, [138] 1829-1922...Recollections: 1829-1922. Cleveland: Arthur H. Clark, 1928. 299 p. WHi. Minnesota lawyer, politician and member of the U.S. diplomatic service.

Andrews, Edwin Alvia, b. 1833. [139] Reminiscent musings. Spring Arbor, Mich.: E. A. Andrews, 1926. 113 p. DLC. Free Methodist missionary in Nebraska, Kansas, Oklahoma and Texas.

Andrews, Emerson, 1806-1884. [140] Living life...Boston: James H. Earle, 1872. 336 p. WHi. Baptist clergyman in the New England and Middle Atlantic states.

Andrews, Joel, b. 1777. Sketch of [141] the life of Joel Andrews of Bethany: written by himself. New Haven: Storer & Store, printers, 1850. 48 p. Mid-B. Methodist clergyman in Connecticut.

Andrews, John D., b. 1860. Eight [142] years in the toils; sketches from a gambler's life. Butte City, Mont.: 1890. 225 p. MoKU. A fantastic account, in Louisiana and South Carolina.

Andrews, Marietta Minnigerode, [143] 1869-1931. Memoirs of a poor relation...N.Y.: E.P. Dutton, 1927. 455 p. WHi. A painter tells of her first twenty-five years in Virginia.

Andrews, Marietta Minnigerode, [144] 1879-1931. My studio window; sketches of the pageant of Washington life. N.Y.: E.P. Dutton & co., 1928. 450 p. WHi. A painter's life in Washington, D.C.

Andrews, Robert W., b. 1790. [145] The life and adventures of Captain Robert W. Andrews of Sumter, North Carolina...Boston: Printed for the author, 1887. 87 p. MiD-B. Teamster, farmer, hotel owner in South Carolina in pre-Civil War days.

Andrews, Roy Chapman, b. 1884. [146] Ends of the earth. N.Y., London: G.P. Putnam's sons, 1929. 355 p. DLC. Naturalist.

Andrews, Roy Chapman, b. 1884. [147] Under a lucky star...N.Y.: Viking, 1943. 300 p. WHi. Naturalist.

Andros, Thomas, 1759-1845. [148] The old Jersey captive...on board the old Jersey prison ship at New York, 1781. Boston: Wm. Peirce, 1833. 80 p. WHi. Privateer.

Angell, Frank Capron. Looking [149] backward, four score years, 1845-1925...Centredale, R.I.: Centredale press, 1925. 178 p. DLC. Rhode Island harness maker, real estate agent and town treasurer.

Angell, George Thorndike, 1823- [150] 1909... Autobiographical sketches and personal recollections by Geo. T. Angell...Boston: 1892? 37 p. WHi. Reformer who was interested in the treatment of animals and in public health.

Angell, James Burrill, 1829-1916. [151] Reminiscences. N.Y.: Longmans, 1911. 258 p. WU. Professor of Literature, college president and diplomatic officer.

Anonsen, Andrew E., b. 1863. [152] Autobiographical sketches. Kerkhoven: 1939. 23 leaves. MnHi. A Norwegian lumber camp worker in Washington tells mainly of his early days as a sailor.

Another voice from the grave... [153] exemplified in the dying confession and exercises of an unfortunate female. Written down by Thomas H. Skinner. Phila.: Published by the Religious tract society of Phila.: 1819. 24 p. MiU-C. Prostitute.

Anson, Adrian Constantine, 1852- [154] 1922. A ball player's career, being the personal experiences and reminiscences of Adrian C. Anson, late manager and captain of the Chicago Baseball Club. Chicago: Era publishing co., 1900. 339 p. NN. As described by the title.

Antheil, George. Bad boy of [155] music. Garden City, N.Y.: Doubleday, 1945. 368 p. WU. Composer.

Anthony, Adam. New England [156] Quakerism illustrated. Or facts relative to the expulsion of Adam Anthony from the Society of Friends. North Providence: Author, 1843. 71 p. MWA. As described by the title.

Anthony, James D., b. 1825. [157] Life and times of Rev. J. D. Anthony; an autobiography... Atlanta: C. P. Byrd, 1896. 404 p. Auto., p. 1-264. NjMD. Methodist clergyman in Georgia and Alabama.

Antin, Benjamin. The gentleman [158] from the 22nd; an autobiography by Senator Benjamin Antin. N.Y.: Boni & Liveright, 1927. 301 p. WHi. A Russian Jewish immigrant who became a state senator in New York.

Antin, Mary, b. 1881. From Plotzk [159] to Boston. Second edition. Boston, Mass.: W. B. Clarke & co., 1899. 80 p. NN. Experiences on the way from Russia to America. Written by the future author of the Promised Land, at the age of eleven.

Antin, Mary, b. 1881. Promised [160] land. Boston & N.Y.: Houghton Mifflin, 1912. 373 p. WHi. The story of an immigrant from Russia.

Antin, Mary, b. 1881. At school [161] in the promised land. Boston: Houghton Mifflin co., 1928. 112 p. DLC. In New York and Boston.

Antoine. See Cierplikowski, Antoine.

Antone, Abram, 1750-1823. [162] The life...taken in part from

his own mouth. Morrisville: Pr.
at the office of the Republican
Monitor, 1823. 12 p. CSmH.
Oneida Indian relates a life of
crime.

Apauk (Piegan Indian), b. 1822. [163]
Apauk, caller of Buffalo, by
James Willard Schultz. Boston:
Houghton Mifflin, 1916. 226 p.
DLC. His youth in Montana.

Apes, William, b. 1798? A son of [164]
the forest. 2d ed., rev. & corr.
N.Y.: G. F. Bruce, 1831. 214 p.
Auto., p. 7-110. WHI. Missionary to
Indians in Maine and Rhode Island.

Appel, Joseph Herbert, b. 1873. [165]
Growing up with advertising.
N.Y.: Business house, pubs.,
1940. 301 p. DLC. As described
by the title.

Appel, Joseph Herbert, b. 1873. [166]
My own story. N.Y.: Platt & Peck,
1913. 146 p. DLC. Lawyer, editorial writer for McClure's and advertising executive for merchan-
dizing stores.

Applegate, Jesse A., 1835-1919. [167]
Recollections of my boyhood, by
Jesse Applegate, Oregon pioneer
of 1843. Roseburg, Oreg.: Press
of Review publishing co., 1914.
99 p. WHi. Frontier boyhood in
Oregon.

Arbuckle, John William, b. 1864. [168]
In the midst of the years.
Waterloo, Iowa: 1942. 235 p. WHi.
Lawyer in Iowa.

Archer, Herman. Mr. Archer, [169]
U.S.A. N.Y.: Doubleday, Page,
1924. 326 p. WHi. A soldier's
experiences in the war with
Spain, and in France during the
first World War.

Archer-Burton, Sally. Your [170]
mother remembers. Fairmont,
Minn.: Town pump, 1931. 66 p.
MnHi. Operator of hotel and
restaurant in Minnesota who previously was the wife of a farmer.

Arditi, Luigi, 1822-1903. [171]
My reminiscences...N.Y.: Dodd,
Mead & co., 1896. 314 p. NN.
Career of the Italian composer
and orchestra leader both in
Europe and the United States.

Arliss, George, b. 1868. My ten [172]
years in the studios. Boston:
Little, Brown & co., 1940. 349 p.
NN. Experiences in the moving
picture world.

Arliss, George, b. 1868...Up the [173]
years from Bloomsbury. Boston:
Little, Brown, 1927. 312 p. DLC.
Star of stage and screen who was
born in England.

Arms, Hiram Phelps, 1799-1822. [174]
A brief sketch of the life of Rev.
H. P. Arms, D.D. ...Boston: Alfred Mudge & son, printers, 1882.
35 p. CtY. A New England boyhood,
followed by a career as a Congregational clergyman.

Arms, Mrs. Mary L. (Day), b. [175]
1836. Incidents in the life of a
blind girl. Baltimore: James
Young, 1859. 206 p. WHi. Her
life at school for blind in Maryland.

Arms, Mrs. Mary L. (Day), [176]
b. 1836. The world as I have found
it. Baltimore: James Young,
1878. 311 p. DLC. The married
life in Chicago of a blind woman.

Armsby, Mrs. Leonora (Wood). [177]
Musicians talk. N.Y.: Dial press,
1935. 242 p. DLC. By a patron of
music in California.

Armstrong, Benjamin G., b. 1820. [178]
Early life among the Indians.
Reminiscences from the life of
Benj. G. Armstrong. Treaties of
1835, 1837, 1842 and 1854. Habits
and customs of the Red Men of the
forest... Dictated to and written
by Thos. P. Wentworth, Ashland,
Wisconsin. Ashland, Wis.:
Press of A. W. Bowron, 1892.
266 p., NN. By an Indian trader
in the St. Croix valley, beginning
with 1840.

Armstrong, David Maitland, 1836- [179]
1918. Day before yesterday,
reminiscences of a varied life.
N.Y.: C. Scribner's sons, 1920.
333 p. WHi. Painter.

Armstrong, Helen Porter. See
Melba, Nellie.

Armstrong, Louis, b. 1900. [180]
Swing that music. N.Y.: Long-
mans, Green & co., 1936. 136 p.
NN. Negro leader of jazz bands.

Armstrong, Nelson. Nuggets of [181]
experience. San Bernardino: 1906.
257 p. WHi. The author tells of
his frontier mining experiences
in the Dakotas and of his services
in the Union army.

Armstrong, William H. Red-tape [182]
and pigeon-hole generals: as
seen from the ranks during a

campaign in the army of the Potomac. By a citizen soldier. N.Y.: Carleton, 1864. 318 p. CSmH. As described by the title.

Arnold, Edward. Lorenzo goes to Hollywood...N.Y.: Liveright, 1940. 282 p. WU. Screen actor. [183]

Arnold, John Motte, 1824-1884. Selections from the autobiography of Rev. J. M. Arnold, D. D. Ann Arbor, Mich.: Index publishing house, 1885. 113 p. NN. Methodist minister serving in Michigan. Also engaged in religious journalism. [184]

Arnold, L.V. A true story of southwest Texas fifty years ago. No imprint. TxU. Cowboy life in the sixties and seventies. [185]

Arnold, Samuel Bland, 1834-1906. Defence and prison experiences of a Lincoln conspirator. Hattiesburg, Miss.: The Book farm, 1943. 133 p. DLC. The author was part of the Booth group that plotted the abduction of Lincoln. [186]

Arnold, William Harris, 1854-1923. Ventures in book collecting. N.Y.: Scribner's sons,1923. 356 p. DLC. The experiences of a book collector. [187]

Aronson, Rudolph, b. 1856. Theatrical and musical memoirs. N.Y.: McBride, Nast, 1913. 283 p. DLC. Music conductor and composer of operettas. [188]

Arthur, Timothy Shay, 1809-1885. Brief autobiography. (In his, Lights and shadows of real life. Philadelphia: 1867.) p. 5-9. NN. Journalist in Baltimore and Philadelphia, who is remembered for his Ten nights in a bar-room. [189]

Asbury, Ai Edgar, 1836-1915. My experiences in the War, 1861 to 1865...Kansas City: Berkowitz, 1894. 45 p. MoK. In the Confederate army. [190]

Asbury, Herbert. Up from Methodism...London: Knopf, 1926. 174 p. LU. In Missouri, where as a young man he revolts against Methodism. [191]

Ash, George. His adventures and life story as cowboy, ranger, and soldier...London: Drane,1923. 234 p. NN. In Texas and California as well as in various foreign countries. The period covered is from 1880. The author was born in Canada. [192]

Ashbridge, Elizabeth, 1713-1755. Some account of the early part of the life of Elizabeth Ashbridge ...Concord, N.H.: 1810. 38 p. WHi. Member of the Society of Friends, in New Jersey. [193]

Ashby, Newton B., b. 1856. The Ashbys in Iowa...N. p.: 1925. 53 p. IaHi. An editor of a farm journal tells also of his life on an Iowa farm in the sixties. [194]

Asher, Jeremiah, 1812-1865. Incidents in the life of the Rev. J. Asher, pastor of the Shiloh (colored) Baptist church, Philadelphia...London: Gilpin, 1850. 80 p. DLC. Negro Baptist clergyman in Conn. and Pa. [195]

Asher, Jeremiah, 1812-1865. Autobiography...Phila.: The author, 1862. 227 p. Auto., p. 1-211. DLC. See the preceding item. [196]

Ashford, Bailey Kelly, 1873-1934. A soldier in science...N.Y.: Morrow, 1934. 425 p. WHi. Army doctor. [197]

Ashley, George Thomas. From bondage to liberty in religion; a spiritual autobiography. Boston: Beacon press, 1919. 226 p. DLC. From Methodist to Unitarianism. [198]

Ashley, George Thomas. Reminiscences of a circuit rider, being a true record of some of the experiences, incidents and observations of a Methodist circuit rider in the late eighties and early nineties of the last century. They cover a period of six years and extend from the swamps of Louisiana to the Ozark Mountains of Missouri, with character sketches of some of the notable men of Methodism at that time. Hollywood, Calif.: 1941. 128 p. NN. The same author who wrote the preceding item. [199]

Ashley, John. The notorious Ashley gang...by Hix C. Stuart. Stuart, Florida: St. Lucie pr. co., 1928. 80 p. MoKU. Florida bank robber. A dictated account. [200]

Ashmead, John. Voyages... between the years 1758 and 1782. No imprint. 16 p. WHi. Merchant sailor. [201]

Askevold, Bernt, b. 1846. Trang vei. Fortälling af Bernt Askevold. Fergus Falls, Minn.: Trykt i Red River tidendes trykkeri, [202]

1899. 106 p. PPLT. Lutheran clergyman in Minn. and Iowa.

Aten, Ira. Six and one-half years [203] in the Ranger service. The memoirs of Ira Aten, Sergeant, Company D, Texas Rangers. Bandera: Frontier times, 1945. 64 p. InU. As described by the title.

Atherton, Mrs. Gertrude Franklin [204] Horn, 1857-1948. The adventures of a novelist. N.Y.: Liveright, 1932. 598 p. WU. Largely in San Francisco, New York and London.

Atkeson, Thomas Clark, 1852- [205] 1935. Pioneering in agriculture; one hundred years of American farming and farm leadership. N.Y.: Orange Judd publishing co., 1937. 222 p. NN. Early agricultural experiences in W.Va.; leader in agricultural education and the National Grange.

Atkins, Edwin Farnsworth, 1850- [206] 1926. Sixty years in Cuba... Cambridge: Riverside press, 1926. 362 p. DLC. Sugar industry.

Atkins, Rebecca Crittenden, b. [207] 1829. "Truth stranger than fiction" Lincoln: 1896. 154 p. DLC. Her unhappy life in Nebraska. A story of domestic disappointments.

Atkinson, Benjamin Franklin, [208] b. 1870. The life ministry of... Louisville: Herald press, n.d. 218 p. LND. Methodist clergyman in Kentucky.

Atkinson, Carroll, b. 1896. [209] "An educational nugget"; true confessions of a Ph.D. Edinboro, Pa.: Edinboro educational press, 1939. 89 p. DLC. On the acquisition of a Ph.D.

Atkinson, Frederick Grant, 1864- [210] 1940. A fascinating game... Minneapolis: 1940. 84 p. DLC. Advertising, by the man who made "Gold Medal Flour" famous.

Atkinson, Lulu (Hurst). b. 1869. [211] Lulu Hurst, (the Georgia wonder), writes her autobiography, and for the first time explains and demonstrates the great secret of her marvelous power... Rome, Ga.: Lulu Hurst book co., 1897. 267 p. NN. The author tells of her various feats of strength performed on the stage and the means by which she accomplished them.

Atkinson, Wilmer, 1840-1920. [212] Wilmer Atkinson, an autobiography. Phila.: Wilmer Atkinson co., 1920. 375 p. WHi. By the editor of Farm Journal.

Atwater, Francis, b. 1858. [213] Memoirs of Francis Atwater. Meriden, Conn.: Horton pr. co., 1922. 313 p. NN. Newspaper proprietor and businessman in Connecticut.

Atwater, George Parkin, 1874- [214] 1932. Annals of a parish; a chronicle of the founding and of the growth and development of the Church of Our Saviour, Akron, Ohio, together with a personal narrative. Akron: 1928. 67 p. Auto., p. 1-35. DLC. By an Episcopalian clergyman.

Atwell, William Hawley, b. 1869. [215] Autobiography...Dallas: Warlick Law pr. co., 1935. 107 p. DLC. Lawyer, judge and politician in Texas.

Audubon, John James, 1785-1851. [216] Audubon and his journals, by Maria R. Audubon...N.Y.: C. Scribner's sons, 1897. 2 vols. Auto., vol. I, p. 7-38. DLC. Covers his life to 1820. This is the autobiography which originally appeared in Scribner's.

Auer, Leopold, 1845-1930. My [217] long life in music. N.Y.: Frederick A. Stokes company, 1923. 377 p. NN. Violinist. Devoted principally to his European career before coming to America after the Russian revolution but has a chapter, p. 357-371, "Musical life in America."

Auffray, Mrs. Edith O'Gorman, See O'Gorman, Edith.

Aughey, John Hill. The iron [218] furnace: or, Slavery and secession. Phila.: Martien, 1863. 296 p. WHi. His experiences in the South during the Civil War, by a sympathizer of the North.

Aughinbaugh, William Edmund, [219] 1870-1940. I swear by Apollo; a life of medical adventure. N.Y.: Farrar & Rinehart, 1938. 420 p. NN. Early life; medical experiences in the U.S. and Cuba; leprosy in Venezuela; bubonic plague in Indian.

Augustin, August E. In the [220] Master's vineyard...tr. from the original German...Chicago: Wartburg, 1923. 183 p. DLC. Lutheran clergyman in Kansas and Nebraska who came from Germany.

Augustus, John, 1785-1859. [221] A report of the labors of John Augustus for the last ten years in the aid of the unfortunate... Boston: Wright & Hasty, printers, 1852. 104 p. MiD-B. A Boston shoe maker who provided bail for unfortunates.

Austin, Emily M. Mormonism; [222] or, life among the Mormons. Madison, Wis.: M.J.Cantwell, 1882. 253 p. CU-B. After leaving the Mormons she became a milliner in the middlewest.

Austin, John Osborne, 1849-1918. [223] Impressions and reflections of sixty years, 1857-1917. Providence, R.I.: 1917. 4 leaves. NN. Author of genealogical works.

Austin, Mary (Hunter), 1868-1934. [224] Earth horizon; autobiography. N.Y.: Literary guild, 1932. 381 p. WU. Novelist.

Autobiography of a landlady of the old school. See Wyatt, Sophia Hayes.

Autobiography of a Neurasthene, [225] as told by one of them and recorded by Margaret A. Clegues. Boston: Badger, 1910. 246 p. DLC. A midwestern physician.

Autobiography of a shaker. See Evans, Frederick William.

Autolyeus (pseud.). See Bacon, Leonard, b. 1887.

Avery, Giles Bushnell, 1815-1890. [226] Autobiography...East Canterbury, N.H.: 1891. 34 p. WHi. Shaker minister in New Hampshire.

Awes, Addison (pseud.). See Cubery, William M.

Ayer, Frederick, 1822-1918. [227] Reminiscences...Boston: 1923. 84 p. DLC. Mill owner.

Ayers, James J. Gold and [228] sunshine...Boston: Richard G. Badger, 1922. 359 p. DLC. Miner, editor, printer and newspaper publisher in California.

# B

Babb, Thomas Earle. The [229] "Ebenezer" of a minister at eighty-five. Holden, Mass.: 1925. 141 p. MWA. Congregational clergyman in Massachusetts.

Babcock, John Martin Luther, [230] 1822-1894. Autobiography... Boston?: C. W. Bryan, printers, 1894. 82 p. Auto., p. 5-63. DLC. By a clergyman who moved from Free Will Baptist, to Unitarian, to "Free Rover".

Babson, Roger Ward, b. 1875. [231] Actions and reactions; an autobiography. N.Y.: Harper, 1935. 404 p. NN. Business executive and educator.

Bacheller, Irving, b. 1859. [232] Coming up the road. Memories of a North country boyhood. Indianapolis: Bobbs-Merrill, 1928. 316 p. WU. The youthful days of an author in New York state.

Bacheller, Irving, b. 1859. [233] From stores of memory. N.Y.: Farrar & Rinehart, 1938. 306 p. WU. His youth and his progress as a writer.

Bacon, Leonard, 1802-1881. [234] Four commemorative discourses ...New Haven: T. J. Stafford, printer, 1866. 66 p. MiD-B. Clergyman in Connecticut of a minor sect.

Bacon, Leonard, b. 1887. [235] Semi-centennial...by Autolyeus (pseud.). N.Y.: Harper, 1939. 273 p. WU. Poet and professor at the University of California.

Bacon, Louisa (Crowninshield), [236] b. 1842. Reminiscences. Salem: 1922. 117 p. DLC. Massachusetts socialite.

Badger, Mrs. Ellen. Memory [237] links of seventy years, 1853-1923. No imprint. 9 p. IaHi. Pioneer life on a farm in Iowa in the fifties and sixties.

Badger, Joseph, 1757-1846. [238] A memoir...containing an autobiography...Hudson, Ohio: Sawyer, Ingersoll & co., 1851. 185 p. WHi. By a clergyman of the Disciples of Christ.

Badger, Joseph, b. 1848? Roving [239] Joe...By A.H. Post. N.Y.: 1882. 15 p. NN. Actually written by Badger? Hunter, trapper and Indian fighter who wrote western stories for Beadle.

Bagger, Eugene Szekeres, b. 1892. [240] For the heathen are wrong; an impersonal autobiography. Boston: Little, Brown & co., 1941. 370 p. NN. Journalist in Europe and America, including Europe at the beginning of the second World War.

**Bagwell, James.** Thrilling [241] narrative of the life...of James Bagwell; who was tried at... Somerset, Pa., for the murder of Solomon Jones... Cinc.: Rev. William Miller, 1851. 42 p. DLC. As described by the title.

**Bahler, John F.,** b. 1840. [242] Thrilling incidents...N.Y.: Pub. for the author, 1884. 88 p. CU-B. A clergyman's testimonial to the kindness of God and the Seventh Day Adventists. The author was a blind grocer in New York.

**Baierlein, Eduard Raimund,** 1819- [243] 1921. Im urwalde bei den roten Indianern. Dresden: Justus Naumann, 1895? DLC. Lutheran missionary to the Indians in Mich.

**Bailey, A.S.,** b. 1835. The story [244] of an ordinary life...No imprint. IaHi. Newspaper printer and editor in Iowa and Pennsylvania.

**Bailey, Mrs. Abigail (Abbot),** 1746 [245] -1815. Memoirs...Boston: S.T. Armstrong, 1815. 275 p. Auto., p. 11-196. WHi. The story of her unfortunate domestic life.

**Bailey, Appleton R.,** b. 1786. [246] The life of Appleton R. Bailey, embracing a narrative of his adventures, imprisonments and sufferings. 3d ed. Rochester: Shepard & Reed, 1848. 24 p. MiD-B. Forger.

**Bailey, Daniel B.,** b. 1852. [247] Historic sketch and incidents... Altoona, Ala.: Priv. pr., 1922. 52 p. DLC. Alabama farmer.

**Bailey, Emma E.,** 1844-1921. [248] Happy day, or the confessions of a woman minister. N.Y.: European pub. co., 1901. 480 p. DLC. Universalist in New York, Pa., and Ohio.

**Bailey, Frank,** b. 1865. [249] It can't happen here again. N.Y.: Knopf, 1944. 177 p. WU. Real estate development in New York.

**Bailey, Margaret Emerson,** [250] b. 1880. Good-bye, proud world. N.Y.: Charles Scribner's sons, 1945. 408 p. NN. Childhood and youth in Providence, R.I., college days at Bryn Mawr and the Univ. of Chicago, revolt against the conventional society of Providence.

**Bailey, Mrs. Margarett Jewett.** [251] The grains, or, passage in the life of Ruth Rover. Portland, Oreg.: Carter & Austin printers, 1854. p. 103-189. Or. School teacher in Oregon, who had much trouble with her drunkard husband. The first 102 pages could not be found in any library in Oregon.

**Bailey, Robert,** b. 1773. The life [252] and adventures...Richmond: 1822. 348 p. WHi. Gambler, drunkard.

**Bailey, Thomas** (pseud.) See Partridge, Bellamy.

**Bainbridge, Lucy (Seaman).** [253] Yesterdays. N.Y. & Chicago: Revell, 1924. 127 p. WHi. Civil War nurse and Superintendent, Woman's Branch, New York City Mission Society.

**Baird, Adam,** b. 1846. Autobiography...Oakland: Scofield [254] printery, n.d. 20 p. NvHi. Railroad worker on the Union Pacific in the sixties. Miner in Nevada in the seventies. Rancher in California in the eighties.

**Baker, Daniel,** 1791-1857. [255] The life and labours of the Rev. Daniel Baker, D.D., pastor and evangelist. Third edition. Phila.: Presbyterian board of publication, 1858. 560 p. NN. Presbyterian clergyman in Virginia, Georgia, Alabama, Mississippi and Texas.

**Baker, Daniel B.,** b. 1842. [256] A soldier's experience in the Civil War. Long Beach, Calif.: Graves & Hersey, 1914. 55 p. Or. Union army.

**Baker, James Hutchins,** 1848- [257] 1925. Of himself and other things. Denver: Priv. pr. 1922. 191 p. NN. President of the Univ. of Colorado, 1892-1914.

**Baker, Josephine,** b. 1906. [258] Las memorias... Paris: Paul Colin, n.d. 125 p. MoHi. American born Negro singer who, after early experiences in Missouri and New York, moved to France.

**Baker, Louisa.** See Webb, Mrs. Eliza (Bowen).

**Baker, Ray Stannard,** 1870-1946. [259] Native American, the book of my youth, by David Grayson (pseud.). N.Y.: Scribner, 1941. 336 p. WHi. A journalist, and confidant of

Pres. Wilson, tells of his youth in Michigan and Wisconsin, and of his days as a cub reporter in Chicago.

Baker, Ray Stannard, 1870–1946. [260] American chronicle...by David Grayson (pseud.) N.Y.: Scribner, 1945. 516 p. WHi. Journalist, adviser to Pres. Wilson.

Baker, Ray Stannard, 1870–1946. [261] Adventures in contentment, by David Grayson (pseud.). N.Y.: Grosset & Dunlap, 1906. 249 p. WU. His experiences as a farmer.

Baker, Sara Josephine. [262] Fighting for life. N.Y.: Macmillan, 1939. 264 p. WU. A physician engaged in public health work.

Balaban, Abe J. Continuous [263] performance. N.Y.: G. P. Putnam's sons, 1942. 240 p. NN. Theatre chain owner in Chicago and motion picture magnate.

Balch, George Washington, 1832– [264] 1908. Compiled in memory... Reminiscences–autobiography–travel–letters–testimonials. N.p.: 1909. 243 p. Auto., p. 9–43. MiD-B. Public utilities and politics in Michigan and Tennessee.

Baldwin, Mrs. Alice (Blackwood), [265] b. 1845. "Memoirs" (In her, Memoirs of the late Frank D. Baldwin. Los Angeles: Wetzel, 1929.) p. 109–198. CSmH. The wife of a soldier in the southwestern states.

Baldwin, George Colfax, 1817–1899.[266] Notes of a forty-one year's pastorate. Phila.: American Baptist publication society, 1888. 287 p. PCC. Baptist clergyman in New Jersey and New York, 1840–85.

Baldwin, Harold. "Holding the [267] line". Chicago: McClurg, 1918. 305 p. NjP. First World War.

Baldwin, James, b. 1841. [268] In my youth. Indianapolis: Bobbs–Merrill, 1914. 493 p. DLC. In Indiana.

Baldwin, James Mark, 1861–1921. [269] Volume I: Memories. Boston: Stratford, 1926. 302 p. WHi. By a professor of philosophy and psychology at Princeton and Johns Hopkins.

Baldwin, Summerfield, 1832–1924. [270] Summerfield Baldwin, his autobiography, his ancestry, with editorial and newspaper comments. Baltimore: Munder, 1925. 89 p. Auto., p. 7–19. DLC. Wholesale dry goods merchant and president of the Baltimore Utility Company.

Ball, Mrs. Alfred Lathrop. See Tempski, Arnive von.

Ball, Charles. Slavery in the [271] United States; a narrative of the life and adventures of Charles Ball, a black man, who lived forty years in Maryland, South Carolina and Georgia, as a slave... N.Y.: John S. Taylor, 1837. 517 p. MWA. The author later escaped to Pennsylvania.

Ball, Frank Clayton, b. 1857. [272] Memoirs... Muncie, Ind.: Priv. pr., 1937. 294 p. ICN. Manufacturer and philantropist who lived in New York and Indiana.

Ball, John, 1794–1884. Autobio- [273] graphy...Grand Rapids: Dean-Hicks, 1925. 230 p. WHi. Land speculator and politician in Michigan. Hunter and trapper in Oregon.

Ball, John, b. 1847. Baptism [274] of fire, an autobiographical sketch, by Lucifer. Boston: 1877. 83 p. DLC. A story of unhappy domestic relations.

Ball, Nicholas, 1828–1896. Voy- [275] ages...1838 to 1853...Boston: L. Barta & co., printer, 1895. 38 p. Auto., p. 5–9. DLC. New England merchant mariner and California miner.

Ball, Thomas, 1819–1911. My [276] threescore years and ten. An autobiography. 2d edition. Boston: Roberts brothers, 1892. 379 p. NN. Sculpture who for many years lived in Italy.

Ballard, Harlan H., 1853–1934. [277] Adventures of a librarian. N.Y.: Walter Neale, 1929. 201 p. DLC. In Massachusetts.

Ballenstedt, C.W.T., [278] Beschreibung meiner reise nach den goldminen Californiens... Schöningen: Druck von J. C. Schmidt, 1851. 103 p. DLC. Forty-niner.

Ballentine, George, b. 1812? [279] Autobiography of an English soldier in the United States army. N.Y.: Stringer & Townsend, 1853. 288 p. WHi. War with Mexico.

Ballon, Adin, 1803-1890. [280]
Autobiography...Lowell, Mass.:
Vox populi, 1896. 586 p. WU.
Abolitionist and Universalist
clergyman who founded Hopedale
Community.

Bancroft, Hubert Howe, 1832- [281]
1918. Literary industries. (In,
The works of Hubert Howe Bancroft. San Francisco: 1891. vol.
39.) WHi. Publisher of histories.

Bangs, Herman, 1790-1869. [282]
The autobiography and journal
of Rev. Herman Bangs. Edited
by his daughters. N.Y.: N. Tibbals,
1872. 385 p. NN. Methodist minister serving mostly in New York
and Connecticut. This account
closes with 1817.

Bangs, John, 1781-1849. [283]
Autobiography...N.Y.: Priv. pr.,
1846. 319 p. Auto., p. 11-224. WHi.
Methodist clergyman in New York.

Banks, Elizabeth L. The [284]
autobiography of a "newspaper
girl." N.Y.: Dodd, Mead, 1902.
317 p. WU. Reporter in New
York and Washington.

Banks, Elizabeth L., The remaking [285]
of an American. Garden City,
N.Y.: Doubleday, Doran, 1928.
297 p. WHi. The author tells
of her efforts, upon returning
from abroad, to accustom herself to America.

Banning, Jeremiah, 1733-1798. [286]
Log and will of Jeremiah
Banning...N.Y.: 1932. 72 p. DLC.
Merchant mariner, and colonial
political figure.

Banta, William, b. 1827. [287]
Twenty-seven years on the
Texas frontier. N.p.: 1933. TxU.
Hunter, Indian fighter.

Baragwanath, John, b. 1888. [288]
Pay streak. Garden City, N.Y.:
Doubleday, Doran & co., 1936.
274 p. NN. Adventures of a mining engineer in both the Americas.

Barber, Daniel, 1756-1834. [289]
Catholic worship and piety, explained and recommended; in
sundry letters, to a very near
friend, and others. By Daniel
Barber, A.M. and not long since
a minister of the Protestant
Episcopal Church, in Claremont,
state of New Hampshire. Washington City: E. DeKrafft, printer,
1821. 40 p. NN. As described by
the title.

Barber, Mary, b. 1848. The true [290]
narrative of the five years' suffering and perilous adventures...
Phila.: Barclay, 1873. 108 p. WHi.
A missionary to the Sioux Indians
in the Dakotas who married one
of the braves.

Barbour, Thomas, b. 1884. [291]
Naturalist at large. Boston:
Little, Brown, 1943. 314 p. WU.
By the Director of the Agassiz
Museum.

Bare, D. M. Looking eighty [292]
years backward. Findlay, Ohio:
College press, 1920. 247 p.
PHuJ. Miller in Pennsylvania.

Baring, Alexander, 1848-1932. [293]
My recollections, 1848-1931.
Santa Barbara, Calif.: Schauer,
1933. 204 p. DLC. The author
was American born, but educated
in England. Upon return to America he engaged in various financial
enterprises.

Barker, Albert Smith, 1843-1916. [294]
Everyday life in the Navy...
Boston: R. G. Badger, 1928.
422 p. WHi. By an officer who
served from 1861.

Barker, Fred C., b. 1852. Lake [295]
and forest as I have known them.
Boston: Lee & Shepard, 1903.
230 p. Auto., p. 9-216. DLC.
Owner of resort camps, logger
and guide, in Maine.

Barker, George, b. 1852. [296]
Thrilling adventures of the
whaler Alcyone...Peabody, Mass.:
George Barker, 1916. 99 p. DLC.
Whaler, Boston policeman, and
music teacher.

Barker, Jacob, 1779-1871. [297]
Incidents in the life of Jacob
Barker, of New Orleans, La.
Washington: 1855. 285 p. WHi.
Financier.

Barker, James K. P., b. 1844. [298]
Through the Civil War in the
Confederate Army. Hillsdale,
Kan.: Pub. by Edgar R. Barker,
n.d. 24 p. KKc. As described by
the title.

Barker, Lewellys Franklin, [299]
b. 1867. Time and the physician...
N.Y.: Putnam, 1942. 350 p. WU.
A physician and professor at
Johns Hopkins and the Univ. of
Chicago.

Barkley, John Lewis. [300]

No hard feelings, N.Y.: Cosmopolitan book co., 1930. 327 p. DLC. Soldier in the first World War.

Barler, Miles, b. 1833. [301] Early days in Llano. No imprint. 68 leaves. TxU. Confederate soldier who later fought Indians and cattle thieves and hunted in Texas.

Barnabee, Henry Clay, 1833-1917. [302] Reminiscences of Henry Clay Barnabee; being an attempt to account for his life, with some excuses for his professional career, ed. by George Leon Varney...Boston, Chapple publishing co., 1913. 461 p. WU. Actor and opera singer.

Barnard, Evan G., b. 1865. [303] A rider of the Cherokee strip. Boston: Houghton Mifflin, 1936. 224 p. WHi. Cowboy.

Barnard, Inman, Cities and men. [304] N.Y.: Dutton, 1940. 256 p. WHi. Newspaper man who was for many years a foreign correspondent in France. He was also secretary to the publisher of the N.Y. Tribune.

Barnes, Al G. [305] Al G. Barnes, Master showman. Calowell, Idaho: Caxton, 1936. 460 p. WHi. Circus life.

Barnes, James 1866-1936. [306] From then till now; anecdotal portraits and transcript pages from memory's tablets. New York: D. Appleton-Century, 1934. 535 p. NN. Writer and war correspondent; student days at Princeton; literary work in New York; World War I experiences.

Barnes, William Croft, 1858- [307] 1936. Apaches and longhorns. Los Angeles: Ward Ritchie, 1941. 210 p. WHi. Frontier soldier, cowboy in Arizona who became a political figure.

Barnett, Bion H. Reminiscences [308] of fifty years in the Barnett bank. Jacksonville: Arnold pr. co., 1927? 24 p. KU. In Kansas, 1875-1925.

Barnett, Luke, b. 1877. [309] Between the ribs; the story of a ticklish business as told to George E. Kelley. Phila.: Dorrance & co., 1945. 296 p. NN. The professional career of a practical joker.

Barnum, James Harvey. The [310] traveller's guide, or the life of James H. Barnum. Gt. Barrington: 1847. 52 p. CSmH. Great Lakes merchant seaman, hunter. Doubt has been cast on the authenticity of at least part of this account.

Barnum, Phineas Taylor, 1810- [311] 1891. Life of P. T. Barnum... Buffalo: Pr. by the Courier co., 356 p. WHi. Showman.

Barnwell, Robert Habersham, b. [312] 1854. Gentle pioneers. Boston: Four seas, 1921. 363 p. CU-B. A 20th century account of ranching and farming in the Rockies.

Barr, Amelia Edith Huddleston, [313] 1831-1919. All the days of my life...N.Y.: Appleton, 1913. 528 p. WU. Novelist.

Barr, Amelia Edith Huddleston, [314] 1831-1919. Three score and ten; a book for the aged. N.Y. & London: Appleton, 1915. 326 p. DLC. In later years.

Barr, John, 1749-1831. History of [315] John Barr...Phila.: George Latimer, 1833. 91 p. DLC. Lay worker for the Presbyterian church who was also a farmer in North Carolina.

Barrett, Benjamin Fiske, 1808- [316] 1892. Benjamin Fiske Barrett, an autobiography. Phila.: Swedenborg pub. ass'n., 1890? 201 p. PPP. Clergyman of the New Church in New England and in the Middle Atlantic states. He was also a writer.

Barrett, Edward John Boyd, [317] b. 1883. The magnificent illusion. N.Y.: Ives Washburn, 1930. 321 p. NN. Story of the gradual disillusionment of the author, a former Jesuit of Irish nationality.

Barrett, Fred W., b. 1858. [318] From a diary. Springfield, Ohio: F. W. Barrett, 1934. 103 p. WHi. Travelling salesman.

Barrett, John Pressley, b. 1852. [319] Forty years on the firing line... Dayton: Christian pub. ass'n., 1914. 351 p. DLC. Clergyman of the Christian Church in Virginia, North Carolina and Ohio. The author was also the editor of religious journals

Barrie, Robert, b. 1866. [320]

My log. Phila.: The Franklin press, 1917. 152 p. DLC. Philadelphia publisher.

Barrows, John Rumsey, b. 1864. [321] Ubet. Caldwell, Idaho: Caxton, 1934. WHi. Montana cattle rancher in the eighties.

Barry, James Buckner, b. 1821. [322] A Texas ranger and frontiersman...Dallas: Southwest press, 1932. 221 p. WHi. As described by the title.

Barry, Joseph Gayle Hurd, 1858- [323] 1931. Impressions and opinions; an autobiography. By J.G.H. Barry, D.D., rector emeritus of S. Mary the Virgin, N.Y. N.Y.: Edwin S. Gorham, 1931. 302 p. NN. Protestant Episcopal clergyman of the High Church party. Early life in Connecticut; church work in Chicago, Wisconsin, and New York.

Barry, William Jackson, b. 1819. [324] Up and down...London: Sampson Low, etc., 1879. 307 p. DLC. An English adventurer who spent some time in the California gold mines.

Barrymore, John. Confessions [325] of an actor. Indianapolis: Bobbs-Merrill, 1926. WU. Star of stage and screen.

Barschak, Erna. My American [326] adventure. N.Y.: Ives Washburn, 1945. 248 p. NN. Reactions of a German refugee to her new American environment.

Bartek, John Francis. Life out [327] there. N.Y.: Scribner, 1943. 117 p. DLC. Army flyer who served with Rickenbacker.

Bartelle, J.P. Forty years on [328] the road. Cedar Rapids: Torch press, 1925. 161 p. DLC. The author represented an Ohio lumber company.

Bartholdt, Richard, 1855-1932. [329] From steerage to Congress. Phila.: Dorrance, 1930. 441 p. DLC. Journalist and member of the U.S. House of Representatives from Missouri who was born in Germany.

Bartlett, George Leighton. [330] Through the mill by "4342". St. Paul: McGill-Warner, 1915. 140 p. MnHi. Forger who was sent to a prison in Minnesota.

Bartlett, Willard. [331] Bartlett's recollections... St. Louis: Mound City press, n.d. 119 p. MWA. A surgeon who taught at Washington University and who was the author of medical texts. A 20th century account.

Bartlett, William Sylvester, [332] b. 1851. My foot's in the stirrup. Dallas, Texas: Dealey and Lowe, 1937. 202 p. NN. Courier for the Confederates in the Civil War and scout and messenger in Texas during the Indian wars.

Barton, Charles Vaden, b. 1862. [333] Romance and reality in the life of Earl Count Courtney. Washington, D.C.: Pr. by C.V. Barton, 1903. 116 p. DLC. By an adventurer.

Barton, Clara Harlowe, 1821-1912. [334] The story of my childhood. N.Y.: Baker & Taylor, 1907. 125 p. NN. Recollections of a Massachusetts girlhood, by the founder of the American Red Cross.

Barton, Thomas H., b. 1828. [335] Autobiography of...the self-made physician of Syracuse, Ohio...Charleston, W.Va.: W.Va. printing co., 1890. 340 p. WHi. The author also served as soldier in the Civil War.

Barton, William Eleazar, 1861- [336] 1930. Autobiography... Indianapolis: Bobbs-Merrill, 1932. 314 p. WHi. Congregational clergyman, religious journalist, and biographer of Lincoln, who for many years lived in Illinois.

Barzee, Clark Louis. Oregon [337] in the making...Salem, Oreg.: Statesman pub. co., 1936. 140 p. NN. Teacher in Oregon, 1860-90.

Bascom, John, 1827-1911. [338] Things learned by living. N.Y.: G. P. Putnam's, 1913. 228 p. WU. Professor and president of the University of Wisconsin.

Basil, George Chester, b. 1902. [339] Test tubes and dragon scales. Chicago, etc.: Winston, 1940. 316 p. DLC. Physician in China.

Bassett, Edward Murray, b. 1863. [340] Autobiography...N.Y.: Harbor press, 1939. 185 p. DLC. Lawyer and member of the U.S. House of Representatives from New York.

Batchelder, George W., b. 1803. [341] Narrative of the life, travels and religious experience...Phila.:

Barret & Jones, printers, 1843. 192 p. Auto., p. 7-102. DLC. Itinerant Methodist clergyman in the Middle Atlantic states.

Batchelor, Charles William, b.1823. [342] Incidents in my life...N.p.: Joseph Eichbaum, 1887. 262 p. OClWHi. Pilot, steamship captain on Ohio and Mississippi rivers.

Bates, Mrs. D.B. Incidents on [343] land and water; or, four years on the Pacific coast...Boston: James French, 1858. 336 p. CSmH. The wife of a hotel operator in California, beginning with 1850.

Bates, Joseph, 1792-1872. The [344] autobiography...Battle Creek: Seventh Day Adventist pub. ass'n, 1868. 306 p. WHi. Merchant sailor who became a Seventh Day Adventist clergyman.

Bates, Onward, b. 1850...Memor- [345] abilia of an engineer. Augusta, Ga.: Mimeographed by Ruth I. Hill, 1933. 40 p. MoHi. The author tells of his railroad experiences in Australia.

Batten, John Mullin, 1837-1916. [356] Around and around. Downingtown, Pa.: Priv. pr., 1906. 226 p. DLC. Pennsylvania physician who served the Union cause in the Civil War.

Battey, George M. 70,000 miles [357] on a submarine destroyer. Atlanta: Webb & Vary, 1920. 348 p. DLC. First World War.

Battey, Thomas Chester. [358] The life and adventures of a Quaker among the Indians. N.Y.: Lee & Shepard, 1875. 339 p. WHi. In the Office of Indian Affairs.

Battle, Augustus Allen, 1864-1928. [359] A synopsis...Washington, D.C.: 1927. 15 p. DLC. Negro Baptist in Alabama, Mississippi and the District of Columbia.

Battle, Jesse Mercer, 1850-1914. [360] Tributes to my father and mother and some stories of my life. St. Louis, Mo.: The Mangan press, 1911. 230 p. NN. Early experiences as a lightning rod salesman and later as a salesman and manufacturer of patent medicines.

Battle, Kemp Plummer, 1831-1919. [361] Memories of an old-time tarheel. Chapel Hill: Univ. of N.C. press, 1945. 296 p. WHi. Lawyer and politician in North Carolina who from 1876-1801 served as president of the University of North Carolina.

Baughman, Theodore, b. 1845. [362] The Oklahoma scout. Chicago: W. B. Conkey, n.d. 216 p. CSmH. Scout and Indian fighter, to about 1885.

Baxter, John M., b. 1859. [363] Life...written by himself. Salt Lake City: Deseret News press, 1932. 234 p. USlGS. Mormon bishop who had been a merchant and cattle rancher.

Baxter, William, 1820-1880. [364] Pea Ridge and Prairie Grove; or...the war in Arkansas. Cinc.: Poe & Hitchcock, 1864. 262 p. WHi. The president of Arkansas College tells of his civilian experiences.

Bayley, John, 1814-1880. [365] Confessions of a converted infidel ...N.Y.: Dodd, 1854. 408 p. DLC. By a Methodist clergyman.

Baylis, Frederic J. From the [366] breadline to the pulpit... N.Y.: Ravell, 1914. 43 p. NbLU. An English-born alcoholic who became a Mission worker in Alaska and Colorado and in 1900 a clergyman.

Bayne, Joseph Breckinridge, [367] b. 1880. Bugs and bullets. N.Y.: Richard R. Smith, 1944. 256 p. DLC. Physician who served in Rumania during the first World War.

Bayne, Samuel Gamble, b. 1844. [368] Derricks of destiny...N.Y.: Brentano's, 1924. 259 p. WHi. The author was an oil magnate in Pa.: and a banker in New York.

Bazemore, Thomas Jefferson, [369] Autobiography and book of sermons. Greenfield, Ind.: D. H. Goble, printer, 1901. 280 p. NRCR-S. Baptist minister in Georgia.

Beach, David Nelson, 1848-1926. [370] Beach family reminiscences... Meriden, Conn.: The Journal press, 1931. 244 p. Auto., p 9-182. DLC. New England Congregational clergyman, college president and author of religious works.

Beach, Rex Ellingwood, b. 1877. [371] Personal exposures. N.Y.: Harper, 1940. 303 p. NN. Novelist, screen writer.

Beadle, William Henry Harrison, [372] 1838-1915. Autobiography... Pierre, S.D.: State historical society, 1938. 160 p. SdU. South Dakotan who was Superintendent of Public Instruction, a college president, and a member of the state legislature.

Beal, Fred E. Proletarian [373] journey: New England, Gastonia, Moscow. N.Y.: Hillman-Curl, 1937. 352 p. NN. Communist and labor leader in textile strikes in New England; condemned for murder in the Gastonia, N.C., textile strike; fled to Russia; returned completely disillusioned with Communist Russia.

Beale, George William. [374] A lieutenant of cavalry in Lee's army. Boston: Gorham press, 1918. 231 p. WHi. As described by the title.

Beals, Carleton, b. 1893. [375] Glass houses, ten years of free-lancing. Phila.: J. B. Lippincott co., 1938. 413 p. DLC. A roving journalist, especially in Mexico.

Beals, Carleton, b. 1893. [376] The great circle; further adventures in free-lancing. Phila.: J. B. Lippincott, 1940. 358 p. NN. Adventures in Mexico, Spain, Russia, and elsewhere of a roving journalist.

Bean, Charley, b. 1879. Boy's life [377] in the West. No imprint. 125 p. DLC. Boyhood in Utah, miner and cattle rancher in Idaho.

Bean, Ellis Peter, 1783-1846. [378] Memoir...Houston: The book club of Texas, 1930. 110 p. DLC. An account of an adventurer and soldier in Mexico, the veracity of which has been questioned.

Bean, George Washington, b. 1831. [379] Autobiography...Salt Lake City: Utah pr. co., 1945. 377 p. Auto., p. 13-259. WHi. Utah pioneer; Indian fighter, farmer, judge, political figure, patriarch in the Mormon Church.

Beane, Joshua Fillebrown. [380] From forecastle to cabin... N.Y.: Editor pub. co., 1905. 341 p. DLC. Whaler.

Bear, John W., b. 1800. The life [381] and travels of...Baltimore: Binswanger, 1873. 299 p. DLC. Well travelled political speaker who held several minor federal political posts.

Bear, Luther Standing. See Standing Bear, Chief Luther.

Beard, Daniel Carter, 1850-1941. [382] Hardly a man is now alive... N.Y.: Doubleday, Doran, 1939. 361 p. WHi. The founder of the Boy Scout movement tells mainly of his youth and work as illustrator.

Beard, Mrs. Ida May (Crumpler), [383] b. 1862. My own life...2d ed. Winston-Salem: Winston pub. co., 1900. DLC. A sad tale of domestic life in North Carolina.

Bearden, Clyde. Here we rest. [384] N.p.: 1941. 102 p. AU. A 20th century high school teacher in Alabama who became a chiropractor.

Beardsley, Isaac Haight, b. 1831. [385] Echoes from peak and plain... N.Y.: Eaton & Mains, 1898. 605 p. CoD. Methodist clergyman in Ohio and Colorado who during the Civil War served as a chaplain.

Beardsley, Levi, b. 1785. [386] Reminiscences...N.Y.: Pr. by Charles Vinten, 1852. 567 p. WHi. New York lawyer and politician.

Bearse, Austin. Reminiscences [387] of fugitive slave law days in Boston. Boston: Pr. by W. Richardson, 1880. 41 p. WHi. Abolitionist in New England.

Beasley, Gertrude. My first [388] thirty years. Paris: Three mountains press, 1925. 321 p. NN. Early life and schooling in Texas; college experiences at Simmons College, Abilene, Texas; teaching experiences; University of Chicago.

Beauchamp, Jereboam O., d. 1826. [389] The confession of Jereboam Beauchamp...who was executed at Frankfort, Ky., for the murder of Col. Solomon P. Sharp...Kentucky: H. T. Goodsell, 1854. 100 p. NN. As described by the title.

Beaudry, Louis Napoleon, 1833- [390] 1892. Spiritual struggles of a Roman Catholic: an autobiographical sketch. N.Y.: Nelson & Phillips, 1875. 275 p. NN. Story of a Roman Catholic convert to Protestantism.

Beaumont, Mrs. Betty (Bentley). [391] Twelve years of my life: an autobiography. Phila.: T. B. Peterson, 1887. 366 p. WHi. An Englishwoman's account of her life in a small merchandising store in Mississippi, 1854-1866.

Beaux, Cecilia, 1863-1942. [392] Background with figures; autobiography of Cecilia Beaux. Boston & N.Y.: Houghton Mifflin co., 1930. 356 p. NN. A portrait artist tells of her early life and education in Pa., and of her many sitters.

Beck, Christian. Reise um die [393] welt. Elfte aufl. Dresden: W. Reuter, 1907. 307 p. MH. German traveller who for several years worked as a blacksmith in Louisville, Cincinnati, New Orleans, Texas and Louisiana.

Beck, Fannie Davis (Veale), [394] b. 1861. On the Texas frontier ...St. Louis: Britt printing co., 1937. 295 p. DLC. A domestic account which includes Iowa as well as Texas.

Beck, Mrs. Henry Harrison. See Beck, Fannie Davis (Veale).

Beck, Joseph Clark, b. 1870. [395] Fifty years in medicine. Chicago: McDonough, 1940. 329 p. Auto., p. 60-95, 103-58. DLC. Physician on the staff of the Cook County hospital who came from Austria.

Beck, Levi Garrett, 1812-1888. [396] Reminiscences of fifty years in the gospel ministry...Phila.: Wagenseller, 1883. 19 p. NRCR-S. Baptist clergyman in Pennsylvania.

Beck, Stephen C., b. 1842. [397] A true sketch of his army life. No imprint, 1912? OClWHi. Union army.

Becker, John P., 1765-1837. [398] Sexagenary, or Reminiscences of the American Revolution... Albany: W. C. Little & O. Steele, 1833. 203 p. NN. The author served in the northern part of New York State.

Becker, Mathias Birne, b. 1859. [399] Dawn of light...Chicago: M. B. Becker, 1931. 220 p. DLC. Religious experiences of a Christian Scientist practicioner.

Beckham, E.C. War reminiscen- [400] ces. Batesville, Ark.: Trevathan, 1908. 42 p. ArLH. Confederate soldier.

Beckley, John, b. 1833. The [401] Honorable John Beckley: an autobiography. Beckley, W.Va.: 1910. 10 p. Wv-Ar. School teacher in what is now West Virginia.

Beckwourth, James P., 1798?- [402] 1867. The life and adventures of James P. Beckwourth...N.Y.: Harper, 1856. 537 p. WHi. White hunter who became a Crow chief.

Beebe, Charles William. [403] Pheasant jungles. N.Y.: Putnam's sons, 1927. 248 p. WU. A naturalist tells of his experiences in various countries in Asia.

Beecher, Catharine Esther, 1800- [404] 1878. Educational reminiscences and suggestions. N.Y.: J. B. Ford & co., 1874. 275 p. NN. An early advocate of the higher education of women. A sister of Henry Ward Beecher and Harriet Beecher Stowe. Had schools in Hartford, Conn., and Cincinnati.

Beecher, Henry Ward, 1813-1887. [405] Henry Ward Beecher...by Lyman Abbott. Hartford, Conn.: Am. pub. co., 1887. 670 p. Auto., p. 604-616. DLC. A brief account of his religious development by a Congregational clergyman.

Beers, Clifford Whittingham, b. [406] 1876. A mind that found itself... Rev. ed. Garden City: N.Y.: Doubleday, Doran, 1931. 399 p. WU. The story of a mentally ill person.

Beers, Mrs. Fannie A. [407] Memories...Phila.: J. B. Lippincott, 1891. 336 p. WHi. A nurse serving the Southern cause.

Beggs, Stephen R., b. 1801. [408] Pages from the early history of the West and Northwest...Cinc.: Methodist book concern, 1868. 325 p. WHi. A Methodist pioneer clergyman in Missouri and the old Northwest.

Begley, John. The western [409] missionary priest. No imprint. 205 p. KHi. Catholic priest in Kansas.

Belden, George P. [410] Belden the white chief; or, twelve years among the wild Indians of the plains. From diaries and manuscripts. Ed. by Gen. James S. Brisbin. Cinc.: C. F. Vent, 1872. 513 p. WHi. As described by the title.

Belding, Mollie. [411] Mollie Belding's memory book. Long Beach, Cal.: Pr. by Ward Ritchie press, n.d. 105 p. OrP.

School teacher in Oregon.

Belew, Pascal Perry, b. 1894. [412]
My old Kentucky home, or experiences from life. Kansas City, Mo.: Nazarene pub. house, 1925? 48 p. KyU. Nazarene preacher in Kentucky.

Bell, Horace. Reminiscences [413] of a ranger; or, early times in southern California. Los Angeles: priv. pr., 1881. WHi. As described by the title.

Bell, Horace. On the old West [414] coast; being further reminiscences of a ranger Ed. by Lanier Bartlett. N.Y.: William Morrow, 1930. 307 p. NHi. Pioneer sailor who became a lawyer and newspaper editor.

Bellamy, John Dillard, b. 1854. [415] Memoirs of an octogenarian. Charlotte, N.C.: Observer pr. house, 1942. 201 p. DLC. Lawyer and state senator in North Carolina who also served in the U.S. House of Representatives.

Bellingall, P.W., b. 1845. [416] (Private memoirs). No imprint, 1922? 162 p. CU-B. Title lacking. After serving in the Union army the author removed to California where he was a stock broker, customs official, and politician.

Bellinger, Lucius, b. 1806. [417] Stray leaves from the portfolio of a Methodist local preacher. Macon: Pr. by J. W. Burke, 1870. 311 p. DLC. In South Carolina, North Carolina and Georgia.

Belmont, Perry, b. 1850. [418] An American democrat...N.Y.: Columbia univ. press, 1940. 705 p. WHi. New York lawyer who served in the U.S. House of Representatives.

Belo, Alfred Horatio, 1893?–1901. [419] Memoirs...dictated...to... Charles Peabody... Boston: Alfred Mudge & son, 1904. 75 p. MWA. After serving in the Confederate army, the author became a newspaper editor in Texas.

Bemelmens, Ludwig, b. 1898. [420] Life class. N.Y.: Viking, 1938. 260 p. DLC. The popular humorist from Austria tells of his experiences while working in the restaurants of New York City.

Bemelmans, Ludwig, b. 1898. [421] My war with the United States. N.Y.: Viking, 1937. 151 p. NN. While serving in the U.S. army during the first World War.

Bemis, Stephen Allen, b. 1828. [422] Recollections...St. Louis: 1932. 92 p. MtHi. After mining in California in the fifties, the author became a cotton mill owner in Missouri.

Benchley, Belle J. My life in a [423] man-made jungle. Boston: Little, Brown, 1940. 293 p. WU. Director of a zoo in San Diego.

Bender, Daniel Henry, 1866–1945. [424] A brief sketch of my life. Albany, Oregon: 1943. 44 p. Addenda 1944. 14 p. InGo. Mennonite clergyman in Pa., Kansas and Indiana. He was also an editor of religious journals and president of a college in Indiana.

Benedict, Carl Peters. [425] Tenderfoot kid on gyp water... Austin: Texas folklore soc., 1943. 115 p. WHi. Texas cowboy.

Benedict, George, b. 1887. [426] Christ finds a rabbi...Phila.: 1932. 399 p. DLC. A spiritual account by a rabbi who was converted to Christianity. Locale: the Middle Atlantic states.

Benedict, Jennie Carter, b. 1860. [427] The road to Dream Acre. Louisville: Standard printing co., 1928. 115 p. DLC. Journalist in Kentucky who also was a caterer.

Benedict, Leopold. See Winchevsky, Morris.

Benedict, Mother. Woman's work [428] for woman. Des Moines: Iowa pr. co., 1892. 223 p. IaHi. The author, who lived in Iowa, sought homes for "fallen" women.

Benham, W. E., b. 1820. [429] The life and writings of W. E. Benham...Meriden, Conn.: 1882. 240 p. MiD-B. Connecticut temperance worker, peddler of religious books and lay church worker.

Benjamin, Samuel Green Wheeler,[430] 1837–1914. The life and adventures of a free lance...Burlington, Vt.: Free press co., 1914. 430 p. WHi. Painter, writer on art, and diplomatic officer in Persia.

Bennett, Edwin Clark, b. 1840. [431] Musket and sword, or the camp, march and firing line in the army of the Potomac. Boston: Coburn,

1900. 337 p. NN. As described by the title.

Bennett, Estelline. Old Deadwood [432] days. N.Y.: J. H. Sears, 1928. 300 p. DLC. A story of youth in a frontier mining town in South Dakota.

Bennett, Fred E. Fred Bennett, [433] the Mormon detective; or adventures in the wild west. Chicago: Laird & Lee, 1887. 283 p. CU-B. A brutal account of his search for polygamists.

Bennett, John Oscar. Ship ahoy... [434] San Francisco: Bennett, 1913. 47 p. CSfSP. The author served in the U.S. Navy.

Bennett, William B., b. 1839. [435] Life story of a plain American... No imprint, 1914? 23 p. WHi. Editor and newspaper publisher in Wisconsin.

Benneville, George de, 1703- [436] 1793. Some remarkable passages ...Tr. from the French. Germantown, Pa.: Converse Cleves,1890. 55 p. DLC. Universalist clergyman who came to the U.S. because of persecution in France.

Benoist, Mary Hunt. Memories. [437] N.p.: 1930. 46 p. MoSM. A story of youth on a Missouri farm.

Benson, B. Ketcham. Who goes [438] there?...N.Y.: Macmillan, 1910. 485 p. WHi. Spy for the Union army.

Benson, Ben. 500,000 miles [439] without a dollar...N.Y.: Hobo news, 1942. 96 p. Ia-HA. Hobo.

Benson, Henry Clar, b. 1815. [440] Life among the Choctaw Indians ...Cinc.: Swormstedt & Poe, 1860. 314 p. WHi. By a Methodist clergyman.

Benson, John, 1744-1818. [441] A short account of the voyages, travels and adventures of John Benson; comprising seven voyages to different parts of the world...N.p.: John C. Benson, n.d. 120 p. MWA. Merchant sailor from Rhode Island.

Benson, Luther. Fifteen years [442] in Hell...Indianapolis: Tilford & Carlon, 1877. 208 p. DLC. Indiana lawyer, committed to asylum, tells of his alcoholism and temperance work.

Benson, N.P. The log of the [443] El Dorado. San Francisco: Barry, 1915. 66 p. CHi. Merchant mariner.

Benson, Samuel Benney, b. 1884. [444] Up from a sod hut...Grand Rapids: Zondervan pub. house, 1936. 256 p. DLC. Clergyman of the Dutch Reformed Church in New York, who served as a chaplain in the first World War.

Bent, George Payne, b. 1854. [445] Tales of travel, life and love; an autobiography. Los Angeles: The Times-Mirror press, 1924. 362 p. NN. Manufacturer of pianos.

Benton, Jesse James. [446] Cow by the tail. Boston: Houghton Mifflin co., 1943. 225 p. NN. Cowboy and pioneer life in Texas and Arizona.

Benton, Roger. Where do I go [447] from here? The life story of a forger. N.Y.: Lee Furman, 1936. 314 p. WU. As described by the title.

Benton, Thomas Hart,1782-1858. [448] "Autobiographical sketch". (In his, Thirty years' view. N.Y.: 1866.) Vol. I, p. i-vi. WHi. Lawyer, United States Senator from Missouri. The body of this book contains much autobiographical information.

Benton, Thomas Hart, b. 1889. [449] An artist in America. N.Y.: Halcyon house, 1939. 276 p. WU. Missouri painter.

Bercovici, Konrad, b. 1882. [450] It's the gypsy in me. N.Y.: Prentice-Hall, 1941. 337 p. NN. An immigrant from Rumania tells of his experiences in New York and of his literary efforts.

Berdahl, Andrew J., b. 1848. [451] Autobiographies of Andrew J. and Erick J. Berdahl. No imprint. 29, 46 p. SdSifA. Andrew Berdahl was a school teacher and farm laborer in Minn., who in 1872 took up a homestead in Dakota. He was born in Norway.

Berdahl, Erick J., b. 1850. [452] Autobiographies of Andrew J. and Erick J. Berdahl. No imprint. 29, 46 p. SdSifA. Railroad and farm laborer in Wisconsin and Iowa. He engaged also in lumbering in Wisconsin, beginning with 1872. He was born in Norway.

Beresford, Walter S., b. 1857? [453] From wealth and happiness to misery and the penitentiary.

Kramer, Ga.: Pub. by author, 1893. 338 p. DLC. Englishman who was engaged in illegal financial transactions and was jailed in Georgia.

Berger, Mrs. Mary Frances. [454] In and out of Catholicism... Dayton: United Brethren pub. house, 1913. 77 p. NbLU. The story of her conversion to the United Brethren faith.

Berkman, Alexander, 1870-1936. [455] Prison memoirs of an anarchist. N.Y.: Mother Earth pub. co., 1912. 512 p. WHi. Life in prison by a radical reformer who was convicted of illegal activities during the Homestead strike.

Berkwitz, William Leonard. [456] Reminiscences. N.Y.: W. L. Berkwitz, 1908. 50 p. OCl. Mail order merchant in New York.

Bernard, John, 1768-1828. [457] Retrospections of America, 1797-1811. N.Y.: Harper & brothers, 1887. 380 p. NN. American experiences of the English actor and manager in New York, Philadelphia, and Boston.

Bernhardt, Sarah, 1844-1923. [458] Memories of my life. N.Y.: D. Appleton, 1907. 456 p. DLC. A French actress who played often in the U.S.

Bernheim, Isaac Wolfe, b. 1848. [459] The closing chapters of a busy life. No imprint. 123 p. CoD. A German born Jew in Kentucky who established a recreation area.

Bernstein, Mrs. Aline (Frankau), [460] b. 1881. An actor's daughter. N.Y.: Knopf, 1941. 228 p. WU. A novelist tells of her childhood in New York in the home of a Jewish actor.

Berry, James Henderson, 1841- [461] 1913. An autobiography... Bentonville: Democrat printing co., 1913. 24 p. DLC. After serving in the Confederate army the author turned to law and politics. He was Governor of Arkansas and for 22 years he was a member of the U.S. Senate

Berry, Thomas Franklin, b. 1832. [462] Four years with Morgan and Forrest. Oklahoma City: Harlow-Ratliff, 1914. 476 p. WHi. Confederate cavalry officer.

Bertram, Charles A. Magician [463] in many lands. N.Y.: Dutton, 1911. 315 p. DLC. English magician who toured the U.S.

Beston, Henry, b. 1888. [464] A volunteer poilu. Boston & N.Y.: Houghton Mifflin, 1916. 217 p. DLG. American who served in the French army during the first World War.

Betts, Frederick William. [465] Forty fruitful years. Boston: Murray press, 1929. 384 p. NBuG. Clergyman of the Universalist faith who labored in New York, New Hampshire and Mass.

Betts, Isaac Smith, b. 1872. [466] Chips from the log of a lifetime voyage. Berkeley: 1943. 190 p. DLC. Banker, and executive officer of several large business firms.

Bevens, W. E. Reminiscences of [467] a private, Company G, First Arkansas regiment infantry. No imprint. 58 p. TxU. In the Confederate army.

Bibb, Henry, b. 1815. Narrative...[468] N.Y.: 1849. 204 p. WHi. Slave.

Bickerdyke, Mrs. Mary Ann (Ball)[469] b. 1817. Mary A. Bickerdyke, "Mother", written by Julia A. Chase. Lawrence, Kan.: Woman's Relief corps, 1896. 145 p. KU. Nurse in the Union army who operated the "Home for the Friendless" in Kansas. Later she operated a hotel in the same state.

Bicknell, Ernest Percy, 1862- [470] 1935. Pioneering with the Red cross; recollections of an old Red crosser. N.Y.: Macmillan, 1935. 281 p. WHi. Indiana newspaper reporter who became an executive in the American Red Cross.

Bicknell, Ernest Percy, 1862- [471] 1935. In war's wake, 1914-1915; the Rockefeller foundation and the American Red cross join in civilian relief. Washington, D.C.: American national Red cross, 1936. 276 p. WHi. The experiences in Europe of an American Red Cross executive during the first World War.

Bicknell, Ernest Percy, 1862- [472] 1935. With the Red cross in Europe, 1917-1922. Washington, D.C.: The American national Red

cross, 1938. 500 p. DLC. Red
Cross executive in Europe following the first World War.

Biddle, Charles, 1745-1821. [473]
Autobiography...Phila.: E. Claxton, 1883. 423 p. WHi. Merchant sailor and Pennsylvania political figure.

Biddle, Ellen (McGowan), b. 1841. [474]
Recollections. Boston: Small, Maynard, 1920. 80 p. DLC. The wandering childhood of the daughter of a naval officer and the early years of her marriage to an officer in the Union army.

Biddle, Ellen (McGowan), b. 1841. [475]
Reminiscences of a soldier's wife. Phila.: J. B. Lippincott, 1907. 256 p. WHi. The period covered is 1865-1900.

Biddle, George, b. 1885. [476]
An American artist's story. Boston: Little, Brown & co., 1939. 326 p. NN. Career of an American painter; youth in Pa., education at Groton School and Harvard; World War I; Tahiti; artistic life in France and America; mural painting; Federal Art Project.

Bidwell, Austin Biron. From [477]
Wall Street to Newgate... Hartford: Bidwell, 1895. 535 p. WU. Swindler.

Bidwell, Benson, b. 1835. [478]
Benson Bidwell, inventor... Chicago: Henneberry press, 1907. 258 p. MoKU. Indiana lawyer who claimed that his inventions (trolley car, electric fan) were stolen.

Bidwell, George, 1837?-1899. [479]
Forging his chains...Hartford: S. S. Scranton, 1888. 560 p. DLC. Forger who was sentenced to prison in England.

Bidwell, John, 1819-1900. [480]
Addresses, reminiscences, etc. of General John Bidwell. Compiled by C. C. Royce. Chico, Calif.: 1907. 113 leaves. DLC. Early California pioneer and prohibition candidate for President.

Bidwell, John, 1819-1900. [481]
...Echoes of the past about California. Ed. by Milo M. Quaife. Chicago: R. R. Donnelley, 1928. 377 p. Auto., p. 1-111. WHi. The author tells of pioneer life in California in the 1840's.

Bierce, Ambrose Gwinett, 1842- [482]
1914? "Bits of autobiography (In his, Collected works. N.Y.: 1909). Vol. 1, p. 225-401. WU. Random recollections of war, travel, journalism.

Bigelow, John, 1817-1911. [483]
Retrospections of an active life. N.Y.: The Baker & Taylor co., 1909-1913. 5 vols. WU. Journalist, historian, diplomat in France.

Bigelow, Mrs. L. Adda (Nichols), [484]
b. 1849. Reminiscences. Chula Vista, Calif.: Denrich press, 1917. DLC. Teacher and saleslady in Tennessee, who later became a prolific poet in California and New York.

Bigelow, Poultney, b. 1855. [485]
Prussian memories, 1864-1914. N.Y.: Putnam's sons, 1915. 197 p. DLC. An American journalist who was educated in Germany and worked there for many years prior to the first World War.

Bigelow, Poultney, b. 1855. [486]
Seventy summers. N.Y.: Longmans, Green, 1925. 2 vols. NN. Journalist and world traveller; education in Germany; newspaper work and politics; Russian experiences.

Biggar, J. H., b. 1854. [487]
These eighty-one years. Chicago: Prairie press, 1935. 32 p. SdHi. Farm laborer in Iowa and Nebraska in the seventies. Farmer in Dakota in the eighties. He emigrated from Canada.

Biggs, Asa, b. 1811. Autobiography [488]
...Raleigh, N.C.: Edwards & Broughton, 1915. 51 p. KHi. North Carolina lawyer, Congressman, U.S. Senator and U.S. district judge.

Bigly, Cantell A. (pseud.). See Peck, George Wilbur.

Bilbie, Edward Normanton, b.1865.[489]
Experiences of a violinist at home and abroad. Pittsburgh: Manchester pr. co., 1921. 77 p. Auto., p. 1-16. DLC. Violinist, music teacher in Pennsylvania.

Billings, Mrs. Katharine (Fowler)[490]
Lunn, b. 1902. The gold missus; a woman prospector in Sierra Leone. N.Y.: W. W. Norton, 1938. 309 p. DLC. As described by the title.

Binder, Jacob William, b. 1866. [491]

All in a lifetime...Hackensack, N.J.: Priv. pr., 1942. 354 p. DLC. Business executive and public relations man chiefly in the middle Atlantic region.

Bingham, Anna E., Added reminiscences of sixteen years on a Kansas farm. No imprint. 4 p. KHi. The period covered is 1870-75. The earlier years of her life are described in the Collections of the Kansas Historical Society for 1923. [492]

Bingham, Hiram, b. 1875. [493] An explorer in the air service. New Haven: Yale univ. press, 1920. 260 p. DLC. Service with the U.S. Army Air Service in France and Washington, D.C. during the first World War.

Binns, John, 1772-1860. [494] Recollections of the life of John Binns: twenty-nine years in Europe and fifty-three in the United States. Phila.: Printed and for sale by the author, 1854. 349 p. NN. Journalist and Democratic politician in Northumberland, Pa., and Philadelphia, who came to America in 1801 after a career as an English radical.

Birch, Chess. Reminiscences [495] of Chess Birch, the musical evangelist. Hannibal, Mo.: Standard pr. co., 1891. 70 p. MoHi. YMCA worker in Missouri, evangelist in Louisiana and Alabama.

Bird, Hiram Thornton. Memories [496] of the Civil war. No imprint. 67 p. IaHi. In an Iowa regiment.

Birdwell, Russell. Ringing [497] doorbells. N.Y.: Julian Messner, 1939. 253 p. NN. Recollections of a newspaper reporter.

Birks, Richard Elliott, b. 1846. [498] The story of my life. Derby: Pr. by J. Harwood, 1923. 168 p. MBUn. Unitarian minister in Mass. The author was born in England.

Bisbee, William Haymond, b. 1840. [499] Through four American wars. Boston: Meador, 1931. 281 p. DLC. Civil War; Indian fighting; Cuba; Philippines.

Bishop, Joseph, b. 1770. [500] The life of...the celebrated old pioneer in the first settlements of middle Tennessee...By John W. Gray. Nashville: The author, 1858. 236 p. DLC. A dictated account by a fur trapper and Indian fighter.

Bishop, Josiah Goodman, 1833- [501] 1922. Autobiography...No imprint. 191 p. Auto., p. 11-130. MoCanD. Clergyman in the Christian Church in Missouri, Iowa and New York

Bishop, Sereno Edwards, 1827- [502] 1909. Reminiscences of old Hawaii. Honolulu: Hawaiian gazette co., 1916. 64 p. CU-B. Recollections of the first thirteen years of his life by the son of a missionary.

Bispham, David Scull, 1857-1921. [503] A Quaker singer's recollections. N.Y.: Macmillan, 1921. 401 p. WHi. By an opera singer.

Bittle, Celestine Nicholas Charles [504] b. 1884. Soldiering for cross and flag; impressions of a war chaplain. Milwaukee: Bruce, 1929. 331 p. DLC. Catholic priest who served as chaplain in France during the first World War.

Bivins, David Francis, b. 1842. [505] Sketch of the life of David Francis Bivins who murdered... Adrian, Mich.: 1865. 40 p. MiD-B. As described by the title.

Bivins, Mrs. Viola (Cobb), [506] b. 1863. Memoirs. No imprint, 1942? 138 p. Auto., p. 82-98. TxU. Wife of sawmill operator in Texas.

Bixby, Sarah. See Smith, Mrs. Sarah Hathaway (Bixby).

Black, A. P. The end of the [507] longhorn trail. Selfridge, N.D.: Selfridge journal, n.d. 59 p. WHi. Cowboy in Texas.

Black, Alexander, 1859-1940. [508] Time and chance; adventures with people and print. N.Y.: Farrar & Rinehart, 1937. 338 p. NN. New York newspaper man and novelist.

Black, Jack. The big break at [509] Folsom...with a sequel by the same author out of prison. San Francisco: The Bulletin, 1903? 71 p. CSmH. The story of his early career as a thief, and of his unsuccessful attempt to escape from Folsom. Upon release from Folsom, he continued his career of crime on the Pacific Coast.

Black, Jack. You can't win. [510] N.Y.: Macmillan, 1927. 394 p. WU. Story of crime and prison life.

Black, Jennie (Prince). [511]
I remember. N.p.: 1938. 112 p.
DLC. A story of childhood and
of married life in New York City.

Black, Martha Louise (Munger), [512]
b. 1866. My seventy years. London, N.Y.: Thomas Nelson, 1939.
317 p. DLC. After spending her
childhood in Chicago, the author
marries a member of the Canadian parliament and upon his death
becomes a member herself.

Black, Samuel. A soldier's [513]
recollections of the Civil war.
Minco: Minco minstrel, 1911.
117 p. PHi. Union army.

Black, Warren Columbus, 1843- [514]
1915. God's estimate of man...
Nashville: M. E. Church, South,
1915. 204 p. Auto., p. 13-27. DLC.
Methodist clergyman in Mississippi.

Black Elk, b. 1863. [515]
Black Elk speaks...N.Y.:
Morrow, 1932. 280 p. WHi. Sioux
Indian.

Black Hawk, 1767-1838. [516]
The life of Black Hawk. Chicago:
R. R. Donnelley, 1916. 181 p. WHi.
Sauk Chief.

Blackford, William Willis, 1831- [517]
1905. War years with Jeb Stuart.
N.Y.: Scribner's, 1945. 322 p.
WHi. By an officer.

Blackman, William, b. 1840. [518]
The boy of Battle Ford, and the
man. Marion, Ill.: Egyptian
press, 1906. 192 p. IU. Illinois
farmer and preacher who served
in the Union army.

Blackmar, Joseph. Autobiography [519]
and memoirs of Rev. Joseph
Blackmar...Dayton, Ohio: Croy,
McFarland, 1879. 111 p. KU. The
period covered is 1800-1878.

Blackwell, Elizabeth, 1821-1910. [520]
Pioneer work in opening the
medical profession to women;
autobiographical sketches. London: Longmans, Green, and co.,
1895. 265 p. NN. Career of the
first woman to receive a medical
degree in America.

Blair, Norvel. Life of Norvel [521]
Blair, a Negro citizen of Morris,
Grundy County, Illinois. Joliet?
Joliet Daily Record steam print,
1880. 32 p. NNC. A story of
political frauds by an Illinois
Negro.

Blair, Walter Acheson, b. 1856. [522]
A raft pilot's log...on the upper
Mississippi. Cleveland: A. H.
Clark, 1930. 328 p. WHi. As
described by the title.

Blakley, Christina. Some [523]
characteristics of the life of
Christina Blakely... St. Louis:
Bockius pr. co., 1914. 81 p. DLC.
A sad tale of domestic tribulations.

Blanchard, Charles Albert, [524]
b. 1848. President Blanchard's
autobiography...Boone, Iowa:
Western Christian alliance, 1915.
199 p. WHi. Professor and president of Wheaton College in Illinois.

Blanding, Stephen F. In the [525]
defences of Washington...
Providence: 1889. 54 p. WHi.
Union army.

Blanding, Stephen F. [526]
Recollections of a sailor boy;
or, The cruise of the gunboat
Louisiana. Providence: E. A.
Johnson & co., 1886. 330 p. NN.
Service along the North Carolina
coast in the Civil War.

Blankenburg, Lucretia M. [527]
(Longshore). "The autobiography
..." (In her, The Blankenburgs
of Philadelphia. Phila.: John C.
Winston, 1928). p. 99-166. DLC.
A socialite whose husband was
mayor of Philadelphia.

Blatch, Mrs. Harriot (Stanton), [528]
1856-1940. Challenging years
...N.Y.: Putnam's, 1940. 347 p.
WHi. Woman suffragist.

Bliss, Arthur Ames, 1859-1913. [529]
Blockley days; memories and
impressions of a resident physician, 1883-1884. Springfield:
Springfield pr. co., 1916. 94 p.
DLC. At Philadelphia City
Hospital.

Bliss, Daniel, 1823-1916. [530]
The reminiscences of Daniel
Bliss. Edited and supplemented
by his eldest son. N.Y. & Chicago:
Fleming H. Revell co., 1920. 259
p. NN. Congregational missionary
and educator in Syria, founder of
Syrian Protestant College.

Bliss, Mrs. Olive Irene Hills. [531]
The miles of yesterday. The
life story of a Minnesota woman.
St. Paul: 1935. 43 leaves. MnHi.
After spending her youth on a
farm in the seventies, the author
married a Minnesota businessman.

Bliss, Theodore, 1822-1910. [532]
Theodore Bliss, publisher and bookseller...N.p.: 1941. 92 p. WU. As described by the title.

Blitz, Antonio, 1810-1877. [533]
Fifty years in the magic circle; being an account of the author's professional life; his wonderful tricks and feats; with laughable incidents, and adventures as a magician, necromancer, and ventriloquist... Hartford: Belknap & Bliss, 1871. 432 p. DLC. As described by the title.

Block, George M. [534]
These memories...St. Louis: Mound City press, 1929. 63 p. MoSHi. Youth on a pioneer farm in Missouri in the fifties and sixties.

Blodgett, Henry W., b. 1821. [535]
Autobiography...Waukegan: 1906. 102 p. WHi. Lawyer, U.S. District judge, and member of the state legislature in Illinois.

Bloodgood, James Henry, b. 1853. [536]
Sailor Jim...Tampa: Empire letter and pr. co., 1941. 156 p. DLC. Merchant sailor on clipper ships, and member of the U. S. Navy.

Bloomfield, Obadiah Benjamin Franklin, b. 1770. Life and adventures...Phila.: 1818. 210 p. WHi. A dubious tale of adventure. [537]

Bloor, Charles Phillip, b. 1894. [538]
A different story in the history of life. Boston: Meador, 1933. 144 p. DLC. A victim of infantile paralysis who became a successful merchant.

Bloor, Ella Reeve, b. 1862. [539]
We are many. N.Y.: International publishers, 1940. 315 p. WHi. Member of the Communist party in America, labor leader.

Blotzman, Sidney. [540]
"Sidney's own story" (The natural history of a delinquent career, by Clifford R. Shaw. Chicago: The University of Chicago press, 1931. 280 p.). p. 51-223. DLC. In Chicago.

Blumenfeld, Ralph David, b. 1864. [541]
Home town. London: Hutchinson, 1944. 116 p. DLC. Wisconsin boyhood days, followed by a career in journalism in New York and in England.

Blumenthal, George, 1862-1943. [542]
My sixty years in show business; a chronicle of the American theater, 1874-1934, as told by George Blumenthal to Arthur H. Menkin. N.Y.: Frederick C. Osberg, 1936. 336 p. NN. The writer was for many years associated with Oscar Hammerstein.

Blythe, Samuel G. [543]
Making of a newspaperman. Phila.: H. Altemus, 1912. 230 p. WU. Small town newspaper reporter.

Bobjerg, Anders Pedersen, b. 1861. En Dansk nybygd i Wisconsin; 40 aar i Storskoven (1869-1909). Kobenhavn: Gad, 1909. 72 p. MoHi. Farmer. [544]

Bodfish, Hartson Hartlett. [545]
Chasing the bowhead...Cambridge: Harvard univ. press, 1936. 281 p. DLC. Merchant captain who engaged in whaling in the Arctic for 31 years.

Bodholdt, Knud C. [546]
Paa praerien og i nybyggertiden. Cedar Falls: Dansk boghandel, 1916. 128 p. MoHi. Lutheran clergyman in Nebraska who came from Denmark in 1882.

Boehm, Henry, 1775-1875. [547]
Reminiscences, historical and biographical, of sixty-four years in the ministry. N.Y.: Carlton & Porter, 1866. 493 p. WHi. Methodist clergyman in Pennsylvania, New York, and Maryland.

Boehm, Henry, 1775-1875. [548]
The patriarch of one-hundred years. N.Y.: Nelson & Phillips, 1875. 587 p. CSmH. The same as the preceding item plus a few new chapters.

Bogen, Boris D., 1869-1929. [549]
Born a Jew. N.Y.: Macmillan, 1930. 361 p. WU. Born in Russia, the author in America became a social service worker in Ohio. Later, he was employed by the Joint Distribution Committee which sought to bring relief in the years after 1919 to Jews in Holland, Poland, Russia and Israel.

Boggess, Francis Calvin Morgan, b. 1833. Veteran of four wars... Arcadia, Florida: pr. at the Champion job rooms, 1900. 87 p. DLC. Participant in Mexican War, filibusters in Yucatan and Cuba, War [550] with Indians in Florida, and Civil War on the Confederate side. The author was also a member of the Florida legislature.

Boggs, William Robertson. [551] Military reminiscences...Durham: Trinity college historical society, 1913. 115 p. WHi. Officer in the Confederate army.

Bogigian, Hagop. In quest of the [552] soul of civilization. Washington, D.C.: The author, 1925. 255 p. DLC. Oriental rug importer of Boston who came to this country from Armenia.

Bohemian life; or, the auto- [553] biography of a tramp. San Francisco: J. Dewing, 1884. 451 p. C. A dubious tale of adventures, including the Chicago fire.

Bohun, Edmund, 1645-1699. [554] The diary and autobiography... Beccles, England: Priv. pr., 1853. 148 p. WHi. Chief justice of South Carolina.

Boicourt, Samuel L., b. 1807. [555] Life of Dr. Samuel L. Boicourt, of Louisville, Kentucky... Louisville: 1857. 50 p. DLC. Kentucky physician.

Bok, Edward William, 1863-1930. [556] The Americanization of Edward Bok...N.Y.: Scribner's, 1920. 461 p. WHi. Newspaper writer and magazine editor who was born in the Netherlands.

Bok, Edward William, 1862-1930. [557] America, give me a chance. N.Y.: Scribner, 1926. 345 p. DLC. See the preceding item.

Bok, Edward William, 1863-1930. [558] Twice thirty; some short and simple annals of the road. N.Y., London: C. Scribner's sons, 1925. 539 p. WHi. See the preceding entries. This work was written for his children.

Bokhoff, Ella M. [559] Revelations of a nurse. Boston: Christopher, 1928. 41 p. DLC. An account dealing chiefly with her religious experiences.

Bokum, Hermann, 1807-1878. [560] Wanderings north and south... Phila.: King & Baird, 1864. 73 p. WHi. A Civil War chaplain who served in a hospital in Philadelphia.

Bolden, Harry T., b. 1845. [561] History...N.p.: 1913. 11 p. MoHi. A slave who became a farmer and a Methodist clergyman in Missouri.

Bolton, Mrs. Sarah (Knowles), [562] 1841-1916. Sarah K. Bolton; pages from an intimate autobiography. Ed. by her son. Boston: Thomas Todd, 1923. 155 p. WHi. Author and social reformer in Ohio.

Boltwood, Edmund, b. 1839. [563] Some events of my busy life. No imprint. 38 p. Auto., p. 1-14. KHi. The author served in the Union army and in the National Guard of Mass. and Kansas.

Bond, Mrs. Carrie (Jacobs), 1862-[564] 1946. The roads of melody. N.Y.: Appleton, 1927. 223 p. DLC. Composer of songs.

Bond, Elias. [565] Father Bond of Kohola; a chronicle of pioneer life in Hawaii. Put together by Ethel M. Damon. Honolulu: The Friend, 1927. 284 p. Auto., p. 3-47. MWA. By a Congregational missionary.

Bond, Isabella (Bacon), 1859- [566] 1931. Memoirs. Boston: 1934. 187 p. DLC. Socialite, philanthropist and civic worker in Boston and Washington.

Bond, John, b. 1844. [567] Handcarts west in '56. N.p.: Priv. pr., 1945. 47 leaves. IdP. English born boy travels to Utah in 1856.

Bond, Sarah (Rider), b. 1847. [568] Following the upward trail... Cinc.: God's Revivalist press, 1925. 287 p. DLC. Lay church worker, and advocate of temperance in the use of alcohol.

Bondi, August, 1833-1907. [569] Autobiography...Galesburg, Ill.: Wagoner pr. co., 1910. 178 p. KHi. Jew, abolitionist who served John Brown, Civil War soldier, and Kansas farmer.

Bonebright, Mrs. Sarah (Brewer), [570] b. 1837. Reminiscences of Newcastle, Iowa...written by her daughter Harriet Bonebright-Closz. Des Moines: Historical Department of Iowa, 1921. 307 p. IaHi. A story of youth on a pioneer farm in the forties and early fifties.

Bonney, Benjamin Franklin, [571]

b. 1838. Recollections...Eugene, Oreg.: Koke-Tiffany, 1923. 20 p. OrU. A young boy in pioneer California during the 1840's.

Bononcini, Eugene, 1835-1907. [572]
Autobiography...St. Paul, Kansas: Journal press, 1942. 120 p. DLC. Italian born priest who became a Catholic missionary in Kansas.

Bonsal, Stephen, b. 1865. [573]
Heyday in a vanished world. N.Y.: W. W. Norton, 1937. 445 p. NN. Foreign correspondent of the New York Herald in the Balkans, Asia, and Africa.

Book, William Henry, b. 1863. [574]
Real life and original sayings. Richmond: Ware & Duke, printers, 1900. 192 p. MoCanD. Clergyman of the Disciples of Christ in Virginia.

Boomer, James McClellan, [575]
b. 1831. Autobiography. N.p.: 1911. 51 p. KHi. Laborer on railroads, bridges, farms and owner of farms in Illinois and Kansas.

Boone, Daniel, 1734-1820. [576]
The discovery, settlement, and present state of Kentucke...to which is added...the adventures of Col. Daniel Boon..., by John Filson. Wilmington: James Adams, 1784. 33 p. WHi. According to the DAB, this is a work "purporting to be told by Boone himself, but given in words that Boone could not have possibly used." An abridged version was published by John Trumbull in Norwich, Conn., in 1786, under the title "The adventures of Colonel Daniel Boon..."

Booth, Ernest. Stealing through [577] life. N.Y.: Knopf, 1929. 308 p. WU. Thief, prisoner.

Booth, Ewing E., b. 1870. [578]
My observations and experiences in the United States Army. Los Angeles: 1944. 301 p. DLC. Served in Cuba, Philippines, France.

Booth, George Wilson, 1844- [579]
1914. Personal reminiscences of a Maryland soldier in the War between the states, 1861-1865. Baltimore: For private circulation only, 1898. 177 p. MdBP. Confederate soldier.

Borcke, Heros von, 1835-1895. [580]
Memoirs of the Confederate war for independence. Edinburgh: Wm. Blackwood, 1866. 2 vols. WHi. A German who served as Chief of Staff to General Stuart.

Borgenicht, Louis. [581]
The happiest man; the life of Louis Borgenicht as told to Harold Friedman. N.Y.: G. P. Putnam's, 1942. 414 p. DLC. This Galician-born Jew tells of his rise in the infants' and children's wear industry, also of his earlier career in Galicia and Hungary.

Borland, James Brown, 1861- [582]
1939. Fifty years in the newspaper game, by James B. Borland, managing editor of The News-Herald, Franklin, Pennsylvania. Boston: Press of Chapple pub. co., 1928. 235 p. NN. As described by the title.

Borthwick, J. D. Three years [583]
in California...Edinburgh: Blackwood, 1857. 384 p. DLC. An artist tells of his three years in the California gold mines.

Borton, Benjamin. On the [584]
parallels, or chapters of inner history...Woodstown: 1903. 333 p. WHi. Union soldier.

Bosqui, Edward, b. 1832. [585]
Memoirs. San Francisco: 1904. 281 p. CU-B. Canadian born pioneer miner and farmer in California. Later he engaged in the real estate business, and in bookbinding. He was employed in the Customs House and was head of a school for juvenile delinquents.

Bostwick, Arthur Elmore, b. 1860. [586]
A life with men and books. N.Y.: H. W. Wilson, 1939. 358 p. DLC. Teacher in New Jersey, librarian in St. Louis, editor.

Boswell, Ira Matthews, b. 1866. [587]
Recollections of a red-headed man. Cinc.: Standard, 1915. 144 p. DLC. Student experiences at the Bible College of Transylvania University.

Boucher, Jonathan, 1737/38-1804. [588]
Reminiscences of an American loyalist, 1738-1789. Ed. by Jonathan Bouchier. N.Y.: Houghton Mifflin, 1925. 201 p. WHi. Anglican clergyman who upheld the British cause during the American revolution.

Boughton, Jennie. Forty years [589] of library service. No imprint, 1943? 8 p. WaSp. In Spokane.

Bourg, Otto V., b. 1869. [590] Recollections of a society clairvoyant. London: E. Nash, 1911. 206 p. DLC. A French clairvoyant tells of her brief experiences in the U.S.

Bours, William M., b. 1857. [591] Memories incident to a ministry ...San Francisco: 1939. 38 p. CU-B. Episcopalian clergyman in California.

Bouscaren, Pierre, 1889-1927. [592] Father Pierre Bouscaren, S.J. A spiritual autobiography. Milwaukee: Bruce, 1935. 142 p. DLC. As described by the title.

Bouton, Nathaniel, 1799-1878. [593] Autobiography of Nathaniel Bouton, D.D., former pastor of the first Congregational Church of Concord and late state historian of New Hampshire...N.Y.: A.D.F. Randolph, 1879. 87 p. WHi. As described by the title.

Boutwell, George Sewall, 1818- [594] 1905. Reminiscences of sixty years in public affairs. N.Y.: McClure, Phillips & co., 1902. 2 vols. WHi. Abolitionist, member of the U. S. House of Representatives, and member of the President's Cabinet.

Bowden, J. W., b. 1842. [595] Autobiography...Meridian: Dunlap pr. co., 1924. 138 p. Auto., p. 9-86. TxU. Methodist clergyman in Texas.

Bowe, John, b. 1869. [596] Soldiers of the Legion. Chicago: Paterson linotyping co., 1918. 281 p. DLC. The author was a member of the French Foreign Legion during World War I.

Bowen, Benjamin B., b. 1819. [597] A blind man's offering...2d ed. N.Y.: 1850. 432 p. Auto., p. 9-23. MiD-B. Music teacher in New England.

Bowen, Herbert Wolcott, 1856- [598] 1927. Recollections, diplomatic and undiplomatic. N.Y.: F. H. Hitchcock, 1926. 320 p. WHi. Lawyer and diplomatic officer in Spain, Persia, Venezuela.

Bowen, Louise De Koven. [599] Growing up with a city. N.Y.: Macmillan, 1926. 226 p. WHi. Social worker, suffragist worker in Chicago.

Bowen, Thomas Jefferson, 1814- [600] 1875. Central Africa: adventures and missionary labors in several countries in the interior of Africa from 1849 to 1856. Charleston: Southern Baptist pub. soc., 1857. 359 p. Auto., p. 27-216. WU. As described by the title.

Bowen, Thomas Jefferson, 1814- [601] 1875. Meroke: or, missionary life in Africa. Rev. by Rev. T. J. Bowen. Phila.: American Sunday school union, 1858. 207 p. NRCR. As described by the title.

Bowers, Benjamin. A narrative, [602] or youth's mirror...containing the trials and sufferings that flowed from inconstant and falsehearted women...Swanton, Vt.: The author, 1847. 424 p. MWA. The marital difficulties of a Vermonter.

Bowman, John Gabbert, b. 1877. [603] The world that was. N.Y.: Macmillan, 1926. 81 p. NN. Reminiscences of an Iowa boyhood, by the president of the University of Pittsburgh.

Bowman, Thornton Hardie, b. 1843[604] Reminiscences of an ex-Confederate soldier; or, forty years on crutches. Austin, Tex.: Gammel-Statesman pub. co., 1904. 126 p. DLC. After the war the author was a teacher in Louisiana and Texas, a sheep rancher in Texas, and the holder of various political offices in Texas.

Bowyer, Mrs. Edith M. (Nicholl). [605] Observations...N.Y.: Macmillan, 1898. 271 p. DLC. Life on a New Mexico farm by a woman born in England.

Box-car Bertha. Sister of the [606] road...as told to Ben L. Reitman. N.Y.: Gold Label books, 1937. 314 p. WU. Hobo, shoplifter, prostitute in Chicago.

Boyce, Anson Augustus, b. 1812. [607] Auto-biography...Santa Barbara: 1904. 199 p. CSmH. Newspaper editor and member of state legislature in New York. Real estate dealer in California.

Boyd, Belle. *See* Hardinge, Belle (Boyd).

Boyd, Joseph Hyatt, b. 1842. [608] Reminiscences...recorded and arranged by William S. Lewis. Seattle: Univ. of Washington press, 1924. 23 p. DLC. English born miner and merchant in Idaho and Oregon.

Boyd, Mrs. Orsemus Bronson. [609] Cavalry life in tent and field. N.Y.: J. Selwin Tait, 1894. 376 p. DLC. The wife of a cavalry officer.

Boyd, Robert, b. 1792. [610] Personal memoirs...Cinc.: R. P. Thompson, printer, 1868. 239 p. Auto., p. 15-151. TxDaM. Methodist clergyman in Pa.

Boyden, Elbridge. [611] Reminiscences of Elbridge Boyden, architect. Worcester, Mass.: 1890. 13 p. MiD-B. As described by the title.

Boylston, Edward Dudley, b. 1814. [612] Sketch of a busy life...Amherst, N.H.: The author, 1892. 184 p. MiD-B. New England journalist.

Brackenridge, Henry Marie, [613] 1786-1871. Recollections of persons and places in the West. 2d ed., enlarged. Phila.: J. B. Lippincott, 1868. 331 p. NN. Early life in Pittsburgh and Missouri; law practice in Baltimore; return to Missouri. This edition narrates the author's career until his departure for Louisiana.

Brackett, Albert G. [614] General Lane's brigade in central Mexico. Cinc.: H. W. Derby, 1854. 336 p. WHi. Volunteer officer in the Mexican War.

Brackett, George Augustus, [615] 1836-1921. A winter evening's tale. N.Y.: Pr. for the author, 1880. 31 p. MnHi. Indian troubles in Minnesota, 1862, and Little Crow at Devil's Lake.

Bradford, Mary D. [616] Memoirs...Evansville, Wis.: Antes press, 1933. 521 p. WHi. Teacher and superintendent of schools in Kenosha, Wis.

Bradford, Samuel, b. 1803. [617] Some incidents in the life of Samuel Bradford, senior, by his son; also the autobiography or a brief narrative of the life of Samuel Bradford, junior, to January 1, 1879. Phila.: printed not published, 1880. 79 p. Auto., p. 35-79. DLC. Pennsylvania merchant and railroad figure.

Bradford, Ward, b. 1809. [618] Biographical sketches...No imprint, 1891? 92 p. DLC. Farmer in the middle west tells of his youth in Oregon. Land speculator on the West Coast. Operator of hotels in Iowa, Missouri and California.

Bradish, Cyrus, b. 1811. [619] Reminiscences of a nonagenarian. Woodsville, N.H.: News print, 1903. 25 p. DLC. District school master in New Hampshire.

Bradlee, Caleb Davis, 1831-1897. [620] Recollections of a ministry of forty years, Dec. 11, 1854-Dec. 11, 1894... Boston: Geo. H. Ellis, 1895. 36 p. NN. Unitarian minister of Boston and vicinity.

Bradley, Floyd N., b. 1904. [621] Ten years behind the sacred desk. Cinc.: Printed by God's Bible school & revivalist, 1932. 208 p. DLC. Methodist minister in New Jersey.

Bradley, Ora (Lewis), b. 1869. [622] The country doctor's wife. N.Y.: Field, 1940. 212 p. DLC. In Georgia.

Bradley, Stephen H. [623] A sketch...Madison: 1830. 12 p. MiD-B. A spiritual account, covering the years five to twenty-four.

Bradshaw, DeEmmett. [624] My story. Omaha: Priv. pr., 1941. 335 p. WHi. Lawyer connected with the Woodmen of the World Life Insurance Society.

Brady, Cyrus Townsend, 1861- [625] 1920. Recollections of a missionary in the great west. N.Y.: Scribner's, 1900. 200 p. WHi. Episcopal clergyman in Missouri, Colorado, Kansas during 1890-1895.

Brady, William A., b. 1863. [626] Showman. N.Y.: E. P. Dutton, 1936. 278 p. WU. Producer of theatricals and ring fighting in New York.

Bragdon, Claude Fayette, 1866- [627] 1946. More lives than one. N.Y.: Alfred A. Knopf, 1938. 368 p. NN. New York architect, stage designer, author; experiences with occultism.

Bragg, Arial, b. 1772. Memoirs.. [628] Milford: Pr. by G. W. Stacy, 1846. 86 p. WHi. Manufacturer and merchant in Massachusetts.

Brainerd, Edith Hubbard. [629]
Some events of my childhood.
N.p.: Priv. pr., 1943. 15 p. OkHi.
In Indian territory (later Oklahoma) in period following 1887.

Brainerd, John, 1720-1781. [630]
A genuine letter from Mr. John Brainard, employed by the Scotch Society for Propagating the Gospel, a missionary to the Indians in America, and minister to a congregation of Indians, at Bethel in East Jersey, to his friend in England. Giving an account of the success of his labours, as well as the difficulties and discouragements that attend his mission among those savages. London: Printed for J. Ward, 1753. 16 p. NN. As described by the title.

Brake, Hezekiah, b. 1814. [631]
On two continents...Topeka: The author, 1896. 240 p. DLC. English born farmer and rancher in New Mexico, Kansas, Minnesota.

Braley, Berton, b. 1882. [632]
Pegasus pulls a hack; memoirs of a modern minstrel. N.Y.: Minton, Balch, 1934. 329 p. NN. Newspaper man and free-lance writer; early newspaper experiences in Montana; literary life in New York; special correspondent World War I.

Braly, John Hyde. Memory [633]
pictures...Los Angeles: Neuner, 1912. 263 p. CSmH. To Pacific Coast in 1847. Operator of boarding school in California, 1860-1880, then planter and banker.

Braman, Isaac, b. 1770. [634]
Semi-centennial discourse... on the fiftieth anniversary of his ordination. Georgetown: Charles Nason, 1847. 39 p. ICN. Congregational clergyman in Mass.

Branch, Erskine B. [635]
A brief sketch of the experience of a Union soldier in the late war. Washington: Chronicle print, 1870. 8 p. CSmH. New York State Volunteers.

Branch, Mary Jones (Polk). [636]
Memoirs of a southern woman "within the lines"...Chicago: Branch, 1912. 107 p. WHi. Civil War experiences, p. 7-53.

Branch, Stephen H., b. 1813. [637]
The life of Stephen H. Branch, (written by himself), and dedicated to those who rove in virtue's grove. N.Y.: 1857. 32 p. NN. An eccentric author who published a number of short-lived periodicals in New York.

Brand, James, 1834-1899. [638]
James Brand, twenty-six years pastor of the First Congregational Church, Oberlin... Oberlin: L.D. Harkness, 1899. 48 p. DLC. As described by the title.

Brandrup, J.R., b. 1864. [639]
Saga of a commerical educator. No imprint. 142 p. MnHi. Dane in Minnesota who operated a business school.

Branstetter, Peter L., b. 1825. [640]
Life and travels. St. Joseph: Messenger of peace, 1913. 203 p. Auto., p. 103-129. MoHi. Clergyman of the "Primitive Baptist" Church in Missouri.

Brashear, John Alfred, 1840- [641]
1920. The autobiography of a man who loved the stars. Boston: Houghton Mifflin, 1925. 262 p. WU. Astronomer.

Bratt, John, 1842-1918. [642]
Trails of yesterday. Chicago: University pub. co., 1921. 302 p. WHi. Pioneer cattleman in Nebraska.

Bray, Henry Truro, 1846-1922. [643]
Evolution of a life...Chicago: Holt, 1890. 436 p. DLC. Mid-Western Episcopal priest who left the priesthood in 1889 because of his evolving ideas.

Breakenridge, William M, 1846- [644]
1931. Helldorado. Boston &N.Y.: Houghton Mifflin, 1928. 256 p. DLC. Wisconsin boyhood. Member 3d Colorado Cavalry, Civil War. Railroad brakeman, prospector, and deputy sheriff in Southwest.

Breaux, Daisy (pseud.). See Calhoun, Cornelia Donovan (O'Donovan).

Breck, Samuel, 1771-1862. [645]
Recollections...Phila.: Porter & Coates, 1877. 316 p. WHi. Boston merchant. The pages relating to Philadelphia (213-316) are scarcely autobiographical.

Bredow, Paul. Erinnerungen [646]
aus dem leben und wirken eines amerikanisch-lutherischen pastors. Waterloo, Iowa: Im Selbstverlage des verfassers, 1904. 231 p. NN.

Lutheran minister in Iowa.

Breed, J. Howard, b. 1849. [647] A narrative...Norristown: 1932. 23 p. Ia-HA. Pennsylvania merchant and salesman.

Breitmann, Hans (pseud.). See Leland, Charles Godfrey.

Brekhus, Edward, 1872-1921. [648] Edward Brekhus...Minneapolis: 1897. 28 p. DLC. Lutheran lay preacher in Minnesota beginning with 1890. The author was born in Norway.

Brent, Joseph Lancaster, 1826- [649] 1905. Memoirs of the war between the states. New Orleans: Fontana, 1940. 238 p. DLC. Louisiana lawyer moves to California in 1850 and becomes member of the legislature. Served in 1862 under Johnston as officer in Army of Northern Virginia.

Brent, Linda. See Jacobs, Mrs. Harriet (Brent).

Brereton, Robert Mailland, [650] b. 1834? Reminiscences of an old English civil engineer, 1858-1908. Portland, Oreg.: Irwin-Hudson co., 1908. 111 p. Auto., p. 7-46. DLC. In the United States 1871-86 and from 1889-1908.

Bretz, Alice. I begin again. [651] N.Y.: McGraw-Hill, 1940. 201 p. WU. The experiences of a woman who was struck by blindness.

Brevig, Peder C., b. 1840. [652] En nordmands oplevelser i Norge og i Amerika. Decorah: Anundsen, 1927. 15 p. MnSL. Minnesota farmer.

Brewer, Charles, 1804-1885. [653] Reminiscences. N.p.: Jamaica Plains, 1884. 67 p. CSmH. Merchant in Mass. and Hawaii. Sea captain.

Brewer, Lucy. See Webb, Mrs. Eliza (Bowen).

Brewer, Nicholas Richard, [654] 1857-1949. Trails of a paintbrush. Boston: Christopher, 1938. 372 p. NN. Landscape and portrait painter in Minnesota and New York.

Brewer-Bonebright, Mrs. Sarah. See Bonebright, Mrs. Sarah (Brewer).

Brice, James. Reminiscences [655] of ten years experience on the western plains...Kansas City, Mo.: 1905? 24 p. TxU. Mail carrier on the Santa Fe trail.

Bridge, Norman. The marching [656] years. N.Y.: Duffield, 1920. 292 p. WU. Editor and publisher of medical journals. Chicago physician.

Bridgman, Helen (Bartlett), [657] 1855-1935. Within my horizon. Boston: Small, Maynard & co., 1920. 262 p. NN. Peoples and places seen by a woman journalist; literary and social life of New York.

Briggs, Caroline Clapp, 1822- [658] 1895. Reminiscences and letters. Boston: Houghton Mifflin, 1897. 415 p. Auto., p. 1-55. WU. The story of her youth in the days before the Civil War.

Briggs, Edward Page, b. 1839. [659] Fifty years on the road. Phila.: Lyon & Armor, 1911. 147 p. DLC. New York travelling salesman (hardware) in the south and west to Missouri.

Briggs, Joshua Ely, 1841-1939. [660] A pioneer Missourian. Boston: Christopher, 1939. 150 p. DLC. Civil War experiences. Missouri farmer and stock raiser.

Briggs, Lloyd Vernon, 1863-1941. [661] Experiences of a medical student in Honolulu, and on the island of Oahu, 1881. Boston: David D. Nickerson, 1926. 251 p. NN. The writer served as Deputy Vaccination Officer.

Briney, William Newton, b. 1865. [662] The years of yesterday, a sermon...Louisville: 1945. 8 p. MoCanD. Member of the Christian Church in Kentucky and Missouri.

Brinkerhoff, Roeliff, 1828-1911. [663] Recollections of a life-time. Cinc.: Robert Clarke co., 1900. 448 p. WHi. Ohio lawyer, banker, penologist. Officer with the Northern forces during the Civil War.

Brinton, John Hill, 1832-1907. [664] Personal memoirs of John H. Brinton...N.Y.: Neale, 1914. 361 p. WHi. Surgeon in the Union army.

Brisbane, Albert, 1809-1890. [665] Albert Brisbane: a mental biography...Boston: Arena, 1893. 377 p. WU. Author, lecturer, social reformer, chiefly in New York.

Bristol, Sherlock, b. 1815. [666] The pioneer preacher...N.Y. & Chicago: Revell, 1887. 330 p. WHi. Congregational clergyman in Ohio, Wisconsin, Idaho, Oregon and especially California.

Bristow, Gwen, b. 1903. [667] Gwen Bristow...Phila.: Crowell, 1940. 13 p. WHi. A publisher's blurb written by a novelist.

Britten, Emma Hardinge. [668] Autobiography...London: John Heywood, 1900. 275 p. MWA. English spiritualist who spent considerable time in the United States prior to and during the Civil War.

Britton, Nan, b. 1896. [669] The President's daughter. N.Y.: Elizabeth Ann Guild, 1927. 437 p. WHi. Harding's alleged mistress.

Britton, Nan, b. 1896. [670] Honesty or politics. N.Y.: Elizabeth Ann Guild, 1932. 374 p. Auto., p. 3-337. MWA. An explanation of why she wrote her first book and a description of her life since that time.

Brockway, Beman, b. 1815. [671] Fifty years in journalism... Watertown: Daily times pr. & pub. house, 1891. 426, 67 p. WHi. Autobiography found in the supplementary pages 1-67. New York State journalist.

Brockway, Sylvia. Sarah and I. [672] N.Y.: E. P. Dutton, 1944. 243 p. NN. Sketches of life in New York, London, and Littleton, N.H. by the author of "Respectfully Yours, Annie".

Brockway, Zebulon Reed, 1827- [673] 1920. Fifty years of prison service...N.Y.: Charities publication committee, 1912. 437 p. WHi. Prison reformer in New York and Michigan.

Broderick, Henry. First person [674] singular. Seattle: pr. by Frank McCaffrey, 1943. 55 p. Wa. Publisher of Seattle directory. Mining in Alaska in 20th century.

Brolaski, Harry. Easy money. [675] Cleveland: Searchlight press, 1911. 328 p. DLC. Gambler.

Bromfield, Louis, b. 1896. [676] Pleasant valley. N.Y.: Harper, 1943. 302 p. WU. A novelist tells of his life as a farmer in Ohio.

Bromley, George Tisdale. The [677] long ago and the later on... San Francisco: A. M. Robertson, 1904. 289 p. WHi. U. S. Consul at Tien-tsin. Port Warden, San Francisco.

Bromley, Joseph. Clear the [678] tracks. N.Y.: Whittlesey, 1943. 288 p. WHi. Locomotive engineer, Lackawanna Road.

Bronson, Edgar Beecher, 1856- [679] 1917. Reminiscences of a ranchman. New rev. ed. Chicago: A. C. McClurg, 1910. 370 p. WHi. In Wyoming.

Brooke, Francis Taliaferro, 1763-[680] 1851. A narrative of my life... Richmond: MacFarlane & Fergusson, printers, 1849. 90 p. WHi. Soldier in the War of the Revolution. Lawyer and state judge.

Brooke, Mary Coffin, b. 1833. [681] Memories of eighty years. N.Y.: Knickerbocker press, 1916. 232 p. WHi. School teacher in Maryland.

Brooke, Mildred Crewe. See Hoover, Mrs. Mildred (Brooke).

Brookes, George S. Thank you, [682] America. The tribute of an Englishman. N.Y.: Dodd, Mead, 1940. 199 p. WHi. Congregational clergyman, born in England.

Brooks, Bryant Butler, b. 1861. [683] Memoirs...cowboy, trapper, lumberman, stockman, oilman, banker, and Governor of Wyoming. Glendale: 1939. 370 p. WHi. Frontier account.

Brooks, Elisha, b. 1841. "Sketch [684] of the life of Elisha Brooks (In his. A pioneer mother in California. San Francisco: Harr Wagner, 1922). p. 37-61. CSmH. An account of a pioneer youth in California.

Brooks, James J., The [685] adventures of a United States detective...Phila.: Souder, 1876. 348 p. MnU. Among the whiskey stills. Fictional?

Brooks, John, b. 1792. [686] The life and times...Nashville: William Cameron, printer, 1848. 175 p. Auto., 7-110. TxDaM. Methodist clergyman in Tennessee.

Brooks, Josephine (Hayden), 1836-[687] 1919. Memories of a busy life. N.p.: 1921. 19 p. Whi. Farmer's wife on the Wisconsin frontier in the fifties.

Brooks, Virginia, b. 1886. [688] My battles with vice. N.Y.: Macaulay, 1915. 248 p. DLC. Crusader against vice in Chicago area.

Brooks, Walter, 1856-1933. [689] A child and a boy. N.Y.: Brentano's, 1915. 127 p. DLC. Story of youthful days, evidently in New England.

Brooks, William Myron, b. 1835. [690] Glimpses of four score years. Los Angeles: 1915. 59 p. CSmH. Founder of the Tabor Literary Institute, 1857. (Location of the Institute not given).

Brotherhead, William. [691] Forty years among the old booksellers at Philadelphia... Phila.: A. P. Brotherhead, 1891. p. 3-21. WHi. Bookseller.

Brougham, John, 1810-1880. [692] Life, stories and poems of John Brougham. Boston: James Osgood, 1881. 461 p. WHi. Pages 15-62 contain a fragmentary autobiography of his life in Ireland. Later experiences as a New York actor and playwriter summarized, p. 63-66.

Broun, William Leroy, 1827- [693] 1902. Dr. William Leroy Brown. Comp. by Thomas C. Brown, N.Y.: Neale, 1912. 247 p. DLC. Pages 3-11 contain his experiences up to 1885. Teacher of mathematics in southern colleges. President of Alabama Polytechnic Institute.

Brower, Charles D., b. 1863. [694] Fifty years below zero...N.Y.: Dodd, Mead, 1942. 310 p. DLC. Whaler, hunter, trader in the Arctic Circle in Alaska.

Brown, Allen Henry, b. 1820. [695] A pioneer of southern New Jersey...Phila.: Allen, Lane & Scott, 1901. 233 p. Auto., p. 13-26. WHi. Presbyterian clergyman in New Jersey.

Brown, Alonzo F., b. 1836. [696] Autobiography. No imprint, 1922? OrHi. Merchant in Mass. and N.Y. Farmer, freighter, rancher, merchant in Oregon.

Brown, Andrew, 1748-1813. [697] A letter concerning family history. Albany: J. Munsell, 1860. 12 p. DLC. Farmer in Pennsylvania who left New England in 1788.

Brown, Azariah. A life sketch [698] of King Azariah Brown...Hudson, N.Y.: Published by the author, 1898. 69 p. Auto., 3-58. DLC. Negro itinerant preacher in New York.

Brown, Belle (Scott). [699] Grandmother Belle remembers. San Antonio: Naylor, 1941. 119 p. DLC. On a Texas ranch.

Brown, Benjamin, b. 1794. [700] Testimonies for the truth: a record of manifestations of the power of God, miraculous and providential, witnessed in the travels and experience of Benjamin Brown, high priest in the Church of Jesus Christ of Latter-Day Saints...Liverpool: S. W. Richards, 1853. 32 p. NN. Experiences of a Mormon elder in New Brunswick, Nauvoo, and Utah, until his departure on a mission to England.

Brown, Burdette Boardman, [701] b. 1871. Brown goes. N.Y.: Fleming H. Revell, 1936. 144 p. NN. A Methodist minister in Connecticut and New York, who was also active in charitable work of the demonimation.

Brown, Charles E., 1813-1901. [702] Personal recollections, 1813-1893...Ottumwa: Stamp works press, 1907. 222, 21 p. Auto., p. 1-101. WHi. Baptist clergyman in Iowa and Illinois.

Brown, Charles P. The life [703] story of...a Boomer railroad man. Whittier, Calif.: priv. pr., 1929. 450 p. DLC. As described by the title.

Brown, Charles Reynolds. [704] My own yesterdays. N.Y.: Century, 1936. 332 p. WHi. California Congregational clergyman, later Dean of the Divinity School at Yale.

Brown, Charles William, 1858- [705] 1928. My ditty bag. Boston: Small, Maynard, 1925. 282 p. DLC. New England sea captain.

Brown, Ebenezer Lakin, 1808- [706] 1899. Autobiographical notes... Schoolcraft, Mich.: 1906. 56 p. MiU-H. Michigan farmer, banker and politician. Life on the frontier.

Brown, Elijah P., b. 1842. [707]
From nowhere to Beulahland...
Chicago: Winona, 1904. 167 p.
DLC. Publisher of religious
newspaper in Midwest. Record
of his conversion.

Brown, Mrs. Frank Townley. [708]
Society's mountaineer, by Brown
Glasgow (pseud.). Louisville:
Morton, 1931. 162 p. KyBgW.
Social life in Kentucky mountains
in the years 1900-1930.

Brown, Frederic Kenyon, b. 1882. [709]
Through the mill...Boston:
Pilgrim press, 1911. 289 p. DLC.
English immigrant's life as a
mill hand in Massachusetts.

Brown, Frederic Kenyon, b. 1882. [710]
Through the school, the experience of a mill boy in securing
an education. By Al Priddy
(pseud.). Boston: Pilgrim press,
1912. 404 p. DLC. In Massachusetts. The names of persons and
places are fictitious.

Brown, George, b. 1792. [711]
Recollections of itinerant life
...2d ed. Cinc.: R. W. Carroll,
1866. 456 p. WHi. Methodist in
Maryland, Ohio and Pennsylvania.

Brown, George Washington, [712]
b. 1828. Old times in oildom.
Being a series of chapters in
which are related the writer's
many personal experiences, during fifty years of life in the oil
regions. Youngsville, Pa.: The
author, 1909. 196 p. NN. By a
lumber dealer in Oil City.

Brown, Glenn, 1854-1932. [713]
1860-1930; memories by Glenn
Brown. Washington: Press of
W. F. Roberts, 1931. 585 p. NN.
Architect who devoted his energies to the development of Washington. Personal reminiscences
of artists and officials participating in the campaign for the
improvement of the city.

Brown, Harriett Marshall. See
Brown, Mrs. Frank Townley.

Brown, Henry Billings, 1836- [714]
1913. Memoir...by Charles A.
Kent. N.Y.: Duffield, 1915. 136 p.
Auto., p. 1-33. WHi. Michigan
lawyer and Supreme Court
justice.

Brown, Henry Collins. A mind [715]
mislaid. N.Y.: Dutton, 1937. 219 p.
WU. Story of recovery from a
nervous breakdown.

Brown, Horace F. The inventions [716]
of Horace F. Brown. San Francisco?: n.d. 27 p. MtHi. Mining
engineer, metallurgist, in California, Nevada, Montana.

Brown, Jacob, b. 1843. [717]
Jakey Brown...Denver: Acme,
1909. 52 p. Auto, p. 5-27, CoD.
Lay worker in the Methodist
Church. Railroad engineer in
middle Atlantic states.

Brown, James Stephens, b. 1828. [718]
California gold...Oakland:
Pacific press, 1894. 20 p. DLC.
At Sutter's Mill when gold was
discovered.

Brown, James Stephens, b. 1828. [719]
Life of a pioneer...Salt Lake
City: Pr. by Cannon & sons, 1900.
510 p. WHi. Mormon missionary.
Gold mining with Sutter in California. Indian fighter, and military
service in the War with Mexico.

Brown, John (slave). [720]
Slave life in Georgia...London:
W. M. Watts, 1855. 250 p. WHi.
Probably fictitious, and surely
ghost written.

Brown, John, 1800-1859. [721]
The public life...with an autobiography of his childhood and
youth. Boston: Thayer & Eldridge,
1860. p. 24-35. NN. As described by
the title.

Brown, John, b. 1817. [722]
The mediumistic experiences of
the medium of the Rockies...Des
Moines: Moses Hull, 1887. 167 p.
CSmH. Spiritualist.

Brown, John, 1820-1896. [723]
Autobiography of pioneer...
Salt Lake City: John Zimmerman
Brown, 1941. 468 p. DLC. Mormon
missionary in South. Member
territorial legislature of Utah.

Brown, John, b. 1843. [724]
Twenty-five years a parson in
the wild west, by Ralph Riley
(pseud.). Fall River: 1896. 215 p.
WHi. Presbyterian clergyman
in Nevada and Texas.

Brown, John E., b. 1869. [725]
From outcast to pastor. Brooklyn:
1908. 200 p. NBLiHi. Clergyman
in New York.

Brown, Kate (Montrose) Eldon. [726]
An autobiography. Sacramento:
Russell & Winterburn, printers,
1866. 24 p. CLU. Housewife in

New York and California. Covers 1815-1865.

Brown, Louisa, 1812-1886. [727]
Reminiscences...Nevada, Iowa: Representative print, 1898. 60 p. IaDm. Early life on a farm in New York.

Brown, Maria Dean (Foster), [728] 1827-1929. Grandmother Brown's hundred years, 1827-1927, by Harriet Connor Brown...Boston: Little, Brown &co., 1929. 369 p. WHi. The life of a farm family in Iowa as related by Grandmother Brown.

Brown, Olympia. See Willis, Mrs. Olympia Brown.

Brown, Philip F. [729]
Reminiscences of the war, 1861-1865. Blue Ridge Springs: 1912. 53 p. WHi. Confederate soldier.

Brown, Phillip Perry, 1790-1862. [730]
"Extracts from the autobiography of Rev. Phillip Perry Brown" (In Personal Recollections of Charles E. Brown. Ottumwa: 1907).p. 179-209. WHi. Baptist clergyman in New York.

Brown, Sanford Miller, b. 1855. [731]
The school of experience. Kansas City, Mo.: The Western Baptist pub. co., 1933. 217 p. MoK. Baptist clergyman in Missouri.

Brown, Tarleton, 1757-1846. [732]
Memoirs of...a captain in the Revolutionary army, ed. by Charles I. Bushnell. N.Y.: 1862. 65 p. WHi. As described by the title.

Brown, Thomas Henderson, [733] 1837-1922. The romance of everyday life. Mitchell, South Dakota: Educator supply co., 1923. 155 p. DLC. Service as secret service man in Civil War. Banker and railroad executive in South Dakota.

Brown, William. America. A [734] four year's residence...Leeds: 1849. 108 p. DLC. Englishman's experiences as tavern keeper in Ohio.

Brown, William. The [735] adventures of an American doughboy. Tacoma: Smith-Kinney, 1919. 77 p. DLC. World War I.

Brown, William Adams, b. 1865. [736]
Teacher and his times...N.Y.: Scribner, 1940. 375 p. WHi. Teacher at Union Theological Seminary.

Brown, William Carey, b. 1859. [737]
Abstract of military record... No imprint. 52 p. CoU. West Pointer. Indian fighting in Arizona, Montana, Idaho, Oregon, Washington. War with Spain. In Mexico in 1914.

Brown, William J.,b. 1814. [738]
The life of William J. Brown, of Providence, R.I. Providence: Angell & co., prtrs., 1883. 230 p. NN. The writer was a free colored man, active in Negro Baptist church affairs in Rhode Island.

Brown, William Montgomery, [739] b. 1855. My heresy...Galion: Bradford-Brown, 1926. 273 p. WHi. The story of his conviction. By a Bishop in the Episcopal church in Arkansas.

Brown, Willis M., b. 1856. [740]
From infidelity to Christianity. Moundsville, W.Va.: Gospel trumpet co., 1904. 349 p. DLC. Member of a pentacostal sect in Kentucky, West Virginia, Illinois. Evangelist.

Browne, Junius Henri, 1833-1902. [741]
Four years in Secessia...Hartford: O. D. Case, 1865. 450 p. WHi. War correspondent for the N.Y. Tribune tells of his military experiences and imprisonment in the South.

Brownell, Thomas Church, 1779- [742] 1865. Autobiography of the Bishop elect (Eben Edwards Beardsley, History of the Episcopal church in Connecticut. N.Y.: Hurd & Houghton, 1868.) Vol. II, p. 189-199. MiD-B. Covers to 1858. Episcopalian minister in Conn. and professor in New York.

Browning, Meshach, b. 1781. [743]
Fourty-four years of the life of a hunter...Phila.: Lippincott, 1864. 400 p. WHi. In the Allegheny Mountains.

Browning, William Garritson, [744] 1825-1910. Grace magnified; incidents in the life, ministry, experiences and travels... N.Y.: Published for the author by Palmer & Hughes, 1887. 451 p. DLC. Methodist clergyman in New York.

Browning, William Garritson, [745]

1825-1910. A few more words. Poughkeepsie: A. V. Haight, 1902. 173 p. NjMD. See the previous entry.

Browning, William Garritson, [746] 1825-1910. Once again. Poughkeepsie: A. V. Haight, 1905. 198 p. NN. See the two previous entries.

Brownlow, William G., 1805- [747] 1877. Helps to the story of Presbyterianism, to which is added a brief account of the life and battles of the author. Knoxville: 1834. 299 p. NcWatC. Methodist clergyman and later governor of Tennessee.

Brownson, Orestes Augustus, [748] 1803-1876. The convert; or, leaves from my experience. N.Y.: Dunigan, 1857. 450 p. WU. A literary figures tells of his conversion to Catholicism.

Bruce, Henry Clay. The new [749] man. Twenty-nine years a slave. Twenty-nine years a free man. York, Pa.: P. Anstadt, 1895. 172 p. NN. Merchant and government employee in Kansas and the District of Columbia.

Bruce, William Cabell, 1860- [750] 1946. Recollections, by William Cabell Bruce, former United States senator from Maryland ... Baltimore: King bros., 1936. 195 p. NN. Early life in Virginia; education at the University of Virginia; law practice in Baltimore.

Bruce, William George, b. 1856. [751] I was born in America. Milwaukee: Bruce, 1937. 405 p. WHi. Advertising manager of the Milwaukee Sentinel, and publisher of the American School Board Journal. Unsuccessful candidate for political office.

Bruell, James D. Sea memories. [752] Biddeford Pool, Me.: Pub. by author, 1886, 67 p. DLC. Fisherman off the coast of Maine. Naval service during the Mexican campaign.

Bruffey, George A., b. 1842. [753] Eighty-one years in the West. Butte, Mont.: The Butte miner co., printers, 1925. 152 p. WHi. Gold mining in Nevada and Montana.

Bruner, Peter, b. 1845. [754] A slave's adventures toward freedom...Oxford, Ohio: 1930? 54 p. KyBgW. From slavery in Kentucky to janitor at Miami University in Ohio.

Brunson, Alfred, 1793-1886. [755] A western pioneer. Cinc.: Hitchcock & Walden, 1872-79. 2 vols. WHi. Chaplain in the Civil War. Pioneering Methodist clergyman in the midwest.

Brunt, Jonathan, b. 1760. [756] A few particulars of the life of Jonathan Brunt...3d ed. Printed by the author, 1797. 8 p. DLC. Travelling bookseller.

Brunt, Jonathan, b. 1760. [757] The little medley...Knoxville: 1809. 16 p. DLC. See the preceding item.

Brunton, David William, b. 1849. [758] Technical reminiscences...N.Y.: 1915. 23 p. NN. The writer in his early days was a mining engineer in Colorado.

Brush, Daniel Harmon, 1813-1890. [759] ...Growing up with Southern Illinois, 1820 to 1861...ed. by Milo Milton Quaife...Chicago: The Lakeside press, 1944. 265 p. DLC. Business (milling, banking) and politics. One of the founders of what is today Southern Illinois University.

Brush, Katharine, b. 1902. [760] This is on me. N.Y.: Farrar & Rinehart, 1939. 436 p. WU. Novelist, chiefly in New York.

Bryan, Mary (Norcott), 1841-1925. [761] A grandmother's recollection of Dixie. New Bern: Owen G. Dunn, printer, 1912? 43 p. Nc. Life on a North Carolina plantation prior to and during the Civil War.

Bryan, Mary (Norcott), 1841-1925. [762] Echoes from the past. New Bern: Priv. pr., 1921. 48 p. NcU. Family life of a North Carolina matron.

Bryan, Roger Bates, b. 1860. [763] Average American army officer. San Diego: Buck-Molina co., printers, 1914. 166 p. DLC. Army officer who served at various frontier posts in the West, and in the War with Spain.

Bryan, William Jennings, 1860- [764] 1925. The memoirs of William Jennings Bryan...Phila.: J. C. Winston, 1925. 560 p. Auto., p. 15-208. DLC. Early law practice in Illinois and Nebraska, and political activities to the election of 1912.

Bryant, Billy. Children of Ol' [765] Man River; the life and times of a show-boat trouper. N.Y.: Lee Furman, 1936. 303 p. NN. As described by the title.

Buchanan, James, 1791-1863. [766] Autobiographical sketch, 1791-1828 (In his, Works. Phila.: Lippincott, 1908-11.) Vol. 12, p. 287-320. WHi. Tells of legal training, political experiences in Pa.; election to Congress. Closes about 1830.

Buchanan, Joseph Ray, 1851-1924. [767] The story of a labor agitator. N.Y.: Outlook, 1903. 461 p. WU. Labor leader, editor of labor newspaper in Colorado.

Buck, Beaumont Bonaparte. [768] Memories of peace and war. San Antonio: Naylor, 1935. 238 p. WHi. Army officer tells of war with Spain and his services in the first World War.

Buck, Charles Nicholas, 1775- [769] 1851. Memoirs...Phila.: Walnut house, 1941. 209 p. CU. German born merchant in Philadelphia.

Buck, Frank. All in a lifetime. [770] N.Y.: McBridge, 1941. 277 p. WU. In Chicago as agent for vaudeville shows. Then to his better known career as taker of wild animals.

Buck, J. R., b. 1870. [771] A convert pastor's autobiography. Huntington, Ind.: Our Sunday Visitor press, 1942. 96 p. Or. Teacher in North Dakota, Minnesota. Farm worker in Oregon and Washington. Converted to Catholicism and becomes a priest in Oregon.

Buck, Pearl S., b. 1892. [772] An autobiographical sketch. John Day: n.d. 8 p. Nv. The novelist's life to about 1931.

Buckingham, Goodsell, b. 1810. [773] Autobiography...N.Y.: Wynkoop & Hallenbeck, printers, 1884? 46 p. MoK. Merchant in Ohio, Illinois and Missouri. Abolitionist. Methodist clergyman in Ohio.

Buckingham, Joseph Tinker, [774] 1779-1861. Personal memoirs and recollections of editorial life. Boston: Ticknor, Reed & Fields, 1852. 2 vols. WHi. Editor of the New England Galaxy and of the Boston Courier.

Buckley, George Wright, b. 1850. [775] Evolution of an American. Los Angeles: Wetzel pub. co., 1935. 484 p. NN. Unitarian minister. Comments on life and persons met in the course of his career.

Buckskin Mose. See Hawley, Curtis B.

Buckskin Sam. See Noble, Samuel H.

Buehler, Fannie J. [776] Recollections of the Rebel invasion and one woman's experience during the Battle of Gettysburg. Gettysburg: Star and sentinel pr., 1900. 29 p. CSmH. As described by the title.

Buenzle, Fred J. [777] Bluejacket; an autobiography. N.Y.: W. W. Norton, 1939. 355 p. WHi. Chief yeoman, U.S. Navy. Tells of the last days of sailing ships.

Buford, Harry T. (alias). See Velazquez, Loreta Janeta.

Bulger, J.W. Memoirs and [778] historical jottings. Davenport, Iowa: n.p., 1939. 25 leaves. IaHi. Youth on Iowa farm in fifties and sixties. Catholic priest in Iowa.

Bulkley, L. Duncan. [779] "Ebenezer"...notes on a busy life. N.p.: priv. pr., 1925. 63 p. MWA. New York doctor tells of his lay work for the Presbyterian church.

Bull, Sidney A., b. 1847. [780] Autobiography and genealogy... North Chelmsford, Mass.: Picken printing co., 1937. 230 p. DLC. Postmaster, farmer, storekeeper, insurance agent in Massachusetts.

Bullard, Asa, 1804-1888. [781] Fifty years with the Sabbath schools. Boston: Lockwood, Brooks & co., 1876. 336 p. Auto.,p. 11-28. MWA. Agent of the Massachusetts Sabbath School Society. Congregational minister.

Bullard, Asa, 1804-1888. [782] Incidents in a busy life. Boston & Chicago: Congregational Sunday school & publishing society, 1888. 235 p. DLC. See the previous entry.

Bullene, Lathrop, 1826-1915. [783] Lathrop Bullene...N.p.: priv. pr.,

1916. 73 p. Auto. p.3-43. KHi. Youth in Wisconsin on homestead. To Kansas where he becomes a merchant. The story closes with 1885.

Bullet, Emma, 1842-1914. [784]
Autobiography. Brooklyn: Eagle Library, 1906. 45 p. DLC. Paris correspondent for the Brooklyn Daily Eagle. Teacher of French in Ohio.

Bullitt, Thomas Walker, b. 1838. [785]
My life at Oxmoor. Louisville: Morton, 1911. 132 p. Auto., p. 26-94. WHi. The life of a youth on a Kentucky farm prior to the Civil War.

Bumpass, Mrs. F. M. [786]
Autobiography and journal. Nashville: Publishing house of the M. E. Church, South, 1899. 82 p. Auto., p. 29-39. Nc. Teacher and lay church worker in North Carolina.

Bunce, D. S., b. 1838. [787]
From gambling table to pulpit... Chicago: Christian witness co., 1909. 158 p. Ia-Ha. Evangelical worker in Iowa.

Bunkley, Josephine M. [788]
Miss Bunkley's book. The testimony of an escaped novice from the Sisterhood of St. Joseph, Emmettsburg, Maryland, the mother-house of the Sisters of Charity in the United States. N.Y.: Harper, 1855. 338 p. NN. As described by the title.

Bunn, Mathew, b. 1772? [789]
Narrative...ed. 7, rev. Batavia: 1828. 59 p. WHi. The author fought against the Indians near Ohio; was captured and escaped to the British post in Detroit; finally, he escaped from the British, and in 1795 returned to Massachusetts.

Bunnell, David C., b. 1793. [790]
The travels and adventures of David C. Bunnell...together with ten years' service in the Navy of the United States. Palmyra, N.Y.: E. B. Grandin, 1831. 199 p. DLC. Seaman who served in the War of 1812.

Bunton, Mary Taylor. [791]
A bride on the old Chisholm trail in 1886. San Antonio: Naylor, 1939. 77 p. TxU. The wife of a rancher in Texas.

Burbank, Elbridge Ayer, b. 1858. [792]
Burbank among the Indians. Caldwell, Idaho: Caxton, 1944. 232 p. OkHi. Painter of Indians.

Burbank, Luther, 1859-1926. [793]
The harvest of the years. Boston: Houghton Mifflin, 1927. 296 p. WU. California naturalist. Breeder of plants.

Burge, William, b. 1842. [794]
Through the Civil war and western adventures. Lisbon, Iowa: N.D. 85 p. IaHi. Union army soldier. Freighter on route from Nebraska to Fort Laramie.

Burgess, Daniel Maynard, b. 1828. [795]
Personal and professional recollections. N.Y.: 1911. 100 p. NN. Physician in New York.

Burgess, John, b. 1821. [796]
Pleasant recollections...Cinc.: Printed for the author, 1887. 460 p. WHi. Methodist clergyman in Ohio.

Burgess, John, b. 1821. [797]
A voice from the past; fifty years' echo. Cinc.: Pr. by Cranston & Curts, 1894. 32 p. IaHi. See preceding entry.

Burgess, John William, 1844-1931. [798]
Reminiscences of an American scholar...N.Y.: Columbia Univ. press, 1934. 430 p. WU. Concludes with 1907. Professor of political science at Amherst and Columbia.

Burgess, Mary Curtis, b. 1834. [799]
A true story. Lincoln, Nebr.: priv. pr., 1907? 93 p. WHi. Life on a Virginia plantation during the Civil War.

Burk, Mrs. Martha (Cannary). [800]
Life and adventures...No imprint. 7 p. MtHi. First published about 1896. Scout for Custer in the Dakotas and Wyoming and rider for the pony express.

Burk, William Herbert, 1867-1933. [801]
Making a museum; the confessions of a curator. No imprint, 1926? 86 p. DLC. Founder and curator of the Valley Forge Museum of American History in New Jersey.

Burke, John William, 1826-1898. [802]
Autobiography; chapters from the life of a preacher. Macon: Burne, 1884. 214 p. ICN. Itinerant Methodist clergyman in Georgia.

Burke, Paul, b. 1911. [803]
Adventures of a farm boy. Omaha: 1942. NbU. Farm laborer and salesman in Nebraska and other

Burkholder, Wealthy A. (Clark), [804]
b. 1819. Some things I remember. Rockton, Pa.: Keystone, 1928. 24 p. DLC. Life on a Pennsylvania farm. Lay worker for Brethren Church (Dunkard) including editorship of church newspaper.

Burkman, John. [805]
Old neutriment, by Glendolin Damon Wagner. Boston: Ruth Hill, 1934. 256 p. Found in private library of Robert Griffen of Reno, Nev. Burkman served with Custer.

Burks, Arthur J. [806]
Land of checkerboard families. N.Y.: Coward-McCann, 1932. 278 p. DLC. Marine officer in Dominican Republic, 1921-23.

Burlend, Mrs. Rebecca, 1793- [807]
1872. ...A true picture of emigration, ed. by Milo M. Quaife. Chicago: Lakeside press, 1936. 167 p. WHi. Story of a woman who with her husband and children settled in Illinois in 1831. An account of domestic life on the frontier.

Burn, June. Living high; [808]
an unconventional autobiography. N.Y.: Duell, Sloan & Pearce, 1941. 292 p. NN. Adventures of a happy-go-lucky family; homesteading in Washington; school teaching in Alaska; roaming across the country.

Burnell, W.P. [809]
Recollections of a college beggar by one who was there. Cleveland: 1882. 277 p. DLC. College fund raiser.

Burnett, Peter Hardeman, 1807- [810]
1895. Recollections and opinions of an old pioneer. N.Y.: Appleton, 1880. 448 p. WHi. Pioneer farmer in Oregon. Jurist and political figure in Oregon and California. Governor of California.

Burnham, Frederick Russell, [811]
b. 1861. Scouting on two continents. Garden City: Doubleday, Doran, 1928. 370 p. WHi. Frontier life in the Klondike and in Africa.

Burnham, Jonathan, 1738-1823. [812]
The autobiography of Col. Jonathan Burnham. Salem, Mass.: 1909. 8 p. DLC. Officer in the American revolutionary army. Tavern keeper in Massachusetts.

Burnham, W. H., b. 1839. [813]
Amusing anecdotes...No imprint, 1919? 32 p. MoSHi. Baptist clergyman in Missouri.

Burns, Robert Elliott. [814]
I am a fugitive from a Georgia chain gang. N.Y.: The Vanguard press, 1932. 257 p. NN. As described by the title.

Burris, Martin, b. 1856. [815]
True sketches of the life and travels of Martin Burris on the western plains, the Rocky mountains and the Pacific coast, U.S.A. Salina, Kan.: Padgett, 1910. 67 p. WaS. Pioneer farmer, freighter, logger, railroad laborer.

Burritt, Elihu, 1810-1879. [816]
Ten-minute talks on all sorts of topics. With auto. of the author. Boston: Lee & Shepard, 1874. 360 p. DLC. Blacksmith and farmer in Massachusetts. Active in the peace movement. U.S. Consul in Britain. Author.

Burroughs, John, 1837-1921. [817]
"Autobiographical sketches" (In, Clara Burr's, Our friend John Burroughs. Boston & N.Y.: Houghton Mifflin, 1914). p. 45-147. DLC. His early life on the farm in the Catskills and how he became a nature writer.

Burroughs, John, 1837-1921. [818]
My boyhood. Garden City, N.Y., & Toronto: Doubleday, Page & co., 1922. 247 p. Auto., p. 1-132. NN. Boyhood days in the Catskills.

Burroughs, Stephen. Memoirs... [819]
N.Y.: Dial, 1924. 367 p. WHi. The life of crime in 18th century America.

Burrow, Reuben, 1798-1868. [820]
Medium theology...with autobiographical sketch...Nashville: Cumberland Presbyterian pub. house, 1881. 623 p. Auto., p. 9-18. DLC. Presbyterian clergyman and professor of theology in southeast.

Burrows, John, 1760-1837. [821]
Sketch of the life of Gen. John Burrows...Williamsport, Pa.: 1917. 25 p. DLC. Farmer and County Commissioner in Pa.

Burrows, John McDowell, b. 1814. [822]
Fifty years in Iowa...Davenport, Ia.: Glass & co., printers, 1888. 182 p. WHi. Iowa industrialist.

Burt, Maxwell Struthers. [823]
　The diary of a dude-wrangler.
　N.Y.: Scribner's, 1924. 331 p.
　WHi. In Wyoming.
Burt, Stephen Smith, 1850-1932. [824]
　Recollections and reflections
　chiefly on my boyhood...N.Y.:
　pr. for private distribution,
　1912. 23 p. NN. By a New York
　physician.
Burt, Stephen Smith, 1850-1932. [825]
　Recollections and reflections of
　a quarter of a century. N.Y.:
　Press of Pusey & Troxell, 1899.
　12 p. NN. Medical practice in
　New York City as described by
　a professor of medicine.
Burton, Annie L. [826]
　Memories of childhood's slavery
　days. Boston: Ross, 1909. 97 p.
　DLC. In Alabama during the
　Civil War. Later a cook in Massa-
　chusetts and a restaurant owner
　in Florida.
Burton, Clarence Alan, b. 1857. [827]
　Autobiography...Kansas City,
　Mo.: 1927. 581 leaves. MoK.
　Youth on a pioneer farm in Kan-
　sas. Foundry operator and manu-
　facturer of machinery in Missouri.
Burton, George W., 1858-1941. [828]
　Memoirs...LaCrosse, Wis.:
　priv. pr., 1941. 34 p. WHi. Wis-
　consin banker.
Burton, Gideon, b. 1811. [829]
　Reminiscences...Cinc.: George
　P. Houston, 1895. 152 p. WHi.
　Merchant in Cincinnati and
　Philadelphia.
Burton, James D. (alias). See
　Hanehan, James
Burton, Thomas William, b. 1860. [830]
　What experience has taught me.
　Cincinnati: Press of Jennings
　& Graham, 1910. 126 p. DLC.
　Negro physician and professor
　of medicine in Ohio.
Burton, Warren, 1800-1866. [831]
　The district school as it was, by
　one who went to it. N.Y.: T.Y.
　Crowell, 1928. 171 p. NN. Recol-
　lections of a New Hampshire
　country school in the first quarter
　of the nineteenth century.
Burtscher, William John, b. 1878. [832]
　Romance in a junk shop. Los
　Angeles: Wetzel, 1938. 248 p.
　DLC. Dealer in used goods in
　California.
Burwell, Letita M. [833]
　Plantation reminiscences, by
　Page Thacker (pseud.) N.p.: 1878.
　69 p. WHi. An account of youth
　in Virginia prior to and during
　the Civil War.
Burwick, James Monroe, b. 1853. [834]
　Conductor Jim. N.Y.: Y.M.C.A.
　press, 1908. 172 p. DLC. Railroad
　conductor in the midwest. Evan-
　gelic work among laborers.
Busey, Samuel Clagett, 1828-1901. [835]
　Personal reminiscences and
　recollections of forty-six years'
　membership in the Medical So-
　ciety of the District of Columbia,
　and residence in this city...
　Washington, D.C.: 1895. 373 p.
　NN. As described by the title.
Busey, Samuel Clagett, 1828-1901. [836]
　An autobiographical sketch of
　early life. (In his: A sou-
　venir, with an autobiographical
　sketch of early life and selected
　miscellaneous addresses and
　communications. Washington,
　D.C.: 1896.)p. 18-80. NN.
　Accounts of his boyhood life in
　Maryland.
Bush, Ira Jefferson, b. 1865. [837]
　Gringo doctor. Caldwell, Idaho:
　Caxton, 1939. 261 p. WHi. In
　Texas. Includes his experiences
　in the Mexican revolution.
Bush, Irving T., b. 1869. [838]
　Working with the world. Garden
　City: Doubleday, Doran, 1928.
　315 p. DLC. Operator of ware-
　house terminal in New York.
Bush, Willard C. Pahang. [839]
　N.Y.: Macmillan, 1938. 284 p. NN.
　Adventures of an American rubber
　plantation manager in the Malay
　peninsula.
Butler, Benjamin Franklin, 1818- [840]
　1893. Butler's book...a review
　of his legal, political and military
　career... Boston: Thayer, 1892.
　1037, 1154 p. NN. Mainly his Civil
　War experiences. Also writes of
　legal and political experiences in
　Massachusetts. Congressman,
　governor of Massachusetts.
Butler, Frances L. See
　Leigh, Frances Butler.
Butler, Joseph G., b. 1840. [841]
　Recollections of men & events...
　N.Y.: G. P. Putnam's, 1927. 349 p.
　WHi. Ohio manufacturer of steel.
Butler, Marion Benjamin, [842]
　1834-1914. My story of the Civil

Butler, Nicholas—Byrne, Charles    45    ENTRIES 843-864

war and the under-ground railroad. Huntington, Ind.: United Brethren, 1914. 390 p. WHi. Officer with the Northern forces.

Butler, Nicholas Murray, b. 1862. [843] Across the busy years; recollections and reflections...by Nicholas Murray Butler...N.Y.: C. Scribner's sons, 1939-40. 2 vols. WU. Educator, president of Columbia University.

Butler, Pardee, 1816-1888. [844] Personal recollections of Pardee Butler...Cinc.: Standard, 1889. 346 p. NN. A minister of the Christian Church in Kansas.

Butler, Mrs. Pierce. See Kemble, Frances Anne.

Butler, Richard Joseph, b. 1875. [845] Dock walloper; the story of "Big Dick" Butler. N.Y.: G.P. Putnam's sons, 1933. 276 p. NN. New York City politician and labor leader, particularly of the longshoremen's, ironworkers' and teamsters' unions.

Butler, Smedley D., b. 1881. [846] Old gimlet eye...N.Y.: Farrar & Rinehart, 1933. 310 p. WHi. Officer in the Marine corps.

Butler, William. [847] From Boston to Bareilly and back. N.Y.: Phillips & Hunt, 1885. 512 p. WHi. Methodist missionary in India.

Butler, William Allen, 1825-1902. [848] A retrospect of forty years, 1825-1865. N.Y.: Scribner's, 1911. 442 p. DLC. New York lawyer.

Butler, William R. [849] Behind prison walls. The story of a wasted life. Chicago: M. Stein, 1916. 60 p. KyRE. A life of crime in Kentucky.

Butterfield, A. E., b. 1861. [850] Butterfield, 7 years with the wild Indians. O'Donnell, Texas: 1945. 130 p. TxU. Methodist missionary to Indians in Texas.

Butterfield, Horatio Q. [851] U. S. Christian commission. A delegate's story. No imprint. 8 p. WHi. A chaplain's brief experience with the Union army.

Butterworth, Henry Thomas, [852] b. 1809. Reminiscences and memories of Henry Thomas Butterworth and Nancy Irvin Wales, his wife. Lebanon, Ohio: Lebanon gazette printing company, 1886. 121 p. NN. An Ohio farmer, deeply interested in spiritualism.

Büttner, Johann Carl, b. 1754. [853] Büttner, der Amerikaner... Zweite auflage. Camenz: Krausche, 1828. 137, 126 p. NN. Indentured servant who later fought in the American Revolution.

Butts, D. Gregory Claiborne, [854] b. 1848. From saddle to city by buggy, boat and railway... Richmond: 1922. 549 p. DLC. Methodist itinerant preacher in the southeast.

Buttz, Rachel Q. [855] A hoosier girlhood. Boston: Richard G. Badger, 1924. 208 p. WHi. Begins about 1825, and includes college experiences.

Byers, Samuel Hawkins Marshall. [856] With fire and sword. N.Y.: Neale, 1911. 203 p. WHi. Officer in the Union army.

Byrd, Ann, 1798-1831. [857] Narratives, pious meditations, and religious exercises, of Ann Byrd, late of the city of New York, deceased. 2d ed. Byberry: John Comly, 1844. 138 p. NN. A member of the Society of Friends.

Byrd, Richard Evelyn, b. 1888. [858] Alone. N.Y.: Putnam, 1938. 296 p. WHi. In the Antarctic, 1934.

Byrd, Richard Evelyn, b. 1888. [859] Discovery; the story of the second Byrd antarctic expedition. N.Y.: Putnam, 1934. 405 p. WHi. In 1933.

Byrd, Richard Evelyn, b. 1888. [860] Little America. N.Y.: Putnam, 1930. 422 p. WHi. Antarctic expedition, 1923.

Byrd, Richard Evelyn, b. 1888. [861] Skyward. N.Y.: G. P. Putnam's sons, 1928. 359 p. WHi. Naval aviator and explorer of North Pole.

Byrd, Russell A. [862] Russ's bus; adventures of an American bus driver. Los Angeles: Wetzel, 1945. 200 p. NN. The author was a driver for the Santa Fe Trailways.

Byrne, Bernard James. [863] A frontier army surgeon. Cranford, N.J.: priv. pr., 1935. 160 p. WHi. Colorado in the eighties.

Byrne, Charles Christopher, [864] 1837-1921. Reminiscences of an army surgeon, 1860-1863.

Byrum, Enoch Edwin, b. 1861. [865]
Life experiences. Anderson, Ind.: Gospel trumpet co., 1928. 432 p. DLC. Publisher of newspaper in the midwest. Representative of the United Brethren in Christ.

Byrum, Enoch Edwin, b. 1861. [866]
Travels and experiences in other lands. Moundsville, W.Va.: Gospel trumpet co., 1905. 600 p. DLC. Publisher of a religious newspaper visits the missionaries of the United Brethren in Christ.

Byrum, Isabel Coston, 1870-1938. [867]
Tread of years. Anderson, Ind.: Gospel trumpet co., 1938. 136 p. DLC. Writer for religious periodicals and author of religious books.

## C

Cabell, James Branch, b. 1879. [868]
These restless heads, a trilogy of romantics. N.Y.: R. M. McBride & co., 1932. 253 p. WU. Virginia novelist.

Cady, John Henry, 1846-1927. [869]
Arizona's yesterdays...Priv. pr., 1915. 120 p. WHi. A frontier story of soldiering, cattle raising and farming.

Cahan, Abraham, b. 1860. [870]
Bleter fun mein leben (in Yiddish) N.Y.: Forward association, 1926-31. 5 vols. DLC. Publisher of Yiddish-language newspaper in New York devoted to socialism.

Calamity Jane. See Burk, Mrs. Marthy (Cannary).

Calderwood, George, b. 1848. [871]
Drunk and sober— an autobiography. Columbus, Ohio: Published at the American Prohibitionist steam printing works, 1880. 174 p. NcWatC. Temperance lecturer (Methodist).

Caldwell, Charles, 1772-1853. [872]
Autobiography of Charles Caldwell, M.D. Phila.: Lippincott, Crambo, and co., 1855. 454 p. NN. Practiced medicine in Philadelphia; later founded the Medical Department of Transylvania Univ., Kentucky, and still later taught in the medical department of the present University of Louisville. Editor of the Port Folio, and voluminous writer on medical subjects.

Caldwell, Joseph, 1773-1835. [873]
Autobiography and biography of Rev. Joseph Caldwell, D.D., Ll.D., first president of the University of North Carolina. Chapel Hill: John B. Neathery, 1860. 68 p. NN. Early life in New Jersey and college experiences at Princeton. The autobiography ends with the writer's going to the University of North Carolina.

Calhoun, Cornelia Donovan [874]
(O'Donovan). The autobiography of a chameleon, by Dairy Breaux. Washington: Potomac press, 1930. 407 p. DLC. Social life in Washington, D.C., New Jersey and in the southeast.

Calhoun, Eleanor Hulda. See Lazarovich-Hrebelianovich, Eleanor Hulda (Calhoun).

Calkins, Earnest Elmo, b. 1868. [875]
"Louder please " The autobiography of a deaf man. Boston: Atlantic, 1924. 260 p. WU. As described by the title.

Call, Hughie (Florence), b. 1890. [876]
Golden fleece. Boston: Houghton Mifflin co., 1942. 250 p. DLC. Wife of a Montana sheep rancher.

Callahan, Ethelbert, b. 1829. [877]
The autobiographical sketch of my life... Robinson, Ill.: Argus printing house, 1915. 248 p. IHi. Illinois lawyer.

Callahan, Jack. [878]
Man's grim justice: my life outside the law. N.Y.: J. H. Sears & co., 1928. 296 p. NN. Life of a robber and his efforts to rehabilitate himself.

Callender, William, b. 1838. [879]
Thrilling adventures of William Callender, a Union spy from Des Moines. Des Moines: Mills & co., printers, 1881. 116 p. NN. Scout with Iowa infantry group.

Callison, John James, b. 1855. [880]
Bill James of...Oklahoma... By John James Callison. Kingfisher, Okla.: Priv. pr., 1914. 328 p. WHi. Presumably a dictated autobiography by a cowboy, gold prospector and river pilot.

Calvé, Emma, 1858-1942. [881]
My life...N.Y.: Appleton, 1922.

279 p. DLC. A foreign singer with the Metropolitan opera.

Calvert, Henry Murray. [882]
Reminiscences of a boy in blue. 1862-1865. N.Y.: Putnam's, 1920. 347 p. WHi. As described by the title.

Camden, Charles, b. 1817. [883]
The autobiography...San Francisco: priv. pr., 1916. 173 p. CU-B. Covers 1835 to 1900. English born farmer in Louisiana. Miner in California in fifties. Owner of iron and silver mills.

Cammack, John H., b. 1843. [884]
Personal recollections of Private John Henry Cammack...Huntington, W.Va.: 1923. 164 p. Wv-Ar. Confederate soldier.

Camp, David Nelson, 1820-1916. [885]
...Recollections of a long and active life. New Britain, Conn.: priv. pr., 1917. 96 p. WHi. Connecticut educator.

Camp, Mortimer M. [886]
Life and adventures of a New England boy. New Haven, Conn.: 1893. 129 p. DLC. Youth in New England, including experiences as a whaler in the early 19th century.

Campaigne, Mrs. Edna (Foote), [887]
b. 1888. I'm fifty...Montclair: 1938. 74 p. DLC. Wife of business executive tells of her childhood and of the struggles of early married life in New York and New Jersey.

Campbell, Alexander, b. 1801. [888]
Autobiography of Rev. Alexander Campbell. Watertown, N.Y.: Post printing house, 1883. 288 p. NN. Minister of the Seventh-day Baptist Church, laboring mostly in Rhode Island and New York State.

Campbell, Elgy Vanvoorhis, [889]
b. 1836. A retrospect. No imprint, 1924? 135 p. MnHi. Presbyterian clergyman in Minnesota, beginning with the sixties.

Campbell, George Alexander, [890]
1869-1943. Friends are my story...St. Louis: Bethany, 1944. 252 p. DLC. Prominent clergyman of the Disciples of Christ in the St. Louis area.

Campbell, James Mann, 1840- [891]
1926. Transplanted heather; a Scotch preacher in America.
Garden City, N.Y.: Doubleday, Doran, 1928. 311 p. NN. Congregationalist minister, laboring in Illinois, Wisconsin and California.

Campbell, Malcolm, b. 1839. [892]
Malcolm Campbell, sheriff. By R. B. David. Casper: Wyomingana, inc., 1932. 361 p. DLC. Frontier sheriff in Wyoming during outlaw and rustler days.

Campbell, Sir Malcolm, b. 1885. [893]
My thirty years of speed. London: Hutchinson, 1935. 270 p. DLC. British racer of automobiles some of whose record runs were made in the United States.

Campbell, Mrs. Patrick, 1865- [894]
1940. My life and some letters. N.Y.: Dodd, Mead, 1922. 451 p. DLC. English actress who appeared several times in the United States.

Campbell, Viola (Hutchinson), [895]
b. 1847. Memories of a busy life. Plymouth: Rogers, 1926. 122 p. Auto., p. 11-101. DLC. Member of a family singing group.

Canby, Henry Seidel, b. 1878. [896]
The age of confidence; life in the nineties. N.Y.: Farrar & Rinehart, 1934. 260 p. WU. The literary critic and editor of the Atlantic tells the story of his youth.

Canby, Henry Seidel, b. 1878. [897]
Alma mater; the Gothic age of the American college. N.Y.: Farrar & Rinehart, 1936. 259 p. NN. Life at Yale both as student and teacher.

Canfield, William A. [898]
A history of the army. Experience of William A. Canfield, by himself. Manchester, N.H.: C. F. Livingston, printer, 1869. 34 p. CSmH. Experience in the Union army.

Cannell, Kathleen Biggar (Eaton), [899]
b. 1891. Jam yesterday. N.Y.: Wm. Morrow & co., 1945. 238 p. NN. Reminiscences of childhood in New York City and Ontario.

Cannon, Frank J. [900]
Under the prophet in Utah... Boston: C. M. Clark, 1911. 402 p. CHi. Written down by a second party. The story of his political struggles with the Mormons in Utah by the one-time senator.

Cannon, George Quayle, 1827-1901.[901]

My first mission. Salt Lake City: Juvenile instructor office, 1879. 66 p. DLC. Mormon tells of his experiences on the Sandwich Islands in the fifties.

Cannon, Joseph Gurney, 1836– [902] 1926. Uncle Joe Cannon, the story of a pioneer American... N.Y.: Holt, 1927. 356 p. WHi. Illinois Congressman, Speaker of the House of Representatives.

Cannon, LeGrand Bouton, 1815– [903] 1906. Personal reminiscences of the rebellion, 1861–1866. N.Y.: Burr prntg. house, 1895. 228 p. WHi. Officer in the Union army.

Cannon, Walter Bradford, b. 1871. [904] The way of an investigator, a scientist's experiences in medical research. N.Y.: W. W. Norton, 1945. 229 p. WU. As described by the title.

Canova, Andrew P. [905] Life and adventures in south Florida...Palatka, Florida: The Southern Sun pub. house, 1885. 136 p. DLC. Indian fighter in the fifties, and hunter.

Canright, Dudley Marvin, 1840– [906] 1919. Seventh-Day Adventism renounced...N.Y.: Revell, 1889. 418 p. CBB. Personal experiences (p. 37–58) as a Seventh Day Adventist in New England in the sixties and in the southeastern states in the seventies before becoming a Baptist.

Cantacuzene, Princess, Countess Speransky. See Kantakuzen, Julia Grant.

Canton, Frank M. (pseud.), [907] 1849–1927. Frontier trails. Boston & N.Y.: Houghton Mifflin, 1930. 236 p. DLC. Peace officer's experience with rustlers in Montana and Wyoming.

Cantor, Eddie, b. 1893. [908] My life is in your hands. N.Y.: Harper, 1928. 300 p. NN. Memories of the stage by a singer of popular songs.

Capablanca, José Raúl, 1888– [909] 1942. My chess career. N.Y.: Macmillan, 1920. 212 p. DLC. Cuban chess master. Only about one-third of this book relates to his biography.

Capers, Henry D., 1835–1910. [910] Recollections of the civil service of the Confederate government... Adairsville, Georgia: 1887? 44 p. CSmH. Chief clerk, Confederate government.

Capers, William, 1790–1855. [911] "Recollections"(Life of William Capers, by William M. Wightman. Nashville: Southern Methodist pub. house, 1858). p. 11-228. WHi. Methodist clergyman in the southeast. The account closes with 1820.

Carden, W. Thomas. [912] On the great highway of time (by Tom Noodle, pseud.) Rome: 1942. 120 p. DLC. Boyhood on ranch in Texas. Farmer and teacher in Georgia.

Cardwell, James R., b. 1830. [913] Reminiscences. Portland, Oreg.: 1914. 7 p. OrU. Dentist in Illinois, and after 1852 in Oregon.

Cardwell, Lawrence. [914] Mountain medicine. Caldwell, Idaho: Caxton, 1941. 232 p. DLC. A city dweller's experiences as the owner of a cattle ranch in Arizona.

Carew, Bampfylde-Moore, b. 1693.[915] The life and adventures of the king of the beggars...London: Printed for J. Buckland, 1793. 235 p. WU. A fanciful tale, including experiences in America, by an Englishman.

Cargile, John Abner, b. 1843. [916] The autobiography...Boston: Advent Christian pub. soc., 1891. 477 p. MoS. An Alabama Baptist clergyman who becomes an Adventist and labors in the southeast, Arkansas and Texas.

Carhart, Albert Elijah, b. 1846. [917] A partial life story. N.p.: 1931. 55 p. DLC. Youthful days on Iowa farm, followed by activity as a temperance worker. Methodist clergyman in South Dakota.

Carhart, Alfreda (Post). [918] It happened in Syria. N.Y.: Revell, 1940. 128 p. DLC. The daughter of a missionary relates her youthful days in Syria.

Carhart, John Wesley, 1834–1914. [919] Four years on wheels; or life as a presiding Elder. Oshkosh, Wis.: Allen & Hicks, printers, 1880. 288 p. DLC. Methodist in New York, Wisconsin and Texas.

Carleton, Robert (pseud.) See Hall, Baynard Rush.

Carlson, Earl Reinhold, b. 1897. [920]

Born that way. N.Y.: John Day, 1941. 174 p. WU. By a New York physician who specialized in work with spastic children.

Carmack, George Washington. [921]
My experiences in the Yukon. Seattle: Trade printery, 1933. 16 p. DLC. Gold mining in 1896.

Carnahan, Wallace. [922]
Odd happenings. Jackson, Miss.: Printed for the author by the Tucker printing house, 1915. 149 p. DLC. Episcopalian minister in Kentucky, Mississippi, Arkansas, Alabama and Texas.

Carnegie, Andrew, 1835-1919. [923]
Autobiography...Boston: Houghton Mifflin, 1920. 385 p. WHi. Manufacturer and philanthropist, chiefly in Pennsylvania.

Carnegie, Andrew, 1835-1919. [924]
How I served my apprenticeship as a businessman. Boston: Perry Mason, n.d. 16 p. WHi. His family leaves Scotland. In Pennsylvania he works in factories, delivers telegrams, and then is employed by a railway company where he rises to the position of Division Superintendent.

Carpenter, Albert von Haller, [925]
b. 1822. Glimpses of the life and times of A. v. H. Carpenter. Chicago: Lanward, 1890. 144 p. MiD-B. Manager of passenger department, Chicago, Milwaukee & St. Paul Railway. The author also describes his earlier railroad experiences in New England.

Carpenter, Seymour D., b. 1826. [926]
Genealogical notes...including the autobiography...Springfield, Ill.: Illinois state journal co., printers, 1907. 242 p. Auto., p. 71-172. USIGS. Youthful days in Ohio, and school teaching in Tennessee. Banking, real estate, railroad development in Iowa. Operator of gas works in Illinois.

Carpenter, William W. [927]
Travels and adventures in Mexico ...N.Y.: Harper, 1851. 300 p. DLC. Mexican war experiences.

Carr, Franklin, b. 1846. [928]
Twenty-two years in state prisons. Phila.: Gazette printing house, 1893. 48 p. DLC. Pennsylvania mission worker tells of his life of crime and of his experiences as an Indian fighter in Wyo.

Carr, John, 1827-1896. [929]
Pioneer days in California. Eureka: Times pub. co., 1891. 452 p. WHi. Miner in California in 1850. Later he held various municipal political positions. Most of this book is not autobiographical.

Carr, John, 1827-1896. A vulcan [930] among the Argonauts. San Francisco: G. Fields, 1936. 75 p. DLC. California miner and blacksmith.

Carr, Thomas David, 1846-1879. [931]
Life and confession...St. Clairsville, W.Va.: J. H. Heaton & co., 1870. 46 p. DLC. Service in the Civil War with Union forces. Life of crime in Ohio and West Virginia, leading to his execution for murder.

Carrara, John, b. 1913. [932]
I become an evangelist. West N.Y., N.J.: Landeck press, 1931. 128 p. DLC. Convert from Catholocism tells of his experiences as a Baptist evangelist in New Jersey.

Carrington, Mrs. Frances (Court-[933] ney). My army life. Phila.: J. B. Lippincott, 1910. 318 p. WHi. On the plains in 1866 by the wife of an infantry officer.

Carrington, Mrs. Margaret Irwin. [934]
AB-SA-RA-KA, home of the Crows, being the experiences of an officer's wife on the plains... Phila.: Lippincott, 1869. 284 p. WHi. Indian warfare in the years following 1865.

Carrington, William Thomas, [935]
b. 1854. History of education in Missouri...Priv. pub., 1931. 141 p. Auto., p. 74-141. DLC. Experiences of the state superintendent of schools are related in the second portion of this book.

Carroll, Andrew. [936]
Moral and religious sketches... with incidents of a ten years' itinerancy in the west. Cinc.: pr. for the author, 1857. vol. I. Auto., p. 5-150. TxDaM. The experiences of a Methodist clergyman in Ohio in the years 1835-45.

Carroll, George Ryerson, 1831- [937]
1895. Pioneer life in and around Cedar Rapids, Iowa from 1839 to 1849. Cedar Rapids: 1895. 251 p. DLC. By a farmer in Iowa.

Carson, Mrs. Ann (Baker). [938]
Memoirs of the celebrated and

beautiful Mrs. Anne Carson...
Second ed., rev., enl. ... Phila.:
1838. 2 vols. in 1. DLC. Wife of
naval officer addicted to opium,
and bigamist.

Carson, Christoper, 1809-1868. [939]
Kit Carson's autobiography.
Chicago: R. R. Donnelley, 1935.
192 p. WHi. Frontier trapper,
guide, Indian agent and soldier.
Chiefly in the Mountain and
Pacific states.

Carson, Laura Hardin, b. 1858. [940]
Pioneer trails...as a pioneer
missionary among the Chin tribes
of Burma. N.Y.: Baptist board of
education, 1927. 255 p. CBB.
Baptist missionary in Burma,
beginning with 1883.

Carson, Thomas. Ranching, [941]
sport and travel. N.Y.: Scribner,
1912. 319 p. DLC. An Englishman
tells of his world-wide experiences, including cattle ranching
in the southwest.

Carter, E. S., b. 1836. [942]
The life and adventures of E.S.
Carter, including a trip across
the plains and mountains in 1852,
Indian wars in the early days of
Oregon in the years 1854-5-6.
Life and experience in the gold
fields of California, and five
years' travel in New Mexico.
St. Joseph, Mo.: Combe pr. co.,
1896. 145 p. NN. As described
by the title.

Carter, Jacob, b. 1813. [943]
My drunken life. Boston: printed
for author, 1848. 96 p. DLC.
Seaman, actor. With Indians in
Texas.

Carter, John Franklin, b. 1897. [944]
The rectory family. N.Y.: Coward
-McCann, 1937. 275 p. NN.
Childhood days in Williamstown,
Mass., where the author's father
was an Episcopal clergyman.

Carter, Mrs. Melissa Booth, [945-955]
b. 1845. Beulah land, an autobiography. Boston: Earle, 1888.
258 p. MoS. Methodist church
worker in New York and Mass.

Carter, Peter, 1825-1900. [956]
Peter Carter...N.Y.: DeVinne
press, 1901. 144 p. WHi. New
York publisher, bookseller and
writer of books for children.

Carter, Richard, b. 1786. [957]
A short sketch of the author's
life...Versailles, Ky.: pr. by
J. H. Wilkins, 1825. 499 p. CSmH.
Pioneer physician in the southeast.

Carter, Robert Goldthwaite, [958]
b. 1845. On the border with Mackenzie, or winning west Texas
from the Comanches. Washington:
Eynon pr. co., 1935. 542 p. WHi.
Covers 1870-75. Written by a
professional soldier.

Carter, Robert Goldthwaite, 1845-[959]
1936. Record of the military
service of First Lieutenant and
Brevet Captain Robert Goldthwaite
Carter...1862 to 1876. Washington:
Gibson press, printers, 1904. 48 p.
DLC. Served with Massachusetts
infantry in the Civil War. After
graduation from West Point, he
served on the Texas border.

Carter, Walter, 1823-1897. [960]
Walter Carter; autobiography and
reminiscence, 1823-1897. N.Y.:
Baker & Taylor, 1907. 197 p. Auto., p.
7-73. DLC. An unfinished autobiography covering to 1845 when
he established himself as a New
York publisher of books.

Cartlidge, Oscar. [961]
Fifty years of coal mining.
Oregon City: Oregon city enterprise, 1933. 63 p. DLC. In Illinois
and West Virginia as mine inspector and engineer.

Cartwright, David W. [962]
Natural history of western wild
animals...Narratives of personal
aventure. Toledo: Blade printing
and paper co., 1875. 280 p. Auto.:
p. 139-255, 271-280. DLC.
Hunter, trapper in the midwest.
Overland to California in 1852.
Dictated account, written down by
Mary F. Bailey.

Cartwright, Peter, 1785-1822. [963]
Autobiography...N.Y.: Carlton &
Porter, 1857. 525 p. WHi. Methodist backwoods clergyman in Kentucky, Tennessee, Illinois and
Ohio.

Cartwright, Peter, 1785-1872. [964]
"Incidents of early life" (Fifty
years as a presiding elder...ed.
by W. S. Hooper. N.Y.: Nelson &
Phillips, 1871). p. 61-79. WHi.
His early preaching career in
Kentucky.

Case, Alden Buell, 1851-1932. [965]
Thirty years with the Mexicans...
N.Y.: Fleming H. Revell, 1917.

285 p. Auto.: p. 15-185. DLC. Congregational missionary.

Case, Frank, d. 1946. [966]
Tales of a wayward inn. N.Y.: Garden City pub. co., 1940. 390 p. DLC. By the owner and manager of the Algonquin hotel in New York.

Case, Frank, d. 1946. [967]
Do not disturb. N.Y.: Frederick A. Stokes co., 1940. 326 p. NN. Random reminiscences of the owner and manager of the Iroquois Hotel, New York City.

Casement, Dan Dillon, b. 1868. [968]
The abbreviated autobiography of a joyous pagan. Manhattan, Kansas: 1944. 74 p. CoHi. Cattle rancher in Kansas and Colorado.

Casey, Thomas G. [969]
Reminiscences of a packer man. N.Y.: 1923. 89 p. MoKU. Newspaper reporter and editor in Missouri, beginning with 1898.

Cash, Jacob. What America [970]
means to me...N.Y.: United States patriotic society, 1925. 125 p. DLC. Jewish immigrant from Tsarist Russia who served in the Spanish-American War and who became Marshall of New York City.

Caskey, Thomas W., 1816-1896. [971]
Caskey's last book containing an autobiographical sketch of his ministerial life. Nashville: Messenger pub. co., 1896. 275 p. Auto.: p. 1-78. TxU. Began as Methodist clergyman in Mississippi. Served with the Confederate forces, and then was clergyman in Texas representing the Disciples of Christ.

Casler, John Overton, b. 1838. [972]
Four years in the Stonewall Jackson brigade. 2d ed. Girard, Kansas: Appeal pub. co., 1906. 365 p. WHi. As described by the title.

Cassler, LaFayette. [973]
Thrilling experiences of frontier life in...Oklahoma. Cinc.: pub. for the author, 197 p. OkU. By a Methodist clergyman, covering the years 1890-1915.

Castanis, Christophoros Plato, [974]
b. 1814. The Greek exile, or A narrative of the captivity and escape of Christophorus Plato Castanis, during the massacre on the island of Scio, by the Turks, together with various adventures in Greece and America. Phila.: Lippincott, Grambo, & co., 1851. 272 p. NN. Brought to this country first by Dr. S. G. Howe, the writer returned again in 1837 and spent a number of years lecturing on Greek affairs.

Castle, N. My experience. [975]
N.p.: Holiness association, n.d. 8 p. OrU. An account of conversion.

Castleman, John Breckenridge, [976]
1841-1918. Active service. Louisville: Courier-Journal job pr. co., 1917. 269 p. DLC. Served with Morgan in the Confederate forces, followed by political activity in Kentucky and military service in the Spanish-American War.

Caswell, Harriett S. [977]
Our life among the Iroquois. Boston: Congregational pub. soc., 1892. 321 p. WHi. Missionary to the Indians in New York.

Catlin, George, 1796-1872. [978]
Life amongst the Indians. A book for boys. London: Sampson, Low, Son & co., 1861. 366 p. NN. Adventures among the Indians of the western United States and the northern portion of South America by the noted painter and ethnologist.

Catlin, George, 1796-1872. [979]
Last rambles amongst the Indians of the Rocky Mountains and the Andes. London: Sampson Low, Son, & Marston, 1868. 361 p. NN. Adventures in South America and on the Pacific Coast of North America by the noted painter and ethnologist.

Cattell, Edward James, b. 1856. [980]
Fighting through. Phila.: Dunlop pr. co., 1936. 416 p. DLC. Mining operator in Colorado and writer for popular magazines who became expatriate in England.

Cazneau, Mrs. William Leslie. [981]
Eagle pass; or, life on the border, by Cora Montgomery (pseud.) N.Y.: George P. Putnam, 1852. 188 p. DLC. Life on the Texas-Mexican border by a frontier settler.

Cedarholm, A., 1822-1867. [982]
Biography of Rev. A. Cedarholm, with a sketch of his labors among the Scandinavian population of the

United States, and as first missionary of the M.E. Church in Sweden. Piqua, Ohio: Helmet steam printing house, 1878. 84 p. DLC. As described by the title.

Chace, Mrs. Elizabeth (Buffum), [983] 1806-1899. Two Quaker sisters...N.Y.: Liveright, 1937. 183 p. Auto., p. 1-48. WHi. The noted abolitionist tells of her youth in Connecticut.

Chaille-Long, Charles, 1842-1917. [984] My life in four continents. London: Hutchinson, 1912. 2 vols. WHi. Service in the Union army, and with "Chinese" Gordon in Africa. U.S. Consul in Korea.

Chaliapin, Fedor Ivanovich. [985] Pages from my life...N.Y.: Harper, 1927. 345 p. WU. There are two chapters on his American experiences by the Russian operatic star.

Chamberlain, Hope (Summerell). [986] This was home. Chapel Hill: The Univ. of N.C. press, 1938. 328 p. NN. Memories of a childhood and youth, spent largely in Salisbury, N.C.

Chamberlin, Clarence Duncan, [987] b. 1893. Record flights. Phila.: Dorrance, 1928. 286 p. WHi. By a noted aviator.

Chamberlin, Mrs. Maria Louise [988] (Barrett), b. 1841. Looking back from eighty-five. Chicago: Federal printing co., 1926. 202 p. DLC. Wife of Y.M.C.A. worker and businessman reminiscences of her years in New York, Washington and Chicago.

Chamberlin, William Fosdick, [989] b. 1870. "I remember." Newark, Ohio: Advocate press, 1942. 104 p. DLC. Reminiscences of boyhood and college days in Ohio, and of insurance business in Conn.

Chamberlin, William Henry. [990] The confessions of an individualist. N.Y.: Macmillan, 1940. 320 p. WU. By an American newspaper reporter specializing in foreign affairs.

Chambers, Mrs. Andrew J. [991] (White). Reminiscences. N.p.: 1903. 48 p. OrHi. The life of a young girl in Oregon in the years following 1851, including her experiences during the Indian War of 1855-56.

Chambers, Mrs. Elizabeth [992] Harrison, b. 1828. From memory's pages. No imprint. 11 p. OrHi. To Oregon in 1845 where she settles on farm with her husband.

Chambers, James Julius, 1850- [993] 1920. Book of New York...N.Y.: priv. pub., 1912. 444 p. WHi. A New York journalist tells of himself and others.

Chambers, James Julius, 1850-1920 [994] News hunting on three continents. N.Y.: Mitchell Kenerley, 1921. 397 p. DLC. Reporter in Europe, Asia and the U.S. who among other posts was editor of the Herald and World in New York City.

Chambers, John, 1780-1852. [995] Autobiography of John Chambers. Iowa City, Ia.: The State historical soc. of Iowa, 1908. 49 p. WHi. Iowa political figure. Member of state legislature. Governor of Territory of Iowa.

Chambrun, Clara Longworth [996] Comtesse de, b. 1873. Shadows like myself. N.Y.: Scribner's, 1936. 348 p. WHi. An American woman, wife of a French general, tells of her experiences in France and Morocco during the first World War. Later her husband was attached to the French embassy in Washington.

Champlin, James, b. 1821. [997] Early biography...2d ed., rev. Columbus, Ohio: priv. pr., 1842. 206 p. WHi. Told by a blind teacher and Methodist lay preacher.

Champney, Benjamin, 1817-1907. [998] Sixty years' memories of art and artists. Woburn, Mass.: The News Print, Wallace & Andrews, 1900. 178 p. NN. The writer, a landscape painter, tells of his studies in Europe and makes many comments on American artists of the first two-thirds of the nineteenth century.

Chanler, Margaret (Terry), 1862- [999] 1934. Autumn in the valley. Boston: Little, Brown, 1936. 293 p. WU. Travel, hunting and social life in the Genesee Valley and abroad.

Chanler, Margaret (Terry), 1862- [1000] 1934. Roman spring, memoirs by Mrs. Winthrop Chanler. Boston: Little, Brown & co., 1934. 324 p.

NN. Early life in Italy; New York and European social life.

Channing, Elizabeth Parsons, [1001] 1818-1906. Autobiography and diary...Boston: American Unitarian ass'n., 1907. 304 p. Auto., p. 1-13. DLC. Unitarian author and lecturer, niece of William Ellery Channing.

Chapin, Adele Le Bourgeois, [1002] b. 1862. "Their trackless way," a book of memories. N.Y.: Holt, 1932. 330 p. WHi. The social life in America, Canada, South Africa and Europe of an American born woman.

Chapin, Charles E. [1003] Charles E. Chapin's story, written in Sing Sing prison. N.Y.: Putnam, 1920. 334 p. WU. By a journalist who murdered his wife.

Chapin, Eugene, b. 1832. [1004] By-gone days... Boston: priv. pr., 1898. 120 p. WHi. Pioneer of the forties in the old Northwest. Assistant Paymaster in the U.S. Navy during the Civil War.

Chaplin, Charles, b. 1888. [1005] Charlie Chaplin's own story. Indianapolis: Bobbs-Merrill, 1916. 257 p. DLC. By the famous comedian.

Chapman, Frank Michler, 1864- [1006] 1945. Autobiography of a birdlover. N.Y.: Appleton-Century, 1933. 420 p. WU. By a curator in the American Museum of Natural History.

Chapman, George Whitefield, [1007] 1780-1875. Brief history of Gilead. Portland, Me.: The author, 1867. 139 p. Auto.: p. 15-23. DLC. Maine farmer and writer of verses.

Chapman, H. L., b. 1832? [1008] Memoirs of an itinerant...No imprint. 331 p. MH. Methodist clergyman in Pennsylvania and Ohio who retired in 1906.

Chapman, Joseph. [1009] Fifty years of skating. Coconut Grove, Fla.: Palms publishing co., 1944. 52 p. DLC. Philadelphia figure skater.

Chapman, Mrs. Lavinia (Gates), [1010] 1835-1919. Short stories of pioneer days. No imprint. 36 p. KHi. Life on a farm in Kansas beginning with 1860.

Charles, John H., b. 1826. [1011] Reminiscences...Sioux City: 1906. 34 p. IaHi. Justice of the Peace and real estate business in Iowa in the late fifties, following upon mining experiences in California. Operator of steamboat business on Missouri River.

Charlton, John B., 1848-1922. [1012] The old Sergeant's story...1870 to 1876. N.Y.: Hitchcock, 1926. 220 p. WHi. Indian fighter and experiences with outlaws.

Charpentier, Henri, b. 1880. [1013] Life á la Henri...N.Y.: Simon & Schuster, 1934. 328 p. NN. Memoirs of a famous restauranteur, both in France and New York.

Chase, Abner, 1784-1854. [1014] Recollections of the past. N.Y.: 1846. 147 p. DLC. Methodist itinerant preacher in New York state.

Chase, Charles, 1841-1867. [1015] Life and confessions of Charles Chase, executed...for the murder of Mrs. Elizabeth McDonald. Pittsburgh: A. A. Anderson, 1867. 35 p. DLC. As described by the title.

Chase, Fred W., b. 1853. [1016] A brief historical sketch...N.p.: 1925. 24 p. NbHi. Story of a farmer in Nebraska following upon boyhood days on a farm in Vermont.

Chase, Ilka. Past imperfect. [1017] Garden City, N.Y.: Blue Ribbon books, 1945. 278 p. WU. By a star of stage and radio.

Chase, Mary Ellen, b. 1887. [1018] A goodly heritage. N.Y.: Holt, 1932. 298 p. WU. A noted literary figure tells of her youth in Maine and of her college career.

Chase, Mary Ellen, b. 1887. [1019] A goodly fellowship. N.Y.: Macmillan, 1940. 305 p. WU. The story of her experiences as a teacher in schools for girls and in universities.

Chase, Philander, 1775-1852. [1020] Bishop Chase's reminiscences: an autobiography. 2d ed. Boston: J.B. Dow, 1848. 2 vols. WHi. Episcopalean Bishop in the middlewest.

Chase, Warren. Forty years [1021] on the spiritual rostrum. Boston: Colby & Rich, 1888. 324 p. WHi. By a lecturer on spiritualism.

Chase, Warren. The life-line [1022]

of the lone one...2d ed. Boston: Bela Marsh, 1858. 310 p. WHi. The early life of a lecturer on spiritualism.

Chaumonot, Pierre Joseph Marie, [1023] 1611-1693. La vie du R. P. Pierre Joseph Marie Chaumonot... Nouvelle York: Presse de Jean-Marie Shea, 1858. 104 p. WHi. Jesuit missionary in new France.

Cheever, Ezekiel, 1783-1862. [1024] Sketches of his life...Northampton: J. Metcalf, 1835. 297 p. DLC. Baptist clergyman in Massachusetts and New York.

Cheney, Ednah Dow (Littlehale), [1025] 1824-1904. Reminiscences. Boston: Lee & Shepard, 1902. 254 p. Auto., p. 1-172. WHi. Abolitionist author.

Cherrie, George Kruck, b. 1865. [1026] Dark trails; adventures of a naturalist. N.Y.: Putnam, 1930. 322 p. WU. As described by the title.

Chester, Samuel Hale, b. 1851. [1027] Memoirs...Richmond: 1934. 235 p. DLC. Secretary of foreign missions of the Presbyterian Church. Clergyman in the southeastern states.

Chetlain, Augustus Louis, 1824- [1028] 1914. Recollections of seventy years. Galena: Gazette pub. co., 1899. 304 p. WHi. Union soldier. Consul to Brussells, and Assessor of the Internal Revenue Department.

Chidlaw, Benjamin Williams. [1029] The story of my life. Cleves, Ohio: priv. pr., 1890. 382 p. WHi. Presbyterian clergyman and missionary with the American Sunday-School Union.

Child, Maude Parker. See Parker, Maude.

Childs, George William, 1829- [1030] 1894. Recollections. Phila.: J.B. Lippincott, 1890. 404 p. NN. Philadelphia publisher and owner of the Philadelphia Public Ledger.

Chiniquy, Charles Pascha [1031] Telesphore, 1809-1899. Fifty years in the Church of Rome. Chicago: Craig & Barlow, 1885. 832 p. DLC. Catholic priest who with his flock in Illinois turns to Presbyterians.

Chisholm, William H. [1032] Vivid experiences in Korea. Chicago: Moody press, 1938. 136 p. WU. Medical missionary in Korea.

Choate, Joseph Hodges, 1832- [1033] 1917. The boyhood and youth of Joseph Hodges Choate. N.Y.: 1917. 153 p. WHi. His education, and early legal experiences in New York.

Christeen (pseud.). See Geier, Christeen.

Christian, George Llewellyn. [1034] Confederate memories and experiences...Richmond: Clayton pr. co., 1914. 32 p. Vi. His experiences at the University of Virginia during the Civil War.

Christowe, Stoyan. This is [1035] my country...N.Y.: Carrick & Evans, 1938. 320 p. WHi. A Bulgarian immigrant tells the story of his Americanization.

Chrysler, Walter Percy, 1875- [1036] 1940. Life of an American workman. Phila.: Curtis pub. co., 1938. 45 p. WHi. Manufacturer of automobiles.

Churchill, Mrs. Caroline (Nichols), [1037] b. 1833. Active footsteps. Colorado Springs: the author, 1909. 258 p. DLC. Author and operator of printing shop in Colorado, active in the suffragette movement.

Churchman, John, b. 1705. [1038] An account of the gospel labours... of a faithful minister of Christ. Phila.: Joseph Crukshank, 1779. 249 p. Whi. Member of the Society of Friends in Pennsylvania.

Cierplikowski, Antoine, b. 1884. [1039] Antoine. N.Y.: Prentice-Hall, 1945. 243 p. NN. Recollections of a famous hair dresser, both in Paris and America.

Cisneros, Evangelina. [1040] The story of... N.Y.: Continental pub. co., 1898. 257 p. DLC. Cuban revolutionist who was rescued by an American journalist and brought to this country.

Claiborne, John Herbert, b. 1828. [1041] Seventy-five years in old Virginia... N.Y.: Neale, 1904. 329 p. WHi. The experiences of a physician in the Confederate army.

Clampitt, Frank T., b. 1860. [1042] Some incidents in my life; a saga of the "unknown" citizen. Ann Arbor, Mich.: Edwards, 1936. 174 p. NN. Farmer, school teacher and

Clampitt, John Wesley, b. 1839. [1043] Echoes from the Rocky Mountains... Chicago: Bedford, Clarke, 1889. 671 p. DLC. A lawyer who was employed by the U.S. Justice Dept. to track down mail robbers in the far west.

Clap, Roger, 1609-1691. Memoirs [1044] ...Boston: pr. for W.T.Clap, 1807. 39 p. WHi. Spiritual account by a colonist.

Clapp, Charles, b. 1899. The big [1045] bender. N.Y.: Harper, 1938. 171 p. NN. The story of the author's downfall through drink and his rehabilitation through the Oxford Movement.

Clapp, Theodore, b. 1792. [1046] Autobiographical sketches and recollections during a thirty-five years' residence in New Orleans. 4th ed. Boston: Phillips, Sampson, 1859. 419 p. WHi. By a Presbyterian clergyman.

Clark, Alvan, 1804-1887. [1047] Autobiography...No imprint. 8 p. MiD-B. Maker of telescopes.

Clark, Amasa Gleason, b. 1825. [1048] Reminiscences of a centenarian. ...Bandera: priv. pr., 1930. 112 p. TxH. By a veteran of the Mexican War.

Clark, Austin S., 1852-1865. [1049] Reminiscences of travel. Middletown, Conn.: priv. pr., n.d. 54 p. CSmH. Thirteen years in the mines of California.

Clark, Champ, 1850-1921. [1050] My quarter century of American politics. N.Y.: Harper, 1920. 2 vols. WHi. Teacher in Kentucky, lawyer and Speaker of the House of Representatives from Missouri.

Clark, Charles A., 1841-1913. [1051] Campaigning with the Sixth Maine ...Des Moines: Kenyon press, 1897. 53 p. CU. The Civil War.

Clark, Charles Edgar, 1843- [1052] 1922. My fifty years in the navy. Boston: Little, Brown, 1917. 337 p. WHi. By a Rear Admiral.

Clark, Charles L., b. 1866. [1053] Lockstep and corridor; thirty-five years of prison life. Cinc.: Univ. of Cincinnati press, 1927. 177 p. DLC. By a man who served eight sentences in the penitentiary.

Clark, D.L. The roving artist... [1054] High Point: 1895. 127 p. NcU. North Carolina artist.

Clark, Ellery Harding, b. 1874. [1055] Reminiscences of an athlete; twenty years on track and field. Boston: Houghton Mifflin, 1911. 196 p. DLC. As described by the title.

Clark, Francis Edward, 1851- [1056] 1927. Memories of many men in many lands...Boston: United society of Christian endeavor, 1922. 698 p. WHi. Congregational minister in New England, president of the United Society of Christian Endeavor.

Clark, Mrs. Francis Edward. [1057] The little girl that once was I. Boston: International society of Christian endeavor, 1936. 52 p. WHi. Christian Endeavor worker tells of her first twelve years in the home of a New England clergyman.

Clark, G. W. (alias). See Strong, George W.

Clark, George, b. 1841. [1058] A glance backward. Houston: Rein, n.d. 93 p. TxU. Confederate soldier and prominent political figure in Texas during the period of reconstruction.

Clark, George Edward. Seven [1059] years of a sailor's life. Boston: Adams, 1867. 358 p. NN. Shipwrecked in Africa; Civil War experiences.

Clark, George Whitefield, 1831- [1060] 1911. Struggles and triumphs of a long life...Phila.: Griffith & Rowland, 1914. 192 p. WHi. Baptist clergyman in New York and New Jersey.

Clark, Isaac Newton, b. 1833. [1061] A personal sketch...Kansas City: Kansas City Baptist theological seminary, 1917. 167 p. WHi. Missionary worker in the middle-west for the American Baptist Missionary Union.

Clark, James Max. [1062] Colonial days. Denver: Smith-Brooks, 1902. 148 p. DLC. Colorado farmer.

Clark, James Samuel, b. 1841. [1063] Life in the middle west. Chicago: Advance pub. co., 1916? 226 p. WHi. Lawyer and manager of the Des Moines Free Insurance Company.

Clark, Leonard Francis. [1064]

A wanderer till I die. N.Y.: Funk & Wagnalls, 1937. 246 p. DLC. The life of a flyer and photographer in China, Java and Mexico.

Clark, Lewis Garrard, 1812-1897. [1065] Narrative of the sufferings of Lewis and Milton Clarke...during a captivity of more than twenty years among the slaveholders of Kentucky...Boston: B. Marsh, 1846. 144 p. DLC. As described by the title. A dictated account by a slave.

Clark, O. S. "Recollections [1066] of Colorado, New Mexico and the Texas Panhandle" (In his, Clay Allison of the Washita. N.p.: 1922) p. 49-90. CLSM. Cowboy, ranchman.

Clark, Mrs. Olive A. [1067] In the new country. No imprint. 13 p. KHi. To Kansas as a child in 1867 where she lived on a farm until her marriage in 1878.

Clark, Thomas March, 1812-1903. [1068] Reminiscences. 2d ed. N.Y.: Thomas Whittaker, 1895. 222 p. WHi. Episcopal clergyman in New England. Bishop of Rhode Island.

Clark, Walter A. [1069] Under the stars and bars...with the Oglethorpes, of Augusta, Georgia. Augusta: Chronicle pr. co., 1900. 239 p. WHi. An account of the Civil War.

Clark, Walter Leighton, 1859- [1070] 1935. Leaves from an artist's memory. Camden, N.J.: Haddon craftsmen, 1937. 270 p. NN. Mechanical engineer and businessman in New York. Painter and patron of art.

Clark, William H. The [1071] soldier's offering. Boston: 1875. 76 p. Auto., p. 11-44. WHi. Union army.

Clarke, Herbert Lincoln, b. 1867. [1072] How I became a cornetist...St. Louis: J. L. Huber, 1934. 74 p. DLC. His life as a bandsman and bandmaster.

Clarke, James Freeman, 1810- [1073] 1888. James Freeman Clarke: autobiography, diary and correspondence, ed. by Edward Everett Hale. Boston & N.Y.: Houghton, Mifflin, 1891. 430 p. Auto., p. 1-80. WHi. The story of a Unitarian minister, covering to the year 1840, during which time he served in Kentucky.

Clarke, Joseph Ignatius [1074] Constantine, 1846-1925. My life and memories. N.Y.: Dodd, Mead, 1925. 404 p. WHi. Immigrant from Ireland. Journalist and playwright in New York.

Clarke, Lewis. See Clark, Lewis Garrard.

Clarke, Mrs. Olive Cleaveland, [1075] b. 1785. Things that I remember. N.p.: priv. pr., 1881. 14 p. WHi. A Massachusetts school teacher tells of her youth in New England.

Clarke, Sarah (Summers), b. 1844. [1076] Then we came to California... a biography...written in the first person by Ralph LeRoy Milliken. Merced, Calif.: Merced Express, 1938. 95 p. CHi. Civil War experiences in Virginia. With husband, she farms in California following 1870.

Clarke, William Newton, 1841- [1077] 1912. Sixty years with the Bible; a record of experience. N.Y.: Scribner's, 1912. 259 p. NN. The author, a Baptist minister and professor of theology, tells about his changing views of the Bible as brought about by modern Biblical criticism.

Clarkson, Robert H. [1078] The tenth anniversary sermon preached in St. James Church, Chicago, 1859. Chicago: Scott & co., printers, 1859. 20 p. MnHi. Covers 1849-59.

Clary, Anna (Lathrop), b. 1859. [1079] Reminiscences...Los Angeles: Bruce McCallister, 1937. 107 p. DLC. Days of a girl in a small Minnesota community.

Clavers, Mrs. Mary (pseud.) See Kirkland, Mrs. Caroline Matilda (Stansbury).

Claxton, Timothy, b. 1790. [1080] Memoir of a mechanic. Boston: George W. Light, 1839. 179 p. NN. An Englishman who resided in this country, 1823-36; a manufacturer of scientific equipment, who was also interested in the education of the working classes. Founder of the Boston Mechanics' Institution.

Clay, Cassius, 1810-1903. [1081] The life of Cassius Marcellus Clay...Cinc.: J.F. Brennan, 1886.

600 p. WHi. Kentucky abolitionist, politician, U.S. Minister to Russia. Covers to 1885.

Clay, Mrs. Clement Claiborne. [1082] Belle of the fifties; memoirs of Mrs. Clay of Alabama...N.Y.: Doubleday, Page, 1904. 379 p. WHi. The wife of a Confederate officer tells of her war-time experiences.

Clay, John, b. 1851. [1083] My life on the range. Chicago: priv. pr., 1924. 366 p. WHi. Cattle rancher in Wyoming. For the experiences of this Scotsman in other countries, see his Old Days Recalled (1915) and My Recollections of Ontario (1918).

Clay-Clopton, Virginia (Tunstall). See Clay, Mrs. Clement Claiborne.

Clayton, Daniel Bragg, b. 1817. [1084] Forty-seven years in the Universalist ministry...Columbia, S.C.: priv. pub., 1889. 370 p. ScU. In various South Atlantic states, 1835-1889.

Clayton, Edward Hyers, 1886- [1085] 1946. Heaven below. N.Y.: Prentice-Hall, 1944. 282 p. DLC. Missionary in China for 20 years.

Cleaveland, Agnes Morley, b.1874. [1086] No life for a lady. Boston: Houghton Mifflin, 1941. 356 p. WU. Life on a cow ranch in New Mexico.

Cleghorn, Sarah Norcliffe, b. 1876. [1087] Threescore...N.Y.: Harrison Smith, 1936. 310 p. WU. New England poet.

Cleland, Charles S., b. 1863. [1088] The Clelands, Phila.: 1939. 16 leaves, MnHi. Mimeographed. Youth on a Minnesota farm in the sixties and seventies.

Cleland, Thomas, b. 1778. [1089] Memoirs.. Cinc.: Moore, Wilstach, Keys, 1859. 199 p. PPPrHi. Presbyterian clergyman in Virginia, Maryland and Kentucky.

Clem, Mrs. Charlotte Martin, [1090] b. 1845. Experiences...Dallas: Wilkinson pr. co., 1916. 95 p. DLC. Wife of Baptist preacher and farmer in Texas and Arkansas.

Clem, John. [1091] Experiences...by Mrs. Charlotte Martin Clem. Dallas: Wilkinson pr. co., 1916. p. 54-62. DLC. Baptist clergyman and farmer in Texas and Arkansas.

Clemens, Katharine (Boland). [1092] Gardens and books; the autobiography of Katharine Clemens. Webster Groves, Mo.: International Mark Twain Society, 1938. 352 p. NN. Missouri of the eighteen-eighties; life in France and England. The author's husband was a doctor.

Clemens, Samuel Langhorne, [1093] 1835-1910. Mark Twain's autobiography. N.Y.: Harpers, 1924. 2 vols. WHi. America's humorist tells of his experiences in the new west as a miner and journalist, and of his later career as a comic writer. There is, of course, autobiographical material in his other writings.

Clement, Samuel Spottford, b. 1861. [1094] Memoirs...Steubenville, Ohio: Herald pr. co., 1908. 67 p. DLC. A former slave tells of his varied life as laborer in Pennsylvania and the Virginias and as constable and owner of hauling concern in Ohio.

Clendenin, Henry Wilson. [1095] Autobiography...Springfield, Ill.: State register co., 1926. 421 p. WHi. Newspaper editor in Illinois.

Clevenger, Shobal Vail, 1843- [1096] 1920. Fun in a doctor's life, being the adventures of an American Don Quixote in helping to make the world better...Atlantic City, N.J.: Evolution pub. co., 1909. 291 p. NN. Specialist in nervous and mental diseases; experiences in the Civil War and on the frontier; medical career in Illinois.

Clews, Henry, 1834-1923. [1097] Fifty years in Wall Street. N.Y.: Irving pub. co., 1908. 1062 p. NN. The author, a Wall Street banker and financier, makes many comments on the financial figures and events of the period covered.

Cline, Isaac Monroe, b. 1861. [1098] Storms, floods and sunshine... New Orleans: Pelican pub. co., 1945. 289 p. LNHT. Meteorologist in Louisiana and Texas.

Clinkscales, John George. [1099] On the old plantation; reminiscences of his childhood. Spartanburg, S.C.: Band & White, 1916. 142 p. WHi. A story of youth.

Clinton, Henry Lauren, 1820- [1100] 1899. Extraordinary cases. N.Y.: Harper, 1896. 403 p. NN.

Experiences of a New York criminal lawyer.

Clise, James William. [1101]
Personal memoirs, 1855-1935. N.p.: 1935. WaU. Investment banker in Washington. Includes his earlier experiences in lumber business and ranching in Colorado, and his boyhood on a farm in Wisconsin.

Cloman, Flora (Smith), b. 1869. [1102]
I'd live it over. N.Y.: Farrar & Rinehart, 1941. 380 p. WHi. Wife of an American diplomat tells of her experiences in London, Berlin, Mexico, Turkey and the Philippines, as well as of her girlhood in Minnesota and Wisconsin.

Clough, John Everett, 1836-1910. [1103]
Social Christianity in the Orient; the story of a man, a mission and a movement. Written down for him by his wife, Emma Rauschenbusch Clough. N.Y.: Macmillan, 1914. 409 p. NN. Baptist missionary to the Telegus of southern India.

Clouse, Demas Letherman. [1104]
The story of a boy's life who went through poverty, perserverence and grace arose to the gospel ministry...Shell Rock, Iowa: 1892. 129 p. OClWHi. Baptist clergyman in Ohio, who in 1850 removed to Pennsylvania and later served in Illinois and Iowa.

Clune, Frank, b. 1894. [1105]
Try anything once...6th ed. London: Angus & Robertson, 1940. 243 p. CHi. A British born lumberjack in the Rockies in the 20th century.

Cluverius, Thomas J., 1861-1887. [1106]
Cluverius. My life, trial and conviction...2d ed. enl. Richmond: Andrews, Baptist & Clemmitt, prtrs., 1887. 128 p. NN. Murderer.

Clyman, James, 1792-1881. [1107]
James Clyman, American frontiersman, 1792-1881...ed. by Charles L. Camp. San Francisco: California historical soc., 1928. 247 p. WHi. Trapper.

Coan, Frederick Gaylord, b. 1859. [1108]
Yesterdays in Persia and Kurdistan. Claremont, Calif.: Saunders studio press, 1939. 284 p. DLC. Presbyterian missionary.

Coan, Titus, 1801-1882. [1109]
Life in Hawaii...1835-1881. N.Y.: Randolph, 1882. 325 p. WHi. Missionary.

Coates, Alexis Urial, b. 1858. [1110]
Life story. No imprint. 23 p. IaDm. Iowa merchant and political figure who ran on the prohibitionist ticket for governor in 1901. The story of his boyhood days on a farm in Iowa is included.

Cobb, Elijah, 1768-1848. [1111]
Elijah Cobb, 1768-1848, a Cape Cod skipper, ed. by Ralph D. Paine. New Haven: Yale Univ. press, 1925. 83 p. WHi. Sea captain.

Cobb, Enos. An exposition... [1112]
to which is added an autobiographical sketch...Montpelier: 1846. 32 p. Auto., p. 6-12. DLC. Physician, lawyer and editor in Mass. and Vermont.

Cobb, Irvin Schrewsbury, 1876- [1113]
1944. Exit laughing. Indianapolis: Bobbs-Merrill, 1941. 572 p. WU. Journalist in Kentucky and New York, humorist.

Cobb, Irvin Schrewsbury, 1876- [1114]
1944. Stickfuls. N.Y.: Doran, 1923. 355 p. DLC. Journalist in Kentucky and New York, humorist.

Cobb, Sylvanus, 1798-1866. [1115]
Autobiography...Boston: Universalist pub. house, 1867. 552 p. WHi. Universalist clergyman and author in New England.

Cobbett, William, 1763-1835. [1116]
Life and adventures of Peter Porcupine...London: Nonesuch press, 1927. p. 17-63. WU. Includes the American experiences of the English journalist.

Cober, Alvin Alonzo, b. 1861. [1117]
Telling on myself. Berlin, Pa.: Berlin pub. co., 1934. 286 p. DLC. Baptist missionary to Central America.

Coburn, Mrs. Fordyce. See Abbott, Eleanor Hallowell

Cocannover, Joseph A. [1118]
Trampling out the vintage. Norman: Univ. of Okla. press, 1945. 221 p. OkU. Student and teacher of agriculture in Oklahoma, Philippines and China.

Cochran, Charles Blake, b. 1872. [1119]
The secrets of a showman. London: Heineman, 1925. 422 p. DLC.

English and American experiences of an actor and producer.

Cocking, George, b. 1862. [1120]
From the mines to the pulpit... Cincinnati: pr. for the author by Jennings & Pye, 1903. 177 p. DLC. From the mines of Colorado to a Methodist pulpit in Indiana.

Cody, William Frederick, 1846- [1121] 1917. Autobiography of Buffalo Bill. N.Y.: Cosmopolitan book corp., 1920. 328 p. DLC. Trapper, scout, buffalo hunter on the plains and in the Rockies. Served as scout in the Civil War with Kansas Volunteers. Showman.

Coe, Charles Francis, b. 1890. [1122] Never a dull moment. N.Y.: Hastings house, 1944. 326 p. DLC. Writer of fiction and movie stories. He tells also of his legal experiences in New York and Florida.

Coe, George Washington, b. 1856. [1123] Frontier fighter...Boston: Houghton Mifflin, 1934. 220 p. DLC. His life as an outlaw in the southwest with Billy the Kid.

Coe, Urling Campbell, b. 1881. [1124] Frontier doctor. N.Y.: The Macmillan co., 1939. 264 p. DLC. Oregon physician on the frontier.

Coffey, Henry Davis, b. 1861. [1125] My life with God...Roanoke: Economy pr. co., n.d. 156 p. MoCanD. Served for many years with the Virginia Christian Missionary Society. Member of the Christian Church.

Coffin, Addison, 1822-1897. [1126] Life and travels...Cleveland: William G. Hubbard, 1897. 570 p. DLC. North Carolina abolitionist, later farmer in Indiana. After the Civil War, he promoted emigration to the West from North Carolina.

Coffin, Elijah, b. 1798. [1127] The life of Elijah Coffin... ed. by Mary C. Johnson. N.p.: E. Morgan, 1863. 307 p. Auto., p. 2-22. WHi. Farmer, teacher in North Carolina. Merchant in Ohio, banker in Indiana. This account closes with 1834.

Coffin, Elizabeth Wood. [1128]
A girl's life in Germantown. Boston: Sherman, French, 1916. 72 p. WHi. As described by the title.

Coffin, George. [1129]
A pioneer voyage to California and around the world, 1849 to 1852. Chicago: G. B. Coffin, 1908. 235 p. WHi. Merchant sailor.

Coffin, Levi, 1789-1877. [1130]
Reminiscences of Levi Coffin, the reputed president of the Underground Railway... Cinc.: R. Clarke, 1876. 712 p. WHi. Indiana abolitionist.

Coffin, Rhoda M. (Johnson), 1826- [1131] 1909. Rhoda M. Coffin; her reminiscences, addresses, papers and ancestry, ed. by Mary Coffin Johnson. N.Y.: Grafton press, 1910. 291 p. WHi. Religious worker in the Society of Friends.

Coffin, Robert, 1833-1914. [1132]
The last of the Logan...Ithaca: Cornell univ. press, 1941. p. 29-187. WU. Merchant sailor.

Coffin, Robert Peter Tristram, [1133] b. 1892. Lost paradise, a boyhood on a Maine coast farm. N.Y.: Macmillan, 1938. 284 p. WU. By the noted literary figure.

Coffin, Robert Stevenson, 1797- [1134] 1827. Life of the Boston bard, written by himself. Mount Pleasant, N.Y.: Stephen Marshall, 1825. 203 p. DLC. Maine poet who served at sea during the War of 1812.

Coggin, William S. [1135]
Discourse delivered at Boxford, Mass., May 10th, 1863...on the twenty-fifth anniversary of his settlement...Augusta: pr. at Kennebec journal office, 1864. 81 p. Auto., p. 3-32. WHi. Congregational minister.

Coghlan, Mrs. John. [1136]
Memoirs...N.Y.: Morrell, 1864. 158 p. WHi. The daughter of Major Moncrieffe who was seduced by Burr tells of the influences which led to her difficulties.

Cohan, George Michael, 1878- [1137] 1942. Twenty years on Broadway and the years it took to get there. N.Y. & London: Harper, 1925. 264 p. NN. Reminiscences of the actor and playwright.

Cohen, Rose (Gallup), b. 1880. [1138]
Out of the shadow. N.Y.: George H. Doran co., 1918. 313 p. NN. A Russian Jewish girl's early experiences in Russia and her gradual adaptation to a N.Y. environment.

Cohen, Mrs. S. J. [1139]
Henry Luria; or, The little Jewish convert...N.Y.: Trow, printer, 1860. 215 p. Auto., p. 17-151. DLC. A Protestant who married a Rabbi and was converted to the Jewish faith, who later came back to the Christian faith.

Cohn, Henry, b. 1831. [1140]
Jugenderinnerungen. Stettin, Germany: 1914. 55 p. CU-B. Peddler in New York and St. Louis in the fifties, then to California where he prospected for gold. The author returned to Europe in 1864.

Cohn, Leopold, b. 1862. [1141]
The story of a modern missionary to an ancient people, being the autobiography of Leopold Cohn, missionary to the 250,000 Jews of Brooklyn, N.Y. 2nd ed. Brooklyn: 1911. NcWAtC. As described by the title.

Coker, Mrs. Hannah Lide. [1142]
A story of the late war. Charleston: Walter, Evans & Cogswell, printers, 1887. 47 p. WHi. Life in the South behind the lines.

Colburn, Zerah, 1804-1839. [1143]
A memoir of Zerah Colburn; written by himself. Springfield, Mass.: 1833. 204 p. WHi. A mathematics prodigy who later became a Congregational clergyman and still later a professor of languages, both in Vermont.

Colby, Albert, 1827-1890. [1144]
Incidents in the life of Albert Colby...Portland, Maine: pr. by Albert Colby's sons, 1875. 32 p. DLC. New England printer and bookseller.

Colby, Mrs. Julia A. (Hovey), [1145]
b. 1837. Reminiscences... Springfield, Mo.: 1916. 104 p. MoKU. Missouri school teacher, beginning with 1852.

Colby, Mrs. Nathalie Sedgwick [1146]
Washburn. Remembering. Boston: Little, Brown, 1938. 308 p. WHi. A New York author tells of her life as wife of Wilson's Secretary of State.

Cole, Cornelius, 1822-1924. [1147]
Memoirs of Cornelius Cole, ex-senator of the United States from California. N.Y.: McLoughlin bros., 1908. 354 p.WHi. Senator from California who earlier was a forty-niner.

Cole, Cyrenus. [1148]
I remember, I remember... Iowa City: State historical society of Iowa, 1936. 525 p. WHi. Member of the House of Representatives from Iowa, who earlier was a journalist.

Cole, Emma. See
Hanson, Mrs. Emma (Cole).

Cole, George Edward, 1826-1906. [1149]
Early Oregon...Spokane: Shaw & Borden, 1905. 95 p. WHi. Politician, farmer in Oregon in the fifties.

Cole, Haydn Samuel, b. 1861. [1150]
Haydn Samuel Cole and his ancestry...St. Paul: priv. pr., 1935. 214 p. Auto., p. 133-188. DLC. St. Paul lawyer and financier tells of his earlier career as a West Point officer in the first World War and against the Indians in the Dakotas.

Cole, Henry G., b. 1851. [1151]
Confessions of an American opium eater. Boston: J. H. Earle, 1895. 241 p. Auto., p. 1-157. DLC. As described by the title.

Cole, Jacob H. [1152]
Under five commanders... Paterson: News pr. co., 1906. 253 p. WHi. Union soldier with Army of the Potomac.

Cole, James Reid, b. 1839. [1153]
Seven decades of my life. Dallas: John F. Worley pr. co., 1913. 212 p. DLC. Member of the Texas legislature who was also a college professor and president. In the Civil War he served in a North Carolina outfit.

Cole, Mary, b. 1853. [1154]
Trials of triumphs of faith. Anderson, Indiana: Gospel trumpet co., 1914. 300 p. DLC. Mission worker in Chicago who earlier was Holiness preacher in Missouri.

Cole, Thomas R., b. 1881. [1155]
Learning to be a school master. N.Y.: Macmillan, 1922. 60 p. Wa. Superintendent of schools in Seattle tells of his days as a high school teacher and principal.

Coleman, Harry J. [1156]
Give us a little smile, baby. N.Y.: E. P. Dutton, 1943. 258 p. NN. Adventures of a newspaper photographer for the Hearst publications in New York, San Francisco and Chicago.

Coleman, Seth, 1740-1816. [1157]
Memoirs of Doctor Seth Coleman, A.M. of Amherst, (Mass.) containing I. A biographical sketch of his life and character. II. Extracts from his journal, taken by himself. III. His letters upon religious subjects. IV. His farewell address to his children. V. Sermon delivered at his funeral, by the Rev. Nathan Perkins. New Haven: Printed by Flagg & Gray, 1817. 288 p. NN. As described by the title.

Coles, George, 1792-1858. [1158]
My youthful days...N.Y.: Lane & Scott, 1852. 267 p. DLC. An English Methodist preacher tells of his early life and of his settling in New York state.

Coles, George, 1792-1858. [1159]
My first seven years in America. N.Y.: Carlton & Phillips, 1854. 314 p. NN. Experiences of a Methodist minister, born in England, among the churches in New York state.

Coles, George, 1792-1858. [1160]
Incidents of my later years. N.Y.: Carlton & Phillips, 1855. 315 p. DLC. Methodist in Mass., New Jersey and New York. He was also a missionary to the Indians in New York.

Collier, Constance, b. 1878. [1161]
Harlequinade; the story of my life. London: John Lane, 1929. 294 p. OCl. English actress who several times appeared in the U.S.

Collings, Kenneth Brown, 1898-1941. [1162]
Just for the hell of it. N.Y.: Dodd, Mead, 1938. 373 p. NN. Adventures of a marine aviator, free-lance writer, and war correspondent in Haiti, Abyssinia, and elsewhere. His experiences in Czechoslovakia as a correspondent are told in his book, These Things I Saw. (1939).

Collins, Asa Weston, b. 1875. [1163]
Doctor Asa. Los Angeles: Ward Ritchie, 1941. 172 p. CHi. Surgeon in California.

Collins, Dennis. The Indians' [1164]
last fight...Girard, Kansas: Press of the Appeal to Reason, 1915. 326 p. Auto., p. 28-166. DLC. Canadian born cattle rancher in Texas and Kansas.

Collins, Elizabeth (Ballinger) [1165]
Mason, 1755-1831. Memoirs... Phila.: N. Kite, 1833. 144 p. DLC. A minister in the Society of Friends in New Jersey.

Collins, Hubert Edwin, b. 1872. [1166]
Warpath and cattle trail. N.Y.: William Morrow co., 1928. 296 p. DLC. Story of youth on ranch in Oklahoma.

Collins, James, 1904-1935. [1167]
Test pilot. Garden City: Doubleday, Doran & co., 1935. 178 p. DLC. As described by the title.

Collins, James Potter, 1763-1844. [1168]
Autobiography of a revolutionary soldier. Clinton, La.: pr. by Feliciana Democrat, 1859. 176 p. WHi. He was also a frontier farmer, horse trader and tailor in Georgia and Tennessee.

Collins, John Sloan, b. 1839. [1169]
Across the plains in '64: incidents of early days west of the Missouri. Omaha: National printing co., 1911. 2 vols. in 1, 151, 152 p. DLC. Trader, cattleman, Sioux Indian commissioner.

Collins, Mrs. Libby (Smith). [1170]
The cattle queen of Montana... Rev. and ed. by Alvin E. Dyer. Spokane: Dyer pr. co., n.d. 260 p. OkU. Ranch woman on the frontier including troubles with Indians.

Collins, Loren Warren, b. 1838. [1171]
The story of a Minnesotan. No imprint, 1912? 86 p. WHi. Lawyer, politician and state judge in Minnesota, including pioneer experiences as a teacher.

Collins, Lorin Cone, 1848-1940. [1172]
Autobiography. Chicago: Lincoln pr. co., 1934. 201 p. DLC. Member of the Isthmian Canal Commission tells of his experiences as lawyer, federal judge and state legislator in Illinois.

Collins, Mary C. [1173]
Winona...N.Y.: American missionary ass'n., 1918? 11 p. SdHi. Missionary to the Indians in the Dakotas beginning with 1875.

Collins, Mary S. (pseud.). See Amos, Mary Jane (Davies).

Collins, Mrs. Nat. See Collins, Mrs. Libby (Smith).

Collins, W. M. [1174]
Lights by the way...Kansas City,

Mo.: Hudson-Kimberly pub. co., 1899. 201 p. OrMcL. A story of conversion by a lay Baptist.

Collis, Mrs. Charles. H. T. See Collis, Mrs. Septima Maria (Levy).

Collis, Mrs. Septima Maria [1175] (Levy), 1842-1917. A woman's war record, 1861-1865. N.Y.: Putnam, 1889. 78 p. DLC. The wife of a Union army officer.

Collyer, Robert, 1823-1912. [1176] Some memories. Boston: American Unitarian association, 1908. 248 p. NN. Unitarian minister in Chicago and New York; early life in England and early days in America; work during the Civil War with the Sanitary Commission. These memoirs close before Dr. Collyer came to New York.

Collyer, Robert H. [1177] Lights and shadows of American life. Boston: Brainard & co., 1838? 40 p. NN. Experiences of an English practitioner of mesmerism who came to the United States in 1836.

Colman, Lucy Newhall (Danforth), [1178] b. 1817. Reminiscences. Buffalo: H. L. Green, 1891. 86 p. NN. Experiences of a religious liberal, advocate of the abolition of the slaves, and worker for women's rights.

Colquitt, Oscar Branch, 1861- [1179] 1940. Gov. O. B. Colquitt... No imprint. 29 p. TxU. Texas newspaper publisher and state senator.

Colton, Eleanora Garner, b. 1845. [1180] Memories...No imprint. 25 p. IaHi. Girlhood days on a farm in Iowa in the forties and fifties.

Colton, Gardner Quincy, 1814- [1181] 1898. Boyhood and manhood recollections; the story of a busy life...N.Y.: printed by A. G. Sherwood & co., 1897. 26 p. NN. Anesthetist, who introduced the use of nitrous oxide in dentistry; also made the first application of electric propulsion to cars. Experiences in early California.

Colton, Gardner Quincy, 1814- [1182] 1898. Boyhood recollections. A story with a moral. N.Y.: Press of E. M. Day, 1891. 13 p. NN. A boyhood in Vermont.

Colton, Sarah (Tarleton), b. 1865. [1183] A rebel in thought. N.Y.: Island press, 1944. 245 p. NN. Life in Alabama and Baltimore in post-Civil War days; training as a nurse at Johns Hopkins Hospital; life and politics in Minnesota; activities in the woman suffrage movement; member of the Minnesota State Board of Education.

Coman, Mrs. Martha (Seymour), [1184] 1826-1911. Memories...Boston: Fort Hill press, 1913. 310 p. Auto., p. 1-98, 113-310. DLC. A story of family life on a farm in New Jersey and Ohio, with travels in in the South and in Europe.

Combs, George Hamilton, b. 1864. [1185] I'd take this way again...St. Louis: The Bethany press, 1944. 256 p. MoK. Clergyman of the Disciple faith in Missouri and Kentucky.

Comerford, William Turpin. [1186] My first 14 wives. N.Y.: Alliance press, 1935. 320 p. NN. Narrative of the author's experiences as a marine engineer officer and of the women encountered during his career.

Comfort, Will Levington, 1878- [1187] 1932. Midstream...N.Y.: Doran, 1914. 320 p. WU. Novelist war correspondent, Spanish-American War.

Comings, Herbert C., b. 1863. [1188] Years of an old Vermonter... No imprint, 1940? 29 p. WHi. Vermont political figure, banker and manufacturer.

Commons, John Rogers, b. 1862. [1189] Myself. N.Y.: Macmillan, 1934. 201 p. WHi. Professor of economics, chiefly at the University of Wisconsin. Noted author.

Comstock, Andrew, 1795-1864. [1190] Autobiography of A. Comstock, M.D., in trochaic verse. Phila.: C. G. Henderson, 1857. 28 p. Auto., p. 3-9. DLC. Physician and elocutionist in Philadelphia.

Comstock, Joshua, b. 1790. [1191] A short history...Providence: 1822. 8 p. CSmH. A New York school teacher tells of his conversion to the faith.

Conant, Thomas, b. 1785. The [1192] autobiography of Thomas Conant. Boston: Andrew F. Graves, 1861. 180 p. MWA. Baptist minister in Mass.

Conboie, Joseph A. [1193]

Lincoln Slim from the golden West. San Francisco: 1943. 346 p. WHi. Drunkard, gambler and college student of respiratory diseases.

Cone, John Philip. Told out of school. No imprint. 25 p. KHi. Service with a Kansas outfit in the Civil War. [1194]

Confessions of a Negro preacher. Chicago: Canterbury press, 1928. 297 p. DLC. After studying with Booker T. Washington, he becomes a Methodist itinerant preacher, mainly in Indiana. [1195]

Congdon, Charles Taber, 1821–1891. Reminiscences of a journalist. Boston: James R. Osgood, 1880. 386 p. DLC. Journalist, editor and publisher in Boston, N.Y. and Washington. [1196]

Congdon, George Edward, b. 1869. Sugar Grove and the class of 1886...Hiawatha, Kansas: Ewing Herbert, printer, 1911. 50 p. IHi. Teacher tells of his student days in Illinois. [1197]

Conklin, George, b. 1845. The ways of the circus, being the memories and adventures of George Conklin, tamer of lions ...N.Y.: Harper, 1921. 308 p. NN. As described by the title. [1198]

Connelly, Howard Wallace. Fifty-six years in the New York post-office... N.Y.: Printed by C. J. O'Brien, 1931. 140 p. DLC. By the Assistant Superintendent of Mails, New York City. [1199]

Connolly, James Brendan, b. 1868. Sea-borne; thirty years a voyaging. Garden City, N.Y.: Doubleday, Doran, 1944. 246 p. NN. Adventures of a free-lance journalist and writer of sea tales, especially of the Gloucester fishing fleets. Contender in the first Olympic games; soldier in the Spanish-American war. [1200]

Connolly, John, 1743?–1813. A narrative of the transactions, imprisonment and sufferings of John Connolly, an American Loyalist. London: priv. pr., 1783. 62 p. WHi. As described by the title. [1201]

Connolly, Stephen. Four trips around the world; or, twenty-eight years on the sea. Isle La Motte, Vt.: C. W. Ross, 1895. 99 p. MWA. By the skipper of whaling and clipper ships. [1202]

Connor, Benjamin M., d. 1922. Rekindling camp fires...(as told to Lewis F. Crawford). Bismarck: Capital book co., 1926. 324 p. DLC. Indian fighter, gold miner, cowboy hunter and army scout. During the Civil War he served with an Ohio outfit. [1203]

Conover, George W., 1848–1936. Sixty years in southwest Oklahoma...Anadarko, Oklahoma: N. T. Plummer, 1927. 129 p. DLC. After serving in the Civil War with a New Jersey outfit, he joined the regular army and saw service in Texas and Oklahoma. Later he became a cattleman. [1204]

Conrad, Thomas Nelson. The rebel scout...Washington: National pub. co., 1904. 220 p. WHi. Confederate soldier. [1205]

Conrad, William, b. 1797. Life and travels of Elder William Conrad. Cinc.: Wrightson & co., 1876. 422 p. KyU. Baptist in Kentucky. [1206]

Conser, Solomon L. M., b. 1812. Virginia after the war. An account of three years experience in reorganizing the Methodist Episcopal church in Virginia at the close of the Civil war. Indianapolis: Baker-Randolph, 1891. 82 p. DLC. Clergyman in Pennsylvania, Maryland and Virginia who after the Civil War gives his efforts to the reorganization of the church in Virginia. [1207]

Contant, George C. (alias George Sontag), b. 1861. A pardoned lifer. Written by Opie L. Warner. San Bernardino: Index print, 1909. 211 p. CHi. Train robber in California whose alias was George Sontag. [1208]

Conway, Moncure Daniel, 1832–1907. Autobiography, memories, and experiences...Boston: Houghton Mifflin, 1904. 2 vols. WHi. Abolitionist, Methodist, Congregational, Unitarian clergyman, and author. Many years spent in England. [1209]

Conwell, Russell H., b. 1843. "Fifty years on the lecture platform" (In his, Acres of Diamonds, N.Y.: Harper, 1915). p. 173–181. WU. Redpath lecturer and founder [1210] of Temple University.

Cook, Charles A. [1211]
Ways of sin; or, experiences of convict life. Des Moines, Ia.: The Patterson-Brown printery, 1894. 145 p. DLC. As described by the title.

Cook, Charles H. [1212]
"Mr. Cook's narrative..." (In, Among the Pimas...Albany: pr. for the Ladies union mission school ass'n., 1893). p. 18-45. CLSM. Methodist missionary to the Indians in Arizona about 1870.

Cook, David. J., b. 1840. [1213]
Hands up; or twenty years of detective life in the mountains and on the plains...Denver: Republican pub. co., 1882. 285 p. DLC. Frontier officer in Colorado, 1866-1882.

Cook, Harry George, b. 1869. [1214]
Boomer—Sooner, a life story. Norman, Okla.: Cooperative books, 1939. 56 p. OkHi. Oklahoma farmer in frontier days who made his claim in 1889.

Cook, James Henry, b. 1857. [1215]
Fifty years on the old frontier as cowboy, hunter, guide, scout and ranchman. New Haven: Yale univ. press, 1923. 291 p. WHi. In Texas, Wyoming and New Mexico.

Cook, James Henry, b. 1857. [1216]
Longhorn cowboy. N.Y.: Putnam, 1942. 241 p. WU. See the preceding entry.

Cook, James M., b. 1858. [1217]
Lane of the Llano. Boston: Little, Brown, 1936. 269 p. WHi. Cowboy on the plains.

Cook, James Wade, b. 1838. [1218]
Forty-five years a minister. South Gifford, Mo.: pub. at the Comet office, n.d. 80 p. MoHi. Member of the Missionary Baptist Church in Missouri.

Cook, John, 1823-1916. [1219]
Reminiscences of John Cook, Kamaaina and forty-niner. Honolulu: New freedom press, 1927. 27 p. CHi. Englishman in Hawaii, 1844-1916, where he was carpenter, whaler.

Cook, John Atkins, 1857- 1937. [1220]
Pursuing the whale...in the Arctic. Boston: Houghton Mifflin, 1926. 344 p. DLC. By the captain of a whaling ship.

Cook, John R., 1844-1917. [1221]
The border and the buffalo... Topeka: pr. by Crane & co., 1907. 351 p. DLC. Buffalo hunter in the southwest.

Cook, Nilla Cram. [1222]
My road to India. N.Y.: Furman, 1939. 462 p. WU. By a person who lived there as an observer.

Cooke, Mrs. Harriet B., b. 1786? [1223]
Memories of my life work. N.Y.: Robert Carter, 1858. 356 p. NN. The writer conducted schools for young women in Vermont and New Jersey. The work is pervaded by a deep religious atmosphere.

Cooke, Philip St. George, 1809- [1224]
1895. Scenes and adventures in the army...Phila.: Lindsay & Blakiston, 1857. 432 p. WHi. Professional soldier tells of his experiences, including the Black Hawk war, to the year 1845.

Cookson, Charles William. [1225]
After fifty years. Troy, Ohio: Montgomery pr. co., 1942. 143 p. DLC. Superintendent of Schools in Ohio.

Coolen, James Sewell, b. 1904. [1226]
We're sailing in the morning. Brattleboro, Vt.: Stephen Daye press, 1937. 199 p. DLC. Merchant sailor from Maine.

Cooley, Byron. Memoirs, [1227]
compiled from his papers and conversations, while under sentence of death. Cinc.: R. P. Brooks, printer, 1837. 42 p. MnHi. A Pennsylvania youth who went to sea and who then lived a life of crime.

Cooley, Winifred (Harper). [1228]
I knew them when... N.Y.: The Saravan house, 1940. 250 p. NN. Journalist and lecturer.

Coolidge, Calvin, 1872-1935. [1229]
The autobiography... N.Y.: Cosmopolitan book co., 1929. 247 p. WHi. His earlier political and legal experiences in Massachusetts.

Coombes, Charles E., b. 1875. [1230]
The prairie dog lawyer. Dallas: Texas folklore society, 1945. 286 p. DLC. Texas lawyer, Federal judge, district attorney.

Cooney, Tom, b. 1853. [1231]
Meet Tom Cooney. Minneapolis: Lund press, 1945. 164 p. MtU. Written in the first person by Mildred H. Comfort. English-born farmer and engineer in the

mountain states.

Coontz, Robert Edward, 1864- [1232] 1935. From the Mississippi to the sea. Phila.: Dorrance, 1930. 483 p. WHi. Naval officer, including experiences in the war with Spain.

Coope, Anna, b. 1854. [1233] Anna Coope, sky pilot of the San Blas Indians; an autobiography. N.Y.: American tract society, 1931. 193 p. NN. Protestant missionary to the West Indies, Venezuela, and the San Blas islands off the coast of Panama.

Cooper, Elwood, 1829-1918. [1234] The life...No imprint. 29 p. CU-B. Ranching and farming in California following 1851. Earlier he had taught in Pennsylvania.

Cooper, Joseph W., b. 1848. [1235] Life and adventures of Joseph W. Cooper among the North American Indians. Albany, Georgia: Albany advertiser, 1879. 39 p. DLC. Soldier in the Confederate army and in the Dakota and Montana territories.

Cooper, Peter, b. 1791. [1236] "The early days and business life of Peter Cooper" (A sketch of the life and opinions of Mr. Peter Cooper, comp. from original sources by John C. Zachos. N.Y.: M. Hill, 1876) p. 11-23. WHi. Inventor and manufacturer, president of North American Telegraph Company. His activities were centered in New York, Maryland and New Jersey.

Cooper, Stephen, b. 1797. [1237] Sketches. Oakland: Pacific press, 1888. 19 p. WHi. Forty-niner. Minor California political figure.

Cope, Samuel W. [1238] The story of a happy life. Chillicothe, Mo.: Johnson & Kiergan, printers, n.d. 168 p. MoK. Methodist clergyman in Missouri.

Copeland, James. [1239] Life and confession of the noted outlaw... By J. R. S. Pitts. N.p.: 1909. 237 p. Auto., p. 31-125. MoKu. In the southeastern and southwestern states.

Copeland, Jonathan, b. 1817. [1240] A brief sketch...Springfield, Colorado: L. A. Wikoff, printer, 1894. 44 p. KU. Congregational clergyman in Michigan, Kansas and Iowa.

Copland, Aaron, b. 1900. [1241] "Composer from Brooklyn: an autobiographical sketch" (In his, Our new music. N.Y.: 1941) p. 212-230. WU. As described by title.

Copp, Elbridge J. [1242] Reminiscences of the War of the rebellion...Nashua: Telegraph pub. co., 1911. 536 p. WHi. Union army officer.

Coppin, Levi Jenkins, b. 1848. [1243] Unwritten history, an autobiography. Phila.: African Meth. Episcopal book concern, 1919. 375 p. WHi. Negro Methodist clergyman.

Copway, George, 1818-1863?. [1244] The life, history and travels of Kah-Ge-Ga-Gah-Bowh (George Copway) 2d ed. Albany: pr. by Weed & Parsons, 1847. 224 p. WHi. Chippewa chief who became a Methodist missionary to his people in the area now known as the Midwest.

Corbett, Elizabeth Frances, [1245] b. 1887. Out at the soldiers' home; a memory book. N.Y.: Appleton-Century, 1941. 266 p. WHi. Memories of her childhood in an old soldiers' home in Wisconsin, by a novelist.

Corbett, James John, 1866-1933. [1246] The roar of the crowd; the true tale of the rise and fall of a champion. Garden City, N.Y.: Garden City pub. co., 1926. 329 p. NN. Adventures of a prizefighter.

Corby, William, 1833-1897. [1247] Memoirs of chaplain life... Three years chaplain in the famous Irish Brigade, "Army of the Potomac." Chicago: La Monte, O'Donnell & co., prtrs., 1893. 391 p. NN. As described by the title.

Cordley, Richard, 1829-1904. [1248] Pioneer days in Kansas. N.Y.: Pilgrim press, 1903. 274 p. WHi. A member of the Kansas Band, formed at Andover 1856, tells of his missionary work in Kansas for the cause of abolition.

Cordley, Richard, 1829-1904. [1249] A quarter centennial sermon. Lawrence: Young people's society of Christian endeavor, 1891. 24 p. KU. In Kansas, 1857-75 and 1884-91.

Cordua, Theodor, 1796-1857. [1250]
The memoirs of Theodor Cordua, the pioneer of New MecKlenberg in the Sacramento Valley. Ed. and tr. by Erwin G. Guddle. San Francisco: California historical society, 1933? 33 p. DLC. A German immigrant who became a rancher in California, 1842-52.

Corey, Charles Henry, 1834-1899. [1251]
A history of the Richmond theological seminary with reminiscenses of thirty years' work among the colored people of the South. Richmond: J. W. Randolph co., 1895. 240 p. WHi. A Negro tells mainly of his service with the U.S. Christian Commission during the Civil War, and among the Negroes of South Carolina. Corey was a Baptist, born in Canada.

Corey, Francis Edwin, 1804-1892. [1252]
Autobiography...Chicago: priv. pr., 1892. 118 p. Auto., p. 15-43. WHi. Merchant in New England and in the Midwest.

Corey, James Benijah, b. 1832. [1253]
Memoir and personal recollection ...Pittsburgh, Pa.: Pittsburgh pr. co., 1914. 405 p. Auto., p. 27-225. DLC. Owner of Pennsylvania coal mine.

Corlett, William Thomas, b. 1854. [1254]
Early reminiscences, 1860-1904. Cleveland: 1920. 420 p. IU-M. A physician tells of his visits to clinics, attendance at scientific meetings, and of his career as Professor of Dermatology at Western Reserve University.

Cornaby, Hannah (Hollingsworth), [1255]
b. 1822. Autobiography and poems ...Salt Lake City: pr. by J. C. Graham & co., 1881. 158 p. Auto., p. 9-64. NN. An Englishwoman who became a Mormon; her trip from England to Utah and later life in that state.

Cornelius, Friedrick Caspar, [1256]
b. 1850. Biography and personal reminiscences. No imprint. 16 p. TxU. A German born Texas farmer.

Cornelius, Samuel, 1795-1871. [1257]
Autobiographical letters...Detroit: O. S. Gulley's steam press, 1871. 43 p. MWA. Baptist clergyman in Virginia, New York, Michigan, and agent for American Colonization Society in New Jersey and Connecticut.

Cornell, C. S. [1258]
A Knoxville physician's part in the World war...1917-1919. Knoxville, Iowa: 1935. IaHi. As described by the title.

Cornell, John J., b. 1826. [1259]
Autobiography...containing an account of his religious experiences and travels in the ministry. Baltimore: The Lord Baltimore press, 1906. 498 p. Auto., p. 9-63; 127-224. DLC. Minister of the Society of Friends in New York, Pennsylvania and Maryland.

Cornell, Katharine, b. 1898. [1260]
I wanted to be an actress...N.Y.: Random House, 1939. 361 p. WU. Actress.

Cornell, Mary Emily, b. 1847. [1261]
Autobiography...Ithaca, N.Y.: The Cayuga press, 1929. 169 p. DLC. The daughter of Ezra Cornell tells of her work for church and charity.

Corning, James Leonard, 1828- [1262]
1903. Recollections of a life. N.Y.: The Knickerbocker press, 1898? 100 p. DLC. Presbyterian and Congregational clergyman who eventually became a Unitarian. He served in Connecticut, New York, New Jersey and in the Midwest.

Cornwell, John Jacob, b. 1867. [1263]
A mountain trail. Phila.: Dorrance, 1939. 106 p. DLC. Governor of West Virginia, lawyer, who began as a school teacher.

Corrigan, Douglas. [1264]
That's my story. N.Y.: Dutton, 1938. 221 p. WU. "Wrong-way" aviator.

Corrothers, James David, 1869- [1265]
1917. In spite of the handicap... N.Y.: Doran, 1916. 238 p. WHi. Negro minister and writer of poetry tells mainly of his white friends.

Corser, Elwood Spencer, 1835- [1266]
1917. Record of the life of Elwood Spencer Corser. Minneapolis: W.F. Black & co., printers, 1911. 23 p. MnHi. Minor political figure in Minneapolis, who served with a New York outfit in the Civil War.

Corsi, Edward. [1267]
In the shadow of liberty. N.Y.:

Macmillan, 1935. 321 p. WHi. Commissioner of Immigration in the New York district.

Cortesi, Salvatore, 1864-1947. [1268] My thirty years of friendships. N.Y.: Harper, 1927. 296 p. NN. The author, an Italian who was the Rome representative of the Associated Press, tells of many of his journalistic experiences.

Cory, Herbert Ellsworth, 1883- [1269] 1947. The emancipation of a freethinker. Milwaukee: Bruce, 1941. 304 p. DLC. From agnosticism to Catholicism, by a university professor.

Coston, Mrs. Martha J. [1270] A signal success...Phila.: Lippincott, 1886. 333 p. WHi. Widow of inventor tells of her efforts to sell his night signals for naval vessels.

Cotten, Bruce. [1271] An adventure in Alaska...1897-98. Baltimore: Sun pr. office, 1922. 107 p. DLC. Gold miner.

Cotter, William Joseph, b. 1823. [1272] My autobiography. Nashville: Publishing house, Methodist Episcopal Church, South, 1917. 190 p. TxU. Methodist clergyman in Georgia, Tennessee and North Carolina.

Cotting, Benjamin Eddy. [1273] Professional reminiscences. Boston: Press of David Clapp & son, 1888. 112 p. MiD-B. Physician in Massachusetts.

Cotton, Alfred Johnson, b. 1800. [1274] Cotton's sketch-book. Autobiographical sketches...Portland: B. Thurstan, 1874. 216 p. DLC. Methodist clergyman in Indiana, who became attorney, judge and Assistant U. S. Marshall. As a clergyman he also lived in Illinois.

Cotton, Alfred Johnson, b. 1800. [1275] ...Poems...to which is appended a short autobiographical sketch. Cinc.: Pub. for the author, 1858. 562 p. Auto., p. 283-366. MoSM. See the previous annotation.

Coughlin, Eugene Francis Paul. [1276] Assistant hero...N.Y.: Crowell, 1944. 133 p. DLC. Hollywood publicity man tells of his services in the second World War.

Coulter, David, b. 1808. [1277] Memoirs...St. Louis: Presbyterian pub. co., n.d. 551 p. Auto., p. 13-62. MoKU. Presbyterian clergyman tells of a portion of his life in Missouri.

Cournos, John. [1278] Autobiography. N.Y.: G. P. Putnam, 1935. 344 p. WU. A Russian born Jew tells of his experiences in America (p. 61-194) as a literary figure during the years 1891-1912.

Coursey, O.W., b. 1873. [1279] Pioneering in Dakota. Mitchell, South Dakota: Educator supply co., 1937. 160 p. MtHi. Covers the years 1883-1896 and tells of his farm, school and church experiences.

Courtney, Abram V., b. 1802. [1280] The adventures of a blind man and his faithful dog...Boston: William White, printer, 1856. 112 p. MiD-B. Sailor, who suffering blindness, becomes a travelling merchant in New York, Pennsylvania and Maryland.

Courtney, Abram V., b. 1802. [1281] Anecdotes of the blind...with a memoir of the author...Boston: The author, 1835. 52 p. Auto., p. 3-27. MWA. A blind peddler in Boston.

Courtney, Charles, d. 1947. [1282] Unlocking adventure. N.Y.: Whittlesey house, 1942. 335 p. NN. The author, the leading American authority on locks and safe combinations, tells of his many interesting experiences, including deep-sea diving exploits.

Courtney, Earl Count (pseud.). See Barton, Charles Vaden.

Cowan, Bud. [1283] Range rider. Garden City: Doubleday, Doran, 1930. 289 p. WHi. In Idaho, Montana and Wyoming.

Cowan, John F. [1284] The you-ought-to-buy-ography of an ink-slinger. Kohala, Hawaii: Midget press, 1915. 132 p. MoKU. Writer for Christian Endeavor World and Methodist Recorder. As a clergyman he served in West Virginia and in Hawaii. The book begins with the year 1860.

Cowell, Joe. [1285] Thirty years passed among the players in England and America. N.Y.: Harper, 1844. 103 p. WHi. British actor whose American experiences are related in p.55-103.

Cowen, Philip, b. 1853. [1286]
Memories of an American Jew. N.Y.: International press, 1932. 438 p. WHi. New York publisher of the magazine, American Hebrew.

Cowherd, Philip Henshaw, b. 1869. [1287]
Sketch of my life. Cynthia, Ky.: Hobson book press, 1944. 135 p. DLC. Baptist clergyman in Kentucky, Virginia and South Carolina.

Cowles, Mrs. Lucy Gillmore. [1288]
Lucy Gillmore Cowles, 1833-1914. No imprint. 37 p. WHi. Story of her youth in Ohio and Illinois.

Cowles, Virginia. [1289]
Looking for trouble. N.Y.: Harper, 1941. 447 p. WU. American journalist tells of her European experiences during 1937-1941.

Cowley, Malcolm. [1290]
Exile's return...N.Y.: W. W. Norton, 1934. 308 p. WU. Literary reminiscences of life in post-World War I Europe and the United States, chiefly in New York.

Cox, Jacob Dolson, 1828-1900. [1291]
Military reminiscences of the Civil war. N.Y.: Scribner's, 1900. 2 vols. WHi. Officer in the Union army, who was later governor of Ohio.

Cox, John E. [1292]
Five years in the U.S. army. Reminiscences and records of an ex-regular. Owensville, Indiana: General Baptist pub. house, 1892. 171 p. ICN. In the Dakota territory 1872-77.

Cox, Mahala Jane (Holland), [1293]
b. 1845. Mother M. J. Cox...an autobiography. Oklahoma City: Black dispatch, 1929. 20 p. DLC. Lay missionary worker (Negress) among Baptists.

Cox, Ross, b. 1793. [1294]
Adventures on the Columbia River including...six years on the western side of the Rocky mountains... N.Y.: Harper, 1832. 335 p. WHi. Frontier trader and Indian fighter in the service of Astor. Cox was an Irishman who returned to Dublin.

Cox, Samuel Sullivan, 1824-1889. [1295]
Three decades of Federal legislation. 1855 to 1885. Personal and historical memories of events preceding, during and since the American Civil War. Providence: J. A. & R. A. Reid, 1886. 726 p. NN. Journalist and member of Congress from Ohio and later from New York.

Cox, W. D., b. 1856. [1296]
The country preacher...by "Ajax". Henderson: Gleaner book and job print, 1897. 164 p. KyRE. Baptist in Kentucky.

Cox, W. T., b. 1835. [1297]
Out of the depths. Sycamore, Ill.: Baker & Arnold, 1876. 80 p. DLC. Printer, editor and publisher of newspapers in Mass. and Illinois, who was cured of alcoholism.

Cox, William Edward, b. 1870. [1298]
Southern sidelights...Raleigh, N. C.: Edwards & Broughton, 1942. 170 p. WHi. His life to the age of 32 when he entered the ministry.

Coyne, Frederick Eugene, b. 1860. [1299]
In reminiscence. Chicago: priv. pr., 1941. 336 p. DLC. Collector of internal revenue in Illinois, postmaster, and restaurant owner.

Coyne, William M. [1300]
A sailor's log of facts; not fables. Boston: The Christopher pub. house, 1934. 228 p. DLC. Twelve years on merchant ships and in the U.S. Navy.

Cozzens, Frederick Swartwout, [1301]
1818-1869. "Autobiographic sketch." (In his: Sayings, wise and otherwise. N.Y.: American book exchange, 1880) p. xiii-xxii.) NN. New York author and wine merchant.

Crabtree, James William, 1864- [1302]
1945. What counted mo. t. Lincoln, Chicago: The Univ. pub. co., 1935. 174 p. NN. Educational leader and college president, largely in Nebraska and Wisconsin.

Craig, John D., b. 1903. [1303]
Danger is my business. N.Y.: Simon & Schuster, 1938. 309 p. NN. Adventures in Africa and India; moving-picture camera man; deep-sea diver.

Craig, Nute, b. 1849. [1304]
Thrills 1861 to 1887. Oakland: priv. pub., n.d. 62 p. WyHi. Mainly of his experiences as a telegrapher in Wyoming, but there is additional material on his political and mercantile activities.

Crain, John Dean, b. 1881. [1305]
A mountain boy's life story. Greenville, S.C.: Baptist Courier

co., 1914. 65 p. DLC. Baptist clergyman and educator in South Carolina.

Craine, Jeremiah V., d. 1855. [1306] The conspirators' victims... Sacramento: 1855. 39 p. C. Murderer.

Cram, Ralph Adams, b. 1863. [1307] My life in architecture. Boston: Little, Brown, 1937. 325 p. WU. Architect.

Crane, Charles Judson. [1308] The experience of a colonel of infantry. N.Y.: The Knickerbocker press, 1923. 578 p. TxWB. In Texas, New Mexico and Arizona, by an officer who left West Point in 1872. His services in the War with Spain are also related.

Crane, George B., b. 1806. [1309] A life history...San Jose: Mercury print, 1886. 243 p. CLU. Physician in New York, Alabama and California. The account closes with 1882.

Crane, Leo, b. 1881. [1310] Indians of the enchanted desert. Boston: Little, Brown, 1925. 364 p. DLC. Indian agent in Arizona.

Crane, Richard Teller, 1832- [1311] 1912. The autobiography of Richard Teller Crane. Chicago: pub. priv., 1927. 247 p. WHi. Illinois manufacturer of bathroom facilities.

Crane, William H., 1845-1928. [1312] Footprints and echoes. N.Y.: E.P. Dutton, 1925. 232 p. NN. Recollections of the American stage by a veteran actor.

Crane, William Whiting, 1805- [1313] 1896. Autobiography...Syracuse: A.W. Hall, 1891. 480 p. Auto., p. 1-149. NN. Methodist minister in New York and Michigan.

Cranfill, James Britton, 1858- [1314] 1942. Dr. J. B. Cranfill's chronicle. A story of life in Texas. N.Y.: Fleming H. Revell, 1916. 496 p. TxU. Texas physician who became a Baptist clergyman and editor of religious journals. Also active in prohibition movement.

Cranfill, James Britton, 1858- [1314A] 1942. From memory; reminiscences, recitals, and gleanings from a bustling and busy life. Nashville, Tenn.: Boardman press, 281 p. NN. See preceding entry.

Crapo, Thomas, b. 1842. [1315] Strange but true...New Bedford: priv. pr., 1893. 151 p. WHi. Service afloat on merchant ships and in the U.S. Navy.

Crapsey, Algeron Sidney, 1847- [1316] 1927. The last of the heretics. N.Y.: Knopf, 1924. 297 p. WHi. By an Episcopal clergyman.

Crary, Albert M., b. 1834. [1317] The A. M. Crary memoirs and memoranda. Herington, Kansas: Herington Times, 1915. 164 p. DLC. Boyhood on a farm in Vermont and Wisconsin, service in the Civil War, followed by farming in Kansas.

Crashing Thunder. Autobiography [1318] of an American Indian. N.Y.: D. Appleton, 1926. 203 p. WHi. The story of a Winnebago Indian living in a white man's civilization.

Crawford, C. M., b. 1860. [1319] Pioneer recollections. No imprint. 19 p. CU-B. California lawyer and politician, who began as a teacher.

Crawford, Charles Howard. [1320] Scenes of earlier days in crossing the plains to Oregon, and experiences of western life. Petaluma, Calif.: Studdert, printer. 1898. 186 p. DLC. Presbyterian clergyman on the frontier in Oregon and California.

Crawford, Isabel Alice Hartley, [1321] b. 1865. A jolly journal. N.Y.: Fleming H. Revell, 1932. 158 p. DLC. Baptist missionary to Indians in Oklahoma.

Crawford, Mary M. The Nez [1322] Perces since Spalding. Experiences...at Lapwai, Idaho. Berkeley: 1936. 64 p. DLC. Presbyterian missionary to the Indians.

Crawford, Mrs. Mattie. [1323] On mule back through Central America with the gospel. Indianapolis: priv. printed, 1922. 224 p. DLC. Missionary representing the church of the Pentacostal Holiness.

Crawford, Samuel Johnson, 1835- [1324] 1913. Kansas in the sixties. Chicago: A. C. McClurg, 1911. 441 p. WHi. Lawyer and governor of Kansas tells of his life to 1910.

Crawford, Thomas. The life and [1325] adventures of Thomas Crawford, a native of England... Concord, N.H.: A. Taylor & Charles Parker, 1849. 176 p. MWA. Itinerant life in New England, including that of a hostler, school teacher.

Crawford, Walter M., b. 1873. [1326] Life and travels... N.p.: J. H. Hoogenakker, 1906. 261 p. TxU. Manual worker, poet and singer in Iowa, Kansas and the southwest.

Crawshaw, William Henry, 1861- [1327] 1940. My Colgate years. Hamilton, N.Y.: priv. pr., 1937. 285 p. WU. By a professor of literature.

Creath, Jacob, 1799-1886. [1328] Memoir...by P. Donan. Cinc.: Chase & Hall, 1877. 212 p. TxU. Baptist clergyman who turned to Campbellites tells of his life in Kentucky, Missouri, Illinois and Iowa.

Creevey, Mrs. Caroline A. [1329] Stickney. A daughter of the Puritans, an autobiography. N.Y.: Putnam, 1916. 272 p. WHi. Writer on gardens tells of her youth to the year 1866.

Crehore, Albert Cushing, b. 1868. [1330] Autobiography. Gates Mills, Ohio: Wm. G. Berner, 1944. 175 p. WU. Physicist who taught at Dartmouth.

Cremong, John C. [1331] Life among the Apaches. San Francisco: A. Roman, 1868. 322 p. WHi. Indian fighter on the southwest frontier.

Cribben, Henry, b. 1834. [1332] The military memoirs...Ed. by J. Clayton Youker. N.P.: priv. pr., 1911. 154 p. WHi. Union army officer.

Critchell, Robert Siderfin, [1333] b. 1844. Recollections of a fire insurance man, including his experience in the U.S. Navy (Mississippi squadron) during the Civil war. Chicago: 1909. 164 p. DLC. In Ohio, Missouri and Illinois.

Critchlow, Edward Coe, b. 1860. [1334] Three-score and ten plus. Los Angeles: Suttonhouse, 1937. 163 p. NN. Experiences in the public utilities field, particularly with natural and artificial gas, and with the Union Oil Company of California.

Crittenden, Thomas Theodore, [1335] 1832-1909. The autobiography of the late Thomas T. Crittenden, governor of Missouri. (In: H. H. Crittenden, compiler, The Crittenden memoirs. N.Y.: G. P. Putnam's sons, 1936.)p. 25-82. NN. Lawyer, Union officer in the Civil War, attorney general and governor of Missouri, and congressman from that state. His outstanding achievement as governor was the breaking up of the James gang of outlaws.

Crittenton, Charles Nelson, 1833- [1336] 1909. The brother of girls. Chicago: World's events, 1910. 247 p. WHi. New York merchant who founded a national group of missions for women. See also his Around the World with Jesus (1893).

Crocker, Aimee, d. 1941. And [1337] I'd do it again. N.Y.: Coward-McCann, 1936. 291 p. NN. In Hawaii, the South Seas, Japan, China and India by a woman who sought adventure.

Crocker, Uriel, 1796-1887. [1338] Memorial of Uriel Crocker. Boston: 1891. 124 p. WHi. Boston publisher.

Crockett, David, 1786-1836. [1339] An account of Col. Crockett's tour to the North and down East... Phila.: E. L. Carey, 1835. 234 p. WHi. Written with Crockett's help. The celebrated tour took place during Crockett's tenure as a Congressman from Tennessee.

Crockett, David, 1786-1836. [1340] A narrative of the life of David Crockett, of the state of Tennessee. Phila.: pr. by E. L. Carey, 1834. 113 p. WHi. Life of the famous frontier hunter and Indian fighter but not written by him. See Parrington and the D.A.B. for a discussion of the authenticity of the Crockett literature.

Cromwell, Emma (Guy). [1341] Woman in politics. Louisville: The Standard pr. co., 1939. 330 p. DLC. Librarian and political figure in Kentucky.

Cronin, David Edward. See Eyland, Seth (pseud.)

Crook, Wiley M., b. 1842. [1342] Autobiography and reminiscences. Starr City, Ark.?: 1917? 70 p. USIGS. Microfilm copy. After service with the Confederate forces, the author lived as a farmer in Tennessee, Missouri and Texas.

Crooks, James, b. 1825. [1343]
The autobiography...Terre Haute:
1900. 228 p. CoD. Physician and
manufacturer of patent medicines
in Indiana.

Crosby, Elisha Oscar, b. 1818. [1344]
Memoirs...San Marino: Huntington
library, 1945. 105 p. WHi. United
States minister to Guatemala.
Lawyer and politician in California.

Crosby, Enoch. [1345]
The spy unmasked...taken from
his own lips...by H. L. Barnum.
N.Y.: J. L. J. Harper, 1828.
206 p. WHi. Secret Service agent
during the Revolutionary War.
Cooper's Harvey Birch may have
been patterned after Crosby.
Barnum is supposed to have
attributed fictitious deeds to
Crosby.

Crosby, Fanny. See
Van Alystyne, Francis Jane (Crosby).

Cross, F. M., b. 1834. [1346]
A short sketch-history from personal reminiscences of early
days in central Texas. N.p.:
1910. 115 p. TxU. Ranching and
farming, from about 1845 to 1870.

Cross, Joseph, 1813-1893. [1347]
Days of my years. N.Y.: Thomas
Whittaker, 1896. 319 p. DLC. His
experiences as a Civil War chaplain by a Methodist clergyman
who came here from England.

Cross, Wilbur Lucius, b. 1862. [1348]
Connecticutt Yankee, an autobiography. New Haven: Yale univ.
press, 1943. 428 p. WHi. Professor
of English at Yale who became
governor of Connecticut.

Croswell, Joseph, 1712-1799. [1349]
Sketches...ed. by Jacob Norton.
Boston: Lincoln & Edmands,1809.
96 p. DLC. An itinerant preacher
in the New England states.

Crowe, Pat, b. 1869. [1350]
Pat Crowe; his story, confession
and reformation. N.Y.: G. W.
Dillingham, 1906. MoK. Thief
and kidnapper who operated in
the Middle Western states.

Crowe, Robert, b. 1823. [1351]
The reminiscences of Robert
Crowe, the octogenarian tailor.
N.Y.: 1901? 32 p. NN. Experiences
in England where the author was
connected with the Chartist movement; came to the U.S. in 1854;
active in the labor movement and
in New York politics.

Crowell, Mrs. Evelyn (Miller) [1352]
Pierce. Texas childhood. Dallas:
The Kaleidograph press, 1941.
91 p. DLC. On a large farm in
Texas.

Croy, Homer, b. 1883. [1353]
Country cured. N.Y.: Harper,
1943. 282 p. DLC. Journalist in
N.Y. and Chicago who also wrote
plays and movies, including
scenarios for the movies.

Croy, Homer, b. 1883. [1354]
Wonderful neighbor. N.Y.: Harper,
1945. 204 p. DLC. Early life on a
Missouri farm by one who later
became a writer.

Crummer, John, 1816-1890. [1355]
Sketch...by Wilbur F. Crummer.
Pub. by his sons, 1916. 81 p. Auto.,
p. 9-25. MoHi. Methodist clergy-
man in Illinois, Wisconsin and
Iowa.

Crump, Thomas G., 1836-1918. [1356]
Recollections of a Minnesota
missionary. No imprint, 1903?
24 p. MnHi. From 1870 to 1874.

Crumpton, Hezekiah John and [1357]
Washington Bryan. The adventures of two Alabama boys.
Montgomery: Paragon press,
1912. 238 p. WHi. Hezekiah tells
of his life as a forty-niner while
Washington tells of his services
with the Confederate army.

Crumpton, Washington Bryan. [1358]
A book of memories, 1842-1920.
Montgomery: Baptist mission
board, 1921. 339 p. AU. Baptist
clergyman in Alabama. Includes
his Civil War experiences. See
also the item by Hezekiah J.
Crumpton.

Cruse, Thomas, b. 1857. [1359]
Apache days and after. Caldwell,
Idaho: Caxton, 1941. 328 p. WHi.
By an army officer.

Crutcher, Samuel W., d. 1909. [1360]
My experience with the liquor
traffic. St. Louis: Christian pub.
co., 1891. 91 p. MoCanD. A Kentucky clergyman tells of his fight
against the whiskey interests.

Cubery, William M., b. 1838. [1361]
Fifty years a printer. No imprint,
1907? p. 5-15. CSmH. His apprenticeship from 1850 to 1857 in Mass.

Cudahy, Patrick, 1849-1919. [1362]
Patrick Cudahy, his life. Milwaukee:
Burdick & Allen, 1912. 290 p. DLC.

Cudmore, Patrick, b. 1831. [1363]
Autobiography. No imprint. 10 p.
WHi. Lawyer in Wisconsin and
Minnesota who was also a novelist, historian and poet.

Culbertson, Ely. The strange [1364]
lives of one man. Phila.: Winston,
1940. 693 p. WHi. Anarchist in
Spain, gambler and revolutionist
in Russia and Mexico, hobo in
California, and bridge teacher.

Culleton, John, b. 1858. [1365]
Ten years a priest, an open confession. Louisville: published by
the author, 1893. 295 p. KyBgW.
A Kentucky Catholic priest in
the seventies and eighties who
left the priesthood.

Culley, John Henry, b. 1864. [1366]
Cattle, horses and men of the
Western range. Los Angeles:
Ward Ritchie press, 1940. 337 p.
Auto., p. 3-90. DLC. An Englishman on a New Mexico ranch,
1890-1916.

Cullinan, Howell. [1367]
Of all places. Norwood, Mass.:
The Plimpton press, 1935. 258 p.
NN. Experiences of a newspaper
man; student days at Cornell;
adventures as a sailor on the
Great Lakes; travel experiences
in various parts of the world.

Cullom, Shelby Moore, 1829-1914. [1368]
Fifty years of public service.
Chicago: A. C. McClurg, 1911.
467 p. WHi. Lawyer and U.S.
Senator from Illinois.

Culver, Newell. [1369]
Methodism forty years ago and
now: embracing many interesting
reminiscences and incidents...
N.Y.: Nelson & Phillips, 1873.
309 p. NN. By a Methodist
clergyman in New Hampshire.

Cumming, Kate, b. 1835. [1370]
A journal of hospital life in the
Confederate army of Tennessee...
Louisville: J. P. Morton, 1866.
199 p. NjP. Covers 1862-1865.

Cummings, Charles L., b. 1848. [1371]
The great war relic...Together
with a sketch of my life, service
in the army...No imprint. 48 p.
Auto., p. 2-12. DLC. Served
with a Michigan outfit in the Civil
War.

Cummings, Florence Amelia. [1372]
Yesterday. Boston: Marshall Jones,
1936. 108 p. NN. Recollections of
a New England childhood.

Cummings, Lewis Vance. [1373]
I was a head-hunter...Boston:
Houghton Mifflin, 1941. 338 p. DLC.
An explorer in South America,
1921-23.

Cummins, H. E. [1374]
A mission man in Michigan.
Frankfort: Victor press, 1935.
63 p. MiD-B. Evangelist.

Cummins, Jim. [1375]
Jim Cummins' book...A true but
terrible tale of outlawry. Denver:
Reed pub. co., 1903. 191 p. TxU.
After serving in the Confederate
forces, the author lived as a robber
in Arkansas and Missouri.

Cummins, Margaret. [1376]
Leaves from my portfolio. St.
Louis: Wm. E. Foote, printer,
1860. 181 p. MoSHi. A spiritual
account by an author who lived
in Missouri during the forties
and fifties.

Cummins, Sarah J. Walden [1377]
(Lemmon), b. 1828. Autobiography
and reminiscences...Cleveland:
Arthur H. Clark, 1914. 63 p. WHi.
A story of frontier life in Ohio,
Missouri and Oregon.

Cunningham, Mrs. Anna M. Lowry.
See Lowry, Anna M.

Cunningham, John Henry, b. 1877. [1378]
As the twig is bent; being chronicles and anecdotes of juvenile
and medical memories. Norwood,
Mass.: priv. pr. at the Plimpton
press, 1936. 205 p. DLC. A
surgeon tells mainly of his boyhood in Massachusetts.

Cunningham, John Lovell, b. 1840. [1379]
Three years with the Adirondack
regiment, 118th New York volunteer infantry...Norwood, Mass.:
Plimpton press, 1920. 286 p. DLC.
Civil War account. Also described
are his activities in New York law
and politics after the War.

Curran, G. W., b. 1886. [1380]
My conversion. N.p.: 1938. 32 p.
CU-B. A layman tells of his conversion from Catholicism to
Mormonism.

Curran, Henry Hastings, b. 1877. [1381]
Pillar to post. N.Y.: Scribner's,
1941. 387 p. WU. Politician in
New York City who among other
posts held that of U.S. Commissioner
for Immigration for the port of N.Y.

Currier, Solon. [1382]
The wonderful wheel of fortune...
Laconia, N.H.: pr. by John H.
Brewster, 1867. 128 p. MWA.
Freewill Baptist preacher in
New Hampshire.

Curtin, Jeremiah, 1835-1906. [1383]
Memoirs of Jeremiah Curtin.
Madison: State historical society
of Wisconsin, 1941. 901 p. WHi.
American minister to Russia
who was also an ethnologist.

Curtis? [1384]
Five years at Anamosa. Anamosa
prison: 1899. 42 p. Ia-HA.
A bigamist tells of his life in
an Iowa prison.

Curwood, James Oliver, 1878- [1385]
1927. Son of the forests; an autobiography, as completed by
Dorothea A. Bryant. Garden City,
N.Y.: Doubleday, Doran, 1930.
243 p. NN. Newspaper man and
novelist of the great out-of-doors.

Cusack, May Frances Clare, [1386]
d. 1899. Nun of Kenmare; an
autobiography. Boston: Ticknor,
1888. 558 p. DLC. Irish born
Mother Superior who left Catholics and went over in 1891 to the
Baptists while in New York City.

Cushing, Frank Hamilton, 1857- [1387]
1900. My adventures in Zuñi.
Santa Fe, N.M.: The Peripatetic
press, 1941. 178 p. NN. Experiences of an anthropologist while
living with the Zuñi Indians of
New Mexico, 1879-1884.

Cushing, S. W., b. 1818. [1388]
Wild oats sowings...N.Y.: Daniel
Fanshaw, 1857. 483 p. DLC.
Naval life.

Cushman, Mrs. Mary (Ames), [1389]
b. 1865. She wrote it all down.
N.Y.: Scribner, 1936. 226 p.
MoS. The story of girlhood
while living in Europe, 1876-80.

Cushman, Mary Floyd, b. 1870. [1390]
Missionary doctor; the story of
twenty years in Africa. N.Y.:
Harper, 1944. 279 p. WU. The
story begins in 1922.

Cushman, Pauline. [1391]
Life of Pauline Cushman, the
celebrated Union spy and scout...
by F. L. Sarmiento. Phila.: J. E.
Potter, 1865. 374 p. WHi. The
writer claimed to have gotten
this account from Miss Cushman,
and to have used her memoranda.
A high-flown tale.

Custer, Edgar A., 1861-1937. [1392]
No royal road. N.Y.: H. C. Kinsey,
1937. 428 p. NN. Mechanical engineer and industrialist; early life
in Altoona, Pa.; work with the
Pennsylvania Railroad and with
the Baldwin Locomotive Company;
first European War experiences.

Custer, Mrs. Elizabeth (Bacon). [1393]
"Boots and saddles," or life in
Dakota with General Custer. N.Y.:
Harper, 1885. 269 p. WHi. As
described by the title.

Custer, Elizabeth (Bacon). [1394]
Tenting on the plains...N.Y.:
C. L. Webster, 1887. 702 p. WHi.
The wife of General Custer tells
of their life in Kansas and Texas
following the Civil War. Covers
1866-67.

Custer, George Armstrong, [1395]
1839-1876. My life on the plains.
Or, personal experiences with
Indians. N.Y.: Sheldon & co., 1874.
256 p. WHi. Indian fighter.

Cutler, Helen R. [1396]
Jottings from life...Cinc.: Poe
& Hitchcock, 1866. 282 p. TxDaM.
By the wife of a Methodist clergyman. The locale is not revealed.

Cuyler, Theodore Ledyard, 1822- [1397]
1909. Recollections of a long
life, an autobiography by Theodore
Ledyard Cuyler...N.Y.: The Baker
& Taylor co., 1902. 356 p. WHi.
Presbyterian clergyman in New
York and New Jersey who was a
temperance worker and who wrote
for the religious press.

# D

Daffan, L. A., 1845-1907. [1398]
My father... by Katie Daffan,
including autobiographical sketch
...Houston: Press of Gray &
Dillaye, n.d. 110 p. Auto., p. 37-
50. TxU. Train master in Texas
who during the Civil War served
with the Confederate forces.

Dagg, John Leadley, 1794-1884. [1399]
Autobiography...Rome, Ga.:
J. F. Shanklin, 1886. 53 p. NcD.
Microfilm copy. Baptist clergyman in the South who was also
president of Mercer University.

Dahl, Borghild Margrethe. [1400]
I wanted to see. N.Y.: Macmillan,

1944. 210 p. WU. A school teacher tells of her final victory over eye disease.

Daily, Starr. [1401]
Love can open prison doors. 7th rev. ed. Melrose, Mass.: Melrose press, 1943. 144 p. WU. A story of prison life by a convict.

Dale, Sam, 1772-1841. [1402]
The life and times of Gen. Sam Dale, the Mississippi partisan, by John F. H. Claiborne. N.Y.: 1860. 233 p. DLC. Mississippi political figure tells also of his military experiences in the Creek War, 1813-14. Based on Dale's own account.

Dall, Caroline Wells (Healey), [1403] 1822-1912. "Alongside;" being notes suggested by "A New England boyhood" of Doctor Edward Everett Hale. Boston: Thomas Todd, 1900. 100 p. NN. An author, reformer tells of her girlhood in Boston.

Dallinger, Frederick William, [1404] b. 1871. Recollections of an old fashioned New Englander. N.Y.: Round table, 1942. 277 p. WHi. Lawyer, judge and U.S. Congressman from Mass.

Dallman, William, b. 1862. [1405]
My life...St. Louis: Concordia pub. house, 1945. 152 p. WHi. Lutheran clergyman in the Ozarks, Maryland, New York, Wisconsin and Illinois.

Dally, Nathan, b. 1848. [1406]
Tracks and trails...Walker: Cass County pioneer, 1931. 138 p. DLC. Early Minnesota settler, operator of steamboat in Minnesota.

Dalton, Emmett, b. 1871. [1407]
Beyond the law...N.Y.: J. S. Ogilvie pub. co., 1916. 190 p. CU. In California and on the plains.

Dalton, Mrs. Hanah Daphne Smith, [1408] b. 1857. Pretty is as pretty does. 2d ed. Mowbray, South Africa: South Africa mission of the Church ...of Latter-Day Saints, n.d. 64 p. UU. After the death of her husband, a Mormon, she opens a hotel in Colorado.

Dalton, James. [1409]
Life and actions of James Dalton, a noted street robber...with account of...the tricks he played in New York, the Bermudas, Virginia, Carolina, and other parts of America, taken from his own mouth while in Newgate. London: 1730. BM. As described by the title.

Dalton, John Call, 1825-1889. [1410]
John Call Dalton, M.D., U.S.V. Cambridge, Mass.: The Riverside press, 1892. 105 p. NN. Experiences of a military surgeon in the Civil War.

Dalton, Kit, b. 1843. [1411]
Under the black flag. Memphis: Lockard, n.d. 251 p. WHi. With Quantrell in the Civil War, and then a border outlaw with Jesse James.

Dalzell, James M. [1412]
James Dalzell...Cinc.: Robert Clarke, 1888. 242 p. Auto., p. 5-64. WU. Writer of sketches of the Civil War who served with an Ohio outfit.

Dame, William Meade. [1413]
From the Rapidan to Richmond and the Spottsylvania campaign. Baltimore: Green-Lucas co., 1920. 213 p. WHi. Confederate soldier.

Dameron, George W., b. 1815. [1414]
Early recollections. Huntsville, Mo.: Herald print, 1898. 54 p. MoHi. Mainly the story of his youth on a farm in Missouri.

Dameron, James Palatine, b. 1828.[1415]
Autobiography...No imprint. 31 p. DLC. Rancher and lawyer in California, beginning with 1849.

D'Amico, Ishmael, b. 1890. [1416]
My testimony. Rochester, N.Y.: 1945. 36 p. UHi. A Catholic who was converted to the Church of Jesus Christ and became an evangelical minister in Colorado, Michigan, Ohio, Pa., and New York.

Damon, Bertha (Clark). [1417]
A sense of humus. N.Y.: Simon & Schuster, 1943. 250 p. DLC. A city dweller who turned to rural living in New Hampshire, especially gardening.

Damon, C.M. [1418]
Sketches and incidents...Chicago: Free Methodist pub. house, 1900. 366 p. KHi. Free Methodist clergyman in Iowa and Kansas in the second half of the 19th century.

Damrosch, Walter Johannes, [1419] b. 1862. My musical life. N.Y.: C. Scribner's sons, 1930. 390 p. DLC. By the noted orchestra conductor.

Dana, Charles Anderson, 1819- [1420]
1897. Recollections of the Civil
war. N.Y.: D. Appleton & co.,
1898. 296 p. DLC. Assistant
Secretary of War, 1863-65.

Dana, Richard Henry, 1815-1882. [1421]
Two years before the mast. A
personal narrative of life at sea
...N.Y.: Harper & bros., 1840.
483 p. WU. The noted author
writes of his trip round Cape
Horn undertaken to rest his eyes
from study.

Dane, John, of Ipswich, b. 1612? [1422]
Declarations of remarkable
providences in the course of my
life. Boston: Samuel G. Drake,
1854. 14 p. MnHi. Farmer and
tailor in Mass.

D'Angelo, Pascal, b. 1894. [1423]
Pascal D'Angelo, son of Italy.
N.Y.: The Macmillan co., 1924.
185 p. DLC. Italian born laborer
who became a poet in New York.

Daniel, Ferdinand Eugene. [1424]
Recollections of a rebel surgeon
...Austin: Von Boeckmann, 1899.
264 p. WHi. As described by the
title.

Daniels, Mrs. Addie Worth [1425]
(Bagley). Recollections of a
cabinet minister's wife, 1913-
1921. Raleigh: Mitchell, 1945.
199 p. NcGW. The wife of
Josephus Daniels tells of her
participation in community
affairs.

Daniels, Bradford Kempton. [1426]
The outer edge. Caldwell, Idaho:
Caxton, 1943. 326 p. DLC. Rancher
in Washington who came for his
health.

Daniels, Josephus, b. 1862. [1427]
Tar heel editor...Chapel Hill:
The Univ. of N.C. press, 1939.
544 p. WHi. North Carolina
journalist.

Daniels, Josephus, b. 1862. [1428]
Editor in politics...Chapel Hill:
The Univ. of N.C. press, 1941.
664 p. WHi. This volume covers
the years 1893-1912.

Daniels, Josephus, b. 1862. [1429]
The Wilson era; years of peace,
1910-1917...Chapel Hill: The Univ.
of N.C. press, 1944. 615 p. WHi.
Member of the Wilson cabinet.

DaPonte, Lorenzo, 1749-1838. [1430]
Memoirs...Phila.: J.B. Lippincott,
1929. 512 p. WU. Poet, librettist.

Dargan, Edwin Charles, 1852- [1431]
1930. Harmony Hall; recollections
of an old southern home. Columbia,
S.C.: State pub. co., 1912. 118 p.
ViU. Baptist clergyman. The
story ends with 1882.

Darley, George Marshall, b. 1847. [1432]
Pioneering in the San Juan. Personal reminiscences...Chicago:
Revell, 1899. 225 p. DLC. Presbyterian missionary in the gold
mining regions of Colorado.

Darling, Flora (Adams), 1840- [1433]
1910. Founding and organization
of the Daughters of the American
Revolution and the Daughters of
the Revolution. Phila.: Independence
pub. co., 1901. 207 p. NN. By the
founder of both organizations.

Darrow, Clarence Seward, 1857- [1434]
1938. The story of my life, by
Clarence Darrow, illustrated from
photographs. N.Y.: C. Scribner's
sons, 1932. 495 p. WHi. Criminal
lawyer.

Dashiell, Thomas Grayson, 1830- [1435]
1893. A pastor's recollections.
N.Y.: Appleton, 1875. 208 p.
ICMILC. Episcopalian minister
in Virginia.

Daugherty, Harvey Harrison, [1436]
b. 1841. A conglomerate...
Indianapolis: The author, 1912.
422 p. Auto., p. 359-422. DLC.
Indiana lawyer and minor political
figure.

Davenport, Homer Calvin, 1867- [1437]
1912. The country boy...N.Y.:
G.W. Dillingham, 1910. 191 p. Or.
A cartoonist tells of his boyhood
in Oregon. See also his, My Quest
of the Arab Horse, owned by Or.

Davenport, John Gaylord. [1438]
Experiences and observations by
the way...Boston: Pilgrim press,
1917. 211 p. DLC. Congregational
clergyman in Connecticut.

David, Elizabeth (Harbison). [1439]
I played their accompaniments.
N.Y.: D. Appleton-Century, 1940.
246 p. WU. Pianist.

Davidge, William Pleator, 1814- [1440]
1888. Footlight flashes. N.Y.:
American news, 1866. 274 p. NN.
Random recollections of the English actor, who came to America
in 1850, remaining here the remainder of his life.

Davidson, Hannah Frances, [1441]
b. 1860. South and south central

Africa; a record of fifteen years'
missionary labors... . Elgin,
Ill.: pr. for the author by Brethren pub. house, 1915. 481 p. DLC.
By a member of the Brethren
in Christ's Church.

Davidson, Henry Damon. [1442]
"Inching along"...Nashville:
National publication co., 1944.
177 p. WHi. Negro educator in
the South.

Davidson, John, 1750-1835. [1443]
Reminiscences. Boston: Stanhope
press, 1916. 16 p. DLC. Colonial
farmer in Maine who refused to
take oath of loalty to the Crown
during Revolution.

Davidson, Mrs. Josie (Martin), [1444]
b. 1857...Her life & work.
Prestonsburg, Ky.: 1922. 258 p.
WHi. Story of everyday married
life by a worker for the Eastern
Star lodge.

Davidson, Lorenzo D., b. 1856. [1445]
Down through eighty years.
Hopkins, Minn.: Hennepin county
review, 1938. 149 p. DLC. Min-
nesota journalist, and Illinois and
North Dakota businessman.

Davidson, Wilson Thompson, [1446]
1868-1944. Years of an army
doctor. San Antonio, Tex.: Naylor,
1944. 189 p. NN. Service in Cuba
during the occupation; life in the
Philippines and among the Moros;
first European War.

Davie, John L., b. 1850. [1447]
My own story. Oakland: Post
enquirer, 1931. 174 p. WU. Frontier cowboy, cattle rancher, merchant and political figure in
California.

Davies, Mrs. Eliza. [1448]
The story of an earnest life...
Cinc.: Central book concern,
1881. 570 p. DLC. A Scottish
Baptist lay missionary worker
in Australia, Virginia and Kentucky.

Davies, William Henry. [1449]
The autobiography of a super-
tramp. N.Y.: Alfred A. Knopf,
1917. 345 p. WHi. Englishman
who spent five years in the U.S.
as a hobo and beggar.

Daviess, Maria Thompson, [1450]
1872-1924. Seven times seven,
an autobiography. N.Y.: Dodd,
Mead, 1924. 321 p. NN. Personal
record of the experiences of an
artist and writer.

Davis, Andrew Jackson, 1826-1910.[1451]
The magic staff; an autobiography.
N.Y.: J. S. Brown, 1857. 552 p. NN.
Mesmerist and spiritualist in
New York.

Davis, Andrew Jackson, 1826- [1452]
1910. Beyond the valley...Boston:
Colby & Rich, 1885. 402 p. DLC.
A sequel to his Magic Staff.

Davis, Arthur Paul, b. 1841. [1453]
Life...Rochester?: 1878. 60 p.
DLC. A physician in New York
whose criminal past led to his
arrest.

Davis, Caleb Forbes, 1829-1898 [1454]
and James Cox Davis, b. 1857.
The autobiographies of an Iowa
father and son. Reprinted from
Annals of Iowa, vol. XIX, 1935.
56 p. Ia-HA. Merchant in Iowa.
His son James was a lawyer in
Iowa.

Davis, Carlyle Channing. [1455]
Olden times in Colorado. Los
Angeles: 1916. DLC. Editor and
owner of newspaper in Colorado
who also had newspaper experience in Missouri and who during
the Civil War served with an
Iowa outfit.

Davis, Clyde Llewellyn, 1884-1919.[1456]
A Kansan at large. Forest Hills,
N.Y.: Bernice Carter Davis,
1924. 143 p. Auto., p. 3-29. DLC.
Lecturer for U.S. Department of
Agriculture and editor of agri-
cultural publications.

Davis, Edward, b. 1830. [1457]
He leadeth me; or the personal
narrative, religious experience,
and Christian labors of Edward
Davis. N.Y.: Nelson & Phillips,
1873. 239 p. NjMD. Methodist
clergyman in New York and in
New England.

Davis, Esmé, b. 1906. [1458]
Esmé of Paris. N.Y.: D. Appleton-
Century, 1944. 444 p. NN. The
writer was a ballet dancer and
circus performer.

Davis, Frances. [1459]
My shadow in the sun. N.Y.:
Carrick & Evans, 1940. 318 p.
WU. Reporter in Spain during
the Revolutionary fighting.

Davis, Fred W. [1460]
The new day. Portland, Oreg.:
1925. 240 p. DLC. A wastrel who
is converted and becomes an

evangelist to lumberjacks in Minnesota.

Davis, George, b. 1821. [1461]
Recollections of a sea wanderer's life; an autobiography of an old-time seaman who has sailed in almost every capacity before and abaft the mast, in nearly every quarter of the globe, and under the flags of four of the principal maritime nations...N.Y.: A. H. Kellogg, prtr., 1887. 408 p. NN. As described by the title.

Davis, George Turnbull Moore, [1462] Autobiography, N.Y.: 1891. 395 p. WHi. Lawyer, newspaper editor (Louisville Courier), and Mayor of Alton, Illinois. Most of the book relates to his experiences in the War with Mexico.

Davis, Henry Turner, b. about [1463] 1833. Solitary places made glad. Cinc.: p r. for the author by Cranston & Stowe, 1890. 422 p. NN. Methodist clergyman in Nebraska.

Davis, Henry Winter, 1817-1865. [1464] Life of Henry Winter Davis, by Bernard C. Steiner. Baltimore: John Murphy co., 1916. 416 p. Auto., p. 7-63. DLC. Member of the House of Representatives during the Civil War who supported the right of Negroes to vote.

Davis, Mrs. Isabella E., b. 1842. [1465] Some recollections of a busy life. Phila.: pr. for private circulation by Dresel Biddle, 1903. 130 p. Auto., p. 9-15. DLC. Experimental farming in New Jersey.

Davis, J. L., b. 1865. [1466]
Mountain preacher...Cinc.: F.L.Rowe, 1909, 75 p. DLC. Member of the Church of Christ in Kentucky.

Davis, James Cox. See Davis, Caleb Forbes.

Davis, James Harvey, b. 1853. [1467] Memoir by Cyclone Davis. Sherman, Texas: The Courier press, 1935. 327 p. NN. Populist congressman from Texas.

Davis, James John, b. 1873. [1468] The iron puddler; my life in the rolling mills and what came of it. Indianapolis: The Bobbs-Merrill co., 1922. 275 p. WHi. Labor leader, founder of the Mooseheart School for Workers.

Davis, John, 1774-1854. [1469]
"A memoir of the author" (In his, The first settlers of Virginia. N.Y.: pr. by Southwicke & Hardcastle, 1805). p. 215-84. DLC. Englishman who came to the U.S. in 1788. Teacher and author.

Davis, John, 1774-1854. [1470]
Personal adventures and travels of four years and a half in the United States of America... London: for J. Davis, 1817. 96 p. DLC. Teacher and writer who visited many places in this country.

Davis, Joshua, b. 1760. [1471]
A narrative of Joshua Davis, an American citizen who was pressed on board six ships of the British Navy...Boston: pr. by B. True, 1811. 72 p. MiU-C. Covers 1779-87.

Davis, Nelle Portrey. [1472]
Stump ranch pioneer. N.Y.: Dodd, Mead, 1942. 245 p. DLC. Grain and stock farming in Idaho during the great drought.

Davis, Noah, b. 1804. [1473]
A narrative...Baltimore: J. F. Weishampel, jr., 1859. 86 p. WHi. Negro Baptist clergyman in Maryland.

Davis, Owen, b. 1874. [1474]
I'd like to do it again. N.Y.: Farrar & Rinehart, 1931. 233 p. WU. Dramatist and screen writer.

Davis, Rebecca Blaine Harding, [1475] 1831-1910. Bits of gossip. Boston: Houghton Mifflin, 1904. 233 p. WU. Pennsylvania novelist tells mainly of her youth in the South.

Davis, Reuben, 1813-1890. [1476]
Recollections of Mississippi and Mississippians. N.Y.: Houghton Mifflin, 1889. 439 p. WHi. Lawyer and political figure in Mississippi.

Davis, Robert Hobart, 1869-1942. [1477] Tree toad; the autobiography of a small boy. N.Y.: Frederick A. Stokes, 1935. 276 p. NN. Reminiscences of a childhood in California. See also the next two items.

Davis, Robert Hobart, 1869-1942. [1478] Over my left shoulder. N.Y.: D. Appleton, 1926. 350 p. NN. Episodes in the life of a New York newspaper man and magazine editor.

Davis, Robert Hobart, 1869-1942. [1479]

Bob Davis again in many moods. N.Y.: D. Appleton, 1928. 348 p. NN. See the description of the previous item.

Davis, Samuel D., 1842-1907. [1480] Autobiography...Plainfield: American Sabbath tract soc., 1942. 98 p. WHi. Clergyman of the Seventh Day Baptist church, mainly in the Southeast and in Pennsylvania.

Davis, William Ellsworth, b. 1896.[1481] Ten years in the Congo. N.Y.: Reynal & Hitchcock, 1938. 301 p. DLC. Baptist medical missionary.

Davis, William Heath, 1822-1909. [1482] Seventy-five years in California. San Francisco: John Howell, 1929. 422 p. WHi. Merchant and ship owner. The story begins with 1831.

Davison, Francis B., b. 1827. [1483] Sketch of the life of F. B. Davison, M.D. 2d ed. West Pittston, Pa.: LaBarre, printer, 1903. 22 p. CSmH. Surgeon in Pennsylvania.

Dawson, Francis Warrington, [1484] 1840-1889. Reminiscences of Confederate service, 1861-1865. Charleston, S.C.: The News & Courier book presses, 1882. 180 p. NN. As described by the title.

Day, Dorothy, b. 1899. From [1485] Union Square to Rome. Silver Springs, Md.: Preservation of the Faith press, 1938. 173 p. DLC. The story of her development from a non-religious childhood to her conversion to Catholicism.

Day, Mary L. See Arms, Mary L. (Day).

Dayton, George Draper, b. 1857. [1486] An autobiography. N.p.: priv. pr., 1933. 329 p. DLC. Minnesota merchant tells also of his lay work for the Presbyterian church.

Dean, Anna (pseud.). See Morris, Anna.

Dean, Gardner, 1816-1882. The [1487] life, experiences and incidents... New Bedford, Mass.: Paul Howland, jr., 1883. 307 p. U$1GS. Non-sectarian clergyman in Mass.

Dean, Harry, b. 1864. The Pedro [1488] Gorino; the adventures of a Negro sea-captain in Africa and on the seven seas in his attempts to found an Ethiopian empire... Written with the assistance of Sterling North. Boston & N.Y.: Houghton Mifflin, 1929. 262 p. DLC. As described by the title.

Deane, Joseph, b. 1829. Sketch of [1489] the life and travels of Joseph Deane, by himself. 2d ed. Lancaster: pr. by J. H. Pearsol, 1854. 35 p. CSmH. Negro sailor.

Deane, Martha (pseud.). See McBride, Mary Margaret.

De Angelis, Jefferson, 1859-1933. [1490] A vagabond trouper. N.Y.: Harcourt, Brace, 1931. 325 p. WU. The life of an actor.

Deason, Beacher. 7 years in [1491] Texas prisons. No imprint. 29 p. TxU. A life of 20th century crime in Texas.

Deaton, E.L. Indian fights on the [1492] Texas frontier. Fort Worth: Pioneer pub. co., 1927. 161 p. TxH. In the sixties. The personal element in this book is not strong.

Debs, Eugene Victor, 1855-1926. [1493] Walls and bars. Chicago: Socialist party, 1927. 248 p. NN. Prison experiences of the Socialist leader, 1919-21, in the Federal Penitentiary at Atlanta.

Decker, Edward W., b. 1869. Busy [1494] years. Minneapolis: Lund press, 1937. 95 p. MnHi. Minnesota broker and banker tells of his youth on a farm.

Deems, Charles Force, 1820-1893.[1495] Autobiography...N.Y., Chicago: Fleming H. Revell, 1897. 365 p. Auto., p. 17-89. DLC.Methodist clergyman in the South, who was also professor and president of several southern colleges.

Deere, George M., b. 1827. Auto- [1496] biography. Riverside, Calif.: Press pr. co., 1908. 387 p. CSmH. Universalist clergyman in New England, the Middle Atlantic states, Wisconsin, Louisiana and California.

DeJong, David Cornel, b. 1905. [1497] With a Dutch accent; how a Hollander became an American. N.Y.: Harper, 1944. 306 p. NN. Early life in Holland; experiences as an immigrant in Michigan.

DeKoven, Anna (Farwell), b. 1860. [1498] A musician and his wife. N.Y.: Harper, 1926. 259 p. DLC. Wife of a pianist and composer.

DeKoven, Louise. See Bowen, Louise DeKoven.

DeLaFontaine, Oliver Roberts, [1499] b. 1857. The great understander. Aurora, Ill.: Walter, 1931. 315 p. DLC. California miner, messenger for Wells Fargo in California and Nevada.

Deland, Mrs. Margaret Wade [1500] (Campbell), b. 1857. Golden yesterdays. N.Y.: Harper, 1940. 351 p. WU. Literary career of a novelist.

Deland, Mrs. Margaret Wade [1501] (Campbell), b. 1857. If this be I, as I suppose it be, by Margaret Deland. N.Y., London: D. Appleton-Century co., 1935. 227 p. WU. The childhood of a novelist.

Delaney, Lucy A. From the darkness cometh light; or, struggles [1502] for freedom. St. Louis: J. T. Smith, n.d. 64 p. MoKU. A Missouri Negress tells of her efforts to escape slavery.

Delano, Alonzo, 1806-1874. Life [1503] on the plains and among the diggings...Auburn: Miller, Orton & Mulligan, 1854. 384 p. IdB. Tells of his life as a miner in California.

Delano, Reuben, b. 1809. The wanderings & adventures of Reuben [1504] Delano. N.Y.: H. Long, 1846. 100 p. WHi. Whaler.

Delany, Selden Peabody, 1874-1935.[1505] Why Rome. N.Y.: The Dial press, 1930. 231 p. DLC. An Episcopal clergyman, living in Wisconsin, Mass. and New York, is converted to Catholicism.

De Lenoir, Cecil. The hundredth [1506] man; confessions of a drug addict. London: Jarrolds, 1933. 288 p. NN. Story of his experiences as an addict and how he was finally cured. The author, an Englishman, also tells of his adventures in the United States and Mexico.

DeLeon, Edwin, 1828-1891. Thirty[1507] years of my life on three continents. London: Ward & Downey, 1890. 2 vols. TxU. Diplomatic service in Egypt and England, in the latter as representative of the Confederate States. In Asia he was connected with efforts to build railroads.

Delevan, Jones. Notes on California and the placers...by one [1508] who has been there. N.Y.: H. Long, 1850. 128 p. CSmH. By a Forty-niner.

Dell, Floyd, b. 1887. Homecoming;[1509] an autobiography. N.Y.: Farrar & Rinehart, 1933. 368 p. WU. Novelist, dramatist.

Delong, Mrs. Emma J. (Wotton). [1510] Explorer's wife. N.Y.: Dodd, Mead, 1938. 252 p. WHi. A 19th century account by the wife of a naval officer and naval explorer.

Delong, Lewis S., b. 1857. 40 years[1511] a peace officer...No imprint. 61 p. TxU. Fighting the Texas desperadoes.

DeMar, Clarence, b. 1888. Marathon. Brattleboro, Vt.: Stephen [1512] Daye press, 1937. 156 p. NN. Career of a long distance runner.

DeMilt, Alonzo Pierre, b. 1831. [1513] The life travels and adventures of an American wanderer...by Franklin Y. Fitch. N.Y.: John W. Lovell, 1883. 228 p. DLC. Adventures among the Indians in Florida and the miners in California.

DeMonbrun, Sarah Ann, 1861-1912. [1514] Honey out of the rock. Elk City, Kansas: God's Messenger pub. co., 1912. 193 p. DLC. A religious account by a member of the Free Methodist Church in Kentucky and Illinois.

Dempsey, Jack, b. 1895. Round [1515] by round; an autobiography. N.Y.: McGraw-Hill, 1940. 285 p. NN. Early life in Colorado and Utah; career as a prize fighter.

Dempster, Joseph S. From Romanism to Pentecost; or, the [1516] spiritual autobiography of Rev. Joseph S. Dempster, the converted Roman Catholic evangelist. Cinc.: M. W. Knapp, 1898. 105 p. DLC. As described by the title.

Denieffe, Joseph. A personal narrative of the Irish Revolutionary [1517] Brotherhood, giving a faithful report of the principal events from 1855 to 1867, written at the request of friends. N.Y.: The Gael pub. co., 1906. 293 p. NN. The author was an Irish-American who returned to Ireland in 1855 to aid in the foundation of the Brotherhood.

Denison, Daniel, 1613-1682. Autobiography of Major-General Daniel Denison. Ed. by Daniel Denison [1518] Slade. Boston: Press of David Clapp, 1892. 9 p. DLC. Officer in the Massachusetts militia. The author came to this country from England in 1631.

Dennis, J.J. A history...No imprint, 1903? 20 p. TxU. Farming in Texas, beginning with 1848. [1519]

Denny, Arthur Armstrong. Pioneer days on Puget Sound. Seattle: C. B. Bagley, printer, 1888. 83 p. WaU. A historical account in which the writer's personal experiences in farming, ranching and lumbering in Washington are included. [1520]

Denny, Emily Inez. Blazing the way...Seattle: Ranier pr. co., 1909. 492 p. DLC. Childhood on Puget Sound by the daughter of one of the founders of Seattle. [1521]

De Nogales, Rafael. See Nogales y Mendez, Rafael.

Densmore, David C., b. 1813. The halo; an autobiography...Boston: Voice of angels pub. house, 1876. 359 p. DLC. New England whaler and shipbuilder, who also published a newspaper for followers of spiritualism. [1522]

Denton, B. E. A two-gun cyclone, by Cyclone (pseud.). Dallas: Denton, 1927. 145 p. DLC. Hunter, ranch hand, member of wild west show. The locale is Montana, Kansas, Wyoming and the southwest. [1523]

De Paolo, Peter. Wall smacker; the saga of the speedway. Cleveland, Ohio: Thompson products, 1935. 271 p. NN. Career of an automobile racing driver. [1524]

Depew, Albert N. Gunner Depew. Chicago: Reitly, 1918. 312 p. NjP. First World War. [1525]

De Remusat, Jean T. Autobiography of Jean T. de' Remusat. Boston: Meador pub. co., 1935. 230 p. NN. Story of a French orphan who arrived in this country at the age of eight; experiences as a tailor in various sections of the country; life in Oregon and Washington. [1526]

Dergan, Bridget, 1843-1867. The life and confession of Bridget Dergan, who murdered Mrs. Ellen Coriell. Phila.: Barclay, 1867. 49 p. DLC. Murderess in New Jersey. [1527]

De Saussure, Mrs. Nancy Bostick. Old plantation days...N.Y.: Duffield, 1909. 123 p. WHi. Including her [1528]
memoirs of the Civil War.

D'Esque, Jean Louis. A count in the fo'c'sle. N.Y.: Brentano's, 1932. 298 p. DLC. Seaman. [1529]

Deterding, Sir Henry W., 1866-1939. An international oilman. N.Y.: Harper, 1934. 126 p. DLC. Dutch oilman who had considerable business dealings in the U.S. [1530]

Detweiler, Jacob, 1833-1922. Autobiography...Wadsworth, Ohio: 1922. 20 p. DLC. Miner and businessman in California. [1531]

Deuel, John Vanderveer. Speed wings. N.Y.: Century, 1930. 223 p. DLC. Army Air Corps. [1532]

De Varila, Osborne. The first shot for liberty. Phila.: Winston, 1918. 223 p. DLC. World War I. [1533]

De Veny, William, b. 1852. The establishment of law and order on western plains...Portland, Oreg.: 1915. 120 p. DLC. Chiropodist, photographer, real estate promoter in Nebraska and Kansas, 1871-92. [1534]

Devereux, Hyacinthe Daly. Roughing it after gold, by Rux (pseud.). London: Sampson, Low, Marston, etc., 1891. MdBE. An Irish adventurer in America about 1875. Only a small part of the book relates to mining. The jobs he held and the places he visited are too numerous to mention. See also his Through the mill, or Rambles in Texas (1892) of which TxU has a copy. [1535]

De Vighne, Harry Carlos. The time of my life; a frontier doctor in Alaska. Phila.: Lippincott, 1942. 336 p. WHi. As described by the title. [1536]

De Vilbiss, John Wesley, 1819-1885. Reminiscences of a superannuated preacher. (In: H. A. Graves, compiler, Reminiscences and events in the ministerial life of Rev. John Wesley De Vilbiss. Galveston: W. A. Shaw & co., 1886.) p. 29-62. NN. Life of a Methodist preacher in Texas. [1537]

Devine, Edward Thomas. When social work was young. N.Y.: Macmillan, 1939. 163 p. WU. Editor of Survey. The years covered are 1900-1910. [1538]

De Vinne, Daniel, b. 1793. Recollections of fifty years in the ministry. N.Y.: N. Tibbals, 1869. 54 p. WHi. Methodist clergyman in [1539]

Mississippi, Louisiana and New York.

Devoe, Elmore E. Autobiography. [1540] N.p.: 1941. 40, 11 leaves. NbHi. Teacher, homesteader and banker in Kansas and Nebraska. The period covered is from about 1865.

Devol, George H., b. 1829. Forty [1541] years a gambler on the Mississippi. Cinc.: Devol & Haines, 1887. 300 p. DLC. As described by the title, except that during the Mexican war he operated on the Rio Grande.

Devoy, John, 1842-1928. Recol- [1542] lections of an Irish rebel. N.Y.: C. P. Young co., printers, 1929. 491 p. WHi. Irish born leader of the Fenian movement in the U. S.

De Waltoff, Dayve Boris, b. 1865. [1543] Life links; tales by an international physician. N.Y.: G. Dobsevage, 1931. 338 p. DLC. Russian born Jew who practiced in New York City.

Dewees, Daniel S. Recollections [1544] of a life time. Parkersburg, W.Va.: Globe pr. and binding co., 1904. 72 p. MWA. Farmer in West Virginia.

Dewees, Samuel, b. 1760. A histo- [1545] ry of the life and services of Captain Samuel Dewees...compiled by John Smith Hanna. Baltimore: Robert Neilson, 1844. 360 p. DLC. A military chronicle, including the Revolutionary War and the War of 1812.

Dewey, George, 1837-1917. Auto- [1546] biography of George Dewey, admiral of the navy. N.Y.: C. Scribner's sons, 1913. 337 p. WHi. Includes the Civil War and the War with Spain.

Dewey, Orville, 1794-1882. Auto- [1547] biography and letters of Orville Dewey, ed. by Mary E. Dewey. Boston: Roberts, 1883. 126 p. WHi. Congregational clergyman who became a Unitarian. He served in Massachusetts and New York.

Dewey, Richard Smith, 1845-1933. [1548] Recollections of Richard Smith, pioneer in American psychiatry. An unfinished autobiography with an introduction by Clarence B. Farrar. Ed. by Ethel L. Dewey.
Chicago: The Univ. of Chicago press, 1936. 173 p. NN. Surgeon in the Franco-Prussian war; superintendent of State Hospital for the Insane at Kankakee, Ill., 1879-1893.

De Wolfe, Elsie. See Mendl, Elsie (De Wolfe), Lady.

Dexter, A. Hersey. Early days in [1549] California. Denver: Tribune-Republican press, 1886. 214 p. DLC. Miner.

Deyneka, Peter. Peter Deyneka: [1550] twice-born Russian; an autobiography. By Peter Deyneka, Russian gospel minister, missionary, evangelist, founder and general director of the Russian Gospel Association, Inc. Grand Rapids: Zondervan, 1944. 131 p. NN. Experiences in Russia, the United States, and South America.

Dickerson, George Holland. [1551] Climbing, a life experience. Denver: Acme, 1898. 120 p. CoD. A laborer and miner tells of his religious conversion. The locale is Missouri, New Mexico and Colorado.

Dickey, Herbert Spencer, b. 1876. [1552] The misadventures of a tropical medico. N.Y.: Dodd, Mead, 1929. 304 p. DLC. Physician and anthropologist in South America.

Diehl, Charles Sanford. The staff [1553] correspondent...San Antonio: Clegg, 1931. 297 p. WU. With the Associated Press.

Dietrichson, Johannes Wilhelm [1554] Christian, 1815-1883. Reise blandt de norske emigranter...Madison: Amerika's bogtrykkeri, 1896. 124 p. WHi. Lutheran clergyman in Wisconsin, 1844-50.

Dietterich, H. A. A wonder of [1555] grace...York, Pa.: P. Anstadt, 1892. 413 p. MoSC-H. Lutheran clergyman in Pennsylvania in the second half of the 19th century.

Dietz, Arthur Arnold. Mad rush [1556] for gold in frozen North. Los Angeles: Times-Mirror pr. house, 1914. 281 p. DLC. Gold miner in the Alaskan Klondike.

Dille, Elbert Riley, 1848-1933. [1557] Then and now...Oakland: Kennedy co., 1923. 22 p. CU-B. Methodist clergyman in Indiana, Oregon, California.

Dillen, Lena (Davidson). Life [1558] history...No imprint. 35 p. DLC.

Forced into prostitution by white slavers, she escapes and operates restaurants in the southwest.

Dillon, William Austin, b. 1877. [1559] Life doubles in brass. Ithaca, N.Y.: The House of Nollid, 1944. 234 p. NN. Reminiscences of a vaudevillian and song writer.

Diman, George Waters, b. 1823. [1560] Autobiography and sketches of my travels by sea and land. Bristol: Bristol phoenix, 1896. 64 p. MH. Merchant sailor.

Dimnet, Ernest, b. 1866. My new [1561] world. N.Y.: Simon & Schuster, 1937. 396 p. NN. About half of the book deals with the French author's experiences in America after the first World War when collecting funds for French relief and also with his various lecture trips.

Dimock, Anthony W. Wall street [1562] & the wilds. N.Y.: Outing, 1915. 469 p. WHi. His business experiences, and how he turned to writing about outdoor life.

Dingle, Aylward Edward, b. 1874. [1563] Rough hewn; the autobiography of a modern Sinbad. N.Y.: D. Appleton-Century, 1933. 383 p. NN. An English sailor who seeks a career in America as a writer.

Dingley, Nelson, 1832-1894. An [1564] autobiography...Lewiston, Maine: Journal office, 1874. 66 p. NNC. Lawyer, temperance leader, newspaper publisher, governor of Maine.

Dinkins, James. Personal recol- [1565] lections and experiences in the Confederate army. Cinc.: Robert Clarke co., 1897. 280 p. WHi. As described by the title.

Dinsmore, R. J., b. 1875. "Hoss" [1566] doctor. Boston: Waverly house, 1940. 311 p. WU. Veterinarian.

Diomedi, Alexander, b. 1843. [1567] Sketches of modern Indian life. Woodstock, Md.: 1894? 79 p. DLC. A missionary who lived in the Rockies, 1876-79.

Ditmars, Raymond Lee, 1876- [1568] 1942. The making of a scientist. N.Y.: Macmillan, 1937. 258 p. NN. Episodes in the life of the Curator of Reptiles of the New York Zoölogical Park.

Dix, John Adams, 1798-1879. Auto-[1569] biography". (In: Memoirs of John Adams Dix, comp. by Morgan Dix. N.Y.: Harper, 1883.) Vol. 1, p. 1-62. WHi. Soldier, politician, tells of his life in New Hampshire to the year 1821.

Dix, Mark H., b. 1878. An Ameri- [1570] can business venture...N.Y.: Harper, 1928. 181 p. DLC. Clothing manufacturer in New York and New Jersey. The author was a Russian-born Jew.

Dixon, Billy, 1850-1913. Life and [1571] adventures of "Billy" Dixon, of Adobe Walls, Texas panhandle... Guthrie, Okla.: pr. by the Cooperative pub. co., 1914. 320 p. WHi. Pioneer on the Plains, including Texas.

Dixon, J. M. The valley and the [1572] shadow...N.Y.: Russell, 1868. 336 p. WHi. Newspaper man in Iowa.

Dixwell, Epes Sargent, 1807-1899. [1573] Autobiographical sketch...Boston: George H. Ellis co., 1907. 69 p. DLC. Schoolmaster in Boston.

Doak, John M., b. 1858. "Mostly [1574] on the range". (In, Life on the range and on the trail, as told by R. J. (Bob) Lauderdale and John M. Doak. Ed. by Lela Neal Pirtle. San Antonio: Naylor, 1936.) p. 1-93. WHi. TxU. In Texas.

Dodd, John Morris, b. 1866. The [1575] autobiography of a surgeon. N.Y.: Walter Neale, 1928. 164 p. WHi. As described by the title.

Dodd, Martha, b. 1908. Through [1576] embassy eyes. Garden City, N.Y.: Garden City pub. co., 1940. 373 p. DLC. Seven years in Germany by the daughter of the U. S. Ambassador.

Dodge, Chester C., b. 1852. Rem- [1577] iniscences of a schoolmaster. Chicago: Ralph F. Seymour, 1941. 114 p. WHi. In Chicago.

Dodge, David Low, 1774-1852. [1578] Memorial of Mr. David L. Dodge... Boston: pub. only for the family, by S. K. Whipple & co., 1854. 325 p. Auto., p. 2-116. WHi. Merchant in Massachusetts, New York and Connecticut.

Dodge, Frank B., b. 1891. The [1579] saga of Frank B. Dodge; an autobiography. Tucson: 1944. 73 p. DLC. Rancher in Arizona and Washington who was born in Hawaii.

Dodge, Grenville M. The Indian [1580]

campaign of winter of 1864-65...
No imprint. 21 p. WyU. By the
commanding officer.

Dodge, Harry P., b. 1812. Fifty [1581] years at the card table. Syracuse: 1885. 111 p. DLC. As described by the title.

Dodge, Theodore Ayrault, b. 1842. [1582] Forty years of hard & happy work. Boston: 1899. 403 p. DLC. By an officer in the U. S. Army.

Doe, Stephen, 1826-1889. Narra- [1583] tive, life, and trials...San Francisco: pub. by the author, 1872. 57 p. DLC. A life of frustration from coast to coast.

Doering, Bertha-Charlotta, b.1890.[1584] Romance of a heavenly princess ...Los Angeles: The "Trust in God" pub. house, 1921. 167 p. DLC. Swedish immigrant to California who founded an interdenominational missionary society.

Doggett, Lawrence Locke, b. 1864.[1585] Man and a school; pioneering in higher education at Springfield College. N.Y.: Association press, 1943. 302 p. DLC. Educator in the Y.M.C.A. college at Springfield, Massachusetts.

Doherty, Edward J. Gall and [1586] honey...N.Y.: Sheed & Ward, 1941. 300 p. WU. Journalist in Chicago and New York.

Doherty, Martin W., b. 1899. The [1587] house on Humility Street; memories of the North American college in Rome. N.Y.: Longmans, Green, 1943. 269 p. WU. Police reporter tells of his preparation for the Catholic priesthood.

Dohoney, Ebenezer Lafayette, [1588] b. 1832. An average American. Paris, Texas: E. L. Dohoney, 1907. 312 p. NN. Texas lawyer, journalist and politician.

Dolbow, Andrew J., b. 1846. The [1589] dark and the bright side of life. Elmer, N.J.: Elmer Times print, 1895. 37 p. DLC. Lay preacher for the Methodist church at camp meetings in various Eastern states.

Dole, Charles Fletcher, 1845- [1590] 1927. My eighty years. N.Y.: Dutton, 1927. 469 p. WHi. Congregational clergyman in Maine and Mass.

Dole, Mary Phylinda, b. 1862. A [1591] doctor in homespun; autobiography ...Greenfield, Mass.: 1941. 165 p. WU. In New England.

Dollar, Robert, 1844-1932. Mem- [1592] oirs...San Francisco: priv. pub. for the author, 1917-1928. 4 vols. WHi. California ship owner who emigrated from Canada.

Dollard, Robert. Recollections...[1593] Scotland, S.D.: 1906. 296 p. WHi. Union Army officer, and Attorney-General of South Dakota.

Dolman, William Hickman, 1830- [1594] 1913. Before the Comstock, 1857-1858...Ed. by Austin E. Hutcheson. Reno: 42 p. CHi. Miner in Nevada.

Domenech, Emmanuel Henri [1595] Dieudonne. Missionary adventures in Texas and Mexico. London: Longman (etc.), 1858. 366 p. WHi. In the forties. French Catholic missionary.

Donaghey, George W., 1856-1937. [1596] Autobiography. Benton, Ark.: L. B. White pr. co., 1939. TxU. Railroad contractor and Governor of Arkansas, 1909-1913. See also his earlier autobiographical sketch (1924).

Donaghy, John, b. 1837. Army [1597] experience. Deland, Fla.: Painter pr. co., 1926. 244 p. WHi. Officer with the Union army.

Donahue, Arthur Gerald, b. 1913. [1598] Tally-Ho. Yankee in a Spitfire. N.Y.: Macmillan, 1941. 190 p. DLC. American pilot with the R.A.F. over England.

Doney, Carl Gregg, b. 1867. Cheer-[1599] ful yesterdays and confident tomorrows. Portland, Oreg.: Binfords & Mort, 1942. 190 p. NN. Methodist minister in Ohio; president of West Virginia Wesleyan College, and later of Willamette University, Oregon.

Donnelly, Edward, 1775-1803. [1600] Confession...Baltimore: pr. by Fryer & Rider, 1803? 7 p. WHi. Drunkard who was executed for the murder of his wife.

Doolittle, Mary Antoinette, b. 1810.[1601] Autobiography...Mt. Lebanon: 1880. 48 p. WHi. A spiritual account by a Shaker.

Dooman, Isaac. A missionary's [1602] life in the land of the Gods. Boston: Richard G. Badger, 1914. MoSC. Methodist missionary to Japan, 1888-1913.

Doran, George Henry, b. 1869. [1603]

Chronicles of Barabbas, 1884-1934. N.Y.: Harcourt, Brace & co., 1935. 416 p. Auto., p. 3-48. WHi. Publisher of books.

Dored, John. I shoot the world. [1604] N.Y.: Lippincott, 1938. 61 p. DLC. Newsreel photographer.

D'Orelli, Gabriel. The story of [1605] my life; embracing experiences material and spiritual. N.Y.: pr. by C. Day co., 1918. 84 p. DLC. A Swiss immigrant tells of his mining experiences in Alaska and California, of farming in Tennessee, and of his religious thoughts.

Dornblaser, Thomas Franklin, [1606] b. 1841. My life-story for young and old. Phila.: 1930. 222 p. DLC. Lutheran itinerant clergyman in Kansas.

Dornblaser, Thomas Franklin, [1607] b. 1841. Sabre strokes of the Pennsylvania Dragoons...Interspersed with personal reminiscences. Phila.: Lutheran publication society, 1884. 264 p. WHi. Union army.

Dornin, George D., 1830-1907. [1608] Thirty years ago. No imprint, 1879? 62 p. CSmH. Gold miner, restaurant owner, wholesale grocer in California, 1849-56.

Dorr, Rheta Louise (Childe), [1609] b. 1872. A woman of fifty. N.Y.: Funk & Wagnalls, 1924. 451 p. DLC. Newspaper writer in New York and in Europe who was also active in the cause of women's political rights.

Dorsey, Theodore Hooper, b. 1899. [1610] From a far country. Huntington, Ind.: Our Sunday visitor press, 1939. DLC. Episcopal priest who was converted to Catholicism.

Dosch, Henry Ernst, b. 1841. [1611] Vigilante days...by Fred Lockley. Portland: Fred Lockley, 1924. 19 p. DLC. With Fremont during Civil War, pony express rider, and merchant in California and Oregon.

Doster, William Émile, b. 1837. [1612] Lincoln and episodes of the Civil war. N.Y. & London: G. P. Putnam's sons, 1915. 282 p. NN. By the Provost Marshal of Washington.

Doty, Bennett Jeffries, b. 1900. [1613] The Legion of the damned... N.Y.: The Century co., 1928. 298 p. DLC. Native of Tennessee who joined the Foreign Legion in 1925 and deserted a year later.

Doty, Madeleine Zabriskie, b. 1879. [1614] Short rations...N.Y.: Century, 1917. 274 p. DLC. Journalist, worker for peace.

Doty, Silas, 1800-1876. The life.. [1615] comp. by J.G.W. Colburn. Toledo: Blade pr. co., 1880. 269 p. CU-B. In New York, and then to the northern midwestern states where he lived the life of a thief.

Doubleday, Charles William, [1616] b. 1829. Reminiscences of the "Filibuster" war in Nicaragua. N.Y.: Putnam, 1886. 225 p. DLC. Member of the Walker expedition, 1855.

Douglas, Emilius Clark, 1850-1928. [1617] The medicine man, being the memoirs of fifty years of medical progress. By E. C. Dudley, ex-president American Gynecological Society; president emeritus of Northwestern University Medical School. N.Y.: J. H. Sears, 1927. 369 p. NN. Medical career in New York and Chicago.

Douglas, Emma (Stoner), b. 1863? [1618] My life and I. Dallas, Texas: Mathias, Van Nort, 1938. 246 p. NN. American living in France for the purpose of providing her children with a European education. During the World War, she did volunteer war work.

Douglas, George Anson, b. 1833. [1619] The experiences of a veteran salesman of memorial monuments. Cinc.: The Chas. O. Ebel pr. co., 1908. 96 p. DLC. In New York, Conn., and the northern midwestern states.

Douglas, George Mellis. Lands [1620] forlorn; a story of an expedition to Hearne's Coppermine river. N.Y.: Putnam, 1914. 285 p. DLC. Three years in the copper areas of Northern Canada.

Douglas, Henry Kyd, 1840-1903. [1621] I rode with Stonewall; being chiefly the war experiences of the youngest member of Jackson's staff from the John Brown raid to the hanging of Mrs. Surratt. Chapel Hill: The Univ. of N. C. press, 1940. 401 p. NN. As described by the title.

Douglas, Stephen Arnold, 1813- [1622]

1861. Autobiography of Stephen A. Douglas. With an introduction by Frank E. Stevens...Springfield, Ill.: Ill. state journal co., 1913. 22 p. WHi. Written in 1838, by the noted Illinois political figure.

Douglas, Thomas, b. 1790. Auto- [1623] biography. N.Y.: Calkins & Stiles, 1856. 132 p. WHi. Lawyer and U.S. District Attorney in Florida.

Douglass, Frederick, 1817-1895. [1624] Narrative of the life of Frederick Douglass, an American slave. Written by himself. Boston: pub. at the Anti-slavery office, 1845. 125 p. WHi. Abolitionist.

Douglass, Frederick, 1817-1895. [1625] My bondage and my freedom... N.Y.: Miller, Orton & Mulligan, 1855. 464 p. WHi. Abolitionist.

Douglass, Frederick, 1817-1895. [1626] Life and times of Frederick Douglass, written by himself. His early life as a slave, his escape from bondage, and his complete history to the present time, including his connection with the anti-slavery movement... Hartford, Conn.: Park pub. co., 1881. 516 p. WHi. Abolitionist. An enlarged version of the preceding title.

Douthit, Jasper Lewis, b. 1834. [1627] Jasper Douthit's story. Boston: American Unitarian assoc.: n.d. 225 p. DLC. Unitarian minister in southern Illinois.

Doutney, Mrs. T. Narcisse. I [1628] told you so...N.p.: 1873. 240 p. MWA. A life of tribulations in Massachusetts, including the operation of a boarding house.

Doutney, Thomas Narcisse, [1629] b. 1845. Thomas N. Doutney: his life-struggles and triumphs... Battle Creek: W. C. Gage, prtrs., 1893. 544 p. DLC. Gambler, liquor store operator who turned to temperance work.

Dow, Daniel, 1772-1849. A remin- [1630] iscence of past events. A semi-centennial sermon...New Haven: pr. by B. L. Hamlen, 1846. 31 p. MiD-B. Congregational clergyman in Connecticut.

Dow, Mary Larcom (Ober). Old [1631] days at Beverly farms. Beverly, Mass.: North shore pr. co., 1921. 81 p. Auto., p. 25-62. WHi. A teacher tells of her childhood in New England.

Dow, Neal, 1804-1897. Reminis- [1632] cences...Portland, Me.: Evening express, 1898. 769 p. WHi. His activities in Portland, Maine, on behalf of the temperance movement.

Dow, Peggy, 1780-1820. Vicissi- [1633] tudes, or the journey of life. (In: History of the cosmopolite...6th ed. by Lorenzo Dow. Cinc.: Rulison, 1857.) p. 607-661. WHi. Wife of Lorenzo Dow tells of her travels with him during his ministerial duties in the U. S. and Europe. This account begins with 1805.

Dowie, John Alexander, 1847- [1634] 1907...American first fruits... 2d, and enl. ed. San Francisco: "Leaves of Healing" office, 1889. 133, 11 p. CU-B. Australian "Divine healer" who did missionary work in California during 1888.

Dowkontt, George D., 1842?-1909. [1635] Tell them; or, the life story of a medical missionary. N.Y.: Office of the Medical missionary record, 1898. 249 p. DLC. Editor of the Medical Missionary Record.

Downen, Mrs. Lula Laney, b. 1867.[1636] Covered wagon days in the Palouse country. Pullman: Pullman herald, 1937. 32 p. Wa. Her early life on a farm in Washington, beginning with 1877. Later she became a school teacher.

Downie, David, b. 1838. From the [1637] mill to the mission field...Phila.: Judson press, 1928. 194 p. Auto., p. 3-100. OrMcL. Baptist missionary in India who came to the U. S. from Scotland.

Downie, William, b. 1819. Hunting [1638] for gold...San Francisco: California pub. co., 1893. 407 p. WHi. In California.

Doy, John. The narrative of [1639] John Doy. N.Y.: pr. for the author, 1860. 132 p. DLC. Farmer and abolitionist in Kansas, beginning with 1854.

Doyle, Mrs. Helen (MacKnight), [1640] b. 1872. A child went forth...N.Y.: Gotham house, 1934. 364 p. DLC. Childhood on a homestead in South Dakota, after which she moved to California where became a physician.

Doyle, Mary (pseud.). See Hitchcock, Mary Evelyn (Martin).

Drake, Daniel, 1785-1852. Pioneer [1641]

life in Kentucky, a series of reminiscential letters...ed. by Charles D. Drake. Cinc.: R. Clarke, 1870. 245 p. WHi. The story of his boyhood by a physician.

Drake, John H., b. 1814. Thirty- [1642] two years of the life of an adventurer. N.Y.: priv. pr., 1847. 122 p. WHi. Sailor, unfortunate business experiences.

Drake, Richard. Revelations of [1643] a slave smuggler, being the autobiography of Capt. Rich'd Drake, African trader for fifty years - from 1807 to 1857, during which period he was concerned in the transportation of half a million blacks from African coasts to America. N.Y.: Robert M. De Witt, 1860. 98 p. NN. As described by the title.

Drannan, William F., b. 1832. [1644] Thirty-one years on the plains and in the mountains; or, the last voice from the plains. An authentic record of a life time of hunting, trapping, scouting and Indian fighting in the Far West. Chicago: Rhodes & McClure, 1903. 586 p. NN. As described by the title.

Drannan, William F., b. 1832. [1645] Chief of scouts...Chicago: Rhodes & McClure, 1910. 407 p. WHi. A supplement to the previous title.

Draper, Elias Johnson, b. 1830. [1646] An autobiography...Fresno: Evening democrat, 1904. 76 p. CL. A midwestern farmer and merchant goes to California in 1863 where he becomes a hog and cattle rancher.

Draper, William Franklin, 1842– [1647] 1910. Recollections of a varied career. Boston: Little, Brown, & co., 1908. 411 p. WHi. Union army soldier, manufacturer of textile machinery, member of the U. S. House of Representatives from Massachusetts, and ambassador to Rome.

Drayton, Daniel, b. 1802. Person- [1648] al memoir of Daniel Drayton, for four years and four months a prisoner...in Washington jail...N.Y.: Am. and foreign anti-slavery soc., 1855. 122 p. WHi. Abolitionist.

Dreiser, Theodore, b. 1871. Dawn. [1649] N.Y.: H. Liveright, 1931. 489 p. WU. Story of his youth in Indiana.

Dreiser, Theodore, b. 1871. A [1650] book about myself. N.Y.: Boni & Liveright, 1922. 502 p. WU. In Chicago, St. Louis and New York as a journalist.

Dressler, Marie, 1873-1934. The [1651] eminent American comedienne Marie Dressler in the life story of an ugly duckling; an autobiographical fragment in seven parts... N.Y.: Robert M. McBride , 1924. 234 p. NN. Reminiscences of a popular American actress.

Dressler, Marie, 1873-1934. My [1652] own story. Boston: Little, Brown, 1934. 290 p. NN. Has much concerning her later career in moving pictures.

Drew, Daniel, 1797–1879. The [1653] book of Daniel Drew...N.Y.: Doubleday, Page, 1937. 423 p. WHi. New York financier, speculator, especially in railroads.

Drew, John, 1853–1927. My years [1654] on the stage. N.Y.: E. P. Dutton & co., 1922. 242 p. WU. As described by the title.

Drew, Louisa (Lane), 1820–1897. [1655] Autobiographical sketch of Mrs. John Drew...N.Y.: Scribner, 1899. 200 p. WU. English born actress who played many times in this country.

Drips, Joseph H. Three years [1656] among the Indians in Dakota. Kimball, S.D.: Brule, 1894. 139 p. NjP. Indian fighter, 1863–65.

Drumheller, Daniel Montgomery, [1657] 1840–1925. "Uncle Dan" Drumheller tells thrills of western trails in 1854. Spokane: Inland-American pr. co., 1925. 131 p. DLC. Miner, rancher, banker on the Pacific coast, especially in Washington. Prior to the Civil War he rode for the pony express.

Drury, Marion Richardson, 1849– [1658] 1939. Reminiscences of early days in Iowa. Toledo: Toledo chronicle press, 1931. 51 p. ICN. Boyhood days on a pioneer farm in Iowa.

Drury, Wells. An editor on the [1659] Comstock Lode. N.Y.: Farrar & Rinehart, 1936. 295 p. WHi. Nevada frontier journalist.

DuBois, Guy P. Artists say the [1660] silliest things. N.Y.: Duell, Sloan, & Pearce, 1940. 304 p. WU. Art critic and editor of art magazine.

DuBois, Silvia, b. 1868. Silvia [1661]

Dubois...by C. Wilson Larison. Ringos, N.J.: C. W. Larison, 1883. 124 p. Auto., p. 43-91. DLC. A dictated account by an ex-slave.

DuBois, William Edward Burghardt, b. 1868. Dusk of dawn... N.Y.: Harcourt, Brace, 1940. 334 p. WHi. Negro historian, novelist, and editor of magazine Crisis. [1662]

DuBose, Horace Mellard, 1858-1941. Through two generations ...N.Y.: Fleming H. Revell, 1934. 160 p. DLC. Methodist clergyman and editor of religious newspapers in the southern states. [1663]

DuBose, William Porcer, 1836-1918. Turning points in my life. N.Y.: Longmens, Green, 1912. 143 p. Auto., p. 1-93. DLC. Professor of theology at the University of the South. [1664]

Duden, Gottfried. Bericht über eine reise nach den westlichen Staaten Nordamerika's und einen mehrjaehrigen aufenthalt am Missouri (in den jahren 1824, 25, 26 und 1827)...Elberfeld: Sam. Lucas, 1829. 348 p. DLC. Farmer in Illinois and Missouri. [1665]

Dudley, Emilius Clark. Medicine man. N.Y.: J. H. Sears, 1927. 369 p. WU. Gynecologist in New York and Illinois, 1870-1927. [1666]

Dudley, Henry Wolbridge, b.1840. Autobiography...Menasha, Wis.: Banta,1913. 189 p. ICHi. Wholesale grocer in Michigan, who tells also of his experiences in the Civil War. [1667]

Dudley, Robert (pseud.). See Baldwin, James.

Dudley, Walter Lee, 1866-1944. Footprints on the sands of time ...Winchester, Va.: 1943. 354 p. MoCanD. Church of Christ clergyman in Virginia, West Virginia and Pennsylvania. [1668]

Duer, William Alexander, 1780-1858. Reminiscences of an old New Yorker. By the late William A. Duer, LL.D., president of Columbia College. N.Y.: pr. for W. L. Andrews. 102 p. NN. As described by the title. [1669]

Duffield, George C. Memories of frontier Iowa. Des Moines: Bishard bros., pr., 1906. 54 p. WHi. A boy's experiences on a homestead in the thirties. [1670]

Duganne, Augustine Joseph Hickey, 1823-1884. Camps and prisons: twenty months in the Department of the Gulf. 2d. ed. N.Y.: Robens, 1865. 424 p. WHi. A poet tells of his Civil War experiences. [1671]

Duggan, Stephen Pierce Hayden, b. 1870. A professor at large. N.Y.: Macmillan, 1943. 468 p. DLC. Director of the Institute of International Education. [1672]

Dugmore, Arthur Radclyffe, b. 1870. The autobiography of a wanderer. London: Hurst & Blackett, 1930. 287 p. DLC. English photographer of wild animals who worked for some years in the U.S. [1673]

Duke, Basil Wilson, 1838-1916. Reminiscences of General Basil W. Duke, C.S.A. Garden City, N.Y.: Doubleday, Page, 1911. 512 p. WHi. As described by the title. [1674]

Dulaney, William H., b. 1818. Biographical sketch...Hannibal, Mo.: 1910. 34 p. MoSHi. Tobacco trader in Missouri who after the Civil War entered the lumber business. [1675]

Dulles, John Welsh, 1823-1887. Life in India...Phila.: Am. Sunday school union, 1855. 528 p. DLC. By a Protestant missionary. [1676]

Dummer, Mrs. Ethel (Sturges). Why I think so...Chicago: Clark-McElroy, 1937. 274 p. DLC. An associate of Jane Addams at Hull House in Chicago. [1677]

Dumond, Annie (Hamilton) Nelles, b. 1837. ...Life of a book agent. Cinc.: priv. pr., 1868. 385 p. WU. Door to door saleswoman. [1678]

Dunaway, Thomas Sanford, 1829-1915. Personal memoirs, sermons and addresses...Lynchburg, Va.: J. P. Bell co., 1900. 383 p. Auto., p. 1-98. Vi. Virginia Baptist clergyman and religious educator. [1679]

Dunaway, Wayland Fuller. Reminiscences of a rebel. N.Y.: Neale, 1913. 133 p. WHi. Confederate soldier. [1680]

Duncan, Isadora, 1878-1927. My life, by Isadora Duncan...N.Y.: Boni & Liveright, 1927. 359 p. WU. The life of the dancer to 1921. [1681]

Duncan, Lee. Over the wall. N.Y.: E. P. Dutton, 1936. 368 p. WU. Thief. [1682]

Duncan, Nehemiah, b. 1746. Extraordinary conversion of Nehemiah [1683]

Duncan, late of Charleston... in the year 1797. Phila.: Crukshank, 1806. 24 p. ICU. The writer lived in New Hampshire.

Duncan, Robert Samuel, b. 1832. [1684] Life story...Kansas City, Mo.: Western Baptist pub. co., 1910. 262 p. MoHi. Baptist clergyman in Missouri.

Duncan, Mrs. S. A. Life story of [1685] a Kansas pioneer woman, 1857-1919. N.p.: 1919. 43 p. KU. Homesteader.

Dunham, Austin Cornelius, 1834- [1686] 1918. Reminiscences of Auston C. Dunham. Hartford, Conn.: The Case, Lockwood & Brainard co., 1913? 151 p. NN. Boyhood days in South Coventry, Conn.; reminiscences of Hartford, Conn., in the forties and fifties.

Dunham, Donald Carl, b. 1908. En-[1687] voy unextraordinary. N.Y.: John Day, 1944. 166 p. DLC. Member U.S. Foreign Service in Germany, Hong Kong, Greece and Aden.

Dunham, E. Allene (Taylor). [1688] From Iowa to California in a covered wagon. No imprint. 20 p. Ia-HA. In the early sixties in California she lived on a dairy ranch.

Dunham, Henry Morton, 1853- [1689] 1929. The life of a musician woven into a strand of history of the New England Conservatory of music. N.Y.: 1931. 235 p. DLC. Organist.

Dunham, Samuel, 1835-1914. Ret- [1690] rospect of a happy ministry... Binghamton: Vail-Ballou co., 1914. 259 p. Auto., p. 1-34. PPPrHi. Presbyterian in New York.

Duniway, Mrs. Abigail (Scott), [1691] 1834-1915. Path breaking...Portland: James, Kerns & Abbott co., 1914. 291 p. DLC. Oregon business woman and newspaper publisher tells of her work for woman's suffrage.

Dunkelberger, Charles. Random [1692] recollections of rebeldom. Phila.: 1890. 23, 21 p. CSmH. Union army. These are two publications with the same title but the contents are different.

Dunlap, George Terry, b. 1864. [1693] The fleeting years; a memoir. N.Y.: priv. pr., 1937. 205 p. NN. The author, partner in the reprint publishing house of Grosset & Dunlap, tells the story of the gradual growth of the concern, together with the story of his earlier career.

Dunlap, William, 1766-1839. "Auto-[1694] biography". (In his: History of the rise and progress of the arts of design...Boston: Goodspeed, 1918.) Vol. I, p. 288-369. WU. Painter.

Dunlap, William, 1766-1839. "Auto-[1695] biographical sketch". (In his: History of the American theatre. N.Y.: J. and J. Harper, 1832.) p. 232-247. DLC. The early story of a playwright and manager to the year 1798.

Dunn, Esther Cloudman. Pursuit [1696] of understanding; autobiography of an education. N.Y.: Macmillan, 1945. 229 p. WU. The story of her school and college days by a professor of English at Smith College.

Dunn, John Beamond, b. 1851. [1697] Perilous trails of Texas. Dallas: Southwest press, 1932. 163 p. WHi. Service with Rangers in expedition against Mexico, 1916.

Dunn, Joseph Bragg, b. 1868. In [1698] the service of the King; a parson's story. N.Y.: Putnam, 1915. 158 p. DLC. Episcopal clergyman in Virginia.

Dunn, Michael, b. 1826. Biography [1699] ...San Francisco: Bacon & co., pr., 1884. 69 p. C. British born thief who was imprisoned at Sing Sing.

Dunn, Musa. Sideways and back- [1700] ward. Waxahachie, Texas: Enterprise pub. co., n.d. 34 p. TxH. Texas poetess.

Dunn, R. Five fronts. N.Y.: Dodd, [1701] Mead, 1915. 308 p. NjP. Personal narrative of the first World War.

Dunn, William E., b. 1882. Travel-[1702] ing under orders. N.Y.: Harper, 1918. 79 p. NjP. First World War.

Dunne, Brian Ború. Cured! [1703] Phila.: Winston, 1914. 240 p. DLC. Maryland reporter who for eight years suffered from dyspepsia.

Dupre, Louis J. Fagots from the [1704] camp fire...Washington, D.C.: Emily Thornton Charles, 1881. 199 p. DLC. Confederate soldier who was chief of scouts for Johnston's army, 1863.

Durand, James, b. 1786. James [1705] Durand, an able seaman of 1812...

New Haven: Yale univ. press, 1926. 86 p. WHi. Covers 1801-1816. This is a reprint of the original of 1820.

Durand, Silas Horton, 1833-1918. [1706] Fragments. Phila.: Biddle press, 1920. 353 p. Auto., p. 1-30. DLC. Baptist minister in New York and Pennsylvania.

Duss, John S. The Harmonists; [1707] a personal history. Harrisburg: Pa. book service, 1943. 425 p. WHi. Member of the New Harmony social experiment. His occupation was that of musician.

Dutton, Charles Judson, b. 1888. [1708] Saints and sinners. N.Y.: Dodd, Mead & co., 1940. 303 p. DLC. New England clergyman who resigned from ministry and became a parole worker for the Pennsylvania Board of Pardons.

Duval, B. R. A narrative of life [1709] and travels in Mexico and British Honduras. Richmond: Clemmitt & Jones, 1878. 80 p. CSmH. Methodist clergyman in Virginia who left for Mexico after the Civil War.

Dwight, Timothy, 1828-1916. Mem-[1710] ories of Yale life and men, 1845-1899. N.Y.: Dodd, Mead, 1903. 500 p. NN. The writer was connected with Yale University from the time of his graduation in 1849, first with the Yale Theological Seminary and later as president of the University, 1886-1899.

D'Wolf, John, 1779-1872. A voy- [1711] age to the North Pacific and a journey through Siberia...Cambridge: Welch, Bigelow and co., 1861. 147 p. DLC. Merchant skipper. The voyage took place 1804-08.

Dye, William Milburn. High lights.[1712] Etawah, Tenn.: 1941. 320 p. WHi. Methodist clergyman in the South.

Dyer, Mrs. D. B. "Fort Reno"... [1713] N.Y.: G. W. Dillingham, 1896. 216 p. DLC. Wife of Indian agent and mayor of Oklahoma City.

Dyer, David Patterson, b. 1838. [1714] Autobiography and reminiscences. St. Louis: William Harvey Miner co., 1922. 357 p.   WHi. Lawyer, U.S. District Attorney and member of the U.S. House of Representatives from Missouri.

Dyer, Heman, b. 1810. Records of [1715] an active life. N.Y.: Whittaker, 1886. 422 p. WHi. Episcopal clergyman who was employed by the American Church Missionary Society, and by the American Sunday School Union.

Dyer, John Lewis, b. 1812. The [1716] snow-shoe itinerant...Cinc.: Cranston & Stowe, 1890. 362 p. CSmH. Methodist clergyman in Colorado, Minnesota and Wisconsin.

Dyer, John Will. Reminiscences [1717] of four years in the Confederate army. Evansville: Keller pr. and pub. co., 1898. 323 p. WHi. As described by the title.

Dyer, Mrs. Mary (Marshall). See Marshall, Mary.

Dyer, William, b. 1844. Memories [1718] of the past...Warrenton, Mo.: Press of Banner pub. co., 1919. 170 p. MoSM. After boyhood on a farm in Missouri, the author became a merchant and newspaper publisher.

Dymond, John, 1836-1922. An ap- [1719] preciation...New Orleans? 1917? 45 p. Auto., p. 9-12. AU. Sugar planter, publisher of farm journals and member of the Louisiana Senate (early 20th century).

# E

Eadie, Thomas, b. 1887. I like [1720] diving; a professional's story. Boston & N.Y.: Houghton Mifflin, 1929. 245 p. NN. Diver for the U. S. Navy.

Eagan, Eddie, b. 1898. Fighting [1721] for fun; the scrap book of Eddie Eagan, amateur heavyweight champion of the world. N.Y.: Macmillan, 1932. 300 p. NN. As described by the title.

Eakin, Harvey Ellis. Thinking my [1722] way out of hell. Baltimore, Md.: The Harmony co., 1936. 199 p. NN. Account of the author's attainment of physical health and spiritual peace through Christian Science.

Eames, Emma, b. 1865. Some [1723] memories and reflections. N.Y.: D. Appleton, 1927. 310 p. DLC. Opera singer.

Earhart, Amelia, 1898-1937. 20 [1724] hours, 40 min.; our flight in the Friendship...N.Y., London: G. P. Putnam's sons, 1928. 314 p. DLC. The life of the aviatrix including her youth in Kansas.

Earhart, Amelia, 1898-1937. The [1725] fun of it...N.Y.: Harcourt, Brace, 1932. 218 p. WU. See the preceding item.

Earl, James J., b. 1845. Earl's [1726] memoirs. Los Angeles: 1916. 24 p. KHi. Farm life in Kansas and Illinois beginning with 1859.

Earle, Absolam. Bringing in [1727] sheaves. Boston: James H. Earle, 1868. 384 p. WHi. Revivalist.

Earle, Horatio Sawyer, b. 1855. [1728] The autobiography of "By Gum" Earle. Lansing: State review pub. co., 1929. 360 p. DLC. State senator in Michigan known especially for his advocacy of a county road system.

Early, Jubal Anderson, 1816-1894. [1729] Lieutenant General Juban Anderson Early, C.S.A. ... Phila.: Lippincott, 1912. 496 p. WHi. As described by the title.

Eastlick, Mrs. Lavina (Dat). [1730] Thrilling incidents in the Indian war of 1862...Minneapolis: Atlas, 1864. 37 p. MnHi. In Minnesota.

Eastman, Charles Alexander, [1731] b. 1858. Indian boyhood. N.Y.: McClure, Phillips & co., 1902. 289 p. WHi. Life with the Sioux Indians in the Dakotas to the age of 15.

Eastman, Charles Alexander, [1732] b. 1858. From the deep woods to civilization...Boston: Little, Brown, 1916. 206 p. WHi. An Indian who became a physician tells of his public services to his people.

Eastman, Edward Roe. See Ladd, Carl Edwin.

Eastman, Zebina. Eight years in [1733] a British consulate from 1861 to 1869. Chicago: Drovers journal press, 1919. 31 p. IHi. U.S. consul at Bristol, England.

Eaton, Edward Dwight, b. 1851. [1734] Along life's pathway...Chicago: R. R. Donnelley & sons, 1941. 251 p. DLC. Congregational clergyman and President of Beloit College in Wisconsin.

Eaton, James Demarest, b. 1848. [1735] Life under two flags. N.Y.: A. S. Barnes, 1922. 297 p. WHi. Congregational clergyman in New Jersey and missionary to Mexico.

Eaton, James Randell, b. 1841. Six- [1736] teen years on the dark blue sea. Indianapolis: Pub. for author, 1894. 152 p. DLC. The life of a sailor.

Eaton, M. Five years on the Erie [1737] canal... Utica: Bennett, Backus, & Hawley, 1845. 156 p. DLC. Missionary for the American Bethel Society.

Eaton, Mrs. Margaret (O'Neil), [1738] 1796-1879. Autobiography of Peggy Eaton. N.Y.: Scribner, 1932. 211 p. WHi. Wife of John Eaton who was Secretary of War under Jackson.

Ebbutt, Percy G. Emigrant life in [1739] Kansas. London: Swan, Sonnenschein & co., 1886. 237 p. DLC. Six years of a young Englishman's life in farming, cattle ranching and lumbering.

Eberhart, Uriah, b. 1821. History [1740] of the Eberharts...with an autobiographical sketch of the author, including many reminiscences of his ministerial and army life. Chicago: Donohue & Henneberry, 1891. 263 p. Auto.,p. 199-263. DLC. Evangelical Lutheran clergyman in Pennsylvania who became a Methodist and served in Illinois and Iowa. During the Civil War he was a chaplain.

Eby, Henry Harrison, b. 1841. Ob- [1741] servations of an Illinois boy in battle, camp and prison-1861 to 1865...N.p.: pub. by the author, 1910. 284 p. NN. As described by the title.

Echols, John Wicker. A certain [1742] country doctor. Boston: Christopher, 1922. 98 p. DLC. In Oklahoma.

Echols, Obadiah, b. 1785. The [1743] autobiography of Rev. Obadiah Echols...Memphis: pr. for the author, 1870. 199 p. DLC. Baptist in Georgia, Alabama and Mississippi.

Eckel, Lizzie (St. John). See Harper, Lizzie (St. John).

Edbrooke, Frank E., b. 1840. Re- [1744] viewing the events of my life. Denver: Egan pr. co., 1921? 57 p. CoHi. Building contractor in Nebraska, Illinois, Texas and Colorado tells chiefly of his services in the Union forces.

Eddy, Frank Marion, b. 1856. Way [1745] back yonder...No imprint. 43 p. MnHi. Republican politician in Minnesota at end of 19th century.

Eddy, George Sherwood, b. 1871. [1746]

A pilgrimage of ideas; or the re-education of Sherwood Eddy... N.Y. Farrar & Rinehart, 1934. 336 p. NN. Leader in the Young Men's Christian Association in India and other parts of Asia; later a leader in liberal movements, including socialism and pacificism.

Eddy, Mary Baker, 1821-1910. Retrospection and introspection. [1747] Boston: Allison V. Stewart, 1916. 95 p. WHi. A spiritual autobiography by the noted Christian Scientist.

Eddy, Thomas, 1758-1827. The [1748] life of Thomas Eddy...by Samuel L. Knapp. N.Y.: Conner Cooke, 1834. 394 p. Auto., p. 42-55. WHi. New York philanthropist and prison reformer tells of his life as broker to the year 1797.

Edgerly, Asa Sanborn, b. 1834. He [1749] did it...San Francisco: H. S. Crocker, co., 1909. 139 p. DLC. A New Englander who made his fortune in the construction business in California.

Edgett, Edwin Francis, b. 1867. [1750] I speak for myself. An editor in his world. N.Y.: Macmillan, 1940. 385 p. WU. Editorial writer for the Boston Transcript.

Edman, Irwin. Philosopher's holiday. N.Y.: Viking press, 1938. [1751] 270 p. WU. A disconnected account of portions of his life by a professor of philosophy.

Edmond, Clementine E'Damie. See Taylor, Mrs. Clementine E'Damie (Edmond).

Edmonds, Jean S. Leaves from a [1752] nurse's life's history. Rochester, N.Y.: Press of the Democrat & Chronicle, 1906. 75 p. DLC. In Africa as a missionary nurse and then with the American troops in the Spanish-American War. The author was born in Canada.

Edmonds, S. Emma E. Nurse and [1753] spy in the Union army; comprising the adventures and experiences of a woman in hospitals, camps and battle-fields. Hartford, Conn.: W.S. Williams, 1865. 384 p. NN. As described by the title.

Edsall, John, b. 1788. Incidents.. [1754] Catskill: the author, 1831. 156 p. DLC. The life of a sailor including service in the War of 1812.

Edson, Charles Leroy, b. 1881. [1755] "The great American ass"... N.Y.: Brentano's,1926. 316 p. DLC. Newspaper columnist and reporter in the New York and in the midwest.

Edstrom, David, b. 1873. The testament of Caliban. N.Y.: Funk & Wagnalls, 1937. 340 p. WU. The life of a Swedish sculptor in the U.S. and abroad. [1756]

Edwards, Agnes (pseud.). See Rothery, Agnes Edwards.

Edwards, Mrs. Benjamin S. Some [1757] incidents...Springfield: 1908. 25 p. RPB. Her childhood and youth in New York and Connecticut; her married life in Illinois.

Edwards, Jonathan. "Personal [1758] narrative". (The works of President Edwards. N.Y.: Carvill,1830.) Vol. I, p. 58-62, 64-67. WU. A spiritual account, closing with 1723.

Edwards, Samuel E., b. 1810. The [1759] Ohio hunter...Battle Creek: Review & Herald steam press, 1866. 240 p. WHi. A frontier account.

Edwards, William, 1770-1851. [1760] Memoirs. Washington, D.C.: 1897. 123 p. DLC. Tanner in Mass., New Jersey and New York.

Edwards, William James, b. 1869. [1761] Twenty-five years in the black belt. Boston: Cornhill, 1918. 126 p. WHi. Negro educator, founder of Snow Hill Normal and Industrial Institute for Negroes.

Edwin, Morton R., b. 1869. "The [1762] autobiography". (In his: Half a century with tobacco. N.Y.: J. B. Hall, 1928.) p. 77-111. DLC. Tobacco merchant and cigar manufacturer who lived in New York.

Egan, Howard Ransom, 1840-1916. [1763] Pioneering the West, 1846 to 1878 ...Richmond, Utah: priv. pr., 1917. 302 p. CSmH. Hunting, Indian fighting and carrying the mail in the Salt Lake region.

Egan, Maurice Francis, 1852-1924.[1764] Recollections of a happy life. N.Y.: George H. Doran co., 1924. 374 p. WHi. Professor of English at Notre Dame and Catholic University of America who was appointed U.S. Minister to Denmark.

Egan, Michael, 1826?-1888. The [1765] flying, gray-haired Yank; or, the adventures of a volunteer...A true narrative of the Civil War.

Phila.: Hubbard bros., 1888. 414 p. DLC. He served mainly in West Virginia.

Eggleston, George Cary, 1839–1911. [1766] Recollections of a varied life. N.Y.: H. Holt & co., 1910. 354 p. WHi. By a journalist and novelist.

Einarsen, Oscar, b. 1867. Life [1767] sketch...Chicago: Life Savior book concern, 1913. 16 p. DLC. Founder of Life Savior Apostolic Social Church in Illinois.

Einstein, Isador. Prohibition agent [1768] no. 1. N.Y.: Frederick A. Stokes co., 1932. 261 p. DLC. In New York.

Eisenberg, Daniel M. I find the [1769] missing; as told to John Nicholas Beffel. N.Y.: Farrar & Rinehart, 1938. 300 p. NN. The author was founder of Skip Tracers, Inc., an organization which specialized in finding missing persons.

Eisenschiml, Otto. Without fame, [1770] the romance of a profession... Chicago: Alliance book corp., 1942. 368 p. WU. Industrial chemist and writer on American history.

Elaw, Mrs. Zilpha. Memoirs. [1771] London: pub. by authoress, 1846. 172 p. DLC. Negro Methodist missionary who worked in Pennsylvania, New Jersey, the southern states, and in England.

Elder, Mrs. P. P. Personal nar- [1772] rative of a woman emigrant. 2d ed. N. p.: 1927. 24 p. KHi. The author moved to Kansas in 1858 where she and her husband took up a homestead.

Elderkin, James D., b. 1820. Bio- [1773] graphical sketches and anecdotes of a soldier of three wars... Detroit: 1899. 202 p. DLC. The three wars were the Mexican War, the war with the Seminole Indians in Florida, and the Civil War (Union army). The writer also mined gold in California.

Eldredge, Charles Q., b. 1845. [1774] The autobiography of the museum man. Albany, N.Y.: The Hamilton pr. co., 1929. 205 p. DLC. The story of a Connecticut businessman who opened a curio museum.

Eldridge, Elleanor, b. 1785. Mem- [1775] oirs of Elleanor Eldridge. Providence: Albro, printer, 1838. 128 p. MWA. The story of a Negro servant in Rhode Island.

Eldridge, Elleanor, b. 1785. [1776] Elleanor's second book...Providence: Albro, printer, 1839. 128 p. RPB. Her later career in which she describes her business activities.

Eldridge, Kathleen (Tamagawa). See Tamagawa, Kathleen.

Elkins, Hervey. Fifteen years in [1777] the senior order of Shakers; a narration of facts, concerning that singular people. Hanover: Dartmouth press, 1858. 136 p. NN. The author's experiences in the Shaker colony at Enfield, N.H.

Elkins, John M., b. 1841. Indian [1778] fighting on the Texas frontier. Amarillo: Russell & Cockrell, 1929. 96 p. TxU. As described by the title.

Ellet Mary (Israel), 1780–1870. [1779] Memoirs... ed. by Herbert Pickens Gambrell. Doyleston, Pa.: Bucks County historical soc., 1939. 76 p. DLC. The experiences of the wife of a farmer and merchant in Pennsylvania.

Ellett, Frank Gates, b. 1860. Mak- [1780] ing the up grade. Detroit: Press of Frank H. West, 1909. 105 p. DLC. Presbyterian clergyman in Michigan.

Elliot, James Wilkinson, b. 1857. [1781] Adventures of a horticulturist. Point Loma: priv. pr., 1935. 229 p. PSew. In Pennsylvania and California.

Elliott, Charles, 1792–1869. Indian [1782] missionary reminiscences... N.Y.: Lane & Scott, 1850. 216 p. WHi. Methodist among the Wyandot Indians in the twenties.

Elliott, Mrs. Ellen Coit (Brown). [1783] It happened this way...Stanford: Stanford univ. press, 1940. 332 p. DLC. By the wife of the Registrar of Stanford University.

Elliott, Mrs. Maud (Howe), b. 1854. [1784] Three generations. Boston: Little, Brown & co., 1923. 418 p. WU. By a New England literary figure.

Elliott, Richard Smith, b. 1817. [1785] Notes taken in sixty years... St. Louis: R. P. Studley & co., printers, 1883. 336 p. WHi. Lawyer, businessman and political journalist in Missouri.

Elliott, Robert G. Agents of death. [1786] N.Y.: Dutton, 1940. 315 p. WU. By an executioner.

Ellis, Anne, b. 1875. The life of [1787] an ordinary woman. Boston & N.Y.: Houghton Mifflin, 1929. 301 p. NN. Pioneer life in the mining districts of Colorado by a woman who was a dressmaker and a cook in a sheep camp.

Ellis, Anne, b. 1875. "Plain Anne [1788] Ellis"; more about the life of an ordinary woman. Boston & N.Y.: Houghton Mifflin, 1931. 265 p. NN. The author enters local politics in Colorado.

Ellis, Anne, b. 1875. Sun- [1789] shine preferred...Boston: Houghton Mifflin, 1934. 249 p. DLC. Her life as an asthmatic in the southwest.

Ellis, Daniel. Thrilling adven- [1790] tures...N.Y.: Harper, 1867. 430 p. WHi. Guide for the Union forces in East Tennessee.

Ellis, John, 1812-1894. Autobio- [1791] graphy and poems...Springfield: New Era co., 1895. 99 p. MoCanD. Clergyman in the Disciple of Christ Church in many parts of the country.

Ellis, John Breckinridge, b. 1870. [1792] Adventure of living. Cedar Rapids: Torch press, 1933. 310 p. NN. Reminiscences of a literary life spent largely in Missouri.

Ellis, Mary (Crispin), b. 1859. [1793] The life story. No imprint. 14 leaves. IaDm. After moving with her parents to Iowa in the seventies, she lives the life of a housewife on a farm in the eighties.

Ellis, Thomas T. Leaves from [1794] the diary of an army surgeon... N.Y.: John Bradburn, 1863. 312 p. WHi. In the Union army.

Ellis, William B. Sanity for sale. [1795] ...Advance: Advance pub. co., 1928. 179 p. NcD. Owner of tobacco factory in North Carolina loses his property to the "tobacco trust" and is "falsely" convicted of insanity.

Ellis, William Turner, b. 1866. [1796] Memories...Eugene: Univ. of Oreg., 1939. 308 p. WHi. Member of the State of California Reclamation Board, who was also in the mercantile business.

Ellison, Mrs. Edith Nicholl Brad- [1797] ley. The desert and the rose. Boston: The Cornhill co., 1921. 215 p. DLC. A literary figure tells of her life as a ranchwoman in New Mexico.

Ellsworth, Lincoln. Search. N.Y.:[1798] Brewer, Warren & Putnam, 1932. 179 p. WHi. The life of an explorer.

Ellsworth, Lincoln. Beyond hori- [1799] zons. N.Y.: Doubleday, Doran, 1940. 403 p. WU. A famous explorer relates his experiences, including his early training for a career in civil engineering.

Elman, Saul. Memoirs of Mischa [1800] Elman's father. N.Y.: 1933. 201 p. DLC. His experiences in Europe and America while traveling with his famous musical son. The author was a Jew born in Russia.

Elpizon (pseud.). See Hoffman, John Jacob.

Elting, Victor, b. 1871. Recollec- [1801] tions of a grandfather. Chicago: A. Kroch, 1940. 232 p. NN. A Chicago lawyer active in civic and philanthropic affairs.

Elworth, Thomas, b. 1816. Sketches[1802] of incidents and adventures... Boston: pr. for the author, 1844. 68 p. DLC. An account of his walking feat in 1842 during which time he walked 1,000 miles in 1,000 consecutive hours.

Ely, Edwin A. Personal memoirs [1803] ...N.Y.: Charles Francis press, 1926. 517 p. WHi. Merchant in N.Y. City.

Ely, Richard Theodore, b. 1854. [1804] Ground under our feet; an autobiography. N.Y.: Macmillan, 1938. 330 p. WU. Teacher of economics at Johns Hopkins, Wisconsin and Northwestern.

Ely, Sally Frothingham (Akers). [1805] A singer's story. Stanford: priv. pr., n.d. 151 p. C. The brief singing career of a New York girl who was trained abroad. This autobiography was written in 1913.

Emerson, George Barrell, 1797- [1806] 1881. Reminiscences of an old teacher. Boston: Alfred Mudge & son, printers, 1878. 153 p. WU. In the English Classical School in Boston.

Emmert, David. Reminiscences of[1807] Juanita College...1876-1901. Huntington, Pa.: priv. pr., 1901. 183 p. DLC. By a teacher in a school supported by the Brethren Church.

Emmet, Thomas Addis, 1828-1919.[1808]
Incidents of my life...N.Y.:
Putnam, 1911. 416 p. WU. Physician
in New York.

Emmet, William LeRoy, b. 1859. [1809]
Autobiography of an engineer.
2d ed. N.Y.: Am. soc. of mechanical engineers, 1940. 233 p. WU.
Mechanical engineer.

Emmett, Chris, b. 1886. Give way [1810]
to the right. San Antonio: Naylor,
1934. 295 p. DLC. A soldier's
experiences in the first World
War.

Emmons, Nathanael, 1745-1840. [1811]
Memoir of Nathanael Emmons,
D.D. written by himself. (In his:
Works. Boston, 1842.) v. 1, p.
ix-xxxvii. NN. Congregational
minister and theologian who
spent most of his adult life in
Franklin, Mass.

Empey, Arthur Guy, b. 1883. [1812]
"Over the top". N.Y.: Putnam,
1917. 315 p. DLC. An American
who served with the British
forces in the first World War.

Enders, Gordon Bandy. Foreign [1813]
devil. N.Y.: Simon & Schuster,
1942. 307 p. DLC. An Iowa boy
who was raised in India in a
missionary family, and who
served in the French army during the first World War. After
the war he was an instructor in
flying for the Chinese forces led
by Chiang Kai-shek.

Enders, Gordon Bandy. Nowhere [1814]
else in the world. N.Y.: Farrar
& Rinehart, 1935. 434 p. NN.
Story of the author's experiences
in Thibet, including his work as
advisor to the Panchan Lama.

Endicott, William, b. 1826. [1815]
Reminiscences of seventy-five
years. Boston: 1913. 27 p. MiD-B.
Dry goods merchant in Mass.

England, W. A., b. 1831. Life and [1816]
travels. Athens, Georgia: 1902.
74 p. G. Minister and sexton
in Georgia.

English, Mrs. Mary Katharine [1817]
(Jackson). Prairie sketches...
Cheyenne: 1918? 76 p. DLC.
The life of the daughter of an
army officer in Wyoming at the
turn of the century.

Enmegahbowh, John Johnson, [1818]
1812?-1902. ...Story. Minneapolis:
Woman's auxiliary, St. Barnabas
hospital, 1904. 56 p. MnHi. A
Chippewa Indian in Minnesota tells
of the troubles of 1857 and 1862
and how he sought to work with
the whites.

Enters, Angna, b. 1907. First [1819]
person plural. N.Y.: Stackpole,
1937. 386 p. DLC. The career
of a dancer and painter.

Enters, Angna, b. 1907. Silly girl. [1820]
Boston: Houghton Mifflin, 1944.
322 p. WU. Dancer and painter.

Epperson, Harry A., b. 1880. [1821]
Colorado as I saw it. Kaysville,
Utah: priv. pr., 1943. 137 p. CoD.
Life on the ranch.

Eppes, Susan (Bradford). Through [1822]
some eventful years. Macon:
J.W. Burke, 1926. 378 p. WHi.
Life in the South before and during the Civil War.

Epstein, Jacob. Let there be [1823]
sculpture. N.Y.: Putnam, 1940.
393 p. WU. An American born
sculptor who moved to England.

Equiano, Oluadah. See Vassa,
Gustavus.

Erath, George Bernard, b. 1813. [1824]
Memoirs...arranged by Lucy A.
Erath. Austin: Texas state historical association, 1923. 105 p.
TxBea. Texas state assemblyman
tells also of his Indian fighting in
the thirties and forties. The
author was born in Austria.

Ericsson, Henry, b. 1861. Sixty [1825]
years a builder; the autobiography
of Henry Ericsson, written in collaboration with Lewis E. Myers.
Chicago: A. Kroch & son, 1942.
388 p. WHi. In Chicago.

Ernst, Anna Catharine, 1726-1816. [1826]
Road to Salem; by Adelaide L.
Fries. Chapel Hill: Univ. of N. C.,
1944. 316 p. WHi. A lay worker
for the Moravian Church in North
Carolina whose manuscript biography is quoted from liberally.

Erpenstein, John, 1812-1852. Life, [1827]
and dying confession of John
Erpenstein, convicted of poisoning his wife...Tr. from the German. Newark: Daily Advertiser
office, 1852. 18 p. DLC. In New
Jersey.

Erskine, Charles. Twenty years [1828]
before the mast...Phila.: the
author, 1896. 311 p. OCl. A sailor
who was with Admiral Wilkes,
1838-42, on his trip around the world.

Erwin, James, b. 1813. Reminis- [1829] cences of early circuit life. Toledo: Spear, Johnson & co., printers, 1884. 378 p. TxDaM. Methodist clergyman in New York.

Esmeralda, Aurora (pseud.). See Mighels, Ella Sterling (Clark).

Espenschied, Charles. Some ran- [1830] dom recollections. N.p. Reprinted from the Northwestern Miller, 1926. 46 p. MoSHi. The life of a miller in Minnesota from about 1870.

Espey, John J. Minor heresies. [1831] N.Y.: Knopf, 1945. 202 p. WU. The story of a youth spent in the home of an American missionary in China.

Estabrooks, Henry L. Adrift in [1832] Dixie...N.Y.: Carleton, 1866. 224 p. WHi. A Union soldier's account of his experiences as a prisoner and of his escape.

Estill, Joe Garner, b. 1863. Epi- [1833] sodes in the life of a commonplace man. Lakeville, Conn.: 1939. 140 p. DLC. Teacher at private school in Connecticut.

Estradas de Mina, Carolino [1834] Amalio, 1809-1832. The life and confession of Carolino Estrades de Mina. Executed at Doylestown ...for poisoning with arsenic, William Chapman. Written by himself in the Spanish language ...translated...by C. G. Phila.: Robert Desilver, 1832. 50 p. DLC. Cuban.

Etan, Raymond (pseud.). See Melharn, Nathan Raymond.

Ethridge, Willie (Snow). This [1835] little pig stayed home. N.Y.: Vanguard, 1944. 240 p. NcGW. A woman's wartime life on the home front in Kentucky, 1942-1943.

Etter, Mrs. Maria Beulah (Under- [1836] wood), b. 1844. Acts of the Holy Ghost...Dallas: Worley pr. co., 1912? 581 p. CU-B. Evangelist of the United Brethren Church who did much of her work in Indiana, Missouri and Iowa.

Eubank, Reuben Blakey, b. 1858. [1837] Twenty years in hell; or, the life, experience, trials and tribulations of a morphine fiend... Kansas City, Mo.: The Revelation pub. co., 1903. 154 p. DLC. Missouri lawyer.

Eulich, Margaret Sally. White [1838] mother in Africa. N.Y.: Richard R. Smith, 1939. 220 p. NN. Experiences of an American woman, married to a mining engineer, in the diamond fields of central Africa.

Eustis, William Henry, b. 1845. [1839] Autobiography...N.Y.: James T. White, 1936. 281 p. MnHi. New York lawyer who came to Minnesota in 1881 where he promoted railroads and telegraph. During 1893-95 he was mayor of Minneapolis.

Evans, Charles, b. 1890. Chick [1840] Evans' golf book...N.Y.: pub. for Thomas E. Wilson, 1921. 343 p. DLC. Amateur golfing champion.

Evans, Frederick William, 1808- [1841] 1893. Autobiography of a Shaker, and revelation of the apocalypse. Mt. Lebanon, N.Y.: F. W. Evans, 1869. 162 p. Auto., p. 9-88. NN. Political and economic reformer, and one of the Shaker leaders in New York. The author was born in England.

Evans, Holden A., b. 1871. One [1842] man's fight for a better Navy. N.Y.: Dodd, Mead, 351 p. WHi. Naval officer and shipbuilder.

Evans, Hugh Davey, 1792-1868. [1843] Hugh Davey Evans. A memoir founded upon recollections written by himself. By the Rev. Hall Harrison. Hartford: pr. by the Church press co., 1870. 182 p. NN. A Baltimore lawyer, active in the Protestant Episcopal Church, and a writer on the theology and ecclesiastical law of the Church.

Evans, Joshua, 1731-1798. A jour- [1844] nal of the life, travels, religious exercises, and labours in the work of the ministry, of Joshua Evans, late of Newton township, Gloucester county, New Jersey. Byberry: John & Isaac Comley, J. Richards, pr., Phila., 1837. 212 p. NN. In most of the Atlantic seaboard states.

Evans, Richard C., b. 1861. Auto- [1845] biography...Lamoni: Herald pub. house, 1909, 284 p. USlC. Mormon of the Reorganized Church who preached in Illinois, Michigan and Ohio. The author, born in Canada, became a minister in England, and preached in the U. S. as an itinerant.

Evans, Robley Dunglison, 1846– [1846]
1912. A sailor's log; recollections
of forty years of naval life. N.Y.:
D. Appleton, 1901. 467 p. WHi.
Naval officer who saw action in the
Civil War and Spanish-American
War.

Evans, Robley Dunglison, 1846– [1847]
1912. An admiral's log; being continued recollections of naval life.
N.Y.: D. Appleton, 1911. 467 p. NN.
The author's career from the
close of the Spanish-American
War until his retirement in 1909.

Evans, Warren F. Autobiography [1848]
of a Shaker...Mount Lebanon,
N.Y.: the author, 1869? 162 p.
MBAt. The story of his conversion.

Evarts, John W., b. 1837. Light of [1849]
life...Oklahoma City: the author,
1909. 485 p. OkHi. Itinerant
printer and apostle of "scientific
religion".

Everett, Syble (Byrd). Adventures [1850]
with life; an autobiography of a
distinguished Negro citizen.
Boston: Meador, 1945. 182 p.
WHi. School teacher and director of physical education, in
Kansas and Oklahoma.

Everton, Walter Marion, b. 1876. [1851]
"Autobiography". (In his: Everton
Knowles book. Logan: 1942.) p. 1–
47. USlC. Utah teacher and merchant, including his missions for
Mormons to North Carolina and
Georgia.

Evstifeef, Alexander. The traitor. [1852]
N.p.: 1938. 112 p. WaS. An account
of his efforts to combat Communism
in the twenties by a man who fled
Russia.

Ewell, Samuel Holbrook, 1819– [1853]
1908. Original poems. Romeo,
Mich: 1901. 146 p. Auto., p. i–iv.
MiU-C. Michigan farmer and
businessman.

Eyland, Seth (pseud.), b. 1839. [1854]
The evolution of a life. N.Y.:
S.W. Green, 1884. 336 p. WHi.
Includes his experiences as a
soldier in the Union army. The
remainder deals with journalism
in New England and business in
Texas. The Library of Congress
assigns the authorship to David
E. Cronin. Halkett names Silas
E. Reynolds as the author.

Eytinge, Rose, 1838–1911. The [1855]
memories of Rose Eytinge, being
recollections and observations of
men, women, and events, during
half a century. N.Y.: Frederick A.
Stokes co., 1905. 311 p. NN. Theatrical reminiscences and memories of her years in Egypt as the
wife of the American consul-general.

Ezzell, Samuel R., 1834–1910. [1856]
"Autobiographic sketch". (In his:
Great legacy. Cinc.: Central book
concern, 1883.) p. 292–311. CSmH.
Clergyman of the Disciples of
Christ church in Missouri, Texas
and Arkansas.

# F

F., M.T. My Chinese marriage. [1857]
N.Y.: Duffield, 1922. 169 p. MtBu.
The life in China of an American
girl, who tells of her family life,
farming, etc.

Fackler, Samuel A. Ups and [1858]
downs of a country editor, mostly
downs. N.p.: Collins job print,
n.d. 103 p. DLC. In Georgia, Alabama and Florida.

Fagan, James Octavius, b. 1859. [1859]
The autobiography of an individualist. Boston & N.Y.: Houghton
Mifflin, 1912. 290 p. NN. Author of
Confessions of a railroad signalman. Youthful adventures in Brazil
and South Africa; telegraph operator and tower signalman on New
England railroads; intellectual development and opinions on railroad
and labor problems.

Fagots from the camp fire. See
Depre, Louis J.

Fairback, Henry, b. 1839. A wan- [1860]
derer...St. Louis: Commercial
prntg. co., 1912. 63 p. MoKu.
German born building contractor
and banker in Missouri tells also
of his early days as a carpenter
in Illinois and a deck hand on the
Mississippi. During the Civil War
he served with an Illinois outfit.

Fairbank, Calvin, b. 1816. Rev. [1861]
Calvin Fairbank during slavery
times...Chicago: R. R. McCabe,
1890. 207 p. ViHaI. By a Methodist
clergyman who lived in New England and in the South. Abolitionist.

Fairchild, David Grandison, [1862]
b. 1869. The world was my garden.
N.Y.: Scribner's, 1938. 494 p. WU.

Explorer of plants.

Fairclough, Henry Rushton, 1862- [1863] 1938. Warming both hands; the autobiography of Henry Rushton Fairclough, including his experiences under the American Red Cross in Switzerland and Montenegro. Stanford univ., Calif.: Stanford univ. press, 1941. 629 p. NN. Experiences at Stanford University, where the author taught Latin and Greek, 1893-1927; also teaching experiences elsewhere as a visiting professor; war relief work during the first World War.

Fairfax, Beatrice (pseud.). See Manning, Marie.

Fairfield, Harrison, 1812-1855. [1864] The wreck and the rescue...Ed. by Enoch Pond. Boston: Massachusetts Sabbath school society, 1858. 157 p. Auto., p. 11-131. MWA. New England Congregational clergyman.

Fairfield, Jane (Frazee), b. 1810. [1865] The autobiography of Jane Fairfield; embracing a few select poems by Sumner Lincoln Fairfield. Boston: Bazin & Ellsworth, 1860. 328 p. NN. Account of her life with her husband, Sumner Lincoln Fairfield, the poet, and of her family troubles, beset with poverty and insanity.

Falk, Louis, 1848-1925. Across [1866] the little space; the life story of Dr. Louis Falk as told to his great-grand-daughter Dorothy Cara Strong. Written by his daughter Francesca Falk Miller (Mrs. Franklin Miller). Chicago: The W.D. Bauman co., 1933. 95 p. NN. Organist, composer and music teacher, who lived in Chicago.

Fanning, David, 1756?-1825. The [1867] narrative of Colonel David Fanning, (a Tory in the Revolutionary War with Great Britain;) giving an account of his adventures in North Carolina, from 1775 to 1783. Richmond, Va.: printed for private distribution only, 1861. 92 p. NN. As described by the title.

Fanning, Edmund, 1769-1841. Voy- [1868] ages and discoveries...1729-1832. Salem: Marine research society, 1924. 330 p. WHi. New England sea-captain and explorer.

Fanning, Nathaniel, 1755-1805. [1869] Fanning's narrative...1778-1783. Ed. by John S. Barnes. N.Y.: Naval historical soc., 1912. 258 p. WHi. Officer in the U.S. Navy who served with John Paul Jones.

Fanning, Thomas W. The hair- [1870] breadth escapes and humorous adventures of a volunteer in the cavalry service. Cinc.: P.C. Browne, 1865. 200 p. CSmH. Civil War.

Farley, Edwin. Experience of a [1871] soldier, 1861-1865. Paducah: Billings pr. co., 1918. 111 p. IHi. In a Wisconsin outfit.

Farley, James Aloysius. Behind [1872] the ballots, the personal history of a politician. N.Y.: Harcourt, Brace, 1938. 376 p. WHi. By the famous New York politician who was associated with F. D. Roosevelt.

Farley, Joseph Pearson. West [1873] Point in the early sixties...Troy, N.Y.: Pafraets, 1902. 201 p. WHi. The story of his student days, followed by his experiences as an officer in the Union army.

Farnham, Eliza Woodson, 1815- [1874] 1864. California, in-doors and out; or, how we farm, mine and live... N.Y.: Dix, Edwards & co., 1856. 508 p. Auto., p. 1-247. DLC. California about 1851.

Farnham, Joseph E. C., b. 1840? [1875] Brief historical data and memories of my boyhood days in Nantucket. 2d ed. Providence: priv. pr., 1923. 319 p. WHi. A boyhood story, including his days as an apprentice to a printer in the sixties.

Farnham, Ralph, 1756-1861. A [1876] biographical sketch of...the sole survivor of the glorious battle of Bunker Hill, by C. W. Clarence. Boston: 1860. 48 p. DLC. From conversations gleaned by the writer describing the life of a farmer in Maine.

Farnsworth, Floyd Forney, b.1869.[1877] Saga of a country doctor among the West Virginia hills. Milton? W.Va.: 1940? 130 p. DLC. Includes his experiences in the first World War and in the U.S. Public Service.

Farquhar, Arthur B. The first [1878] million the hardest...Garden City, N.Y.: Doubleday, Page, 1922. 316 p. WHi. Manufacturer in Pa. The period covered is 1850-1920.

Farrar, Geraldine, b. 1882. Ger- [1879] aldine Farrar, the story of an

American singer, by herself. Boston & N.Y.: Houghton Mifflin, 1916. 115 p. NN. This includes the story of her childhood which is not in the item that follows.

Farrar, Geraldine, b. 1882. The [1880] autobiography of Geraldine Farrar: Such sweet compulsion. N.Y.: The Greystone press, 1938. 303 p. NN. Memories of an American singer and opera star.

Farrell, Sister Mary Xavier, [1881] b. 1849. Happy memories of a sister of Charity. St. Louis: B. Herder, 1941. 190 p. DLC. In Pennsylvania.

Farrington, Harry Webb, 1880- [1882] 1930. Kilts to togs; orphan adventures. N.Y.: Macmillan, 1930. 358 p. NN. Recollections of an orphan boyhood in Maryland, largely in Baltimore.

Farrow, W. Milton. How I became [1883] a crack shot. Newport: Davis & Pitman, 1882. 204 p. Auto., p. 3-155. DLC. An account of the matches in which he engaged, and the tours made on behalf of the sport of marksmanship.

Farson, Negley. The way of a [1884] transgressor. London: V. Gollancz, 1935. 639 p. WHi. A foreign newspaper correspondent. There is a little additional biography in his Transgressor in the Tropics.

Faulconer, Albert. A bundle of [1885] roots. No imprint, 1941? 151 p. KHi. Missouri farmer and teacher who becomes a Kansas lawyer about 1900.

Faulkner, Arthur Lincoln, b.1864. [1886] Fifty years' recollections... Cleveland: The Electric printing co., 1919. 53 p. DLC. Labor union leader who among other positions was president of the Amalgamated Window Glass Workers of America.

Faulkner, Joseph P. Three years [1887] on a whaler. Bath, N.Y.: A. L. Underhill, 1875. 72 p. DLC. As described by the title.

Faunce, Hilda. Desert wife. Boston: Little, Brown, 1934. 305 p. [1888] WHi. In Arizona on an Indian reservation as the wife of a trader.

Fear, John Carey, b. 1855. Recollections of a country doctor. [1889] Lyndon, Kansas: O.J. Rose, printer, 1938. 52 p. KHi. In Kansas.

Fearn, Anne (Walter), b. 1867. My [1890] days of strength; an American woman doctor's forty years in China. N.Y.: Harper, 1939. 297 p. WU. As described by the title.

Featherston, Edward Baxter, [1891] b. 1850. A pioneer speaks. Dallas: Cecil Baugh, 1940. 239 p. DLC. Baptist clergyman in Texas who was also a Justice of the Peace.

Fedric, Francis. See Frederick, Francis.

Fee, John Gregg, 1816-1901. Auto- [1892] biography of John G. Fee, Berea, Kentucky. Chicago, Ill.: National Christian assoc., 1891. 211 p. NN. Minister, abolitionist and founder of Berea College, who labored mostly in Kentucky.

Fee, William Ingram, 1817-1900. [1893] Bringing the sheaves; gleanings from harvest fields in Ohio, Kentucky and West Virginia. Cinc.: Cranston & Curts; 663 p. NN. Methodist minister.

Fellows, Corabelle. Blue star... [1894] by Kunigunde Duncan. Caldwell, Idaho: Caxton printers, 1938. 211 p. KHi. Teacher and missionary who during 1881-88 was located in Nebraska and the Dakota territory.

Fellows, Dexter William, 1871- [1895] 1937. This way to the big show. N.Y.: The Viking press, 1936. 362 p. NN. Reminiscences of the famous press agent for Buffalo Bill and for the Barnum & Bailey and Ringling circuses.

Felton, Rebecca (Latimer), 1835- [1896] 1930. Country life in Georgia in the days of my youth. Atlanta: 1919. 248 p. WHi. A story of youth by a U.S. Senator and writer.

Fenger, Christian, 1840-1902. [1897] "Autobiography". (In his: Collected works. Phila.: W. B. Saunders, 1912.) Vol. 1, p. 1-5. WU. Surgeon, pathologist and professor of medicine in Chicago.

Fennell, James, 1766-1816. An [1898] apology for the life of James Fennell. Phila.: Moses Thomas, 1814. 510 p. NN. English actor who spent the latter part of his life in the United States. He also engaged unsuccessfully in the business of extracting salt from seawater.

Ferber, Edna, b. 1887. A peculiar [1899]

treasure, by Edna Ferber. N.Y.: Doubleday, Doran & co., 1939. 398 p. WU. Novelist.

Ferber, Nat Joseph, b. 1889. I [1900] found out; a confidential chronicle of the twenties. N.Y.: The Dial press, 1939. 351 p. NN. Reporter on the New York American. As described by the title.

Ferebee, L. R. Brief history of [1901] the slave life of L. R. Ferebee... and four years of his ministerial life...Raleigh: Edwards, Broughton, 1882. 24 p. Nc. In North Carolina.

Ferguson, Charles D., b. 1832? [1902] The experiences of a forty-niner... in California and Australia. Cleveland: Williams, 1888. 507 p. DLC. A miner in California and Australia.

Ferguson, Edward Alexander, [1903] b. 1826. Founding of the Cincinnati southern railway. Cinc.: Robert Clarke co., 1905. 163 p. Auto., p. 1-5. DLC. Ohio lawyer and state senator.

Fergusson, Harvey, b. 1890. [1904] ...Home in the West, an inquiry into my origins. N.Y.: Duell, Sloan & Pearce, 1845. 247 p. WU. A novelist tells of his boyhood in New Mexico.

Fernald, Mark, 1784-1851. Life of [1905] Elder Mark Fernald. Newburyport: Geo. Moore Payne & D. P. Pike, 1852. 405 p. NN. Minister of the Christian denomination, laboring mostly in New Hampshire and Maine.

Fernandez-Azabal, Lilie (Bouton) [1906] de. The countess from Iowa. N.Y.: G. P. Putnam's sons, 1936. 263 p. NN. Recollections of the author's stage career; later of social life in Europe, especially in Germany and Russia.

Ferris, David, 1707-1779. Mem- [1907] oirs...Phila.: Merrihew & Thompson, 1855. 106 p. OrNeGF. Minister of the Friends in Connecticut and Delaware.

Ferris, Isaac, 1798-1873. Mem- [1908] orial discourse; or fifty years's ministry in the Reformed Church of America, N.Y.: pr. by Edward O. Jenkins, 1871. 38 p. WHi. Reformed clergyman in New York and New Jersey.

Ferris, Warren Angus, 1810-1873. [1909] Life in the Rocky Mountains... Denver: 1940. 365 p. WHi. By an employee of the American Fur Company.

Fesperman, Joseph Hamilton, [1910] 1841-1892. The life of a sufferer... Utica: Young Lutheran co., 1892. 127 p. NcU. Lutheran pastor in North Carolina.

Fetterhoff, John, 1798-1822. The [1911] life...Chambersburg, Pa.: United Brethren in Christ print., 1883. 284 p. DLC. Itinerant preacher in the United Brethren in Christ Church in the state of Pennsylvania.

Ficke, Charles August, b. 1850. [1912] Memories of fourscore years. Davenport: 1930. 508 p. DLC. German born businessman, lawyer and politician in Iowa.

Field, Alfred Griffith, b. 1852. [1913] Watch yourself go by. Columbus, Ohio: pr. by Spohr & Glenn, 1912. 593 p. DLC. Minstrel and circus performer.

Field, Benjamin F. Reminiscences [1914] of a Boston merchant. Boston: Rand Avery co., The Franklin press, 1887. 136 p. MWA. Story of his youthful days when he shipped as supercargo to the Orient.

Field, Charles D. Three years in [1915] the saddle from 1861 to 1865... Goldfield? Iowa: 1898. 74 p. CSmH. With Illinois cavalry in Missouri and Arkansas.

Field, Charles Kellogg, b. 1873. [1916] The story of Cheerio. Garden City, N.Y.: Garden city pub. co., 1937. 382 p. DLC. Radio actor in California.

Field, Eugene, 1850-1895. ...An [1917] autoanalysis. Chicago: 1896. n.p. WU. A brief statement by the well known literary figure.

Field, George. Memoirs, incidents [1918] and reminiscences of the early history of the New Church in Michigan, Indiana, Illinois and adjacent states...N.Y.: Swinney, 1879. 368 p. WHi. By one of their clergymen. While intended as a history, much personal material is included.

Field, Mrs. Isobel (Osbourne). [1919] This life I've loved. N.Y.: Longmans, Green, 1937. 353 p. WU. Literary stepdaughter of R. L. Stevenson tells of her life among intellectuals.

Field, Joseph E. Three years in [1920]
Texas...Boston: Abel Tompkins,
1836. 47 p. Auto., p. 41-47. DLC.
His experiences in the War with
Mexico.

Field, Richard, b. 1843. Richard [1921]
Field. Lexington, Mo.: 1930. 38 p.
MoK. Missouri lawyer and judge
tells also of his youth on a farm.

Field, Stephen Johnson, 1816-1899.[1922]
Personal reminiscences of early
days in California, with other
sketches. San Francisco? 1880.
248 p. WHi. By a judge and member of the state legislature.

Fifer, Joseph Wilson, b. 1840.    [1923]
"Private Joe" Fifer. Memories
of war & peace. Bloomington, Ill.:
Pantagraph pr. co., 1936. 104 p.
WHi. Civil War soldier and
governor of Illinois.

Finch, Edwin Ward, b. 1831. The [1924]
frontier, army and professional
life of Edwin W. Finch...N.Y.:
Press of Simmonds, Manning &
Dawson, 1909. 119 p. Auto., p. 1-64.
DLC. A New York physician tells
of his boyhood on a Michigan
homestead and of his service
with the Union forces as a surgeon.

Finck, Henry Theophilos, 1854-   [1925]
1926. My adventures in the golden
age of music. N.Y.: Funk & Wagnalls, 1926. 462 p. WU. Music
critic.

Finerty, John Frederick, 1846-   [1926]
1908. War-path and bivouac...
the Big Horn and Yellowstone
expedition. Chicago: 1890. 460 p.
DLC. Newspaper correspondent
with Crook, 1866-67, in the
campaigns against the Indians
in the West.

Finley, James Bradley, 1781-1856.[1927]
Autobiography of Rev. James B.
Finley; or, pioneer life in the
West. Cinc.: pr. at the Methodist
book concern, for the author,
1853. 455 p. WHi. Methodist in
the old Northwest.

Finley, James Bradley, 1781-1856.[1928]
Life among the Indians...Cinc.:
Hitchcock & Walden, 1868. 507 p.
WHi. An enlarged version of the
preceding item.

Finn, Francis James, 1859-1928. [1929]
Father Finn, S.J.; the story of
his life told by himself for his
friends young and old. N.Y.:
Benziger bros., 1929. 236 p. NN.
Teacher in St. Louis and Cincinnati.
A pioneer promoter of juvenile literature for Catholics.

Finney, Charles Grandison, 1792- [1930]
1875. Charles G. Finney. An autobiography. Popular ed. London,
N.Y.: The Slavation army book department, 1903. 401 p. WHi. Presbyterian, later Congregational, clergyman in the middle western states.

Finney, Charles Grandison, d.1875.[1931]
The inner and outer life...London: S. W. Partridge, 1882. 32 p.
WHi. The author left the Presbyterian church to become a member
of the Salvation Church in New
York City.

Finney, John Miller Turpin,      [1932]
b. 1863. A surgeon's life. N.Y.:
Putnam, 1940. 400 p. WU. In
Massachusetts and Maryland.

Firestone, Harvey S. Men and    [1933]
rubber...Garden City: Doubleday,
Page, 1926. 279 p. WU. Manufacturer of rubber products.

Fischer, Augusta Catherine,      [1934]
b. 1891. Searchlight; an autobiography. Seattle 1937. 233 p. NN.
The story of the causes leading
to the author's mental breakdown
and her experiences in insane
hospitals in the state of Washington.

Fisher, Clara. See Maeder, Mrs.
Clara (Fisher).

Fisher, Daniel Webster, 1838-1913.[1935]
A human life...N.Y.: Revell, 1909.
325 p. PU. Presbyterian clergyman who was also president of
Hanover College in Indiana.

Fisher, Elizabeth (Munro), b. 1759.[1936]
Memoirs, of Mrs. Elizabeth Fisher,
of the city of New York,...giving
a particular account of a variety
of domestic misfortunes, and also
of her trial, and cruel condemnation to the state's prison for six
years, at the instance of her brother Peter Jay Munro...N.Y.: 1810.
48 p. DLC. By an American Tory.

Fisher, George Adams, b. 1835.   [1937]
The Yankee conscript, or eighteen
months in Dixie. Phila.: J. W.
Daughaday, 1864. 251 p. WU. By
a Union soldier.

Fisher, Hugh Dunn, b. 1824. The [1938]
gun and the gospel...4th ed. Kansas
city: Hudson-Kimberly, 1902. 347 p.
WHi. Methodist clergyman in
Kansas, Nebraska, Utah, Idaho and
Montana. Chaplain in the Union army.

Fisher, Mary Frances Kennedy, [1939] b. 1908. The gastronomical me. N.Y.: Duell, Sloan & Pearce, 1943. 295 p. DLC. Cook book writer.

Fisher, Milton Metcalf. Autobio- [1940] graphy...Concord: Rumford press, 1902. 85 p. WHi. Abolitionist, banker and dealer in real estate in Massachusetts.

Fisher, Orion Paul, b. 1867. Auto- [1941] biography of Orion Paul Fisher, banker and financier...San Francisco: San Francisco pub. co., 1921. 347 p. DLC. In Ohio, New York, Massachusetts, and on the west coast.

Fisk, J.H. Two years before the [1942] mast, and ten behind it...Portland, Oreg.: Madden & Crawford, printers, 1892. 48 p. WaU. Conn. sailor (19th century) in the Pacific on a whaler.

Fiske, Bradley Allen, b. 1854. [1943] From midshipman to rear-admiral. N.Y.: Century, 1919. 688 p. WHi. U. S. Naval officer.

Fitz, Frances Ella. Lady sour- [1944] dough. N.Y.: Macmillan, 1941. 319 p. WHi. Gold miner in Alaska.

Fitzgerald, Oscar Penn, 1829- [1945] 1911. Sunset views...Nashville & Dallas: Pub. house of the M.E. Church, South, 1901. 343 p. Auto., p. 3-145. DLC. Methodist clergyman.

Fitz-James, Zilla, b. 1827. Zilla [1946] Fitz James, the female bandit of the Southwest...An autobiographical narrative, ed. by Rev. A. Richards...Little Rock: A. R. Orton, 1852. 31 p. CtY. As described by the title.

Fitzsimmons, Fred. His career [1947] of crime and his nemesis. Pittsburgh: Mooar & Hill, 1892. 64 p. PSew. In Pennsylvania.

Five years in the west, by a Texas preacher. See Allen, William M.

Flake, Jacob. Christian miscel- [1948] lany...Phila.: 1844. 106 p. Auto., p. 7-14. MH. Clergyman in Pa., belonging to a Baptist sect founded by John Winebrenner, known as the Church of God in America.

Flake, William H. From crime [1949] to Christ. Binghampton, N.Y.: Business-art-press, 1915. 62 p. DLC. He turns to religion after a life of crime and prison in New York and Michigan.

Fleming, E. B. Three years in [1950] a mad house...Chicago: Donohue, Henneberry & co., 1893. 234 p. DLC. A once successful Texas merchant tells of his life in an asylum, 1886-89, from which he escaped.

Fleming, George Thornton, 1855- [1951] 1928. ...My high school days, including a brief history of the Pittsburgh Central High School from 1855 to 1871 and addenda. Pittsburgh, Pa.: 1904. 257 p. NN. As described by the title.

Fletcher, Daniel Cooledge. Rem- [1952] iniscences of California and the Civil war. Ayer, Mass.: Press of H.S. Turner, 1894. 196 p. WHi. Union soldier who from 1852 to 1860 had been a miner in California.

Fletcher, Ebenezer, 1761-1831. [1953] The narrative of Ebenezer Fletcher, a soldier of the Revolution, written by himself. N.Y.: priv. pr., 1866. 86 p. NN. As described by the title.

Fletcher, John Gould, b. 1886. [1954] Life is my song; the autobiography of John Gould Fletcher. N.Y.: Toronto, Farrar & Rinehart, 1937. 406 p. WU. Literary figure.

Fletcher, Philip Cone, b. 1871. [1955] The story of my heart. San Antonio: Alamo pr. co., 1929. 344 p. TxDaM. Methodist clergyman in Arkansas, Missouri and Texas.

Fletcher, William Andrew, b.1839. [1956] Rebel private front and rear... Beaumont: Press of Greer print, 1908. 193 p. DLC. With a Texas outfit.

Flexner, Abraham, b. 1866. I re- [1957] member...N.Y.: Simon & Schuster, 1940. 414 p. WU. A Jewish physician who served for many years on the General Educational Board, his most notable achievement perhaps being the organization of the Institute for Advanced Study at Princeton.

Flexner, Mrs. Helen (Thomas). [1958] A Quaker childhood. New Haven: Yale univ. press, 1940. 335 p. WHi. In Baltimore.

Flickinger, Daniel Kumler, 1824- [1959] 1911. Fifty-five years of active ministerial life...Dayton: United Brethren pub. house, 1907. 261 p. DLC. Missionary of the United Brethren Church in West Africa.

He later became a bishop.

Flinn, Charles (Alias). See Mortimer, Charles.

Flint, Charles Ranlett, 1850-1934. Memories of an active life. N.Y.: Putnam, 1923. 322 p. WHi. Industrial capitalist, known as the "Father of trusts". [1960]

Flipper, Henry Ossian, 1856-1940. The colored cadet at West Point. Autobiography of Lieut. Henry Ossian Flipper, U.S.A.: first graduate of color from the U.S. Military Academy. N.Y.: Homer Lee & co., 1878. 322 p. NN. As described by the title. [1961]

Flying Hawk, Chief, b. 1852. Chief Flying Hawk's tales. N.Y.: Alliance press, 1936. 56 p. MtHi. By a participant of the Custer fight. [1962]

Flynt, Josiah Willard. See Willard, Josiah Flynt.

Fogarty, Tom (alias). The story of Tom Fogarty; the autobiography of a criminal (written down by Thomas Sullivan). Chicago: Cannon: 1900. 280 p. DLC. Thief in Illinois. In the Joliet prison he used the name of John Smith. [1963]

Folger, Allen, b. 1827. Twenty-five years as an evangelist. Boston: James H. Earle & co., 1905. 339 p. DLC. Secretary of the New Hampshire Y.M.C.A. for which he did evangelical preaching. [1964]

Folwell, William Watts, 1833-1929. The autobiography and letters of a pioneer of culture, ed. by Solon J. Buck. Minneapolis: Univ. of Minn. press, 1933. 287 p. WHi. Historian, teacher and president of the University of Minnesota. [1965]

Fontaine, Lamar, b. 1829. My life and my lectures. N.Y. & Wash.: Neale, 1908. 361 p. Auto., p. 1-280. TxU. A Texas school teacher tells mainly of his services with the Confederate army. He was with Perry in 1858. [1966]

Foot, Samuel Alfred, 1790-1878. Autobiography. N.Y.: Electrotyped by Smith & McDougal, 1872. 436 p. WHi. Lawyer in the state of New York. A second volume is made up of his speeches. [1967]

Foote, Julia A.J., b. 1823. A brand plucked from the fire. An autobiographical sketch. Cleveland, O.: pr. for the author by Lauer & Yost, 1886. 124 p. NN. The author was a Negro evangelist of the African Methodist Episcopal Church. [1968]

Foraker, Joseph Benson, 1846-1917. Notes of a busy life. Cinc.: Stewart & Kidd co., 1916. 2 vols. WHi. U. S. Senator from Ohio. [1969]

Foraker, Julia (Bundy), b. 1847. I would live it again, memories of a vivid life. N.Y.: Harper, 1932. 351 p. WHi. The wife of the U.S. Senator from Ohio tells of her social and political life. [1970]

Forbes, John Murray, 1813-1898. Letters and recollections. Boston & N.Y.: Houghton Mifflin, 1899. 2 vols. MH. This was intended for the public, while the next item was intended for the family. This one contains more editorial comment, while the second contains the greater number of letters. [1971]

Forbes, John Murray, 1813-1898. Reminiscences of John Murray Forbes. Boston: George H. Ellis, 1902. 3 vols. MH. New England industrialist who developed railroads in the midwest. The author was also a prominent advisor to the Lincoln administration. Much of these volumes is made up of letters. [1972]

Forbes, Robert Bennet, 1804-1899. Personal reminiscences. Boston: priv. pr., 1876. 382 p. DLC. Boston sea merchant in the China trade, who during the Civil War was Commodore of the Mass. Coast Guard. [1973]

Ford, Arthur P. Life in the Confederate army...N.Y.: Neale, 1905. 136 p. Auto., p. 7-71. WHi. As described by the title. [1974]

Ford, Charles Albert, 1845-1933. Tales of the civil war... Chicago: Floyd Boys, 1931. 47 p. MiU-H. By a resident of Michigan. [1975]

Ford, Henry, b. 1863. My life and work...Garden City, N.Y.: Doubleday, Page & co., 1922. 289 p. WHi. Parts of this work are autobiographical, and relate the early efforts of Mr. Ford in the manufacturing of automobiles. [1976]

Ford, Henry, b. 1863. Henry Ford's own story...as told to Rose W. Lane. N.Y.: E. O. Jones, 1917. 184 p. WHi. Manufacturer. [1977]

Ford, James L. Forty-odd years [1978]

in the literary shop. N.Y.: E. P. Dutton, 1921. 362 p. WU. Newspaper writer, contributor to Puck, tells of his experiences, especially with people of the theatre.

Ford, O. B., b. 1845. Biography...[1979] Yale, Okla.: Yale record job print, n.d. 64 p. OkHi. Union soldier and Iowa farmer.

Ford, Thomas J. With the rank [1980] and file...Milwaukee: Evening Wisconsin co., 1898. 95 p. WHi. Union army soldier.

Forder, Archibald, b. 1863. Ventures among the Arabs. Boston: [1981] W. N. Hartshorn, 1905. 292 p. DLC. By a protestant missionary.

Fordham, Daniel. Three years [1982] with a farmer; or, misfortunes in youth. A thrilling account of the cruel and unnatural treatment of a child nine years of age, written by himself. Islip: Long Island Herald print, 1874. 14 p. NSmB. In New York.

Forgan, James Berwick, 1852- [1983] 1924. Recollections of a busy life. N.Y.: Bankers pub. co., 1924. 335 p. WHi. Banker in Minneapolis and Chicago.

Forman, Harrison, b. 1904. Horizon hunter...N.Y.: Robert M. [1984] McBride, 1940. 314 p. DLC. Aviator, adventurer in the Far East, technical director of motion pictures dealing with Chinese-Japanese warfare.

Formes, Karl Johann Franz, 1815- [1985] 1889. My memoirs...San Francisco: Barry, 1891. 240 p. DLC. German born opera singer who sang in this country and eventually settled in California.

Forrest, Mrs. Elizabeth Chabot. [1986] Daylight moon. N.Y.: Stokes, 1937. 340 p. DLC. The author was employed by the U.S. Bureau of Education to teach in Alaska.

Forster, Minnie Jay. He led me [1987] through the wilderness. No imprint. 139 p. KHi. Wife of a farmer who was also an inventor of farm machinery. The period covered is the late 19th and early 20th century. The locale is Missouri, New Mexico, Oklahoma and Kansas.

Forsyth, George Alexander, 1837-[1988] 1915. Thrilling days in army life. N.Y. & London: Harper & bros., 1900. 196 p. DLC. With Sheridan during the Civil War, later a Commander of a scout detachment for Sheridan, and on Apache raid in 1882 in the Territory of New Mexico.

Fort, John Porter, 1841-1917. [1989] Memorial and personal reminiscences. N.Y.: The Knickerbocker press, 1918. 103 p. DLC. After service in the Confederate army, the author turned to fruit growing, irrigation and drainage problems in Georgia.

Fortescue, Granville. Front line [1990] and deadline...N.Y.: Putnam's, 1937. 310 p. WU. A personal account by a war correspondent, covering 1897-1936.

Foss, James Henry, b. 1841. Gen- [1991] tleman from everywhere. Boston: priv. pr., 1902. 318 p. DLC. Promoter of Florida real estate ventures who previously was a travelling book agent.

Foss, Joe. Joe Foss, flying mar- [1992] ine...N.Y.: E. P. Dutton, 1943. 160 p. WU. The author flew against the Japanese in the second World War.

Foster, Bert. A Rocky mountain [1993] parson. Upland, Calif.: 1940. 96 p. CBCh. From about 1890, mainly in Wyoming and Colorado.

Foster, John, b. 1847. Memoirs [1994] of John Foster, company G, Freeman's regiment, February, 1863-March, 1865, C.S.A. Little Rock: United Daughters of the confederacy, Arkansas Division, 1918? 18 leaves. DLC. As described by the title.

Foster, John Watson, 1836-1917. [1995] Diplomatic memoirs. Boston & N.Y.: Houghton Mifflin, 1909. 2 vols. WHi. In Russia, Spain, Mexico and Japan, 1872-1905.

Foster, William Zebulon. Pages [1996] from a worker's life. N.Y.: International publishers, 1939. 314 p. WHi. American Communist leader. See also his From Bryan to Stalin.

Foulke, William Dudley, 1848-1935.[1997] A Hoosier autobiography. N.Y.: Oxford univ. press, 1922. 252 p. WHi. Historian and politician. The author served as State Senator in Indiana, and was a member of the U.S. Civil Service Commission. He was also interested in civil service and monopoly reforms, and in the cause of peace.

Fowle, Charles H., b. 1852. The [1998] life and career of...N.p.: 1925. 219 p. Auto., p. 5-22. MWA. Mass. amateur journalist, founder of the "Eastern Amateur Press Association".

Fowler, A. Richard, b. 1868. [1999] From the pulpit to the penitentiary. Fountain Inn, S.C.: Mrs. Maggie L. Fowler, 1900? 135 p. DLC. Presbyterian clergyman in Georgia and South Carolina, imprisoned for forgery.

Fowler, Gene, b. 1890. ...A solo [2000] in tom-toms. N.Y.: Covici, Friede, 1931. 30 p. DLC. Journalist. See also the later work of the same title, published in 1946.

Fowler, Smith, b. 1829. Autobio- [2001] graphical sketch. Manistee, Mich.: Times & standard steam power print, 1877. Auto., p. 1-36. WHi. Lawyer and member of the State Senate of Michigan.

Fowler, Theodosius. Memoir... [2002] N.Y.: pr. by W. H. Tinson, 1859. 15 p. WHi. Soldier who served in the Revolutionary War.

Fox, Ebenezer, 1763-1843. The [2003] adventures of Ebenezer Fox, in the Revolutionary War. Boston: Charles Fox, 1848. 240 p. NN. As described by the title.

Fox, George Henry, 1846-1937. [2004] Reminiscences. N.Y.: Medical life press, 1926. 248 p. NN. New York doctor and professor at the College of Physicians and Surgeons.

Fox, John, b. 1831. Life... written [2005] by Hollis Kellogg. Meadville, Pa.: Truran & sons, 1921. 95 p. DLC. Pennsylvania farmer, mail carrier and carpenter. A dictated account.

Fox, Wells B. What I remember [2006] of the great rebellion...Lansing: D. D. Thorp, 1892. 278 p. MiU-H. Surgeon with Michigan outfit.

Foy, Eddie, 1856-1928. Clowning [2007] through life. N.Y.: E. P. Dutton, 1928. 331 p. WU. Vaudeville star (comedian, dancer).

Frackelton, William, 1870-1943. [2008] Sagebrush dentist...Chicago: A. C. McClurg, 1941. 246 p. DLC. In Wyoming, beginning about 1890.

Frame, Nathan T. and Esther [2009] (Gordon). Reminiscences... N.p.: 1907. 673 p. WHi. Ministerial work by Evangelical Friends, mainly in Ohio and Indiana.

France, George W. The struggles [2010] for life and home in the northwest ...1865-1889. N.Y.: I. Goldmann, printer, 1890. 607 p. DLC. Miner in Nevada who then went to a homestead in Idaho.

Francis, Charles, 1848-1936. [2011] Printing for profit...N.Y.: Bobbs-Merrill, 1917. 404 p. Auto., p. 15-26. DLC. By an outstanding business executive in printing.

Francis, Charles Lewis. Narra- [2012] tive of a private soldier in the volunteer army of the United States. Brooklyn: William Jenkins & co., 1879. 185 p. DLC. Union army, 1861-63.

Franck, Rachel (Latta). I married [2013] a vagabond; the story of the family of the writing vagabond. N.Y.: D. Appleton-Century co., 1939. 241 p. NN. Travels in the West Indies, Japan, China, Korea, Scandinavia, England, and France.

Frank, Herman W. Scrapbook of [2014] a western pioneer. Los Angeles: Times-mirror press, 1934. 132 p. WHi. California merchant and civic leader.

Frank, William Hamilton, b. 1852. [2015] Eighty years of my life...Detroit: Northwestern pr. co., 1933. 119 p. Auto., p. 9-77. DLC. Banker, businessman in W.Va.

Franklin, Benjamin, 1706-1790. [2016] Autobiography. N.Y.: John Bigelow, 1868. WHi. Covers to 1775. Printer, book publisher, political figure.

Franklin, Samuel Rhoads. Mem- [2017] ories of a rear-admiral... N.Y.: Harper, 1898. 398 p. WHi. U.S. Navy.

Franko, Sam, 1857-1937. Chords [2018] and discords; memoirs and musings of an American musician. N.Y.: Viking press, 1938. 186 p. DLC. Concert performer, teacher, composer.

Fraser, James Duncan. The gold [2019] fever; or, two years in Alaska... N.p.: 1923. DLC. As described by the title.

Fraser, Mary (Crawford). A dip- [2020] lomatist's wife in many lands. N.Y.: Dodd, Mead, 1910. 2 vols. WHi. American wife of a British diplomat.

Fraser, Mary (Crawford). Rem- [2021] iniscences of a diplomatist's wife in many lands. N.Y.: Dodd, Mead, 1912. 395 p. WHi. See the preceding item.

Fraser, Robert, b. 1906. Over- [2022] coming obstacles; the autobiography of a blind evangelist. Conshohocten, Pa.: printed by the Recorder pub. co., 1936. 175 p. Auto., p. 17-74. DLC. Presbyterian.

Frasier, Isaac, 1740-1768. A [2023] brief account of the life and abominable thefts of the notorious Isaac Frasier...New London: Timothy Green, 1768. 16 p. MWA. As described by the title.

Frazier, Harry, 1868-1937. Rec-[2024] ollections. Huntington, W.Va.: The Chesapeake & Ohio railway co., 1938. 93 p. KyU. Engineer, Chesapeake and Ohio Railway.

Frear, James A. Forty years [2025] of progressive public service... Washington: Associated writers, 1937. 315 p. WHi. Member of the U.S. House of Representatives from Wisconsin, and Wisconsin Secretary of State.

Frederick, Francis. Slave life [2026] in Virginia and Kentucky; or, fifty years of slavery in the Southern states of America. London: Wertheim, Macintosh & Hunt, 1863. 115 p. DLC. As described by the title.

Frederics, Diana: (pseud.). [2027] Diana; a strange autobiography. N.Y.: Dial press, 1939. 284 p. WU. Lesbian.

Freeman, George D. Midnight [2028] and noonday...giving twenty years experience on the frontier ...in and around Caldwell, Kansas from 1871 until 1890...Caldwell: 1892. 406 p. DLC. Farmer, hunter, miner, photographer, law officer.

Freeman, Joseph. An American [2029] testament...N.Y.: Farrar & Rinehart, 1936. 668 p. WHi. Jewish social reformer, co-editor of New Masses.

Freeman, Lewis Ransome. Many [2030] rivers. N.Y.: Dodd, Mead, 1937. 368 p. WHi. Explorer.

Freeman, Merrill P. A justifi- [2031] cation as shown by a life's experiences. Tucson: 1914. 5 p. CLSM. In California in the sixties as miner, postmaster, telegrapher, and railroader.

Freer, Mrs. Eleanor (Everest), [2032] 1864-1942. Recollections and reflections of an American composer. N.Y.: pr. by the Musical advance pub. co., 1929. 122 p. DLC. As described by the title.

Fremont, Elizabeth Benton. [2033] Recollections...N.Y.: F. H. Hitchcock, 1912. 184 p. WHi. The daughter of John C. Fremont tells of frontier social life in California and Arizona.

Fremont, John Charles, 1813- [2034] 1890. Memoirs of my life... Chicago: Belford, Clarke, 1887. 655 p. WHi. Deals only with his life as explorer to the year 1846.

French, Chauncey Del, b. 1890. [2035] Railroadman. N.Y.: Macmillan, 1938. 292 p. DLC. The author was employed in various capacities on railroads in the mid and far west.

French, George Hazen, b. 1841. [2036] Life retrospect...Rangoon, Burma: Am. Baptist mission press, 1936. 139 p. Auto., p. 1-64. MoCanC. Entomologist at Illinois Agricultural College. The author also taught in the grade schools of Wisconsin and New York.

French, Jonathan, 1778-1856. [2037] Reminiscences of a fifty-years pastorate. A half-century discourse, delivered in North-Hampton, N.H. November 18, 1851, by Jonathan French, D.D. pastor of the Congregational Church. Portsmouth: C. W. Brewster & son, prtrs., 1952. 46 p. NN. As described by the title.

French, Mary. Memories of a [2038] sculptor's wife. Boston: Houghton Mifflin, 1928. 294 p. WU. As described by the title.

French, Samuel Gibbs, 1818- [2039] 1910. Two wars: an autobiography of Gen. Samuel G. French...Mexican war; war between the states; a diary; reconstruction period, his experience; incidents, reminiscences, etc. Nashville, Tenn.: Confederate veteran, 1901. 404 p. WHi. As described by the title.

French, William, b. 1854. Some [2040] recollections of a Western ranchman; New Mexico, 1883-1899. N.Y.: F.A. Stokes, 1928. 283 p. WHi.

Englishman in New Mexico.

Frewen, Moreton, b. 1853. Melton [2041] Mowbray and other memories. London: Herbert Jenkins, 1924. DLC. An Englishman on a cattle ranch in Wyoming.

Frey, Hugo Evon, b. 1883. Hugo's [2042] odyssey; the lure of the South Sea islands. Los Angeles: Institute press, 1942. 161 p. NN. The author's "experiences in the South Seas (Samoa) and on the last of the wooden sailing ships in the United States Navy."

Frey, Joseph Samuel Christian [2043] Frederick, 1771-1850. Narrative: N.Y.: W. B. Gilley, 1817. 480 p. Auto., p. 1-139. WHi. The author was a German born Jew who was converted to Protestantism, later becoming a Baptist clergyman. The period covered is to 1810, prior to author's coming to America. The work covers the author's missionary work among the Jews in England.

Friedemann, Lera-Biddena [2044] (Elliot), b. 1890. Under five flags; experiences of the Friedemanns, missionaries to Central Europe. Grand Rapids: Zondervan, 1940. 287 p. DLC. Baptist missionary.

Fritz, John, 1822-1913. The auto- [2045] biography...N.Y.: Wiley, 1912. 326 p. WU. Iron master in Pennsylvania.

Frohman, Daniel, b. 1851. Daniel [2046] Frohman presents...N.Y.: Kendall & Sharp, 1935. 397 p. WU. New York producer of plays. See also his Memories of a Manager, and Encore.

Frost, Edwin Brant, 1866-1935. [2047] An astronomer's life. Boston: Houghton Mifflin, 1933. 286 p. WHi. As described by the title.

Frost, William Goodell, 1854- [2048] 1938. For the mountains; an autobiography. N.Y.: Fleming H. Revell co., 1937. 352 p. NN. Account of the author's labors as president of Berea College, Ky., 1892-1920, for the education of the Southern mountaineers and the Negroes and for the advancement of the idea of vocational education.

Frothingham, Eugenia Brooks, [2049] b. 1874. Youth and I. Boston: Houghton Mifflin, 1938. 167 p. NN. Memories of a girlhood spent in Boston, France, and Italy.

Frothingham, Octavius Brooks, [2050] 1822-1895. Recollections and impressions, 1822-1890. N.Y.: G. P. Putnam's sons, 1891. 302 p. DLC. Unitarian clergyman in New England, New York and New Jersey who founded a new group of Unitarians in 1867.

Fry, Henry, b. 1738. "The auto- [2051] biography". (In: Memoir of Col. Joshua Fry, by P. Slaughter. No imprint.) p. 84-105. WHi. Methodist lay preacher. The account covers to 1792.

Fuchs, Emile, 1866-1929. With [2052] pencil, brush and chisel; the life of an artist. N.Y. & London: G.P. Putnam's sons, 1925. 254 p. NN. Austrian-born painter and sculptor, who came to the United States in 1905.

Fuchs, Mrs. Louise (Romberg). [2053] Erinnerungen. No imprint, 1928. 131 p. TxU. German born wife of a pioneer farmer in Texas who came here in 1847.

Fuerbringer, Ludwig Ernest, [2054] 1864-1947. 80 eventful years; reminiscences. Saint Louis: Concordia pub. house, 1944. 267 p. NN. Evangelical Lutheran theologian and educator, connected for over fifty years with Concordia Theological Seminary, St. Louis, as student, professor, and president; also editor of denominational periodicals.

Fulkerson, B.H. From the gutter [2055] to the ministry. N.p.: 1895. 136 p. TxU. Methodist in Texas, following upon a life of gambling and drinking.

Fulkerson, Horace Smith, 1818- [2056] 1891. A civilian's recollections of the war between the states. Baton Rouge: Otto Claitor, 1939. 253 p. DLC. The author was engaged in securing supplies abroad for the Confederacy.

Fuller, Arthur Franklin, b. 1880. [2057] An odd soldiery...9th ed. Fort Worth: Anchor pub. co., 1914. 151 p. C. Composer of songs and poems tells of his experiences as a beggar cripple.

Fuller, Arthur Franklin, b. 1880. [2058] Wrestling the wolf...Sequel to an Odd soldiery...Los Angeles: 1919. 121 p. C. Further experiences

Fuller, Charles Augustus, [2059] b. 1841? Personal recollections of the war of 1861. Sherburne, N.Y.: 1906. 108 p. DLC. With a New York regiment.

Fuller, Frederick Lincoln, [2060] b. 1861. My half century as an inventor. N.Y.: Mail & express pr. co., 1938. 241 p. Auto., p. 1-67. DLC. And as a manufacturer, in New Jersey and Ohio.

Fuller, Harvey Austin, b. 1834. [2061] Trimsharp's account of himself: a sketch of his life, together with a brief history of the education of the blind...Ann Arbor: Ann Arbor pr. and pub. co., 1873. 150 p. DLC. Blind manufacturer of brooms in New York, who lectured widely on religious topics.

Fuller, Loie, 1870-1928. Fifteen [2062] years of a dancer's life, with some account of her distinguished friends. Boston: Small, Maynard & co., 1913. 288 p. NN. Memories of a life spent largely in Europe.

Fuller, Margaret. See Ossoli, Sarah Margaret (Fuller).

Fuller, Richard Frederick, 1824-[2063] 1869. Recollections...Boston: priv. pr., 1936. 102 p. DLC. The author, a lawyer, was brother to Margaret Fuller.

Fuller, Thomas Oscar, b. 1867. [2064] Twenty years in public life, 1890-1910...Nashville: National Baptist pub. board, 1910. 279 p. DLC. Negro Baptist clergyman, prominent in educational circles in North Carolina and Tennessee. In 1898 he was elected to the U.S. Senate from North Carolina.

Fullerton, James, b. 1853. Auto-[2065] biography of Roosevelt's adversary. Boston: Roxbaugh pub. co., 1912. 162 p. DLC. Homesteader in Minnesota and rancher in Montana who was placed in an insane asylum.

Fulton, Ambrose C. A portion [2066] of a life's voyage...Davenport, Iowa: Osborn-Skelly, printers, 1902. 144 p. Ia-HA. Promoter of highways and railroads in Iowa and Illinois, and owner of lumber mill in Illinois. This account begins with the year 1840.

Fulton, David Bryant, b. 1863. [2067] Recollections of a sleeping-car porter. Jersey City: Doan & Pilson, printers, 1892. 45 p. DLC. Porter and author.

Funk, Henry. The true life at the [2068] Last Chance; or, seven years... in a human slaughter house. San Francisco: Bruce's printing house, 1878. 16 p. CSmH. The author was a patient in a hospital.

Funston, Frederick, 1865-1917. [2069] Memories of two wars. Cuban and Philippine experiences. N.Y.: Scribner's, 1911. 451 p. WHi. As described by the title.

# G

G., C. See Christeen.

GT-99. Labor spy. Indianapolis:[2070] Bobbs-Merrill, 1937. 309 p. DLC. Factory worker who operated as a labor spy.

Gabriel, Charles Hutchinson, [2071] 1854-1932. Personal memoirs. Chicago: 1918. 51 p. WHi. Writer of religious songs.

Gaddis, Maxwell Pierson, [2072] b. 1811. Footprints of an itinerant. Cinc.: 1856. 546 p. WHi. Methodist clergyman.

Gade, John Allyne, b. 1875. All [2073] my born days; the experiences of a Naval intelligence officer in Europe. N.Y.: Scribner, 1942. 408 p. WU. As described by the title.

Gaebelein, Arno Clemens. Half [2074] a century. N.Y.: Publication office "Our hope", 1930. 261 p. MnSC. Methodist itinerant clergyman who left his church to speak on religious subjects from coast to coast. The author came to the United States from Germany in 1879.

Gage, Lyman Judson, 1836-1927. [2075] Memoirs...N.Y.: Field, 1937. 253 p. WHi. Illinois banker and secretary of the Treasurer under McKinley.

Gage, William Leonard. Light in [2076] darkness; or, Christ discovered in his true character by a Unitarian. Boston: Gould & Lincoln, 1864. 123 p. MWA. New England Unitarian who became a Congregational clergyman.

Gailor, Thomas Frank, 1856- [2077] 1935. Some memories, by Thomas

Frank Gailor, third bishop of Tennessee, first president of the National Council of the Episcopal Church, chancellor of the University of the South, 1908-1935. Kingsport, Tenn.: Southern publishers, 1937. 339 p. NN. As described by the title.

Gainard, Joseph A. Yankee [2078] skipper. N.Y.: Stokes, 1940. 265 p. WHi. Officer in the U.S. Navy and merchant mariner.

Gaisberg, F. W. The music [2079] goes round.. N.Y.: Macmillan, 1942. 273 p. WU. The author was engaged in recording music.

Galbreath, Thomas Crawford. [2080] Chasing the cure in Colorado... Denver: pub. by the author, 1908. 60 p. CoD. The author suffered from tuberculosis.

Gale, James. A long voyage in a [2081] leaky ship; or, a forty years' cruise on the sea of intemperance .., Cambridgeport: P.L. & H.S. Cox, 1842. 144 p. MWA. By a drunkard who reformed.

Gale, Zona, 1874-1938. When I [2082] was a little girl. N.Y.: Macmillan, 1925. 390 p. WU. A novelist writes of her early days in Wisconsin.

Galer, Roger S., b. 1863. Recol- [2083] lections of busy years. Iowa City: 1944. 72 p. IaHi. Teacher, lawyer and farm laborer in Iowa.

Galitzine, Princess. See Crocker, Aimee.

Gallaher, James, 1792-1853. [2084] The western sketch book. Boston: Crocker & Brewster, 1850. 408 p. DLC. Presbyterian clergyman in the southern states, Wisconsin and Missouri.

Gallatin, E. L., b. 1828. What [2085] life has taught me. Denver: n.d. 215 p. CoD. Saddle maker, trader in Montana and Wyoming. The author was one of the founders of a cooperative land development project in Colorado.

Gallenga, Antonio Carlo Napo- [2086] leone, 1810-1895. Episodes of my second life, by L. Mariotti (pseud.). London: Chapman & Hall, 1884. 2 vols. DLC. Italian born historian and travel writer tells of his experiences in the United States.

Gallier, James, 1798-1868. Auto- [2087] biography...Paris: pr. by E. Briere, 1864. 150 p. LNHT. Louisiana architect.

Galpin, Charles Josiah, b. 1864. [2088] My drift into rural sociology. University, La.: Louisiana state univ. press, 1938. 151 p. WU. Professor of Sociology at the University of Wisconsin and employee of the U.S. Department of Agriculture.

Gambier, James, b. 1723. A nar- [2089] rative of facts relative to the conduct of Vice-Admiral Gambier during his late command in North America. London: M. Scott, 1782. 73 p. RPJCB. Naval officer. The period covered is 1778-1782.

Gamble, Anna Dill. My road to [2090] Rome. No imprint. 56 p. PV. A 20th century spiritual autobiography.

Gann, Mrs. Dolly (Curtis). Dolly [2091] Gann's book. Garden City, N.Y.: Doubleday, Doran, 1933. 241 p. WHi. Social and political account by the sister of Vice-President Curtis.

Gannett, Mrs. Lucy Ellen (White-[2092] head). Lucy Ellen's girlhood days. Denver: n.d. 15 p. CoD. The social life of a merchant's wife in Wyoming. As a girl she grew up in the home of a Kansas lawyer who moved to Colorado in 1866.

Gano, John, 1727-1804. Bio- [2093] graphical memoirs...N.Y.: pr. by Southwick & Hardcastle, 1806. 151 p. WHi. Baptist clergyman in North Carolina and New York. He was also a chaplain in the Continental Army. After the war he served in Kentucky.

Ganz, Marie. Rebels...N.Y.: [2094] Dodd, Mead, 1920. 282 p. WHi. Jewish anarchist tells of her work and prison life.

Ganzhorn, John W. I've killed [2095] men. London: Robert Hale, n.d., 288 p. DLC. Gambler in Arizona, 1880-1910.

Gardiner, Charles Fox. Doctor [2096] at timberline. Caldwell, Idaho: Caxton, 1938. 315 p. WHi. In the Rocky Mountains.

Gardiner, Henry. The Anglo- [2097] American; or, memoirs of Captain Henry Gardiner. London: A. K. Newman, 1813. 249 p. DLC.

Merchant mariner who among other experiences was impressed by the British in 1792.

Gardiner, Lion. The papers and [2098] biography...ed. by Curtiss C. Gardiner. St. Louis: pr. for the editor, 1883. 106 p. MoSM. A 17th century account of Indian warfare in Mass. by an engineer in charge of fortifications.

Gardiner, Robert Hallowell, [2099] 1782-1864. Early recollections ...Hallowell, Me.: pr. for R. H. & W. T. Gardiner by White & Horne, 1936. 226 p. DLC. Real estate dealer and owner of lumber mills in Maine.

Gardner, Benjamin Howard, [2100] b. 1854. Memoirs...Palestine, Texas: 1944. 531 leaves. TxU. Compiled by John and Flossie Carpenter from material furnished by Mr. Gardner, who was a Texas lawyer and judge.

Gardner, James Peter, b. 1873. [2101] Reminiscences of a Scottish laddie. Boston, Bruce Humphries, 1940. 134 p. DLC. A banker tells mainly of his youth in Scotland and America.

Gardner, Leonard Marsden, [2102] 1831-1925. Sunset memories... Gettsburg, Pa.: Time & news pub. co., 1941. 155 p. DLC. Methodist clergyman in Baltimore, Washington, D.C. and Pennsylvania.

Gardner, Matthew, 1790-1873. [2103] The autobiography of Elder Matthew Gardner, a minister in the Christian Church sixty-three years. Dayton, Ohio: Christian pub. assoc., 1874. 286 p. NN. The writer served mainly in Ohio and Kentucky.

Gardner, Robert Winslow, 1835- [2104] 1911. Autobiography...Orange, N.J.: 1911. 101 p. DLC. Pharmaceutical chemist in New Jersey.

Garland, Augustus Hill, 1832- [2105] 1899. Experience in the Supreme Court of the United States... Wash.: John Byrne & co., 1898. 100 p. Auto., p. 3-45, 72-97. DLC. By the U.S. Attorney-General, who previously was Governor of Arkansas and U.S. Senator.

Garland, Hamlin, 1860-1940. A [2106] son of the middle border. N.Y.: Macmillan, 1917. 467 p. WHi. Covers 1865-1893. Tells of his early life in frontier Wisconsin and Iowa, his life in New England and return to Wisconsin.

Garland, Hamlin, 1860-1940. A [2107] daughter of the middle border. N.Y.: Macmillan, 1921. 405 p. WHi. Covers 1893-1913. Literary life in Illinois and Wisconsin.

Garland, Hamlin, 1860-1940. [2108] Back-trailers from the middle border. N.Y.: The Macmillan co., 1928. 379 p. WHi. Covers 1914-1928. In this volume he leaves for New York.

Garnett, S. Ann. Autobiograph- [2109] ical sketch. (In her: Cursory family sketches. Albany: Johns Munsell, 1870.) p. 57-140. In. Wife of Mississippi physician.

Garrett, Alfred Cope, 1867-1946. [2110] One mystic...Phila.: Harris & Partrigge, 1945. 322 p. DLC. Member of the Society of Friends who was active in religious education in Pennsylvania.

Garrettson, Freeborn, 1752- [2111] 1827. The experience and travels of Mr. Freeborn Garrettson, minister of the Methodist-Episcopal Church in North-America...Philadelphia: pr. by Parry Hall and sold by John Dickins, 1791. 276 p. NN. As described by the title.

Garrison, Abraham Elison, [2112] b. 1810. Life and labour...N.p.: priv. pr., 1943. 130 p. WHi. Pioneer farmer and Methodist clergyman in Oregon.

Garrison, James Harvey, 1842- [2113] 1931. Memories and experiences ...St. Louis: Christian board, 1926. 269 p. CBB. Publisher of religious journals in St. Louis. The author belonged to the Disciples of Christ Church.

Garver, John H., b. 1826. Rem- [2114] iniscences.. N.p.: 1906. 34 p. CLU-C. A Dakota pioneer who dealt in real estate, and who earlier was a justice of the peace. The author tells also of his mining experiences in California.

Gaskins, John, b. 1816? Life and [2115] adventures...Eureka Springs, Ark.: 1893. 113 p. DLC. Lifelong farmer in Arkansas who served with Union forces.

Gass, Patrick, 1771-1870. The [2116]

life and times of Patrick Gass...
by John G. Jacob. Wellsburg, Va.:
Jacob & Smith, 1859. Auto., p. 9–
193. DLC. Based on journals and
other sources. Gass was with
Lewis and Clarke, and served in
the War of 1812.

Gatchell, Joseph. Disenthralled: [2117]
being reminiscences in the life
of the author...2d ed. Troy: Press
of N. Tuttle, 1844. 59 p. NNC.
Irish seaman tells of intemperate
drinking habits and life as railroad worker in N.Y.

Gates, Bill. The true life story [2118]
of Swiftwater Bill Gates. Written
by Mrs. Iola Beebe. N.p.: 1908.
139 p. WaS. A dictated tale of a
gold strike in the Yukon at the
turn of the century and of various
troubles with his wife.

Gates, Caleb Frank, b. 1857. Not [2119]
to me only. Princeton: Princeton
univ. press, 1940. 340 p. WU.
Congregational missionary to
Turkey, and president of Robert
College in Turkey.

Gates, Isaac Edgar. Watching [2120]
the world go by. Nashville: Sun-
day school board of the Southern
Baptist convention, 1930. 184 p.
TxWB. Baptist clergyman in
Texas.

Gates, Theophilus R., b. 1786. [2121]
The trials, experience...and
first travels...Poughkeepsie:
pr. for the author, 1810. 214 p.
TxU. A clergyman in Georgia,
Virginia, Maryland, New Jersey
and New York. He was leader
of a sect known as the Battle-
Axes.

Gatti-Casazza, Giulio. Memories [2122]
of the opera. N.Y.: Scribner's,
1941. 326 p. WU. General manager of the "Met", 1908–35.

Gause, Isaac, b. 1843. Four years [2123]
with five armies: Army of the
Frontier, Army of the Potomac,
Army of the Missouri, Army of
the Ohio, Army of the Shenandoah. By Isaac Gause, late of
Co. E, Second Ohio Cav. N.Y. &
Washington: The Neale pub. co.,
1908. 384 p. NN.

Gautier, George R., b. 1839. Har- [2124]
der than death...N.p.: 1902. 62 p.
TxGR. Sheep rancher on frontier
Texas who served in the Confederate forces.

Gauvreau, Emile Henry. My last [2125]
million readers. N.Y.: Dutton,
1941. 488 p. WU. Journalist in
New York City.

Gavitt, Elnathan Corringto. [2126]
Crumbs from my saddle bags.
Blade pr. co., 1884. 298 p. WHi.
Methodist clergyman in the middle
western states.

Gay, Mary Ann Harris, b. 1823. [2127]
Life in Dixie during the war...
4th ed., enl. Atlanta: Foote &
Davis, 1901. 404 p. WHi. The
Civil War as experienced by a
civilian.

Gay, Walter, b. 1856. Memoirs.. [2128]
N.Y.: priv. pr., 1930. 87 p. KHi.
After experiencing life on a ranch
in Nebraska (1872–73), the author,
a painter, moved to Europe.

Gayarre, Charles Etienne Arthur [2129]
1805–1895. Biographical sketch
by a Louisianian. New Orleans:
1889. 24 p. Location unknown.
Historian. On the authorship of
this work, see the Louisiana
Historical Quarterly, January,
1929, p. 5–8.

Gaylord, Augustus. In and out of [2130]
the Wisconsin Adjutant-General's
office, 1862–1866. N.Y.: priv. pr.,
1894. 24 p. WHi. As described
by the title.

Geannopulos, James Nicholas, [2131]
b. 1883. Mother's wish...St. Louis:
A. B. Smith pr. co., 1936. 122 p.
DLC. The author escaped from
prison in Greece to America
where he became a restaurant
owner in Missouri.

Geer, John J. Beyond the lines, [2132]
or a Yankee prisoner loose in
Dixie. Phila.: J. W. Daughaday,
1863. 285 p. WHi. As described
by the title.

Geer, Theodore Thurston, b.1851. [2133]
Fifty years in Oregon; experiences, observations, and com-
mentaries upon men, measures,
and customs in pioneer days and
later times. N.Y.: The Neale pub.
co., 1912. 536 p. WHi. Political
figure.

Geers, Edward Franklin, b.1851. [2134]
Ed Geers' experience with the
trotters and pacers. Embracing
a brief history of his early life
in Tennessee, with descriptions
of some of the customs peculiar
to that state, and a general

description of the most noted horses he has driven...Buffalo, N.Y.: The Matthews-Northrop co., 1901. 146 p. NN. The author's experiences in training and driving light-harness horses.

Geier, Christeen. Forty years of [2135] life...by Christeen. Evansville, Ind.: Keller pr. co., 1891. 573 p. DLC. The story of her unfortunate life as a domestic worker.

Gelashmin, Hatto. See James, George.

Gelett, Charles Wetherby, b.1813. [2136] A life on the ocean...Honolulu: Hawaiin gazette, 1917. 119 p. DLC. Merchant mariner whose vessels engaged in trade and whaling.

Genthe, Arnold, 1869-1942. As I [2137] remember. N.Y.: Reynal & Hitchcock, 1936. 290 p. NN. Memories of the famous photographer of San Francisco, New York, and of his famous sitters.

Geoffrey, Theodate (pseud.). See Wagman, Dorothy (Godfrey).

George, Mrs. Alice Mendenhall. [2138] The story of my childhood. Whittier, Calif.: 1923. 88 p. WHi. In Minnesota in the fifties and sixties.

George, Charles B. Reminis- [2139] cences of a veteran conductor; forty years on the rail. 2d ed. Chicago: R. R. Donnelley, 1887. 262 p. CU. As described by the title.

Gerard, James W. My four [2140] years in Germany. N.Y.: Doran, 1917. 432 p. WU. As ambassador.

Gerberding, George Henry, 1847- [2141] 1927. Reminiscent reflections of a youthful octogenarian. Minneapolis: Ausberg pub. house, 1928. 294 p. DLC. Lutheran itinerant clergyman in the Dakotas.

Geronimo, 1829-1909. Geroni- [2142] mo's story of his life, taken down and edited by S.M. Barrett. N.Y.: Duffield, 1906. 216 p. WHi. Apache chief tells of his warfare against the white man.

Gerrish, Theodore, b. 1846. [2143] Army life; a private's reminiscences of the Civil war. By Rev. Theodore Gerrish, late a member of the 20th Maine Vols. Portland: Hoyt, Fogg & Donham, 1882. 372 p. NN. As described by the title.

Gerster, Arpad Geyza, 1848-1923. [2144] Recollections of a New York surgeon. N.Y.: Hoeber, 1917. 347 p. WU. As described by the title.

Gibbon, John, 1827-1896. Per- [2145] sonal recollections of the Civil war. N.Y.: Putnam, 1928. 426 p. WHi. Union army officer.

Gibbons, Alfred R. The recol- [2146] lections of an old Confederate soldier. Shelbyville, Mo.: n.d. 31 p. MoK. As described by the title.

Gibbons, James Joseph. In the [2147] San Juan, Colorado...Chicago: 1898. 194 p. CoD. Clergyman in Colorado. The denomination is not stated. The years covered are 1888-98.

Gibbs, Archie, b. 1906. U-boat [2148] prisoner; the life story of a Texas sailor. Boston: Houghton Mifflin, 1943. 208 p. WHi. The author tells of his experiences in reform school, as a hobo, member of the merchant marine in the second World War, and as a prisoner.

Gibbs, Charles, 1794?-1831. [2149] Mutiny and murder...Providence: Israel Smith, 1831. 36 p. Auto., p. 5-17. DLC. Based on conversations with Gibbs, who was a pirate.

Gibbs, Commodore Perry. "My [2150] old Kentucky home." Louisville: Pentecostal pub. co., 1919? 44 p. KyBC. Minister in Indiana.

Gibbs, Mifflin Wister, b. 1823. [2151] Shadow and light...Washington, D.C.: the author, 1902. 372 p. WHi. Negro lawyer, judge and politician in Arkansas. Miner and merchant in California. U.S. Consul to Madagascar.

Giblin, Charles. Saved from the [2152] scaffold...Worcester, Mass.: Charles Giblin, 1896. 119 p. MWA. The author was accused of robbery and murder in New York but was pardoned by the Governor.

Gibson, J. Watt, b. 1829. Recol- [2153] lections of a pioneer. St. Joseph, Mo.: Press of Nelson-Hanne pr. co., 1912. 216 p. WHi. Gold miner in California, cowboy on the plains, and soldier in the Confederate Army.

Gibson, Mrs. Katharine. With [2154] Custer's cavalry. Caldwell, Idaho: Caxton, 1940. 285 p. WHi. The widowed wife of a frontier soldier tells of her life in Dakota and of the Custer massacre.

Gibson, William Thomas, 1822- 1896. Adulescentiae folia, or reminiscences of a school boy's development. Utica: Church Eclectic, 1895. 12 p. NUt. By a New York Episcopal clergyman. See also the next item. [2155]

Gibson, William Thomas, 1822- 1896. Some notes of clerical and editorial life. Utica: L. C. Child's, 1895. 86 p. Auto., p. 3-47. DLC. New York Episcopal minister and editor of the Church Eclectic. [2156]

Giddens, Tandy Key, b. 1868. Tandy Key Giddens. Shreveport?: Journal pr. co., 1929. 63 p. DLC. Farmer, timber dealer and banker in Louisiana. [2157]

Giddings, Sarah Powell, b. 1847. In the enemies' land; a personal experience. Chicago: Regan pr. house, 1899. 259 p. DLC. A story of domestic unhappiness. [2158]

Gielgud, John, b. 1904. Early stages. London: Macmillan, 1939. 313 p. DLC. English actor who many times played in America. [2159]

Gilbert, Alfred West, b. 1816. Colonel A. W. Gilbert. Cinc.: Historical and philosophical soc. of Ohio, 1934. 122 p. Auto., p. 17-49. WHi. Engineer in Cincinnati. [2160]

Gilbert, Anne (Hartley), 1821-1904. The stage reminiscences of Mrs. Gilbert; ed. by Charlotte M. Martin. N.Y.: Scribner's, 1901. 247 p. WHi. Actress, dancer. [2161]

Gilbert, F. C. From Judaism to Christianity...Concord, Mass.: 1911. 384 p. NbLU. Evangelist in Mass., working among Jews. [2162]

Gilbert, George Blodgett, d.1948. Forty years a country preacher. N.Y.: Harper, 1939. 319 p. WHi. Episcopal clergyman. [2163]

Gilder, Jeannette Leonard, 1849-1916. The tomboy at work. N.Y.: Doubleday, Page, 1904. 252 p. WHi. Reporter in New York City. [2164]

Gilder, Jeanette Leonard, 1849-1916. The autobiography of a tomboy. N.Y.: Doubleday, Page, 1901. 349 p. WU. A newspaper reporter tells of her youth. [2165]

Giles, Charles, b. 1783. Pioneer ...N.Y.: G. Lane & P. P. Sandford, 1844. 333 p. WHi. Methodist clergyman on the frontier in New York. [2166]

Giles, Nell. Punch in, Susie... N.Y.: Harper, 1943. 143 p. NcGW. The author undertook to do factory work during the second World War. [2167]

Gilfillan, Mrs. Andrew Kertesz. I went to pit college, by Lauren Gilfillan (pseud.). N.Y.: Viking, 1934. 288 p. WU. Her experiences among miners, by a writer. [2168]

Gilfillan, Lauren (pseud.). See Gilfillan, Mrs. Andrew Kertesz.

Gilfond, Mrs. Duff, b. 1902. I go horizontal. N.Y.: The Vanguard press, 1940. 281 p. DLC. Her experiences with sleeping sickness. [2169]

Gill, John, 1841-1912. Reminiscences of four years as a private soldier. Baltimore: Sun pr. office, 1904. 136 p. DLC. With a Virginia regiment in the Civil War. [2170]

Gillespie, Elizabeth (Duane), b. 1821. Book of remembrance. Phila. & London: J. B. Lippincott co., 1901. 393 p. DLC. By a woman who was active in the social, civic and musical life of Philadelphia. [2171]

Gillett, C. E., b. 1857. Pioneering. Elgin, Ill.: pub. for the author, 1929. 218 p. CoD. Pioneer farmer and United Brethren clergyman in Missouri, Texas and Arizona. [2172]

Gillett, James B., b. 1856. The Texas Ranger...Chicago: World book co., 1927. 218 p. DLC. Same as his book of 1921 with different title. His experiences with outlaws, Indians, Mexicans. [2173]

Gilliland, James Hiram, 1855-1912. Twenty-five years of religious life in Bloomington, Ill. Bloomington: 1912. 53 p. MoCanD. Clergyman of the Christian Church. [2174]

Gillis, O. J., b. 1855. To Hell and back again...or life in the penitentiaries of Texas and Kansas. Little Rock: 1906. 112 p. CoD. How the convict lives, by one who committed murder and robbery. [2175]

Gilliss, Walter, 1855-1925. Recollections of the Gilliss press and its work during fifty years, 1869-1919. N.Y.: Grolier club, 1926. 134 p. WHi. Printer in New York City. [2176]

Gilman, Charlotte (Perkins), 1860-1935. The living of Charlotte [2177]

Perkins Gilman...N.Y.: D. Appleton-Century, 1935. 341 p. DLC. Poet, social reformer.

Gilman, Daniel Coit, 1831-1908. [2178] The launching of a university... N.Y.: Dodd, Mead, 1906. 386 p. WU. First president of Johns Hopkins.

Gilmer, George R., 1790-1859. [2179] Sketches of some of the first settlers of upper Georgia, of the Cherokees and the author. Americus: Americus book co., 1926. 458 p. WHi. Autobiographical passages written by the Governor of Georgia, and member of the U.S. Congress.

Gilmor, Harry, 1838-1883. Four [2180] years in the saddle. London: Longmans, Green & co., 1866. 310 p. WHi. Confederate soldier.

Gilson, Mary Barnett. What's [2181] past is prologue. Reflections on my industrial experience. N.Y.: Harper, 1940. 307 p. WU. By an expert on labor relations.

Ginn, Edwin, 1838-1914. Outline [2182] of the life of Edwin Ginn, including his preparation for the publishing business...Boston: Ginn, 1908. 24 p. DLC. Publisher.

Girdler, Tom Mercer, b. 1877. [2183] Boot straps. N.Y.: Scribner, 1943. 471 p. WHi. Ohio steel manufacturer.

Girl, Christian, b. 1825. Human [2184] depravity; or Sixty-two years of my life, showing the trials and persecutions of a once happy family...Decatur, Ill.: J. W. Franks & sons, 1888. 283 p. DLC. Illinois farmer who tells of how his home was broken by his enemies.

Gitlow, Benjamin, b. 1891. I confess; [2185] the truth about American communism. N.Y.: Dutton, 1940. 611 p. WU. American communist.

Gladden, Washington, 1836-1918. [2186] Recollections. Boston: Houghton Mifflin, 1909. 445 p. WU. Congregational clergyman in New York, Mass., and Ohio. He was known especially for his ideas on social reform.

Glasgow, Brown (pseud.). See Brown, Mrs. Frank T.

Glaspell, Kate (Eldridge). Incidents [2187] in the life of a pioneer. Davenport, Iowa: Sawden bros., 1943. 64 p. DLC. Wife of a farmer, lawyer and judge in pioneer Dakota territory.

Glaspell, Susan, 1882-1948. The [2188] road to the temple. N.Y.: Stokes, 1941. 445 p. DLC. By a writer of fiction and drama in Iowa.

Glass, Alexander, b. 1850. Sixty- [2189] five years of iron and steel in Wheeling, by Robert L. Plummer. Personal reminiscences of a long and active career, as related by Alexander Glass. Wheeling, 1938? 72 p. Auto., p. 5-38. DLC. Steel executive in West Virginia.

Glasscock, Lemuel, b. 1801. The [2190] life...Maysville, Ky.: 1841? 27 p. DLC. Pioneer homesteader in Kentucky, Ohio, Illinois. The author was sentenced to prison for murder.

Glaum, Ellen Brant, b. 1866. On [2191] creaking wheels. No imprint. 147 p. MnHi. Youth on farm in seventies and eighties in Minnesota and Montana.

Gleig, George Robert. A sub- [2192] altern in America, comprising his narrative of the campaigns of the British army, at Baltimore, Washington...during the late war. Phila.: E. L. Carey & A. Hart, 1833. 266 p. WHi. Experiences of an English chaplain during the War of 1812.

Glendinning, William, 1747-1816. [2193] The life of William Glendinning, preacher of the gospel...Phila.: pr. at the office of W.W. Woodward, 1795. 154 p. DLC. Clergyman of the Christian Church in Virginia and the middle Atlantic states.

Glenn, Archibald Alexander, [2194] 1819-1901. Auto-biography... N.p.: 1901. 12 p. DLC. Lawyer and politician in Illinois and Kansas.

Glenroy, John H., b. 1828. Ins [2195] and outs of circus life; or forty-two years travel of John H. Glenroy, bareback rider...Compiled by Stephen Stanley Stanford. Boston: M. M. Wing & co., printers, 1885. 190 p. DLC. As described by the title.

Glyn, Elinor. Romantic adventure [2196] ...N.Y.: Dutton, 1937. 350 p. WU. Novelist.

Goble, Benjamin, b. 1813. Narrative [2197] of...the life of an Illinois pioneer. Moline: Kennedy steam & job printer, 1881. 35 p. ICHi. Farmer.

Godbey, John Emory, b. 1839. [2198] Lights and shadows of seventy years. St. Louis: Nixon-Jones pr. co., 1913. 312 p. MoK. Methodist clergyman in Missouri and Arkansas, who was also editor of religious journals.

Godbey, William B., b. 1833. [2199] Autobiography...Cincinnati: God's revivalist office, 1909. 509 p. MoHi. Evangelist minister in Kentucky, Tennessee and Georgia.

Goddard, Nathaniel, 1767-1853. [2200] A Boston merchant, 1767-1853. Cambridge: 1906. 272 p. Auto., p. 44-135. MH. The first 30 years of his life.

Goddard, Paul R., b. 1865. My [2201] life story. Washington, Ill.: 1937. NN. Newspaper editor in South Dakota, Iowa and Illinois.

Godfrey, Samuel E. A., 1782- [2202] 1818. A sketch...Windsor, Vt.: 1818. 35 p. MWA. Murderer.

Godoy, Mercedes. When I was [2203] a girl in Mexico...Boston: Lothrop, Lee & Shepard, 1919. 139 p. DLC. The daughter of a Mexican diplomat tells of her life in Mexico and Washington, D.C.

Goebel, Arthur C., b. 1895? Art [2204] Goebel's own story. Kansas City, Mo.: 1929 36 p. DLC. Pilot, stunt flyer.

Goebel, Gert. Laenger als ein [2205] menschenleben in Missouri. St. Louis: C. Witter, 1877. 233 p. DLC. Farmer in Missouri, 1832-76.

Goeth, Mrs. Ottilie (Fuchs), [2206] b. 1836. Was grossmutter erzaehlt. San Antonio: Passing show pr. co., 1915. 140 p. TxU. The author came to Texas from Germany in 1845 and later was married to a pioneer Texas farmer.

Goff, Florence. Text and tri- [2207] umphs. Falcon, N.C.: 1924. 96 p. NcWatC. Holiness preacher in North Carolina.

Going, William, b. 1768. Memoir [2208] of William Going, formerly keeper of the state prison, Charlestown, Mass. Boston: pr. for the author, 1841. 51 p. MH-L. As described by the title.

Gold, Michael. Jews without [2209] money. Garden City, N.Y.: Sun dial press, 1930. 209 p. WU. His boyhood on the East Side of New York.

Golden, John, b. 1874. Stage- [2210] struck John Golden. N.Y.: French, 1930. 324 p. WU. Playwright, producer.

Goldie, John R., b. 1853. Pioneer-[2211] ing in the west. Sioux City: Goldie, 1931. 102 p. WHi. A commercial printer in Sioux City who as a boy lived on a homestead.

Goldman, Emma, 1869-1940. Liv-[2212] ing my life. N.Y.: Knopf, 1931. 2 vols. WU. Anarchist, social reformer.

Goldman, Raymond Leslie, [2213] b. 1895. The good fight. N.Y.: Coward-McCann, 1935. 194 p. DLC. A writer of mystery stories tells of his fight for health.

Goldsmith, William Marion, [2214] b. 1888. Stones in a life. Springfield, Mo.: Jewell, 1908. 154 p. DLC. College student in Missouri.

Goldstein, David, b. 1870. Auto- [2215] biography of a campaigner for Christ. Boston, Mass.: Catholic campaigners for Christ, 1936. 416 p. NN. Story of a Jewish Socialist who became a member of the Catholic Church and campaigned against Socialism.

Goldwyn, Samuel, b. 1882. Be- [2216] hind the screen. N.Y.: George H. Doran co., 1923. 263 p. NN. Career of a motion picture producer.

Gompers, Samuel, 1850-1924. [2217] Seventy years of life and labor... N.Y.: E. P. Dutton, 1925. 2 vols. WHi. Labor leader. The author was a Jew.

Gonsalves, M.J. The testimony.[2218] ...Boston: The author, 1859. 102 p. CSmH. After leaving the Catholic Church the author, a clergyman, labored among sailors on the Atlantic coast. The writer was born in Madeira.

Good, Milt, b. 1889. Twelve [2219] years in a Texas prison. Amarillo: pr. by Russell stationery co., 1935. 88 p. TxH. By a Texas cowboy who was convicted of murder. This is mainly his account of prison life.

Goodbird, Edward, b. 1869? [2220] Goodbird, the Indian, his story, told...to Gilbert L. Wilson. N.Y.: Revell, 1914. 80 p. DLC. Hidatsa Indian who became a farmer and interpreter on a reservation in South Dakota.

Goode, John, 1829-1909. Recol- [2221] lections of a lifetime. N.Y. & Washington: The Neale pub. co., 1906. 266 p. WHi. Lawyer and member of the U.S. House of Representatives from Virginia.

Goode, John Gordon, 1864-1904. [2222] The life story of John Goode, criminal. Red hell. By Thelma Roberts...N.Y.: Rae D. Henkle, 1934. 320 p. NN. The career of a life-time criminal and his final regeneration at the Bowery Mission, New York. Based upon his notes as worked up by Miss Roberts.

Goode, William Henry, 1807- [2223] 1879. Outposts of Zion, with limnings of mission life. Cinc.: Poe & Hitchcock, 1863. 464 p. Auto., p. 23-395. DLC. Methodist missionary to the Indians in Kansas and Nebraska, 1854-59.

Goodell, Charles LeRoy, b. 1854. [2224] My ministry. N.Y.: Revell, 1938. 185 p. DLC. Methodist clergyman in Rhode Island, Mass., and New York, who from 1918 to 1937 was on the staff of the Federal Council of Churches of Christ in America.

Goodell, William, 1792-1867. [2225] Forty years in the Turkish empire...6th ed. N.Y.: Robert Carter & bros., 1883. 489 p. Auto., p. 1-60. DLC. Congregational missionary. The autobiographical portion covers only to 1822. The remainder is made up of journals and letters.

Goodhart, George Walter, 1842- [2226] 1927. The pioneer life of George W. Goodhart, and his association with the Hudson's bay and American fur company's traders and trappers; Trails of early Idaho, as told to Abraham C. Anderson. Caldwell, Id.: The Caxton printers, ltd., 1940. 368 p. WHi. Frontiersman in Idaho.

Goodkind, Ben. A poor Ameri- [2227] can in Ireland and Scotland. San Francisco: W.S. van Cott, 1913. 286 p. US1C. Hobo who spent some time in Utah, California and New York.

Goodlander, Charles W. Mem- [2228] oirs and recollections...of the early days of Fort Scott...Fort Scott: Monitor pr. co., 1900. 145 p. DLC. Carpenter, builder and hotel operator in early Kansas.

Goodloe, Albert Theodore. Con- [2229] federate echoes: a voice from the South in the days of secession and of the Southern Confederacy. Nashville, Tenn.: Pub. house of the M. E. Church, South. Smith & Lamar, 1907. 452 p. NN. The author was a clergyman who had served in the armed forces of the Confederacy.

Goodman, Benny, b. 1909. The [2230] kingdom of swing. N.Y.: Stackpole, 1939. 265 p. DLC. Jewish musician.

Goodman, Philip, 1885-1940. [2231] Franklin Street. N.Y.: Alfred Knopf, 1942. 277 p. NN. Recollections of a Philadelphia childhood in the latter part of the nineteenth century.

Goodrich, Caspar F., 1847-1925. [2232] Rope yarns from the old Navy. N.Y.: Naval history soc., 1931. 167 p. WHi. By a naval officer.

Goodrich, Ezra, b. 1826. Auto- [2233] biography...N.p.: 1908. 13 p. DLC. Pioneer Wisconsin farmer.

Goodrich, Samuel Griswold, [2234] 1793-1860. Recollections of a lifetime...Auburn: Miller, Orton, 1857. 2 vols. WHi. Publisher and author of children's literature.

Goodson, Mrs. E.F. Fifty [2235] golden years of kingdom building. Nashville: pr. for the author, 1924. 194 p. KyRE. A lay worker with the Woman's Missionary Society of the M.E. Church, South in Kentucky.

Goodspeed, Charles Eliot, b.1867. [2236] Yankee bookseller...Boston: Houghton Mifflin, 1937. 305 p. WHi. Publisher in Boston.

Goodwin, Elijah, 1807-79. Life [2237] of Elijah Goodwin, by James M. Mathes. St. Louis: John Burns, 1880. 314 p. DLC. Itinerant clergyman of the Christian Church in Indiana who was publisher of the Christian Monitor. This book is largely autobiographical.

Goodwin, John West. A golden [2238] anniversary. No imprint. 4 p. MoHi. By a newspaper publisher in Missouri in the second half of the ninettenth century.

Goodwin, Nathaniel Carl, 1857- [2239] 1919. Nat Goodwin's book. Boston: R. G. Badger, 1914. 366 p. WU. Actor.

Goodyear, Charles, 1800-1860. [2240] Gum-elastic and its varieties, with a detailed account of its applications and uses, and of the discovery of vulcanization. New Haven: 1853-55. 2 vols. NN. Contains much autobiographic material on the author's discovery of the process of vulcanizing rubber.

Gordon, Andrew, 1828-1887. [2241] 1855-1885. Our India mission. Phila.: Andrew Gordon, 1886. 511 p. DLC. By a United Presbyterian clergyman.

Gordon, Elizabeth Southall [2242] Clarke. Days of now and then. Phila.: Dorrance, 1945. 259 p. DLC. Reminiscences of social life in Baltimore and Philadelphia.

Gordon, George Angier, 1853- [2243] 1929. My education and religion ...Boston: Houghton Mifflin, 1925. 352 p. WHi. Congregational clergyman in Conn. and Mass.

Gordon, George Henry, 1825?- [2244] 1886. Brook Farm to Cedar Mountain...Boston: Osgood, 1883. 376 p. WHi. Officer in the Union army.

Gordon, George Henry, 1825?- [2245] 1886. A war diary of events in the war of the great rebellion. 1863-1865. By George H. Gordon, late colonel Second Massachusetts Infantry, brigadier-general, and brevet major-general U.S. Volunteers in the war... Boston: Osgood, 1882. 437 p. NN. As described by the title.

Gordon, Henry C., b. 1835. Auto-[2246] biography of Henry C. Gordon, and some of the wonderful manifestations through a medium persecuted from childhood to old age. By Thomas R. Hazard. Ottumwa, Iowa: Spiritual offering, 1884? 30 p. NN. Spiritualism.

Gordon, John Brown, 1832-1904. [2247] Reminiscences of the Civil war. By General John B. Gordon of the Confederate army...N.Y.: Chas. Scribner's sons, 1904. 474 p. NN. As described by the title.

Gordon, Marquis Lafayette, 1843-[2248] 1900. An American missionary in Japan. Boston: Houghton Mifflin, 1892. 276 p. WHi. A medical missionary.

Gordon, Marquis Lafayette,1843-[2249] 1900. M.L. Gordon's experiences in the Civil war from his narrative, letters and diary...Boston: priv. pr., 1922. 72 p. DLC. The author served with a Pennsylvania regiment.

Gordon, Mary Jane. See How, Mrs. Mary Jane (Gordon).

Gordon, Taylor, b. 1893. Born to [2250] be. N.Y.: Covici-Friede, 1929. 238 p. NN. The writer, a Negro singer, tells of his experiences as a youth in Montana, as a pullman porter, a chauffer for John Ringling, the circus man, and of his later career as a singer.

Gorham, Harry M., b. 1859. My [2251] memories of the Comstock. Los Angeles: 1939. 222 p. WHi. Nevada miner in frontier times.

Goritzina, Kyra. ...Service [2252] entrance; memoirs of a Park Avenue cook. N.Y.: Carrick & Evans, 1939. 315 p. NN. Experiences of a Russian emigré couple in domestic service in New York City.

Goss, Mrs. Caroline (Martin), [2253] 1834-1936. Memoirs. N.p.: 1934? 87 p. WHi. Wisconsin housewife.

Goss, Cornelia A., b. 1850. [2254] 'Neath the waters; from modiste to Salvation Army officer... Cinc.: Monford, 1923. 63 p. DLC. In the middle Atlantic states.

Gottschall, Amos H. Travels...[2255] Harrisburg: The author, 1894. 287 p. DLC. The author was engaged in many occupations, including farming, ranching, newspaper reporting.

Gough, John Bartholomew,1817- [2256] 1886. Autobiography...Springfield: Bill, Nichols, 1870. 552 p. WHi. Lecturer on temperance.

Gould, John Thomas, b. 1908. [2257] Farmer takes a wife. N.Y.: Morrow, 1945. 153 p. DLC. In Maine.

Gould, Roland F., b. 1817. The [2258] life of Gould an ex-man-of-war's man...Claremont, N.H.: priv. pr.,

1867. 239 p. WHi. His experiences included three years on the ship Ohio with Hull.

Goulder, William Armistead, [2259] b. 1821. Reminiscences; incidents in the life of a pioneer in Oregon and Idaho. Boise: Timothy Regan, 1909. 376 p. NN. By a miner on the Idaho frontier and a member of the Idaho Territorial Legislature.

Gouverneur, Mrs. Marian. [2260-2261] As I remember; recollections of American society during the nineteenth century. N.Y.: Appleton, 1912. 416 p. WHi. Social life.

Graber, Henry W., b. 1841. The [2262] life record of a Terry Texas ranger, 1861-1865. N.p.: 1916. 492 p. WHi. The author, after serving in the Confederate forces, was a merchant in Louisiana and Texas.

Grace, Dick, b. 1898. Squadron [2263] of death; the true adventures of a movie plane-crasher. Garden City, N.Y.: Doubleday, Doran & co., 1929. 304 p. NN. Adventures of a movie stunt man.

Grace, Dick, b. 1898. I am still [2264] alive. Chicago: Rand McNally & co., 1931. 255 p. NN. Additional adventures of the author.

Gracie, Constance Elise Schack. [2265] Personal experiences in life's journey. Wash.: Press of Charles H. Potter, 1919. 245 p. DLC. New York socialite.

Graffenried, Christopher von, [2266] 1661-1743. Christopher von Graffenried's account of the founding of New Bern...Raleigh: Edwards & Broughton pr. co., 1920. 417 p. DLC. Founder of the Swiss colony in New Bern.

Grafton, Charles Chapman, 1830-[2267] 1912. A journey Godward...New ed. N.Y.: Longmans, Green, 1914. 332 p. DLC. Episcopal clergyman in the District of Columbia, Massachusetts and Wisconsin.

Graham, Andrew J., b. 1854. [2268] Autobiographical notes, verses and other writings. Charles River, Mass.: The Runnymede co., 1936. 267 p. NN. Protestant Episcopal clergyman in Nebraska, Minnesota, The District of Columbia, Indiana, and Rochester, N.Y., who later became a Christian Scientist.

Graham, Balus Joseph Winzer, [2269] b. 1862. A ministry of fifty years. Atlanta: 1939. 360 p. DLC. Baptist clergyman who was one of the founders of the Christian Index.

Graham, James Stevenson. A [2270] Scotch-Irish-Canadian Yankee. N.Y.: Putnam's, 1939. 269 p. WHi. Salesman, text book writer.

Graham, Jaret Benedict, b. 1839. [2271] Handset reminiscences; recollections of an old-time printer and journalist. Salt Lake City: Century pr. co., 1915. 307 p. DLC. Newspaper publisher in Michigan, Colorado and Utah. The author was also a printer and journalist in New York and California.

Graham, John, b. 1794. Autobio- [2272] graphy and reminiscences... Phila.: W. S. Rentoul, 1870. 206 p. DLC. Presbyterian clergyman in New York.

Graham, Martha Morgan, b. 1825. [2273] An interesting life history...San Francisco: Women's cooperative pr. union, 1875. 67 p. CLSU. A housewife who lived in various parts of the country.

Graham, Tom. Twice born. [2274] Denver: pub. by the author, 1904. 74 p. CoHi. The author, born in Scotland, was a lay mission worker in various states during the years 1870-1900.

Gramp, W. E. H. See Hughes, William Edgar.

Grandy, Moses. Narrative of [2275] the life of Moses Grandy, late a slave...2d Am. ed. Boston: O. Johnson, 1844. 46 p. WHi. As described by the title.

Grant, J. W. The flying regi- [2276] ment. Providence: S. S. Rider, 1865. 152 p. WHi. Union army.

Grant, Robert, 1852-1940. Four- [2277] score; an autobiography...Boston & N.Y.: Houghton Mifflin, 1934. 413 p. NN. Novelist and probate judge in Boston.

Grant, Ulysses Simpson, 1822- [2278] 1885. Personal memoirs...N.Y.: Webster, 1885-86. 2 vols. WHi. A soldier's account, ending with 1865, by a former President of the United States.

Graves, Alonzo. The eclipse of [2279] a mind. N.Y.: Medical journal press, 1942. 722 p. WU. Recorded by his attending physician.

Graves, Anson R., b. 1842. The [2280]

farmer boy who became a bishop. Akron: New Werner co., 1911. 220 p. WHi. Episcopalian in various states west of the Mississippi River. He was bishop of Nebraska.

Graves, David William, 1837- [2281] 1918. Life history...No imprint. 65 leaves. MoHi. Baptist clergyman in Missouri who also was a farmer and teacher.

Graves, Jackson A. My seventy [2282] years in California 1857-1927. 2d ed. Los Angeles: Times-Mirror, 1928. 478 p. WHi. Lawyer and banker.

Gravis, Peter W., b. 1828. [2283] Twenty-five years...Comanche, Texas: Exponent, 1892. 67 p. TxU. Methodist clergyman in Texas.

Gray, Asa, 1810-88. "Autobio- [2284] graphy, 1810-1843". (In: Letters of Asa Gray, ed. by Jane Loring Gray. Boston: Houghton Mifflin, 1893.) Vol. 1, p. 1-28. WHi. His experiences as a teacher, hunter of botanical specimans and writer on botanical subjects.

Gray, Charles Martin, b. 1800. [2285] The old soldier's story...Edgefield, S.C.: Edgefield advertiser print, 1868. 63 p. TxU. A tale of Indian warfare in the territories of Georgia and Florida in the years 1820-29.

Gray, Edna. One woman's busy [2286] life. Baltimore: Summers, 1907. 350 p. MoCanC. A story of an unfortunate marriage, blindness and the struggle to bring up her children.

Gray, George M., b. 1856. Fifty [2287] years in the practice of medicine. Kansas City: 1932. 9 p. KHi. In Kansas, beginning with 1880.

Gray, Henry Judd, 1892-1928. [2288] Doomed ship; the autobiography of Judd Gray. N.Y.: Horace Liveright, 1928. 251 p. NN. Life story of the author, who was executed with Mrs. Ruth Snyder for the murder of the latter's husband.

Gray, John Franklin Fowler, [2289] b. 1849. Story of my life. Hagerstown: 1924. 40 p. DLC. Itinerant Methodist minister in Maryland and Virginia.

Graydon, Alexander, 1752-1818. [2290] Memoirs of a life, chiefly passed in Pennsylvania, within the last sixty years. Harrisburgh: pr. by John Wyeth, 1811. 378 p. DLC. Officer in the American Revolutionary army and member of the constitutional convention.

Grayson, David (pseud.). See Baker, Ray Stannard.

Great American Ass. See Edson, Charles Leroy.

Grebenc, Lucile. Under green [2291] apple boughs. Garden City, N.Y.: Doubleday, Doran & co., 1936. 280 p. NN. The author retreats from the depression to a Connecticut farm and finds a new way of life.

Greeley, Horace, 1811-1872. Rec-[2292] ollections of a busy life: including reminiscences of American politics and politicians, from the opening of the Missouri contest to the downfall of slavery. N.Y.: J.B. Ford, etc., 1868. 624 p. WHi. Journalist and national political figure.

Greely, Adolphus Washington, [2293] 1844-1935. Reminiscences... N.Y.: Scribner, 1927. 338 p. WHi. Officer in the U.S. Army, explorer.

Green, Mrs. A. M. Sixteen years [2294] on the Great American desert... Titusville, Pa.: Frank W. Truesdell, printer, 1887. 84 p. CoHi. The wife of a Colorado miner, farmer and rancher, beginning with 1870.

Green, A. V., b. 1795. The life [2295] and experience of...Wooster: D. N. Sprague, 1848. 72 p. DLC. Reformed drunkard who became a Methodist clergyman and temperance leader in Ohio.

Green, Adam Treadwell, 1831- [2296] 1921. Seventy years in California. San Francisco: pr. by Taylor & Taylor, 1923. 42 p. CSmH. Merchant. This account concludes with the year 1859.

Green, Ashbel, 1762-1848. The [2297] life of Ashbel Green. N.Y.: Robert Carter, 1849. 477 p. WHi. Presbyterian clergyman in Pa., and the District of Columbia, and president of the College of New Jersey, later Princeton.

Green, Beriah, 1795-1874. Ser- [2298] mons and other discourses. With brief biographical hints. N.Y.: S. W. Green, 1860. 556 p. NN. Congregational clergyman, abolitionist and educational reformer, who labored principally in Ohio and New York State.

Green, Elisha Winfield. Life... [2299] Maysville, Ky.: The Republican pr. co., 1888, 60 p. DLC. After attaining his freedom from slavery, the author became a Baptist minister, prominent in the educational and political affairs of Kentucky.

Green, Ella Jane (Williams), [2300] b. 1853. "Big-Geen". No imprint, 1936? 60 p. WaPS. After spending her youthful days on a farm in Indiana, Ohio, and Missouri, the author married. Her husband was a California farmer in the seventies and a rancher in the Washington Territory beginning with 1883.

Green, Gretchen. The whole [2301] world & company. N.Y.: Reynal & Hitchcock, 1936. 313 p. NN. Varied experiences of a world traveller, in America, Africa, Europe, and Asia, where she worked with Rabindranath Tagore.

Green, H. H., b. 1839. The simple [2302] life of a commoner. Decorah: Press of Public opinion, 1911. 184 p. IaHi. The author lived on a pioneer Iowa farm in the fifties, served in the Union forces, and then served as a Methodist clergyman in Iowa.

Green, Jacob D. Narrative of [2303] the life of S. D. Green, a runaway slave from Kentucky...Huddersfield, England: pr. by Henry Fielding, 1864. 43 p. NN. As described by the title.

Green, John E. John E. Green [2304] and his forty years in Houston. Houston: Dealy-Adey-Elgin, 1928. 176 p. WHi. Methodist clergyman.

Green, John Paterson, b. 1845. [2305] Facts stranger than fiction. Cleveland, Ohio: Riehl pr. co., 1920. 368 p. NN. The writer, a free negro born in North Carolina, tells of his life as a lawyer in Cleveland, Ohio; also of his early participation in reconstruction politics in South Carolina as well as later political career in Ohio.

Green, John Paterson, b. 1845. [2306] Recollections of the...KuKlux outrages...N.p.: 1880. 205 p. DLC. A Negro's farm life in South Carolina during the period of reconstruction.

Green, Julien, b. 1900. Memories [2307] of happy days. N.Y. & London: Harper, 1942. 320 p. WU. American born novelist who lived mainly in France.

Green, Samuel, d. 1822. Life of [2308] Samuel Green, executed at Boston...for the murder of Billy Williams...Boston: David Felt, 1822. 47 p. DLC. Robber, murderer.

Green, Wharton Jackson, b. 1831. [2309] Recollections and reflections... N.p.: Edwards & Broughton, 1906. 221 p. WHi. Student at the University of Virginia; Civil War soldier; member of the U. S. House of Representatives from North Carolina.

Green, William. Narrative of [2310] events in the life of William Green (formerly a slave). Springfield, Mass.: L. M. Guernsey, 1853. 23 p. DLC. In Maryland.

Greene, Jonathan Harrington, [2311] b. 1812. Twelve days in the Tombs ...N.Y.: W. Taylor, 1850. 80 p. WHi. Gambler who became a social reformer.

Greene, Jonathan Harrington, [2312] b. 1812. The reformed gambler... Phila.: T. B. Peterson, 1858. DLC. The later years of a gambler who turned to reform.

Greenhow, Rose O'Neal, d. 1864. [2313] My imprisonment and the first year of abolition rule at Washington. London: Richard Bentley, 1863. 352 p. NN. Secret Service worker for Beauregard.

Greenleaf, A. B. Ten years in [2314] Texas. Selma: William G. Boyd, 1881. 131 p. DLC. A varied life, including horse thievery, salesman of patent medicines, service in the Mexican army.

Greenslet, Ferris, b. 1875. Under [2315] the bridge. Boston: Houghton Mifflin, 1943. 237 p. WU. Writer for Nation, free lance reviewer, sub-editor of the Atlantic, editor for publishing firm.

Greenwalt, Leonidas Lorenzo, [2316] b. 1864. Seventy-five years of progress. Hastings, Iowa: 1944. 260 p. DLC. Iowa farmer.

Greenwood, Mrs. Annie (Pike). [2317] We sagebrush folks. N.Y.: Appleton-Century, 1934. 483 p. WHi. Life on a farm in Idaho, roughly from

1890 to 1920.

Greenwood, Bernard, b. 1827. [2318] Dealings of God with a laborer; or the experience of Bernard Greenwood. Raleigh: Edwards, 1884. 222 p. Nc. Minister in Ohio and North Carolina.

Greenwood, John, 1760-1819. The [2319] Revolutionary services of John Greenwood. N.Y.: 1922. 155 p. DLC. Officer.

Gregg, John Chandler. Life in [2320] the army...with an account of the author's life and experience in the ministry. 2d ed. Phila.: Perkinpine & Higgins, 1868. 271 p. WHi. Methodist clergyman in Delaware and Pennsylvania. Chaplain in the Union army.

Gregg, Josiah, 1806-1850? [2321] Commerce of the prairies... N.Y.: Langley, 1844. 2 vols. WHi. By a Santa Fe trader, in which general and personal history are combined.

Gregg, William Cephas, b. 1862. [2322] Hackensack, N.J.: priv. pr., 1933. 364 p. DLC. Lumberman, manufacturer of textiles, and of railroad equipment in Minnesota. He was also interested in the preservation of national parks.

Gregory, Mrs. Adeline Hibbard, [2323] b. 1859. A great-grandmother remembers. Chicago: A. Kroch, 1941. 238 p. WHi. Wife of Chicagoan tells of her social life and club activities.

Gregory, Elizabeth (Hiatt). Show [2324] window of life. Los Angeles: 1944. 160 p. WU. Pioneer woman writer on aviation.

Gregory, U.S. Recollections of [2325] U. S. Gregory, old time sheriff, resident of California sixty years. San Francisco: pr. by Pernau-Walsh, n.d. 47 p. CSfSP. Lumberman in Nevada, miner in Alaska, and sheriff in California.

Gregson, Mrs. Eliza (Marshall), [2326] b. 1824. The Gregson memoirs... reprinted from the California historical society Quarterly, June, 1940. 31 p. C. Story of everyday life on a pioneer ranch in California, 1845-50.

Gregson, James. See Gregson, Mrs. Eliza (Marshall).

Grellet, Stephen, 1773-1855. [2327] Memoirs...Phila.: Henry Longstreet 1860. 2 vols. DLC. French born missionary of the Society of Friends, who travelled widely in the U. S.

Grey, Frederick William. Seek- [2328] ing a fortune in America. London: Smith, Elder & co., 1912. 307 p. CtY. An Englishman in the southwest in the nineties who tried his hand at farming, and who had various adventures.

Grierson, Francis, 1848-1927. [2329] The valley of shadows. Recollections of the Lincoln country, 1858-1863. Boston: Houghton Mifflin, 1909. 315 p. DLC. Boyhood memories of life in Illinois and Missouri. The writer later became a musician.

Griffin, A. A., b. 1866. A mis- [2330] spent life. Hutchinson, Kan.: Wholesale pr. co., 1914. 48 p. DLC. A house painter tells of his previous life of crime in the southeastern and southwestern states.

Griffin, Thomas Ancel, 1832- [2331] 1910. Semi-centennial sermon. A personal retrospect of fifty years in the Troy conference...Troy: Henry Stowell & son, 1906. 44 p. NjMD. Methodist clergyman in New York and Vermont.

Griffis, Joseph K. Tahan; out of [2332] savagery into civilization...N.Y.: Doran, 1915. 263 p. WHi. A Presbyterian missionary in Oklahoma tells of his mixed parentage and of his early life with the Osage Indians.

Griffis, William Elliott, 1843- [2333] 1928. Sunny memories of three pastorates...Ithaca: Andrus & Church, 1903. 310 p. WHi. Congregational clergyman in Ithaca, Boston and Schenectady.

Griffith, George Washington [2334] Ewing, b. 1833. My ninety-six years in the great West. Los Angeles: 1929. 284 p. WHi. California merchant and banker who spent his earlier days pioneering in Kansas and Indiana.

Griffith, John. A journal of the [2335] life, travels and labours in the work of the ministry...Phila.: reprinted by Joseph Crukshank, 1780. 426, 112 p. MiU-C. English born Quaker who served in Pennsylvania and New Jersey, 1726-1746.

Griggs, Edward Howard, b. 1868.[2336] The story of an itinerant teacher. Indianapolis & N.Y.: The Bobbs-Merrill co., 1934. 231 p. NN. The author taught at the University of Indiana and at Leland Stanford.

Grigsby, Melvin, b. 1845. The [2337] smoked Yank. Rev. ed. Sioux Falls: M. Grigsby, 1911? 251 p. NN. Civil War experiences.

Grimes, Absolam Carlisle, [2338] 1834-1911. ...Confederate mail runner. New Haven: Yale univ. press, 1926. 216 p. WHi. As described by the title.

Grimes, Helen Mills. Meet the [2339] Mills. No imprint. 87 p. IaDm. The story of her youth, beginning about 1900, in the family of a small town Iowa doctor.

Grimes, William, b. 1784. Life of [2340] William Grimes, the runaway slave. N.Y.: 1825. 68 p. WHi. Connecticut barber, servant, tells of his former life as a slave in Virginia and Georgia.

Grimes, William W., b. 1824. [2341] Thirty-three years' experience of an itinerant minister of the A.M.E. Church. Lancaster, Pa.: E. S. Speaker, printer, 1887. 30 p. TNF. In New England and the Middle Atlantic states.

Grimm, George, jr. The public [2342] service...Red Wing, Minn.: 1945. 74 p. MoS. A 20th century account by an engineer employed by the city of St. Louis.

Grinde, Mrs. Bertha. See Grinde, Carl and Bertha.

Grinde, Carl. Souvenir auto- [2343] biographies by Carl and Bertha (Gutterson) Grinde. Colton, S.D.: n.d. n.p. MtHi. Farmer and his wife tell of their lives in Wisconsin and the Dakota Territory, beginning about 1879.

Gringo, Harry. See Wise, Henry Augustus.

Grinnell, George Bird, 1849- [2344] 1938. When buffalo ran. New Haven: Yale univ. press, 1920. 114 p. DLC. Youth and early manhood of an Indian on the Plains.

Grinnell, Joseph, b. 1877. Gold [2345] hunting in Alaska. Elgin: Cook pub. co., 1901. 96 p. OrHi. A year in Alaska.

Grinnell, Josiah Bushnell, 1821- [2346] 1891. Men and events of forty years. Boston: Lothrop, 1891. 426 p. WHi. Congregational clergyman, abolitionist, Iowa State Senator, and member of the U.S. House of Representatives.

Griscom, John, 1774-1852. Mem-[2347] oir of John Griscom, LL.D. late professor of chemistry and natural philosophy; with an account of the New York High School; Society for the Prevention of Pauperism; the House of Refuge; and other institutions. Compiled from an autobiography, and other sources, by John H. Griscom, M.D. N.Y.: Robert Carter & bros., 1859. 427 p. NN. Teacher, educational reformer, chemist and social reformer.

Griscom, Lloyd C. Diplomatic- [2348] ally speaking. Boston: Little, Brown, 1940. 476 p. WU. The author served in England, Turkey, Persia, Japan, Brazil and Italy.

Griswold, Frank Gray, 1854- [2349] 1937. After thoughts. N.Y. & London: Harper & bros., 1936. 202 p. NN. Reminiscences of sport, racing and fishing; social life of New York City; the opera.

Griswold, Frank Gray, 1854- [2350] 1937. Race horses and racing. Norwood, Mass.: Plimpton press, 1925. 216 p. NN. By a socialite.

Groff, Spencer. Diamond dust, [2351] by the salvager. Kansas City, Mo.: Brown-White co., 1936. MoK. Missouri farmer who lost his money speculating. The period covered is 1900-35.

Gronniosaw, James Albert [2352] Ukawsaw, b. 1714? A narrative... Newport: reprinted and sold by S. Southwick, 1774. 48 p. DLC. The author was taken as a slave to New York. He eventually moved to England.

Gross, Samuel David, 1805-1884.[2353] Autobiography...Phila.: George Barrie, 1887. Vol. I, 907 p. WU. Prof. of Medicine in Ohio and Kentucky. The second volume is a journal.

Gross, William, 1796-1823. The [2354] last words...Phila.: 1823. 20 p. DLC. Murderer in Pennsylvania.

Grouard, Frank, b. 1850. Life [2355] and adventures of Frank Grouard, chief of the scouts (told to Joe

DeBarthe). Buffalo, Wyoming: reprinted by the Buffalo Bulletin, n.d. 326 p. WHi. Frontier Indian fighter.

Grout, Josiah, b. 1841. Memoir [2356] of General William Wallace Grout and autobiography of Josiah Grout. Newport, Vt.: Bullock press, 1919. 402 p. Auto., p. 195-364. WHi. Member of the state legislature and Governor of Vermont.

Grout, Lewis, 1815-1905. The [2357] autobiography of the Rev. Lewis Grout; or a brief outline, supplement, and appendix, of his eighty-eight years of life and labors in Africa and America... Brattleboro, Vt.: for sale by Clapp & Jones, 1905? 63 p. DLC. Congregational missionary.

Grow, Galusha Aaron, 1823- [2358] 1907. Galusha A. Grow, by S. T. DuBois...Boston: Houghton Mifflin, 1917. 305 p. WHi. A dictated account by a Pennsylvania lawyer and politician.

Grow, William B., b. 1816. 85 [2359] years of life and labor. Carbondale, Pa.: pub. by the author, 1902. 299 p. MiU-H. Baptist clergyman in Michigan.

Grubbs, Samuel Bates, 1871- [2360] 1942. By order of the Surgeon-General; thirty-seven years active duty in the Public Health service. Greenfield, Ind.: press of William Mitchell, 1943. 332 p. DLC. As described by the title.

Guerin, Eddie, b. 1860. Crime... [2361] London: John Murray, 1928. 319 p. WU. British born, the author lived the life of a thief in Chicago.

Guernsey, Charles Arthur. Wyo- [2362] ming cowboy days. N.Y.: Putnam's sons, 1936. 288 p. KHi. Cattle rancher, iron ore miner, member of the Wyoming State Senate. The period covered is 1880-1935.

Guggenheim, William, 1868- [2363] 1941. William Guggenheim, by Gatenby Williams (pseud.) in collaboration with Charles Monroe Heath. N.Y.: Lone voice pub. co., 1934. 252 p. DLC. Philanthropist who engaged in industrial mining ventures in the West.

Guitry, Sacha, b. 1885. If mem- [2364] ory serves. Garden City, N.Y.: Doubleday, Doran, 1935. 312 p. DLC. French playwright, actor, comedian who toured the U.S.

Gull, Caroline, b. 1859. The [2365] story of my life. Phila.: 1935. 197 p. DLC. Nurse, physical therapist in Pa., born in Switzerland.

Gulley, Samuel Samson, b. 1859. [2366] Happy Sam, the converted miner; the reminiscences of a Salvation Army captain. Louisville, Ky.: Pentacostal pub. co., 1918. 68 p. DLC. As described by the title.

Gumpert, Martin, b. 1897. First [2367] papers. N.Y.: Duell, Sloan & Pearce, 1941. 310 p. NN. Reactions to, and reflections upon the American scene by a refugee German physician who came to this country in 1936.

Gunder, Claude A. Life of [2368] Claude A. Gunder, saved by the blood from a drunkard's hell. Now in Taylor University, Upland, Ind., preparing for temperance work. Marion, Ind.: The author, 1909. 70 p. MWA. As described by the title.

Gunnison, Nathaniel, 1811-1872. [2369] An autobiography...2d ed. Brooklyn: 1910. 61 p. Auto., p. 7-22. WHi. Universalist clergyman in New England.

Guthrie, Woody, b. 1912. Bound [2370] for glory. N.Y.: E. P. Dutton, 1943. 428 p. DLC. Hobo singer.

Guttersen, Granville, 1897- [2371] 1918. Granville. Tales and tail spins from a flyer's diary. N.Y.: Abingdon press, 1919. 176 p. DLC. The author tells of his training for flying a plane in the first World War.

Guyton, Boone T. This exciting [2372] air; the experiences of a test pilot. N.Y.: Whittlesey, 1943. 219 p. DLC. Test pilot for the U.S. Navy and the French government.

# H

Haas, John Jacob, b. 1853. Along [2373] the way...Los Angeles: 1938. 117 p. Auto., p. 1-97. DLC. Farmer, banker, member of state legislature in Missouri.

Habersham, Alexander Wylly. [2374] The North Pacific surveying and exploring expedition...Phila.:

Hackenburg, Frederick L. A [2375] solitary parade. N.Y.: Thistle, 1929. 339 p. WHi. New York political figure who fought privilege and corruption. The author was born in Germany.

Haddad, George. Mt. Lebanon [2376] to Vermont...Rutland: 1916. 187 p. WHi. By a merchant who came from Syria.

Hadden, Ida May. First and [2377] second chronicles. N.Y.: Fleming H. Revell, 1937. 96 p. NN. School teacher on an Indian reservation in South Dakota; later, the writer was a nurse.

Haddock, William J. The [2378] prairies of Iowa...Iowa City: 1901. 71 p. IaHi. A school teacher and lawyer tells mainly of his feelings towards the prairielands of Iowa.

Hadley, Harold. Come see [2379] them die. N.Y.: Julian Messner, 1934. 237 p. DLC. Newspaper reporter in Denver, New York, Omaha, and Detroit.

Hadley, Henry Harrison. The [2380] blue badge of courage. Akron, Ohio: The Saalfield pub. co., 1902. 468 p. DLC. Temperance worker.

Hadley, Samuel Hopkins, 1842- [2381] 1906. Down in Water Street. N.Y.: Fleming H. Revell, 1902. 242 p. DLC. Mission worker in New York.

Hafen, Mary Ann (Stucki), b.1854.[2382] Recollections of a handcart pioneer of 1860...Denver: 1938. 117 p. DLC. Wife of Morman who describes her activity on behalf of the church in Utah and Nevada, and her family life.

Hagen, Mrs. Lois (Denley). Par-[2383] ish in the pines. Caldwell: Caxton printers, 1938. WHi. An account of childhood in a missionary family in Minnesota.

Hagerty, T. H. A reminiscent [2384] discourse...St. Louis: 1912. 20 p. MoK. Methodist clergyman in Missouri, beginning with the sixties.

Hagood, Johnson, 1829-1898. [2385] Memoirs of the War of Secession, from the original manuscripts of Johnson Hagood, brigadier-general C.S.A. Columbia, S.C.: The State co., 1910. NN. As described by the title.

Hague, Parthenia Antoinette [2386] (Vardaman), b. 1838. A blockaded family; life in southern Alabama during the Civil War. N.Y.: Houghton, Mifflin, 1888. 176 p. NN. As described by the title.

Hague, William, 1808-1887. Life [2387] notes...Boston: Lee & Shepard, 1888. 326 p. WHi. Baptist clergyman in New York, Mass., and Rhode Island; editor of Christian Watchman.

Hahn, Emily, b. 1905. China to [2388] me. A partial autobiography. Garden City, N.Y.: Doubleday, Doran, 1944. 429 p. WU. Foreign correspondent in China in the thirties and forties.

Haight, Austin D. The biography[2389] of a sportsman. N.Y.: Thomas Y. Crowell co., 1939. 209 p. NN. Hunting and fishing reminiscences.

Haight, Mrs. W. A. Some rem- [2390] iniscences...No imprint, 1900? 16 p. CU-B. Manager of orphan asylum in San Francisco, operated by a Protestant church. Her story begins about 1853.

Haines, Aaron Watson, b. 1842. [2391] Sacred memories of a circuit rider, by Octo. Rockford, Ill.: Buss pr. co., 1930. 48 p. IaHi. Methodist clergyman in Iowa.

Halbleib, Augustus J. The auto-[2392] biography of a fallen "Christ". Richmond: Haltina pub. co., 1927. 143 p. DLC. The story of a priest who left the Catholic church.

Haldeman-Julius, Emanuel, [2393] b. 1889. The first hundred million. N.Y.: Simon & Schuster, 1928. 340 p. DLC. Publisher of books.

Hale, Edward Everett, 1822- [2394] 1909. A new England boyhood. N.Y.: Cassell pub. co., 1893. 267 p. DLC. Unitarian clergyman who wrote the "Man without a country".

Hall, Arethusa, 1802-1891. [2395] Arethusa Hall. A memorial...ed. by Francis E. Abbot. Cambridge, Mass.: 1892. 167 p. Auto., p. 9-73. DLC. Teacher in New England and New York academies.

Hall, Baynard Rush, 1798-1863. [2396] The new purchase...by Robert Carleton (pseud.). N.Y.: Appleton:

1843. 2 vols. DLC. Presbyterian minister and educator in pioneer Indiana.

Hall, C. W. Threescore years [2397] and ten. Cinc.: Elm street pr. co., 1884. 303 p. DLC. Lawyer and District Attorney in Tennessee. This account begins about 1860.

Hall, Daniel Weston, b. 1841. [2398] Arctic rovings...Boston: Abel Tompkins, 1861. 171 p. DLC. Whaler who jumped his ship in Siberia.

Hall, Mrs. Florence Marion [2399] (Howe), 1845-1922. Memories grave and gay. N.Y.: Harper & bros., 1918. 341 p. WHi. The daughter of Julia Warde Howe, who was a minor literary figure.

Hall, George Lyman, b. 1913. [2400] Sometime again...Seattle: Superior pub. co., 1945. 218 p. CU-B. The peaceful side of army life during the second World War in Alaska.

Hall, Granville Stanley, 1844- [2401] 1924. Life and confessions of a psychologist. N.Y.: D. Appleton & co., 1923. 622 p. WU. Professor of psychology at Johns Hopkins and president of Clark University.

Hall, Isaac Freeman, b. 1847. [2402] In school from three to eighty... Pittsfield, Mass.: Eagle pr. & binding co., 1927. 246 p. DLC. Superintendent of schools in Massachusetts.

Hall, J. Sonora...Narrative of a [2403] residence of fifteen years. Chicago: Jones pr. co., 1881. 331 p. CSmH. A story of mining and Indian trouble in Mexico, Arizona and California beginning with 1850.

Hall, James Augustus. Starving [2404] on a bed of gold...Santa Cruz: press of the Sentinel, 1909. 149 p. DLC. Miner and lawyer in Alaska. A 20th century account.

Hall, James Norman, b. 1887. [2405] Kitchener's mob; the adventures of an American in the British army. Boston & N.Y.: Houghton Mifflin, 1916. 201 p. DLC. First World War.

Hall, James Norman, b. 1887. [2406] High adventures. A narrative of air fighting in France. Boston: Houghton Mifflin, 1918. 237 p. DLC. Member of Lafayette Escadrille during the first World War.

Hall, James Norman, b. 1887. [2407] Flying with Chaucer. Boston: Houghton Mifflin, 1930. 56 p. DLC. Flyer tells of his imprisonment by the Germans, his escape and his further experiences during the first World War.

Hall, James Norman, b. 1887. [2408] On the stream of travel. Boston: Houghton Mifflin, 1926. 365 p. DLC. Novelist tells of his midwest boyhood, his service in the first World War, and his world travels.

Hall, Robert, b. 1814. Life of [2409] Robert Hall...Also, sketch of Big Foot Wallace. Austin: Ben J. Jones, 1898. 103 p. Auto., p. 1-91. TxU. Soldier who fought against Mexico; with the Confederate Army; and against the Indians. This account was written down by "Brazos".

Hall, Thomas Wakeman, 1818- [2410] 1895. Recollections of a grandfather. No imprint. 48 p. CSmH. Miner and merchant in California about 1850 who in the sixties was a farmer in Wisconsin.

Hallet, Richard Matthews, b.1887.[2411] The rolling world. Boston: Houghton Mifflin, 1938. 346 p. NN. The Maine writer tells of his adventurous life in Australia, on the high seas, in the mines, and as a hobo.

Hallock, Charles, 1834-1917. An [2412] angler's reminiscences. A record of sport, travel and adventure. With autobiography of the author. Cinc.: Sportsmen's review pub. co., 1913. 135 p. NN. Newspaper man and writer on sports, founder of the sporting periodical Field and Stream.

Halloran, Matthew Francis, [2413] 1865-1940. Romance of the merit system...Wash., D.C.: Judd & Detweiler, 1928. 314 p. DLC. A personal history, interwoven with the history of the civil service system.

Hallowell, Benjamin, 1799-1877. [2414] Autobiography of Benjamin Hallowell. Phila.: Friends' book association, 1883. 394 p. WHi. Maryland and Virginia educator who was president of Maryland Agricultural College (1859).

Halls, William, b. 1834. Selec- [2415] tions . . . with an autobiographical sketch...Salt Lake City: Deseret news, 1911. 149 p. Auto., p. 1–6. USlC. Mormon Patriarch in Utah, who was also a farmer, stock raiser, carpenter and school teacher.

Halper, Albert, b. 1904. On the [2416] shore; young writer remembering Chicago. N.Y.: The Viking press, 1934. 257 p. NN. Story of the author's childhood.

Halsell, Harry H., b. 1860. Cow- [2417] boys and cattleland. Nashville, Tenn.: Parthenon press, 1937. 276 p. DLC. Texas cowboy and cattleman.

Halsey, Gaius Leonard, 1819– [2418] 1891. Reminiscences of village life and of Panama and California from 1840 to 1850...(In: The pioneers of Unadilla village... by Francis Whiting Halsey. Unadilla, N.Y.: 1902. 323 p.) DLC. Physician in California who served a gold mining company.

Hamblen, Herbert Elliott, [2419] b. 1849. On many seas; the life and exploits of a Yankee sailor, by Frederick Benton Williams (pseud.). Edited by his friend William Stone Booth. N.Y.: Macmillan, 1897. 417 p. NN. As described by the title.

Hambleton, Chalkley J. A gold [2420] hunter's experience. Chicago: 1898. 116 p. WHi. In Colorado, 1860–62.

Hamblin, Jacob, b. 1819. Jacob [2421] Hamblin, a narrative of his personal experiences as a frontiersman, missionary to the Indians. Salt Lake City: Deseret news, 1909. 151 p. DLC. After his conversion, the author served the Mormons as missionary of peace to the Indians.

Hambourg, Mark, b. 1879. From [2422] piano to forte...London, etc.: Cassell, 1931. 310 p. DLC. Rumanian born musician who played several tours in the U.S.

Hamburger, Estelle. It's a [2423] woman's business. N.Y.: Vanguard press, 1939. 300 p. WU. The author was in charge of advertising for a department store in New York City.

Hamilton, Alice. Exploring the [2424] trades...Boston: Little, Brown, 1943. 433 p. WU. Physician who served at Hull House tells of her experiences in industrial medicine.

Hamilton, Allan McLane, 1848– [2425] 1919. Recollections of an alienist, personal and professional. N.Y.: George H. Doran, 1916. 416 p. NN. As described by the title.

Hamilton, Henry Raymond, [2426] b. 1861. Footprints. Chicago, 1927. 188 p. WHi. A Chicagoan tells of the early phases of his career: education, travelling salesman in the West.

Hamilton, Henry S., b. 1836. [2427] Reminiscences of a veteran. Concord, N.H.: Am. press assoc., 1897. 180 p. DLC. Soldier who saw service in the west during troubles with the Indians and the Mormons. Later, the author settled in New Hampshire as a printer.

Hamilton, James Alexander, [2428] 1788–1878. Reminiscences... N.Y.: Scribner, 1869. 647 p. WHi. The son of Alexander Hamilton, who was a district attorney under Jackson, tells of his political activities within the Democratic Party in New York and Washington.

Hamilton, Mrs. S. Watson. A [2429] pioneer of fifty-three. Albany, Oreg.: Herald press, 1905. 139 p. OrU. A ryhming account of her pioneer youth in Iowa, and of crossing the plains.

Hamilton, Mrs. Sarah, b. 1745. [2430] A narrative...Greenwich: John Howe, printer, 1806. 26 p. CSmH. The author relates her troubles with a Catholic family in South Carolina, in which she was raised, when she became a Protestant. The writer was born in Germany.

Hamilton, Thomas Marion. The [2431] young pioneer. Wash., D.C.: Library press, 1932. 284 p. DLC. After his youth on a farm in Wisconsin, the author mined, hunted, and "punched" cows in Wyoming and New Mexico.

Hamilton, William Douglas, 1832–[2432] 1915. Recollections of a cavalryman of the Civil War after fifty years, 1861–1865. Columbus, Ohio: The F. J. Heer pr. co., 1915. 309 p. NN. By an officer.

Hamilton, William Thomas, [2433]

Hamlin, Cyrus. My life and [2434] times. 2d ed. Boston & Chicago: Congregational sunday-school & pub. soc., 1893. 538 p. WHi. Missionary and president of Robert College in Turkey who later became president of Middlebury College in Vermont.

Hamlin, Cyrus, 1811-1900. [2435] Among the Turks. N.Y.: R. Carter, 1878. 378 p. NjP. Missionary and President of Robert College in Turkey.

Hammon, Briton. A narrative. [2436] Boston: pr. by Green & Russell, 1760. 14 p. DLC. Slave who was permitted to leave Mass. for Jamaica. The author experienced shipwreck, captivity among the Florida Indians and imprisonment by the Spaniards. An 18th century account.

Hammond, Isaac B. Reminiscences of frontier life. Portland: [2437] 1904. 134 p. WaU. Surveyor and miner in Kansas, Wyoming, Oregon and Alaska.

Hammond, John Hays, b. 1855. [2438] Autobiography...N.Y.: Farrar & Rinehart, 1935. 2 vols. WU. The author was a business associate of Rhodes in Africa, and a political figure in the Republican party of the 20th century.

Hampel, Mrs. Elizabeth (Coffey).[2439] Yankee bride in Moscow. N.Y.: Liveright, 1941. 319 p. DLC. The author was the wife of a diplomatic official.

Hampton, Noah Jasper. An eye- [2440] witness to the dark days of 1861-65; or, a private soldier's adventures and hardships during the war. Nashville: pr. for the author, 1898. 80 p. CSmH. Confederate soldier.

Hance, Charles Hewitt, b. 1837. [2441] Reminiscences of one who suffered in the lost cause. Los Angeles: n.d. 22 p. DLC. After serving the Confederate cause as a soldier, the author engaged in the drug business and in politics in Missouri and then California.

b. 1822. My sixty years on the plains trapping, trading, and Indian fighting. N.Y.: Forest & stream pub. co., 1905. 244 p. WHi. As described by the title.

Hance, Gertrude Rachel, b.1844. [2442] The Zulu yesterday and to-day; twenty-nine years in South Africa. N.Y., Chicago, etc.: Fleming H. Revell, 1916. 274 p. DLC. Congregational missionary.

Hancock, Samuel. The narrative [2443] of Samuel Hancock, 1845-1860. N.Y.: Robert M. McBride, 1927. 217 p. WHi. Frontier trader, miner in Oregon and California.

Handsaker, Samuel, b. 1831. [2444] Pioneer life. Eugene: 1908. 104 p. OrU. The author, a farm laborer, Indian fighter and merchant, came to Oregon in 1853. He was born in England.

Handshaw, James E., b. 1855. [2445] Looking backward...Smithtown Branch, N.Y.: J. E. Handshaw, 1923. 322 p. DLC. New York stamp dealer.

Handy, William C., b. 1873. [2446] Father of the blues...N.Y.: Macmillan, 1942. 317 p. WU. Composer of music, and musician.

Hanehan, James, alias James [2447] D. Burton. A thrilling story. St. Louis: 1912 32 p. MoHi. Murderer and thief in the Tenn., Ky., Ohio area who in 1869 became an auctioneer in Missouri and in 1911 confessed to his crimes.

Haney, M. L., b. 1825. Pente- [2448] costal possibilities...Chicago: Christian witness co., 1906. 398 p. WHi. Methodist clergyman who served mainly in Illinois. During the Civil War he was a Chaplain with the Union Army.

Hankins, Samuel W. Simple [2449] story of a soldier. Nashville: Confederate veteran, 1912. 63 p. CSmH. The author served in a Mississippi regiment.

Hanks, N. C. Up from the hills. [2450] N.p.: Deseret news press, 1921. 32 p. UU. A Utah miner, blinded in an accident, tells of his fight to overcome despair.

Hanley, William. Feelin' fine. [2451] by Anne S. Monroe, Garden City, N.Y.: Doubleday, Doran, 1930. 304 p. WHi. Frontier cattleman in Oregon, known for his wit.

Hannibal, Peter M. [2452] Halvhundredaar i Amerika... Blair, Nebraska: Danish Lutheran pub. house, 1906. 105 p. MoHi. Teacher in Nebraska.

Hansen, A. H. Tundra, romance [2453] and adventure on Alaskan trails... N.Y.: Century, 1930. 334 p. DLC. U.S. Deputy Marshal in Alaska.

Hanser, Carl Johann Otto. [2454] Irrfahrten und heim fahrten... Buffalo: Lutheran pub. co., 1910. 291 p. MoSC-H. After attempts at business, the author becomes a sailor, and then in sixties he becomes a Lutheran clergyman, serving in Missouri, Mass., and Indiana. He was born in Germany.

Hanson, Mrs. Emma (Cole). [2455] The life and sufferings of Miss Emma Cole. 2d ed. Boston: M. Aurelius, 1844. 36 p. WHi. A Maine servant girl flees the country disguised as a sailor, is captured by pirates, but manages to return to the U.S. where she marries.

Hanson, Miles. Out of old paths. [2456] Boston: Beacon press, 1919. 103 p. DLC. Congregational clergyman in Texas who became a Unitarian, serving in Mass. He was born in England.

Hanus, Paul Henry, b. 1855. Ad- [2457] venturing in education. Cambridge, Mass.: Harvard univ. press, 1937. 259 p. DLC. After teaching in Colorado, the author founded the Department of Education at Harvard.

Hanway, J. Edwin. The mem- [2458] oirs...Caspar: 1942. 246 p. WyU. After trailing cattle from Kansas to Texas, the author turned to a newspaper career which he followed in Kansas, Utah, Colorado, Wyoming, Texas and New Mexico.

Hapgood, Hutchins, b. 1869. A [2459] Victorian in the modern world. N.Y.: Harcourt, Brace, 1939. 604 p. WU. Journalist (dramatic critic and editorial writer) in New York, and writer of books on various subjects.

Hapgood, Norman, 1868-1937. [2460] The changing years; reminiscences of Norman Hapgood. N.Y.: Farrar & Rinehart, 1930. 321 p. NN. Newspaperman in New York City, editor of Colliers; social reformer.

Harden, William, b. 1844. Recol-[2461] lections of a long and satisfactory life. Savannah: Review pr. co., 1934. 150 p. DLC. After serving in the Confederate Army the author held minor public posts in Savannah, Georgia.

Hardin, John Wesley, 1853-1895. [2462] The life of John Wesley Hardin. Bandera, Texas: Frontier Times, 1925. 54 p. WHi. Gambler and murderer who served time in a Texas prison.

Harding, Chester, 1792-1866. [2463] My egotistography. Cambridge: press of John Wilson, 1866. 185 p. WHi. Portrait painter. This same book was published in 1890 under another title.

Hardinge, Belle (Boyd), 1843- [2464] 1900. Belle Boyd in camp and prison. London: Saunders, Otley, 1865. 2 vols. DLC. Confederate spy.

Hardy, Arthur Sherburne, 1847- [2465] 1930. Things remembered. Boston & N.Y.: Houghton Mifflin, 1923. 311 p. WU. Professor of mathematics at Dartmouth, novelist, minister in Persia (1897-1901), Switzerland (1901-1903), and Spain (1903-1905).

Hardy, Edwin. A pioneer's [2466] recollections of Ottowa country. No imprint. 46 p. KHi. Indian troubles, hunting in Kansas in the sixties and seventies.

Hare, Joseph, d. 1818. The life [2467] and dying confession...of the noted robber in Auburn: pr. by D. Rumsey, 1818. 16 p. CSmH. Mail robber who operated in the southeastern states.

Hare, William Hobart, 1838- [2468] 1909. Reminiscences...Phila.: pr. by Wm. F. Fell, 1888. 25 p. WHi. Episcopalian missionary among the Indians in South Dakota.

Hargraves, Edward Hammond, [2469] 1816-1891. Australia and its gold fields...London: H. Ingram, 1855. 240 p. DLC. Includes gold mining in California, 1849-50, p. 69-96.

Hargrove, Marion. See here, [2470] private Hargrove. N.Y.: Holt, 1942. 211 p. WHi. The author's experiences in a training camp, World War II.

Harker, Joseph R. Eventide [2471] memories...Jacksonville, Illinois: A. B. Press, 1931. 343 p. DLC. President of Illinois Woman's College, 1893-1925.

Harlan, Jacob Wright, b. 1828. [2472] California, '46 to '88. San

Francisco: Bancroft, 1888. 242 p. CSmH. After serving with Fremont in Mexico the author removed to California where he kept store, operated a hotel and speculated in land.

Harland, Mrs. Hester Ann (Lam- [2473] bert), 1857-1940. Reminiscences. No imprint (mimeographed). C. California suffragist, wife of a mining engineer.

Harland, Marion (pseud.). See Terhune, Mrs. Mary Virginia.

Harland-Edgecumbe, Francis [2474] Willis, b. 1898? The man who fooled a continent...London: John Long, 1935. 253 p. DLC. An Englishman who posed as a Lord in the U.S., and who was eventually exposed.

Harlow, Frederick Pease. The [2475] making of a sailor...Salem: Maine research society, 1928. 377 p. WHi. Life on a square rigger in the seventies.

Harmon, J. C., b. 1848. Crazy- [2476] the kid, or the cowboy scout. Sioux City?: 1921? 90 p. CoD. Cowboy and government scout in Kansas, Wyoming, Colorado and the Southwest. Rancher in South Dakota.

Harmon, Thomas Dudley, b.1919. [2477] Pilots also pray. N.Y.: Thomas Y. Crowell, 1944. 184 p. NN. Pilot in the second World War, principally with General Chennault's squadron in China.

"Harold". Rebel without a [2478] cause; the hypnoalysis of a criminal psychopath. By Robert M. Lindner. N.Y.: Grune & Stratton, 1944. 284 p. WU. As described by the title.

Harpending, Asbury. The [2479-2480] great diamond hoax...San Francisco: 1913. 283 p. CU-B. With Walker in Nicaragua. Mining in California in fifties, and in Mexico. Served with Confederate forces during Civil War, and after the War he engaged in California real estate, railroading and politics. The account closes with the year 1870.

Harper, Angelo, b. 1865. Auto- [2481] biography and essays. Takoma Park, D.C.: 1929. 8 p. DLC. Western Union telegrapher employed in Illinois.

Harper, Joseph Henry, b. 1850. [2482] I remember. N.Y.: Harper, 1934. 281 p. WHi. Publisher of books.

Harper, Lizzie (St. John), 1836- [2483] 1916?. Maria Monk's daughter; an autobiography. By Mrs. L. St. John Eckel. N.Y.: pub. for the author by the United States pub. co., 1874. 604 p. NN. Career of an American adventuress, both in the United States and France.

Harper, Samuel N., 1882-1943. [2484] The Russia I believe in...Chicago: University of Chicago press, 1945. 279 p. Auto., p. 1-80. WU. The Chancellor of the University of Chicago tells of his life as a student and teacher and of his trips to Russia.

Harrer, William. With drum and [2485] gun in '61; a narrative of the adventures of William Harrer, of the fourteenth New York state volunteers...in the war for the Union from 1861 to 1863. Greenville, Pa.: pub. for the author by the Beaver pr. co., 1908. 119 p. NUt. As described by the title.

Harriman, Florence Jaffray [2486] (Hurst), b. 1870. From pinafores to politics. N.Y.: H. Holt, 1923. 359 p. WHi. Member of Federal Industrial Relations Commission, and woman suffragist. The author played a prominent part as a civilian war worker in the first World War.

Harriman, Florence Jaffray [2487] (Hurst), b. 1870. Mission to the north. Phila.: J. B. Lippincott, 1941. 331 p. WU. The author was U.S. Minister to Norway.

Harrington, Daniel, b. 1860. [2488] Memoirs...N.p.: 1939. 27 p. UU. County school superintendent in Utah who in 1885 became a newspaper editor. The author was also engaged in politics.

Harrington, Estelle (Messenger), [2489] b. 1878. Ida Amelia. N.p.: 1940. 79 p. DLC. Her childhood experiences on a farm in Illinois.

Harrington, Gardner. A short [2490] epitome on the life, sufferings and travels of Gardner Harrington...commencing at the termination of the second volume of the history of his life. Troy: J. C. Kneeland & co., 1849. 50 p. MPiB. Baptist clergyman in New England in the forties.

Harris, Branson L., b. 1817. [2491] Some recollections of my boyhood. Indianapolis: The Hollenbeck press, 1908? 70 p. NN. Pioneer days on a farm in Indiana.

Harris, Charles J. Reminis- [2492] cences of my days with Roland Hayes. Orangeburg, S.C.: 1944. 27 p. DLC. Negro pianist, accompanist to Roland Hayes.

Harris, Charles Kassell, 1864- [2493] 1930. After the ball...N.Y.: Frank-Muaurice, 1926. 376 p. DLC. New York song writer and music publisher.

Harris, Corra May (White), [2494] 1869-1935. My book and heart. Boston & N.Y.: Houghton Mifflin, 1924. 318 p. NN. Novelist and wife of a southern Methodist clergyman.

Harris, Credo Fitch, b. 1874. [2495] Microphone memoirs of the horse and buggy days of radio. Indianapolis: Bobbs-Merrill, 1937. 281 p. DLC. Operator of early radio station in Kentucky. The period covered is 1922-37.

Harris, Elmo Golightly. Brief [2496] autobiography...Ann Arbor, Mich.: Edwards, 1939. 41 p. MoHi. Professor in the Missouri School of Mines and Metallurgy, 1891-1931.

Harris, Mrs. Evelyn. The Barter [2497] lady...N.Y.: Doubleday, Doran, 1934. 338 p. WU. Woman farmer in Maryland.

Harris, Frank, b. 1855. My life [2498] and loves. Paris: Obelisk press books, n.d. 4 vols. WU. Volume I contains his early American experiences in the southwest as a cowboy, his student days at the University of Kansas, his law practice in Kansas to about 1875. He was born in Ireland.

Harris, Frank, b. 1855. My [2499] reminiscences as a cowboy. N.Y.: Boni, 1930. 217 p. WHi. His life in the southwest, prior to leaving for the University of Kansas.

Harris, Harry Jasper, b. 1847. [2500] My story. Higginsville, Mo.: Jefferson pub. co., 1923. 14 p. KHi. Pioneer farmer in Kansas.

Harris, John Howard. Thirty [2501] years as president of Bucknell... Wash., D.C.: 1926. 545 p. Auto., p. 7-107. WU. From 1889.

Harris, Louisa. Behind the [2502] scenes; or, Nine years at the four courts of Saint Louis. St. Louis, Mo.: A. R. Fleming, 1893. 220 p. NN. Police matron.

Harris, Lucien Montalvin, [2503] b. 1858. Random recollections of seventy-nine years. N.Y.: 1937. 113 p. DLC. Owner of newspaper in Alabama.

Harris, Marcus. Fifty years in [2504] wool trading. St. Louis: 1944. 26 p. MoSHi. In Missouri, beginning with about 1875.

Harris, Nathaniel E., b. 1846. [2505] Autobiography...Macon, Georgia: J. W. Burke, 1925. 522 p. WHi. Lawyer, and Governor of Georgia, 1915-1917.

Harris, Samuel, b. 1836. Per- [2506] sonal reminiscences...Chicago: Rogerson press, 1897. 172 p. WHi. Officer in the Union army.

Harris, Mrs. Sarah Fisk (Bacon), [2507] 1821-1874. Sarah Fisk Harris. N.p.: 1914. NbHi. The author tells of her youth in Vermont in the family of a lawyer, and of her life in Indiana where her husband was a merchant.

Harrison, Carter Henry, b. 1860. [2508] Stormy years, the autobiography of Carter H. Harrison, five times mayor of Chicago. Indianapolis, N.Y.: The Bobbs-Merrill co., 1935. 361 p. WHi. As described by the title.

Harrison, Carter Henry, b. 1860. [2509] Growing up with Chicago, sequel to "Stormy years". Chicago: R. F. Seymour, 1944. 375 p. WHi. See description of preceding item.

Harrison, Constance (Cary), [2510] 1843-1920. Recollections grave and gay. N.Y.: C. Scribner's sons, 1911. 386 p. WHi. A novelist tells mainly of her social life and of her experiences in the South during the Civil War.

Harrison, Elizabeth, 1849-1927. [2511] Sketches along life's road. Boston: The Stratford co., 1930. 227 p. NN. Pioneer in the American kindergarten movement; president of the National Kindergarten College, Chicago, 1890-1920.

Harrison, Juanita. My great [2512] wide beautiful world. N.Y.: Macmillan, 1936. 318 p. DLC. A Negro domestic servant who worked her way around the world, 1927-1935.

Harrison, Marguerite Elton [2513] (Baker). There's always tomorrow; the story of a checkered life. N.Y.: Farrar & Rinehart, 1935. 664 p. NN. A woman newspaper correspondent tells of her travels and experiences in Germany, Russia, where she was imprisoned by the Russians, and in Asia after the first World War. The first part of the book tells of her earlier career in Baltimore.

Harrison, Paul Wilberforce, [2514] b. 1883. Doctor in Arabia. N.Y.: The John Day co., 1940. 303 p. NN. Career of a medical missionary.

Harrison, Thomas G. Career [2515] and reminiscences of an amateur journalist...Indianapolis: The author, 1883. 330 p. Auto., p. 87-330. WHi. In Indiana, beginning with 1875.

Harshberger, John William, [2516] 1869-1929. The life and work of John W. Harshberger, Ph.D., an autobiography. Phila.: 1928. 40 p. NN. Professor of botany at the University of Pennsylvania.

Harshman, Samuel Rufus, 1841- [2517] 1912. Memoirs...Sullivan, Illinois: 1914. 295 p. Auto., p. 1-208. DLC. Methodist clergyman in the midwest.

Hart, Bob (pseud.). See Sutherland, James Monroe.

Hart, Henry Martyn, 1838-1920. [2518] Recollections and reflections. N.Y.: Gibb bros. & Moran, prtrs., 1917. 205 p. NN. The writer, an Episcopal clergyman, was Dean of St. John's Cathedral, Denver. He tells of his experiences in Denver and of his earlier career in England.

Hart, James Morgan, 1839-1916. [2519] German universities: a narrative of personal experience. N.Y.: Putnam's, 1874. 398 p. WU. His student days, beginning with 1861, by a philologist.

Hart, William Surrey. My life [2520] east and west. Boston & N.Y.: Houghton Mifflin, 1929. 346 p. WU. Motion picture actor.

Hartman, Howard, b. 1868. The [2521] seas were mine...N.Y.: Dodd, Mead & co., 1935. 330 p. DLC. Merchant mariner and adventurer.

Hartshorn, Edmund F., b. 1843. [2522] Experiences of a boy. Newark: Baker prntg. co., 1910. 131 p. DLC. After serving with the Union army the author shipped out on a whaler. In Hawaii he took up his early trade of printer.

Hartshorn, Edmund F., b. 1843. [2523] Sequel to Experiences of a boy. Newark: Baker printing co., 1911. 124 p. DLC. Sailor, printer and manufacturer in California.

Hasanovitz, Elizabeth, b. 1892. [2524] One of them; chapters from a passionate autobiography. Boston & N.Y.: Houghton Mifflin, 1918. 333 p. NN. Experiences of a Russian Jewish immigrant in the New York garment trade and her efforts to organize the industry.

Hasey, John F. Yankee fighter; [2525] the story of an American in the Free French Foreign Legion. Boston: Little, Brown, 1942. 293 p. WHi. A World War II account.

Haskell, George, b. 1809. A nar- [2526] rative...Ipswich: 1896. 156 p. WHi. Horticulturist, and member of the State Legislature in Mass.

Haskell, J. Stickney. Autobio- [2527] graphy. San Francisco: A. L. Bancroft, 1874. 80 p. CU-B. After a career in the circus, the author became a temperance lecturer in California in the seventies.

Haskell, Mrs. Joseph. "Early [2528] days in Minnesota". (In: Hiram A. Haskell, Joseph Haskell of Afton. Winsor, Calif.: 1941. 21 p.) p. 15-17. MnHi. Wife of a farmer in the Minnesota Territory beginning about 1848.

Haskins, C.W. The Argonauts [2529] of California...N.Y.: Fords, Howard & Hulbert, 1890. 501 p. DLC. California miner.

Hastings, Frank Stewart. A [2530] ranchman's recollections... Chicago: Breeder's gazette, 1921. 235 p. WU. Texas cattle trader and breeder.

Hasty, John Eugene. Done with [2531] mirrors; admissions of a freelance writer. N.Y.: Ives Washburn, 1943. 337 p. NN. Adventures in radio, television, advertising, press agenting, and ghost writing.

Hatch, Rebecca (Taylor), 1818- [2532]

1904. Rebecca Taylor Hatch, 1818-1904; personal reminiscences and memorials. N.Y.: 1905. 111 p. Auto., p. 1-52. DLC. Brooklyn social leader who was active in Sunday school and church work.

Hatcher, Green Waggener. A [2533] pilgrim and his pilgrimage. Columbia, Missouri: 1916. 263 p. DLC. Baptist clergyman in Missouri.

Hatcher, William Eldridge, [2534] 1834-1912. Along the trail of the friendly years. N.Y.: Fleming H. Revell co., 1910. 359 p. NN. Experiences of a Baptist clergyman in Virginia and Maryland; also active in educational work of the denomination.

Hatfield, John T., b. 1851. Thirty-[2535] three years a live wire...Cinc.: God's revivalist office, n.d., 317 p. Nv. Methodist evangelical preacher in Indiana, Illinois, Kansas, Oklahoma, Iowa and in the Rocky Mountain states.

Hathaway, Levi, b. 1790. Narra- [2536] tive...Providence: 1820. 140 p. WHi. Clergyman of the Christian Church, called Smithites, in New England, New York and New Jersey.

Hauberg, Max D., b. 1837. Mem- [2537] oirs. Rock Island, Ill.: 1923. 193 p. WHi. Illinois farmer who was born in Schleswig-Holstein.

Haugen, Nils Pederson, 1849- [2538] 1931. Pioneer and political reminiscences. Madison: State historical society of Wisconsin, n.d., 198 p. WHi. State Tax Assessor in Progressive era and member of the U. S. House of Representatives from Wisconsin at the end of the nineteenth century.

Hauk, Minnie, 1852-1929. Mem- [2539] oirs of a singer...London: A. M. Philpot, 1925. 295 p. DLC. The author grew up on a Kansas farm, After singing in New York, she continued her career abroad.

Haven, Erastus Otis, 1820-1881. [2540] Autobiography...N.Y.: Phillips & Hunt, 1883. 329 p. DLC. Methodist clergyman in New York, president of the University of Michigan and of Northwestern, and Chancellor of Syracuse University.

Haven, Violet Sweet. Many [2541] ports of call. N.Y.: Longmans, Green, 1940. 250 p. NN. Experiences of a young woman journalist with an urge to see the world.

Haviland, Emma Hillmon, [2542] b. 1863. Under the Southern cross, or A woman's life work for Africa. Cinc.: God's Bible school and revivalist, 1928. 461 p. DLC. Free Methodist missionary.

Haviland, Mrs. Laura (Smith), [2543] b. 1808. A woman's life work... 3d ed. Chicago: C. V. Waite, 1887. 554 p. WHi. Abolitionist.

Hawes, Elizabeth, b. 1903. [2544] Fashion is spinach. N.Y.: Random house, 1938. 336 p. Auto., p. 25-330. DLC. Fashion designer in New York.

Hawie, Ashad G., b. 1890. The [2545] rainbow ends. N.Y.: Gaus, 1942. 165 p. DLC. Syrian tells of his experiences as a salesman in New York and Alabama, and of his army services in the first World War.

Hawks, Clarence, b. 1869. Hit- [2546] ting the dark trail; starshine through thirty years of night. N.Y.: Henry Holt, 1915. 176 p. NN. The author, who is blind, tells the story of his fight to overcome his handicap and how he became a well-known nature writer.

Hawkes, Clarence, b. 1869. The [2547] light that did not fail. Boston: Chapman & Grimes, 1935. 178 p. NN. Additional details of the author's life, bringing it up to date.

Hawkins, Edward W., d. 1857. [2548] The history and confession of the young felon Edward W. Hawkins... Beattyville, Ky.: pr. for Edward Kincaid, n.d. 56 p. KyU. Kentucky felon.

Hawkins, Thomas Samuel, [2549] b. 1836. Some recollections of a busy life. San Francisco: 1913. 160 p. WHi. Real estate, banks, public utilities in California.

Hawks, Frank, 1897-1938. Speed.[2550] N.Y.: Warren & Putnam, 1931. 314 p. DLC. Aviator who set cross-country speed records.

Hawley, Curtis B. Buckskin [2551] Mose...N.Y.: Worthington, n.d. 285 p. UHi. A dubious western tale of experiences as actor, circus rider, detective, ranger, gold digger,

Indian scout, guide.

Hawley, Henry W. The life [2552] story...No imprint. 101 p. USlC. A Mormon tells of his homestead in Utah, and of being a sheriff. He then mines in Alaska and becomes a building contractor in Washington; finally he founds a gravel company in California. The period covered is roughly the late 19th century and early 20th century.

Hawley, Robert Emmett, b. 1862. [2553] Skqee mus, or pioneer days on the Nooksack. Bellingham, Wash.: Miller & Sutherlen, 1945. 189 p. WaHi. In early seventies to the Washington Territory where his father took up a homestead. The author became a farmer, rancher and owner of a lumber mill.

Hawthorne, Julian, 1846-1934. [2554] The memoirs of Julian Hawthorne ...N.Y.: Macmillan, 1938. 299 p. WU. Novelist, journalist and poet tells of his New England youth and of college days at Harvard.

Hawthorne, Julian, 1846-1934. [2555] Shapes that pass...Boston: Houghton Mifflin, 1928. 364 p. WU. See the preceding item. In this book Hawthorne tells of his experiences in England, beginning about 1870.

Hayden, Mrs. Dorothea Hoaglin. [2556] These pioneers. Los Angeles: 1938. 287 p. WHi. Teacher of speech and drama.

Hayden, Herbert Hiram, 1850- [2557] 1907. The Rev. Herbert H. Hayden, an autobiography. The Mary Stannard murder. Tried on circumstantial evidence...Hartford: Press of the Plimpton mfg. co., 1880. 164 p. NN. Methodist minister tried for murder. Written while in prison.

Hayden, Mary Jane, b. 1830. [2558] Pioneer days. San Jose: Murgotten's press, 1915. 49 p. OrHi. To Oregon in the fifties where the author raised stock and engaged in farming. Included is an account of Indian fighting, 1855-1856.

Hayden, William, b. 1785. Nar- [2559] rative...Cinc.: pub. for author, 1846. 156 p. DLC. The life of a slave.

Hays, Arthur Garfield. City [2560] lawyer...N.Y.: Simon & Schuster, 1942. 470 p. WHi. New York Jewish lawyer, famous for his defence of civil liberty cases.

Hays, Harold Melvin, b. 1880. [2561] Personality and other things... N.Y.: American physician, 1937. 163 p. DLC. New York physician.

Haywood, William Dudley, 1869- [2562] 1928. Bill Haywood's book... N.Y.: International publishers, 1929. 368 p. WHi. Labor leader of the Industrial Workers of the World.

Hazelett, George A. Ten years [2563] hustling without feet...Weston, Nebr.: 1899. 20 p. CoD. Salesman of books, knives, etc., in many parts of the country.

Hazen, Daniel L., b. 1835. The [2564] story of my life. Los Angeles: 1910. 108 p. CSmH. Merchant in Massachusetts, school teacher in New Jersey; farmer in California.

Hazen, Edward Adams, b. 1824. [2565] Salvation to the uttermost. Lansing, Mich.: Darius D. Thorp, 1892. 340 p. DLC. Methodist clergyman in California and in the states of the midwest.

Hazen, Jacob A. Five years be- [2566] fore the mast...Phila.: Willis P. Hazard, 1854. 444 p. DLC. Whaler, and service in the U.S. Navy. The period covered is 1837-42.

Heacock, Annie, b. 1838. Rem- [2567] iniscences...N.p.: 1926. 40 p. DLC. Pennsylvania suffragist who in the sixties taught Negro children in South Carolina, and who helped found a high school in Pennsylvania.

Healy, George Peter Alexander, [2568] 1813-1894. Reminiscences of a portrait painter. Chicago: A. C. McClurg, 1894. 221 p. Auto., p. 13-73. WHi. In Boston, Chicago, Paris, Rome.

Heard, William H., b. 1850. [2569] From slavery to the bishopric in the A.M.E. Church...Phila.: African Methodist Episcopal pub. house, 1924. 104 p. NcD. Methodist clergyman in Pennsylvania; slave in Georgia.

Heath, Herman H., d. 1874. Let- [2570] ter from Gen'l H. H. Heath. Washington, D.C.: 1870. 8 p. DLC. Union army, Indian fighter in Nebraska, acting governor of New

Mexico, newspaper editor, member of state legislature of Nebraska.

Heath, S. Burton. Yankee report- [2571] er. N.Y.: W. Funk, 1940. 391 p. WU. In New York City, and in the New England states.

Hebert, Frank. 40 years pros- [2572] pecting and mining in the Black Hills of South Dakota. Rapid City: Rapid city daily journal, 1921. 199 p. DLC. As described by the title.

Heckel, George Baugh, b. 1858. [2573] The paint industry; reminiscences, St. Louis, Mo.: American paint journal co., 1931. 679 p. DLC. Sales manager, executive manager for paint firms in Chicago.

Hecker, Frank Joseph. Activities [2574] of a lifetime 1864-1923. Detroit: priv. pr., 1923. 53 p. DLC. The author was connected with the railroad industry for many years. During the war with Spain he was an Army officer charged with army transport, and later he was a member of the Isthmian Canal Commission.

Heckman, Helen, b. 1898. My [2575] life transformed. N.Y.: Macmillan, 1928. 202 p. DLC. Interpretive dancer who was born deaf.

Hedges, Henry Parsons, 1817- [2576] 1911. Memories of a long life... East Hampton: E. S. Boughton, 1909. 59 p. NBLiHi. Lawyer, District Attorney and County Judge in New York.

Hedley, James. Twenty years [2577] on the lecture platform. Cleveland: Mary Hedley, 1901. 239 p. DLC. A physician who turned to the national lecture platform speaking on moral uplift.

Heffelfinger, Christopher B., [2578] 1834-1915. Memoirs...Comp. by Lucia L. Peavey Heffelfinger. Minn.: 1922. 101 p. MnHi. The author came to Minnesota in 1857 where he was a painter, shoe merchant, and dealer in real estate. During the Civil War he served in the Union Army.

Heffernan, W. T. Personal rec- [2579] ollections...N.p.: 1930. 22 p. CSmH. A physician who went to California in 1892, and who engaged in real estate development.

Hein, Otto Louis, b. 1847. Mem- [2580] ories of long ago...N.Y.: Putnam, 1925. 310 p. WHi. Army officer who served on the frontier, in the Philippines, as Military Attache in Vienna, and as Commandant of West Point.

Heinzen, Karl Peter, 1809-1880. [2581] Erlebtes...Boston: 1864-74. 2 vols. (Gesammelte schriften, band 3-4.) WU. A German revolutionist who tells of his journalistic work in this country. Only the second volume relates to his American experiences.

Heiser, Ellinor (Stewart). Days [2582] gone by. Baltimore: Waverly press, 1940. 117 p. Auto., p. 1-110. DLC. Reminiscences of childhood on a Maryland plantation.

Heiser, Harvey Michael, b. 1883. [2583] Memories of the fire service. Fresno: Fresno lithograph co., 1941. 177 p. DLC. In Sacramento. The autobiographical references are widely scattered.

Heiser, Victor George, b. 1873. [2584] An American doctor's odyssey... N.Y.: Norton, 1936. 544 p. WHi. The author was employed by the Rockefeller Foundation.

Helbrant, Maurice. Narcotic [2585] agent. N.Y.: Vanguard, 1941. 319 p. DLC. The author, born in Rumania, served as a Federal narcotics agent from 1924 to 1939.

Heller, Isaac, d. 1836. The life [2586] and confession of Isaac Heller, alias Isaac Young...Liberty, Ind.: C. V. Duggins, printer, 1836. 22 p. In. Indiana resident who murdered his wife and three children.

Hellier, Thomas, d. 1678. The [2587] vain prodigal life and tragical penitent death of Thomas Hellier ...who for murdering his master, mistress, and a maid, was executed according to law at Westover in Charles City, in the county of Virginia...London: pr. for Sam Crouch, 1680. 40 p. CSmH. As described by the title.

Hellman, Andrew, b. 1792. Con- [2588] fession of Adam Horn, alias Andrew Hellman...Baltimore: pr. by J. Young, 1843. 31 p. PP. Murderer.

Hellman, George Sidney, b. 1878. [2589] Lanes of memory...N.Y.: Alfred A. Knopf, 1927. 241 p. NN. Autobiographical sketches of personalities encountered in the author's career as a writer and bookman.

Hellyer, Henry Leon, b. 1880. [2590] From the Rabbis to Christ; a personal narrative...Phila.: Westminister press, 1911. 87 p. DLC. A Jew's conversion to Christianity.

Helm, Mary (Sherwood) Wight- [2591] man, b. 1807. Scraps of early Texas history...Austin: pr. for the author, 1884. 198 p. DLC. A Texas teacher tells of the building of Matagorda in 1828, and of the war with Mexico.

Helmbold, Henry T. Am I a [2592] lunatic?...N.Y. 1877. 137 p. DLC. A Philadelphia businessman who was confined in a number of asylums.

Helms, Edgar James, b. 1863. [2593] Pioneering in modern city missions. Boston: Morgan memorial pr. dep't., 1927. 136 p. CtMW. Methodist clergyman in Mass.

Hemenway, Charles W., b.1860. [2594] Memories of my day; in and out of Mormondom...Salt Lake City: Deseret news co., 1887. 265 p. DLC. Newspaper editor in Oregon and Utah who travelled extensively.

Henderson, James, 1859-1942. [2595] An autobiography...N.p.: 1944. 194 p. PHC. Minister of the Society of Friends in Ohio.

Henderson, Joseph Lindsey, [2596] b. 1869. Educational memoirs... Austin: Boeckman-Jones, 1940. 335 p. DLC. Texas educator: principal, superintendent, professor of Education.

Hendricks, William Quinett, [2597] b. 1849. Stranger than fiction... Wooster, Ohio: 1928. 66 p. DLC. Circus performer.

Hendrickson, Ford, b. 1875. [2598] The "Livingstone" of the Orinocco ...Wauseon, Ohio: 1942. 212 p. DLC. Evangelistic missionary to Central and South America.

Hendrickson, Henry, b. 1843. [2599] Out from the darkness; an autobiography...Chicago: Western Sunday school pub. co., 1879. 394 p. WHi. Blind broom manufacturer in Wisconsin and Illinois who was born in Norway.

Henie, Sonja, b. 1912. Wings on [2600] my feet. N.Y.: Prentice-Hall, 1940. 177 p. NN. The famous Norwegian born skater tells of her career.

Henry, Alexander, 1739-1824. [2601] Alexander Henry's travels and adventures in the years 1760-1776. Ed. by Milo M. Quaife. Chicago: R. R. Donnelley, 1921. 318 p. WHi. Fur trader whose travels brought him to the Lake Superior region.

Henry, George W., b. 1801. [2602] Incidents...Utica: R. W. Roberts, printer, 1846. 305 p. NUt. Blind Methodist clergyman and businessman who lived in New York.

Henry, George W., b. 1801. [2603] Trials and triumphs...2d ed. Oneida: 1861. 349 p. MH. A spiritual account by a blind Methodist clergyman of New York and Pennsylvania.

Henry, Katherine (pseud.). See Krebs, Mrs. Katherine (Stauffer).

Henry, Theodore C. An address. [2604] No imprint, 1902? 15 p. KHi. Farmer in Kansas and Colorado.

Henschel, George, b. 1850. Mus- [2605] ings and memories of a musician. N.Y.: Macmillan, 1919. 400 p. WU. German born conductor of the Boston Symphony Orchestra.

Hensey, Andrew Fitch, b. 1880. [2606] My children of the forest. N.Y.: George H. Doran, 1924. 221 p. DLC. Disciples of Christ missionary in Belgian Congo.

Henson, Josiah, 1789-1881. The [2607] life of Josiah Henson, formerly a slave, now an inhabitant of Canada, as narrated by himself. Boston: A. D. Phelps, 1849. 76 p. DLC. As described by the title.

Henson, Matthew A., b. 1866. [2608] A Negro explorer at the North pole. N.Y.: F. A. Stokes, 1912. 200 p. WHi. With Peary.

Hentschke, Max. A California [2609] dream come true. No imprint, 1936? 8 p. CHi. Laborer, farmer in California in the 1880's. The author was born in Germany.

Hergesheimer, Joseph, b. 1880. [2610] The Presbyterian child. N.Y.: Alfred A. Knopf, 1923. 66 p. NN. Recollections of a Pennsylvania childhood.

Hergesheimer, Joseph, b. 1880. [2611] From an old house. N.Y.: Alfred A. Knopf, 1925. 211 p. NN. Literary memories of the author, interspersed with accounts of his reconstruction of the house in Pennsylvania which became his home.

Hermann, Isaac. Memoirs of a [2612] veteran...Atlanta: Byrd pr. co., 1911. 285 p. WHi. Confederate.

Herndon, Angelo, b. 1913. Let [2613] me live. N.Y.: Random house, 1937. 409 p. NN. The writer, a Negro labor leader, tells of his conviction in Georgia on charges of inciting the Negroes to revolt and of distributing Communist literature, and of his sentence to the chain gang.

Herne, Peregrine. Perils and [2614] pleasures of a hunter's life... Boston: L. P. Crown, 1854. 336 p. DLC. Fur hunter on the plains and in the Rockies.

Herr, Horace D., b. 1852. Harvey [2615] Vonore, or the making of a minister...Fort Meyers, Fla.: Geddes pr. co., 1933. KU. Congregational clergyman in Kansas beginning with 1880.

Herr, John, 1782-1850. Life of [2616] John Herr. LaSalle, N.Y.: David N. Long, 1890? 30 p. InGo. Farmer and clergyman of the Reformed Mennonite Church in Pennsylvania.

Herrick, John P. Founding a [2617] country newspaper 50 years ago. Olean, N.Y.: 1936. 19 p. NN. Newspaper experiences in northern Pennsylvania near the New York State line.

Herrick, Myron Timothy, 1854- [2618] 1929. Myron T. Herrick...by Thomas Bentley Mott. N.Y.: Doubleday, Doran, 1929. 377 p. WHi. Lawyer, banker, Governor of Ohio and Ambassador to France.

Herrick, William W., b. 1848. [2619] Life and deeds of William Herrick, hermit...2d ed. N.p.: 1903. 59 p. MnHi. After serving in the Union army, the author turned to trapping in the Black Hills, the Big Horn country and the Powder Horn country. When his health broke down he became a hermit.

Herring, Donald Grant. Forty [2620] years of football. N.Y.: Carlyle house, 1940. 308 p. NN. The author played football at Princeton.

Hersey, Lewis Greenleaf, 1828- [2621] 1903. In memoriam...No imprint. 24 p. Auto., p. 5-11. IaHi. After mining in California, in 1863 the author turned to farming in Iowa.

Hertz, Carl. A modern mystery [2622] merchant...London: Hutchinson & co., 1924. 319 p. DLC. Magician who lived much of his life in England.

Hertzler, Arthur Emmanuel, [2623] b. 1870. The horse and buggy doctor. N.Y.: Harper, 1938. 322 p. DLC. In Kansas. See also his Ventures in Science (1944).

Hess, Joseph F., b. 1851. The [2624] autobiography of...Rochester, N.Y.: E. R. Andrews, printer, 1886. 140 p. DLC. Temperance lecturer who had been a prize fighter, and sailor on the Great Lakes.

Hess, Thomas, b. 1863. Life and [2625] experience...Reading, Pa.: 1920. 56 p. Auto., p. 5-16. DLC. Methodist clergyman in New Jersey.

Hesselbein, Alfred T. H., b.1896. [2626] Destiny. Astoria, N.Y.: 1937. 347 p. DLC. German adventurer who entered the U.S. illegally and managed a sports arena in Louisiana.

Heurich, Christian, b. 1842. Aus [2627] meinem Leben...Washington, D.C.: 1934. 141 p. DLC. German immigrant who operated a brewery in Washington, D.C.

Heustis, Daniel D., b. 1806. A [2628] narrative...Boston: Wilder, 1847. 168 p. WHi. American volunteer with Canadian forces during the thirties in the fighting with the British.

Hewitt, Edward Ringwood, [2629] b. 1866. Those were the days. N.Y.: Duell, Sloan & Pearce, 1943. 318 p. WHi. Mechanical engineer, inventor and manufacturer of trucks tells of the early days of aviation and automobiles.

Hewitt, Edward Ringwood, [2630] b. 1866. Secrets of the salmon. N.Y.: Scribner's, 1925. 159 p. DLC. The story of his fishing experiences.

Hewitt, Edward Ringwood, [2631] b. 1866. Telling on the trout... New & rev. ed. N.Y.: Scribner's, 1930. 216 p. DLC. The story of his fishing experiences.

Hewlett, Samuel Mudway, [2632] b. 1818. The cup and its conqueror;

or the triumphs of temperance... Boston: Redding & co., 1862. 124 p. Auto., p. 11-114. DLC. Temperance lecturer who had been a clerk on Mississippi steamboats, and a drunkard.

Hibbard, Angus S., b. 1860. Hello. [2633] Goodbye. My story of telephone pioneering. Chicago: McClurg, 1941. 266 p. WHi. By the General Superintendent of the A.T. & T.

Hibbard, Billy, b. 1771. Mem- [2634] oirs...2d ed. N.Y.: priv. pr., 1843. 474 p. WHi. Methodist clergyman in New York and in the New England States.

Hibernicus, b. 1779. Hibernicus; [2635] or, memoirs of an Irishman now in America...Pittsburgh: pr. by Cramer & Spear, 1828. 251 p. DLC. An Irishman who came to the U.S. in 1819. This book was written for the sales it might net the author, whose economic progress had been unsatisfactory.

Hickman, William A., b. 1815. [2636] Brigham's destroying angel... N.Y.: Geo. A. Crofutt, 1872. 219 p. DLC. Associate of Brigham Young in Utah and member of the Territorial Legislature.

Hicks, Albert W., 1820-1860. [2637] "Story of my life." (The life, trial, confession and execution of Albert W. Hicks the pirate and murderer ...N.Y.: Robert M. DeWitt, 1860.) p. 41-66. WHi. As described by the title.

Hicks, Clarence J. My [2638-2639] life in industrial relations...N.Y.: Harper, 1941. 180 p. WU. As described by the title.

Hicks, Edward, b. 1780. Mem- [2640] oirs...Phila.: Merrihew & Thompson, printers, 1851. 365 p. WHi. Minister of the Society of Friends in Pa.

Hicks, Mrs. Rachel (Seaman), [2641] b. 1789. Memoir of Rachel Hicks (written by herself) late of Westbury, Long Island, a minister in the Society of Friends...N.Y.: Putnam, 1880. 287 p. NN. In New York.

Hicks, Urban East, b. 1828. [2642] Yakima and Clickitat Indian wars, 1855 and 1856. Personal recollections. Portland, Oreg.: n.d. 20 p. IdU. In the Washington Territory.

Higbee, Mrs. Blanche Aurora [2643] (Son), b. 1856. The autobiography of a pioneer woman. Spokane: Knapp book store, 1935. 37 leaves. WaPS. French born teacher in Illinois, Michigan and Washington. Later she marries a Washington farmer.

Higginson, Alexander Henry, [2644] b. 1876. Try back; a huntsman's reminiscences. N.Y.: Huntington press, 1931. 227 p. NN. Experiences in hunting to hounds.

Higginson, Thomas Wentworth, [2645] 1823-1911. Cheerful yesterdays. Boston & N.Y.: Houghton Mifflin, 1901. 374 p. WU. New England abolitionist, historian, biographer.

Hightower, James. Happy hunt- [2646] ing grounds. Colorado Springs: pub. by the author, 1910. 151 p. CoU. The life of an Indian youth in 19th century Indian territory.

Higinbotham, Harlow Niles, [2647] 1838-1919. ...Memoir with brief autobiography...written and ed. by Harriet Monroe. Chicago: priv. pr., 1920. 62 p. ViLxW. Chicago merchant and philanthropist.

Hildebrand, C. D., b. 1840. [2648] Eighteen years behind the bars... 4th ed. Fort Wayne, Ind.: Gazette co., printers, 1884. 157 p. MoHi. The story of a robber outlaw whose career touched many states and extended to Cuba.

Hildebrand, Samuel S., 1836- [2649] 1872. Autobiography of the... renowned Missouri "Bushwhacker" ...Jefferson City: State times book and job printing house, 1870. 312 p. WHi. Robber, fugitive from justice.

Hildreth, James. Dragoon cam- [2650] paigns to the Rocky Mountains... by a Dragoon. N.Y.: Wiley & Long, 1836. 288 p. Auto., p. 2-250. DLC. Indian service, 1833-34.

Hilgard, Theodor Erasmus, [2651] b. 1780. Meine Erinnerungen. Heidelberg: 1860. 379 p. NN. German born lawyer who came to Illinois in 1836 where he became a horticulturist and viniculturist.

Hill, Alonzo. Sermon by Rev. [2652] Dr. Alonzo Hill (The pastor's record, a sermon...on the fortieth anniversary of his settlement...Cambridge: John Wilson, 1867. 66 p.) p. 3-41. MiD-B.

Congregational clergyman in Mass., 1827–67.

Hill, Mrs. Elizabeth (Freeman). [2653] The widow's offering...New London: D. S. Ruddock, printer, 1852. 1752. 179 p. DLC. An unhappy domestic tale of a cruel father, and the early death of her husband, a merchant sailor. Left alone with a child in New York, she opens a boarding house.

Hill, Emma Shepard. A danger- [2654] ous crossing and what happened on the other side. Denver: Bradford-Robinson, 1924. 206 p. DLC. The wife of a farmer in Colorado.

Hill, Frederic Stanhope, 1829– [2655] 1913. Twenty years at sea; or, leaves from my old log-books. Boston & N.Y.: Houghton Mifflin, 1893. 273 p. NN. Includes his experiences in the Navy during the Civil War.

Hill, George Handel, 1809–1849. [2656] Scenes from the life of an actor... by a celebrated comedian. N.Y.: Garrett & co., 1853. 246 p. NN. As described by the title.

Hill, Henry, 1795–1892. Recol- [2657] lections of an octogenarian. Boston: D. Lothrop & co., 1884. 195 p. NN. Early days in Catskill, N.Y.; business experiences in South America, 1817–1821.

Hill, Henry B., b. 1823. Jottings [2658] from memory from 1823 to 1901. Boston?: 1901? 128 p. DLC. Massachusetts cabin boy, cooper, who became a member of the Mass. state legislature.

Hill, James Langdon, b. 1848. [2659] My first years as a boy. Andover: Andover press, 1928. 356 p. DLC. In Iowa.

Hill, Mrs. Laura C. Laure; [2660] history of a blasted life. Phila.: Claxton, Remsen & Haffelfinger, 1872. 371 p. NN. Housewife in Mississippi.

Hill, Robert Greenberry, [2661] b. 1857. Ups and downs...San Diego: Bowman's printing co., 1930. 339 p. Auto., p. 9–77. DLC. Lawyer in Kentucky, banker in Louisiana.

Hill, Walter M., 1865–1952. [2662] Reminiscences...Cedar Rapids, Iowa: The Torch press, 1923. 13 p. DLC. Dealer in rare books.

Hill, William. Col. William [2663] Hill's memoirs of the revolution. Columbia: State historical commission of South Carolina, 1921. 36 p. WHi. As described by the title.

Hill, William B., b. 1843. Experi- [2664] ences of a pioneer evangelist of the northwest. N.p.: 1902. 344 p. NbHi. Seventh Day Adventist in Minnesota, Wisconsin, Nebraska, North Dakota. This is the same as his 1892 book of a similar title.

Hillquit, Morris, 1869–1933. [2665] Loose leaves from a busy life. N.Y.: Macmillan, 1934. 339 p. WHi. Lawyer, socialist in New York politics.

Hills, Oscar Armstrong, 1837– [2666] 1919. An autobiography. Wooster: 1905. 152 p. NN. Clergyman in Indiana, Ohio and California.

Hills, Mrs. Sabrina Ann (Loom- [2667] is), b. 1811. Memories. Cleveland: 1899. 57 p. WHi. Story of youth in New York.

Hillyer, Jane. Reluctantly told. [2668] N.Y.: Macmillan, 1926. 205 p. DLC. A story of mental illness.

Hinchman, Lydia S. (Mitchell), [2669] b. 1845. Recollections of Lydia S. (Mitchell) Hinchman. N.p.: 1929. 113 p. USlGS. The domestic tale of a woman in Pennsylvania who was married to a Quaker.

Hindman, David R., b. 1827. The [2670] way to my golden wedding. St. Joseph, Mo.: pub. by his children, 1908. 200 p. MoK. Presbyterian clergyman and farmer in Illinois, Missouri, Tennessee, Iowa and Kansas. Other experiences include mining in California and service with the Union army.

Hindus, Maurice Gershev, [2671] b. 1891. Green worlds. Garden City, N.Y.: Doubleday, 1938. 359 p. WU. The early life in Russia and in New York City of a noted literary figure.

Hines, David Theodore, b. 1810? [2672] Life, adventures and opinions... N.Y.: Bradley & Clark, 1849. 195 p. WHi. A braggadocio account of larceny and adultery by a man who claimed to have practiced medicine.

Hinkhouse, John F. Forty years [2673] of continuous active Iowa Presbyterian ministry...No imprint. 13 p. IaHi. Beginning with 1886.

Hinkle, James Fielding, b. 1864. [2674] Early days of a cowboy on the

Pecos. Roswell: 1937. 35 p. DLC. Beginning with 1884. The author later became Governor of New Mexico.

Hinley, Holmes, 1793-1866. [2675] Holmes Hinkley, an industrial pioneer, 1793-1866, ed. by Walter S. Hinchman, Cambridge: pr. at the Riverside press, 1913. 42 p. Auto., p. 15-29. DLC. Builder of locomotive steam engines in Boston.

Hinkson, Fred Oscar, b. 1855. [2676] Autobiography. Miami, Florida: 1929. Ia-Ha. A lawyer and member of the Iowa state legislature tells also of his early days, beginning about 1869, on an Iowa farm.

Hinsdale, Elizur Brace, b. 1831. [2677] Autobiography...N.Y.: J. J. Little, 1901. 84 p. WHi. New York lawyer and judge.

Hird, Mary Evan, b. 1873. [2678] Threads of memory...N.Y.: Harbor press, 1932. 317 p. Auto., p. 13-98, 197-317. DLC. An account of youthful days spent in Pennsylvania and Massachusetts.

Hitchcock, Alfred Marshall, [2679] b. 1868. A New England boyhood. N.p.: priv. pr., 1934. 153 p. NN. Boyhood days in New Hampshire and Connecticut, by a literary figure.

Hitchcock, Edward, 1793-1864. [2680] Reminiscences of Amherst College, historical, scientific, biographical, and autobiographical. Northampton, Mass.: 1863. Auto., p. 281-407. WHi. Geologist, teacher, president of Amherst, and Congregational clergyman.

Hitchcock, Embury Asbury, [2681] b. 1866. My fifty years in engineering...Caldwell, Idaho: Caxton printers, 1939. 277 p. WU. Mecanical engineer, professor of Engineering at Ohio State University.

Hitchcock, Mary Evelyn (Martin)[2682] b. 1889. Life was like that, by Mary Doyle (pseud.). Boston & N.Y.: Houghton Mifflin, 1936. 256 p. NN. Experiences as a newsstand girl at the Waldorf and Plaza hotels, an actress (for a little while), and as a New York reporter.

Hoagland, Henry Williamson, [2683] b. 1876. My life. Pomona: 1940.
138 p. DLC. Physician in Colorado and California.

Hoar, George Frisbie, 1826-1904.[2684] Autobiography of seventy years. N.Y.: Scribner's, 1903. 2 vols. WHi. Lawyer, U.S. Senator from Massachusetts.

Hoar, George Frisbie, 1826- [2685] 1904. A boy sixty years ago. Boston: Perry Mason, n.d. 40 p. WHi. A U. S. Senator tells of his boyhood in Concord.

Hobart, Chauncey, b. 1811. Recol-[2686] lections of my life. Fifty years of itinerancy in the Northwest. Red Wing, Minn.: Red Wing pr. co., 1885. 409 p. WHi. Methodist clergyman in the Old Northwest.

Hobart, Mrs. Garret A. Mem- [2687] ories. Paterson, New Jersey: 1930. 89 p. DLC. By the wife of a U.S. Vice President (1896), who tells of her life in Washington.

Hobart-Hampden, Augustus [2688] Charles, 1822-1886. Never caught; personal adventures connected with twelve successful trips in blockade-running during the American Civil War, 1863-4. By Captain Roberts (pseud.). London: J. C. Hotten, 1867. 123 p. NN. By an English Naval officer.

Hobbs, James, b. 1819. Wild life [2689] in the far west...Hartford, Conn.: Willey, 1874. 488 p. WHi. Hunter, trapper in the southwest; military service with Doniphan in Mexico; mining in California.

Hobson, Mrs. Elizabeth Christo-[2690] pher (Kimball), 1831-1912. Recollections of a happy life. N.Y.: Putnam, 1916. 253 p. WHi. Social worker who sought to improve hospitals and schools for Negroes in the South.

Hodgdon, Sam K. Town hall, [2691] to-night. N.p.: 1891. 93 p. DLC. An actor who played small towns across the country.

Hodgkins, Samuel, b. 1839. Auto-[2692] biography...compiled by Carrie E. Chatfield. Minneapolis: 1923. 47 p. Auto., p. 9-25. DLC. Union soldier, Minnesota farmer.

Hoffman, J. Jacob. Offener [2693] brief an alle herren pastoren, professoren und lehrer der erwürdigen "Synode von Missouri, Ohio und andern staaten". Milwaukee: Harold, 1881. 45 p. MnSL. Lutheran

Hoffman, John Jacob, b. 1842. [2694]
A true story, by Elpizon (pseud.).
New Orleans: 1915. 18 p. LNHT.
Lutheran clergyman, mission
worker in New Orleans.

Hoffman, Malvina, b. 1887. [2695]
Heads and tales. N.Y.: Scribner's,
1936. 416 p. WU. Sculpture who
sought ethnic types.

Hoffman, Richard, 1831-1909. [2696]
Some musical recollections of
fifty years. N.Y.: Scribner, 1910.
168 p. Auto., p. 61-157. WU. English pianist. The volume includes
a description of his experiences
in the U.S.

Hoffman, Ross John Swartz, [2697]
b. 1902. Restoration. N.Y.:
Sheed & Ward, 1934. 205 p. DLC.
A spiritual account by a convert
to Catholicism.

Hoffman, Ruth and Helen. We [2698]
married an Englishman. N.Y.:
Carrick & Evans, 1938. 314 p.
DLC. Twins, one of whom
married an Englishman, who lived
two years in Iraq.

Hoffman, Ruth and Helen. Our [2699]
Arabian nights. N.Y.: Carrick &
Evans, 1940. 307 p. DLC. See
preceding item. This books tells
of Bedouins, harem life, etc.

Hoffman, Wickham, 1821-1900. [2700]
Camp, court and siege; a narrative of personal adventure and observation during two wars—1861-65;
1870-71. N.Y.: Harper & bros.,
1877. 285 p. NN. Union army
officer. Diplomatic service in
Paris, 1870-71.

Hogan, Benedict, b. 1841? Ben [2701]
Hogan's wild career in both armies.
Bounty jumping, blockade running
and spying. Chicago: Radcliffe
and Manny, printers, 1887. 46 p.
DLC. A boisterous account of
service in the Civil War.

Hogan, Benedict, b. 1841? The [2702]
life and adventures...written by
George Francis Train. N.Y.?1878.
276 p. Auto., p. 1-238. DLC.
See the preceding item. In this
account much is related about
prize fighting, oil drilling, saloon
keeping.

Hogan, John J., b. 1829. On the [2703]
mission in Missouri, 1857-1868.
Kansas City: 1892. WHi. Irish
born Catholic missionary who
later became bishop of Kansas City.

Hogan, John J., b. 1829. Fifty [2704]
years ago...Kansas City, Mo.:
Hudson pub. co., 1907. 108 p. MoK.
Irish born Catholic tells of his
trip down the Mississippi River
as a Catholic missionary.

Hoinville, Charles H. Memories.[2705]
Chicago: 1944. 6 p. KHi. A domestic account of honeymoon, homes
and vacations.

Hoinville, Charles H. Away [2706]
back when. Chicago: 1945. 10 p.
KHi. Youth in Chicago.

Holbrook, Alfred, 1816-1909. [2707]
Reminiscences of the happy life
of a teacher. Cinc.: Elm street
pr. co., 1885. 362 p. NN. A pioneer
in the professional training of
teachers in the Middle West, whose
principal field of labor was in Ohio.

Holbrook, John C. Prairie[2708-2709]
breaking...Boston: Ira Bradley,
1863. 89 p. IaCrM. Congregational
clergyman in Iowa and Wisconsin,
roughly from 1840 to 1863.

Holbrook, John Calvin, 1808- [2710]
1900. Recollections of a nonagenarian of life in New England,
the Middle West, and New York,
including a mission to Great Britain
in behalf of the Southern Freedmen;
together with scenes in California.
Boston: The Pilgrim press, 1897.
351 p. NN. In earlier days a publisher and bookseller; later, a
Congregational minister.

Holbrook, Samuel F. Threescore[2711]
years...Boston: James French,
1857. 504 p. WHi. Sailor in U.S.
Navy, and miner in California in
1849.

Holcomb, James Foote, and [2712]
Helen H. In the heart of India...
Phila.: Westminster press, 1905.
251 p. Auto., p. 97-251. DLC.
Presbyterian missionaries.

Holcomb, Walter, b. 1853. Mem-[2713]
ories...N.p.: 1935. 47 p. DLC.
Minnesota lawyer who previously
had been a civil engineer employed
in railroad construction in the
southwest.

Holcombe, Henry, 1762-1824. [2714]
The first fruits...Phila.: pr. by
Ann Cochran, 1812. 228 p. TxU.
Baptist clergyman in Georgia
and Pennsylvania.

Holcombe, William Henry, 1825-[2715]
1893. How I became a homeopath.

Chicago: Halsey, 1869. 30 p. DLC.
The author practiced medicine in
Chicago, Cincinnati, and New
Orleans.

Holden, Frank Alexander. War [2716]
memories. Athens, Georgia:
Athens book co., 1922. 215 p. DLC.
First World War, in France.

Holden, William Woods, 1818– [2717]
1892. Memoirs...ed. by W. K.
Boyd. Durham: Trinity college
hist. soc., 1911. 199 p. WHi. Governor of North Carolina in period
of reconstruction.

Holder, Charles Frederick, [2718]
1851–1915. The log of a sea
angler; sport and
adventures in many seas with
spear and rod. Boston & N.Y.:
Houghton, Mifflin, 1906. 385 p.
NN. Fishing adventures, largely
in Florida.

Hollandersky, Abraham, b.1888. [2719]
Life story of Abe the newsboy...
N.Y.: 1930. 201 p. DLC. Newsboy
who was also a prize fighter.

Holley, James Arthur, b. 1854. [2720]
Recollections of a country doctor.
Boston: Meador, 1939. 126 p.
DLC. The locale is not indicated.

Holliday, George H. On the [2721]
plains in '65...N.p.: 1883. 97 p.
DLC. With the army on Indian
duty in Nebraska, Colorado,
Wyoming, Montana and the
Dakotas after the Civil War.

Hollister, John Hamilcar. [2722]
Memories of eighty years...
Chicago:1912. 240 p. Auto., p. 11–
161. WHi. Physician in Michigan
and Illinois.

Hollman, Frederick G., 1791– [2723]
1875. Autobiography...No imprint.
42 p. WHi. Lead mining and Indian
fighting on the frontier in Wisconsin and Illinois.

Holman, J. W., b. 1805. The [2724]
faith once delivered to the
saints...to which is added a short
account of the life...of the author
... Phila.: 1830. 144 p. Auto.,
p. 58–85. MWA. Clergyman of
the Church of God in Pennsylvania.

Holmes, Burton, b. 1870. Burton [2725]
Holmes and the travelogue; a
life story as told to Lothrop
Stoddard...Phila.: pr. by George
F. Lasher pr. co., 1939. 48 p.
DLC. World traveller, lecturer.

Holmes, David Eugene, b. 1858. [2726]
From cradle to commencement...
Sarasota, Florida: 1938. 35 p.
IaGG. Farm laborer and tenant
in Iowa in seventies, who later
became a teacher (about which
there is little in this account).
Includes college experiences in
Iowa.

Holmes, Ella Marie. Sowing seed [2727]
in Assam; missionary life and
labours in northeast India. N.Y.:
Revell, 1925. 195 p. DLC. Baptist
missionary worker.

Holmes, Robert D. Yankee in [2728]
the trenches. Boston: Little,
Brown, 1918. 214 p. NjP. First
World War.

Holmes, William Olmstead, [2729]
1894–1945. Time of my youth.
Reno: 1945. 78 p. NvHi. A story
of boyhood memories to which is
added his army experiences in
the first world war.

Holsapple, John Wright, b. 1854. [2730]
Autobiography of an octogenarian.
Temple, Texas: 1937. 166 p.
MoCanD. Kentucky school teacher,
farmer and clergyman of the
Christian Church.

Holsey, Lucius Henry, 1842?– [2731]
1920. Autobiography...Atlanta:
Franklin pr. & pub. co., 1898.
288 p. Auto., p. 9–30. WHi.
Negro Methodist clergyman in
Georgia.

Holstein, Anna Morris (Ellis), [2732]
1824–1901. Three years in field
hospitals of the Army of the
Potomac. Phila.: J. B. Lippincott,
1867. 131 p. NN. Nurse in the Civil
War.

Holstein, Mrs. William. See
Holstein, Anna Morris (Ellis).

Holt, Adoniram Judson, b. 1847. [2733]
Pioneering in the southwest.
Nashville: Sunday school board
of the Southern Baptist convention,
1923. 304 p. TxU. Baptist clergyman, missionary to Seminole
Indians in Southeastern and
Southwestern states.

Holt, Miss C. E. An autobio- [2734]
graphical sketch of a teacher's
life, including a residence in the
northern and southern states,
California, Cuba and Peru.
Quebec: pr. by J. Carrel, 1875.
104 p. DLC. Canadian who taught
some years in the U.S.

Holt, Clarence Eugene, b. 1874. [2735]

One life in Maine. Portland: Forest City pr. co., 1940. 190 p. DLC. Dentist and lumber operator.

Holt, Henry, 1840-1926. Garruli- [2736] ties of an octogenarian editor... Boston & N.Y.: Houghton Mifflin, 1923. 406 p. WHi. Book publisher in New York.

Holter, A. M. Pioneer lumber- [2737] ing in Montana. Portland, Ore.: The Timberman, n.d. 23 p. MnHi. Owner of timber lands and sawmill. The period covered is 1863-1898.

Holton, David Parsons. Remin- [2738] iscences. N.Y.?: 1874? 29 p. MiD-B. Physician in New York, beginning about 1830.

Holton, Isaac Farwell. New [2739] Granada; twenty months in the Andes. N.Y.: Harper, 1857. 605 p. DLC. A botanist tells of his trip to Colombia, 1852-54.

Holtzclaw, William Henry. The [2740] black man's burden. N.Y.: Neale, 1915. 232 p. WHi. Negro educator in New York. The period covered is the late 19th and early 20th century.

Home, Daniel D., b. 1833. Inci- [2741] dents in my life. N.Y.: Carleton, 1863. 315 p. Nv. English born medium who in the fifties was in New York and Massachusetts. Most of the book concerns his experiences abroad.

Homer, Sidney, b. 1864. My wife [2742] and I...N.Y.: Macmillan, 1939. 269 p. WU. Teacher of music tells of his life with an opera singer.

Hood, John Bell, 1831-1879. Ad- [2743] vance and retreat; personal experiences in the United States and Confederate armies. by J. B. Hood, lieutenant-general in the Confederate Army. New Orleans: pub. for the Hood orphan memorial fund, 1880. 358 p. NN. Covers 1849-1865.

Hooker, John, b. 1816. Some [2744] reminiscences of a long life. Hartford: Belknap & Warfield, 1899. 351 p. WHi. Lawyer, recorder of the State Supreme Court of Connecticut.

Hooker, Rufus W. Ship's doctor. [2745] N.Y.: McGraw-Hill, 1943. 279 p. NN. As described by the title.

Hooker, William Francis, 1846- [2746] 1938. Glimpses of an earlier Milwaukee. Milwaukee: The Milwaukee journal, 1929. 106 p. DLC. The author sold newspapers in Wisconsin, and for three years was a hunter and trader in Wyoming.

Hooker, William Francis, 1856- [2747] 1938. The prairie schooner. Chicago: Saul bros., 1918. 156 p. DLC. Ox-team driver in Wyoming who transported supplies from railroad to frontier settlements. Reissued later as the Bullwhacker.

Hooper, James, 1769-1842. Life [2748] and sentiments of James Hooper, minister of the gospel. Paris, Maine: G. W. Millett, printer, 1834. 72 p. MeWaC. In Maine.

Hooper, James W., b. 1827. [2749] Three score and ten in retrospect... Syracuse, N.Y.: C. W. Borden, 1900. 80 p. DLC. Educator in New York.

Hoopes, Grace Gertrude. Out [2750] of the running. Springfield: C.C. Thomas, 1939. 158 p. WU. The author suffered from congenital cerebral palsy.

Hoover, David, 1781-1866. Mem- [2751] oir...Richmond, Indiana: James Elder, 1857. 44 p. Auto., p. 9-20. DLC. Indiana pioneer who for 14 years was clerk of Wayne County.

Hoover, Mrs. Mildred (Brooke), [2752] 1872-1940. Mildred Crew Brooke, an unfinished manuscript of reminiscences. Casa del Oso: 1940. 110 p. CU-B. A domestic account. The author's husband was employed in California and in Europe.

Hope, Ben (pseud.). See Love, James Stanhope.

Hope, Bob, b. 1903. I never left [2753] home. N.Y.: Simon & Schuster, 1944. 207 p. DLC. The star of radio and movies tells of his entertaining servicemen in England and North Africa during the second World War.

Hopkins, Anson Smith, b. 1851. [2754] Reminiscences of an octogenarian. New Haven, Conn.: The Tuttle, Morehouse & Taylor co., 1937. 120 p. NN. Boyhood in Vermont; in the tile and ceramics business in Chicago; casualty insurance business in the East.

Hopkins, Arthur Warren. Pep, [2755] pills and politics. Brattleboro: Vermont pr. co., 1944. 239 p. WHi.

Physician in New England.

Hopkins, Claude C., b. 1866. My [2756] life in advertising. N.Y.: Harper & bros., 1927. 206 p. WU. As described by the title.

Hopkins, Frank Easton, 1863- [2757] 1933. The DeVinne & Marion presses; a chapter from the autobiography...Meriden: The Columbiad club , 1936. 61 p. DLC. Printer in New York.

Hopkins, John Henry, 1792-1868. [2758] Autobiography in verse...Cambridge: Riverside press, 1866. 121 p. WHi. Episcopal clergyman in Vermont.

Hopkins, Samuel, 1721-1803. [2759] Sketches...Hartford: Stephen West, 1805. 240 p. DLC. New England Congregational clergyman, chiefly remembered for his influence on New England theology. He was a voluminous writer on religious subjects.

Hopkins, Mrs. Sarah Winne- [2760] mucca, 1844?-1891. Life among the Piutes: their wrongs and claims; ed. by Mary T. P. Mann. N.Y.: G. P. Putnam's, 1883. 268 p. DLC. Life on an Indian reservation in Oregon and Washington, by a Piute Indian. As a young girl she lived in Nevada.

Hoppe, Willie, b. 1887. Thirty [2761] years of billiards...N.Y.: G. P. Putnam's sons, 1925. 255 p. Auto., p. 3-181. DLC. By the world's leading player of billiards.

Hopper, DeWolf, 1858-1935. [2762] Once a clown, always a clown: reminiscences...Boston: Little, Brown, 1927. 238 p. WU. Stage and screen actor.

Hopwood, Josephus, 1844-1935. [2763] A journey through the years; an autobiography. St. Louis, Mo.: The Bethany press, 1932. 206 p. NN. Teacher, college president, minister of the gospel, laboring in the Appalachian Mountain regions of Virginia, Tennessee, and North Carolina. The author was a member of the Disciples of Christ.

Horlacher, James Levi. A year [2764] in the oil fields. Lexington: Press of the Kentucky kernel, 1929. 68 p. DLC. In Texas, 1926-27.

Horn, Adam (alias). See Hellman, Andrew.

Horn, Henry Harcourt, b. 1845. [2765] An English colony in Iowa. Boston: Christopher pub. house, 1931. 91 p. DLC. English born farmer in Iowa in the period following 1865.

Horn, Robert Cannon, 1844- [2766] 1936. The annals of Elder Horn... N.Y.: Richard R. Smith, 1930. 225 p. WHi. Disciples of Christ, in Tennessee and Texas.

Horn, Tom, 1860-1903. Life of [2767] Tom Horn...Denver: Coble, 1904. 317 p. WHi. Scout for Chaffee, Crook and Miles in the southwest (Arizona), and Indian interpreter. Later he became a stock detective in Wyoming.

Horn, William, 1839-1917. Auto- [2768] biography of Bishop William Horn, 1839-1917. Cleveland: 1920. 23 p. DLC. Minor sect clergyman in the midwest.

Hornaday, William Temple, 1854-[2769] 1937. Thirty years war for wild life; gains and losses in the thankless task. N.Y.: C. Scribner's sons, 1931. 292 p. NN. Tells of his efforts in the movement for the protection of wild life.

Hornaday, William Temple,1854- [2770] 1937. Two years in the jungle. N.Y.: Charles Scribner's sons, 1885. 495 p. DLC. A naturalist in India, Ceylon, Borneo and the Malayan peninsula.

Hornby, Harry Paulson. Going [2771] around. Uvalde, Texas: Hornby press, 1945. 158 p. MoHi. Englishman in Texas, beginning with 1889. The author was a rancher, and editor and publisher of a newspaper.

Horner, John Meirs, b. 1821. [2772] Personal history...Honolulu: Hawaiian gazette co. print, 1898. 276 p. Auto., p. 247-76. CLSM. After his arrival in California in 1846, the writer became a farmer and then a flour manufacturer. After the business depression of the fifties, he became a sugar planter in Hawaii.

Horowitz, David, b. 1903. Thirty-[2773] three candles. N.Y.: World union press, 1949. 506 p. DLC. Jewish mystic who participated in the movement to provide a new translation of the Old Testament.

Horowitz, Louis Jay, b. 1875. [2774] The towers of New York; the memoirs of a master builder. N.Y.: Simon & Schuster, 1937. 277 p. NN. The author was one of the leading building construction men in the country, president of the Thompson-Starrett Company.

Horsley, Albert E., b. 1866. The [2775] confessions and autobiography of Harry Orchard (pseud.). N.Y.: McClure, 1907. 255 p. WU. Labor spy on the west coast.

Horst, Henry W. Homesteading [2776] in western Kansas, 1885-1892. Rock Island, Ill.: n.d. 157 p. KHi. As described by the title.

Horton, Emily McGowan. Our [2777] family. N.p.: 1922. CSfSP. Prior to crossing the plains to California, the author's youth in the fifties was spent in the midwest.

Horton, George. Recollections, [2778] grave and gay...Indianapolis: Bobbs-Merrill, 1927. 321 p. WHi. Diplomatic officer in Germany, Greece and Turkey, 1893-1924.

Horton, James P., b. 1769. A [2779] narrative...N.p.: 1839. 216 p. DLC. Methodist clergyman in New York.

Horton, Rufus Landon, b. 1861. [2780] Philosophy of modern life; an autobiography of a lawyer. Los Angeles: Time-Mirror press, 1929. 303 p. DLC. In California.

Horwich, Bernard, b. 1861. My [2781] first eighty years. Chicago: Argus, 1939. 426 p. WHi. A Lithuanian Jew tells of the life of an immigrant in America. The writer was a merchant in Chicago.

Hoshour, Samuel Klinefetter, [2782] 1803-1883. Autobiography... St. Louis: John Burns pub. co., 1884. 233 p. NN. Educator and clergyman of the Christian Church who labored mostly in Indiana.

Hostetler, Mrs. Martha Luella [2783] (Doggett). Sketches here and there along the way from the year 1856. Lincoln: 1938. 197 p. WHi. Wife of Nebraska businessman tells of her early days as a teacher, and then of her activities as a club-woman.

Hotchkiss, Willis Ray, b. 1873. [2784] Sketches from the dark continent. Cleveland: Friends Bible, 1901. 160 p. DLC. Quaker missionary in Africa for a period of four years.

Hotchkiss, Willis Ray, b. 1873. [2785] Then and now in Kenya Colony; forty adventurous years in East Africa. N.Y.: Fleming H. Revell, 1937. 160 p. NN. A record of missionary labors.

Hough, Emerson, 1857-1923. [2786] Getting a wrong start, a truthful autobiography. N.Y.: Macmillan, 1915. 234 p. DLC. A Virginian goes west to practice law, but turns to journalism and to the writing of of novels.

Hough, Henry Beetle. Country [2787] editor. N.Y.: Doubleday, Doran, 1940. 325 p. WU. In Massachusetts.

Hough, Jesse W. Fifty years of [2788] my life; a sermon preached... Nov. 26, 1882. Jackson: Daily citizen pr. house, n.d. 16 p. MiD-B. Congregational minister in Michigan.

Houghton, Mrs. Hadwin. See Wells, Carolyn.

Houghton, Mitchell B. See Houghton, William Robert.

Houghton, William Robert and [2789] Mitchell B. Houghton. Two boys... Montgomery: Paragon press, 1912. 242 p. OClWHi. Confederate soldiers. The autobiography of the first author is found within pages 57-152, and that of the second within pages 16-56.

House, Abigail, 1790-1861. [2790] Memoirs...Jefferson, Ohio: Ashtabula sentinel steam press, 1861. 264 p. Auto., p. 5-70. WHi. Spiritual account.

House, Mrs. Susan Adeline [2791] (Beers), b. 1850. A life for the Balkans...N.Y.: Revell, 1939. 208 p. WU. By the wife of a missionary in Turkey.

Houston, David Franklin. Eight [2792] years with Wilson's cabinet, 1913 to 1920...Garden City, N.Y.: Doubleday, Page, 1926. 2 vols. WHi. By Wilson's Secretary of Agriculture and Secretary of the Treasury.

Hovey-Colby, Mrs. Julia A. See Colby, Mrs. Julia A. (Hovey).

How, David D., 1776-1824. Life [2793] and confession of David H. How... by Joseph Badger, N.Y.?: 1824. 24 p. Auto., p. 5-12. DLC. Murderer in New York.

How, Mrs. Mary Jane (Gordon), [2794] 1816-1847. Life and confession... by J. S. Calhoun. Augusta: 1847. 32 p. DLC. Murderess in Maine.

Howard, Frances Thomas. In [2795]

and out of the lines...N.Y.: Neale, 1905. 238 p. NjP. A confederate soldier tells of his experiences in Georgia while that state was occupied by Federal troups.

Howard, Guy Wesley, b. 1891. [2796] Walkin' preacher of the Ozarks. N.Y.: Harper, 1944. 273 p. WHi. Itinerant clergyman.

Howard, James W., b. 1848. The [2797] life story...No imprint, 1931? 24 p. CoD. The author fought Indians on the plains, 1867-72; then he was a policeman in Wyoming and a teamster in Colorado; finally, he joined a cooperative community in Colorado.

Howard, Jennie E. In distant [2798] climes and other years. Buenos Aires: The American press, 1931. 136 p. DLC. An American who taught in Argentina.

Howard, John Raymond. Remem- [2799] brance of things past...N.Y.: Crowell, 1925. 405 p. WHi. Officer in Union Army.

Howard, Joseph, b. 1815. Life [2800] of Major Joseph Howard, an American dwarf. N.p.: 1854. 24 p. DLC. As described by the title. The author lived in Maine.

Howard, Kathleen. Confessions [2801] of an opera singer. N.Y.: Knopf, 1918. 273 p. DLC. As described by the title.

Howard, Leland Ossian. Fighting [2802] the insects...N.Y.: Macmillan, 1933. 333 p. WU. Entomologist.

Howard, McHenry. Recollec- [2803] tions of a Maryland Confederate soldier...Baltimore: Williams & Wilkins, 1914. 423 p. WHi. As described by the title.

Howard, Oliver Otis, 1830-1909. [2804] My life and experiences among our hostile Indians...Hartford: Worthington, 1907. 570 p. DLC. In Florida, Arizona, New Mexico, Oregon, Washington.

Howard, Oliver Otis, 1830-1909. [2805] Autobiography...N.Y.: Baker & Taylor, 1907. 2 vols. WHi. Indian fighter, officer in Union army and Commissioner of the Freedman's Bureau.

Howard, Robert Milton, b. 1834. [2806] Reminiscences. Columbus, Ga.: Gilbert pr. co., 1912. 346 p. DLC. Construction engineer in Alabama who later fought with the Confederacy.

Howbert, Irving, b. 1846. Mem- [2807] ories of a lifetime in the Pike's peak region. N.Y.: Putnam, 1925. 298 p. WHi. Banker, mining industrialist and Colorado State Senator.

Howe, Charles Oliver, 1822- [2808] 1915. What I remember. Macon: 1928. 91 p. DLC. Son of a farmer tells of his youth in Massachusetts.

Howe, Eber D., b. 1798. Auto- [2809] biography...No imprint. 59 p. NbHi. After serving in the war of 1812 the writer became a newspaper publisher in Ohio.

Howe, Edgar Watson, 1854-1937. [2810] Plain people. N.Y.: Dodd, Mead & co., 1929. 317 p. WHi. Kansas journalist and novelist.

Howe, Frederic Clemson, [2811] 1867-1940. The confessions of a reformer. N.Y.: Scribner, 1925. 343 p. WHi. A lawyer who engaged in political and economic movements.

Howe, Julia (Ward), 1819-1910. [2812] Reminiscences, 1819-1899. Boston & N.Y.: Houghton Mifflin, 1899. 465 p. WHi. New England abolitionist, woman suffragist, author of the Battle Hymn of the Republic.

Howe, Mark Antony DeWolfe, [2813] b. 1864. A venture in remembrance. Boston: Little, Brown & co., 1941. 319 p. NN. The author, writer of histories and biographies, tells of his literary career and of literary Boston.

Howell, Peter, b. 1805. The life [2814] and travels...Newbern: W. H. Mayhew, 1849. 320 p. DLC. Itinerant clergyman in Virginia, West Virginia and North Carolina.

Howells, William Cooper, 1815- [2815] 1894. Recollections of life in Ohio, 1813-1840. Cinc.: Robert Clarke, 1895. WHi. Journalist.

Howells, William Dean, 1837- [2816] 1920. My year in a log cabin. N.Y.: Harper, 1893. 62 p. WU. In 1850 on the Little Miami River.

Howells, William Dean, 1837- [2817] 1920. My literary passions. N.Y.: Harper & bros., 1895. 261 p. NN. A record of his reading and its influence on his own literary career.

Howells, William Dean, 1837- [2818] 1920. Literary friends and acquaintance...N.Y.: Harper, 1902. 291 p.

WU. The experiences of a literary man.

Howells, William Dean, 1837-1920. Boys town. N.Y.: Harper, 1904. 247 p. WU. The author's life from three to eleven. [2819]

Howells, William Dean, 1837-1920. Years of my youth. N.Y.: Harper, 1916. 239 p. WU. His college days and the years of the Civil War. [2820]

Howes, Osborn, 1806-1893. An autobiographical sketch. Boston: Barta, 1894. 53 p. WHi. Merchant sailor, and Boston merchant. [2821]

Hoxse, John, b. 1774. The Yankee tar...Northampton: pr. by John Metcalf, 1840. 200 p. DLC. Naval life, including engagements against the French in the period 1797-98. [2822]

Hoyt, Henry Franklin, 1854-1930. A frontier doctor. N.Y.: Houghton Mifflin, 1929. 260 p. DLC. The author was a cowboy and bartender in the Southwest. Later he was head of the Department of Health of St. Paul, and surgeon with the U.S. Army in the Philippines. [2823]

Hrdlicka, Ales, b. 1869. Alaska diary, 1926-1931. Lancaster: Catell press, 1943. 406 p. DLC. By an anthropologist. [2824]

Huard, Frances (Wilson), b.1885. My home in the field of honour. N.Y.: Doran, 1916. 302 p. DLC. The author's experiences in France during World War I. Her home was used by the Germans as an outpost. [2825]

Huard, Frances (Wilson), b.1885. My home in the field of mercy. N.Y.: Doran, 1917. 269 p. DLC. An American woman physician who during the first World War turned her French home into a hospital. [2826]

Huard, Frances (Wilson), b.1885. With these who wait. N.Y.: Doran, 1918. 249 p. DLC. The author's experiences in France during the first World War. [2827]

Hubbard, George, 1780-1853. George Hubbard's autobiography... New London: D.S. Duddock, 1852. 35 p. DLC. Lawyer, member of state legislature in Connecticut. [2828]

Hubbard, Gurdon Saltonstall, 1802-1886. Incidents and events... Chicago: Rand McNally, 1888. DLC. [2829] Fur trader in the Illinois area, 1818-1830.

Hubbard, Jeremiah. A teacher's ups and downs from 1858 to 1879. Richmond, Ind.: Palladium steam prntg. house, 1879. 216 p. KHi. In Indiana, Missouri and the Indian Territory. [2830]

Hubbard, Jeremiah, b. 1837. Forty years among the Indians... Miami, Florida: pr. by Phelps bros., 1913. 200 p. OkU. Quaker clergyman in the Indian territory west of the Mississippi. [2831]

Hubbard, John Milton. Notes of a private. Memorial ed. St. Louis: Nixon-Jones, 1913. 205 p. WHi. Confederate soldier. [2832]

Hubbard, Mary Ann, 1820-1909. Family memories. Pr. for private circulation, 1912. 146 p. DLC. A story of youth in Vermont, and of domestic life in Illinois and Iowa. [2833]

Hubbell, Charles Bulkley, 1853-1939. The recollections of an inconsequential man. Williamstown: 1928. 109 p. DLC. New York lawyer, member of the Public Service Commission. [2834]

Hubbell, R. M., b. 1840. Personal reminiscences. No imprint. 21 p. CoD. Confederate soldier. [2835]

Hubbell, Seth. A narrative of the sufferings of Seth Hubbell and family in his beginning a settlement in the town of Walcott, in the state of Vermont. Danville: E. & W. Eaton, printers, 1826. 24 p. WHi. As described by the title. [2836]

Huber, Samuel, 1782-1868. Autobiography of the Rev. Samuel Huber, elder in the church of the United Brethren in Christ... Chambersburg, Pa.: M. Kieffer, printer, 1858. 256 p. DLC. In Pennsylvania. [2837]

Hubert, Philip Gengembre, 1852-1925. Liberty and a living... N.Y.: Putnam's sons, 1889. 239 p. DLC. A city dweller tells of his life in the country. [2838]

Hudson, Bannus, 1848-1935. The memoirs...Sedalia, Mo.: Hurlbut, n.d. 57 p. KHi. Soldier in the Union army. [2839]

Hudson, Bell. A Pecos pioneer, by Mary Hudson Brothers. Albuquerque: Univ. of New Mexico [2840] press, 1943. 169 p. NmU. New Mexico pioneer, from 1878, who was a rancher, Indian fighter and hunter of outlaws.

Hudson, James, d. 1825. The life [2841] and confession of James Hudson ...written and published at the request of the deceased. By Samuel Woodworth. Indianapolis: pr. at the Gazette office, 1825. 24 p. In. Indiana farmer, executed for murder.

Hudson, John B., b. 1770. Nar- [2842] rative...Rochester: pr. by Wm. Alling, 1838. 176 p. CSmH. A Methodist clergyman, formerly a Baptist, in New York and Pa.

Hudson, Joshua Hilary, b.1832. [2843] Sketches and reminiscences. Columbia, S.C.: The State co., 1903. 198 p. DLC. Confederate soldier, later a lawyer and judge in South Carolina.

Hueston, Mrs. Ethel (Powelson), [2844] b. 1887. Preacher's wife. Indianapolis: Bobbs-Merrill, 1941. 308 p. DLC. Life in the home of a Methodist clergyman in Iowa, by the daughter of the "wife".

Huffman, James, 1840-1922. [2845] Ups and downs of a Confederate soldier. N.Y.: William E. Rudge's sons, 1940. 175 p. NN. As described by the title.

Hughes, Dan de Lara. South [2846] from Tombstone, a life story... London: Methuen, 1938. 311 p. DLC. Miner and cattleman in Arizona and northern Mexico.

Hughes, Edwin Holt. I was [2847] made a minister...Nashville: Abingdon Cokesbury, 1943. 328 p. WHi. Methodist clergyman in California, Massachusetts, Illinois and the District of Columbia.

Hughes, Henry, b. 1833. Auto- [2848] biography. Tr. from the Welsh. No imprint. 36 leaves. MnHi. Welshman who came to America in 1851. He was a coal miner in Ohio, and a farmer in Minnesota beginning 1855.

Hughes, John Wesley. The auto- [2849] biography of John Wesley Hughes, D.D. Louisville: Pentecostal pub. co., 1923. 295 p. KyU. Methodist clergyman in Kentucky who founded Asbury College, and Kingswood College.

Hughes, Langston. The big sea; [2850] an autobiography. N.Y.: Knopf, 1940. 335 p. WU. A Negro poet and novelist tells of his life to the age of 27. The account covers his struggles to make a living in Paris during the twenties, his life in Harlem, college days, and early success as a poet.

Hughes, Louis, b. 1832. Thirty [2851] years a slave. Milwaukee: South side pr. co., 1897. 210 p. DLC. After gaining his freedom, the author went North where he was first a laborer and then the owner of a laundry in Wisconsin.

Hughes, Nannie Worley, b.1842. [2852] Memories...No imprint. 85 p. IaHi. The author tells of her youth in Ohio and of her married life with a judge.

Hughes, William Edgar, b. 1840. [2853] The journal of a grandfather. St. Louis: 1912. CoD. After serving in the Confederate army, the writer became a banker and president of a railroad in Texas.

Hulbert, Mary (Allen), d. 1939. [2854] The story of Mrs. Peck...N.Y.: Minton, Balch & co., 1933. 286 p. NN. The life story of the author, whose name was associated with that of Woodrow Wilson in public rumor. This account tells much about her social life in Bermuda.

Hull, William, 1753-1825. Mem- [2855] oirs of the campaign of the North Western army of the United States, A.D. 1812...Boston: True & Greene, 1824. 229 p. WHi. An officer defends his military record.

Hume, Sophia, 1701-1774. An ex- [2856] hortation...Phila.: pr. by William Bradford, 1747. 158 p. DLC. Quaker in South Carolina.

Hummel, William, b. 1832. Auto- [2857] biography. No imprint, 1939? 3 leaves. MnHi. German who came as a child in forties to the U.S., where he was a farmer and merchant in the state of Minnesota.

Humphrey, James Lorenzo, [2858] b. 1829. Twenty-one years in India. Cinc.: Jennings & Graham, 1905. 283 p. DLC. By a medical missionary.

Humphrey, Seth King, 1864-1932. [2859] Following the prairie frontier. Minn.: Univ. of Minnesota, 1931. 264 p. WHi. The writer was a land inspector for a mortgage company in the Dakotas and Nebraska in the eighties.

Humphreys, Charles Alfred, [2860] b. 1838. Field, camp, hospital and prison in the Civil War, 1863–1865. Boston: press of Geo. H. Ellis, 1918. 428 p. NN. Chaplain, Union army.

Hundley, Will M. Squawtown, [2861] my boyhood among the last Miami Indians. Caldwell, Idaho: Caxton, 1939. 209 p. WHi. The locale is Indiana during the last quarter of the nineteenth century.

Huneker, James Gibbons, 1860– [2862] 1921. Steeplejack. N.Y.: Scribner's, 1921. 2 vols. WU. By a music critic in New York.

Hunt, Frazier, b. 1885. One [2863] American and his attempt at education. N.Y.: Simon & Schuster, 1938. WU. Newspaper reporter, chiefly abroad.

Hunt, George W., b. 1831. A his- [2864] tory of the Hunt family. Boston: press of McDonald, Gill & co., 1890. 79 p. Auto., p. 12–79. DLC. To Oregon with his father, where he became a farmer on the frontier.

Hunt, Harriet Kezia, 1805–1875. [2865] Glances and glimpses...including twenty years' professional life. Boston: John P. Jewett, 1856. 418 p. WHi. Social reformer who was especially interested in medical education for women.

Hunt, Isaac H. Astounding dis- [2866] closures. Three years in a mad house...Skowhegan: pr. for A.A. Mann, 1851. 84 p. Auto., p. 3–25. DLC. In Maine, 1844–47.

Hunt, Marion Palmer, b. 1860. [2867] The story of my life. Louisville: Herald press, 1941. 171 p. DLC. Baptist clergyman, mainly in Kentucky.

Hunt, Nancy A. By ox-team to [2868] California...No imprint. 14 p. CSmH. A story of youth in a pioneer Illinois family in the thirties.

Hunt, Thomas Poage, 1794–1876. [2869] Life and thoughts...an autobiography...Wilkes-Barre, Pa.: R. Baur, 1901. 400 p. DLC. Presbyterian clergyman in New England, New York and Pennsylvania who was active in the temperance movement.

Hunt, Una Atherton (Clarke), [2870] b. 1876. Una May; the inner life of a child. N.Y.: Scribner's, 1914. 268 p. NN. A childhood in Cincinnati and Washington. The account ends with the author's fourteenth year.

Hunt, Una Atherton (Clarke), [2871] Young in the "nineties." N.Y.: Scribner's, 1927. 313 p. NN. A continuation of the preceding item. Her youth in Washington.

Hunter, Dard, b. 1883. Before [2872] life began, 1883–1923. Cleveland: The Rowfant club, 1941. 115 p. DLC. Book designer, manufacturer of paper.

Hunter, George, b. 1835. Remin- [2873] iscences of an old-timer...3d. ed. Battle Creek: Review & Herald, 1888. 454 p. WHi. Hunter, miner, scout in the Pacific Northwest.

Hunter, Jane Edna (Harris), [2874] b. 1882. A nickel and a prayer. Nashville, Tenn.: The Parthenon press, 1940. 198 p. NN. The author, a Negro, tells of her early career as a nurse and of her later work in Cleveland, Ohio, where she founded the Phillis Wheatley Association for helping Negro girls.

Hunter, John. Strange incidents [2875] in Mexico, Hawaii, and the United States. La Feria, Texas: n.d. 142 p. TxH. Physician in Texas and Mexico.

Hunter, John Dunn, 1798–1827. [2876] Manners and customs of several Indian tribes located west of the Mississippi...Phila.: pub. for the author, 1823. 402 p. Auto., p. 9–142. DLC. After leaving the Indians, the author was a hunter and trapper.

Hunter, John Warren. A story of [2877] the Civil war period; heel-fly time in Texas. Bandera: Frontier Times, n.d., 47 p. TxU. By a Confederate soldier.

Hunter, Robert Hancock, 1813– [2878] 1902. Narrative...Austin: Cook pr. co., 1936. 41 p. KHi. An account of experiences in the war with Mexico, including the Battle of San Jacinto.

Hunter, Ruth. Come back on [2879] Tuesday. N.Y.: Scribner's sons, 1945. 265 p. NN. Career of a young American actress.

Hunter, Thomas, 1831–1915. [2880]

The autobiography...N.Y.: Knickerbocker press, 1931. 377 p. WU. New York educator.

Huntington, Daniel, 1774-1864. [2881] Memories, counsels and reflections...Cambridge: Metcalf, 1857. 119 p. MnHi. Calvinist clergyman in Massachusetts.

Huntington, Henry G. Memories; [2882] personages, people, places. London: Constable, 1911. 379 p. NN. An account of social life in Europe.

Huntington, William Reed, 1838- [2883] 1909. Twenty years of a Massachusetts rectorship. Worcester: press of Charles Hamilton, 1883. 39 p. NN. Episcopalian.

Huntington, Zebulon, 1766-1851. [2884] The exile of Connecticut...Enfield? 1845? 28 p. DLC. Vermont farmer tells of his disillusionment with the Shakers.

Huntington-Wilson, Francis [2885] Mairs, b. 1875. Memoirs of an ex-diplomat. Boston: Bruce Humphries, 1945. 373 p. WHi. Diplomatic officer in Far East and Europe who was also Assistant Secretary of State in the Taft administration.

Hunton, Addie D. and Johnson, [2886] Kathryn Magnolia. Two colored women with the American expeditionary forces. Brooklyn: Eagle press, 1920. 256 p. DLC. Y.M.C.A. workers during the first World War.

Hunton, Eppa, 1822-1908. Auto- [2887] biography...Richmond: William Byrd press, 1933. 268 p. DLC. Virginia lawyer and member of the U.S. House of Representatives. During the Civil War he was an officer in the Confederate army.

Hurst, Carlton Bailey, b. 1867. [2888] The arms above the door. N.Y.: Dodd, Mead & co., 1932. 377 p. DLC. Consul General in Europe, South America and the Caribbean area.

Hurst, I. S. Reminiscences... [2889] Los Angeles: Times-Mirror press, 1923. 170 p. WHi. Private detective who did much work for the Mexican government under Diaz.

Hurst, Lulu. See Atkinson, Lulu (Hurst).

Hurston, Zora Neale. Dust [2890] tracks on a road...Phila.: Lippincott, 1942. 294 p. WU. Anthropologist (Negress).

Huse, Caleb, 1831-1905. The sup- [2891] plies for the Confederate army... Boston: pr. by T. R. Marvin, 1904. 34 p. WHi. Confederate officer who was purchasing agent in England for the Confederacy.

Husing, Edward Britt, b. 1901. [2892] Ten years before the mike... N.Y.: Farrar & Rinehart, 1935. 298 p. NN. Career of a radio broadcaster.

Hussey, Tacitus, b. 1832. Begin- [2893] nings; reminiscences of early Des Moines. Des Moines: Am. lithographing co., 1919. 221 p. Auto., p. 187-197. IaHi. By a printer and newspaper publisher.

Huston, George, b. 1821. Mem- [2894] ories of eighty years. Morganfield: Sun print, 1904. 153 p. MoHi. Kentucky lawyer tells of his youth on a pioneer farm.

Hutcheson, Joseph. Autobio- [2895] graphical letter. (European school days...by Jane Hutcheson Windom. Princeton: 1931.) p. 1-17. DLC. Ohio banker.

Hutchins, Elias, b. 1783. The [2896] old sailor...Biddeford: Eastern journal job office, 1854. 47 p. DLC. Merchant sailor and member of U.S. Navy for a period of 40 years.

Hutchins, Jere Chamberlain, [2897] b. 1851. Jere C. Hutchins, a personal story. Detroit: 1938. 372 p. NN. Newspaper work in Texas; railroad construction in the Southwest; street railways in Detroit, Michigan.

Hutchins, Levi, 1761-1855. Auto- [2898] biography...Cambridge: 1865. 188 p. WHi. Manufacturer of clocks in New England.

Hutchinson, Edward Howard, [2899] b. 1852. Eighty years of activity. Buffalo: priv. pr., 1932. 181 p. DSI. Banker, builder, local political figure in Buffalo. Only 6 pages of this work are autobiographical.

Hutchinson, Forney, b. 1875. My [2900] treasure chest...Atlanta: Banner press, 1943. 213 p. DLC. Methodist clergyman who served mainly in Arkansas and Oklahoma.

Hutchinson, John W. The book [2901] of the Brothers (second series) being a history of the adventures of John W. Hutchinson and his family in the camps of the Army of the Potomac. Boston: S. Chism, 1864. 24 p. WHi. The author and his family sang for the entertainment of the soldiers.

Hutchison, Mrs. Eloise Paxton, b. 1874. Out of the past. Shreveport: 1943. 193 p. WHi. A lay worker for the Baptists, wife of a businessman tells of her domestic life in Arkansas and Louisiana. [2902]

Hutchison, James Lafayette. China hand. Boston, N.Y.: Lothrop, Lee & Shepard, 1936. 418 p. DLC. Sales representative for American firm in China in twentieth century. [2903]

Hutchison, Thomas S. An American soldier under the Greek flag at Bezanie...Nashville: Greek-American pub. co., 1913. 261 p. WU. An American in the Balkans during the first World War. [2904]

Hutslar, Charles Frederick, b. 1877. Along the way...Pasadena: 1942. 219 p. MoCanD. Clergyman of the Christian Church in California and West Virginia. [2905]

Hutton, Laurence, b. 1843. A boy I knew...8th ed. N.Y.: Harper, 1901. 116 p. WU. A bibliophile tells of his youth in New York. [2906]

Hutzel, Emerson E., b. 1890? Memories of days that were. St. Louis?: 1944? 54 p. MiU-H. The story of youth spent in Michigan. [2907]

Hyde, Charles Leavitt, b. 1860. Pioneer days...N.Y.: Putnam, 1939. 286 p. WHi. Cowboy, rancher, real estate promoter in South Dakota. [2908]

Hylan, John F. Autobiography. N.Y.: Rotary press, 1922. 93 p. WHi. Lawyer and politician in New York. [2909]

Hynes, William Francis. Soldiers of the frontier. Denver: 1943. 208 p. CoHi. Indian fighting by a soldier in the Dakota Territory. [2910]

Hyrew, Frederic, b. 1812. The dispensation...Boston: Alfred Mudge, 1870. 59, 56 p. Auto., p. 1-59. MH. Story of visions seen by a Russian born religious fanatic who lived in New York. [2911]

# I

Ickes, Harold Le Claire. Autobiography of a curmudgeon. N.Y.: Reynal & Hitchcock, 1943. 343 p. WHi. Chicago journalist who served with the propaganda office in the first World War, and later became a member of the cabinet of F.D.R. [2912]

Ide, Jacob. A pastor's review.. on the fifteenth anniversary of the author's ordination...Boston: Congregational board of publications, 1864. 72 p. WHi. Congregational clergyman in Mass. [2913]

Ide, William Brown, 1796-1852. Who conquered California?... Claremont: 1882. 137 p. Auto., p. 17-125. CSmH. In which the author presents his claim to be known as the organizer and leader in the conquest of California. This is a reprint of the same material published under another title in 1880. [2914]

Iles, Elijah, b. 1796. Sketches of early life and times in Kentucky, Missouri and Illinois. Springfield: Springfield pr. co., 1883. 64 p. KHi. The writer tells of his youth on a Kentucky farm, of clerking in a Missouri store, and of dealing in livestock in Illinois. He also saw military service in the Black Hawk War, 1832. [2915]

Imbs, Bravig. Confessions of another young man. N.Y.: Henkel-Yewdale, 1936. 302 p. WU. Poet, novelist. [2916]

Ingalls, Joshua King, b. 1816. Reminiscences of an octogenarian in the fields of industrial and social reform. Elmira: Gazette co., 1897. 198 p. IaGG. New York reformer, interested mainly in land ownership and temperance. [2917]

Ingersoll, Ernest, b. 1852. Knocking round the Rockies. N.Y.: Harper, 1883. 218 p. DLC. The writer served four years with U.S. geological surveyors in Colorado and Wyoming. [2918]

Ingerson, Carl Alfred, b. 1884. Musings of a coroner. St. Paul: Metropolitan print shop, 1927. [2919]

MnHi. Minnesota physician and coroner tells of his life in poetry.

Ingham, William Harvey, 1827- [2920] 1914. Ten years on the Iowa frontier. No imprint. IaHi. In the fifties on a farm.

Ingraham, Charles Anson. The [2921] years of my pilgrimage... Cleveland, Ohio: Central pub. house, 1927. 139 p. USlGS. Physician in New York, 1878-83, who became a newspaper writer and lay worker for the Congregational Church, and a social reformer.

Ingram, Orrin Henry, b. 1830. [2922] Autobiography...Eau Claire, Wis.: 1912. 83 p. WHi. The author was part of the lumber industry in New York, Canada and Wisconsin.

Irelan, Elma. Fifty years with [2923] our Mexican neighbors. St. Louis: Bethany press, 1944. 131 p. DLC. Missionary for the United Christians in Mexico.

Ireland, James, 1748-1806. The [2924] life of the Rev. James Ireland. Winchester, Va.: pr. by J. Foster, 1819. 232 p. Auto., p. 6-197. DLC. Baptist preacher in Virginia who was born in Scotland.

Irvine, Alexander Fitzgerald, [2925] 1863-1941. From the bottom up; the life story of Alexander Irvine. N.Y.: Doubleday, Page & co., 1910. 304 p. NN. Early life in Ireland and England; early struggles in this country; work as a Congregational minister with the down and out; gradual conversion to Socialism, and efforts to further the social aspects of religion. Ends with his connection with the Church of the Ascension, New York City.

Irvine, Alexander Fitzgerald, [2926] 1863-1914. A Yankee with the soldiers of the King. N.Y.: Dutton, 1923. 225 p. DLC. Irish born American Congregational clergyman who lectured to British troops during the first World War.

Irvine, Alexander Fitzgerald, [2927] 1863-1941. Fighting parson... Boston: Little, Brown, 1930. 289 p. WHi. This account goes over the same ground covered by the two preceding items.

Irving, Frederick Carpenter, [2928] b. 1883. Safe deliverance. Boston: Houghton Mifflin, 1942. 308 p. WU. Boston physician.

Irwin, David, b. 1911. Alone [2929] across the top of the world; the authorized story of the Arctic journey of David Irwin (as told to John Sherman O'Brien). Chicago: Winston, 1935. 254 p. DLC. Explorer in search of a lost expedition.

Irwin, William Henry, 1873- [2930] 1948. Making of a reporter. N.Y.: Putnam, 1942. 440 p. WU. Newspaper reporter in New York, and editor of McClure's.

Isaacs, Nicholas Peter, b. 1784. [2931] Twenty years before the mast... N.Y.: J. P. Beckwith, 1845. 199 p. DLC. Norwegian born sailor who settled in New York and who was impressed into the British Navy during the War of 1812.

Isbell, F. A. Mining and hunting [2932] in the far west, 1852-1870. Burlingame: William P. Wreden, 1948. 36 p. CSmH. In California and Idaho.

Isely, Mrs. Elise Dubach. Sun- [2933] bonnet days, as told to Bliss Isely. Caldwell, Idaho: Caxton, 1935. 219 p. WHi. A Swiss born girl tells of her life as a wife on a pioneer farm in Kansas. The story closes about 1890.

Israelson, Andrew Martin, [2934] b. 1857. Utah pioneering...Salt Lake City: Deseret news press, 1938. 328 p. Auto., p. 17-28. WHi. Cattle farmer born in Norway.

Ives, Ella Gilbert, 1847-1913. [2935] The evolution of a teacher. Boston: Pilgrim press, 1915. 188 p. DLC. In Chicago, and later in New England.

Ives, Frederick Eugene, 1856- [2936] 1937. The autobiography of an amateur inventor. Phila.: press of Innes & sons, 1928. 98 p. NN. Inventor of photoengraving and color photography processes.

Ives, Levi Silliman, 1797-1867. [2937] The trials of a mind in its progress to Catholicism. Boston: Donahoe, 1854. 233 p. ICMILC. Episcopal clergyman in North Carolina who turned to Catholicism.

Ivey, Joseph Benjamin, b. 1864. [2938] My memories. Greensboro, N.C.: The Piedmont press, 1941. 400 p. NN. Career of a leading North

## J

Jacks, Leo Vincent, b. 1896. [2939] Service record, by an artilleryman. N.Y.: Scribner, 1928. 303 p. DLC. In France during the first World War.

Jackson, Andrew, b. 1815. [2940] Narrative...written by a friend. Syracuse: 1847. 120 p. Auto., p. 7-23. MB. Slave in Kentucky who escaped to New York where he delivered lectures on slavery.

Jackson, Chevalier, b. 1865. The [2941] life of Chevalier Jackson... N.Y.: Macmillan, 1938. 229 p. WU. Physician.

Jackson, Daniel, b. 1804. Re- [2942] ligious experiences...Cinc.: Applegate, 1859. 214 p. CSmH. Baptist clergyman in New England and in Tennessee.

Jackson, Drury Wellington, [2943] b. 1836. Autobiography...Fulton: Baptist flag pub. co., 1913. 80 p. DLC. Baptist clergyman in Texas.

Jackson, James Albert, 1840- [2944] 1921. Autobiography. Madison: State historical society of Wis., 1945. 58 p. WHi. Wisconsin physician.

Jackson, James F. Reminis- [2945] cences. Boston: priv. pr., 1932. 121 p. MWA. Lawyer and chairman of the Mass. State Railroad Commission, 1899-1908.

Jackson, Mattie Jane. The story [2946] of Mattie J. Jackson...written... by Dr. L.S. Thompson...as given by Mattie. Lawrence: pr. at Sentinel office, 1866. 34 p. CSmH. Slave.

Jackson, Thomas Jonathan, 1824-[2947] 1863. "Old Jack" and his foot-cavalry; or, a Virginian boy's progress to renown. A story of the war in the Old Dominion. N.Y.: J. Bradburn, 1864. 300 p. NjP. Civil War account.

Jackson, William, b. 1794. The [2948] man of sorrows...3d ed., rev., enl. Boston: priv. pr., 1842. 420 p. MH. English born Methodist who became a Baptist, serving in Mass. and Pa.

Jackson, William Henry, 1843- [2949] 1942. The pioneer photographer; Rocky Mountain adventures with a camera. Yonkers-on-Hudson: World book co., 1929. 314 p. MH. See the entry that follows.

Jackson, William Henry, 1843- [2950] 1942. Time exposure...N.Y.: Putnam, 1940. 341 p. WHi. Photographer employed by U.S. Geological Survey and by Jay Gould.

Jacobs, Mrs. Harriet (Brent). [2951] Incidents in the life of a slave girl...Boston: priv. pr., 1861. 303 p. WHi. As described by the title.

Jacobs, Helen Hull, b. 1908. Be- [2952] yond the game; an autobiography. Phila.: Lippincott, 1936. 275 p. NN. Career of the tennis star.

Jacobs, Orange. Memoirs... [2953] Seattle: 1908. 234 p. Auto., p. 11-138. WHi. Member of the Legislature and Chief Justice in the Washington Territory.

Jacobs, Thomas Jefferson. [2954] Scenes, incidents and adventures in the Pacific...under Capt. Benj. Morrell. N.Y.: Harper, 1844. 372 p. DLC. A description of events during an exploring expedition in the Pacific.

Jacobs, Thornwell, b. 1877. Step [2955] down, Dr. Jacobs...Atlanta: Westminster, 1945. 1094 p. Auto., p. 1-405. DLC. President of Oglethorpe University in Georgia.

Jacobs, Victor, b. 1858. Thirty [2956] years of ups and downs of a commercial traveller...Chicago?: 1911. 82 p. DLC. A German born salesman who became a manufacturer of clothes in Chicago.

James, Doris. My education at [2957] Piney Woods school. N.Y.: Revell, 1937. 85 p. DLC. A white woman, employed as an office worker, tells of her experiences in a Negro school in Mississippi.

James, Frank, d. 1926. The only [2958] true history of the life of Frank James, written by himself. Pine Bluff: Norton pr. co., 1926. 134 p. TxU. The authenticity of this outlaw story has been challenged by R.F. Adams in his, Six-guns &

Saddle Leather.

James, Henry, 1843-1916. A [2959] small boy and others. N.Y.: Scribner, 1913. 419 p. WU. The story of his youth, to 1855.

James, Henry, 1843-1916. Notes [2960] of a son and brother. N.Y.: Scribner, 1914. 515 p. WU. This account covers his education during the years 1855-1870. The early years were spent mainly in Europe. James later attended Harvard.

James, Henry, 1843-1916. The [2961] middle years. N.Y.: Scribner, 1917. 119 p. NN. Early English memories.

James, Henry B. Memories of [2962] the Civil war. New Bedford: F. E. James, 1898. 133 p. WHi. Union Army.

James, Jason W., b. 1843. Memorable events...No imprint, 1911? [2963] 150 p. TxU. The account relates author's experiences in Louisiana during Reconstruction and his later life as a rancher in Texas.

James, Jason W., b. 1843. Memories and viewpoints. Roswell: [2964] priv. pr., 1928. 183 p. Auto., p. 15-85. MoSHi. During 1858-61 the author was a hunter on the plains, after which he served in the Confederate army.

James, Jesse E., b. 1875. Jesse [2965] James, my father. Kansas City: J. James, jr., 1899. 198 p. Auto., p. 5-13, 116-198. DLC. After the death of his famous outlaw father, the author tells of his fight to escape the charge of train robbery in Missouri.

James, John, b. 1852. My experience with Indians...Austin: [2966] Gammel's book store, 1925. 147 p. WHi. A white teacher of Indians in Texas.

James, Marquis, b. 1891. The [2967] Cherokee strip. A tale of an Oklahoma boyhood. N.Y.: Viking, 1945. 294 p. WHi. A writer tells of his early years.

James, Thomas, 1782-1847. [2968] Three years among the Indians and Mexicans. St. Louis: Missouri state historical soc., 1916. 316 p. WHi. Trader and trapper in the Southwest.

James, Will, 1892-1942. Lone [2969] cowboy; my life story...N.Y.: Scribner, 1930. 431 p. WHi. In the West, from north to south.

James, Winton Lee, p. 1858. [2970] Frontier and pioneer recollections of early days in San Antonio and west Texas. San Antonio: 1938. 210 p. Auto., p. 39-86. TxH. Hunter and sheep rancher. This account closes with 1882.

Jamison, James Carson, 1830- [2971] 1916. With Walker in Nicaragua... Columbia, Mo.: 1909. 181 p. WHi. In the fifties.

Jamison, Matthew H., b. 1840. [2972] Recollections of pioneer and army life. Kansas City: Hudson press, 1911. 363 p. WHi. About one-half of this book is an account of his boyhood in the Mississippi Valley. The remainder is the story of his life in the army during the Civil War.

Janis, Elsie, b. 1889. So far, so [2973] good. N.Y.: E. P. Dutton, 1932. 344 p. WU. Star of stage and screen.

Janney, Samuel Macpherson, [2974] 1801-1880. Memoirs...Phila.: Friend's book association, 1881. 309 p. WHi. Quaker minister in Virginia.

Jansen, Peter, b. 1852. Memoirs [2975] ...No imprint, 1921? 140 p. NbHi. Russian born farmer and sheep raiser in Nebraska who in 1898 became a member of the state legislature.

Janson, Kristofer Nagel, 1841- [2976] 1917. Hvad jeg har oplevet... Copenhagen: Gyldendalske, 1913. 276 p. WU. Norwegian born novelist and Unitarian minister who served in Minnesota and Wisconsin, 1881-1893.

Jaques, Mary J. Texan ranch [2977] life...London: Horace Cox, 1894. 363 p. TxU. Much of this is a travel account, but there is also described a stay of 20 months on a ranch in Texas. The author was born in England.

Jaquith, James, b. 1781. The [2978] history of James Jaquith...N.p.: 1830. 36 p. WHi. A frontier account. The author was a farmer in New Hampshire and a teacher in Kentucky and Tennessee.

Jarman, William. ...Uncle [2979] Sam's abscess...Exeter: pr. at H. Leduc's steam printing works, 1884. 194 p. CU-B. By a member of the Mormon priesthood. The author was born in England.

Jarratt, Deveraux, 1773-1801. [2980] The life...Baltimore: 1806. 223 p. WHi. Episcopal clergyman in Virginia.

Jarves, James Jackson, 1818- [2981] 1888. Why and what am I? The confessions of an inquirer. In three parts. Part I. Heart-experience; or, The education of the emotions. Boston: Phillips, Sampson & co., 1857. 320 p. NN. The writer was a well-known art collector.

Jay, Allen, 1831-1910. Autobio- [2982] graphy...Phila.: John C. Winston co., 1910 421 p. DLC. Quaker minister and educational leader whose work took him to Indiana, Maryland and Rhode Island.

Jayson, Lawrence M. Mania. [2983] N.Y.: Funk & Wagnalls, 1937. 263 p. WU. The author's experiences in a mental asylum.

Jefferson, Joseph, 1829-1905. [2984] The autobiography of Joseph Jefferson. N.Y.: The Century co., 1890. 501 p. WHi. Actor.

Jefferson, Thomas, 1743-1826. [2985] Autobiography. (In: The complete Jefferson...assembled by Saul K. Padover. N.Y.: Duell, Sloan & Pearce, 1943.) p. 1119-1194. DLC. Covers to the year 1790.

Jelliffe, Belinda (Dobson), [2986] b. 1892. For dear life. N.Y.: Scribner's, 1936. 355 p. NN. Trials of a woman whose ambition for an education led her to leave her North Carolina home and who finally through perseverance became a trained nurse in in New York City.

Jemison, Mary, 1743-1833. The [2987] narrative...20th ed. N.Y.: Am. scenic and historic preservation society, 1918. 144 p. WHi. The story of a woman who was captured by the Indians and who willingly lived with them her entire life.

Jenkins, A. B. The salt of the [2988] earth. Salt Lake City: Deseret news, 1939. 78 p. UHi. The author developed the Bonneville Salt Flats in Utah, for racing automobiles.

Jenkins, Burris Atkins, 1869- [2989] 1945. Facing the Hindenburg line...N.Y.: Revell, 1917. 256 p. WU. A war correspondent tells of his adventures in 1917.

Jenkins, Burris Atkins, 1869- [2990] 1945. Where my caravan has rested. Chicago: Willett, Clark, 1939. 241 p. WHi. Clergyman of the Disciples of Christ in Kansas City, journalist and teacher.

Jenkins, C. Francis, b. 1867. [2991] The boyhood of an inventor. Wash.,D.C.: 1931. 273 p. OrPU. On a farm in Indiana. The author, who writes in the third person, describes his later inventions in the field of radio and movies. The account closes with the year 1930.

Jenkins, James, b. 1764. Experi- [2992] ence, labours...N.p.: 1842. 232 p. WHi. Methodist clergyman in South and North Carolina.

Jenkins, James, 1809-1885. Auto- [2993] biography. Oshkosh: Hicks print. co., 1889. 110 p. WHi. Merchant sailor.

Jenkins, James Gilbert, 1834- [2994] 1864. Life and confessions... arranged for the press by R. E. Wood. Napa City: C. H. Allen and R. E. Wood, 1864. 56 p. CSmH. Murderer and highway robber who visited many states.

Jenkins, Malinda (Plunkett), [2995] b. 1848. Gambler's wife. Boston & N.Y.: Houghton Mifflin, 1933. 296 p. NN. Life in Indiana, Texas, Washington, Idaho, Oregon, California and Alaska.

Jennings, Alphonso J., b. 1863. [2996] Beating back. N.Y.: Appleton, 1914. 354 p. WHi. Criminal lawyer in Oklahoma who previously had served a prison term for robbery of a train.

Jennings, Alphonso J., b. 1863. [2997] Through the shadows with O. Henry. N.Y.: H. K. Fly co., 1921. 320 p. DLC. An Oklahoma outlaw tells of his life in prison and of his friendship with O. Henry.

Jennings, Henry C. A story of [2998] fifty years, 1871-1921. N.p.: Methodist book concern, 1921. 44 p. WHi. Methodist clergyman in Minnesota.

Jennings, Napoleon Augustus, [2999] 1850-1919. A Texas ranger. Dallas: Southwest press, 1930. 287 p. WHi. In the seventies.

Jensen, Carl Christian. An [3000] American saga. Boston: Little, Brown, 1927. 219 p. WHi. A social worker tells of her life as an immigrant from Denmark.

Jensen, M. C. En dansk- [3001] Amerikansk prästs erindringer fra 1888-94. Copenhagen: Woels, 1927. 127 p. MnHi. Lutheran clergyman in Iowa and Minnesota. The author was born in Denmark.

Jensen, P. Minder gennem [3002] halvfjerd-sindstyve aar. Cedar Falls, Iowa: Dannevirkes trykkeri, 1920. 142 p. MoHi. Pioneer clergyman from Denmark who served in Nebraska, Dakota, Iowa and Wisconsin.

Jenson, Andrew. Autobiography [3003] ...Salt Lake City: Deseret news, 1938. 670 p. WHi. Historian and biographer of the Mormons.

Jerger, Joseph Ambrose, b.1880. [3004] Doctor—here's your hat; the autobiography of a family doctor. N.Y.: Prentice-Hall, 1939. 279 p. NN. Experiences of a general practitioner both in Chicago and in Waterloo, Iowa.

Jeritza, Maria. Sunlight and [3005] song. N.Y. & London: Appleton, 1924. 262 p. DLC. Austrian-born opera star who performed often in the U.S.

Jernigan, Charles Brougher, [3006] b. 1863. From the prairie schooner to a city flat. Brooklyn: 1926. 140 p. DLC. Cowboy, then Methodist evangelist in Texas, Oklahoma and New York.

Jerome, Chauncey, 1793-1868. [3007] History of the American clock business for the past sixty years, and life of Chauncey Jerome, written by himself...New Haven: F. C. Dayton, Jr., 1860. 144 p. NN. The author was a leading clock maker during the first half of the nineteenth century.

Jessel, George Albert, b. 1898. [3008] So help me. N.Y.: Random, 1943. 240 p. NN. Star of the entertainment world.

Jessup, Henry Harris, 1832- [3009] 1910. Fifty-three years in Syria. N.Y.: Revell, 1910. 2 vols. WHi. By a Presbyterian missionary.

Jeter, Henry Norval, b. 1852. [3010] Forty-two years experience as a pastor. No imprint. 48 p. PCA. Negro Baptist clergyman in Rhode Island. The book contains only a few scattered references to the details of his life.

Jeter, Jeremiah Bell, 1802-1880.[3011] The recollections of a long life. Richmond, Va.: The Religious Herald co., 1891. 325 p. NN. Baptist clergyman, Negro, whose principal field of labor was in Virginia.

Jett, Curtis, b. 1875. From [3012] prison to pulpit...Louisville, Ky.: Kentucky Pentacostal pub. co., 1919. 79 p. Auto., p. 5-31. DLC. The author, a student attending a theological seminary in Kentucky, tells of his conversion while in prison.

Jewel, Mrs. Adele M., b. 1834. [3013] A brief narrative of the life of Mrs. Adele M. Jewel, being deaf and dumb...Ann Arbor: Chase's steam pr. house, 1869. 24 p. MiD-B. In Michigan.

Jewett, Albert Henry Clay, [3014] 1841-1898. A boy goes to war. Bloomington, Ill.: 1944. 73 p. MB. Covers 1860-64.

Jewett, Charles, 1807-1879. [3015] A forty years' fight with the drink demon, or A history of the temperance reform as I have seen it, and of my labor in connection therewith. N.Y.: National temperance society & pub. house, 1872. 407 p. NN. Recollections of the early temperance movement.

Jewett, Mary. Reminiscences of [3016] my life in Persia. Cedar Rapids: Torch press, 1909. 187 p. IaU. By a missionary, who went to Persia in 1871.

Jex, Mrs. Eliza (Goodson), [3017] b. 1826. In memoriam. Spanish Fork, Utah: Spanish Fork press, 1921. 55 p. USlGS. A Mormon, born in England, who came to Utah about 1855. The writer accepted the system of plural marriages.

Johonnot, Jackson. The remark-[3018] able adventures of Jackson Johonnet (sic) of Massachusetts... reprinted at Providence, R.I., 1793. 15 p. DLC. The author served under Generals Harmar and St. Clair.

Johns, Clayton, 1857-1932. Rem-[3019]

iniscences of a musician. Cambridge: Washburn & Thomas, 1929. 132 p. DLC. The period covered is 1882-1928.

Johns, Orrick, b. 1887. Time of our lives...N.Y.: Stackpole, 1937. 353 p. WU. A newspaper reporter in St. Louis, New York, Italy and France. [3020]

Johnsen, Birger. Far horizon, twenty years of adventure... on the new air frontier, by Henry W. Lanier. N.Y.: Knopf, 1933. 284 p. DLC. Pilot and inventor of aircraft appliances, who was born in Norway. Presumably, Johnson dictated this account to Lanier. [3021]

Johnson, Adam Rankin, b. 1834. The Partisan Rangers of the Confederate States Army. Ed. by William J. Davis. Louisville, Ky.: Geo. G. Fetter co., 1904. 476 p. Auto., p. 1-226. NN. As described by the title. [3022]

Johnson, Alexander, b. 1847. Adventures in social welfare; being reminiscences of things, thoughts and folks during forty years of social work. Fort Wayne: the author, 1923. 455 p. WU. Especially in connection with the National Conference of Social Work. [3023]

Johnson, Mrs. Anna (French). The making of a minister's wife. N.Y.: Appleton-Century, 1939. 268 p. DLC. The wife of a Presbyterian clergyman in the Dakotas and Wisconsin. [3024]

Johnson, Bengt, b. 1844. Autobiography...Everett, Wash.: n.d. 17 p. WaU. The writer came to the U.S. from Sweden in 1870. He was a railroad laborer in Illinois and Nebraska and a farmer in Washington. [3025]

Johnson, Burges, b. 1877. As much as I dare; a personal recollection. N.Y.: Ives Washburn, 1944. 346 p. WU. Literary adviser to publishers, editor of magazines, professor of English at Vassar. [3026]

Johnson, Charles Beneulyn, b. 1843. Sixty years in medical harness...1865-1925. N.Y.: Medical life press, 1926. 333 p. DLC. Country doctor in Illinois. During the Civil War he was a hospital steward in the Union army. [3027]

Johnson, Charles Beneulyn, b. 1843. Muskets and medicine; or, army life in the sixties. Phila.: F. A. Davis co., 1917. 276 p. NN. By a hospital steward in the Union army. [3028]

Johnson, Edith. The story of my life. Oklahoma City: Oklahoma pub. co., 1940. 22 p. OkHi. Newspaper feature writer in Oklahoma City. [3029]

Johnson, Mrs. Electa Amanda W., b. 1838. The simple story of an uneventful life. Milwaukee: Morehouse, 1924? 206 p. WHi. This account was written by the wife of a Wisconsin political figure, who was a judge and in the sixties a member of the state legislature. [3030]

Johnson, Ella Hicks, b. 1861. Granny remembers. Macon: J. W. Burke co., 1928. 86 p. NNC. Recollections of youthful days in Kentucky. [3031]

Johnson, Emory Richard, b.1864. Life of a university professor, an autobiography. Phila.: 1943. 283 p. WU. Professor and Dean at Wharton School of Finance and Commerce. The writer also served on several federal government commissions. [3032]

Johnson, Erastus, 1826-1912. Autobiography...Los Angeles: Frank Wiggins trade school, 1937. 82 p. DLC. Lumber and farm work in Maine; employed in oil refinery in Pennsylvania; farmer in state of Washington. [3033]

Johnson, Frederick F., b. 1833. Life and works of F. F. Johnson ...Stonefort: Turner pub. co., 1913. 347 p. Auto., p. 1-132, 151-158. KyLoS. Clergyman of the Seventh Day Adventist Church in Illinois, and surgeon in the Union army. [3034]

Johnson, George W., b. 1823. Jottings by the way...St. George: 1882. 36 p. USlC. The author became a Mormon in Ohio in 1833. From there he went to Illinois and then to Utah in 1851, where he became a farmer. [3035]

Johnson, Henry, b. 1867. The other side of Main Street; a history teacher from Sauk Centre. N.Y.: Columbia univ. press, 1943. 256 p. WHi. A professor at Columbia tells of his Minnesota [3036] boyhood, of college, and of his early days as a teacher.

Johnson, Hugh Samuel, 1882– [3037] 1942. The blue eagle, from egg to earth. Garden City, N.Y.: Doubleday, Doran, 1935. 443 p. DLC. Army officer with Pershing in Mexico and in the first World War; industrialist; head of Roosevelt's N.R.A.

Johnson, Isaac. Slavery days in [3037A] old Kentucky. Ogdensburg: Republican & journal print, 1901. KyRE. As described by the title.

Johnson, Ithiel Town, b. 1849. [3038] The story of my life. Burlington: Free press pr. co., 1912. 231 p. Auto., p. 16-160. DLC. New England evangelist.

Johnson, J.B., (alias). Buried [3039] alive...in the Missouri penitentiary...Kansas City, Mo.: Hudson-Kimberly pub. co., n.d. 246 p. Auto., 147-235. MoHi. Gambler, thief in Missouri in the eighties tells of prison life.

Johnson, Jack, b. 1878. Jack [3040] Johnson, in the ring and out. Chicago: National sports pub. co., 1927. 259 p. LNX. Negro prize fighter.

Johnson, James Weldon, 1871– [3041] 1938. Along this way...N.Y.: Viking, 1935. 418 p. WHi. Negro poet and novelist.

Johnson, Jeremiah, b. 1827. [3042] Sparks and flashes of a busy life. N.Y.: J. W. Pratt, 1893. 169 p. DLC. Real estate promoter in Brooklyn.

Johnson, Jeremiah Augustus, [3043] b. 1836. The life of a citizen at home and in foreign service. N.Y.: Vail-Ballou, 1915. 275 p. WHi. U.S. Consul in Syria.

Johnson, John. The life and [3044] confession of John Johnson, the murderer of James Murray... N.Y.: Brown & Tyrell, 1824. 26 p. DLC. Johnson was born in Ireland.

Johnson, John A., b. 1829. My [3045-wife, her lover, and I; auto- 3046] biography. Norfolk: 1883. DLC. A domestic account of a North Carolina businessman who was deserted by his wife.

Johnson, Lewis, b. 1859. One [3047] man's journey...Heron Lake: Heron Lake news, 1934. 24 p. MnHi. The author came to Minnesota from Sweden in 1869. He became a school teacher, owner of a general store, insurance agent and real estate agent.

Johnson, Marshall LaFayette, [3048] b. 1848. Trail blazing...Dallas: Mathis pub. co., 1935. 116 p. TxU. Indian fighter, rancher and hunter in Texas in the sixties and seventies. This is an expanded version of his, True History (1923).

Johnson, Osa Helen (Leighty), [3049] b. 1894. I married adventure... N.Y.: Lippincott, 1940. 376 p. WHi. The wife of Martin Johnson, photographer of wild animals.

Johnson, Osa Helen (Leighty), [3050] b. 1894. Four years in Paradise. N.Y.: J. B. Lippincott, 1941. 345 p. WU. In Africa where she and her husband photographed wild animals.

Johnson, Peter, b. 1862. Mem- [3051] oirs of Captain Peter Johnson. Honolulu: 1937. 107 p. DLC. Swedish born sailor who sailed many American ships and then became a citizen of the U.S.

Johnson, Richard W., 1827-1897. [3052] A soldier's reminiscences in peace and war. Phila.: Lippincott, 1886. 428 p. WHi. Indian warfare, war with Mexico, officer in the Union army, real estate business in St. Paul.

Johnson, Robert Underwood, [3053] 1853-1937. Remembered yesterdays. Boston: Little, Brown, 1923. 624 p. WU. Magazine editor and Ambassador to Italy.

Johnson, Samuel, 1696-1772. [3054] "Autobiography". (In: Samuel Johnson...ed. by Herbert and Carol Schneider. N.Y.: Columbia univ. press, 1929. vol. 1.) p. 3-49. WHi. President of King's College (now Columbia).

Johnson, Thomas L., b. 1836. [3055] Twenty-eight years a slave... London: Christian workers depot, 1909. 266 p. IEN. After obtaining his freedom, the author served as a missionary and evangelist in Africa and England.

Johnson, Tom Loftin, 1854-1911. [3056] My story. N.Y.: B. W. Huebsch, 1911. 326 p. WHi. Ohio industrialist, member of Congress (1890-94) and mayor of Cleveland

Johnston, Annie Fellows, b.1863. [3057]
The land of the little colonel.
Boston: L. C. Page & co., 1929.
133 p. WU. By the author of the
Little Colonel series. The scene
is Kentucky and Indiana.

Johnston, David, b. 1803. Auto- [3058]
biographical reminiscences...
Chicago: 1885. 223 p. CSmH.
Very little of this book relates
to the U.S. The author came
from Scotland, and became a
teacher in Milwaukee about 1858.

Johnston, David E. The story of [3059]
a Confederate boy in the Civil
War. Rev. ed. Portland: 1914.
379 p. Or. As described by
the title.

Johnston, Mrs. Elizabeth [3060]
Lichtenstein, b. 1764. Recollections of a Georgia loyalist. N.Y.:
Mansfield, 1901. 224 p. Auto.,
p. 37-164. WHi. The portion
relating to the U.S. is brief. The
remainder pertains to the writer's
life in Jamaica and Nova Scotia.

Johnston, Harry V. My home [3061]
on the range...St. Paul: 1942.
313 p. WHi. Cowboy and mail
carrier in the Dakotas.

Johnston, James Perry, b. 1852. [3062]
Twenty years of hus'ling. Chicago: Thompson & Thomas, 1887.
659 p. WaU. A kaleidoscopic
account, in Ohio and Michigan, of a
railroad telegrapher, peddler,
insurance agent, merchant, horse
trainer, hotel manager and
auctioneer.

Johnston, James Perry, b. 1852. [3063]
What happened to Johnston.
Chicago: Thompson & Thomas,
1904. 459 p. ICU. Merchant in
Illinois and Indiana.

Johnston, John, 1778-1855. The [3064]
autobiographical and ministerial
life of the Rev. John Johnston,
D.D. N.Y.: M. W. Dodd, 1856.
225 p. DLC. Presbyterian clergyman in New York.

Johnston, Joseph Eggleston, [3065]
1807-1891. Narrative of military
operations, directed during the
late war between the states, by
Joseph E. Johnston, general,
C.S.A. N.Y.: D. Appleton, 1874.
602 p. NN. As described by the
title.

Johnston, N.R. Looking back [3066]
from the sunset land...Oakland:
1898. 624 p. CSmH. Presbyterian
clergyman in Iowa, Minn., Vermont and South Carolina and
California. Later he became an
educator in Pennsylvania, and the
editor of Our Banner, a religious
magazine.

Johnston, Richard Malcolm, [3067]
1822-1898. Autobiography...
Washington: Neale, 1900. 190 p.
WHi. Novelist and teacher at
the University of Georgia.

Johnston, William Andrew, 1871-[3068]
1929. My own Main Street.
Cincinnati: Standard pub. co.,
1921. 238 p. NN. A boy's recollections of a small Pennsylvania
town.

Johnston, William Graham, [3069]
b. 1828. Life and reminiscences
from birth to manhood...Pitts-
burgh: 1901. 303 p. WHi. The
life of a boy in Pittsburgh to the
year 1848.

Johnstone, Abraham. See
Johnstone, Benjamin.

Johnstone, Benjamin, d. 1797. [3070]
The address of Abraham Johnstone, a black man, who was hanged
at Woodbury, in the county of
Glocester, and state of New Jersey,
on Saturday the 8th day of July
last; to the people of colour.
Phila.: 1797. 47 p. NN. Slave, free
laborer in New Jersey, hanged
for murder. Obviously ghost
written.

Johonnot, Jackson. See
Entry 3018.

Jonas, Edward Asher, b. 1865. [3071]
Once upon a time. Louisville:
Wilderness road book shop, 1942.
144 p. DLC. Newspaperman in
Kentucky, born in England.

Jonas, Nathan S. Through the [3072]
years...N.Y.: Business bourse,
1940. 330 p. WHi. Jewish banker,
philanthropist in New York.

Jones, Abner, 1772-1841. Mem- [3073]
oirs. Exeter: pr. by Norris &
Sawyer, 1807. 108 p. N. Clergyman of the Christian Church in
Mass. and Vermont.

Jones, Amanda Theodosia, 1835-[3074]
1914. A psychic autobiography.
N.Y.: Greaves, 1910. 455 p. NN.
Inventor of a process of preserving
fruit. The book is a record of the
author's psychic experiences.

Jones, Anson, 1798-1858. Mem- [3075] oranda and official correspondence relating to the Republic of Texas ...Including a brief autobiography of the author. N.Y.: Appleton, 1859. 648 p. Auto., p. 1-26. TxU. By the president of Texas. This book, concluding with the year 1850, contains an account of politics and war.

Jones, Burr W., b. 1846? Remin- [3076] iscences of nine decades. Evansville, Wis.: Antes press, n.d. 123 p. WHi. Lawyer, justice of the Supreme Court of Wisconsin, and member of the U.S. House of Representatives.

Jones, Burton Renesselaer, [3077] b. 1845. Incidents...Chicago: Free Methodist pub. house, 1909. 315 p. TxDaM. Methodist clergyman in New York, Michigan, Illinois, and Indiana.

Jones, Charles E., 1830-1857. [3078] The life and confessions of Charles E. Jones, convicted of the murder of Isaac Jackson, a Jew peddler...Montpelier, Vermont: pr. by Ballou, Loveland & co., 1860. 168 p. MoU. In New England.

Jones, Charles J., b. 1818. From [3079] the forecastle to the pulpit...N.Y.: 1884. 538 p. CBPac. A sailor, born in England, who became a preacher among the sailors in New York.

Jones, Daniel Webster. Forty [3080] years among the Indians. Salt Lake City: Juvenile instructor, 1890. 400 p. WHi. Mormon "Seventy" in Utah, Arizona and Mexico.

Jones, Evan Rowland, 1840-1920. [3081] Four years in the army of the Republic. London: Tyne pub. co., 1881. 246 p. WHi. In the Union Army.

Jones, George Farquhar, b. 1811. [3082] Myself and others; or, reminiscences, recollections and experiences in a life of seventy-six years, 1811-1887, in public, business and social life, in Providence, Rhode Island, and Philadelphia, Pa.: Phila. Globe pr. house,1887? 252 p. NN. The writer was engaged in the dry-goods business in Philadelphia.

Jones, George Wallace, 1804- [3083] 1896. "Autobiography". (In: John Carl Parish, George Wallace Jones. Iowa City: State historical soc., 1912.) p. 75-247. WHi. Businessman in Wisconsin (lead mining), who was also U.S. Minister to Bogota, and U.S. Senator from Iowa.

Jones, Harry W. A chaplain's [3084] experience ashore and afloat... N.Y.: A. G. Sherwood, 1901. 300 p. TxU. A Baptist clergyman in New York, New Jersey and Conn. There is much about his service on the "Texas" in 1896.

Jones, James Claybourne, 1826- [3085] 1914. Autobiography of Old Claib Jones. Hazard, Ky.: pr. by Hazard book co., 1915. 39 p. NcWAtC. Kentucky mountain feudist.

Jones, Joe, 1847-1932. The life [3086] story of Joe (Daddy) Jones. Waco: Davis, 1937. 79 p. DLC. A New York farmer who was convicted of murder, served 41 years, and was then pardoned when another person confessed.

Jones, John Logan, b. 1859. The [3087] individualist...Kansas City: Brown-White-Lowell press, 1942. 277 p. KHi. Merchant in Kansas, Illinois and Missouri.

Jones, John P. (Slim). Ten years [3088] in the oil fields. Eldorado: Berry's print shop, n.d. 85 p. TxU. In Oklahoma and Texas. A 20th century account.

Jones, John Paul, 1747-1792. [3089] A narrative of the celebrated Commodore John Paul Jones. Phila.: Peter K. Wagner, 1806. 37 p. DLC. Written by the great naval hero, this account is a translation of a work which appeared in French in 1798.

Jones, Laurence C. Up through [3090] difficulties. Braxton, Miss.: Pine torch, 1913. 79 p. IaHi. Founder of an industrial school for Negroes in Mississippi.

Jones, Mary Ann. In old [3091] Mizzoury..N.p.: 1906. 86 p. Auto., p. 47-86. MoK. An account of the author's early life: farm, school, courting in the eighties and nineties.

Jones, Mrs. Mary Cadwalader [3092] (Rawle), 1850-1935. Lantern slides. Boston: Updike, 1937.

129 p. DLC. Social life in Philadelphia and New York.

Jones, Mrs. Mary (Harris), [3093] b. 1830. Autobiography of Mother Jones. Chicago: C. H. Kerr & co., 1925. 242 p. WHi. Social reformer and labor leader in Chicago.

Jones, Nat. H. Memoires (sic) [3094] of...an insurance man. N.Y.: Spectator, 1900. 273 p. CoHi. Country agent in Missouri and Kansas. The names given are obviously fictitious, and this may be a burlesque.

Jones, Oliver F., b. 1896. Fifteen years in a living hell. [3095] N.p.: 1944. 131 p. DLC. A life of crime and imprisonment in Illinois, Oklahoma, Kansas, Wyoming, Idaho and Nevada.

Jones, Rufus Matthew, 1863- [3096] 1948. A small-town boy. N.Y.: Macmillan, 1941. 154 p. NN. Life and education of a boy in rural Maine.

Jones, Rufus Matthew, 1863- [3097] 1948. A boy's religion from memory. Phila.: Ferris & Leach, 1902. 141 p. NN. The purpose of the author, a leading Quaker, "is to tell what a boy's religion is like-to show it growing and developing."

Jones, Rufus Matthew, 1863- [3098] 1948. Finding the trail of life. N.Y.: Macmillan, 1926. 148 p. NN. A re-written version of the preceding item, inclusive of a longer period of time.

Jones, Rufus Matthew, 1863- [3099] 1948. The trail of life in college. N.Y.: Macmillan, 1929. 201 p. DLC. A noted quaker tells of his experiences as a student in college, and of the early years of his teaching career.

Jones, Rufus Matthew, 1863- [3100] 1948. The trail of life in the middle years. N.Y.: Macmillan, 1934. 250 p. DLC. This item covers the years 1893-1914 (see the preceding titles).

Jones, Samuel Milton, 1846- [3101] 1904. "Autobiography". (In his: New right...N.Y.: Eastern book concern, 1899.) p. 37-112. WHi. Political and economic reformer who lived in Ohio.

Jones, Samuel Porter, 1847- [3102] 1906. Living words...Toronto: William Briggs, 1886. 595 p. IaMpI. Methodist clergyman in Georgia and Tennessee who was earlier a drunken lawyer.

Jones, Sylvester. Not by might. [3103] Elgin: Brethren pub. house, 1942. 159 p. DLC. An American Quaker missionary in Cuba.

Jones, Thomas H. The experi- [3104] ence of Thomas H. Jones who was a slave for forty-three years. Written by a friend. Boston: pr. by Bazin & Chandler, 1862. 48 p. WHi. As described by the title.

Jones, Thomas Lewis, b. 1841. [3105] From the gold mine to the pulpit; story of a backwoods Methodist preacher in the Pacific Northwest ...Cinc.: 1904. 169 p. WaU. As described by the title. The period covered is 1865-1900. The author was a miner in Idaho.

Jones, William Frank, b. 1872. [3106] The experiences of a deputy U.S. Marshal of the Indian Territory. No imprint, 1937? 40 p. Auto., p. 4-20. MtHi. In Oklahoma, beginning about 1894.

Jordan, Charles Edward, b.1851. [3107] A letter from Charles Edward Jordan to his family and friends. N.p.: 1932. 47 p. DLC. The author was employed by the Panama Canal Commission in various capacities.

Jordan, David Starr, 1851-1931. [3108] The days of a man...Yonkers-on-Hudson: World book co., 1922. 2 vols. WU. Naturalist, President of Stanford University.

Jordan, Elizabeth. Three rous- [3109] ing cheers. N.Y.: Appleton-Century, 1938. 369 p. WU. Writer of short stories, novels, and plays. Editorial writer for chain of newspapers.

Jordan, Jules, 1850-1927. The [3110] happenings of a musical life. Providence: Palmer press, 1922. 195 p. DLC. Singer, teacher, conductor, composer who lived in Rhode Island.

Jordan, Lewis G. On two hem- [3111] ispheres...No imprint. 80 p. LND. Baptist clergyman, once a slave, who served in Texas and did mission work in Africa.

Jordan, Louis Fenimore, b.1888. [3112] Memoirs of a criminal lawyer. Staunton, Va.: The Beverley press,

1935. 145 p. NN. Experiences of a criminal lawyer in the Blue Ridge section of Virginia.

Jordin, John Franklin, b. 1851. [3113] Memories...Gallatin, Mo.: North Missourian press, 1904. 189 p. MoHi. In Missouri: youthful days on a pioneer farm; his experiences as a constable.

Jorgensen, Frederick E., b.1864. [3114] 25 years a game warden... Brattleboro, Vt.: The Stephen Daye press, 1937. 168 p. NN. Career of a Maine game warden.

Joseph, John. The life... [3115] Wellington: pr. for John Joseph, 1848. 8 p. MoKU. A Negro, born in Africa, is brought to South Carolina from which he escapes in 1843.

Joss, Catherine (Smith), b.1820. [3116] Autobiography...Cleveland: 1891. 464 p. DLC. Housewife, operator of boarding houses, and worker for the Salvation Army. The author lived mainly in Ohio.

Journeycake, Charles, b. 1817. [3117] The Indian Chief, Journeycake, by S. H. Mitchell. Phila.: Am. Baptist pub. soc., 1895. 108 p. NbHi. A Delaware Indian, converted to Christianity, tells of his work for the church in Ohio and Kansas.

Joyce, John Alexander, b. 1842. [3118] A checkered life. Chicago: S.P. Rounds, 1883. 318 p. WHi. The author served in the Union army, was a Federal revenue agent, and a minor political figure in Kentucky.

Joyce, Peggy Hopkins. Men, [3119] marriage and me. N.Y.: The Macaulay co., 1930. 286 p. DLC. Acress, movie star whose chief claim to fame was her numerous marital engagements.

Joyce, W.J., 1826-1918. Life... [3120] San Marlos: San Marlos pr. co., 1913. 126 p. Auto., p. 1-49. TxU. Methodist clergyman in Texas who fought in the Confederate army. An earlier book (1910) contains no material not found in this later one.

Judge, Hugh, 1750?-1834. Mem- [3121] oirs and journal of Hugh Judge; a member of the Society of Friends, and minister of the gospel; containing an account of his life, religious observations, and travels in the work of the ministry. Byberry: Comly, 1841. 396 p. NN. In the Eastern half of the United States.

Judson, Mrs. Emily Chubbuck, [3122] 1817-1854. The life and letters of...by A. C. Kendrick. N.Y.: Sheldon & co., 1860. 426 p. Auto., p. 12-32. MWA. A story of youth in New York.

Judson, Mrs. Phoebe Newton, [3123] 1832-1926. A pioneer's search for an ideal home. Bellingham: 1925. 309 p. CSmH. Life on a farm in the Washington Territory, beginning with 1853.

Jusserand, Jean J. What me be- [3124] fell...Boston: Houghton Mifflin, 1933. 360 p. WHi. French ambassador in the U.S., from 1903 through the administration of T. Roosevelt (see pages 219-346).

Justesen, Peter. Two years' [3125] adventures of a Dane in the California gold mines. Gloucester: pr. for the author, 1865. CU-B. As described by the title. The years referred to are 1850-51. The original of this (Copenhagen, 1863) can be found in MoHi.

Juul, Ole, 1838-1903. Erindringer [3126] Decorah, Iowa: Lutheran pub. house, 1902. 331 p. DLC. Lutheran clergyman in New York, New Jersey and Indiana.

# K

Kachel, Edwin. A quarter of a [3127] century with the traveling public. N.p.: 1937. 113 p. WaU. Dining car steward on run between Seattle and Portland.

Kalbfus, Joseph H., 1852-1918. [3128] Dr. Kalbfus's book...Altoona: Times tribune co., 1926. 342 p. DLC. Secretary of Pennsylvania State Game Commission for 24 years.

Kane, John, 1860-1934. Sky hooks.[3129] Philadelphia, N.Y.: Lippincott co., 1938. 196 p. DLC. Painter.

Kane, Samuel E. Life or death [3130] in Luzon. Indianapolos: Bobbs-Merrill, 1933. 331 p. DLC. Veteran of Spanish-American War, who remained in the Philippines to prospect gold, plant coffee, build roads, and finally to become Governor of Bontoc Province.

Kang, Younghill, b. 1903. East [3131] goes west. N.Y.: Scribner, 1937. 401 p. NN. Experiences of a Korean youth in America.

Kantakuzen, Julia (Grant), [3132] b. 1876. Revolutionary days... Boston: Small, Maynard & co., 1919. 411 p. DLC. American wife of a Russian nobleman tells of her experiences in Russia in the early days of the Bolshevik revolution.

Kantakuzen, Julia (Grant), [3133] b. 1876. My life here and there. N.Y.: Scribner, 1922. 322 p. WHi. See the preceding item. This book covers the years 1889 to 1914. It includes her life in Vienna as the daughter of a U.S. diplomatic official, her marriage, and her life in Russia from 1906 to 1914.

Karr, M. L., b. 1867. Life of [3134] the cowboy preacher. Baxter, Kansas: n.d. 186 p. OkU. Baptist clergyman in Kansas.

Kasovich, Israel Isser, b. 1859. [3135] Days of our years...N.Y.: Jordan pub. co., 1929. 358 p. OCl. The author, born in Lithuania, came to the U.S. to stay about 1900. He was editor of a farm journal; he farmed and taught school in New York, Mass., and Conn.

Kavanagh-Priest, Anne. Mem- [3136] oirs of a Gothic American. N.Y.: Macmillan, 1929. 500 p. NN. The author's life on a New Hampshire farm until she went away to college.

Kay-Scott, C. (pseud.). See Wellman, Frederick Creighton.

Kean, John, b. 1762. Autobio- [3137] graphy...Harrisburg, Pa.: Harrisburg pub. co., 1888. 12 p. Ia-HA. A merchant in Pennsylvania who in the 18th century held various political offices.

Kearney, Belle, b. 1863. A slave-[3138] holder's daughter. N.Y.: Abbet press, 1900. 269 p. DLC. A Southerner tells of her teaching, and of her work on behalf of temperance.

Keating, Cecil A., b. 1850. [3139] ...Reminiscences...Dallas: 1920. Auto., p. 54-133. TxGR. The writer, born in Canada, was clerk for a plow manufacturer in Chicago, and then was a farm machinery merchant in Texas.

Keckley, Elizabeth. Behind the [3140] scenes; or, thirty years a slave and four years in the White House. N.Y.: G. W. Carleton, 1868. 371 p. Auto., p. 17-331. DLC. Most of this book relates to her experiences as modiste to Mrs. Lincoln.

Keeler, Ralph, 1840-1873. Vag- [3141] abond adventures. Boston: Fields, Osgood, 1870. 274 p. CSmH. Minstrel on the Mississippi and Ohio rivers. This account closes with 1862.

Keeley, John, b. 1827. A true [3142] story of the ups and downs and narrow escapes of John Keeley, a native of Maine...Portland: pr. by B. Thurston, 1870. 24 p. MiD-B. Merchant.

Keenan, John L. A steel man [3143] in India. N.Y.: Duell, Sloan & Pearce, 1943. 224 p. WU. The author was General Manager of the Tata Iron & Steel co., beginning with 1913.

Keene, Foxhall. Full tilt; the [3144] sporting memoirs of Foxhall Keene, by Alden Hatch and Foxhall Keene. N.Y.: The Derrydale press, 1938. 170 p. NN. Racing, steeplechasing, foxhunting, polo and golf.

Keene, Moses W., 1801-1841. [3145] The life and confession of Moses W. Keen (sic)...Maysville: 1842. 24 p. DLC. Murderer in Kentucky.

Keesy, William Allen, b. 1843. [3146] War as viewed from the ranks. Norwalk: Experiment & news co., 1898. 240 p. DLC. Union army soldier who later became a clergyman of the United Brethren Church in Ohio.

Kegley, Charles Hill, b. 1859. [3147] Personal memoirs. Los Angeles: priv. pr., 1936. 142 p. WHi. In Iowa, banker; in California, banker, real estate dealer, building contractor.

Keifer, Joseph Warren, 1836- [3148] 1932. Slavery and four years of war. A political history...together with a narrative of the campaigns and battles...in which the author took part, 1861-1865. N.Y. &

London: G.P.Putnam's sons, 1900. 2 vols. WHi. Officer in the Union army.

Keith, Benjamin F., b. 1861. [3149] Memories. Raleigh: Bynum pr. co., 1922. 158 p. NcU. Farmer and politician in North Carolina.

Keith, William, b. 1776. The ex- [3150] perience of William Keith. Utica: pr. by Asahel Seward, 1806. 23 p. NjT. Minister in New York.

Keithley, Jacob Carter, b. 1831. [3151] Autobiography. Marshall, Mo.: Democrat-News print, n.d. 58 p. MoHi. School teacher in Missouri.

Kell, John McIntosh. Recollec- [3152] tions of a naval life. Washington: Neale, 1900. 307 p. WHi. The author served in the Confederate navy, and later was Adjutant-General of Georgia.

Kellar, Harry, 1849-1922. A [3153] magician's tour...Chicago: Donohue, Henneberry, 1886. 214 p. MB. The travels of a magician in this country and abroad to the year 1886.

Keller, Carl. Als "Greenhorn" [3154] in western von Nord-Amerika... Hamburg: Königliche hofbuchhandlung, 1893. 208 p. CU-B. A rather unlikely tale of mining camps, Indians, etc., by a German who was a private detective in Colorado, a barkeeper in Kansas, and a miner in California.

Keller, Helen Adams, b. 1880. [3155] My religion. Garden City, N.Y.: Doubleday, Doran & co., 1927. 208 p. NN. A record of the author's religious experiences.

Keller, Helen Adams, b. 1880. [3156] The story of my life. N.Y.: Doubleday, Page, 1903. 441 p. Auto., p. 3-140. WU. Her early years including student days at Radcliffe.

Keller, Helen Adams, b. 1880. [3157] Midstream: my later life. Garden City, N.Y.: Doubleday, Doran, 1929. 362 p. WHi. This account begins where the preceding item leaves off.

Keller, Julius, d. 1945. Inns and [3158] outs. N.Y.: G. P. Putnam's sons, 1939. 250 p. NN. The author, an immigrant Swiss, tells of his career as one of the prominent restaurant men in New York City.

Kellersberger, Julia Lake [3159] (Skinner), b. 1897. God's ravens. N.Y.: Fleming H. Revell, 1941. 207 p. NN. Missionary experiences in the Belgian Congo.

Kelley, Francis Clement, b.1870. [3160] Bishop sets it down...(by Myles Muredach, pseud.) N.Y.: Harper, 1939. 327 p. WHi. Catholic clerbyman in Oklahoma and Texas.

Kelley, Hall Jackson, 1790-1874. [3161] A history...Springfield, Mass.: Union pr. co., 1868. 128 p. DLC. Promoter of immigration to Oregon in the thirties.

Kellog, Charles. Charles Kellog, [3162] the nature singer...Morgan Hill: Pacific science press, 1929. 243 p. DLC. Vaudeville performer, lecturer on birds, singer of bird songs.

Kellogg, Clara Louise, 1842-1916. [3163] Memoirs...N.Y.: Putnam, 1913. 382 p. WU. Opera singer.

Kellogg, Daniel B., b. 1834. Auto- [3165] biography of Dr. D. B. Kellogg; or explanation of clairvoyance... Ann Arbor: Dr. Chase's steam printing house, 1869. 203 p. MiU. Spiritualist in Michigan.

Kellogg, George Josiah, b. 1828. [3164] Narrative of Geo. J. Kellogg from 1849 to 1915, and some history of Wisconsin since 1835. Alvin, Texas: 1914. 36 p. InU. California gold miner. Horticulturist in Wisconsin.

Kellogg, John Jackson. War ex- [3166] periences...Washington, Iowa: Evening journal, 1913. 64 p. WHi. Union army.

Kells, C. Edmund, 1856-1928. [3167] Three score years and nine. New Orleans: pub. by Edmund Kells, 1926. 563 p. LU. Louisiana dentist.

Kells, David. "The ways of the [3168] world"...Adrian, Mich.: pr. for the author, 1867. 24 p. DLC. The writer as a young boy worked on farms in New York; on the Mississippi river; and on farms in Michigan. During the Civil War he fought with the Union army.

Kelly, Ebenezer Bariah, b. 1783. [3169] Ebenezer Beriah Kelly, an autobiography. Norwich: pr. by John W. Stedman, 1856. 100 p. WHi. Merchant sailor.

Kelly, Mrs. Florence (Finch). [3170]

Flowing stream; the story of 56 years in American newspaper life. N.Y.: Dutton, 1939. 571 p. WU. Novelist, editorial writer who worked in New York, California, Mass., Illinois and Kansas.

Kelly, John B., b. 1860. Born to [3171] battle...Boston: Meadar, 1944. 153 p. DLC. Irish immigrant who came to Mass. in 1881 where he became a manufacturer.

Kelly, Luther Sage, 1849-1928. [3172] "Yellowstone Kelly"; the memoirs of Luther S. Kelly. New Haven: Yale univ. press, 1926. 268 p. NN. Army scout, Indian fighter on the plains.

Kelly, William. A stroll through [3173] the diggings of California. London: Simms & M'Intyre, 1852. 240 p. CHi. By an Englishman.

Kelsey, Albert Warren. Auto- [3174] biographical notes and memoranda, 1840-1910. No imprint. 130 p. DLC. The author was a sailor in the Union navy.

Kemble, Frances Anne, 1809- [3175] 1893. Records of a girlhood. N.Y.: Henry Holt, 1879. 605 p. NN. Early career of the famous English actress and public reader who came to America in 1832. The last sixty pages record her earliest American experiences.

Kemble, Frances Anne, 1809- [3176] 1893. Records of later life. N.Y.: Henry Holt, 1882. 676 p. NN. This volume carries the author from 1834 into the beginning of 1848.

Kemp, Harry, b. 1883. Tramp- [3177] ing on life; an autobiographical narrative. N.Y.: Boni & Liveright, 1922. 438 p. NN. Adventures of the literary vagabond and poet.

Kemp, Robert H., 1820-1897. [3178] Father Kemp and his old folks... Boston: 1868. 254 p. Auto., p. 11-195. DLC. Boston shoe dealer, known for his promotion of concerts of religious songs.

Kendall, Henry, b. 1774. Auto- [3179] biography...Portland, Me.: pub. by the author, 1853. 201 p. DLC. Baptist evangelist in Maine.

Kendall, Hiram. Real life... [3180] San Francisco: 1861. 31 p. RPB. California gold miner, 1853-61.

Kendall, T. D., b. 1822. The life [3181] and anecdotes of T.D. Kendall, the mountain poet of Kentucky... Evansville, Ind.: Journal co., printers, 1879. 234 p. KyU. Methodist clergyman in Kentucky.

Kendall, Walter Gardner, 1854- [3182] 1946. Four score years of sport. Boston: The Stratford co., 1933. 201 p. NN. Recollections of a Boston dentist of his interests in various sports.

Kenderine, Thaddeus S. A Cal- [3183] ifornia tramp...or, Life on the plains and in the golden state thirty years ago...Newton: 1888. 416 p. DLC. Herd driver across plains, and then farmer in California.

Kendig, A. B., b. 1830. Sparks [3184] from my forge...Boston: B.B. Russell, 1879. 183 p. Auto., p. 1-28. IaHi. Spiritual autobiography by a Methodist minister.

Kendrick, Ariel, b. 1772. [3185] Sketches of the life and times of Eld. Ariel Kendrick. Ludlow, Vt.: pr. by Barton & Tower, 1847. 96 p. NN. Baptist minister serving in New Hampshire and Vermont.

Kendricken, Paul Henry, b.1834. [3186] Memoirs...Boston: priv. pr., 1910. 355 p. DLC. Civil War experiences of a Union naval engineer. Later he engaged in business in Mass., where he held various political offices, including that of State Senator.

Kenlon, John, 1860-1940. Four- [3187] teen years a sailor, by John Kenlon, chief of Fire Department of the city of New York. N.Y.: George H. Doran, 1923. 320 p. NN. As described by the title.

Kennedy, Bess Davis. The lady [3188] and the lions. N.Y.: McGraw, 1942. 221 p. DLC. Trapper for the U.S. Bureau of Biological Survey.

Kennedy, George W., b. 1847. [3189] The pioneer campfire...Portland: 1914. 240 p. CSmH. Pioneer farmer, miner and hunter in Oregon who later became a Methodist clergyman and a teacher.

Kennedy, Millard Fillmore, [3190] b. 1863. Schoolmaster of yesterday...N.Y.: McGraw-Hill, 1940. 359 p. Auto., p. 203-359. WU.

District school teacher in the South.

Kenny, Elizabeth. And they [3191] shall walk...N.Y.: Dodd, Mead, 1943. 281 p. WU. Australian nurse, famous for her treatment of paralysis.

Kenoly, Jacob, b. 1876. The life [3192] ...by C. C. Smith. Cinc.: 1912. 160 p. MoCanD. Clergyman in Africa who grew up in Missouri on a farm and went to college in Alabama.

Kent, Mrs. E. C. Life sketches [3193] ...San Antonio: 1884. 64 p. TxU. Texas school teacher in the fourth quarter of the 19th century.

Kent, Mrs. E. C. "Four years [3194] in Secessia". A narrative of a residence at the South previous to and during the Southern rebellion, up to November, 1863, when the writer escaped from Richmond. Second ed. with additions. Buffalo: Franklin pr. house, 1865. 35 p. DLC. As described by the title.

Kent, Lyman Blackmarr, 1830- [3195] 1911. A stalwart of the old guard. ...Chicago: The Christian witness, 1912. 178 p. Auto., p. 9-28. DLC. The author's life to 1847 when he was converted to Methodism.

Kent, Rockwell, b. 1882. This is [3196] my own. N.Y.: Duell, Sloan & Pearce, 1940. 393 p. NN. The artist and writer tells of establishing a home in the Adirondaks and of his particpation in the efforts to reform local politics in Essex county.

Kent, William, 1864-1928. Rem- [3197] iniscences of outdoor life. San Francisco: A. M. Robertson, 1929. 305 p. NN. Early recollections of California, Nevada, and Nebraska; later reminiscences of New Mexico, Lower California and Mexico.

Ker, John, 1673-1726. The mem- [3198] oirs of John Ker...London: pr. by Curl, 1726. 3 vols. in 2. DLC. British secret agent in North America during the French and Indian Wars.

Kerbey, Joseph Orton, d. 1913. [3199] An American consul in Amazonia. N.Y.: Rudge, 1911. 370 p. DLC. In Brazil.

Kerbey, Joseph Orton, d. 1913. [3200] The boy spy...N.Y.: Belford, Clarke, 1889. 556 p. WHi. Union army.

Kercher, John, b. 1863. Fifty [3201] years a doctor. Boston: Meador, 1939. 247 p. NN. Experiences in Chicago and in Alaska.

Kern, Mrs. Corinne (Johnson), [3202] b. 1881. I go nursing. N.Y.: Dutton, 1933. 256 p. DLC. Private nurse in California.

Kern, Mrs. Corinne (Johnson), [3203] b. 1881. Nursing through the years. N.Y.: Dutton, 1939. 340 p. DLC. See preceding description.

Kersey, Jesse, 1768-1845. A [3204] narrative of the early life, travels and gospel labors of Jesse Kersey, late of Chester county, Pennsylvania. Phila.: T. Ellwood Chapman, 1851. 288 p. NN. A member of the Society of Friends, who labored in the eastern portion of the United States and also travelled in England and Ireland.

Kertesz, Mrs. Andrew. See Gilfillan, Mrs. Andrew Kertesz.

Keyes, Elisha Williams, 1828- [3205] 1910. A reminiscent history of the village and town of Lake Mills, Jefferson County...From 1837 to 1847...Madison: 1894. 55 p. WHi. Growing up in rural Wisconsin.

Keyes, Frances Parkinson [3206] (Wheeler), b. 1885. Along a little way. N.Y.: P. J. Kennedy, 1940. 83 p. DLC. A novelist tells of her conversion to Catholocism.

Keyes, Frances Parkinson [3207] (Wheeler), b. 1885. Capital kaleidoscope...N.Y.: Harper, 1937. 358 p. WHi. Social life (1919-37), by the wife of a U.S. Senator.

Kieffer, Henry Martyn, b. 1845. [3208] The recollections of a drummer-boy. By Harry M. Kieffer, late of the one hundred and fiftieth Pennsylvania Volunteers. Rev. & enl. Boston & N.Y.: Houghton Mifflin, 1911. 250 p. NN. As described by the title. Written for boys.

Kildare, Owen Frawley, 1864- [3209] 1911. My Mamie Rose; story of my regeneration. N.Y.: The Bauer & Taylor co., 1903. 303 p. DLC. Bowery bum who became a newspaper and magazine writer.

Kilgo, John Wesley. Campaign- [3210]

ing in Dixie...N.Y.: Hobson book press, 1945. 223 p. WHi. Republican candidate for Governor in Tennessee in 1943.

Kilgore, Elias Gaston, b. 1856. [3211] Trials and triumphs of a young preacher...Nashville: Publishing house of the M.E. Church, South, 1908. 421 p. DLC. Methodist itinerant preacher in the Southern states.

Kimball, Henry D., b. 1841. [3212] Records of a journey...Cinc.: Jennings & Graham, 1911. 280 p. OrSaW. Methodist clergyman in New Hampshire, New York, Mass., Illinois, Washington and Oregon. Also educator in Oregon.

Kimball, Ivory George, 1843- [3213] 1916. Recollections from a busy life, 1843 to 1911. Washington: Carnahan press, 1912. 229 p. DLC. Lawyer and jurist in the District of Columbia.

Kimball, Maria Porter (Brace). [3214] My eighty years. Boston: 1934. 103 p. Auto., p. 7-36, 73-100. DLC. Wife of army doctor in the West who was a voice teacher.

Kimball, S., b. 1852. Thirty [3215] years in captivity, and my rescue from the bondage of sin. Manchester, N.H.: Albert Ruemely, printer, 1904. 28 p. MWA. Evangelist in Mass., New York and New Hampshire.

Kimball, Solomon Farnham. [3216] Thrilling experiences. Salt Lake City: Magazine pr. co., 1909. 157 p. WHi. Mormon religious writer tells of his religious development.

Kimbrough, Emily, b. 1899. How [3217] dear to my heart. N.Y.: Dodd, Mead & co., 1944. 267 p. NN. Recollections of a girlhood in Muncie, Indiana.

Kinel, Lola. This is my affair. [3218] Boston: Little, Brown, 1937. 355 p. WU. Polish born, the writer came to the U.S. in 1916 where she lived in Chicago and then Hollywood. In America she worked on magazines, and began to become a writer. Earlier, her chief experience was personal secretary to Isadora Duncan.

Kiner, Frederick F. One year's [3219] soldiering...Lancaster: E.H. Thomas, printer, 1863. 219 p. CSmH. Chaplain, 14th Iowa infantry.

King, Barnabas. Fiftieth anni- [3220] versary sermon...1848. N.Y.: J. M. Sherwood, 1849. 23 p. MnHi. Presbyterian clergyman in New Jersey, 1808-1848.

King, Basil, 1859-1928. Conquest [3221] of fear. Garden City, N.Y.: Garden City pub. co., 1921. 270 p. WU. A spiritual autobiography by an Episcopal clergyman.

King, Cardenio Flournoy, b.1867. [3222] The light of four candles. Boston: The author, 1908. 510 p. DLC. Newspaper editor and publisher in North Carolina, Mass. Later he was head of a Mass. financial house which crashed. Much about the financier, T.W. Lawson.

King, Caroline Howard, 1822- [3223] 1909. When I lived in Salem, 1822-1866. Brattleboro: Daye, 1937. 216 p. WHi. An account of "everyday" happenings.

King, Charles, 1844-1933. Trials [3224] of a staff officer. Phila.: L. R. Hamersly & co., 1891. 214 p. DLC. Instructor at West Point, ordnance officer in the West.

King, Frank Marion, b. 1863. [3225] Wranglin' the past; being the reminiscences of Frank M. King. Los Angeles: pr. pub. by the author, 1935. 244 p. DLC. Cowboy in the Southwest; sheriff, customs collector, newspaperman in Arizona.

King, Grace Elizabeth, 1851- [3226] 1932. Memories of a Southern woman of letters. N.Y.: Macmillan, 1932. 398 p. WHi. Louisiana novelist and historian.

King, John Anthony. Twenty-four [3227] years in the Argentine Republic; ...by Col. J. Anthony King, an officer in the army of the republic, and twenty-four years a resident of the country. N.Y.: D. Appleton & co., 1846. 324 p. NN. Experiences of the author in the army.

King, John Rufus. My experi- [3228] ence in the Confederate army and in northern prisons. Clarksburg: 1917. 52 p. WHi. As described by the title.

King, Joseph Elijah, 1823-1913. [3229] A reminiscent book. Hempstead: Alumni assoc. of Fort Edward institute, 1915. 151 p. DLC. The writer taught in a number of

New York seminaries.

King, Leonard, b. 1900? From [3230] cattle rustler to pulpit. San Antonio: Naylor, 1943. 216 p. TxU. Son of cattle rustler who became a rancher and Baptist clergyman in Texas.

King, Margaret (Harned), b. 1871.[3231] The autobiography...N.p.: 1945. 21 leaves. USlGS. The author was a secretary and bookkeeper in Kentucky. After embracing the Mormon faith she moved to Utah where she became a lay worker for her church.

King, Marian. The recovery of [3232] myself; a patient's experience in a hospital for mental illness... New Haven: Yale univ. press, 1931. 148 p. MiU. Story of childhood experiences leading to excessive use of the drug "veronal".

King, Mary B. (Allen). Looking [3233] backward; or, memories of the past. N.Y.: Anson D.F. Randolph & co., 1870. 455 p. NN. Recollections of a school teacher in upper New York state. About half of the book is taken up with an account of her trip to Europe in 1859-60.

King, William Fletcher, b.1830. [3234] Reminiscences. N.Y.: Abingdon press, 1915. 716 p. WHi. Teacher of Latin and Greek at Cornell College in Iowa.

Kingman, Henry, b. 1842. The [3235] travels and adventures...in search of Colorado and California gold, 1859-1865. Delavan, Kansas: Herington sun press, 1917. 68 p. CoD. As described by the title.

Kingsbury, Alice Eliza, 1858- [3236] 1937. In old Waterbury...Waterbury: Mattatuck historical soc., 1942. 55 p. DLC. A story of youth in Conn.

Kinney, Mrs. Hannah. A review [3237] of the principal events of the last ten years...Boston: J. N. Bradley, 1841. 87 p. WU. The writer, married to a drunkard, was acquitted of the charge of murdering him.

Kinney, Newcombe, b. 1842. [3238] Reminiscences of the Sioux Indian and Civil wars. No imprint, 1916? 12 p. MnHi. With Minnesota outfit in the Union army which moved against the Sioux in North Dakota.

Kino, Eusebio Francisco, d.1711. [3239] Kino's historical memoir of Pimeria Alta...ed. by H.E. Bolton. Cleveland: Arthur H. Clark, 1919. 2 vols. WHi. Jesuit missionary, explorer in the Southwest.

Kinsman, Frederick Joseph, [3240] 1868-1944. Salve mater. N.Y.: Longmans, Green, 1920. 302 p. NN. Account of the gradual changes in the author's theological views which led him, a bishop of the Protestant Episcopal Church, to embrace Roman Catholicism.

Kinzie, Mrs. John H., b. 1806. [3241] Wau-Bun. The early day in the northwest. Chicago: Rand, McNally & co., 1901. 393 p. WHi. The western shores of Lake Michigan in the thirties. Life on the frontier among the Indians in the family of an Indian trader.

Kip, Francis M. Memoirs of an [3242] old Disciple. N.Y.: Robert Carter, 1848. 309 p. N. Clergyman in New York.

Kip, Herbert Zabriskie, b. 1874. [3243] The boy I knew the best. Boston: Badger, 1932. 284 p. DLC. Boyhood in New York in the family of a clergyman of the Dutch reformed church.

Kip, Leonard, 1826-1906. Cali- [3244] fornia sketches with recollections of the gold mines. Albany: E. H. Pease, 1850. 57 p. WHi. Gold miner.

Kip, William Ingraham, 1811- [3245] 1893. The early days of my episcopate. N.Y.: Thomas Whittaker, 1892. 263 p. WHi. Episcopalian in California 1853-1860.

Kirby, Georgiana Bruce, b.1818. [3246] Years of experience. N.Y.: Putnam, 1887. 315 p. WHi. Reformer: slavery, prisons, communal life at Brook Farm.

Kirby, Terrence, b. 1795? The [3247] life and times...of the adventurous and renowned Capt. Kirby, the hero of the war of 1812. (Dictated to M. Hodges). Cinc.: 1865. 32 p. DLC. Much imagined?

Kirby, William. Mormonism ex- [3248] posed...40 years' experience. Nashville: Gospel advocate, 1893. 500 p. CU-B. By an Englishman who came to Utah in 1860 to work as a laborer. This is his story of disillusionment with Mormonism.

Kirk, Charles, 1800-1890. Recol-[3249] lections of Charles Kirk. Phila.: Friends book assoc., 1892. 63 p. PSC. Pennsylvania farmer.

Kirk, Loren O., b. 1871. The [3250] autobiography...Minneapolis: 1936. 57 leaves. MnHi. Builder and architect in Minnesota who learned his business working with his father in Louisiana.

Kirkland, Mrs. Carolina Matilda [3251] (Stansbury), 1801-1864. A new home...(by Mary Clavers, pseud.) 5th ed. N.Y.: C. S. Francis, 1855. TxU. Wife on Michigan frontier. This book was later issued under a slightly different title.

Kirwan, Thomas, 1829-1911. [3252] Soldiering in North Carolina... Boston: 1864. 126 p. DLC. In 1862-64, by a Union soldier.

Kitchen, Victor Constant, b.1891. [3253] I was a pagan. N.Y.: Harper, 1934. 186 p. DLC. Spiritual autobiography by a New York advertising agent who was converted to the Oxford group.

Klaw, Barbara (Van Doren), [3254] b. 1920. Camp follower. N.Y.: Random house, 1944. 166 p. DLC. Wife of soldier stationed in Missouri.

Klein, Henry H. My last fifty [3255] years. N.Y.: 1935. 460 p. WHi. Jewish lawyer and political figure in New York City.

Kliewer, John W., 1869-1938. [3256] Memoirs...North Newton, Kansas: Bethel College, 1943. 150 p. InGo. President of Bethel College in Kansas, clergyman of the Mennonite Church.

Kline, Samuel J., b. 1859. Recol-[3257] lections and comments. Los Angeles: 1924. 277 p. CoD. Jewish merchant, bookkeeper in Illinois.

Klock, Annie Marie (Brengle). [3258] Some of the reminiscences of a life of struggle. Chattanooga: 1889. 22 p. DLC. Itinerant singer, drummer tells of her unhappy childhood, unfaithful husband, etc.

Klumpke, Anna Elizabeth, b.1856. [3259] Memoirs of an artist...Boston: Wright & Potter pr. co., 1940.

91 p. DLC. Painter who returned to California after many years in France.

Knapp, Emma (Benedict), 1847- [3260] 1907. Hic habitat felicitas; a volume of recollections and letters by Mrs. Shepherd Knapp (Emma Benedict). Compiled by her children. Boston: W. B. Clarke co., 1910. 274 p. NN. "The narrative of the first four chapters [p. 1-47] is compiled from recollections written from time-to-time for her children." Early life in New York City.

Knapp, George Fred, b. 1849. A [3261] brief autobiography. Spokane: mimeographed in Knapp bookstore, 1939. 24 p. WaPS. Farmer and teamster in Michigan.

Knapp, Jacob, 1799-1874. Auto- [3262] biography of Elder Jacob Knapp. N.Y.: Sheldon & co., 1868. 341 p. NN. Baptist clergyman in the middle west, temperance worker.

Knapp, William Henry, b. 1812. [3263] An autobiography...Boston: A. Williams & co., 1873. 307 p. Auto., p. 1-221. DLC. Universalist, later Unitarian minister, in New England.

Knebel, Aaron G., b. 1874. Four [3264] decades with men and boys. N.Y.: Association press, 1936. 244 p. DLC. Y.M.C.A. secretary who lived in various parts of the U.S.

Kneeland, Martin D., b. 1848. [3265] Eighty-one years young. Bangor, Maine: Jordan-Frost pr. co., 1930. 191 p. MWA. Presbyterian clergyman in New England.

Knight, Almena R., b. 1836. Rec-[3266] ollections of a mute...Jackson: 1858. 15 p. MiD-B. In Michigan.

Knight, Jane D. Brief narrative [3267] of events touching various reforms. By Jane D. Knight, who was reared in the Society of Friends, and united with the Shakers at Mt. Lebanon, Columbia co., N.Y., in the year 1826, in the twenty-second year of her age. Albany: Weed, Parsons & co., 1880. 29 p. NN. Events leading to the author's decision to join the Shakers.

Knight, Mary. On my own. N.Y.: [3268] Macmillan, 1938. 374 p. WU. Foreign correspondent of the thirties in Europe and Asia.

Knights, Arthur E. Notes by the [3269] way in a sailor's life. San Francisco: A. M. Robertson, 1905. 61 p. CSmH. Merchant captain in the Pacific, from 1850.

Kniseley, Mrs. C. F. Menninger. See Menninger, Flo V. (Kniseley).

Knoblaugh, H. Edward. Correspondent in Spain. London & N.Y.: Sheed & Ward, 1937. 233 p. DLC. During the Spanish civil war. [3270]

Knott, James, b. 1850. The life [3271] history...Seattle: pr. by Pigott Washington, 1929. 44 p. WaPS. An English stone mason who came to the U.S. in 1872, residing in New York, California, Washington.

Knott, Middleton O'Malley. Gone [3272] away with O'Malley; seventy years with horses, hounds and people. Garden City, N.Y.: Doubleday, Doran & co., 1944. 280 p. NN. Experiences as a veterinarian and as a rider to hounds.

Knower, Daniel. The adventures [3273] of a forty-niner...Albany: Weed-Parsons, printers. 1894. 200 p. WHi. Gold miner in California.

Knowles, Archibald Campbell, [3274] b. 1865. Reminiscences of a parish priest. Milwaukee: Morehouse, 1935. 212 p. NN. Episcopal clergyman in Philadelphia.

Knowlton, William Smith, b.1839. [3275] The old schoolmaster. Augusta: Burleigh & Flynt, 1905. 269 p. DLC. In Maine.

Knox, John Clark, b. 1881. A [3276] judge comes of age. N.Y.: Scribner, 1940. 346 p. WHi. Lawyer, federal judge in New York.

Kober, George Martin, 1850– [3277] 1931. Reminiscences of George Martin Kober, M.D. Washington, D.C.: pub. under the auspices of the Kober Foundation of Georgetown univ., 1930. NN. Account of his service in the Army's Medical Corps and in the Surgeon General's Office.

Kobrin, Leon, 1872–1946. [3278] Erinerungen fun a Yiddishn dramaturg. N.Y.: L. Kobring committee, 1925. NN. Factory worker, writer for Yiddish press in Philadelphia, dramatist.

Koch, Carl G., b. 1817. [3279] Lebenserfahrungen. Cleveland: Evangelischen gemeinschaft, 1871. 411 p. IU. Evangelical minister in Ohio and Pennsylvania.

Koenigsberg, Moses, b. 1878. [3280] King News; an autobiography. N.Y.: F. A. Stokes co., 1941. 511 p. NN. Journalistic exploits of one of Hearst's most prominent editors.

Koerner, Gustave, 1809–1896. [3281] Memoirs...Cedar Rapids: Torch press, 1909. 2 vols., WHi. U.S. Minister to Spain, Lt. Governor of Illinois.

Koerner, Hermann Joseph Aloys.[3282] Lebenskaempfe...N.Y.: L. W. Schmidt, 1865. 2 vols. DLC. Professor in New York, who came to the U.S. from Germany.

Koger, Nannie Elizabeth, b.1862. [3283] My life story. Cinc.: Revivalist, 1940. 70 p. DLC. Domestic tribulations on a Kansas farm.

Kohlsaat, Herman Henry, 1853– [3284] 1924. From McKinley to Harding. N.Y.: Scribner, 1923. 241 p. WHi. Journalist in New York who specialized in political writing.

Kohut, Rebekah (Bettelheim), [3285] b. 1864. My portion. N.Y.: Thomas Seltzer, 1925. 294 p. DLC. A Hungarian born Jew, prominent in welfare work in New York.

Kolb, Charles B., b. 1867. Help- [3286] ing up the man who is down; or, seven years in the slums. 2d ed. Columbus: 1910. 37 p. DLC. Methodist clergyman in Ohio.

Kopeloff, Isidore, 1858–1933. [3287] Amol un shpeter. Vilna: Farlag "altnei", 1932. 407 p. NN. A Russian born factory worker and writer for the Yiddish language press in New York.

Kraus, Adolf, b. 1850. Remin- [3288] iscences and comments... Chicago: 1925. 244 p. DLC. Jewish lawyer, political figure in Chicago who was born in Austria-Hungary.

Krebs, Ebba Victoria. Since [3289] coming to America, 1880–1924. Phila.: Lippincott, 1924. 202 p. WHi. A domestic account of life in Delaware by the wife of an immigrant.

Krebs, Katherine (Stauffer), [3290] b. 1867. Back home in Pennsylvania. Phila.: Dorrance, 1937.

213 p. WHi. A story of girlhood days in Pennsylvania.

Krehbiel, Christian Benjamin, [3291] b. 1840. Errinnerungen und bilder eines irren...Moundridge, Kansas: 1903. DLC. An account of mental illness.

Kress, Daniel Hartman. See Kress, Mrs. Lauretta (Eby).

Kress, John Alexander, b. 1839. [3292] Memoirs...No imprint, 1925? 51 p. WHi. West Point graduate tells of experiences in the Civil War, Indian warfare in the West, and the Spanish-American War.

Kress, Mrs. Lauretta (Eby) and [3293] Daniel Hartman Kress. Under the guiding hand...Washington, D.C.: College press, 1932. 240 p. DLC. Husband and wife medical team in Michigan and Illinois. Mr. Kress was licensed to preach by the Seventh Day Adventists.

Kreymborg, Alfred, b. 1883. [3294] Troubadour. N.Y.: Liveright, 1925. 415 p. WU. A poet and playright tells especially of his early life and growing love of music.

Kring, Charles F. Love and law.[3295] ...St. Louis: pub. by the author, 1882. 200 p. Auto., p. 7-47. MoKU. Arson, murder in Illinois in the seventies. The writer was born in Germany.

Kroll, Harry Harrison. I was a [3296] share cropper. N.Y.: Bobbs-Merrill, 1936. 327 p. WU. From share cropper to school teacher and novelist.

Kromer, Tom. Waiting for [3297] nothing. N.Y.: Knopf, 1935. 187 p. DLC. The story of a bum.

Krout, Mary Hannah, 1857-1927. [3298] A looker-on in London. N.Y.: Dodd, Mead, 1899. 352 p. DLC. Foreign correspondent in London.

Krout, Mary Hannah, 1851-1927. [3299] Hawaii and a revolution. N.Y.: Dodd, Mead, 1898. DLC. Foreign correspondent in Hawaii.

Krueger, Max, 1851-1927. [3300] Pioneer life in Texas...San Antonio: press of the Clegg co., 1930? 225 p. WHi. Cowboy, photographer, cattleman, flour mill operator, industrialist.

Krugg, Albert Arthur, b. 1864. [3301] Facts and fancies. Coffeyville, Kan.; C. C. Drake, 1944. 84 p. KHi. Kansas doctor.

Krüsi, Johann Heinrich Hermann[3302] 1817-1903. Recollections of my life. N.Y.: Grafton press, 1907. 439 p. Auto., p. 7-324. WU. The writer, born in Switzerland, taught in American normal schools in New England, New York and New Jersey.

Kubinyi, Victor von, b. 1875. [3303] Through fog - to light...South Bend, Indiana: The Seemore co., 1914. 140 p. DLC. A Hungarian born Catholic priest who turned to the Episcopal Church. His work was conducted mainly in Indiana.

Kuhls, A. A few reminiscences [3304] of forty years in Wyandotte county, Kansas. Kansas City: Lane pr. co., 1904. 45 p. KHi. Catholic clergyman, beginning with 1864.

Kuhn, Mrs. Irene Corbally. [3305] Assigned to adventure. N.Y.: Lippincott, 1938. 431 p. WU. Journalist in Hollywood, New York, Paris, Far East.

Kulberg, Martha, b. 1880. The [3306] story of my life. Brooklyn: 1930. 143 p. MNSL. Nurse in New York; missionary nurse in Norway and China. The period covered is 1900-1927.

Kumarappa, Bharatan, b. 1896. [3307] My student days in America. Bomba: Padma publications, 1945. 108 p. DLC. A student from India tells of his experiences in the U.S. as a student. The time is the twenties.

Kune, Julian. Reminiscences of [3308] an octogenarian Hungarian exile. Chicago: 1911. 216 p. WHi. A Hungarian immigrant who served in the Union army, and covered the Franco-Prussian War for the Chicago Tribune.

Kurtz, Mrs. Frank. See Kurtz, Margo (Rogers).

Kurtz, Margo (Rogers). My rival,[3309] the sky. N.Y.: G. P. Putnam's sons, 1945. 218 p. NN. Autobiography of an army pilot.

Kurtz, W. H., b. 1870. Forty [3310] years in the service of the Lord. N.p.: 1934. 44 p. IaHi. Lutheran clergyman, born in Germany, who served in Washington, Illinois and Iowa.

Kuykendall, William Littlebury, [3311] b. 1835. Frontier days...N.p.: J.M. and H. L. Kuykendall, 1917. 251 p. WHi. The writer was in the sheep and cattle business in Wyoming and the Dakotas, and was also engaged in politics in the Dakotas.

Kyne, Peter Bernard, b. 1880. [3312] Peter B. Kyne. N.Y.: International magazine co., 1919. 31 p. CHi. A businessman in California tells how he came to be a novelist.

Kyner, James Henry, b. 1846. [3313] End of track...as told to Hawthorne Daniel. Caldwell, Idaho: Caxton printers, 1937. 277 p. DLC. After serving in the Union army, the author settled on a homestead in Nebraska, where he became a member of the Legislature. Beginning with 1880's he was a railroad contractor in the West.

## L

Laberge, Mrs. Agnes N. [3314] (Ozman), b. 1870. What God hath wrought. Chicago: Herald pub. co., n.d. 127 p. CoHi. Pentecostal evangelical worker in Kansas, Nebraska, Missouri, Iowa, Oklahoma, Arkansas, Texas, Wisconsin and Washington.

Ladd, Carl Edwin, and Edward [3315] Roe Eastman. Growing up in the horse and buggy days. N.Y.: Nesterman, 1943. 263 p. WHi. A joint autobiography, in which is described life on a New York farm in the 1890's.

Ladenburger, Theodor, b. 1870. [3316] Forty years, by Theodore Laer, (pseud.) N.Y.: Putnam, 1936. 376 p. WHi. A German tells of his Americanization. Little is told of his importing business.

Laer, Theodor (pseud.). See Ladenburger, Theodor.

Lafarge, Oliver, b. 1901. Raw [3317] material. Boston: Houghton Mifflin, 1945. 213 p. WU. Novelist, ethnologist.

Lafferty, John James. An editor, [3318] 1874-1894. No imprint. 20 p. CSmH. Methodist clergyman and editor of religious periodicals who served in Virginia.

Laflin, Louis Ellsworth. Anxious [3319] bench; or, life at a prep school. Chicago: R. F. Seymour, 1929. 337 p. DLC. In New Jersey, 1913-1918.

LaFollette, Robert Marion, 1855-[3320] 1925. LaFollette's autobiography ...Madison: R. M. LaFollette co., 1913. 807 p. WHi. U. S. Senator from Wisconsin, candidate for President.

Lagergren, Carl Gustaf, b. 1846. [3321] Från strids-och arbetsfältet... Minneapolis: Vecoblad pub. co., 1927. 543 p. MnHi. Professor of Theology in Illinois and Minnesota who was born in Sweden.

Laighton, Oscar, b. 1839. Ninety [3322] years at the Isles of Shoals. Boston: Beacon press, 1930. 154 p. WHi. Hotel owner in Maine.

Lake, Simon. Submarine, the [3323] autobiography of Simon Lake as told to Herbert Corey. N.Y.: Appleton-Century, 1941. 303 p. WU. Inventor.

LaLonde, Leona M. Belgium [3324] was my home. Portland, Oreg.: Binfords & Mort, 1944. 166 p. Or. The writer came to the U.S. at the age of 17. This is the story of her life on a Belgian farm.

Lamar, James Sanford, 1829- [3325] 1908. Recollections of pioneer days in Georgia. Washington,D.C.: 1906. 64 p. NcWAtC. Disciple of Christ preacher.

Lamb, E. J., b. 1832. Memories [3326] of the past...Dayton?: United Brethren pub. house, 1906. 257 p. CoD. Farmer, miner, and United Brethren minister in Kansas, Nebraska and Colorado.

Lambert, Sylvester Maxwell, [3327] b. 1882. A Yankee doctor in paradise. Boston: Little, Brown, 1941. 393 p. WU. In the South Pacific, sent by the Rockefeller Foundation.

Lambie, Thomas Alexander, [3328] b. 1885. A doctor without a country. N.Y.: Revell, 1939. 252 p. DLC. Medical missionary for Presbyterians in Africa.

Lambie, Thomas Alexander, [3329] b. 1885. A doctor carries on. N.Y.: Revell, 1942. 173 p. DLC. Further experiences in Africa.

Lambie, Thomas Alexander, [3330] b. 1885. Boot and saddle in Africa.

Phila.: Blakiston, 1943. 158 p. DLC. See the two preceding items.

Lamey, H. T. Side lights. [3331] Denver: P. J. McIntyre, 1906. 94 p. CoHi. The author lived in California in the last years of the 19th century where he was an insurance agent and examiner.

Lamme, Benjamin Garver, 1864- [3332] 1924. ...An autobiography. N.Y.: Putnam, 1926. 271 p. Auto., p. 3-176. WU. Electrical engineer, inventor.

Lampman, Clinton Parks, b.1862. [3333] The great western trail. N.Y.: Putnam, 1939. 280 p. WHi. Cowboy in Wyoming, merchant in Minnesota, advertising executive in Illinois.

Lamson, David Albert. We who [3334] are about to die; prison as seen by a condemned man. N.Y.: Scribner's, 1935. 338 p. NN. The author spent thirteen months in the death house at San Quentin Penitentiary, California, on a conviction for the murder of his wife.

Lamson, Frank Bailey, b. 1867. [3335] Personal recollections. No imprint, 1943? 32 p. MnHi. School principal, newspaper publisher, minor political figure in Minnesota.

Lamson, Zachary G. Autobio- [3336] graphy...Boston: W. B. Clarke, 1908. p. 152-253. WHi. Merchant sailor, 1797-1814.

Lancaster, Joseph, 1778-1838. [3337] Epitome of some of the chief events and transactions in the life of Joseph Lancaster, containing an account of the rise and progress of the Lancasterian system of education; and the author's future prospects of usefulness to mankind; written by himself, and published to promote the education of his family. New Haven: pr. for the author by Baldwin & Peck, 1833. 54 p. NN. English educational reformer who came to the U.S. in 1818.

Landa, Harry, b. 1860? As I [3338] remember. 3d ed. San Antonio: Carleton pr. co., 1945. 100 p. TxU. Rancher, flour miller, railroad president in Texas.

Landon, Seymour. Fifty years in [3339] the itinerant ministry. N.Y.: N. Tibbals, 1868. 48 p. CtY. Methodist clergyman in New York 1814-1868.

Landrum, William Bibb, b. 1803. [3340] The life and travels of the Rev. William B. Landrum, of the Kentucky Conference, M.E. Church, South. Nashville, Tenn.: Southern Methodist pub. house, 1878. 427 p. NN. As described by the title.

Lane, Dick, b. 1837. Confessions [3341] of a criminal...Chicago: Prairie state pub. co., 1904. 96 p. DLC. Includes prison experiences.

Lane, Horace, b. 1789. The [3342] wandering boy...Skaneateles: pr. by Luther A. Pratt, 1839. 224 p. DLC. Sailor, imprisoned for murder, robbery in New York.

Lane, Isaac, 1834-1937. Auto- [3343] biography...Nashville: M. E. Church, South, 1916. 192 p. Auto., p. 47-142. WHi. Methodist minister (Negro) in Tennessee, who became a Bishop, responsible for Texas and Louisiana.

Lane, Lunsford. The narrative [3344] of Lunsford Lane, formerly of Raleigh, N.C., embracing an account of his early life, the redemption by purchase of himself and family from slavery, and his banishment from the place of his birth for the crime of wearing a colored skin. Published by by himself. Boston: J. G. Torrey, printer, 1842. 54 p. NN. As described by the title.

Lane, Lydia Spencer (Blaney). [3345] I married a soldier. Phila.: Lippincott, 1893. 214 p. DLC. A domestic account of life in Texas and New Mexico.

Lane, Samuel Alanson, b. 1815. [3346] Forty years of Akron and Summit County. Akron: Beacon job department, 1892. 1167 p. Auto., p. 9-30. WHi. Merchant, newspaper publisher and city mayor, in Ohio.

Lane, Walter Paye, 1817-1892. [3347] The adventures...Marshall, Texas: News messenger pub. co., 1928. 180 p. WHi. A military account: Confederate army, Indian fighter, war with Mexico.

Lang, Lincoln Alexander, b.1867. [3348] Ranching with Roosevelt. Phila.: J. B. Lippincott, 1926. 367 p. DLC. Irish born cattle rancher in the Dakotas.

Langewiesche-Brandt, Wolfgang [3349]

Ernst, b. 1907. A student's odyssey. London: F. Muller, 1935. 247 p. DLC. A German student, seeking to further his education in the United States works on a ranch in the Rocky Mountains.

Langley, John W. They tried to [3350] crucify me. Pikeville: 1929. 256 p. WHi. A member of the U.S. House of Representatives from Kentucky tells of his imprisonment for violation of the Prohibition Act.

Langston, John Mercer, 1829- [3351] 1897. From the Virginia plantation to the national capital... Hartford: Am. pub. co., 1894. 534 p. WHi. Ohio Negro educator, U.S. Minister-Resident in Haiti, member of the U.S. House of Representatives.

Langtry, Lillie, 1852-1929. The [3352] days I knew. N.Y.: Doran, 1925. 300 p. DLC. Famous English actress who often played in the U.S.

Lanier, James Franklin Doughty, [3353] 1800-1881. Sketch of the life of J.F.D. Lanier. 2d ed. N.p.: 1877. 87 p. Auto., p. 5-48. WHi. Financier in Indiana.

Lankton, Arba, b. 1835. Incidents [3354] ...Hartford: Arba Lankton's total abstinence society, 1891. 184 p. DLC. Newspaper publisher in New York and Conn., known for his work in the Conn. temperance movement.

Lansing, Robert, 1864-1928. [3355] The peace negotiations, a personal narrative. Boston: Houghton Mifflin, 1921. 328 p. WHi. In which the Secretary of State emphasizes his role in the Paris Peace Conference.

Lansing, Robert, 1864-1928. [3356] War memoirs...N.Y.: Bobbs Merrill, 1935. 369 p. WHi. By the Secretary of State, 1915-1920.

Lapeyrouse, Stanislas de. [3357] Miseres oubliées, Californie, 1850-1853...Paris: Maurice Dreyfus, n.d. 301 p. CU-B. Frenchman in California mines.

Lappin, S. S. Where the long [3358] trail begins. Cinc.: Standard pub. co., 1913. 65 p. MoCanD. On a pioneer farm in the seventies in Missouri and Illinois.

Larcom, Lucy, 1824-1893. A New [3359] England girlhood. Boston: Houghton Mifflin, 1889. 274 p. WU. By a teacher and poet.

Larimer, William Henry Harrison, 1840-1910. Reminiscences [3360] of General William Larimer... Lancaster, Pa.: Press of the New Era pr. co., 1918. 266 p. NN. Pioneer life in Kansas, Nebraska and Colorado.

Lark, Fred A. The lark's nest. [3361] N.Y.: Neale, 1918. 174 p. DLC. The son of an Arkansas farmer tells of his youth.

Larowe, Mrs. Nina (Churchman) [3362] An account of my life's journey so far...Portland: 1917? 68 p. OrU. Actress in California, Nevada and Oregon.

Larpenteur, August Louis, b.1823. [3363] Reminiscences and recollections of St. Paul...1843-1898. No imprint, 1898? 48 p. MnS. By a merchant.

Larpenteur, Charles, 1807-1872. [3364] ...Forty years a fur trader on the upper Missouri; the personal narrative of Charles Larpenteur, 1833-1872. Chicago: The Lakeside press, 1933. 388 p. NN. As described by the title.

Larsen, Oluf Christian, b. 1836. [3365] A biographical sketch (written down by his son). No imprint. 69 leaves. USlGS. Born in Norway, the writer came to Utah in 1862 where he engaged in farming, in Indian fighting, and in lay work for the Mormon church.

Larson, James, 1841-1921. Sergeant Larson, 4th Cav. San [3366] Antonio: Southern literary institute, 1935. 326 p. NN. Experiences as an enlisted man on the frontier before and during the Civil War.

Larson, Laurence Marcellus. [3367] The logbook of a young immigrant. Northfield: Norwegian-American history assoc., 1939. 302 p. WHi. A college professor, born in Norway, tells of his early days in the U.S. as a college student and high school teacher.

Lathers, Richard, d. 1903. [3368] Reminiscences...N.Y.: Grafton, 1907. 425 p. WHi. Merchant and farmer in New York.

Lathrop, Clarissa Caldwell, [3369] 1847-1892. A secret institution.

N.Y.: Bryant pub. co., 1890. 339 p. DLC. The author was committed by her family to an institution treating mentally unbalanced persons.

Lathrop, George, d. 1848. Dark [3370] and terrible deeds...New Orleans: W. Stuart, 1848. 31 p. DLC. Robber, murderer who was hung in New Orleans.

Lathrop, Joseph, 1731-1820. Ser- [3371] mons...with a memoir of the author's life. Springfield: A.G. Tannatt, 1821. 327 p. Auto., p. xi-lx. MiD-B. Baptist clergyman in Mass.

Lathrop, Marvin M., 1830-1915. [3372] Some pioneer recollections, being the autobiography of George Lathrop, one of the first to help in the opening of the West. And a statement made by John Sinclair relative to the rescue of the Donner party, also an extract from a letter written by Geo. McKinstry with reference to the rescue of the Donner party. Phila.: George W. Jacobs & co., 1927. 32 p. NN. Pioneer in Wyoming and Nebraska. Indian fighter, driver of stage coaches, cowboy.

Latimer, Henry Randolph, [3373] b. 1871. The conquest of blindness. N.Y.: Am. foundation for the blind, 1937. 363 p. WU. By a teacher of the blind.

Latta, Morgan London, b.1853. [3374] History of my life and work. Raleigh: 1903. 371 p. DLC. The author founded a school in North Carolina.

Latta, Robert Ray, b. 1836. Rem- [3375] iniscences of pioneer life. Kansas City: F. Hudson, 1912. 186 p. WHi. Forty-niner. In the fifties and sixties he farmed, logged and operated a saw mill in the middlewest.

Lauderdale, Robert Jaspar, [3376] b. 1854. Life on the range and on the trail. San Antonio: Naylor, 1936. p. 96-213. WHi. A Southwestern account of the cattle trail.

Laughlin, Clara Elizabeth, 1873- [3377] 1941. Traveling through life; being the autobiography of Clara E. Laughlin. Boston & N.Y.: Houghton Mifflin, 1934. 319 p. NN. The author, a writer of travel books and magazine articles, who also ran a travel agency, tells of her literary and business career.

Laughlin, Edward Douglas. The [3378] Yaqui gold. San Antonio: Naylor, 1943. 80 p. WHi. Arizona cowhand who about 1900 tried to take gold out of Yaqui territory in Mexico.

Lavayssière, P. Un mission- [3379] naire en Californie. Limoges: Ardant frères, 1863. 119 p. DLC. As described by the title.

Laven, Goat. Rough stuff. The [3380] life story of a gangster. London: Falcon books, 1933. 231 p. NN. Gangster in Illinois in the 20th century.

Lavender, David Sievert, b.1910. [3381] One man's West. Garden City, N.Y.: Doubleday, Doran, 1943. 298 p. DLC. Gold miner in Colorado, cattle rancher in Colorado and Utah.

Lawes, Lewis E. Twenty thou- [3382] sand years in Sing Sing. N.Y.: Ray Long & Richard R. Smith, 1932. 412 p. WU. Prison guard; warden at Sing Sing beginning in 1920.

Lawing, Mrs. Nellie (Trosper) [3383] Neal. Alaska Nellie. Seattle: 1940. 201 p. DLC. Prior to operating restaurants in Alaska, the author was a cook in Colorado mining towns.

Lawler, Benjamin Franklin, [3384] b. 1834. Forty years in the ministry... Boulder, Colo.: Press of Rocky Mountain Baptist, 1902. 187 p. CoD. Baptist in Missouri, Nebraska and Colorado.

Lawlor, David S. The life and [3385] struggle of an Irish boy in America ...Newton: Carroll pub. co., 1936. 274 p. WHi. Newspaper advertising.

Lawrence, Catherine S. Auto- [3386] biography. Sketch of life and labors of Miss Catherine S. Lawrence, who in early life distinguished herself as a bitter opponent of slavery and intemerance...rev. ed. Albany, N.Y.: J. B. Lyon, printer, 1896. 238 p. WHi. Social reformer, hospital worker during Civil War.

Lawrence, Frieda, b. 1879. "Not [3387] I, but the wind..." N.Y.: Viking, 1934. 297 p. DLC. The German born wife of the English novelist, D. H. Lawrence, tells of their life together, including the time spent in the U.S.

Lawrence, Gertrude. A star [3388] danced. Garden City, N.Y.: Doubleday, Doran, 1945. 238 p. DLC. English actress and musical comedy star who played frequently in the U.S.

Lawrence, John Craig, b. 1861. [3389] The story of my life. N.p.: 1925. 69, 16 leaves. Wa. Railroad Commissioner and Superintendent of public instruction for the Territory of Washington.

Lawrence, William, 1850-1914. [3390] Memories of a happy life. Boston: Houghton Mifflin, 1926. 424 p. WHi. Episcopal Bishop of Massachusetts.

Lawrence, William, 1850-1914. [3391] Fifty years. Boston: Houghton Mifflin, 1923. 97 p. DLC. See the preceding item. This is Bishop Lawrence's spiritual autobiography.

Laws, Wallace, b. 1872. Life of [3392] a tramp. Chicago: M.A. Donohue, 1910. 157 p. ICU. As described by the title.

Lawson, Joseph Albert, b. 1859. [3393] Some high spots in the commonplace autobiography of J.A.L. Albany, N.Y.: J. B. Lyon co., 1934. 148 p. DLC. Lawyer in New York.

Lawson, Josephine, b. 1865. [3394] Reminiscences from a simple life...Oakland: Messiah's advocate, 1920. 154 p. WHi. Swedish born lay worker on behalf of the Adventists.

Lawson, Thomas William, 1857- [3395] 1925. Frenzied finance...N.Y.: Ridgway-Thayer, 1906. 559 p. WHi. Banker, broker.

Lawson, William Pinkney. The [3396] log of a timber cruiser. N.Y.: Duffield, 1926. 214 p. CoD. Employee of the U.S. Forest Service in New Mexico (20th century).

Lawton, Ralph Waldo. An engin- [3397] eer in the Orient. Los Angeles: Walton & Wright, 1942. 201 p. DLC. After employment in New York, Pa., and Wisconsin, the author moved to India.

Laylander, Orange Judd, b. 1858. [3398] The chronicles of a contented man. Chicago: A. Kroch, 1928. NN. Schoolteaching in Ohio and Iowa; in the school book publishing business with Ginn & co.

Layton, Christopher, 1821-1898. [3399] Autobiography...Ed. by John Q. Cannon. Salt Lake City, Utah: The Deseret news, 1911. 317 p. NN. Bishop in the Mormon Church; experiences in the Mormon Battalion; life in Nevada, Utah and Arizona.

Lazarovich-Hrebelianovich, [3400] Eleanor Hulda (Calhoun). Pleasures and palaces...N.Y.: Century, 1915. 360 p. DLC. American born actress who married a Serbian and lived most of her life in Europe.

Leach, Frank Aleamon, b. 1846. [3401] Recollections of a newspaperman ...San Francisco: S. Levinson, 1917. 416 p. WHi. Director of the U.S. Mint, and newspaperman in California.

Leach, Frank Willing, 1855- [3402] 1943. Frank Willing Leach, a partial portrait by himself. Lancaster: Wickersham press, 1943. 20 p. DLC. Lawyer who was active in the Republican party on the national level, and who wrote history in his spare time.

Leader, John. Oregon through [3403] alien eyes. Portland, Oreg.: J. K. Gill, 1922. 147 p. Auto., p. 13-81. OrHi. The author, born in England, during the first World War directed the officer training program at the University of Oregon, and helped organize the Oregon Home Guard.

Leader, Pauline. And no birds [3404] sing. N.Y.: Vanguard, 1931. 276 p. WU. A deaf Jewess in New York who had an illegitimate child and was sent to a reformatory.

Leahey, Edward. Seven years in [3405] a monastery...Albany: C. Killmer, 1848. 48 p. N. Trappist monk in N.Y.

Leale, John, 1850-1932. Recollec- [3406] tions of a tule sailor, by John Leale (1850-1932), master mariner, San Francisco bay, with interpolations by Marion Leale. San Francisco: George Fields, 1939. 311 p. NN. Ferryboat captain on San Francisco bay for thirty-six years and before that on the Sacramento and San Joaquin rivers.

Learned, Ellin (Craven). Finding [3407] the way. N.Y.: Parish visitors of Mary Immaculate, 1940. 107 p. Auto., p. 15-79. DLC. The story of the author's conversion to Catholicism.

Leary, Eliza Ferry, b. 1851. [3408] Through historic years... Seattle: Dogwood press, 1934. 93 p. DLC. Club woman and D.A.R. member in the state of Washington.

Leavell, William Hayne, b. 1850. [3409] After fifty years of public service. Houston: n.d. 15 p. TxU. Presbyterian clergyman in New York, New Hampshire, Mass., Mississippi and Texas.

Leavitt, Humphrey Howe, 1796- [3410] 1873. Autobiography of the Hon. Humphrey Howe Leavitt...N.Y.: 1893. 160 p. DLC. The author served in the war of 1812; was a U.S. District Judge in Ohio (1834-71) and represented Ohio in the House of Representatives (1830-34).

Leavitt, Michael Bennett, b.1843. [3411] Fifty years in theatrical management. N.Y.: Broadway pub. co., 1912. 735 p. WU. Mainly in Boston, San Francisco and New York.

Leckband, Theodore Hans Jurgen [3412] b. 1854. Eighty seven years... Clinton: Pinney pr. co., 1941. 58 p. DLC. Iowa building contractor.

Leckenby, Charles H., b. 1872. [3413] The tread of pioneers. Steamboat Springs, Colo.: Steamboat pilot, 1945. 206 p. CoU. Newspaper reporter and publisher in Colorado, and political figure.

LeConte, Joseph, 1823-1901. The [3414] autobiography...N.Y.: Appleton, 1903. 337 p. WU. Geologist, professor who taught in Georgia, South Carolina and California.

Lee, Aaron, b. 1832. From the [3415] Atlantic to the Pacific...Seattle: Metropolitan press, printers, 1915. 190 p. DLC. Iowa fruit farmer, who then took up a homestead in Washington. During the Civil War he served in the Union Army.

Lee, Mrs. Eliza (Buckminster), [3416] 1794-1864. Sketches of a New England village, in the last century. Boston: J. Munroe & co., 1838. 110 p. DLC. The life of a girl who was raised in a minister's home in a New Hampshire village.

Lee, Eugene, b. 1868. Yeggmen [3417] in the shadows. London: A.H. Stockwell, 1935. 78 p. ViU. Hobo, thief, convict. The locale in the main is the area west of the Mississippi.

Lee, George W. Life and travels [3418] of Elder George W. Lee, the converted sailor. Belton, Texas: Embree, 1904. 101 p. TxBel. Printer, sailor, clergyman of the Disciples of Christ who lived in Florida, Alabama and Texas.

Lee, Mrs. Jarena, b. 1783. The [3419] life and religious experience of Jarena Lee, a coloured lady, giving an account of her call to preach the gospel...Phila.: pub. for the author, 1836. 24 p. DLC. Methodist in Pennsylvania.

Lee, John Doyle, 1812-1877. [3420] Mormonism unveiled...St. Louis: Bryan, Brand, 1877. 390 p. DLC. An official of the Mormon Church who was executed for his part in the Mountain Meadows Massacre. In this book, Lee seeks to blame others.

Lee, John Doyle, 1812-1877. The [3421] life and confession of John D. Lee, the Mormon...Phila.: Barclay & co., 1877. 45 p. DLC. See the preceding item.

Lee, Kate, (pseud.) A year at [3422] Elgin insane asylum...N.Y.: The Erving co., 1902. 138 p. DLC. In Illinois, by an inmate.

Lee, Luther, 1800-1889. Auto- [3423] biography...N.Y.: Phillips & Hunt, 1882. 345 p. WHi. Methodist clergyman, editor of religious journal, and professor, best known for his abolitionist activities. His activities were associated mainly with New York, Ohio and Michigan.

Lee, Mrs. Martha A., b. 1842. [3424] Mother Lee's experience in fifteen years' rescue work, with thrilling incidents of her life... Omaha: 1906. 219 p. DLC. Head of a rescue home for women in Nebraska.

Lee, Ping-Quan, b. 1880. To a [3425]

president's taste...as told to Jim Miller. Emmaus, Pa.: Rodale press, 1939. 278 p. Auto., p. 1-30. DLC. Navy chef who served on Presidential yacht for Harding and Coolidge.

Lee, Richard, b. 1747. A short [3426] narrative of the life of Mr. Richard Lee. Kennebunk, Maine: pr. by Stephen Sewall, for the author, 1804. 24 p. DLC. A spiritual account by a lay Baptist preacher in New England.

Lee, William. The true and [3427] interesting travels of William Lee...London: pr. for T. & R. Hughes, 1808. 40 p. DLC. Englishman who came to this country in 1768. He was a trader and plantation owner, living in the middle and southern colonies. He returned to England in 1781.

Lee, William Mack, b. 1835. [3428] History of the life of Rev. Wm. Mack Lee, body servant of General Robert E. Lee, through the Civil war, cook from 1861 to 1865...Norfolk: Smith pr. co., 1918. 6 p. DLC. Servant to General Lee who eventually became a Baptist minister in Washington, D.C. and in other southern cities.

Lee, Yan Phou, b. 1861. When I [3429] was a boy in China. Boston: Lothrop, 1887. 111 p. CBB. A story of youth in China, and in the U.S. The American experience is related in pages 105-111.

Leech, Samuel, 1798-1848. Thir-[3430] ty years from home, or, a voice from the main deck: being the experiences of Samuel Leech, who was for six years in the British and American navies... Boston: Tappan & Dennet, 1843. 305 p. WHi. War of 1812.

Leeper, David Rohrer, 1832- [3431] 1900. The Argonauts of 'forty-nine; some recollections of the plains and the diggings. South Bend: J. B. Stall & co., printers, 1894. 146 p. DLC. Mining and lumbering in California.

Leeth, John, 1755-1832. ...A [3432] short biography...A reprint with illustrative notes by C.W. Butterfield. Cinc.: R. Clarke, 1883. 90 p. DLC. After 18 years with the Indians in the Old Northwest, among whom he was captive, trapper and trader, Leeth became a farmer in Ohio and Pennsylvania.

Leevier, Mrs. Annette. Psychic [3433] experiences of an Indian princess, daughter of Chief Tommyhawk... Los Angeles: Austin pub. co., 1920. 32 p. DLC. Spiritualist medium and healer.

Lefavor, William. Captain Le- [3434] favor's forty years' travels at sea and in foreign countries. With an account of his shipwrecks. Phila.: J. A. Wagenseller, printer, 1877. 189 p. DLC. As described by the title.

Leffingwell, Charles Wesley, [3435] 1840-1928. Early days at St. Mary's, Knoxville, Illinois. Milwaukee: Morehouse pub. co., 1926. 319 p. DLC. Rector of woman's school operated by Episcopal Church.

Leffman, Henry, 1847-1930. Out-[3436] line autobiography of Henry Leffman, A.M., M.D., Ph.D., D.D.S., of Philadelphia, with a reference index of contributions to science and literature. Phila.: 1905. 21 p. NN. A list of dates, positions held, and professional positions and society memberships.

Leforge, Thomas, b. 1850. Mem-[3437] oirs of a white Crow Indian. N.Y.: Century, 1928. 356 p. WHi. The author lived on the Montana frontier among the Indians.

Left-Hand, Chief, b. 1838? Chief [3438] Left-Hand. His life story. N.Y.: Am. Baptist home mission soc., n.d. 15 p. OkHi. Tells of fighting the white man on the plains in the sixties, and of his conversion to Christianity.

Left Handed, b. 1868. Son of Old [3439] Man Hat, a Navaho autobiography. N.Y.: Harcourt, Brace, 1938. 378 p. WHi. As described by the title.

Le Gallienne, Eva, b. 1899. At [3440] 33. N.Y.: Longmans, Green, 1934. 262 p. WU. Actress.

Leggett, Abraham, 1755-1842. [3441] The narrative of Major Abraham Leggett, of the army of the revolution, now first printed from the original manuscript, written by himself. With an introduction and notes, by Charles I. Bushnell. N.Y.:

priv. pr., 1865. 72 p. NN. As described by the title.

Lehman, Leo Herbert, 1895- [3442] 1950. The soul of a priest; my conversion to the Pauline succession. N.Y.: Loizeaux, 1942. 163 p. DLC. Irish born Catholic priest who renounced Catholicism to become an Evangelical minister.

Lehmann, Lilli, 1848-1929. My [3443] faith through life...N.Y.: Putnam, 1914. 510 p. DLC. German opera singer who has appeared in the U.S.

Lehmann, Liza, 1862-1918. The [3444] life of Liza Lehmann...London: T. Fisher Unwin, 1919. 232 p. WU. Austrian born opera singer.

Lehmann, Lotte, b. 1885. [3445] ...Wings of song, an autobiography. London: Kegan Paul, Trench, Trubner & co., 1938. 251 p. DLC. German born opera singer who sang frequently in the U.S.

Lehr, Elizabeth Drexel. "King [3446] Lehr". Phila.: Lippincott, 1935. 322 p. WHi. The story of her marriage to a notorious social figure of the nineties.

Leigh, Mrs. Frances Butler, [3447] 1838-1910. Ten years on a Georgia plantation since the war. London: R. Bentley, 1883. 347 p. WHi. The story of her relations with Negroes after the Civil War by a plantation owner.

Leighton, Levi, b. 1818. Auto- [3448] biography...written at the age of 72 years. Portland: pr. for the author, n.d. 235 p. MiD-B. Politician, teacher, merchant in Maine.

Leinweber, Martin. One man's [3449] life. Boston: The Christopher pub. house, 1938. 145 p. NN. The author, a German immigrant, tells of his roving life in the United States and the Yukon Territory, Canada.

Leith, John. See Leeth, John.

Lejeune, John Arthur, b. 1867. [3450] Reminiscences of a marine. Phila.: Dorrance, 1930. 488 p. WHi. Spanish-American War, and first World War.

Leland, Charles Godfrey, 1824- [3451] 1903. Memoirs...(By Hans Breitmann, pseud.) N.Y.: Appleton, 1893. 439 p. WU. Journalist, poet, essayist, magazine editor, associated mainly with New York and Philadelphia.

Leland, John, 1754-1841. Some [3452] events in the life of John Leland, written by himself. Pittsfield: pr. by Phineas Allen & son, 1838. 44 p. NN. Baptist clergyman in Virginia, 1776-1791, later in Cheshire, Mass., 1791-1841.

Leman, Walter Moore, b. 1810. [3453] Memories of an old actor. San Francisco: A. Roman co., 1886. 406 p. NN. Recollections of actors and plays; nearly half of the book is devoted to author's career on the Pacific Coast.

Lemley, John, b. 1843. Auto- [3454] biography and personal recollections of John Lemley, editor of the Golden Censer, with seven years' experience as editor and public speaker. Rockford, Ill.: Blakely & Brown, printers, 1875. 400 p. WHi. German born editor in Illinois.

Lemley, John, b. 1843. The [3455] weeping pilgrim, or the early life of...the editor of the Golden Censer. Rockford: Golden Censer, 1869. 64 p. WHi. See the preceding item. This account largely covers the same ground, with emphasis on the early years.

Le Moyne de Morgues, Jacques, [3456] d. 1588. Narrative of Le Moyne, an artist who accompanied the French expedition to Florida under Laudonnière, 1564. Tr. from the Latin of DeBry...Boston: J. R. Osgood & co., 1875. 23 p. DLC. As described by the title.

Lemperle, Julius, b. 1874. This [3457] is my life. No imprint. 104 p. UU. The writer, who was born in Germany, lived in many places and engaged in various occupations, including farming in Utah.

Lenk, Margrete (Klee), b. 1841. [3458] Fünfzehn jahre in Amerika. 3 aufl. Zwickau: Johannes Herrmann, 1911. 144 p. MoHi. The wife of a clergyman who came to St. Louis from Dresden.

Lenroot, Mrs. Clara (Clough), [3459] b. 1856. Long, long ago. Appleton: Badger pr. co., 1929. 68 p. WHi. A Wisconsin childhood in the sixties and seventies.

Lent, Henry Bolles, b. 1901. [3460] Sixty acres more or less; the

diary of a week-end Vermonter.
N.Y.: Macmillan, 1941. 194 p. DLC.
An account of rural life.

Leonard, Adna Bradway, 1837– [3461] 1916. The stone of help; autobiography of A. B. Leonard...for twenty-four years corresponding secretary of the missionary society and Board of Foreign Missions of the Methodist Episcopal Church. N.Y., Cinc.: The Methodist book concern, 1915. 349 p. DLC. As described by the title.

Leonard, Eddie (pseud.). See Toney, Lemuel Gordon.

Leonard, William Ellery, b.1876. [3462] The locomotive-God. N.Y.: Century, 1927. 434 p. WU. Professor of literature at the University of Wisconsin who suffered "fear of spatial distance from a centre of safety". Poet.

Leonard, Zenas, 1809–1858. [3463] ...Narrative...Chicago:R.R. Donnelley, 1934. 278 p. WHi. Fur trapper and trader in the Rockies.

Leonardo, Richard Anthony, [3464] b. 1895. American surgeon abroad. N.Y.: Froben press, 1942. 235 p. DLC. The author studied abroad and made several professional visits to western Europe.

Leonhardt, Edmund. Auf den [3465] strassen der west...Ludwigshafen am Rhein: N.S.Z.–Rheinfront, 1940. 418 p. DLC. A wandering musician. For his American experiences see p. 235–303. Written down by Hermann Moos.

Leonhart, Rudolph. Errinerungen [3466] an Neu Ulm. Erlebnisse aus dem Indianer-gemetzel in Minnesota, 1862. Pittsburg: 1880. 46 p. DLC. Teacher in Minnesota, 1860–62, who experienced an attack by Indians.

Lepine, Paul, b. 1865. The life [3467] story of a lumberjack. N.p.: 1924? 164 p. DLC. In the Rockies by a Canadian born lumberjack and railroad worker.

Leslie, Charles Robert, 1794– [3468] 1859. Autobiographical recollections...Boston: Ticknor & Fields, 1860. 363 p. Auto., p. 1–170. WHi. Painter, born in England of American parents, who lived abroad many years.

Leslie, Marjorie (Ide). Childhood [3469] in the Pacific. Samoa-Philippines-Spain. London: Macdonald, 1943. 110 p. DLC. The writer's father was an American diplomat.

Letterman, Jonathan, 1824–1872. [3470] Medical recollections of the Army of the Potomac. N.Y.: Appleton, 1866. 194 p. OU. Written by the surgeon who was Medical Director of the Army of the Potomac.

Levell, Robert O. "War on the [3471] ocean", a sailors souvenir. Newcastle, Ind.: 1937. 56 p. DLC. Convoy duty during the first World War.

Levick, Elizabeth W., b. 1789. [3472] Recollections of her early days... Phila.: priv. pr., 1881. 117 p. Auto., p. 9–79. MWA. Philadelphia Quaker.

Levinger, Lee Joseph, b. 1890. [3473] A Jewish chaplain in France. N.Y.: Macmillan, 1921. 220 p. WU. As described by the title except that the autobiographical element is not strong.

Levison, Jacob Bertha, b.1862. [3474] Memories for my family. San Francisco: pr. by John Henry Nash, 1933. 282 p. CHi. California underwriter, a Jew, writes about his life and his love for music.

Levy, John, b. 1797. The life and [3475] adventures of John Levy. Lawrence, Mass.: pr. by R. Bower, 1871. 82 p. DLC. A carpenter in New York who was born in the West Indies and who was impressed into the British navy.

Levy, Rosalie Marie, b. 1889. [3476] Thirty years with Christ. N.Y.: 1943. 246 p. Auto., p. 5–169. DLC. Jewish convert to Catholicism who wrote a number of religious books.

Lewis, Dai H., b. 1866. America [3477] bid me welcome; the autobiography of Dai H. Lewis, managing director of the Automobile Club of Buffalo. Pub. by the author, 1943. 151 p. NN. Experiences in the cycle business, editor of the American Wheelman, and secretary and director ot the Buffalo Automobile Club, 1904.

Lewis, David, 1783–1867. Recol- [3478] lections of a superannuate; or, sketches of life, labor and experience in the Methodist itinerancy. Ed. by S. M. Merrill. Cinc.: pr. at the Methodist book concern for the author, 1857. 311p. DLC. In New York, Ohio, and New England.

Lewis, David, 1790-1820. The [3479] confession or narrative, of David Lewis. Containing an account of the life and adventures of this celebrated counterfeiter and robber...Carlisle: pr. and pub. by John M'Farland, 1820. 61 p. DLC. In Pennsylvania.

Lewis, Dio, 1823-1886. Gypsies; [3480] or, why we went gypsying in the Sierras. Boston: Eastern book co., 1881. 416 p. DLC. A New England physician who retired and spent several years camping in California.

Lewis, Mrs. Faye Cashatt. The [3481] Doc's wife. N.Y.: Macmillan, 1940. 198 p. DLC. In a rural community in Iowa. Both the writer and her husband were physicians.

Lewis, H. E. Fights and adven- [3482] tures with the Indians; thrilling stories of an American scout on the western plains in the old days. East Chattanooga, Tenn.: Andrews printery, 1922. 94 p. DLC. As described by the title.

Lewis, James Campbell, 1879. [3483] Black Beaver, the trapper... From the Amazon to the Mackenzie rivers. Chicago: pr. by Robert O. Law co., 1911. 58 p. DLC. As described by the title.

Lewis, John, 1727-1760. A nar- [3484] rative of the life...of John Lewis, who was executed at Chester,... 1760, for the...murder of his wife...New Haven: reprinted by James Parker & co., 1762. 9 p. DLC. In Pennsylvania.

Lewis, John I., b. 1834. My gar- [3485] den of roses; or, the footnotes of life. Berkeley?: 1913? 106 p. CSmH. California miner, 1853.

Lewis, Joseph Goold, b. 1824. [3486] Reminiscences of days gone by. Portland, Maine: 1901. 45 p. MWA. Sailing master.

Lewis, Joseph Vance. Out of the [3487] ditch; a true story of an ex-slave. Houston, Texas: Rein & sons co., prtrs., 1910. 154 p. NN. Career of a Negro lawyer both in the North and in Texas.

Lewis, Mary Hammett. An ad- [3488] venture with children. N.Y.: The Macmillan co., 1928. 250 p. DLC. Principal of a school in Ohio.

Lewis, Seth, 1764-1848. Auto- [3489] biographical memoir... N.p.: F. F. Hansell, 1847? LU. U.S. District Judge in the South tells also of his earlier experiences at business and law in Louisiana and Mississippi.

Lewis, Tessie Edna, b. 1886. [3490] Twelve months in an army hospital, by a nurse who didn't go across. Washington, D.C.: The Able printers, 227 p. DLC. During the first World War.

Lewisohn, Ludwig, b. 1882. Up [3491] stream...N.Y.: Boni & Liveright, 1922. 248 p. WU. Professor of literature, critic, novelist. Born in Germany.

Lewisohn, Ludwig, b. 1882. Mid- [3492] channel... N.Y.: Blue ribbon books, 1931. 302 p. DLC. A sequel to the preceding item. In this book the writer discusses his life in Europe, 1924-1934.

Lhamon, William Jefferson, [3493] b. 1855. Twice forty-four. No imprint. 80 leaves. MoHi. Professor of Bible in colleges in Missouri. Clergyman of the Christian Union Church in Ohio, Minnesota and Pennsylvania.

Lienhard, Heinrich, 1821-1904. [3494] A pioneer at Sutter's Fort, 1846-1850; the adventures of Heinrich Lienhard...tr., ed., and annotated by Marguerite Eyer Wilbur from the original German manuscript. Los Angeles: The Calfia society, 1941. 291 p. NN. Frontier gold mining and real estate experiences.

Life in Sing Sing. See Number 1500.

The life of a successful banker, [3495] by his Boswell. San Francisco: Press of Paul Elder, 1905. 8 p. RPB. In California.

Life unveiled, by a child of the [3496] drumlins...Garden City, N.Y.: Doubleday, Page, 1922. 335 p. DLC. A woman tells of her experiences in medical school.

Liggett, Hunter, 1857-1935. [3497] Commanding an American army; recollections of the World War. Boston & N.Y.: Houghton Mifflin, 1925. 207 p. DLC. In France during the first World War.

"Light-fingered Jim". Auto- [3498] biography of a thief. Recorded by

Hutchins Hapgood. N.Y.: Fox, Duffeld, 1903. 349 p. DLC. As described by the title.

Lightcraft, George (pseud.). [3499] Scraps from the log book... Syracuse: Hall & Dickson, 1847. 108 p. NjP. Whaler.

Lightfoot, Captain. See Martin, Michael.

Lighton, William Beebey, b.1805. [3500] Autobiography and reminiscences ...Albany: Munsell, 1854. 311 p. WHi. Escapes from British army. Becomes exhorter, lecturing in New England. Most of this book is not related to his experiences in the U.S. The American period covers 1825-49.

Lighton, William Beeby, [3500-a] b. 1805. Autobiography...New & rev. ed. Albany: Munsell, 1855. 311 p. DLC. Englishman who came to the U.S. in 1825 where he was a Methodist clergyman in Vermont, New Hampshire, Mass., Pa., and New York.

Lighton, William Rheem, [3501] b. 1866. Happy hollow farm. N.Y.: Doran, 1915. 318 p. DLC. Rural life in Arkansas as lived by urbanites from Nebraska.

Lightsey, R. J. The veteran's [3502] story (written down by Ada Christine Lightsey). Meridian: Meridian news, 1899. 51 p. WHi. Confederate soldier.

Liliuokalani, queen of Hawaii, [3503] 1838-1917. Hawaii's story by Hawaii's Queen, Liliuokalani. Boston: Lee & Shepard, 1898. 409 p. DLC. Includes an account of revolution and annexation by the U.S.

Lillehei, Torger August, b. 1870.[3504] Fra sjaelenes verden...Minn.: Augsburg pub. house, 1921. 95 p. MnNS. Lutheran clergyman in Minnesota, Michigan, New York, and New Hampshire.

Lillie, Gordon W., b. 1860. Life [3505] story of Pawnee Bill. N.p.:1916. 22 p. OkHi. Buffalo hunter, Indian fighter.

Lillie, Mrs. R. Shepard. Two [3506] chapters from the book of my life, with poems. Boston: J. Wilson, 1889. 229 p. Auto., p. 1-56. DLC. Spiritualist, medium in New York.

Lilly, Kader, b. 1817. My life [3507] and experience. Williamstown, N.C.: 1903. 27 p. NcWAtC. Layman (Primitive Baptist) tells the story of his conversion.

Linck, James G. ...Paulina pre-[3508] ferred. Portland, Oreg.: Binfords & Mort, 1945. 220 p. DLC. Fisherman and nature lover tells of his experiences in New York, Canada and Oregon.

Lincoln, Abraham, 1809-1865. [3509] "Short autobiography written at the request of a friend..." (In: Abraham Lincoln; complete works ...ed. by John G. Nicolay and John Hay. N.Y.: The Century co., 1894.) Vol. I, p. 638-44. DLC. See also the autobiographical letter to Fell of 1859 in I: 596-7.

Lincoln, John Larkin, 1817-1891. [3510] In memoriam... Boston: Houghton Mifflin, 1894. 641 p. Auto., p. 22-147. DLC. Professor at Brown University.

Lind, Earl (pseud.) Autobio- [3511] graphy of an androgyne. N.Y.: The Medico-legal journal, 1918. 265 p. DLC. As described by the title.

Lindberg, Walter. The winding [3512] road, an autobiography in story form. Burlington, Ia.: The Lutheran literary board, 1933. 279 p. DLC. Finn who sang in many parts of the U.S., and who settled in this country.

Lindbergh, Charles Augustus, [3513] b. 1902. "We". N.Y.: Putnam, 1927. 318 p. Auto., p. 1-230. WHi. Aviator.

Linden, Mrs. Charlotte E., [3514] b. 1859. Autobiography and poems. 3d ed. Springfield, Ohio: 1907? 64 p. DLC. Ohio poet.

Lindevall, Carl August, b. 1863. [3515] Reminiscences of an old clergyman...Rock Island, Ill.: Augustana book concern, 1936. 231 p. DLC. Swedish born Lutheran clergyman in Pennsylvania.

Lindsay, John, b. 1864. Amazing [3516] experiences of a judge...Phila.: Dorrance, 1939. 117 p. Auto., p. 30-45, 49-58. DLC. Lawyer, judge in Montana, born in Scotland.

Lindsay, Nicholas Vachel, 1879- [3517] 1931. Adventures while preaching the gospel of beauty. N.Y.: Mitchell Kennerley, 1914. 186 p. NN. Story of a poetic pilgrimage

Lindsay, Nicholas Vachel, 1879- [3518]
1931. A handy guide for beggars
...N.Y.: Macmillan, 1916. 205 p.
WU. A poet in New Jersey,
Pennsylvania, and in the South on
a tramp voyage.

Lindsey, Benjamin Barr, 1869- [3519]
1943. The dangerous life. N.Y.:
Horace Liveright, 1931. 450 p.
NN. A municipal judge in Denver,
a pioneer in the juvenile courts
movement, and an advocate of
marriage reforms and a worker
for social justice.

Lindsley, Aaron Ladner, 1817- [3520]
1891. Farewell sermon...Portland: 1886. 43 p. OrU. Presbyterian clergyman in Portland,
Oregon.

Linebarger, Paul Myron Wentworth, 1871-1939. Mes mémoires [3521]
abrégés sur les Révolutions de
Sun-Yat-Sen. Paris: Éditions
Mid-nation, 1938. 201 p. DLC.
American born lawyer and judge,
who resigned his federal post to
become legal counsellor to Sun-Yat-Sen.

Linford, James Henry, b. 1836. [3522]
Autobiography. N.p.: 1919. 87 p.
USIGS. Englishman who became
a Mormon priest in Utah, and
who held various offices in the
Mormon Church.

Linhart, George Augustus, [3523]
b. 1884. Out of the melting pot.
Riverside: 1923. 213 p. DLC.
Immigrant from Austro-Hungary
who became a scientist in the U.S.

Linn, Clemen Huntingford Jack, [3524]
b. 1886. Hallelujah Jack, being
the story of a sinner saved by
grace. Louisville: Pentecostal
pub. co., 1917. 120 p. DLC.
Methodist clergyman in Arkansas
and Tennessee; Congregational
minister in Chicago; evangelist.

Linn, John Blair, b. 1777. [3525]
Valerian; a narrative poem...
with a sketch of the life of the
author. Phila.: Palmer, 1805.
97 p. PPPrHi. Presbyterian
clergyman in New York, New
Jersey and Pennsylvania.

Linton, William James, 1812- [3526]
1897. Threescore and ten years,
1820 to 1890; recollections. N.Y.:
C. Scribner's sons, 1894. 236 p.
WHi. Wood engraver, poet, printer
who was born in England.

Lippitt, Francis James, 1812- [3527]
1902. Reminiscences...Providence: Preston & Rounds, 1902.
122 p. WHi. California lawyer.

Lips, Eva. Rebirth in liberty. [3528]
N.Y.: Flamingo, 1942. 304 p.
NN. The process of Americanization of a German intellectual.
For her life in Germany, see her,
Savage Symphony.

Lipscomb, Carl Roscoe, b. 1893. [3529]
My observation oversea. Dyersburg, Tenn.: 1922. 39 p. DLC.
Service with army in first World
War.

Litchfield, Beals Ensign, b.1823. [3530]
Autobiography of Beals E.
Litchfield; or, Forty years intercourse with the denizens of the
spirit world and inspirational
poems by the same author.
Ellicottville, N.Y.: B. E. Litchfield, 1893. 486 p. Auto., p. 17-355. DLC. As described by the
title.

Litchfield, Paul Weeks, b. 1875. [3531]
Autumn leaves; reflections of
an industrial lieutenant. Cleveland:
The Corday & Gross co., 1945.
125 p. DLC. Chemical engineer,
industrialist, long associated with
Goodyear, writes a spiritual
account.

Little, George, 1838-1924. Mem- [3532]
oirs...Tuscaloosa: Weatherford
pr. co., 1924. 125 p. DI. Geologist,
educator in Alabama, Miss. and
Georgia.

Little, James Alexander, b. 1831.[3533]
What I saw on the old Santa Fe
trail...Plainfield: 1904. 127 p.
WHi. Wagon train driver, 1854.

Little, John Andrew, b. 1796. [3534]
The autobiography of a New
Churchman...Phila.: Lippincott,
Grambo, 1852. 258 p. WHi. Swedenborgian in Pennsylvania.

Littlepage, John D. In search [3535]
of Soviet gold. N.Y.: Harcourt,
Brace & co., 1938. 310 p. DLC.
Mining engineer in Alaska, and
from 1928-37 in Soviet Russia.

Livermore, Harriet, 1788-1868. [3536]
A narration of religious experience. In twelve letters...Concord:
pr. by Jacob B. Moore, for the
author, 1826. 282 p. DLC. The
author preached in various New
England and New York cities,

flirting with several churches, finally becoming a member of the Christian Church.

Livermore, Mrs. Mary Ashton [3537] (Rice), 1820-1905. My story of the war: A woman's narrative of four years personal experience as nurse in the union army and in relief work at home, in hospitals, camps, and at the front during the war of the rebellion... Hartford: A. D. Worthington & co., 1888. 700 p. WHi. As described by the title.

Livermore, Mary Ashton (Rice), [3538] 1820-1905. The story of my life ...Hartford, Conn.: A.D. Worthington & co., 1897. 730 p. NN. Army nurse in Civil War, lecturer for temperance and woman's rights.

Livermore, Thomas Leonard, [3539] 1844-1918. Days and events, 1860-1866. Boston & N.Y.: Houghton Mifflin, 1920. 485 p. NN. Union army.

Livingston, John H. "One-two"; [3540] the story of the fifth national air tour as related by the winner... Troy, Ohio: Waco aircraft co., 1930. 31 p. DLC. Aviator.

Livingston, Leon Ray, b. 1872. [3541] Life and adventures of A-no. 1, America's most celebrated tramp. Corry, Pa.: Self mastery press, 1908. 96 p. MoKU. In Mexico, Alaska and various parts of the U.S.

Livingstone, Belle. Belle of [3542] Bohemia...N.Y. & Newark: Barse, n.d. 318 p. KHi. Kansas girl becomes actress, playing in the U.S. and various foreign lands. The period covered is roughly 1875-1925.

Lloyd, Harold Clayton. An [3543] American comedy. N.Y.: Longmans, Green, 1928. 204 p. DLC. Screen star.

Lloyd, John William, b. 1837. [3544] Eneres; or, the questions of Reska. Boston: Houghton Mifflin, 1930. 191 p. DLC. A spiritual account.

Lobdell, Lucy Ann, b. 1824. Narrative of Lucy Ann Lobdell, the [3545] female hunter of Delaware and Sullivan counties, N.Y. N.Y.: The authoress, 1855. 47 p. DLC. A huntress, including her affairs of the heart.

Locke, E. W. Three years in [3546] camp and hospital. Boston: G.D. Russel & co., 1870. 408 p. WHi. Song leader in Union army.

Locke, Jerome G., b. 1882. A [3547] sign of the times...No imprint. 36 p. MtHi. Surveyor General for the state of Montana; an attack upon private power companies.

Lockhart, Mrs. Esther Mehitable [3548] (Selover). Destination, West. By Agnes Ruth (Lockhart) Sengstacken. Portland: Binfords & Mort, 1942. 219 p. NN. A domestic account of pioneer life in the Oregon Territory.

Lockwood, James D. Life and [3549] adventures of a drummer-boy; or, seven years a soldier; a true story. Albany, N.Y.: John Skinner, 1893. 191 p. NN. Experiences during the Civil War, and then four years on the western plains in the regular army.

Lodge, Henry Cabot, 1850-1924. [3550] Early memories. N.Y.: Scribner 1913. 362 p. WHi. This covers the early labors as historian and magazine editor in Mass. of the later U.S. Senator. The account closes with 1880.

Loening, Grover Cleveland, [3551] b. 1888. Our wings grow faster... Garden City, N.Y.: Doubleday, Doran, 1935. 203 p. DLC. Aeronautical engineer in New York.

The Log-cabin lady; an anony- [3552] mous autobiography. Boston: Little, Brown & co., 1922. 108 p. NN. The story of how a woman raised on the western frontier learned the social conventions.

Logan, Deborah (Norris), 1761- [3553] 1839. The Norris house. Phila.: Fair-Hill press, 1867. 12 p. NN. An account of the author's childhood home in Philadelphia.

Logan, Henry M. Fifty-four [3554] years in Kansas, 1867-1921. No imprint. 88 p. KHi. Merchant.

Logan, Mrs. John A. See Logan, Mrs. Mary Simmerson (Cunningham).

Logan, Mrs. Kate Virginia (Cox), [3555] 1840-1915. My Confederate girlhood. Richmond: Garrett & Massie, 1932. 150 p. DLC. The wife of General Logan tells of her courtship, and of her experiences and social life during the Civil War. The period covered is 1860-65.

Logan, Mrs. Mary Simmerson [3556] (Cunningham), 1838-1923. Reminiscences of a soldier's wife. N.Y.: Scribner, 1913. 470 p. WHi. A domestic account, emphasizing social affairs, by the wife of John A. Logan, military figure, and U.S. Senator from Illinois.

Logan, Olive, 1839-1909. Before [3557] the footlights and behind the scenes... Phila.: Parmelee, 1870. 612 p. WU. Actress.

Loguen, Jermain Wesley, 1814- [3558] 1872. The Rev. J. W. Loguen as a slave and as a freeman... Syracuse: J.G.K. Truair, printer, 1859. 454 p. WHi. Slave, abolitionist, who then became a Methodist clergyman in New York. Though written in the third person, the D.A.B. believes this to be autobiographical. See also the book on Negro authors by Loggins.

Lomas, Thomas J. Recollec- [3559] tions of a busy life. No imprint. 220 p. WHi. Pioneer; mining in California in sixties; farming in Wisconsin in seventies.

London, Jack, 1876-1916. Jack [3560] London's "What life means to me". Memorial ed. San Francisco: Socialist Party, 1916. 23 p. CU-B. The story of his early life in California, and how he discovered the evils of capitalism.

London, Jack, 1876-1916. The [3561] road. N.Y.: Macmillan, 1907. 224 p. WU. The author's life when a hobo.

Long, Augustus White. Son of [3562] Carolina. Durham: Duke univ. press, 1939. 280 p. WHi. Professor of English literature at Princeton, 1922-16, who was raised in North Carolina and attended the state university as an undergraduate.

Long, Charles Chaillé. See Chaillé-Long, Charles.

Long, Dwight. Seven seas on a [3563] shoestring. ..N.Y.: Harper, 1939. 310 p. DLC. The author sailed around the world in a ketch.

Long, Francis. Half a world [3564] away; from boarding school to Jap prison. N.Y.: Farrar & Rinehart, 1943. 243 p. DLC. When the war broke out, the author was in Shanghai. He was taken prisoner by the Japanese in the Philippines.

Long, Francis A., 1859-1937. [3565] A prairie doctor of the eighties... Norfolk, Nebr.: Huse, 1937. 223 p. DLC. In Iowa and Nebraska.

Long, Green H., 1817-1851. The [3566] arch fiend...N.Y.: Orton, 1852. 31 p. MoU. Robber, murderer in New York, Missouri, Arkansas and Pennsylvania.

Long, Huey Pierce, 1893-1935. [3567] Every man a king...New Orleans: National book co., 1933. 343 p. WHi. Louisiana governor and U.S. Senator.

Long, James Irvin, 1861-1928. [3568] Pioneering in Mexico. Los Angeles: Long co., 1942. 120 p. DLC. An American youth who worked on Mexican mines and on railroads.

Long, Mrs. Maggie E. (Miller), [3569] 1862-1937. "The prairie doctor's wife". (In: A prairie doctor of the eighties...by Francis A. Long. Norfolk, Nebr.: Huse pub. co., 1937). p. 161-179. DLC. In Nebraska.

Long, Mason, b. 1842. The life [3570] of Mason Long, the converted gambler...Fifth ed. Fort Wayne: 1882. 280 p. NN. Gambler, Union army soldier.

Long, Robert McKee, b. 1853. [3571] Interesting incidents in the life of R. M. Long. Sac City: Sac City sun co., 1939? 131 p. Ia-HA. Teacher and farmer in Iowa.

Long, Sol L. Recollections of a [3572] country lawyer. Winfield, Kan.: Courier pr. co., 1906. 165 p. KKc. In Kansas.

Longfellow, Ernest Wadsworth, [3573] 1845-1921. Random memories. Boston: Houghton Mifflin, 1922. 263 p. WU. Painter. This account closes with 1882.

Longley, William P., d. 1878. [3574] Adventures of Bill Longley. Nocogdoches: n.d. 74 p. DLC. Desperado in Texas and Louisiana.

Longmire, James. Narrative. [3575] No imprint. 14 p. WaU. Longmire came to Washington in 1853 where he engaged in farming and Indian fighting.

Longstreet, James, 1821-1904. [3576]
From Manassas to Appomattox;
memoirs of the Civil war in America. Phila.: J. B. Lippincott co.,
1896. 13-690 p. WHi. A military
account by an officer in the Confederate army.

Longwell, Oliver Henry, 1855- [3577]
1920? Autobiography. Des Moines:
Highland pub. co., 1919. 156 p.
IaDm. College professor and
president in Iowa.

Longworth, Alice (Roosevelt). [3578]
Crowded hours...N.Y.: Scribner,
1933. 355 p. WHi. A political
account by the wife of Nicholas
Longworth, speaker of the U.S.
House of Representatives.

Loomis, Frederic, 1877-1949. [3579]
...Consultation room. N.Y.:
Knopf, 1939. 281 p. DLC.
California physician.

Loomis, Frederic, 1877-1949. [3580]
The bond between us...N.Y.:
Knopf, 1942. 267 p. DLC. California physician tells of his early
experiences in the mines of
Alaska; and of his patients and
their problems.

Loomis, William Isaacs, 1810- [3581]
1888. Incidents and facts in my
life. N.Y.: Holman, printer, 1867.
36 p. DLC. Baptist clergyman,
amateur astronomer in New York.

Lope, Mary E. Clary. Life, [3582]
reminiscences and travels of
M.E.C. Lope...Maysville, Ky.:
F. W. Bauer, printer, 1889.
58 p. DLC. Teacher in West
Virginia who is persecuted,
robbed and jailed.

Lord, Eleanor Louisiana, b. 1866.[3583]
Stars over the schoolhouse...
N.Y.: R. R. Smity, 1938. 239 p.
WU. College professor and dean
at Goucher.

Lord, Mrs. Elizabeth (Laughlin),[3584]
b. 1841? Reminiscences of
eastern Oregon. Portland: The
Irwin-Hodson co., 1903. 255 p.
WHi. Youthful days in a pioneer
Oregon family.

Lord, George A., 1820-1888. [3585]
A short narrative...Troy: 1864.
64 p. Auto., p. 5-14. DLC. Union
army soldier who was born in
Canada.

Lord, John, b. 1846. Frontier [3586]
dust. Hartford: E. V. Mitchell,
1926. 198 p. WHi. Union army
soldier. Ranchman, cowboy in the
West.

Loring, William Wing, 1818-1886.[3587]
A confederate soldier in Egypt,
by W. W. Loring...féreek pacha
and general in the army of the
khedive of Egypt. N.Y.: Dodd,
Mead, 1884. 450 p. NN. A record
of ten years' service, including
the campaign against Abyssinia
in 1875-76.

Lorrain, Alfred M. The helm, [3588]
the sword, and the cross. Cinc.:
Poe & Hitchcock, 1862. 456 p.
LU. Merchant sailor; soldier
in War of 1812; Methodist clergyman in Louisiana and Ohio.

Losche, Albert Carl, b. 1924. [3589]
Washington memoirs. Indianapolis: Indianapolis pr. co., 1940.
200 p. DLC. Page in the U.S.
House of Representatives, 1937-38.

Losee, Almira, b. 1825. Life [3590]
sketches...N.Y.: pr. for the author
by Nelson & Phillips, 1877. 229 p.
MoKU. Non-sectarian missionary
worker in New York.

Lothrop, Samuel Kirkland, 1804-[3591]
1886. Some reminiscences.
Cambridge: J. Wilson, 1888.
266 p. DLC. Unitarian minister
in New Hampshire and Mass. in
the first half of the 19th century.

Lothrop, William Henry. Keep- [3592]
ers of the lighthouse. N.Y.: 1942.
113 p. DLC. Mission worker in
New York City.

Lott, Edson Schuyler, b. 1856. [3593]
A Penn Yan boy...N.Y.: pr. by
Montross & Clarke, 1941. 259 p.
DLC. Insurance agent in New
York.

Loux, DuBois Henry, b. 1867. [3594]
The vicar's excursion...N.Y.:
Workers' press, 1912. 157 p. DLC.
A clergyman (Presbyterian and
Congregationalist) tells of his faith
in Christian socialism.

Love, James Stanhope, b. 1887. [3595]
The story of my life and work,
by Ben Hope (pseud.) Gaffney:
Gaffney ledger, 1909? 38 p. DLC.
Crippled South Carolina poet.

Love, Nat, b. 1854. Life and ad- [3596]
ventures of Nat Love, better known
in the cattle country as "Deadwood
Dick", by himself; a true history
of slavery days, life on the great
cattle ranges...Los Angeles: 1907.
162 p. WHi. A rapid-fire story by

Lovejoy, Daniel B. From youth [3597] to age...Chicago: American authors' protective pub. co., 1894. 272 p. DLC. Union army soldier, pioneer life in the Dakotas.

Lovejoy, Mrs. Esther (Clayson) [3598] Pohl, b. 1870. The house of the good neighbor. N.Y.: Macmillan, 1919. 218 p. WU. Hospital and welfare worker with children in France during the first World War.

Lovell, Thomas, b. 1863. Auto- [3599] biography in education...Ann Arbor: 1928. 48 p. Auto., p. 1-24. DLC. Poet, songwriter in Michigan, born in England.

Low, Charles Porter, b. 1824. [3600] Some recollections...Boston: George H. Ellis, 1905. 179 p. WHi. Merchant sailor in the China trade.

Low, Gorham P., 1806-1880. [3601] The sea made men; the story of a Gloucester lad... N.Y.: Revell, 1937. 280 p. WHi. Merchant sailor. The account closes with 1842.

Low, Will Hicok, 1853-1932. A [3602] chronicle of friendships, 1873-1900. N.Y.: Scribner, 1908. 507 p. WU. Painter.

Low, Will Hicok, 1853-1932. A [3603] painter's progress, being a partial survey along the pathway of art in America and Europe...N.Y.: Scribner's, 1910. 301 p. NN. Much of a personal nature though not entirely autobiographical

Low, William Gilman, b. 1844. [3604] Some recollections for his children and grandchildren. N.Y.: G. P. Putnam's sons, 1909. 242 p. DLC. New York lawyer, brother of Seth Low.

Lowe, Frank Melville, 1859- [3605] 1935. Fifty years at the American bar, a warrior lawyer; the colorful and exciting career of Frank M. Lowe, country editor, criminal lawyer, world traveler, Christian teacher. Based upon his unfinished memoirs, compiled by his son, F.M.L., jr. N.Y.: Fleming H. Revell co., 1942. 215 p. NN. Lawyer and politician of Kansas City, Mo.

Lowe, Percival G., b. 1828. Five [3606] years a Dragoon ('49 to '54) and other adventures on the Great Plains. Kansas City: Franklin Hudson pub. co., 1906. 417 p. WHi. Indian warfare.

Lowell, Alice (King), b. 1852. [3607] Stories of the Kings. Kansas City: The Lowell press, 1930. 67 p. MWA. Story of youth in Iowa. The account closes with 1865.

Lowrie, Donald. My life in pri- [3608] son. N.Y.: Mitchell Kennerley, 1912. 422 p. WU. In San Quentin (California).

Lowrie, Donald. My life out of [3609] prison. N.Y.: Mitchell Kennerley, 1915. 345 p. WU. Prison reform.

Lowrie, Walter Macon, 1819- [3610] 1847. Memoirs of the Rev. Walter M. Lowrie, missionary to China. N.Y.: Robert Carter, 1849. 500 p. DLC. Protestant missionary in China and Formosa.

Lowry, Anna M., b. 1874. The [3611] martyr in black; twenty years of the convent life of "Sister Justina" ...Aurora: Menace pub. co., 1912. 80 p. DLC. As described by the title. The period covered is 1890-1910.

Loy, Matthias, 1828-1915. Story [3612] of my life. Columbus, Ohio: Lutheran book concern, 1905. 440 p. NN. Lutheran clergyman and educator of Ohio.

Lubbock, Francis Richard, 1815- [3613] 1905. Six decades in Texas; or, memoirs of Francis Richard Lubbock, governor of Texas in war time, 1861-63...ed. by C.W. Raines. Austin: B. C. Jones & co., printers, 1900. 685 p. WHi. Rancher, Confederate soldier, political figure in Texas.

Lucas, Frederic Augustus, 1852-[3614] 1929. Fifty years of museum work...N.Y.: American museum of natural history, 1933. 81 p. Auto., p. 3-32. WU. Naturalist.

Lucas, Jim Griffing, b. 1914. [3615] ...Combat correspondent. N.Y.: Reynal & Hitchcock, 1944. 210 p. DLC. An Oklahoma reporter becomes a marine combat correspondent in the second World War, serving in the Pacific area.

Lucas, Orrington, b. 1858. Red [3616] Orrington Lucas. (The experiences of a deputy U.S. marshal... by William Frank Jones. No imprint, 1937?) p. 20-25. MtHi.

U.S. Marshal in Oklahoma, last decade of the 19th century.

Lucas, Mrs. Rachel, b. 1774. [3617] Remarkable account...Boston: pr. by Samuel Avery, 1811. 12 p. MiD-B. An account of healing at the hand of God.

Lucifer. See Ball, John, b. 1847.

Luckey, John. Life in Sing Sing [3618] state prison, as seen in a twelve years' chaplaincy. N.Y.: N. Tibbals & co., 1860. 376 p. NN. As described by the title.

Ludey, Charles Addison, b. 1874.[3619] Decision reserved. Phila.: Dorrance, 1941. 349 p. WHi. Lawyer in Ohio, oil producer in Oklahoma.

Ludlow, Louis, b. 1873. From [3620] cornfield to press gallery; adventures and reminiscences of a veteran Washington correspondent. Wash., D.C.: W. F. Roberts co., 1924. 432 p. DLC. Reporter in Indiana who later covered Washington events for various papers.

Ludlow, Noah Miller, 1795-1886. [3621] Dramatic life as I found it... St. Louis: G. I. Jones, 1880. 733 p. WHi. Actor, manager, mainly in the Mississippi valley.

Luff, Joseph, b. 1852. Autobiography...Lamoni: Herald pub. [3622] house, 1894. 377 p. WHi. One of the Twelve Apostles of the Reorganized Church of Jesus Christ of Latter Day Saints.

Luhan, Mrs. Mabel (Ganson) [3623] Dodge, b. 1879. Intimate memories. N.Y.: Harcourt, Brace, 1933-37. 4 vols. WU. Literary life in Europe and America. Mrs. Luhan was a patron of young writers who contributed much to the fame of Taos.

Lukens, Edward C. A Blue [3624] Ridge memoir. Baltimore: Sun print, 1922. 152 p. DLC. The author served in the Army in France during the First World War.

Lummus, Aaron. The life of [3625] Aaron Lummus...Portland: pr. by Francis Douglas, 1816. 72 p. DLC. Clergyman of the Church of God who served in New England.

Lumpkin, Wilson, 1783-1870. [3626] The removal of the Cherokee Indians from Georgia...together with a sketch of his life and conduct while holding many public offices under the government of Georgia and the United States, prior to 1827, and after 1841... N.Y.: Dodd, Mead, 1907. 2 vols. WHi. U.S. Commissioner who executed the Indian Treaty of 1835. Governor of Georgia and U.S. Senator from Georgia.

Lund, Mrs. Alice Dahlin. Pioneer [3627] memories. N.p.: 1945. 91 leaves. WHi. A story of youth in rural Wisconsin. The period covered is 1870-88.

Lundin, Hjalmar, 1870-1941. On [3628] the mat — and off; memoirs of a wrestler. N.Y.: Albert Bonnier, 1937. 166 p. NN. As described by the title.

Lunsford, Otto. From the foot- [3629] lights of the theatre unto the lights of the cross...Linton, Indiana: 1925. 68 p. DLC. The author prepared for the career of concert pianist, then turned to spiritualism and to evangelical preaching.

Lunt, Cornelia Gray, b. 1843. [3630] Sketches of childhood and girlhood. Chicago, 1847-64. Evanston: 1925. 244 p. ICN. In New England and Illinois.

Luster, Mary R. (Spangler), [3631] b. 1853. The autobiography... Springfield: Cain pr. co., 1935. 196 p. DLC. Pioneer life in Illinois, Missouri and then in Idaho. A domestic account.

Lutes, Della (Thompson), d. 1942.[3632] Home grown. Boston: Little, Brown & co., 1937. 272 p. NN. Recollections of a childhood in southern Michigan.

Lutes, Mrs. Della (Thompson). [3633] Country schoolma'am. Boston: Little, Brown, 1941. 328 p. WU. In Michigan in the eighties.

Lutz, Henry Frey, 1868-1926. [3634] To infidelity and back...Cinc.: Standard pub. co., 1911. 231 p. Auto., p. 1-44. DLC. Spiritual account by an evangelist of the Disciples of Christ.

Lykkejaeger, Hans (pseud.). See Smith, Andrew Madsen.

Lyman, H. H. Memoirs of an [3635] old homestead. Oswego: R. J. Oliphant, 1900. 181 p. MoHi. In the Black River country (Lorraine), 1845-65. A story of youthful days in school and on a farm.

Lyman, Henry M., 1835-1904. [3636] Hawaiian yesterdays...Chicago: A.C. McClurg, 1906. 281 p. WHi. Son of missionary family, born in Hawaii. His education, his job as a surveyor, and departure for the U.S. in 1853, are described.

Lynch, John Fairfield, b. 1845. [3637] The advocate...Portland: G.D. Loring, 1916. 226 p. WHi. Lawyer in Maine.

Lynch, James, 1826-1909. With [3638] Stevenson to California, 1846. No imprint, 1896? 65 p. DLC. Rancher in California.

Lynch, William Francis, 1801- [3639] 1865. Naval life...N.Y.: Scribner, 1851. 308 p. DLC. Naval officer. Much of this is not autobiographical.

Lyon, Mrs. Marguerite, b. 1892. [3640] Take to the hills; a chronicle of the Ozarks...Indianapolis: Bobbs-Merrill, 1941. 305 p. DLC. From Chicago to a farm in Missouri.

Lyon, Mrs. Marguerite, b. 1892. [3641] And green grass grows all around. Indianapolis: Bobbs-Merrill, 1942. 307 p. DLC. Further adventures in the Ozarks.

# M

Mabie, Henry Clay, b. 1847. [3642] From romance to reality... Boston: pr. for the author, 1917. 396 p. WHi. Director of foreign mission work for the Baptists, prior to which he had congregations in New England and in the Midwest.

Mabry, W.S. Some memories.. [3643] Bandera: Frontier times print, 1927. 32 p. TxU. Texas rancher.

MacAdam, Mrs. Madelene Victoria (Brocklebank). Fortune in [3644] my own hands. Boston: Christopher, 1940. 382 p. DLC. Insurance, real estate in California.

MacArthur, Charles, b. 1895. War [3645] bugs. Garden City, N.Y.: Doubleday, Doran, 1929. 301 p. DLC. Army in World War I.

Macartney, William Napier, [3646] 1862-1940. Fifty years a country doctor. N.Y.: E. P. Dutton, 1938. 584 p. WU. In New York.

MacCauley, Clay, b. 1843. Memories...Tokyo: Fukuin pr. co., [3647] 1914. 781 p. MH. A Congregational clergyman turned Unitarian (in Michigan, Minnesota, New York and Mass.). Later he served in a mission in Japan.

MacCorkle, William Alexander, [3648] b. 1857. Recollections of fifty years of West Virginia. N.Y.: Putnam, 1928. 633 p. WHi. Lawyer, governor.

Macdonald, Betty (Bard). The [3649] egg and I. Phila.: Lippincott, 1945. 277 p. DLC. Chicken farmer in Washington.

Macdonald, Charles Blair, 1856- [3650] 1939. Scotland's gift: golf. N.Y.: Charles Scribner's sons, 1928. 340 p. NN. Golfing experiences of the author, who has been responsible for the construction of numerous golf courses.

MacDonald, George Everett [3651] Hussey, b. 1857. Fifty years... N.Y.: Truth seeker, 1929-31. 2 vols. WHi. Editor of religious magazines.

MacDonald, Norman, b. 1911. The [3652] orchid hunters; a jungle adventure. N.Y.: Farrar & Rinehart, 1939. 294 p. DLC. In Colombia, Venezuela from 1934.

Mac Dougall, Mrs. Alice (Foote), [3653] b. 1867. Alice Foote MacDougall, the autobiography of a business woman. Boston: Little, Brown, 1928. 205 p. WHi. Owner of restaurant chain in New York.

MacDowell, Syl, b. 1892. We live [3654] in a trailer. N.Y.: Messner, 1938. 243 p. DLC. While crossing the country.

Macfarland, Charles Stedman, [3655] b. 1866. Across the years. N.Y.: Macmillan, 1936. 367 p. WHi. General Secretary, Federal Council of the Churches of Christ in America.

MacFarlane, C. Reminiscences [3656] of an army surgeon, 1860-1863. Oswego: Lake City print shop, 1912. 82 p. CtY. Union army.

MacIntyre, William Irwin, [3657] b. 1882. Legislative reminiscences. Thomasville, Ga.: Times-enterprise pub. co., printers, 1909. 22 p. DLC. In Georgia.

Mack, Arthur James. Shellproof [3658] Mack...Boston: Small, Maynard, 1918. 224 p. NjP. The author served in the British army during the first World War.

Mack, Solomon, b. 1735. A nar- [3659] raitve of the life of Solomon Mack, containing an account of the many severe accidents he met with during a long series of years, together with the extraordinary manner in which he was converted to the Christian faith ...Windsor: pr. at the expence of the author, 1811? 48 p. NN. Career of an unlettered New Englander with his many unfortunate ups and downs.

Mackay, Malcom Sutherland. [3660] Cow range and hunting trail. N.Y.: Putnam, 1925. 243 p. DLC. Cowboy, big game hunter in Canada, Alaska, North Dakota, Wyoming, Montana.

Mackenzie, Colin, b. 1918. [3661] Sailors of fortune. N.Y.: Dutton, 1944. 190 p. DLC. Merchant seaman, World War II.

Mackin, Sarah Maria Aloisa [3662] (Britton) Spottiswood. A society woman on two continents. N.Y.: Transatlantic, 1896. 327 p. DLC. An account of social life in the U.S. and Europe.

MacLaren, Gay, b. 1886. Mor- [3663] ally we roll along... Boston: Little, Brown & co., 1938. 308 p. NN. Experiences on the Lyceum and Chautauqua circuits.

MacLeish, Andrew, 1838-1928. [3664] The life of Andrew MacLeish. Chicago: priv. pr., 1929. 96 p. ICN. School teacher and executive in department store in Chicago.

MacManus, Seumas, b. 1870. [3665] The rocky road to Dublin. N.Y.: Macmillan co., 1938. 324 p. NN. Born in Ireland. Only the last chapter relates to his American literary experiences.

MacMartin, Daniel Frederick. [3666] Thirty years in Hell; or, the confessions of a drug fiend. Topeka: Capper pr. co., 1921. 274 p. DAFM. The period covered is 1889 to 1921.

MacMillan, Donald Baxter, [3667] b. 1874. Four years in the north. N.Y.: Harper, 1918. 426 p. WHi. Explorer in the Arctic.

MacMillan, Donald Baxter, [3668] b. 1874. How Peary reached the Pole; the personal story of his assistant. Boston & N.Y.: Houghton Mifflin co., 1934. 306 p. DLC. To the Pole with Peary in 1908-09.

MacMillan, Donald Baxter, [3669] b. 1874. Etah and beyond; or, life within twelve degrees of the Pole. Boston: Houghton Mifflin, 1927. 287 p. DLC. Explorer on scientific expedition to Greenland, 1923.

MacMurray, James Edwin, [3670] b. 1862. The man from Missouri ...Los Angeles: Times-Mirror, 1943. 156 p. DLC. Lawyer, steel manufacturer in Illinois.

MacNutt, Francis Augustus, [3671] 1863-1927. A Papal chamberlain ...N.Y.: Longmans, Green, 1936. 398 p. WHi. An American who served in the U.S. Diplomatic corps, and was made a member of the Papal household in the Vatican.

MacNutt, Francis Augustus, [3672] 1863-1927. Six decades of my life. Brixen: Weger press, 1927. 2 vols. ViLxW. An earlier version of the preceding item.

Macon, Mrs. Emma Cassandra [3673] (Riely), b. 1847. Reminiscences of the Civil war. Cedar Rapids: Torch press, 1911. 158 p. DLC. A girl's life in Virginia during the Civil War.

Macy, Jesse, 1842-1919. Jesse [3674] Macy, an autobiography... Springfield: C. C. Thomas, 1933. 192 p. WHi. Teacher, writer of books on government who lived many years in Iowa.

Madden, Joseph Augustin, b.1894. [3675] What'll you have, boys? N.Y.: Farrar & Rinehart, 1934. 138 p. NN. Chronicles of a West Side New York speakeasy owner in prohibition days.

Madeleine, an autobiography. [3676] Hollywood: Hollywood press, 1924. 341 p. WaPS. Prostitute, "madam", drunkard and gambler. Locale: Illinois, Montana and Canada.

Madsen, Christian, b. 1852. Med [3677] sabel og pistol. Omaha: A. H. Andersen, 1921. 166 p. DLC. Norwegian born Indian fighter; U.S. Marshal in Oklahoma.

Maeder, Mrs. Clara (Fisher), [3678] 1811-1898. Autobiography...ed. by Douglas Taylor...N.Y.: The Dunlap society, 1897. 138 p. WU.

Actress, singer.

Magee, Harvey White, b. 1847. [3679] The story of my life. Albany: Boyd pr. co., 1926. 137 p. CSmH. Lawyer and bank commissioner in California who was raised on a Missouri farm.

Magee, James H., b. 1839. The [3680] night of affliction and morning of recovery. An autobiography. Cinc.: The author, 1873. 173 p. TNF. Clergyman in Illinois, Wisconsin and Ohio.

Magill, Edward Hicks, 1825- [3681] 1907. Sixty-five years in the life of a teacher, 1841-1906. Boston: Houghton-Mifflin, 1907. 323 p. WU. President of Swarthmore, and college teacher of French.

Magner, Dennis. The art of [3682] taming and educating the horse... and the story of the author's personal experience...Battle Creek, Mich.: Review & herald pub. house, 1884. 1088 p. Auto., p. 472-536. DLC. Horse trainer who was born in Ireland.

Magner, Dennis. Magner's story [3683] of twenty years a horse tamer... Battle Creek, Mich.: Magner book co., 1895. 320 p. Auto., p. 14-163. DLC. See preceding entry.

Magnus, Maurice, 1876-1920. [3684] Memoirs of the Foreign Legion. London: Secker, 1924. 319 p. Auto., p. 101-319. DLC. A 20th century account.

Magoun, George Frederick, [3685] 1821-1896. A ministry for the Northwest (Minutes of the second and third triennial conventions, held at Chicago, October 1861 and April 1864, in connection with the Chicago Theological Seminary. Chicago: Dunlop, Sewell & Spalding, printers, 1864). p. 31-50. OO. Presbyterian and Congregationalist clergyman in the old Northwest.

Maguire, William Augustus, [3686] b. 1890. Rig for church. N.Y.: Macmillan, 1942. 251 p. WHi. U.S. Navy chaplain. This account closes with 1941.

Maguire, William Augustus, [3687] b. 1890. The captain wears a cross. N.Y.: Macmillan, 1943. 207 p. WHi. U.S. Navy chaplain, 1941-1943.

Mahan, Alfred Thayer, 1840- [3688] 1914. From sail to steam... N.Y.: Harper, 1907. 325 p. WHi. Naval officer.

Mahan, Asa, 1800-1889. Auto- [3689] biography...London: T. Woolmer, 1882. 458 p. DLC. Presbyterian clergyman in New York and Ohio, and President of Oberlin College who later left the U.S. for England.

Mahan, James Curtis, b. 1840. [3690] Memoirs...Lincoln: Franklin press, 1919. 176 p. NbHi. Union soldier. Farmer and dealer in livestock in Nebraska.

Mahan, Phineas Jenks. Remin- [3691] iscences of the war for Texas independence. No imprint, 1872? 9 p. TxU. As described by the title.

Mailliard, Joseph, b. 1857. Auto-[3692] biography...No imprint. 29 p. C. California ornithologist.

Mails, John. Pioneer days in [3693] Kansas. Manhattan, Kan.: Mattie Mails Coons, 1939. 41 p. KHi. Homesteader who came to Kansas in 1855.

Mains, George Preston, b. 1844. [3694] Mental phases in a spiritual biography. N.Y.: Harper, 1928. 256 p. Auto., p. 1-15. DLC. Methodist clergyman.

Mains, Laura A., b. 1847. [3695] Mizpah. Autobiographical sketches. Grand Rapids: Hensen & Reynders, 1892. 107 p. MiU-H. Baptist clergyman in Michigan.

Major, Mrs. Gertrude E. Rem-[3696] iniscences of an elementary teacher...Kansas City, Mo.: Burton pub. co., 1940. 121 p. MoK. In Oklahoma and Missouri.

Majors, Alexander, 1814-1900. [3697] Seventy years on the frontier. N.Y.: Rand, McNally, 1893. 325 p. WHi. Promoter of Pony Express.

M'Allister, Mrs. M. E., b. 1844. [3698] Sunshine among the clouds; or, extracts from experience. Cinc.: Hitchcock & Walden, 1873. 243 p. DLC. A spiritual account of a woman born into a religious family, who marries a clergyman.

Mallory, William, b. 1826. Old [3699] plantation days. Hamilton?: n.d. 56 p. DLC. Slave who escaped and then fought in the Union army. After the war he became a Canadian citizen and went to Africa to do missionary work.

Malone, Thomas H., 1834-1906. [3700] Memoir...Nashville: Baird-Ward, 1928. 227 p. DLC. Lawyer in Tennessee; soldier in the Confederate army.

Maloney, John. Let there be [3701] mercy; the odyssey of a Red Cross man. Garden City, N.Y.: Doubleday, Doran, 1941. 329 p. DLC. A journalist who served as an observer for the Red Cross in the second World War.

Malony, William N. Twice one. [3702] Portland, Me.: The Dirigo editions, 1939. 39 p. DLC. A story of youth (in Iowa?).

Maltby, William J., b. 1829. [3703] Captain Jeff; or, Frontier life in Texas...By one of the nine, a member of Company E, Texas Rangers. Colorado: Whipkeg pr. co., 1906. 161 p. WHi. As described by the title.

Manahan, James, 1866-1932. [3704] Trials of a lawyer...Minneapolis: Farnham pr. co., 1933. 248 p. DLC. Lawyer and politician in Minnesota, known for his activities in the Farmer-Labor party.

Manderson, Charles Frederick, [3705] 1837-1911. The twin seven-shooters. N.Y.: F. Tennyson Neely, 1902. 54 p. WyU. Union army.

Manford, Erasmus. Twenty-five [3706] years in the West. Chicago: 1867. 359 p. WHi. Universalist clergyman in Indiana, Missouri, Kansas, Ohio and Illinois.

Mangasarian, Mangasar Mugur- [3707] pitch, b. 1859. The story of my mind...Chicago: Independent religious society, 1909. 125 p. DLC. Presbyterian clergyman becomes lecturer for Ethical Culture Society in New York and Chicago, and then founds his own society.

Manire, Benjamin Franklin, [3708] 1829-1911. Reminiscences of preachers and churches in Mississippi. Jackson: Messenger pub. co., 1892. 60 p. MoCanD. Member of the Christian Church.

Manly, William Lewis, b. 1820. [3709] Death Valley in '49...San José: Pacific tree & vine co., 1894. 498 p. NN. Pioneer miner in California.

Mann, Mrs. Lucile Quarry. [3710] From jungle to zoo; adventures of a naturalist's wife. N.Y.: Dodd, Mead, 1934. 246 p. DLC. As described by the title.

Mann, Robert, b. 1824. The auto- [3711] biography of Robert Mann... Phila.: J. B. Lippincott co., 1897. 83 p. DLC. Manufacturer of axes in Pennsylvania.

Mannes, David, b. 1866. Music [3712] is my faith...N.Y.: Norton, 1938. 270 p. DLC. Violinist, music teacher, conductor in New York.

Manning, Edwin Cassander, [3713] b. 1838. Biographical, historical and miscellaneous selections. Cedar Rapids: 1911. 194 p. Auto., p. 13-97. DLC. Union army soldier. Owner of newspaper in Kansas.

Manning, Joseph Columbus, [3714] b. 1870. From five to twenty-five, his earlier life as recalled by Joseph Columbus Manning. N.Y.: T. A. Hebbons, 1929. 89 p. DLC. The writer tells of how he came to enter politics in Alabama.

Manning, Marie, d. 1945. Ladies [3715] now and then, by Beatrice Fairfax (Marie Manning). N.Y.: E.P. Dutton, 1944. 254 p. NN. Memories of a woman journalist and columnist for the Hearst publications.

Manship, Andrew, b. 1824. Thir- [3716] teen years' experience in the itinerancy...Phila.: pub. by the author, 1864. 454 p. WHi. The author served in the Southern and Middle Atlantic regions, as well as in England and Ireland. Written by a Methodist clergyman.

Månsson, Evelina. ...Amerika- [3717] minnen...Hvetlanda: Svenska allmogeförlaget, 1930. 109 p. MnHi. A Swedish girl who came to Minnesota in 1901, working at menial tasks.

Manthey-Zorn, Carl. See Zorn, Carl Manthey.

Mapleson, James Henry, 1830- [3718] 1901. The Mapleson memoirs, 1848-1888. 3d ed. N.Y.: Belford, Clarke, 1888. 2 vols. WU. An English impresario who produced numerous operas in the U.S.

Marbury, Elisabeth, 1856-1933. [3719] My crystal ball; reminiscences. N.Y.: Boni & Liveright, 1923. 355 p.

WU. Agent for actors and authors.

Marcosson, Isaac F. Adventures [3720] in interviewing. N.Y.: Dodd, Mead, 1923. 314 p. WU. This covers from the War with Spain to about 1918. Written by a journalist and writer for magazines.

Marcosson, Isaac F. Turbulent [3721] years. N.Y.: Dodd, Mead, 1938. 497 p. WU. This covers from 1919 to 1936; the author tells of the many world personalities he interviewed while employed by the Saturday Evening Post.

Maretzek, Max, 1821–1897. [3722] Crotchets and quavers...N.Y.: S. French, 1855. 346 p. WU. Opera impresario, born in Moravia.

Maretzek, Max, 1821–1897. [3723] Sharps and flats...N.Y.: American musician pub. co., 1890. 87 p. DLC. A sequel to the preceding item.

Mariotti, L. (pseud.). See Gallenga, Antonio Carlo Napoleone.

Markham, Pauline. Life of [3724] Pauline Markham. N.Y.: 1871. 31 p. DLC. English actress who appeared in the U.S. on several occasions.

Marks, David, 1805–1845. The [3725] life of David Marks to the 26th year of his age. Including the particulars of his conversion, call to the ministry, and labours in itinerate preaching for nearly eleven years. Written by himself. Limerick, Maine: pr. at the office of the Morning Star, 1831. 386 p. NcWAtC. Free Will Baptist.

Marks, William Sherman, b.1866. [3726] Brief biographical sketch... N.p.: 1939. 19 p. DLC. Lawyer, member State Board of Education in Utah.

Marlow, Alfred, and his several [3727] brothers. Life of the Marlows... as related by themselves. Ouray: W.S. Olexa, n.d. 160 p. CoD. Brothers in Texas in the nineties, accused of horse stealing.

Marlow, Charles, d. 1872. The [3728] confession of Carl Marlow, convicted of the murder of William Bachmann...Dunkirk: J. Fleischman, 1872. 16 p. DLC. As described by the title.

Marlowe, Dave (pseud.). See Timmins, Arthur Henry.

Marrant, John, b. 1755. A narra- [3729] tive of the Lord's wonderful dealings with John Marrant, a Black, (now going to preach the gospel in Nova-Scotia) born in New-York, in North-America. 2d ed. London: Gilbert & Plummer, 1785. 38 p. NN. Negro clergyman in Mass., and Canada.

Marrs, Elijah P., b. 1840. Life [3730] and history of the Rev. Elijah P. Marrs. Louisville: Bradley & Gilbert, 1885. 146 p. DLC. Confederate soldier (Negro), and Baptist clergyman in Kentucky.

Mars, James, b. 1790. Life of [3731] James Mars... 4th ed. Hartford: Press of Case, Lockwood, 1867. 38 p. DLC. Negro slave and free laborer, both in Connecticut.

Marsh, Charles Wesley, 1834– [3732] 1918. Recollections, 1837–1910. Chicago: Farm implement news co., 1910. 299 p. WHi. Inventor, manufacturer of agricultural machinery in Illinois. The author was born in Canada.

Marsh, James Charlwood. From [3733] printers devil to boss. Los Angeles: J.M. press, 1934. 91 p. DLC. Printer, born in England, who plied his trade in California, Florida, Missouri and New England.

Marsh, John, 1788–1868. Tem- [3734] perance recollections...N.Y.: Scribner, 1866. 356 p. WHi. Abolitionist, editor of the American Temperance Union.

Marsh, Robert. Seven years of [3735] my life...Buffalo: Faxon & Stevens, 1848. 207 p. DLC. American citizen living in Canada, imprisoned for aiding rebellion in 1838.

Marshall, Albert O. Army life [3736] ...2d ed. Joliet, Ill.: pr. for the author, 1883. 410 p. NN. Union soldier.

Marshall, Mrs. Anne James. [3737] The autobiography...Pine Bluff, Ark.: Adams-Wilson, 1897. 232 p. OkU. Teacher in Arkansas, 1840–1870, and marriage to a clergyman. The author was born in England.

Marshall, Frank James, 1877– [3738] 1944. My fifty years of chess. Phila.: David Mackay, 1942. 242 p. Auto., p. 3–26. DLC. As described by the title.

Marshall, John, 1755-1835. An [3739] autobiographical sketch. Ann Arbor: The Univ. of Michigan press, 1937. 48 p. WHi. Chief justice, U.S. Supreme Court, lawyer.

Marshall, Mary. "The life and [3740] sufferings of the author". (In her: Rise and progress of the serpent from the garden of Eden...Concord: 1847.) p. 153-268. WHi. A tale of domestic discord in New England brought about by her Shaker husband, whom she married in 1799.

Marshall, Roujet DeLisle, 1847- [3741] 1922. Autobiography...Madison: Democrat pr. co., 1923. Vol. I. 558 p. WHi. Justice of the Supreme Court, Wisconsin, 1895-1918.

Marshall, Thomas Riley, 1854- [3742] 1925. Recollections...Indianapolis: Bobbs-Merrill, 1925. 383 p. WHi. Governor of Indiana, Vice-president of the U.S.

Marshall, Victor Fred, b. 1873. [3743] Doctor. ...Appleton: C.C. Nelson, 1945. 235 p. DLC. Physician in Wisconsin.

Marshburn, William V., b. 1855. [3744] Spiritual experiences in business life. Richmond, Ind.: Nicholson pr. co., 1929. 141 p. DLC. A physician tells of his religious experiences. The author is a Quaker.

Marsman, Jan Hendrik, b.1892. [3745] I escaped from Hong Kong. N.Y.: Reynal & Hitchcock, 1942. 249 p. DLC. American businessman (insurance, mining, construction), born in Holland, who was captured by Japanese.

Martin, Désirée. Les veillées [3746] d'une soeur; ou le destin d'un brin de Mousse. Nouvelle Orléans: Cosmopolite, 1877. 230 p. DLC. By a sister.

Martin, Franklin Henry, 1857- [3747] 1935. The joy of living, an autobiography...Garden City: Doubleday, Doran, 1933. 2 vols. WHi. Physician in Minnesota with Mayo brothers.

Martin, Franklin Henry, 1857- [3748] 1935. Fifty years of medicine... Chicago: Surgical pub. co., 1934. 444 p. Auto., p. 1-356. DLC. His experiences in Chicago.

Martin, Frederick Townsend, [3749] 1849-1914. Things I remember... N.Y.: John Lane co., 1913. 297 p. NN. Social life in New York, Newport and Europe.

Martin, George Adam. (See his [3750] narrative in Chronicon Ephratense by Lamech and Agrippa. Lancaster: Zahm, 1889. p. 242-262.) WHi. A spiritual account written by the leader of the movement in Pennsylvania in the 18th century which resulted in the split between Baptists and Seventh Day Baptists.

Martin, Isaac, 1758-1828. A [3751] journal...Phila.: pr. by W.P. Gibbons, 1834. 160 p. WHi. Quaker minister on the Atlantic coast from New York to the Carolinas.

Martin, Joseph Plumb, b. 1760. [3752] A narrative...of a revolutionary soldier... Hallowell: pr. by Glazier, Masters, 1830. 213 p. DLC. As described by the title.

Martin, Luther, 1748?-1826. [3753] Modern gratitude. Baltimore: 1802. No. 5, p. 131-153. DLC. Lawyer, Attorney General of Maryland.

Martin, Michael, 1795-1821. Life [3754] of Michael Martin, who was executed for highway robbery... Boston: Russell & Gardner, 1821. 102 p. DLC. In Massachusetts.

Martin, Morgan Lewis, 1805- [3755] 1887. Reminiscences...Madison: 1888. 37 p. DLC. Lawyer, political figure in Wisconsin.

Martindale, Elijah, 1793-1878. [3756] Autobiography and sermons... Indianapolis: Carlon & Hollenbeck, 1892. 173 p. Auto., p. 1-58. WHi. Indiana clergyman belonging to the "Newlights", influenced by the ideas of the Campbellites.

Martingale, Hawser (pseud.). See Sleeper, John Sherburne.

Masliansky, Zebi Hirsh, b. 1856. [3757] Memoirs (in Yiddish). N.Y.: Zerubabel, 1924. 371 p. DLC. Propagandist for a Zionist state.

Maslin, Thomas, 1846-1910. [3758] From saloon to prison, from prison to pulpit. Ashland, Pa.: pr. by G. Kyler, 1912. 96 p. DLC. Robber who served two years in prison. Soldier in the Union army. Methodist clergyman in New Jersey. Temperance worker.

Mason, Arthur, b. 1876. Ocean [3759] echoes...N.Y.: Holt, 1922. 287 p. DLC. Irish born sailor who mined in the West. See also his Ocean boyhood.

Mason, Daniel Gregory, b. 1873. [3760] Music in my time... N.Y.: Macmillan, 1938. 409 p. WU. Composer.

Mason, Francis, 1799-1874. The [3761] story of a working man's life: with sketches of travel in Europe, Asia, Africa, and America, as related by himself. N.Y.: Oakley, Mason & co., 1870. 462 p. NN. Baptist missionary in Burma.

Mason, Isaac, b. 1822. Life of [3762] Isaac Mason as a slave. Worcester: 1893. 74 p. WHi. As described by the title.

Mason, Jeremiah, 1768-1848. [3763] Memoir, autobiography and correspondence...Kansas City: Lawyers' international pub. co., 1917. 491 p. Auto., p. 1-36. DLC. New England lawyer.

Mason, Philip, 1793-1868. A [3763a] legacy to my children...Cinc.: Moore, Wilstach & Baldwin, printers, 1868. 610 p. Auto., p. 91-365. WHi. Merchant, farmer, physician and member of the state legislature in Indiana.

Mason, William, 1829-1908. [3764] Memories of a musical life. N.Y.: Century, 1901. 306 p. WU. Pianist, music teacher.

Massey, John, b. 1834. Reminis- [3765] cences...Nashville: Pub. house of the M.E.Church, south, 1916. 330 p. WHi. Alabama educator.

Massey, John Edward, 1819-1901.[3766] Autobiography...N.Y.: Neale, 1909. 312 p. WHi. Virginia politician, and Baptist clergyman.

Masters, Edgar Lee, b. 1869. [3767] Across Spoon River... N.Y.: Farrar & Rinehart, 1936. 426 p. WU. Poet.

Masters, J.W., 1854-1924. Fol- [3768] lowing the trail of a preacher in the mountains of Virginia and Kentucky...No imprint. 69 p. MoCanD. Disciples of Christ.

Masterson, William. The authen-[3769] tic confession of...the cruel murderer of his father and mother...Richmond, Va.: M.L. Barclay, 1854. 34 p. MWA. As described by the title.

Mathews, Charles Edwin,b.1865.[3770] Reminiscence. Seneca: Courier-Tribune press, 1941. 157 p. DLC. Farm life in Kansas.

Mathews, Edward. Autobiogra- [3771] phy...N.Y.: American Baptist Free mission society, 1866. 444 p. WHi. Abolitionist activities described by a Wisconsin clergyman.

Mathews, John, 1826-1907. Peeps[3772] into life; autobiography of Rev. John Mathews, a minister of the gospel for sixty years. Nashville, Tenn.?: 1904. 394 p. NN. Methodist minister in Tennessee, Missouri, Alabama and Louisiana.

Mathews, John Joseph. Talking [3773] to the moon. Chicago: Univ. of Chicago press, 1945. 243 p. DLC. The life of retirement on the Osage plains of Oklahoma.

Mathews, Shailer, b. 1863. New [3774] faith for old... N.Y.: Macmillan, 1936. 303 p. WHi. Theology professor at the University of Chicago.

Matschat, Mrs. Cecile (Hulse). [3775] Seven grass huts; an engineer's wife in Central and South America. N.Y.: Farrar & Rinehart, 1939. 281 p. DLC. This is mainly a domestic account by a horticulturist.

Matson, Daniel, 1842-1920. Life [3776] experiences...Fowler: Tribune print, 1924. 144 p. WHi. Union soldier.

Matthews, Azel Dennis, 1809- [3777] 1900. Autobiography and memoirs. Brooklyn: 1902. 264 p. WHi. Temperance worker.

Matthews, Brander, 1852-1929. [3778] These many years; recollections of a New Yorker. N.Y.: Scribner, 1917. 463 p. WU. Dramatist, university professor of literature at Columbia.

Matthews, James Thomas, [3779] b. 1864. Turn right to paradise. Portland: Binfords & Mort, 1942. 196 p. DLC. Professor of Mathematics at Willamette University in Oregon.

Matthews, Jeremiah H., b. 1847. [3780] Reminiscences of a life-time experience...Nashville: pr. by the author, 1924. 227 p. WHi. Lumber business (sawmills, transportation)on the Ohio and Tennessee rivers.

Matthews, Joseph Brown,b.1894. [3781]

Odyssey of a fellow traveler. N.Y.: Mount Vernon publishers, 1938. 285 p. DLC. Lecturer, writer who eventually denounced the Communist-front organizations with which he had been associated.

Matthews, Leonard, 1828-1931. [3782] A long life in review. St. Louis: 1928. 178 p. NN. Wholesale drug manufacturer, later a banker and broker, in St. Louis, Mo.

Matthews, Sallie (Reynolds), [3783] b. 1861. Interwoven, a pioneer chronicle. Houston, Texas: The Anson Jones press, 1936. 234 p. NN. Pioneer life in Texas. A domestic account.

Matthews, William Henry, 1872- [3784] 1946. Adventures in giving. N.Y.: Dodd, Mead, 1939. 252 p. NN. Social service worker; Kingsley House, Pittsburgh; investigation of hours of labor in the steel industry; work with the New York Association for Improving the Condition of the Poor; relief work during the depression of the thirties.

Mattson, Hans, 1832-1893. Rem- [3785] iniscences: the story of an emigrant. St. Paul: D. D. Merrill, 1891. 314 p. WHi. Newspaper publisher; Minnesota political figure; Consul General to India; emigration agent in Sweden. Mattson was born in Sweden.

Maude, Cyril, b. 1862. Lest I [3786] forget. N.Y.: J. H. Sears, 1928. 350 p. WU. English actor who appeared in the U.S.

Maule, Joshua, b. 1806. Transac- [3787] tions...Phila.: J.B. Lippincott, 1886. 384 p. OrNeGF. Minister in the Society of Friends, serving in Ohio, New York and Pa. Abolitionist, temperance worker.

Maulsby, Orlando W., b. 1856. [3788] Rolling stone... Los Angeles: 1931. 130 p. DLC. Farmer, fruit grower, rancher, newspaper editor, in Iowa, Kansas and California.

Maurer, James Hudson, b. 1864. [3789] It can be done... N.Y.: Rand school press, 1938. 322 p. WHi. Socialist, labor leader.

Maury, Dabney Herndon, 1822- [3790] 1900. Recollections of a Virginian in the Mexican, Indian and Civil Wars. N.Y.: Scribner, 1894. 279 p. WHi. In addition to his military career, Maury was U.S. Minister to Colombia. When the Civil War began, he resigned his army commission to join the Confederates.

Maverick, Mary Ann (Adams), [3791] 1818-1918. Memoirs of Mary A. Maverick, arranged by Mary A. Maverick and her son Geo. Madison Maverick. San Antonio: Alamo pr. co., 1921. 136 p. NN. Life in pioneer Texas. Indian troubles, Mexican War. Covers to 1860.

Mavity, Henry. History of the [3792] life of Elder Henry Mavity, the pioneer Christian minister of Kentucky. Vanceburg: Sun print, 1901? KyMidF. Covers 1830-1890.

Maxidiwiac (Hidatsa Indian), [3793] b. 1839? Waheenee, an Indian girl's story...St. Paul: Webb, 1921. 189 p. CLSM. A 19th century story, the locale of which is North Dakota. A simple tale of marriage, etc.

Maxim, Hiram Percy, 1869- [3794] 1936. Horseless carriage days. N.Y.: Harper, 1937. 175 p. DLC. New England inventor who worked especially with electric automobiles and combustion engines. Covers 1893-1901.

Maxim, Hiram Stevens, 1840- [3795] 1916. My life. London: Methuen, 1915. 322 p. WU. Inventor, famous for his automatic gun, who lived many years in England and who became a British citizen in 1900.

Maxim, Hudson, 1853-1927. [3796] ...Reminiscences and comments, as reported by Clifton Johnson. Garden City: Doubleday, Page, 1924. 350 p. Auto., p. 1-229. WU. Chemist, inventor of explosives.

Maxwell, Hugh, 1733-1799. The [3797] Christian patriot. N.Y.: S. W. Benedict, 1833. 139 p. N. Soldier, farmer and surveyor in Mass.

Maxwell, James Robert, b.1844. [3798] Autobiography... N.Y.: Greenberg, 1926. 325 p. ICN. Confederate soldier, Alabama farmer.

Maxwell, Thomas. Tom Max- [3799] well. No imprint. 127 p. MoSHi. Horse dealer in Missouri in the second half of the 19th century.

May, Samuel Joseph, b. 1797. [3800] A brief account of his ministry. Syracuse: Masters & Lee, printers,

1867. 52 p. WHi. Unitarian clergyman in New England, abolitionist.

Maybrick, Mrs. Florence Elizabeth (Chandler), b. 1862. Mrs. Maybrick's own story; my fifteen lost years. N.Y. & London: Funk & Wagnalls co., 1905. 394 p. DLC. American girl, married to an Englishman, who was imprisoned for the murder of her husband, of which she was later exonerated. [3801]

Mayer, Edwin Justus, b. 1897. A preface to life. N.Y.: Boni & Liveright, 1923. 252 p. NN. Literary and spiritual apprenticeship of a dramatist, from his 15th to 20th year. [3802]

Mayerberg, Samuel Spier, b. 1892. Chronicle of an American crusader...N.Y.: Bloch, 1944. 148 p. WHi. Rabbi. [3803]

Mayfield, Thomas Jefferson, b. 1843? San Joaquin primeval... Tulare: Tulare times, 1929. 88 p. DLC. California rancher, miner. [3804]

Mayhew, Carroll C. The life and times...Nashville: pr. for the author, 1857. 360 p. TxDaM. Methodist clergyman in Tennessee. [3805]

Maynard, Sampson. The experience of Sampson Maynard... N.Y.: pr. for the author, 1828. 252 p. CtY. Methodist clergyman in New York and Ohio. [3806]

Maynard, Theodore, b. 1890. The world I saw. Milwaukee: The Bruce pub. co., 1938. 313 p. NN. Literary and religious experiences of a Catholic poet and writer, a convert from Protestantism, who spent the first portion of his life in India and England. [3807]

Mayne, Isabella Maud. Maud. N.Y.: Macmillan, 1939. 593 p. DLC. The youth of a girl in Illinois, who was active in local theatre work, and later wrote for women's magazines. [3808]

Mayo, Lucy Ella, b. 1868. Father and daughter. College View: Union college press, 1904. 188 p. NbLU. An account with strong religious overtones. The author, who grew up on a pioneer farm in Nebraska, was an active worker in the Christian Endeavor Society. [3809]

Maze, Katie (Goar), b. 1861. Looking backward. Harrisburg: Evangelical press, 1943. 118 p. DLC. The author and her husband, clergyman of the Evangelical faith, were missionary workers in Nebraska. [3810]

Mazzei, Philip, 1730-1816. Memoirs...tr. by Howard R. Marraro. N.Y.: Columbia univ. press, 1942. 414 p. WHi. An Italian who became a horticulturist in Virginia, and who in 1779 was sent to Italy to borrow money for Virginia. His American career was ended in 1785. [3811]

Mazzuchelli, Samuel Charles, 1806-1864. Memoirs historical and edifying... Chicago: W.F. Hall pr. co., 1915. 375 p. DLC. Roman Catholic missionary, born in Italy, who served in Wisconsin, Iowa and Illinois. The account closes with 1844. [3812]

M'Bride, Robert Ekin, b. 1846. In the ranks: from the Wilderness to Appomattox court-house. The war, as seen and experienced by a private soldier in the Army of the Potomac...Cinc.: Walden & Stowe, 1881. 246 p. NN. Union army. [3813]

McAdoo, William Gibbs, 1863-1941. Crowded years...Boston: Houghton Mifflin, 1931. 542 p. WHi. Secretary of the Treasury in Wilson's cabinet. Previously practiced law in Tennessee and New York. During 1933-39 he was U.S. Senator from California. [3814]

McAllister, Agnes. A lone woman in Africa; six years on the Kroo coast. N.Y.: Hunt & Eaton, 1896. 295 p. DLC. Methodist missionary in Liberia. [3815]

McAllister, Ward, 1827-1895. Society as I have found it. N.Y.: Cassell, 1890. 469 p. NN. For many years the author was the arbiter of Newport and New York society. [3816]

McArthur, Harriet, b. 1851. Recollections of the Rickreall. Portland: Koke-Chapman, 1930. 24 p. NN. Youthful days in Oregon. [3817]

McAuley, Jeremiah, 1839-1884. Transformed; or, The history of a river thief, briefly told. N.Y.:? 1875. 78 p. NN. Upon conversion, he founded a mission in New York City. [3818]

McBride, Herbert Wes, 1873-1933. The Emma Gees. Indianapolis: Bobbs-Merrill, 1918. 218 p. DLC. [3819]

Machine gunner in France, first World War.

McBride, Herbert Wes, 1873– [3820] 1933. A rifleman went to war. Marines, N.C.: Small-arms technical pub. co., 1935. 398 p. DLC. National guardsman in Indiana and Illinois. Upon outbreak of war in 1914 he joined the Canadian army.

McBride, Mary Margaret, [3821] b. 1899. Here's Martha Deane, presented by Mary Margaret McBride. Garden City, N.Y.: Garden City pub. co., 1936. 294 p. NN. Experiences on the radio.

McBride, Mary Margaret, [3822] b. 1899. How dear to my heart. N.Y.: The Macmillan co., 1940. 196 p. NN. Recollections of a Missouri childhood.

McCaleb, J.M. Once traveled [3823] roads. Nashville: Gospel advocate co., 1934. 542 p. MoCanD. American missionary in Japan, beginning with 1892.

McCallie, Samuel Washington. [3824] Autobiographical sketch. Atlanta: 1927. 11p. G. By the State Geologist of Georgia.

McCandless, James Sutton, [3825] b. 1855. A brief history... Honolulu: T. H. Advertising pub. co., 1936. 79 p. DLC. An American who developed a well-digging company in Hawaii.

McCarer, William H. Reminiscences and reflections... [3826] Evansville: 1880. 39 p. Auto., p. 27–39. MnHi. Presbyterian clergyman in Indiana, 1850–1880.

McCartee, Divie Bethune, 1820– [3827] 1900. A missionary pioneer in the Far East. A memorial of Divie Bethune McCartee, for more than fifty years a missionary of the Board of Foreign Missions of the Presbyterian Church in the U.S.A. N.Y.: Revell co., 1922. 224 p. NN. Medical missionary in China and Japan.

McCarter, Robert Harris, 1859– [3828] 1941. Memories of a half century at the New Jersey bar. Camden: N.J.: The Haddon Craftsmen, 1937. 178 p. NN. Largely reminiscences of fellow members of the New Jersey bar. The author was attorney general of New Jersey, 1903–08.

McCarthy, Edward Thomas. Incidents in the life of a mining [3829] engineer. London: Geo. Routledge, 1918. 384 p. NN. The experiences of the author, an Englishman, in North Carolina and Colorado.

McCarthy, Patrick Joseph, 1848– [3830] 1921. Autobiographic memoirs... Providence, R.I.: Visitor press, 1927. 300 p. DLC. Irish born lawyer, and political figure in Rhode Island and Massachusetts.

McCarthy, Peter H. Twenty-two [3831] years on whiskey row...Joliet: Brewster press, 1931. 48 p. DLC. Bartender and prize fighter turned reformer, who founded a mission in Illinois.

McCarthy, Timothy F. A year [3832] at Camp Gordon...Wilkes-Barre: Caxton press, 1920. 156 p. DLC. Welfare worker, 1918–19, in a Georgia training camp.

McCarty, Richard Justin, b. 1851. [3833] Work and play...Kansas City: Empire pr. co., 1925. 253 p. WHi. Civil engineer, connected with transportation in Kansas City.

McCaskey, Townsend H., b. 1908. [3834] Bustin' in'to an education; a new boys "log" of life as it is lived at school. N.Y.: D. McCaskey, 1926. 183 p. DLC. A student at a military academy in Wisconsin.

McCauley, James Emmit, 1873– [3835] 1924. A stove-up cowboy's story. Austin: Texas folklore society, 1943. 73 p. WHi. Texas cowboy.

McClain, Matthew, 1806–1876. [3836] Life and labors of the Rev. Matthew McClain, with recollections and events through a life of seventy years. Indianapolis: J.G. Doughty, printer, 1876. 232 p. DLC. Baptist itinerant preacher in Indiana.

McClellan, George Brinton, [3837] 1826–1885. McClellan's own story: the war for the union, the soldiers who fought it, the civilians who directed it and his relations to it and to them. N.Y.: C. L. Webster & co., 1887. 678 p. WHi. Covers period of his command, to Nov. 1862.

McClintock, Alexander, d. 1918. [3838] Best o' luck; how a fighting Kentuckian won the thanks of Britain's King. N.Y.: George H. Doran, 1917.

171 p. DLC. American with Canadian forces in first World War.

McClintock, Marshall, b. 1906. [3839] We take to bed. N.Y.: J. Cape & H. Smith, 1931. 321 p. DLC. Victim of tuberculosis in New York.

McClune, Hugh H., d. 1835. Miscellanca. York, Pa.: The Gazette co., 1907. 214 p. DLC. Teacher; lecturer on phrenology; lawyer. In New York and Pa. [3840]

McClure, Samuel Sidney, b. 1857. [3841] My autobiography. N.Y.: F. A. Stokes, 1914. 266 p. WHi. Magazine publisher, founder of newspaper syndicate.

McColl, Mrs. Eleanor Evans [3842] (Thomas). Old folks at home. N.Y.: 1921. 186 p. DLC. A civilian's life in South Carolina during the Civil War.

McCollum, Charles Holmes, [3843] b. 1874. Pills and proverbs. Boston: Meador pub. co., 1941. 225 p. NN. Recollections of a Texas doctor.

McComb, Earl Vinton, b. 1883. [3844] Doctor of the north country. N.Y.: Crowell, 1936. 238 p. WU. In Minnesota.

McConaughy, David, b. 1860. [3845] Pioneering with Christ, among the young men of India and the churches of America...N.Y.: Association press, 1941. 101 p. DLC. By a Y.M.C.A. worker.

McConnell, Ethel J., b. 1897. [3846] Out of darkness into His marvelous light. Phoenix, Ariz.: Am. Desert mission, 1944. 6 p. UU. A spiritual account by a person who left the Mormon church.

McConnell, H. H. Five years a [3847] cavalryman; or, sketches of regular army life on the Texas frontier...Jacksboro: J. N. Rogers & co., printers, 1889. 319 p. TxH. In the sixties.

McConnell, J. W. Early Kansas [3848] experiences...No imprint. 5 p. KHi. Beginning with 1858. Farming, hunting, Indian fighting.

McConnell, William John, 1839– [3849] 1925. ...Frontier law; a story of vigilante days...Yonkers-on-Hudson, N.Y.: World book co., 1924. 233 p. NN. Miner, homesteader, in Oregon. Governor of Idaho. Member of the U. S. Congress.

McCorkle, John, b. 1838. Three [3850] years with Quantrell; a true story. Told by his scout, John McCorkle; written by O. S. Barton. Armstrong, Mo.: Armstrong Herald print, 1914. 157 p. NN. A Confederate account.

McCormack, John, 1884–1945. [3851] John McCormack, his own life story, transcribed by Pierre V. R. Key. Boston: Small, Maynard, & co., 1918. 433 p. DLC. Irish singer.

McCormick, John Newton, 1863– [3852] 1939. A small part, by the Rt. Rev. John Newton McCormick, bishop of Western Michigan. Milwaukee, Wis.: Morehouse pub. co., 1934. 165 p. NN. Methodist clergyman, later an Episcopalian. Labors in Maryland and Virginia; religious work in Europe during and after the first World War.

McCormick, Robert Rutherford, [3853] b. 1880. With the Russian army, being the experiences of a national guardsman. N.Y.: Macmillan, 1915. 306 p. DLC. Covers 1914–1918.

McCormick-Goodhart, Mrs. [3854] Henrietta Laura, b. 1857. Hands across the sea...reminiscences of an anglo-American marriage. Chicago: pr. by R. R. Donnelley & sons, 1921. 123 p. DLC. Childhood in Chicago; domestic life in England. An account of social life in America and Europe.

McCosh, James, 1811–1894. [3855] Twenty years of Princeton College. Being farewell address, delivered June 20th, 1888...N.Y.: Scribner's sons, 1888. 68 p. DLC. By the president of Princeton.

McCosh, James, 1811–1894. The [3856] life of James McCosh, a record chiefly autobiographical, by William M. Sloane. N.Y.: Scribner, 1896. 287 p. WHi. Scot who became famous from his metaphysical writings, and who was made president of Princeton.

McCoy, Isaac, 1784–1846. History [3857] of Baptist Indian missions... Wash.: William M. Morrison, 1840. 611p. NbHi. Baptist missionary among Indians in the Mississippi Valley, beginning about 1817.

McCoy, Patrick Terrance. Kiltie [3858] McCoy; an American boy with an Irish name fighting in France as a Scotch soldier. Indianapolis: Bobbs-Merrill co., 1918. 246 p. DLC. World War I.

McCrackan, William Denison, [3859] 1864-1923. An American abroad and at home...N.Y.: M. E. Starr, 1924. 220 p. DLC. Writer and poet, born in Germany of American parents.

McCravy, Edwin Parker, b. 1873.[3860] Memories. Greenville: Observer pr. co., 1941. 375 p. DLC. Businessman (insurance and real estate); member of State Senate of South Carolina; U. S. Senator.

McCue, James, b. 1836. Twenty-[3861] one years in California. Incidents in the life of a stage-driver. San Francisco: 1878? 30 p. CSmH. Miner, merchant, operator of stage business, beginning with 1854.

McCullagh, Archibald. A sermon[3862] commemorative of the twenty-fifth anniversary of the ordination of Rev. Archibald McCullagh, D.D., pastor of Plymouth Congregational church, Worcester, Mass. Worcester: press of Lucius P. Goddard, 1896. 26 p. MWA. As described by the title.

McCullough, A.M., b. 1825. The [3863] experience of seventy years. Minneapolis: Tribune job pr. co., 1895. 199 p. Auto., p. 9-65. MoKU. Irish born missionary who in the seventies served in Minnesota and Ohio.

McDaniel, Charles W., b. 1849. [3864] Telephone reminiscences. No imprint, 1935? 261 p. Auto., p. 1-92. KHi. Promoter of telephone development in Missouri, Nebraska and Kansas.

McDonald, Colin. Personal notes[3865] ...1864-1877. Urbana, Ohio: 1928. 47 p. DLC. The author served with the Union army in the Civil War, and then attended the U.S. Naval Academy.

McDonald, Mrs. Cornelia(Peake)[3866] 1822-1909. A diary with reminiscences of the war. Nashville: Cullow & Ghertner, 1934. 508 p. DLC. A civilian account of life in the south during the Civil War.

McDougall, Alexander, b. 1845. [3867] Autobiography. N. p.: A. Miller, 1932. 238 p. MnHi. Merchant sailor, born in Scotland; later he became a shipbuilder in Duluth.

McDougall, Walter Hugh, 1858- [3868] 1938. This is the life. N.Y.: Knopf, 1926. 330 p. NN. Newspaper cartoonist.

McFarland, Asa, 1804-1879. An [3869] outline biography and recollections. Concord: Republican press, association, 1880. 145 p. Nh. Newspaper publisher in New Hampshire.

McFarland, Bertha Blount. Our [3870] garden was so fair; the story of a mission in Thailand. Phila.: The Blakiston co., 1943. 141 p. NN. Mission work in Siam.

McFarland, Henry, 1831-1911. [3871] Sixty years...Concord: Rumford press, 1899. 331 p. NN. Official of the Union Pacific Railroad. Journalist in New Hampshire. Paymaster in the Union army.

McFee, William, b. 1881. More [3872] harbours of memory. Garden City: Doubleday, Doran, 1934. 339 p. WU. Englishman, after coming to live in the United States, tells of his life on a merchant ship. See also his earlier book, Harbours of Memory.

McGee, Joseph H., b. 1821. Story [3873] of the Grand River country, 1821-1905...Gallatin: North Missourian press, 1909. MoK. After serving in the war with Mexico, the author went to California in 1849, where he mined for gold. In the fifties he taught school in Missouri, and in the sixties he was a county clerk.

McGehee, John Boykin, b. 1833. [3874] Autobiography...Buena Vista: Weaver pr. co., 1915? 162 p. OkHi. Methodist clergyman in Georgia.

McGilvary, Daniel, 1828-1911. [3875] A half century among the Siamese and the Lao...N.Y.: Revell, 1912. 435 p. WU. Presbyterian missionary.

McGinty, Billy, b. 1870. The old [3876] west. N.p.: 1937. 108 p. InU. Cowboy in Texas, Oklahoma and Arizona, 1885-1897.

McGlinchey, Joseph Francis, [3877] b. 1882. Mission tours, India. Boston: Soc. for Propagation of the Faith, 1925. 280 p. DLC. A Catholic mission officer visits Ceylon and India.

McGowan, Edward, 1813-1893. [3878] Narrative of Edward McGowan, including a full account of the author's adventures and perils while persecuted by the San Francisco vigilance committee of 1856...San Francisco: The author, 1857. 240 p. DLC. A frontier account: A California justice is accused of murder.

McGrath, Edward F. I was con- [3879] demned to the chair, by Edward F. McGrath, Sing Sing death-house prisoner no. 60021, recommitted for twenty years to life as no. 61550. N.Y.: Frederick A. Stokes co., 1934. 312 p. NN. Experiences at Sing Sing, Dannemora, and Great Meadows.

McGraw, John Joseph, 1873-1934. [3880] My thirty years in baseball. N.Y.: Boni & Liveright, 1923. 265 p. NN. The author, a noted baseball player, was later manager of the New York Giants.

McHenry, Beth. I had illusions. [3881] N.Y.: The Henkle co., 1935. 286 p. NN. Two years' experiences as a student nurse in a San Francisco hospital.

McIlhany, Edward Washington, [3882] b. 1828. Recollections of a '49er. A quaint and thrilling narrative of a trip across the plains, and life in the California gold fields during the stirring days following the discovery of gold in the Far West. Kansas City: Hailman pr. co., 1908. 212 p. DLC. After his mining experiences, the author settled in Missouri, where he was a stockman and a cattle agent for railroads.

McIlwaine, Richard, b. 1834. [3883] Memories of three score years and ten. N.Y.: Neale, 1908. 383 p. WHi. Presbyterian clergyman and college president in Virginia.

McIlyar, James Jackson, 1816- [3884] 1907. James Jackson McIlyar, preacher, evangelist, Freemason ...Harrisburg? 1912? 311p. Auto., p. 7-274. OClWHi. Methodist clergyman in Ohio and Pennsylvania.

McIntire, James, b. 1846. Early [3885] days in Texas...Kansas City: McIntire pub. co., 1902. 229 p. DLC. Cowboy, ranger, marshal.

McKay, Claude, 1890-1948. A [3886] long way from home. N.Y.: Furman, 1937. 354 p. NN. Negro novelist and poet.

McKay, Robert Henderson, b.1840. [3887] Little pills...Pittsburg: Pittsburg headlight, 1918. 127 p. WHi. Army physician on frontier, 1869-75. The locale is the plains and the Rockies.

McKean, James W. See Snyder, Gerrit.

McKeith, George Robert, [3888] b. 1870. My life and call... Blair: Pilot press, 1912. 64 p. NbHi. Congregational minister in Nebraska.

McKenna, James A. Black [3889] range tales; chronicling sixty years of life and adventures in the southwest. N.Y.: Wilson-Erickson, 1936. 300 p. WHi. Miner on the frontier in New Mexico.

McKenney, Ruth, b. 1911. My [3890] sister Eileen. N.Y.: Harcourt, Brace & co., 1938. 226 p. NN. Episodes in the early life of the author and her sister.

McKenney, Thomas Loraine, [3891] 1785-1859. Memoirs, official and personal; with sketches of travels among the northern and southern Indians; embracing a war excursion, and descriptions of scenes along the western borders. N.Y.: Paine & Burgess, 1846. 2 vols. NN. Superintendent of the Indian Trade, 1816-22, and Chief of the Bureau of Indian Affairs, 1824-30. The second volume is not autobiographical.

McKinney, Edward Pascal. Life [3892] in tent and field, 1861-1865. Boston: R. G. Badger, 1922. 161 p. DLC. Union army officer.

McLane, Robert Milligan, 1815- [3893] 1898. Reminiscences, 1827-1897. N.p.: 1903. 165 p. DLC. Lawyer and political figure in Maryland. U.S. Minister to Mexico and France.

McLaughlin, Daniel, b. 1863. [3894] Chronicles of a Northern Pacific veteran. Spokane: 1930. 56 p. DLC. Railroader.

McLean, Evalyn Walsh. Father [3895] struck it rich. Boston: Little, Brown, 1936. 309 p. WHi. Drug addict whose husband was committed to a mental hospital.

McLean, John Howell, b. 1838. [3896]

Reminiscences...Nashville: pub. for the author by Smith & Lamar, 1918? 322 p. ICU. Methodist clergyman in Texas.

McLean, Kathryn (Anderson), [3897] b. 1909. Mama's bank account. N.Y.: Harcourt, Brace & co., 1943. 204 p. NN. Recollections of a girlhood in San Francisco.

McLean, R. B. Reminiscences [3898] of early days at the head of the lakes. No imprint, 1913? 8 p. MnHi. The writer explored for minerals in Minnesota in the fifties.

McMaster, S.W., b. 1811. 60 [3899] years on the Upper Mississippi ...Rock Island: 1893. 300 p. WHi. Frontier merchant in Illinois, Iowa, Minnesota and Wisconsin.

McMeans, A., b. 1813. Travels [3900] and life...Weatherford: Sun pub. co., 1885. 143 p. TxU. Confederate soldier, who then became a teacher in Texas and Kansas.

McMullen, Daniel Yeoward. The [3901] experiences of a "little" man... Chicago: pr. by Rogers & Wells, 1900. 138 p. DLC. Dwarf who became a banker.

McNeil, Samuel. McNeil's [3902] travels...Columbus: Scott & Bascom, printers, 1850. 40 p. DLC. California trader and miner.

McNeil, Samuel A. Personal [3903] recollections of service in the army of the Cumberland and Sherman's army...No imprint. 76 p. WHi. Union army.

McNemee, Andrew J., b. 1848. [3904] "Brother Mack"...Portland: T. G. Robinson, printer, 1924. 79 p. WHi. Methodist clergyman in Oregon.

McPherson, Mrs. Aimee Semple. [3905] This is that, personal experiences, sermons and writings of Aimee Sample McPherson, evangelist. Los Angeles: Bridal call, 1919. 685 p. DLC. Evangelist tells of her tours in England, China and the U.S.

McPherson, Mrs. Aimee Semple. [3906] In the service of the King...N.Y.: Boni & Liveright, 1927. 316 p. WHi. Evangelist.

McPherson, George Wilson, [3907] b. 1865. A parson's adventures... Yonkers: Yonkers book co., 1925. 298 p. WHi. Baptist revivalist in New York City and Denver.

McQuie, Robert Edwin, b. 1848. [3908] Autobiography...Montgomery City, Mo.: Standard pub. co., n.d. 6 p. MoSHi. Baptist clergyman in Missouri.

McRae, Milton Alexander, 1858- [3909] 1930. Forty years in newspaperdom...N.Y.:Brentano, 1924. 496 p. WU. Newspaper publisher.

McReynolds, Robert, d. 1928. [3910] Thirty years on the frontier. Colorado Springs: El Paso pub. co., 1906. 256 p. WHi. Cowboy and miner in the Black Hills, Colorado and Oklahoma.

McWilliams, John, b. 1832. Rec- [3911] ollectons (sic.)...Princeton: Princeton univ. press, 1921? 186 p. WHi. A youthful miner in early California and Oregon.

Meacham, Henry H. The empty [3912] sleeve...Springfield: 1869? 32 p. DLC. Soldier in the Union army.

Mead, Homer, b. 1847. The [3913] Eighth Iowa cavalry in the Civil war ...Carthage: S.C. Davidson, 1925. 27 p. DLC. Soldier in the Union army.

Meade, David. Autobiography of [3914] David Meade. (In: Chaumiere papers, ed. by Henry J. Peet. Chicago: 1883). p. 9-47. KyU. Landowner in Kentucky and Virginia.

Meade, Edwards Hoag, b. 1863. [3915] Doubling back; autobiography of an actor...Chicago: Hammond press, 1916. 180 p. DLC. Stock company, vaudeville.

Meade, Julian Rutherford. I live [3916] in Virginia. N.Y.: Longmans, Green, 1935. 310 p. WHi. A writer tells of his early efforts to learn his craft.

Meads, Simeon P., b. 1849. In [3917] my own lot and place...No imprint. 102 p. CSmH. School teacher in Maine and California.

Means, George H. God's wonder [3918] of fifty years. Louisville: The Standard pr. co., 1926. 302 p. KyLo. The disjointed reminiscences of a Methodist clergyman who served in Kentucky.

Mears, David Otis, 1842-1915. [3919] David Otis Mears, an autobiography, 1842-1893. Boston: Pilgrim press, 1920. 249 p. WHi. Congregational and Presbyterian clergyman in New England.

Mears, John Henry. Racing the [3920] moon...Being the story of the...circumnavigation of the globe by airplane and steamship in 23 days ...N.Y.: Rae D. Henkle co., inc., 1928. 320 p. DLC. As described by the title.

Mecklin, John Moffatt, b. 1871. [3921] My quest for freedom. N.Y.: Scribner, 1945. 293 p. WU. Professor of Philosophy at Dartmouth tells of his religious development.

Medary, Thomas Corwin, 1840- [3922] 1893. Journalistic adventures... No imprint, 1942? 57 p. WHi. Editor in Iowa.

Medem, Vladimir, 1879-1923. [3923] Zikhroynes. Warsaw: Medem, 1920. 154 p. NN. A writer for the Yiddish language press in New York describes his work for the Bund during the War against Germany in 1918. The writer was born in Latvia.

Meek, Joseph L. River of the [3924] west...by Mrs. Frances Victor. Hartford: Columbian book co., 1870. 602 p. Auto., p. 41-512. DLC. Hunter, trapper, trader in Rocky Mountains, Oregon.

Meeker, Ezra, 1830-1928. Ven- [3925] tures and adventures...Seattle: Ranier pr. co., 1909. 384 p. DLC. Pioneer farmer in Oregon. Published in 1916 as: The Busy Life of Eighty-Five Years...

Meeker, Ezra, 1830-1928. Per- [3926] sonal experiences on the Oregon trail sixty years ago. St. Louis: McAdoo pr. co., 1912. 150 p. DLC. An account similar to the preceding, presumably written for young people. Same as his Ox-Team Days.

Mela, Alvin S. My little part in [3927] a big war. N.Y.: Hella press, 1919. 84 p. DLC. Service with the army in France in the First World War.

Melba, Nellie, b. 1861. Melodies [3928] and memories. London: Butterworth, 1925. 335 p. WU. Australian opera singer who devotes three chapters to her experiences in America.

Meldrum, Andrew Barclay, [3929] b. 1857. Forty years in the ministry. Cleveland: 1924. 27 p. MnHi. A Presbyterian clergyman, born in Scotland, who served in California.

Melharn, Nathan Raymond, [3930] b. 1871. The diary of a deacon, by Raymond Etan (pseud.). Phila.: The Castle press, 1925. 170 p. DLC. A Lutheran deacon in Pa.

Mellish, Mary (Flannery), [3931] b. 1890. Sometimes I reminisce ...N.Y.: Putnam, 1941. 336 p. WU. Opera singer.

Mellon, Thomas, 1813-1908. [3932] Thomas Mellon and his times. Pittsburgh: Johnston & co., printers, 1885. 648 p. DLC. Lawyer, state judge, banker in Pittsburgh.

Melton, William Walter, b.1879. [3933] Stories from life. Dallas: Helms pr. co., 1943. 222 p. TxWB. Baptist clergyman in Texas.

Memoranda of the experience, [3934] labors, and travels of a Universalist preacher. Cinc.: John A. Gurley, 1845. 400 p. MoHi. In New Jersey, Pa., Indiana, Ohio, Missouri, Louisiana and in several states in the South Atlantic region.

Menand, Louis, 1807-1900. Auto-[3935] biography and recollections of incidents connected with horticultural affairs, etc., from 1807 up to this day, 1892... Albany: Weed, Parsons & co., 1892. 200 p. Auto., p. 5-138. DLC. A Frenchborn florist and gardener in New York.

Mencken, Henry Louis, b. 1880. [3936] Happy days, 1880-1892. N.Y.: Knopf, 1940. 313 p. WU. Youthful experiences in Baltimore.

Mencken, Henry Louis, b. 1880. [3937] Newspaper days, 1899-1906. N.Y.: Knopf, 1941. 313 p. WU. Reporter, editor in Maryland.

Mencken, Henry Louis, b. 1880. [3938] Heathen days, 1890-1936. N.Y.: Knopf, 1943. 299 p. WU. Random reminiscences by a journalist and editor of the American Mercury.

Mendl, Elsie (DeWolfe), lady, [3939] b. 1865. After all. N.Y. & London: Harper, 1935. 278 p. NN. This American-born writer tells of her experiences, first as an actress and later as an interior decorator, and of her social life both in New York and in Europe.

Menninger, Flo V. (Kniseley), [3940]
b. 1863. Days of my life, memories of a Kansas mother and teacher. N.Y.: R. R. Smith, 1939. 310 p. DLC. As described by the title.

Mercier, Henry James. Life in [3941] a man of war...by a fore-top man. Phila.: L. R. Bailey, printer, 1841. 267 p. DLC. Covers 1839-41.

Meriwether, Lee, b. 1862. My [3942] yesteryears... Webster Groves: International Mark Twain society, 1942. 436 p. WHi. Lawyer and politician in Missouri. Diplomatic officer in Europe and the Far East. See also his After Thoughts (1945).

Merkley, Christopher, b. 1808. [3943] Biography of Christopher Merkley. Salt Lake City: J. H. Parry, 1887. 46 p. WHi. Mormon minister in the Plains, Rockies and the Far West.

Merriam, Charles Bailey, [3944] b. 1885. Machete...Dallas: Southwest press, 1932. 231 p. DLC. Life on a sugar plantation in Mexico.

Merrick, George Byron, b. 1841. [3945] Old times on the Upper Mississippi ...Cleveland: Clark, 1909. 323 p. WHi. Steamboat pilot, 1854-63.

Merrill, Daniel, 1765-1833. Auto-[3946] biography...Phila.: Baptist general tract society, 1833. 12 p. MeWaC. Baptist clergyman in Maine.

Merrill, Mrs. Frances. Among [3947] the nudists. N.Y.: Knopf, 1931. 246 p. Auto., p. 3-176. DLC. In Europe. The author explains her advocacy of nudism.

Merrill, Marringer Wood,1832- [3948] 1906. Utah pioneer and apostle ...Salt Lake City: Deseret news, 1937. 527 p. Auto., p. 25-61. DLC. Canadian who came to Utah in 1853. Farmer, and Mormon "teacher". This account closes with 1860.

Merrill, Orin S. "Mysterious [3949] Scott"... Chicago: 1906. 210 p. CSmH. Gold hunting in Nevada in the 20th century.

Merrill, Sereno Taylor, b.1816. [3950] Narrative. Milwaukee: Press of the Evening Wisconsin co., 1900. 91 p. WHi. In Wisconsin: manufacturer of paper products; politician.

Merritt, Edwin Atkins, b. 1828. [3951] Recollections, 1828-1911. Albany: J. B. Lyon co., printers, 1911. 188 p. WHi. Politician in New York; collector of the Port of New York; Consul General at London.

Merritt, Henry Clay, b. 1831. [3952] Shadow of a gun. Chicago: F.T. Peterson, 1904. 450 p. DLC. By a man whose business was the hunting of wild animals in the midwestern states.

Merryweather, F. From England [3953] to California...Sacramento City: J. A. Wilson, 1868. 146 p. CU-B. An Englishman's account of trouble with the Indians in the fifties in the Pike's Peak area.

Mersfelder, Louis Calhoun, [3954] b. 1884. Cowboy, fisherman-hunter...Kansas City: Brown-White-Lowell press, 1941. 246 p. DLC. The first 54 pages are about his cowboy experiences in Texas.

Metcalf, Ada. Lunatic asylums: [3955] and how I became an inmate of one. Doctors, incidents, humbugging. Chicago: Ottaway & Colbert, printers, 1876. 75 p. DLC. The period covered is roughly 1868-76.

Metcalf, Anthony, b. 1827. Ten [3956] years before the mast. Malad City: 1888. 81 p. USlC. An Englishman tells of his religious development: he became a Mormon in 1852; went over to the Reorganized branch, and was later excommunicated.

Metcalf, Edwin. Personal inci- [3957] dents in the early campaigns of the Third Regiment Rhode Island Volunteers and the Tenth Army corps. Providence: S. S. Rider, 1879. 31 p. OClWHi. As described by the title.

Metcalf, Mrs. Lucy Williams. [3958] Concerning a career. No imprint. 10 p. LNHT. Louisiana girl who taught music in various parts of the country.

Metcalf, Stanley W. Personal [3959] memoirs; a narrative of the experiences of an American in France and Germany in 1917-1919. Fulton: Morrill press, 1927. 254 p. DLC. Ambulance driver and soldier in the First World War.

Metcalfe, Mrs. John. See Scott, Evelyn.

Metcalfe, V. M., b. 1832. Uncle [3960]
Minor's stories...Nashville:
McQuiddy pr. co., 1916. 256 p.
KyU. Owner of cotton factories,
farmer who lost his fortune during
the Civil War. After the War, he
was a merchant in Tennessee,
and then a traveling salesman.

Metzgar, Judson D. Adventures [3961]
in Japanese prints... Los Angeles:
Dawson's book shop, 1944? 116 p.
Auto., p. 17-70. DLC. Illinois
art collector.

Meyer, Adolph C., b. 1872. [3962]
Travel search for bells. Chicago:
Lightner pub. co., 1944. 197 p.
DLC. The adventures of a collector of bells.

Meyer, Ernest Louis, 1892-1952. [3963]
Hey! Yellowbacks! The war
diary of a conscientious objector.
N.Y.: John Day, 1930. 209 p. DLC.
As described by the title.

Meyer, George. Autobiography. [3964]
Shenandoah, Iowa: Open door,
1908. 28 p. CtY. California
forty-niner.

Meyer, Henry, b. 1859. Life [3965]
staked at cards; a sketch of the
life of Henry Meyer, a converted
gambler. N.Y.: The author, 1895.
26 p. DLC. As described by the
title.

Meyer, Henry A., b. 1860. Look-[3966]
ing through life's window; personal reminiscences. N.Y.:
Coward-McCann, inc., 1930.
236 p. DLC. Grocer; real estate
dealer; and political figure in
New York.

Meyer, Henry Coddington, 1844- [3967]
1935. The story of the Sanitary
Engineer later the Engineering
Record. N.Y.: Press of Jaques
co., 1928. 62 p. NN. The author
founded the periodical in 1877
and conducted it 1877-1902.

Meyer, Henry Coddington, 1844- [3968]
1935. Civil war experiences...
N.Y.: Putnam, 1911. 119 p. WHi.
In Union army.

Meyer, Jacob G., 1846-1930. [3969]
Autobiography...No imprint.
48 p. InGo. Ohio farmer.

Meyers, Augustus. Ten years in [3970]
the ranks, U.S. army. N.Y.:
Stirling press, 1914. 356 p. WHi.
Military service in Indian territory, 1854-64.

Micheaux, Oscar, b. 1884. The [3971]
conquest; the story of a Negro
pioneer, by the pioneer. Lincoln:
Woodruff press, 1913. 311 p. DLC.
Railroad porter, homesteader in
the Dakotas and Nebraska.

Michel, Auguste Marie, b. 1862. [3972]
A mutilated life story;...sketches
of experiences as a nurse and
doctor in an African hospital,
and in the American West. Chicago:
The author, 1911. 171 p. DLC. The
author was born in France.

Michelson, Charles. The ghost [3973]
talks. N.Y.: Putnam's sons, 1944.
245 p. WHi. The author, a newspaperman, undertook publicity for
the Democratic party in 1930.

Michener, Ezra, 1794-1887. [3974]
Autobiographical notes...Phila.:
Friends' book association, 1893.
202 p. Auto., p. 1-62. DLC.
Physician and botanist in Pennsylvania.

Mickwitz, Harold von, b. 1859. [3975]
The memoirs...Dallas: Dealey
& Lowe, 1936. 116 p. TxU. Pianist
and teacher of music in Texas and
Illinois.

Middleton, George. Circus [3976]
memoirs; reminiscences of
George Middleton as told to and
written by his wife. Los Angeles:
Geo. Rice & sons, prtrs., 1913.
118 p. NN. Recollections of the
circus and the dime museums.

Miel, Charles Francis Bonaven-[3977]
ture, 1818-1902. A soul's pilgrimmage; being the personal
and religious experiences of
Charles F. B. Miel, D. D.
Phila.: G. W. Jacobs & co., 1899.
190 p. DLC. A French Jesuit
renounces his church to become
an Anglican in England. He then
came to the U.S. to do missionary
work.

Mifflin, Warner, 1745-1798. The [3978]
defence... Phila.: pr. by Samuel Sanson, 1796. 30 p. Auto., p. 3-
19. DLC. A defence of his activities on behalf of temperance,
peace and abolition of slavery.

Mighels, Mrs. Ella Sterling [3979]
(Clark), b. 1853. Life and letters
of a forty-niner's daughter (by
Aurora Esmeralda, pseud.). San
Francisco: Harr Wagner, 1929.
371 p. DLC. Journalist in California.

Mikkelsen, Amund, 1835-1930. [3980]

Nogle af en prests erfaringer i en af de store byer. Decorah, Iowa: Norske Synodes Bogtrykkeri, 1892. 350 p. MnHi. Lutheran clergyman in Chicago, 1874-88.

Milburn, William Henry, 1823- [3981] 1903. Ten years of preacher life. N.Y.: Derby & Jackson, 1859. 363 p. WHi. Methodist clergyman in the Mississippi Valley, 1843-53.

Miles, Nelson Appleton, 1839- [3982] 1925. Personal recollections and observations... Chicago: Werner, 1896. 590 p. DLC. Soldier in the Union army; Indian fighter.

Miles, Nelson Appleton, 1839- [3983] 1925. Serving the Republic... N.Y.: Harper, 1911. 339 p. WHi. See the preceding item. This one contains, in addition, material on his services in the War with Spain.

Millar, Mrs. Mara (Elder), [3984] b. 1869. Hail to yesterday. N.Y.: Farrar & Rinehart, 1941. 302 p. NN. Memories of life and society in Kansas, Oklahoma, and the East, by a woman who looks back on better days.

Millard, F. S., b. 1863. A cow- [3985] puncher of the Pecos. No imprint. 47 p. TxBea. Texas cowboy.

Millard, Mrs. Shirley. I saw [3986] them die; diary and recollections of Shirley Millard. N.Y.: Harcourt, Brace & co., 1936. 115 p. DLC. Nurse, First World War.

Miller, A. P. Tom's experience [3987] in Dakota: why he went; what he did there; what crops he raised and how he raised them... Minneapolis: Miller, Hale & co., 1883. 146 p. DLC. As described by the title.

Miller, Benjamin S. Ranch life [3988] in Southern Kansas and the Indian Territory...N.Y.: Fless & Ridge pr. co., 1896. 163 p. TxDaM. Beginning with 1878.

Miller, Charles C., b. 1831. Fifty [3989] years among the bees. Medina: A. I. Root co., 1911, 340 p. Auto., p. 9-40. DLC. Bee keeper in Ohio.

Miller, Charlie, b. 1850. Broncho [3990] Charlie...(written down by Gladys Shaw Erskine). N.Y.: Crowell, 1934. 316 p. WHi. Broncho buster, and rider for the Pony Express.

Miller, Christopher Blackburn, [3991] b. 1885. Hudson valley squire. N.Y.: Frederick A. Stokes co., 1941. 339 p. NN. Reminiscences of the author's boyhood in Orange county, New York.

Miller, Emory, 1834-1912. Mem- [3992] oirs and sermons. Cinc.: Jennings & Graham, 1911. 303 p. Auto., p. 11-204. DLC. Methodist clergyman in Iowa.

Miller, George, 1774-1816. Life, [3993] experience and ministerial labors of George Miller, Evangelical preacher. (Jacob Albright and his co-laborers, comp. by Reuben Yeakel. Cleveland: Evangelical association, 1883. 329 p.) p. 173-265. OClWHi. Evangelical clergyman in Pennsylvania.

Miller, George, b. 1794. A Mor- [3994] mon bishop... London: n.d. 91 p. UU. The author did missionary work in Illinois, Kentucky and Texas (roughly at mid-century).

Miller, George Elmer, b. 1881. [3995] In the land of sweepers and kings ...Cinc.: Powell & White, 1922. 194 p. MoCanD. Medical missionary in India. No denomination is mentioned.

Miller, Harry, b. 1864. Footloose [3996] fiddler. N.Y.: Whittlesey house, 1945. 326 p. DLC. A roving musician living the life of a hobo.

Miller, Henry, b. 1891. "Auto- [3997] biographical note". (In his: Cosmological eye. Norfolk: New directions, 1939.) p. 357-63. DLC. Novelist, essayist who lived many years in France.

Miller, Joaquin, 1839-1913. Life [3998] amongst the Modocs...London: R. Bentley, 1873. 400 p. DLC. Frequently reprinted under various titles. A writer tells of his experiences with Indians in California. Has been described as: Romance with a wavering thread of fact.

Miller, Joaquin, 1839-1913. [3999] Overland in a covered wagon; an autobiography. Ed. by Sidney G. Firman. N.Y.: D. Appleton & co., 1930. 130 p. NN. "Recollections of his life from early boyhood until he was about twenty years old." Much skepticism has been expressed as to the authenticity of Miller's memoirs.

Miller, Lizzie E. The true way. [4000]

Life and evangelical works of Lizzie E. Miller, (of Fairview, West Va.) written by herself. Los Angeles: pr. for the author, 1895. 320 p. DLC. Evangelist.

Miller, Mary Esther (Mulford), [4001] b. 1849. An East Hampton childhood. East Hampton: Starr press, 1938. 44 p. MiD-B. In New York.

Miller, Max, b. 1901. The begin- [4002] ning of a mortal. N.Y.: E. P. Dutton & co., 1933. 253 p. NN. Boyhood in Washington and Montana.

Miller, Max., b. 1901. I cover [4003] the waterfront. N.Y.: E. P. Dutton & co., 1932. 204 p. NN. The author covered the waterfront for the San Diego Sun.

Miller, Morris Smith, 1814- [4004] 1870. Memoir of the services of Morris S. Miller...No imprint. 7 p. DLC. An account of military services, 1834-66.

Miller, Neva Pinkham. Behind [4005] convent walls. Newcomerstown: 1929. 89 p. DLC. An account by a sister who gave up her vows.

Miller, Norman Mickey, b.1908. [4006] I took the sky road...as told to Hugh B. Cave. N.Y.: Dodd, Mead, 1945. 212 p. DLC. U.S. Navy flier in the second World War.

Miller, Susan Frances (East), [4007] b. 1851. Sixty years in the Nueces valley, 1870-1930. San Antonio: Naylor pub. co., 1930. 374 p. NN. Life in Texas by the wife of a pioneer settler.

Miller, Webb. I found no peace [4008] ...N.Y.: Simon & Schuster, 1936. 332 p. WU. Foreign correspondent (1917-35) in Europe and Africa.

Miller, Wesson Gage, 1822- [4009] 1894. Thirty years in the itinerancy: 1844-1874. Milwaukee: Hauser, 1875. 304 p. WHi. Methodist clergyman who began his labors in Iowa in the forties and then went on to Wisconsin.

Milligan, James. I didn't stay [4010] honest. London: S. Low, 1936. 256 p. NN. Goldminer and cowboy who turned to peddling of "dope". A 20th century account.

Milliken, Ralph L. See Clarke, Sarah.

Mills, Anson, 1834-1924. My [4011] story. Washington: 1918. 412 p. WHi. Professional soldier who served in the Union army and then in the West; inventor of woven web ammunition carrier.

Mills, Bill. Twenty-five years [4012] behind prison bars. Dallas?: 60 p. TxU. In Georgia, Oklahoma and Texas.

Mills, Frank Moody, b. 1831. [4013] Early days in a college town and Wabash college in early days and now with autobiographical reminiscences. Sioux Falls: Sessions pr. co., 1924. 289 p. DLC. The writer lived many years in Iowa where he was engaged in the printing business. Later he published a newspaper in Illinois, and operated a street railway company in South Dakota.

Mills, Frank Moody, b. 1831. [4014] Something about the Mills family ...with autobiographical reminiscences, compiled and prepared by Frank Moody Mills (April 4, 1911). Sioux Falls: 1911. 219 p. DLC. See the preceding item. See also p. 188-209 of his Notings of a nonogenarian (1926).

Mills, Joe. A mountain boyhood.[4015] N.Y.: Sears, 1926. 286 p. DLC. Hunter, trapper, mountain guide in Colorado.

Mills, John H., b. 1811. Auto- [4016] biography of the Rev. John H. Mills, a local deacon in the Methodist Episcopal Church... N.Y.: J. W. Amerman, printer, 1857. 263 p. DLC. In New York.

Mills, Robert, 1781-1855. "Mills [4017] autobiography." (In: Robert Mills, architect of the Washington monument, by Helen M. (Pierce) Gallagher, N.Y.: Columbia univ. press, 1935. 233 p.) p. 159-166. DLC. Architect who practiced in Philadelphia, Baltimore and Washington, and who was associated with Jefferson and Latrobe. This account closes with 1836.

Mills, William W., 1836-1913. [4018] Forty years at ElPaso, 1858-1898...Chicago: W. B. Conkey, 1901. 166 p. DLC. Trader and storekeeper in Texas; served in Union army; Customs Collector at El Paso.

Minder, Charles Frank, b. 1895. [4019] This man's war, the day-by-day record of an American private on the western front. N.Y.:

Pevensey press, 1931. 368 p. DLC. First World War.

Miner, Amos, 1785-1833. Life [4020] and confession of Amos Miner, who was tried and convicted... of the murder of John Smith... taken from his own mouth...(by Sylvester S. Southworth). Providence: 1833. 24 p. DLC. In Rhode Island.

Mines, Flavel Scott, 1811-1852. [4021] A Presbyterian clergyman looking for the church... N.Y.: Pudney & Russell, 1855. 580 p. DLC. A Presbyterian clergyman becomes an Anglican, serving in New York and California.

Minne, Nils Monson, 1855-1938. [4022] Liv og virke. Menominee, Mich.: 1931. 61 p. IaDL. Lutheran clergyman in Iowa, Illinois, Indiana, Minnesota, Wisconsin and Mich.

Mitchell, Charles Fletcher, [4023] 1869-1945. The story of my life. Habana: Heraldo Cristiano, 1940? 200 p. TxDaM. Methodist clergyman in Oklahoma.

Mitchell, Edward. Five thousand [4024] a year; and how I made it in five years' time, starting without capital. Boston: Loring, 1870. 125 p. DLC. Bookkeeper in New York turns to vegetable and flower gardening.

Mitchell, Edward Page, 1852- [4025] 1927. Memoirs of an editor... N.Y.: Scribner, 1924. 458 p. WU. Editor of the New York Sun.

Mitchell, Mrs. Elizabeth Rand, [4026] b. 1881. Music with a feather duster. Boston: Little, Brown, 1941. 280 p. DLC. Amateur pianist, and music lover, living in New York.

Mitchell, Ewing Young. Kicked [4027] in and kicked out of the President's little cabinet. Washington: Andrew Jackson press, 1936. 371 p. TxU. Missouri political figure who under F.D.R. was Assistant Secretary of Commerce.

Mitchell, Hinckley Gilbert [4028] Thomas, 1846-1920. For the benefit of my creditors. Boston: The Beacon press, 1922. 321 p. NN. Professor of theology at Boston University, suspended by the Methodist Church for heresy.

Mitchell, John, 1794-1870. [4029] Derwent... N.Y.: Anson D.F. Randolph & co., 1872. 365 p. DLC. Childhood on a country estate in Connecticut.

Mitchell, Joseph Everett. Big [4030] Mitch, by Joseph Everett Mitchell, city councilman of Salinas, California. San Francisco: The Recorder pr. & pub. co., 1936. 303 p. NN. The author tells of his varied career: feuds in the Ozarks: peace officer and insurance man in California; political life in Salinas, California.

Mitchell, Mary, 1731-1810. A [4031] short account of the early part of the life of Mary Mitchell, late of Nantucket, deceased, written by herself...New Bedford: Abraham Shearman, Jr., 1812. 74 p. MBNew. Gospel preacher, Society of Friends, in New York, New Jersey, Rhode Island.

Mitchell, Nathan J., b. 1808. [4032] Reminiscences and incidents in the life and travels of a pioneer preacher of the "ancient" gospel ...Cinc.: Chase & Hall, 1877. 479 p. Auto., p. 13-183. NN. Evagelist of the Christian Church, laboring largely in Pennsylvania.

Mitchill, Samuel Latham, 1764- [4033] 1831. Some of the memorable events and occurences in the life of Samuel L. Mitchill of New York from 1786 to 1826. N.Y.: 1826. 8 p. NNC. Physician.

Mix, Jonathon, 1753-1817. A [4034] brief account of the life and patriotic services... New Haven: pr. by Tuttle, Morehouse & Taylor, 1886. 98 p. USlGS. Soldier during the Revolutionary War, mercantile business in New York; inventor.

Mixson, Frank M., b. 1846. Rem-[4035] iniscences of a private. Columbia, S.C.: The State co., 1910. 130 p. DLC. In the Confederate army.

M'Lean, James. Seventeen [4036] years' history of the life and sufferings of James M'Lean... Hartford: The author, 1814. 27 p. DLC. The writer was impressed into the British navy.

Modjeska, Helena, 1840-1909. [4037] Memories and impressions... N.Y.: Macmillan, 1910. 571 p. WU. Polish-American actress.

Moe, Stiles, b. 1834. Family [4038] story. Union Grove: 1921. 47 p.

WHi. A story about boyhood in Wisconsin.

Moennich, Martha L. Pioneer [4039] for Christ in Xingo jungles; adventure in the heart of South America. Grand Rapids: Zondervan pub. house, 1942. 196 p. DLC. In Brazil.

Moffett, Mrs. Dessie Clorene (Allred). See Moffett, Joseph Franklin.

Moffett, Joseph Franklin, b. 1900 [4040] and Mrs. Dessie Clorene (Allred) Moffett, b. 1907. Autobiographies. No imprint. 45 leaves. USIGS. Farmer and school teacher in Texas; on mission for Mormons in Mexico. His wife tells of her youth in a Mormon family in New Mexico, and of mission work in Mass. and Pa.

Molee, Elias, b. 1845. Molee's [4041] wandering...Tacoma: 1919. 122 p. MiD-B. Life in the rural midwest when a boy, including school experiences.

Molineaux, Mrs. Emily E. (Bow-[4042] man), b. 1829. Lifetime recollections...San Francisco: C. W. Gordon, pr., 1902. 98 p. CU-B. Bible agent in California; evangelical worker in California, Arkansas, Nevada, Colorado and Kansas.

Moncrieffe, Margaret. See Coghlan, Mrs. John.

Mondésir, Édouard de. Souvenir [4043] d'Édouard de Mondésir. Baltimore: Johns Hopkins press, 1942. 60 p. DLC. Member of Sulpitian priestly order who helped to found a seminary in Baltimore in 1791.

Monmouth, Mrs. Sarah Elizabeth [4044] (Harper), 1829-1887. Living on half a dime a day...Concord: 1932. 54 p. DLC. How she lived on a pittance; also, her work for the Congregational church as a lay reader. The locale is New England.

Monroe, Anne Shannon, 1877- [4045] 1942. The world I saw. Garden City: Doubleday, Doran, 1928. 331 p. NN. Novelist, and writer of books for the general reader.

Monroe, Harriet, 1860-1936. A [4046] poet's life...N.Y.: Macmillan, 1938. 488 p. WU. As described by the title.

Monteiro, Aristides. War rem- [4047] iniscences by a surgeon of Mosby's command. Richmond: 1890. 236 p. NN. Confederate army.

Montgomery, Mrs. Carrie (Judd) [4048] b. 1858. "Under His wings"; the story of my life. Oakland: Office of triumphs of faith, 1936. 256 p. DLC. "Faith healer" in New York and California.

Montgomery, Cora (pseud.). See Lazneau, Mrs. William Leslie.

Montgomery, Frank Alexander, [4049] b. 1830. Reminiscences of a Mississippian in peace and war. Cinc.: The Robert Clarke co. press, 1901. 305 p. NN. Member of Mississippi legislature in eighties, Federal judge. Most of the book relates to his service in the Confederate army.

Montgomery, Helen. The colonel's [4050] lady. N.Y.: Farrar, 1943. 242 p. NcGW. The author tells of her life at army posts where her husband was stationed.

Montgomery, Helen (Barrett), [4051] 1861-1934. Helen Barrett Montgomery, from campus to world citizenship. N.Y.: Fleming H. Revell co., 1940. 140 p. NN. "Account of her childhood, college days (at Wellesley), and marriage." The author was active in the Baptist church.

Montgomery, Hugh, b. 1839. [4052] Hugh Montgomery; or, experiences of an Irish minister and temperance reformer. N.Y.: Phillips & Hunt, 1883. 416 p. Auto., p. 13-300. CtY. Methodist clergyman, born in Ireland, who served in New Hampshire.

Montgomery, Thomas Johnson, [4053] 1812-1877. Some genealogical data...comp. by John F. Montgomery...Manchester: Journal press, 1933. 25 p. Auto., p. 7-25. DLC. Country doctor in Kentucky and Missouri.

Montrose, Kate. See Brown, Kate (Montrose) Eldon.

Mood, Francis Asbury, 1830- [4054] 1884. Life and labors of Francis Asbury Mood, by Claude Carr Cody. Chicago: F.H.Revell, 1886. 352 p. DLC. Based upon a ms autobiography. Mood was a Methodist clergyman in South Carolina and a college president in Texas.

Moody, Dan W., b. 1853. The life [4055] of a rover, 1865-1926. Chicago: 1926. 116 p. WHi. Indian scout in South Dakota; member of surveying group for United Pacific Railway in Utah.

Moody, Dwight Lyman, 1837- [4056] 1899. Echoes from the pulpit and platform...Hartford: A. D. Worthington, 1900. 640 p. Auto., p. 113-640 IaCrM. Disjointed account by the noted evangelist.

Moody, Granville, 1812-1887. [4057] A life retrospect...Cinc.: Curt & Jennings, 1890. 486 p. WHi. Methodist clergyman in Ohio.

Moody, James, 1744-1809. Narrative...ed. by Charles I. Bushnell. N.Y.: 1865. 98 p. Auto., p. 9-60. WHi. A loyalist tells of his military services. Originally published in 1782. [4058]

Moody, John, b. 1868. The long [4059] road home... N.Y.: Macmillan, 1933. 263 p. WU. The publisher of statistical manuals tells of his spiritual struggles.

Mooney, Mrs. Sue F.(Dromgoule)[4060] My moving tent. Nashville, Dallas: Publishing house Methodist Episcopal Church, South, 1903. 300 p. DLC. Told by the wife of an itinerant Methodist preacher who labored mainly in Tennessee and Alabama.

Moore, Albert Alfonzo, b.1842. [4061] Genealogy and recollections. San Francisco: pr. by Blair-Murdoch co., 1915. 170 p. DLC. Lawyer in the Idaho Territory and California.

Moore, Charles Chilton, b.1837. [4062] Behind the bars; 31498. Lexington: Blue Grass pr. co., 1899. 303 p. MoCanD. An atheistic ex-preacher is jailed in Kentucky for blasphemy.

Moore, Grace, b. 1901. You're [4063] only human once. Garden City: Doubleday, Doran, 1944. 275 p. WU. Opera singer and star of screen.

Moore, James. Two years in the [4064] service; or, the personal recollections of a medical officer. Phila.: S. A. George, 1863. 16 p. CSmH. With the Union army. The autobiographical element is not strong in this account.

Moore, John Henry, 1846-1935. [4065] The boy and the man...Elgin: Brethren pub. house, 1923. 190 p. InGo. Clergyman of the Church of the Brethren, and editor of religious publications. This account closes with 1916.

Moore, John M., b. 1865. The [4066] west. Wichita Falls: Wichita pr. co., 1935. 147 p. DLC. Cowboy who becomes artist, depicting western scenes.

Moore, John Milton. On the [4067] trail of truth. N.Y.: Revell, 1937. 187 p. DLC. Baptist clergyman in Pa., New Jersey, Illinois and New York.

Moore, Kenneth Willoughby. The [4068] romance of an orphan, Ken. Trenton, N.J.: The Smith press, 1911. 293 p. DLC. Author, an orphan, was a successful advertising man who became active in foreign mission work, and a clergyman. Locale and church denomination are not indicated.

Moore, Langdon W., b. 1830. [4069] Langdon W. Moore...Boston: L. W. Moore, 1893. 659 p. WHi. Counterfeiter, bank burglar and gambler.

Moore, Madeline. The lady [4070] lieutenant. A wonderful startling and thrilling narrative of the adventures of Miss Madeline Moore, who, in order to be near her lover, joined the army, was elected lieutenant and fought in western Virginia. Phila.: Barclay, 1862. MWA. As described (?) by the title.

Moore, Mrs. Melissa Genett [4071] (Anderson), b. 1845. The story of a Kansas pioneer...Mt. Vernon: Manufacturing printers co., 1924. 61 p. WHi. Wife of a homesteader.

Moore, Mike, b. 1840. Autobiography of Mike Moore, the jolly Irishman. Owensboro: Stone pr. co., 1908. 93 p. KyLoF. Farmer and tradesman in Kentucky, beginning with the fifties. [4072]

Moore, Robert, b. 1805. Autobiographical outlines of a long life. Cinc.: The author, 1887. 68 p. DLC. The author was raised on a farm in Ohio. Later he became the manufacturer of steam locomotives. [4073]

Moore, Sallie Alexander (Moore)[4074]

b. 1840. Memories of a long life in Virginia. Staunton, Va.: The McClure co., 1920. 183 p. DLC. A member of a prominent social and political family of Virginia tells of her life, including her experiences during the Civil War.

Moore, Samuel Downing, b.1812. [4075] Human life, illustrated in my individual experience...Adrian, Mich.: Times & expositor print, 1887. 29 p. Auto., p. 3-23. MiD-B. Member of Society of Friends, in Pa. and Michigan, tells of his religious beliefs, of his interest in the temperance and abolition movements, and why he left the Friends.

Moore, Thomas, b. 1917. The sky [4076] is my witness. N.Y.: Putnam, 1943. 135 p. DLC. Marine flyer in the second World War.

Moorman, Mrs. Mollie Claire, [4077] b. 1849. An Iowa woman's vindication...Chicago: pr. for the publisher, 1877. 116 p. IaHi. A story of domestic unhappiness.

Mooso, Josiah. The life and [4078] travels of Josiah Mooso...Winfield: Telegram print, 1888. 400 p. WHi. A smoothly written account by a frontiersman; hunter, Indian captive, trapper for American Fur Company on the Yellowstone and Columbia rivers, and flatboat man on the Mississippi River.

Mordecai, Mrs. Ellen(Mordecai)[4079] Gleanings from long ago. Savannah: Braid & Hutton, 1933. 125 p. DLC. Childhood in a country home in North Carolina.

Moré, Charles Albert, chevalier [4080] de Pontgibaud, comte de, 1758- 1837. A French volunteer of the War of Independence (the chevalier de Pontgibaud) tr. & ed. by Robert B. Douglas... N.Y.: J. W. Bouton, 1897. 209 p. DLC. Aide-de-camp to Lafayette.

Morearty, Edward Francis, [4081] b. 1860. Omaha memories... Omaha: Swartz pr. co., 1917. 248 p. NbU. Lawyer, civic and political figure in Nebraska.

Morehouse, Alonzo Church, [4082] b. 1820. Autobiography of A.C. Morehouse, an itinerant minister of the New York and New York East conferences of the Methodist Episcopal Church. N.Y.: Tibbals

book co., 1895. 306 p. NN. As described by the title.

Morehouse, Ward. ...Forty-five[4083] minutes past eight. N.Y.: The Dial press, 1939. 267 p. DLC. Newspaper writer and drama critic in New York.

Morgan, Arthur Ernest, b. 1878. [4084] Finding his world...by Lucy G. Morgan. Yellow Springs: Kahoe & Spieth, 1927. 108 p. CoD. Boyhood on Minnesota farm; surveyor of lumber areas. A dictated account.

Morgan, Daniel E. When the [4085] world went mad. Boston: Christopher pub. house, 1931. 163 p. DLC. Marine in the first World War; then coal miner in Pa.

Morgan, Edwin Denison, 1854- [4086] 1933. Recollections for my family. N.Y.: C. Scribner's sons, 1938. 286 p. DLC. New England sportsman who ranched in Mexico.

Morgan, George L., b. 1857. [4087] Sketch of my life... No imprint. MnM. Evangelist in Minnesota.

Morgan, Henry, 1825-1884. [4088] Shadowy hand... Boston: The author, 1874. 448 p. DLC. Methodist itinerant preacher in New York, New Jersey and New England.

Morgan, James Morris, 1845- [4089] 1928. Recollections of a rebel reefer. Boston: Houghton Mifflin, 1917. 491 p. WHi. Confederate Naval officer; Consul General in Australia.

Morgan, William Henry. Person-[4090] al reminiscences of the war of 1861-5... Lynchburg: J. P. Bell, 1911. 286 p. WHi. Confederate soldier.

Morgenthau, Henry, 1856-1946. [4091] All in a lifetime. Garden City: Doubleday, Page, 1922. 454 p. WHi. Born in Germany of Jewish parentage. New York lawyer, investment business, real estate, worker in the cause of the Democratic party, and Ambassador to Turkey.

Morgenthau, Henry, 1856-1946. [4092] Ambassador Morgenthau's story. Garden City: Doubleday, Page, 1918. 407 p. WU. The story of his activities as Ambassador to Turkey.

Morlae, Edward. A soldier of [4093] the Legion. Boston: Houghton

Mifflin, 1916. 129 p. DLC. In the First World War.

Morley, Mrs. Ione Randolph, [4094] b. 1883. Life, poems, songs and stories of Ione Randolph Morley. White Pigeon, Mich.: 1933. 49 p. DLC. Writer of stories and verse in Michigan.

Morrell, Ed., b. 1869. The [4095] twenty-fifth man; the strange story of Ed. Morrell, the hero of Jack London's "Star rover", by Ed. Morrell, lone survivor of the famous band of California feud outlaws. Montclair, N.J.: New Era pub. co., 1924. 390 p. NN. Life as a prisoner in Folsom and San Quentin prisons in California; work for prison reform.

Morrell, Z., 1803-1883. Flowers [4096] and fruits in the wilderness... Boston: Gould & Lincoln, 1872. 386 p. DLC. Baptist clergyman in Texas.

Morrill, Charles Henry, b. 1843. [4097] The Morrills and reminiscences. Chicago: Univ. pub. co., 1918. 160 p. WHi. Banker in Nebraska.

Morrill, Gulian Lansing, 1857- [4098] 1928. A musical minister. Chicago: M. A. Donohue, 1906. 206 p. MnM. Organist, singer and music teacher who becomes a minister. The ministerial portion of his career is only mentioned.

Morris, Ann (Axtell), b. 1900. [4099] Digging in Yucatan. N.Y.: Junior literary guild, 1931. 279 p. DLC. Archaeologist. This book was written for young people.

Morris, Anna. Drifted out, by [4100] Miss Anna Dean (pseud.) Columbus: 1883. 184 p. DLC. A story of youth (in Ohio?).

Morris, Charles, 1784-1856. [4101] The autobiography of Commodore Charles Morris, U.S.N. Annapolis: The Institute, 1880. 111 p. DLC. As described by the title.

Morris, Clara, 1848-1925...Life [4102] on the stage...N.Y.: McClure, 1901. 399 p. WHi. As described by the title. See also her Stage Confidences.

Morris, F. Baldwin. The pan- [4103] orama of a life, and experiences in associating and battling with opium and alcoholic stimulants... Phila.: Geo.W. Ward, printer, 1878. 107 p. DLC. As described by the title.

Morris, Felix. Reminiscences. [4104] N.Y.: International telegram co., 1892? 176 p. DLC. English comedy actor who appeared several times in the U.S.

Morris, Ira Nelson, b. 1875. [4105] From an American legation. N.Y.: Knopf, 1923. 287 p. Auto., p. 3-240. DLC. Ambassador to Sweden

Morris, James, 1752-1820. [4106] Memoirs... New Haven: pr. by the Yale univ. press, 1933. 65 p. WHi. School master in Conn.

Morris, John Gottlieb, 1803- [4107] 1895. Life reminiscences of an old Lutheran minister. Phila.: Lutheran pub. society, 1896. 396 p. NN. Most of the author's career was spent in Baltimore, Md.

Morris, Lloyd R., b. 1893. A [4108] threshold in the sun. N.Y.: Harper, 1943. 275 p. WU. Writer of history and literary criticism tells of his intellectual development.

Morris, Robert Tuttle, b. 1857. [4109] Fifty years a surgeon. N.Y.: Dutton, 1935. 346 p. WU. And professor of medicine in New York.

Morris, Samuel Leslie, b. 1854. [4110] Samuel Leslie Morris; an autobiography... Richmond, Va.: The Presbyterian committee of publication, 1932. 140 p. DLC. Presbyterian clergyman in South Carolina and Georgia; Secretary of Home Missions in Oklahoma.

Morrison, Adele (Sarpy), b. 1842. [4111] Memoirs...St. Louis: Woodward & Tiernan pr. co., 1911. 206 p. DLC. Social leader in St. Louis, and writer of fiction tells of her social and family activities.

Morrison, Charles, b. 1902. My [4112] battle. Boston: Meador pub. co., 1942. 206 p. DLC. Electrical engineer, born in England of American parents, tells of his fight for Fascism.

Morrison, Harry Steele, b.1880. [4113] How I worked my way around the world. N.Y.: Christian herald, 1903. 424 p. DLC. The author financed his way around the world as a "boy reporter".

Morrison, Henry Clay. Autobio- [4114] graphy. Nashville: Pub. house of the M.E. Church, South, 1917. 256 p. Auto., p. 9-86. TxDaM. Methodist clergyman in Kentucky.

Morrison, Henry Clay, 1857- [4115] 1942. Some chapters of my life story. Louisville: Pentecostal pub. co., 1941. 269 p. DLC. Methodist clergyman in Kentucky, who was one of the founders of Asbury College. The writer also was a missionary in India.

Morrison, William. Horrible [4116] and awful developments...Phila.: E. E. Barclay, 1853. 32 p. CtY. Counterfeiter, robber, murderer who did his work in various states of the Union.

Morrison-Fuller, Berenice, [4117] d. 1947. Plantation life in Missouri. No imprint. 34 p. MoHi. Memories of girlhood in the thirties.

Morrow, Decatur Franklin, [4118] b. 1856. Then and now...Macon: J. W. Burke, 1926. 346 p. DLC. North Carolina boyhood in the sixties.

Morrow, John. A voice from [4119] the newsboys. N.Y.?: 1860. 135 p. DLC. A tale of domestic misfortune by a English born lad who ran away from a cruel father.

Morrow, Nancy Rodelcia (Cam- [4120] eron). Golden years in retrospect, teacher and voyager. Charleston, W.Va.: The author, 1941? 244 p. DLC. Teacher in West Virginia.

Morse, Francis W. Personal [4121] experiences in the war of the great rebellion... Albany: Munsell, printer, 1866. 152 p. MB. In the Union army.

Morse, Richard Cary, b. 1841. [4122] My life with young men...N.Y.: Association press, 1918. 547 p. DLC. Y.M.C.A. worker.

Morse, Virgil, 1861-1937. V.D.'s [4123] stories... Ithaca: R.V. Morse, 1945. 98 p. DLC. Telegraph operator in North Dakota, mill operator, manufacturer, insurance agent in Ohio and New York.

Morse, William Gibbons, b.1877. [4124] Pardon my Harvard accent. N.Y.: Farrar & Rinehart, 1941. 364 p. WU. Student days at Harvard; purchasing agent at Harvard, beginning with 1920.

Morse, William Inglis, b.1874. [4125] Autobiographical records of William Inglis Morse, 1874-1905. Boston: McIver-Johnson co., 1943. 56 p. DLC. Baptist clergyman in Mass. and Conn.

Mortimer, Charles, 1834-1873. [4126] ...Life and career of the most skillful and noted criminal of his day... Sacramento: 1873. 110 p. CSmH. In California.

Mortimer, Maud. A green tent [4127] in Flanders. Garden City: Doubleday, Page, 1917. 242 p. DLC. Nurse in France during first World War.

Morton, Cyrus, b. 1831. Auto- [4128] biography... Omaha: Douglas pr. co., 1895. 46 p. CoD. Nebraska homesteader and freighter. Miner, cattle trader in Montana. In 1869 he returned to Nebraska where he was a farmer.

Morton, John Watson. The artil- [4129] lery of Nathan Bedfort Forrest's cavalry... Nashville: Pub. house of the M.E. Church, South, 1909. 374 p. Auto., p. 19-324. DLC. Confederate soldier.

Morton, Leah (pseud.). See Stern, Mrs. Elizabeth Gertrude (Levin).

Morton, Marmaduke Beckwith, [4130] b. 1859. Kentuckians are different. Louisville: Standard press, 1938. 337 p. DLC. Newspaper reporter and editor in Kentucky, Alabama and Tennessee.

Morton, Mrs. Rosalie (Slaughter) [4131] b. 1876. A woman surgeon... N.Y.: Stokes, 1937. 399 p. WU. As described by the title. Includes her experiences in Europe and Asia.

Mosby, John Singleton, 1833- [4132] 1916. Mosby war reminiscences ...Boston: G. A. Jones, 1887. 256 p. WHI. Confederate army.

Moscheles, Felix Stone. Frag- [4133] ments of an autobiography. London: Nisbet, 1899. 364 p. DLC. English portrait painter who tells of his American experiences, p. 208-45.

Most, Johann Joseph, 1846-1906. [4134] Memoiren. Erlebtes, erforschtes und erdachtes. N.Y.: Selbstverlag des verfassers, 1903-07. 4 pts. DLC. The life of the anarchist prior to his arrival in the United States in 1882.

Moton, Robert Russa, b. 1867. [4135] Finding a way out... Garden City:

Doubleday, Page, 1920. 295 p. WHi. Negro educator.

Mott, D. C. Fifty years in Iowa. [4136] Marengo: Marengo republican, n.d. 21 p. IaHi. Youth on a pioneer farm in Iowa in the sixties.

Mott, Edward, b. 1886. Sixty [4137] years of gospel ministry. Portland, Ore.: n.d. 206 p. OrNeGF. Minister of the Friends in Ohio, California and Oregon.

Mott, Thomas Bentley. Twenty [4138] years as military attaché. N.Y.: Oxford univ. press, 1937. 342 p. WHi. In Paris, London and Constantinople. The author also saw military service against Spain and in the first World War.

Mountford, Mrs. Lydia Mary [4139] Olive, 1855-1917. The life sketch... N.Y.?: 1908. 48 p. OClWHi. Lecturer.

Mounts, Eli. Islands in the [4140] ocean of memory. Whatcom: Boyer-Culver co., 1901. 257 p. WaPS. Sailor, lecturer in Oregon and California.

Mowatt, Mrs. Anna Cora (Ogden). See Ritchie, Mrs. Anna Cora (Ogden) Mowatt.

Mowbray, Harry Siddons, 1858- [4141] 1928. H. Siddons Mowbray; mural painter, 1858-1928. Stamford: 1928. 143 p. Auto., p. 16-117. DLC. Born in Egypt of English parents.

Mower, Henry S., b. 1834. Rem- [4142] iniscences of a hotel man of forty years' service. Boston: Worcester pr. co., 1912. 159 p. DLC. In New York City.

Mowrer, Paul Scott, b. 1887. The [4143] house of Europe. Boston: Houghton Mifflin, 1945. 647 p. WU. Foreign correspondent in Europe and Africa. The account closes with 1934.

Mowry, William Augustus, 1829- [4144] 1917. Recollections of a New England educator, 1838-1908... Silver, Burdett, 1908. 292 p. WU. Mowry was editor of the Journal of Education, and Superintendent of Schools in Providence and Salem.

Muhlenberg, Henry Melchior, [4145] 1711-1787. ...Selbstbiographie, 1711-43. Allentown: Brobst, Diehl & co., 1881. 248 p. DLC. Lutheran clergyman, born in Germany, who served in Pennsylvania.

Mühlmann, Adolf, b. 1867. A [4146] grobber koll; erinnerungen von Adolf Mühlmann. Chicago: Gutenberg press, 1932. 323 p. DLC. German opera singer who sang in this country.

Muir, John, 1838-1914. The story [4147] of my boyhood and youth. Boston: Houghton Mifflin, 1913. 293 p. WHi. By a naturalist who grew up on a Wisconsin farm. This account includes his college experiences.

Muir, Peter. War without [4148] music. N.Y.: C. Scribner's sons, 1940. 262 p. DLC. The writer served in the American Field service in France during the Second World War.

Mukerji, Dhan Gopal. Caste and [4149] outcast. N.Y.: Dutton, 1923. 303 p. DLC. A Hindu Indian tells of his college education in California and of his association with the I. W. W.

Muldoon, William, 1845-1933. [4150] Muldoon, the solid man of sport... N.Y.: Stokes, 1929. 364 p. DLC. N.Y. Wrestler, manager of prize fighters, instructor in physical improvement.

Mulford, Ami French. Fighting [4151] Indians in the 7th U.S. Cavalry, Custer's favorite regiment. 2d ed., rev. Corning: Mulford, 1879. 155 p. CU. As described by the title.

Mulford, Prentice, 1834-1891?. [4152] Prentice Mulford's story... N.Y.: Needham, 1889. 299 p. WHi. Mainly an account of his mining experiences in California in the fifties and sixties, by a journalist on frontier newspapers.

Mulkey, Abe. Abe Mulkey's [4153] budget. Corsicana: Freeman, printer, 1897. 222 p. Auto., p. 171-205. TxU. Methodist evangelist in Texas who formerly had been dishonest in business.

Mullen, Arthur Francis. Western [4154] Democrat. N.Y.: Funk, 1940. 360 p. WHi. Lawyer and political figure in Nebraska.

Mullen, Barbara, b. 1914. Life is [4155] an adventure. London: Faber & Faber, 1937. 319 p. NN. Life of a young Irish-American working girl raised in the tenement districts of Boston and New York.

Mullen, Pat. Man of Aran. Lon- [4156] don: Faber & Faber, 1934. 286 p. DLC. Irishman who was a laborer in the Boston area, active in the labor union movement. See also his Come Another Day, covering later experiences on the island of Aran.

Mullowney, John James, b. 1878. [4157] American gives a chance... Tampa: The Tribune press, 1940. 171 p. NN. Medical missionary in China; public health work in Pennsylvania; teacher in Girard College; president of Meharry Medical School for Negroes.

Munford, Beverley Bland, b.1856.[4158] Random recollections. N.Y.: DeVinne press, 1905. 238 p. DLC. Virginia political figure.

Munger, Hiram, b. 1806. The [4159] life and religious experience of Hiram Munger. Chiopee Falls: 1856. 180 p. MB. Millerite tells of his religious development and of his sawmill business in Mass.

Munk, Joseph Amasa, b. 1847. [4160] Activities of a lifetime. Los Angeles: Times-Mirror press, 1924. 221 p. WHi. Physician who was president of the National Eclectic Medical Association, and book collector.

Munson, Arley Isabel, b. 1871. [4161] Jungle days; being the experiences of an American woman doctor in India. N.Y.: D. Appleton & co., 297 p. 1913. DLC. Medical missionary.

Murdock, Charles Albert, [4162] b. 1841. A backward glance at eighty. San Francisco: Elder, 1921. 275 p. WHi. California printer.

Muredach, Myles (pseud.). See Kelley, Francis Clement.

Murphy, Charles J., b. 1832. [4163] Reminiscences of the war of the rebellion and of the Mexican war. N.Y.: Ficker, 1882. 80 p. DLC. Graduate of West Point who saw service against Mexico and the Confederacy. He later became a merchant in California, and established a commercial firm in China.

Murphy, Charles M. A mile-a- [4164] minute career...Jamaica: Jamaica law print co., n.d. 12 p. NNQ. New York policeman.

Murphy, Harry Williams, b.1878. [4165] Twenty-five years in "Hell's kitchen". Jersey City: Real American, 1931. 120 p. DLC. Presbyterian evangelist in New York's "Hell's Kitchen".

Murphy, Patrick Charles, b.1883.[4166] Behind gray walls...Caldwell: Caxton printers, 1920. 83 p. DLC. A convict tells of his spiritual regeneration.

Murphy, T. J. Four years in the[4167] war. Phila.: 1866. 315 p. DLC. Union army.

Murray, George W. The life and[4168] adventures of Sergt. G. W. Murray...Minneapolis: Manley & Dada, 1872. 45 p. DLC. After serving in the Union army, the author sold books in Wisconsin and Minnesota.

Murray, John, 1741-1815. The life[4169] of Rev. John Murray...Boston: Universalist pub. house, 1869. 307 p. WHi. One of the early leaders among Universalist clergymen, who came to this country from England in 1770. The account closes with 1774.

Murray, Lindley, 1745-1826. [4170] Memoirs... N.Y.: Samuel Wood & sons, 1827. 280 p. Auto., p. 3-130. WHi. The noted grammarian tells of his books, and of his prior experiences in Pennsylvania and New York where he was merchant and lawyer.

Murray, Lois Lovina (Abbott), [4171] b. 1826. Incidents of frontier life... Goshen, Ind.: Ev. United Mennonite pub. house, 1880. 274 p. NN. Pioneer life in Kansas.

Murray, Samuel, b. 1806. Short [4172] autobiography...Mexico, Indiana: 1896. 20 p. PHuJ. Clergyman in Indiana, of the Brethren church.

Murray, William D., b. 1858. [4173] As he journeyed... N.Y.: Association press, 1929. 412 p. WHi. A lawyer tells mainly of his work within the Y.M.C.A. and the Boy Scouts.

Murray, William Henry, b.1869. [4174] Memoirs of Governor Murray... Boston: Meador, 1945. 3 vols. WHi. Of Oklahoma.

Murrill, William Alphonso, [4175]

b. 1869. Billy the boy naturalist; the true story of a naturalist's boyhood in Virginia just after the Civil War. N.Y.: W. A. Murrill, 1918. 252 p. DLC. Written for young people.

Murrill, William Alphonso, [4176] b. 1869. The naturalist in a boarding school. N.Y.: W. A. Murrill, 1919. 276 p. DLC. His experiences while teaching in Kentucky. The autobiographical portions are scattered.

Murrill, William Alphonso, [4177] b. 1869. Autobiography. Gainesville: 1945. 165 p. DLC. Science teacher, officer of the Botanical Gardens in New York.

Musgrove, Richard Watson, [4178] b. 1840. Autobiography...N.p.: Mary D. Musgrove, 1921. 230 p. ICN. Soldier in the Union Army.

Musin, Ouide, 1854-1929. My [4179] memories. N.Y.: Musin pub. co., 1920. 298 p. DLC. Violinist, composer who was born in Belgium and who came to live in the U.S. in 1908.

Myer, William C. Twenty-five [4180] years' experience with Jersey cattle. Ashland, Oreg.: 1896. 12 p. OrHi. In Illinois, California and Oregon.

Myers, Frank. Soldiering in [4181] Dakota...1863-4-5. Huron: Huronite pr. house, 1888. 60 p. NN. Indian fighter.

Myers, Mrs. Harriet (Williams). [4182] We three. No imprint. 145 p. C. The writer devoted herself to the protection of birds and wild life.

Myers, Jerome, b. 1867. Artist [4183] in Manhattan. N.Y.: American artists group, 1940. 263 p. WU. Painter.

Myers, Martin L. Yardbird [4184] Myers, the fouled-up leatherneck. Phila.: Dorrance, 1944. 230 p. DLC. In boot camp.

Myers, Mordecai, b. 1776. Rem- [4185] iniscences, 1780 to 1814, including incidents in the war of 1812-14. Washington: The Crane co., 1900. 56 p. DLC. Political figure in New York, soldier in the War of 1812.

Mylar, Isaac L. Early days at [4186] the Mission San Juan Bautista... Watsonville: Evening Pajoronian, 1929. 195 p. DLC. A youth grows up in the California sheep country and becomes a rancher.

# N

Nadal, Ehrman Syme, 1843-1922.[4187] "Autobiographical notes". (In his: Virginian village. N.Y.: Macmillan, 1917.) p. 1-67. WHi. Essayist on literary and social topics.

Nagel, Charles, b. 1849. A boy's[4188] Civil war story. St. Louis: Eden, 1934. 420 p. WHi. The author, later Secretary of Commerce under Taft, lived in Texas and Missouri when a boy.

Nakashian, Avedis. A man who [4189] found a country. N.Y.: Crowell, 1940. 278 p. DLC. Physician, born in Turkey, who came to the U.S.

Nash, Arthur, 1870-1927. The [4190] golden rule in business. N.Y.: Chicago: Fleming H. Revell co., 1923. 160 p. NN. The author was head of a clothing manufacturing concern in Cincinnati.

Nash, Ide D., b. 1872. My prison [4191] experience in Oklahoma...Hugo: Husonian, 1918. 92 p. Auto., p. 3-64. DLC. Negro bootlegger.

Nash, Leonidas Lydwell,b.1846. [4192] Recollections and observations during a ministry in the North Carolina conference. Raleigh: Mutual pub. co., printers, 1916. 142 p. DLC. Methodist.

Nash, Wallis. A lawyer's life on[4193] two continents. Boston: Badger, 1919. 212 p. WHi. An Englishman who came to live in Oregon.

Nason, William A. With the [4194] ninth army corps in east Tennessee. Providence: Rhode Island Soldiers and Sailors Historical society, 1891. 70 p. DLC. Union army.

Nassau, Robert Hamill, 1835- [4195] 1921. My Ogowe, being a narrative of daily incidents during sixteen years in equatorial West Africa. N.Y.: Neale, 1914. 704 p. NN. Missionary.

Nathan, Mrs. Maud. Once upon [4196] a time and today. N.Y.: Putnam, 1933. 327 p. WHi. Suffragist, and worker in the cause of peace.

Nation, Mrs. Carry Amelia [4197] (Moore), 1846-1911. The use and need of the life of Carry A. Nation. Topeka: Steves, 1904. 184 p. WHi. Temperance agitator.

Natonek, Hans, b. 1892. In search [4198] of myself. N.Y.: Putnam, 1943. 261 p. WU. A Czech novelist who sought exile in the U.S.

Nau, Henry. We move into Africa [4199] St. Louis: Concordia, 1945. 414 p. DLC. A Lutheran helps to establish a mission in Nigeria.

Navarro, Mary (Anderson) de, [4200] b. 1859. A few memories. N.Y.: Harper, 1896. 262 p. WHi. An actress, born in the U.S., most of whose work was done in England. See also her, A Few More Memories.

Nay, Winfield Scott, b. 1850. The [4201] old country doctor; an autobiography. Rutland, Vt.: Tuttle, 1937. 87 p. NN. Country doctor in Underhill, northern Vermont.

Neal, Basil Llewellin McKeen [4202] Green, b. 1837. A son of the American revolution... Washington: The Washington reporter print, 1914. 135 p. DLC. His experiences in the Confederate army.

Neal, John, 1793-1876. Wander- [4203] ing recollections of a somewhat busy life... Boston: Roberts bros., 1869. 431 p. WHi. Novelist, poet, editor of periodicals; lawyer and dealer in real estate in Maine.

Neale, Samuel, 1729-1792. Some [4204] account... A new ed. London: C. Gilpin, 1845. 380 p. DLC. A Quaker from Ireland who labored in New England, the South, and Pennsylvania.

Neill, William, 1778?-1860. [4205] Autobiography... Phila.: Presbyterian board of publication, 1861. 272 p. DLC. Presbyterian clergyman in New York and Pa. President of Dickinson College (in Pa.).

Neill, William, 1778?-1860. A [4206] discourse reviewing a ministry of fifty years... Phila.: J. M. Wilson, 1857. 63 p. WHi. Presbyterian clergyman in New York and Pa.

Nelles, Annie Hamilton. See Dumond, Mrs. Annie (Hamilton) Nelles.

Nelligan, John Emmett, b.1852. [4207] The life of a lumberman...N.p.: 1929. 202 p. WHi. In Maine, Pa., and the Great Lakes region.

Nelson, Battling, b. 1882. Life, [4208] battles and career of Battling Nelson, lightweight champion of the world. Hegewisch: 1909. 265 p. DLC. Born in Denmark.

Nelson, James Horace, 1839- [4209] 1924. Autobiography... Portland: 1944. 149 p. UU. Mormon in Utah: farmer, priest, real estate business. Imprisoned for polygamy.

Nelson, John Young, b. 1826. [4210] Fifty years on the trail... by Harrington O'Reilly. London: Chatto & Windus, 1889. 381 p. DLC. A dictated account. Scout and trapper in California, Colorado, Utah and Wyoming.

Nelson, Oscar Battling Matthew. See Nelson, Battling.

Nelson, Victor Folke, b. 1898. [4211] Prison days and nights. Boston: Little, Brown, 1933. 282 p. DLC. By a convict. This account covers 12 years.

Nesbit, Evelyn. Prodigal days... [4212] N.Y.: Messner, 1934. 315 p. DLC. Model, actress, dancer, wife of Harry K. Thaw who shot one of her friends.

Neutson, K., b. 1851. Memoirs of [4213] a pioneer. New Orleans: Peerless pr. co., 1938. 38 p. MnHi. On the Red River, 1870-1873: trapping, building telegraph lines; transporting lumber on rafts. Very little is said of the author's later career selling fire insurance. Neutson was born in Norway.

Nevens, William, b. 1781. Forty [4214] years at sea. 3d ed. Portland: Colesworthy, Thurston, Finley, printers, 1850. 314 p. DLC. Sailor.

Neville, Amelia (Ransome), [4215] 1837-1927. The fantastic city; memoirs of the social and romantic life of old San Francisco. Boston & N.Y.: Houghton Mifflin, 1932. 285 p. NN. A tale of social life in San Francisco.

Nevius, Mrs. Helen Sanford [4216] (Coan), 1833-1910. Our life in China. N.Y.: R. Carter & bros., 1869. 504 p. DLC. By the wife of a Presbyterian missionary.

Newby, J. F., b. 1915. High spots [4217] ... Randolph, Kan.: 1931. KHi. A story of youth in Kansas.

Newcomb, Mary A., 1817-1893? [4218] Four years of personal reminiscences of the war. Chicago: H. S. Mills, 1893. 131 p. WHi. Union army nurse.

Newcomb, Simon, 1835-1909. The [4219] reminiscences of an astronomer. Boston: Houghton, Mifflin, 1903. 424 p. WU. As described by the title.

Newcome, Louis A. Lincoln's [4220] boy spy. N.Y.: Putnam, 1929. 197 p. WHi. Secret service.

Newcome, Louis A. The post [4221] office burglers of the Shawangunk mountains... N.Y.: Newcome & Traver's detective agency, 1886. 160 p. DLC. Detective in New York and Conn.

Newcomer, Christian. The life [4222] and journal of the Rev. Christian Newcomer. Hagerstown: Knapp, printer, 1834. 330 p. DLC. Clergyman of the United Brethren in Christ in Virginia, Maryland, and Pennsylvania.

Newell, Ebenezer Francis, 1775-[4223] 1867. Life and observations of Rev. E. F. Newell, who has been more than forty years an itinerant minister in the Methodist Episcopal church... Comp. from his own manuscripts... Worcester: C.W. Ainsworth, 1847. 288 p. DLC. In New England.

Newhall, James Robinson, 1809-[4224] 1893. Legacy of an octogenarian. Lynn: Nichols press, 1897. 182 p. WHi. Journalist, printer, historian who lived in New England.

Newman, Alfred. Ups and downs [4225] in America... London: Nicholls, 1868. 83 p. British Museum. An Englishman who during 1855—62 was engaged in a number of occupations while living in the U.S.

Newman, James A., b. 1840. The [4226] autobiography of an old fashioned boy. N.p.: 1923. 100 p. WHi. Union army soldier, Indian fighter in Arizona. This is mainly an account of a frontiersman in California and Oregon.

Newmark, Harris, 1834-1916. [4227] Sixty years in southern California, 1853-1913, containing the reminiscences of Harris Newmark. Ed. by Maurice H. and Marco R. Newmark. 3d ed, rev. & augmented. Boston & N.Y.: Houghton Mifflin, 1930. 744 p. NN. Jewish merchant.

Newsome, J. A., b. 1874. The life [4228] and practice of the wild and modern Indian... Oklahoma City: Harlow, 1923. 212 p. DLC. Evangelist among Indians in Oklahoma.

Newton, Alexander Herritage, [4229] b. 1837. Out of the briars... Phila.: A.M.E. book concern, 1910. 269 p. PP. Clergyman of the African Methodist Episcopal Church in North Carolina, New York and New Jersey.

Newton, John Marshall, 1827- [4230] 1897. Memoirs of John Marshall Newton. Cambridge, N.Y.: Washington county post, 1913. 91 p. DLC. Miner in California, 1850-52. Bank clerk in Ohio.

Newton, William Wilberforce, [4231] 1843-1914. Yesterday with the fathers. N.Y.: Cochrane pub. co., 1910. 210 p. NNG. Episcopal clergyman in Mass., Pa., New Jersey and Rhode Island.

Nibley, Charles W., b. 1849. [4232] Reminiscences. Salt Lake City: 1934. 193 p. USlC. Merchant in Utah, and freight and passenger agent. Lumber business in Idaho and Oregon.

Nicholl, Edith M. See Bowyer, Mrs. Edith M. (Nicholl).

Nichols, Charles, b. 1798. Auto-[4233] biography... New Britain: 1881. 322 p. GEU. Clergyman in Conn.

Nichols, Edwin Seymour, b.1863. [4234] Ed Nichols rode a horse. Austin: Texas folklore society, 1943. 134 p. WHi. Texas cowboy.

Nichols, George, 1778-1865. [4235] George Nichols, Salem shipmaster and merchant: an autobiography dictated by him over fifty years ago, when he was eighty years old. The narrative deals chiefly with his seafaring life at the close of the 18th century and the opening of the 19th... Ed. with introduction and notes by his granddaughter, Martha Nichols. Salem, Mass.: The Salem press co., 1914? 89 p. NN. As described by the title.

Nichols, George C., b. 1824. [4236] Recollections of a pioneer steamboat pilot... LaCrosse: Turner & co., printers, 1883. 40 p. MnHi. On the upper Mississippi River, beginning with 1840.

Nichols, Ira Alfred, b. 1869. [4237]
Forty years of rural journalism
in Iowa. Fort Dodge: Messenger
press, 1938. 260 p. WU. Publisher in Iowa and Nebraska.

Nichols, J. A., b. 1834. A very [4238]
varied life. University Place,
Nebr.: Chaflin pr. co., 1915. 123 p.
NNC. With the Union army.
Methodist clergyman in North
Carolina and Nebraska.

Nichols, William Ford, 1849- [4239]
1924. Days of my age; chimney
corner chats for the home circle...
San Francisco: 1923. 381 p. NN.
Episcopal clergyman in Connecticut and Philadelphia, later
bishop of California.

Nicholson, Peter Edward, b.1820. [4240]
The life of P. E. Nicholson...
LaPorte: pr. at the office of the
Chronicle, 1898. 31 p. TxU. Methodist clergyman in the Southwest.

Nickelson, B. C., b. 1862. A [4241]
brief sketch. Dallas: Stellmacher
& Clark, printers, 1928. 16 p. TxH.
Confederate soldier.

Nickerson, Ansel D. A raw recruit's war experience. Providence: pr. by the Press co., 1888. [4242]
64 p. DLC. Union army.

Nidever, George, 1802-1883. [4243]
The life and adventures of George
Nidever... Berkeley: Univ. of
California press, 1937. 128 p.
WHi. Hunter, trapper and miner
on frontier in California.

Niederkorn, Mrs. Barbara. [4244]
Betty, a pioneer of Idaho. Idaho
Falls: Scott, 1929. 35 p. IdIf.
In the eighties.

Nielsen, Thomas Miller, b. 1875.[4245]
How a Dane became an American; or, hits and misses of my
life. Cedar Rapids, Iowa: The
Torch press, 1935. 305 p. NN.
Career of a Danish immigrant
who became a Methodist minister
in Iowa.

Niemeyer, Mary A. Light in [4246]
darkness; autobiography. Phila.:
Niemeyer, 1873. NN. Story of a
blind woman living in Maryland.

Nifong, Frank G., b. 1867. The [4247]
afterglow. No imprint. 347 p.
MoHi. Youth on a farm; physician.
The locale is Missouri.

Nisbet, Henry Tingley, b. 1845. [4248]
"Foot prints on the road". N.Y.:
M. B. Brown co., printers, 1903?
312 p. DLC. Traveling salesman
(shoes), on the road for 28 years.

Nix, Evett Dumas, b. 1861. Okla- [4249]
hombres... St. Louis: 1929. 280 p.
DLC. Merchant in Kentucky moves
to Oklahoma where he becomes
a U.S. Marshal.

Noble, Carl, d. 1935. Jugheads [4250]
behind the lines... Caldwell:
Caxton printers, 1938. 208 p.
DLC. Soldier in the first World
War, including service in France.

Noble, Samuel H., b. 1838. Life [4251]
and adventures of Buckskin Sam.
(Samuel H. Noble.) Rumford
Falls, Maine: Rumford Falls pub.
co., 1900. 185 p. NN. Adventurer
in South America, India and England, as well as in the U.S.
Largely imaginative?

Nock, Albert Jay, d. 1945. Mem- [4252]
oirs of a superfluous man. N.Y.
& London: Harper, 1943. 326 p.
NN. Described by the author, a
historian and journalist, as "the
autobiography of a mind in relation to the society in which it
found itself".

Noel, Theophilus. Autobiography [4253]
and reminiscences. Chicago:
Noel, 1904. 348 p. WHi. Mainly
an account of services in the
Confederate army, by a Texas
political figure.

Nogales y Mendez, Rafael de, [4254]
b. 1879. Memoirs of a soldier of
fortune. N.Y.: H. Smith, 1932.
380 p. DLC. Venezuelan. For
his mining experiences in Nevada
and Alaska, see p. 59-116.

Noice, Harold, b. 1895. With [4255]
Steffansson in the Arctic. N.Y.:
Dodd, Mead, 1924. 269 p. DLC.
During 1915-17.

Noland, S., b. 1818. Will makes [4256]
way... Nashville: pr. for the
author, 1886. 239 p. MoS. Lawyer,
banker and Methodist clergyman
in Virginia.

Nolte, Vincent Otto, 1779-1856. [4257]
Fifty years in both hemispheres;
or, reminiscences of the life of a
former merchant. By Vincent
Nolte, late of New Orleans. Tr.
from the German. N.Y.: Redfield,
1854. 484 p. NN. The author was
Italian.

Noodle, Tom (pseud.). See
Carden, W. Thomas.

Norbeck, George, b. 1836. The [4258]

Norbecks of South Dakota, by Peter Norbeck...Redfield: 1936. 104 p. Auto., p. 84-104. DLC. Farm laborer in Wisconsin in the sixties; to the Dakotas in 1868 where he was a farmer and clergyman of the Evangelical Lutheran Church in America.

Nord, Sverre. A logger's odyssey. Caldwell: Caxton printers, 1943. 255 p. DLC. In the Pacific Northwest. The author was born in Norway. [4259]

Nordenson, Anton V. As one of the many. Des Moines: E. A. Young, 1899. 313 p. IaHi. Laborer in New York, Iowa and Missouri who came to the U.S. from Sweden. [4260]

Nordhoff, Charles Bernard, b. 1887. The fledgling. Boston: Houghton Mifflin, 1919. 201 p. DLC. American citizen, born in England, who served with the French forces in the first World War. [4261]

Norlin, Nils, b. 1858. Svenska tag i Amerika... Stockholm: Hökerberg, 1936. 200 p. NN. The author was a homesteader in the Indian Territory, beginning with 1889. Later he was a merchant in Wisconsin. [4262]

Norris, George Washington, b. 1864. Ended episodes. Phila.: Winston, 1937. 250 p. WHi. Investment banker, Philadelphia lawyer, member of the Farm Loan Board (1916-20) and Governor of the Federal Reserve Bank (1920-36). [4263]

Norris, George William, b.1861. Fighting liberal... N.Y.: Macmillan, 1945. 419 p. WHi. U.S. Senator from Nebraska. [4264]

Norris, Kathleen (Thompson), b. 1880. Noon; an autobiographical sketch. Garden City, N.Y.: Doubleday, Page, 1925. 86 p. NN. The author tells of her early life in San Francisco and of her career as a novelist. [4265]

Norris, Mary Harriott, 1848-1918. The golden age of Vassar. Poughkeepsie: Vassar college, 1915. 164 p. NN. Recollections of student life in the early days of the college. [4266]

Norris, Septimus Henry, 1830-1917. Autobiography. Phila.: 1917. 33 leaves. DLC. Corporation lawyer and owner of trust companies, in Pa. [4267]

Northup, Herbert W., b. 1858. The prodigal's return...Greensboro: W. R. Cox, 1907. 82 p. DLC. Drunkard who reformed and began to attend a Bible school. [4268]

Norton, Lemuel, b. 1785. Autobiography of Lemuel Norton: including an account of his early life — two years in a printing office—eleven years at sea, in which he was twice shipwrecked, and experienced several narrow escapes from death. Also his Christian experience, and labors in the gospel ministry. Concord: Fogg, Hadley & co., prtrs., 1864. 192 p. NN. Baptist clergyman in Maine. See title for further particulars. [4269]

Norton, Lewis Adelbert, b. 1819. Life and adventures... Oakland: Pacific press, 1887. 492 p. WHi. Veteran of the War with Mexico; lawyer in California in the fifties. [4270]

Norton, Thomas Herbert, b.1851. Reflections... N.Y.: Press of the Chemical, color & oil record, 1921. 32 p. WHi. Professor of Chemistry in Ohio, and minor diplomatic official in Turkey, Persia and Europe. [4271]

Norvell, Saunders, b. 1864. Forty years of hardware. N.Y.: Hardware age, 1924. 443 p. DLC. Salesman, sales manager, executive officer, and then founder of his own company. [4272]

Norwood, Abraham, 1806-1880. The pilgrimage of a pilgrim... 5th & rev. ed. Boston: Pilgrim, 1852. 324 p. DLC. Partialist and Universalist clergyman in New England. [4273]

Norwood, Hal Lee, b. 1871. "Just a book"... Mena: Starco print, 1938. 90 p. Auto., p. 5-68. DLC. Lawyer and political figure in Arkansas. [4274]

Norwood, John Wall, b. 1876. Fifty thousand miles with Uncle Sam's army, by Uncle Dudley (pseud.). Waynesville: Enterprise pub. co., 1912. 95 p. DLC. In the Philippines, 1900-1901. [4275]

Nostitz, Lili. See Fernandez-Azabal, Lilie (Bouton) de.

Noteman, Norman Lester, b. 1877. Reminiscences... Los [4276]

Angeles: Times-Mirror, 1944. 157 p. DLC. Banker, broker in New York who grew up on a farm in Kansas.

Nott, Charles Cooper, 1827- [4277] 1916. Sketches of the war. N.Y.: C. T. Evans, 1863. 174 p. WHi. In the Union army.

Nourse, Charles Clinton, b. 1829. [4278] Autobiography... Cedar Rapids: Torch press, 1911. 235 p. IaHi. Iowa lawyer.

Novello-Davies, Mrs. Clara, [4279] b. 1861. The life I have loved. London: Heinemann, 1940. 323 p. DLC. Organizer of Welsh choir which visited this country several times.

Nowlin, William, b. 1821. The [4280] bark-covered house. Detroit: 1876. 250 p. WHi. Pioneer life in Michigan.

Noyes, Alexander Dana, b. 1862. [4281] The market place; reminiscences of a financial editor. Boston: Little, Brown & co., 1938. 384 p. WU. As described by the title.

Noyes, Alva Josiah, b. 1855. The [4282] story of Ajax... Helena: State pub. co., 1914. 158 p. WaS. Ranchman who came to Montana in the sixties.

Noyes, John Humphrey, 1811- [4283] 1886. Religious experience of John Humphrey Noyes, founder of the Oneida community...N.Y.: The Macmillan co., 1923. 416 p. DLC. Social reformer who in his religious thinking espoused "perfectionism".

Noyes, Nathan, b. 1784. A short [4284] account of the life and experience of Nathan Noyes... Detroit: Bagg & Harmon, printers, 1847. 68 p. Auto., p. 3-36. MiD-B. Baptist minister in New York and Michigan.

Noyes, Pierrepont Burt, b. 1870. [4285] My father's house. An Oneida boyhood. N.Y.: Farrar & Rinehart, 1937. 312 p. WHi. His boyhood within the famous Oneida, N.Y. communal settlement. This account closes with 1886.

Nugent, John Charles, b. 1878. [4286] It's a great life. N.Y.: Dial press, 1940. 331 p. DLC. Broadway actor and playwright. Screen writer in Hollywood.

Number 1500. Life in Sing Sing, [4287] by Number 1500. Indianapolis: Bobbs-Merrill co., 1904. 276 p. DLC. The author served a term of six and one-half years.

Nunez Cabeca de Vaca, Alvar. [4288] The narrative... Washington: 1851. 138 p. WHi. A 16th century Spanish explorer of Florida.

Nutchuk. See Oliver, Simeon.

Nutting, Wallace, b. 1861. Wallace [4289] Nutting's biography. Framingham: Old America co., 1936. 295 p. DLC. Congregational clergyman in New York who became a famous photographer.

Nye, Edgar William, 1850-1896. [4290] Bill Nye, his own life story; continuity by Frank Wilson Nye. N.Y.: Century, 1926. 412 p. NN. Newspaper humorist.

Nye-Starr, Kate, b. 1838. A self- [4291] sustaining woman... Chicago: Illinois printing & binding co., 1888. 161 p. ICN. Railway ticket office worker in New York, Nevada and Illinois.

# O

Oakes, Abbie Buxton. The old [4292] sea chest. No imprint (193-). 61 p. Auto., p. 1-20. DLC. Wife of a sea captain tells of her experiences aboard ship.

Oakes, Charles C. The old sea [4293] chest. No imprint (193-). 61 p. Auto., p. 21-61. DLC. Sea captain.

Oakes, George Washington Ochs, [4294] 1861-1931. The life and letters of George Washington Ochs-Oakes. N.p.: 1933. 452 p. Auto., p. 3-50. DLC. Newspaper publisher in Paris; managing editor of newspapers in Philadelphia and New York. Mayor of Chattanooga, Tenn.

Oakley, Wiley. Roamin' with the [4295] roamin' man of the Smoky Mountains. Gatlinburg: Little pigeon press, 1940. 72 p. DLC. Hunter and guide in the Smoky Mountains.

Ober, Charles Kellog, b. 1856. [4296] Exploring a continent (personal and associational reminiscences). N.Y.: Association press, 1929. 187 p. DLC. Y.M.C.A. worker in administrative and organizational posts.

Ober, Frederick Albion. Camps [4297]

in the Caribbees: the adventures of a naturalist in the Lesser Antilles. Boston: Lee & Shepard, 1880. 366 p. DLC. Leader of ornithological expedition, 1876-78.

Oberholtzer, John H., 1809-1895. [4298] Wahre character...Milford Squer, Pa.: 1860. 115 p. InGo. Mennonite clergyman and school teacher in Pennsylvania.

O'Brien, John, 1837-1917. A cap- [4299] tain unafraid... N.Y.: Harper, 1912. 295 p. DLC. Soldier adventurer in Central and South America (1885-1900).

O'Brien, John Augustine, 1851- [4300] 1931. The sea saga of Dynamite Johnny O'Brien (written by Milton A. Dalby). Seattle: Lowman & Hanford, 1933. 249 p. DLC. Merchant sailor, born in Ireland.

O'Brien, John Emmet, b. 1848. [4301] Telegraphing in battle... Scranton: Raeder press, 1910. 312 p. NN. Telegraph operator in the Union army.

O'Brien, John Sherman. By dog [4302] sled for Byrd... Chicago: Rockwell, 1931. 192 p. WHi. Member of Byrd's Antarctic expedition of 1928-30.

O'Brien, Thomas D., 1859-1935. [4303] There were four of us, or was it five. N.p.: 1936. 105 p. WHi. Minnesota lawyer and judge of state supreme court.

O'Connell, William Henry, b.1859.[4304] Recollections of seventy years. Boston: Houghton-Mifflin, 1934. 395 p. WHi. Catholic clergyman who became a Cardinal.

O'Connor, Elizabeth (Paschal), [4305] d. 1931. I myself, by Mrs. T.P. O'Connor. London: Methuen, 1910. 352 p. NN. The American-born wife of the Irish journalist and politician tells in the first part of her book of her early life in Texas, Washington and New York.

O'Connor, James A. Christ's [4306] mission, New York and its founder ... No imprint. 30 p. Auto., p.6-17. WHi. A Catholic priest decides to found a non-denominational mission.

O'Connor, Mrs. T. P. See O'Connor, Elizabeth (Paschal).

O'Connor, Winfield Scott, b.1884. [4307] Jockeys, crooks and kings... As told to Earl C. May. N.Y.: J. Cape & Harrison Smith, 1930. 219 p. DLC. Jockey.

Octo (pseud.). See Haines, Aaron Watson.

Odegard, J.T. Erindringer. [4308] Oslo: Eget forlag, 1930. 218 p. MnHi. The author came to the U.S. from Norway in 1867. This account, closing with 1881, tells the story of his farm implement business.

Odlum, Hortense (McQuarrie), [4309] b. 1892. A woman's place; the autobiography of Hortense Odlum. N.Y.: Charles Scribner's sons, 1939. 286 p. NN. The author, president of Bonwit Teller, New York, tells how she managed to bring that department store from near failure to success.

Oehler, Andrew, b. 1781. The life [4310] adventures and unparalled sufferings... Trenton: 1811. 226 p. DLC. Tailor, merchant, jack of all trades, born in Germany, who travelled through various states of the South Atlantic region, and Louisiana.

O'Ferrall, Charles Triplett, [4311] 1840-1905. Forty years of active service... N.Y.: Neale, 1904. 367 p. WHi. Service in the Confederate army; lawyer, county judge, congressman and governor of Virginia.

Officer, Morris, b. 1823. The [4312] life of Rev. Morris Officer, by Alex J. Imhoff. Dayton: United Brethren pub. house, 1876. 464 p. Auto., p. 17-31. MoKU. How he came to choose the ministry as a career.

Offley, G.W., b. 1808. Life and [4313] labors...of a colored man and local preacher. Hartford: 1860. 52 p. MnHi. In Delaware, where he teaches prize fighting; in Connecticut where he became a minister.

O'Flaherty, Liam, b. 1896. Two [4314] years. London: Jonathan Cape, 1930. 351 p. NN. The Irish author, in the latter portion of this account, tells of his adventures in Boston & New York.

Ogden, Aaron, 1756-1839. Auto- [4315] biography of Col. Aaron Ogden, of Elizabethtown. Paterson, N.J.: Press pr. & pub. co., 1893. 33 p. NN. New Jersey lawyer and statesman, governor and U.S. Senator; deals mostly with his Revolutionary War experiences.

Ogilvie, James, d. 1820. Supplementary narrative. (In his: Philosophical essays. Phila.: 1816.) p. i-xci. NN. Teacher in Virginia and public lecturer, who tried to establish chairs of oratory in American colleges. The author was born in Scotland. [4316]

O'Gormon, Edith. Convent life unveiled; or, six years a nun: trials and persecutions of Miss Edith O'Gormon, otherwise Sister Teresa de Chantal... Hartford: Conn. pub. co., 1871. 264 p. WHi. As described by the title. [4317]

Ohnstad, Karsten. The world at my finger tips. Indianapolis: Bobbs-Merrill, 1942. 348 p. NN. Story of a young blind man and his struggle for an education and a career. [4318]

O'Keefe, Rufus W., b. 1857. Cowboy life; reminiscences of an early life, early boyhood and experiences as a cowboy on the range, on the trail, as manager of a ranch and then owner and operator in cattle. San Antonio: Naylor co., 1936. 244 p. NN. In Texas. [4319]

O'Kelly, James J. The Mambi-land... Phila.: Lippincott, 1874. 359 p. DLC. Foreign correspondent in Cuba, 1872-73. [4320]

Okumara, Takie. Seventy years of divine blessings. No imprint. Printed in Japan, 1934? 191 p. CBPac. A Japanese woman who came to Hawaii in 1894 to do Christian mission work for the Methodists. [4321]

Olcott, Henry Steel, 1832-1907. Old diary leaves, the true story of the Theosophical society. N.Y.: G. P. Putnam's sons, 1895. 491 p. WHi. By the founder of the society. [4322]

Older, Fremont, 1856-1935. My own story. New ed., rev. N.Y.: Macmillan, 1926. 340 p. WHi. Social and political reformer, newspaper editor and publisher in California. [4323]

Older, Fremont, 1856-1935. Growing up... San Francisco: San Francisco Call-Bulletin, 1931. 168 p. DLC. Compositor in the northern midwestern states, who becomes a crusading newspaper editor and publisher in California. [4324]

Oliphant, J. H., b. 1835. Autobiography. St. Joseph, Mo.: pr. by the Messenger of Peace, 1923. 80 p. NcWAtC. "Primitive" Baptist clergyman in Indiana. [4325]

Oliphant, John, 1771-1831. Memoirs and remains... Auburn: H. Ivison, 1835. 212 p. Auto., p. 17-48. WHi. Presbyterian clergyman in New York. [4326]

Olive, Johnson, 1816-1885. One of the wonders of the age... Raleigh: Edwards, Broughton, 1886. 314 p. Auto., p. 19-206. WHi. Baptist clergyman in North Carolina. [4327]

Oliver, Andrew. Recollections of my life and early days in Illinois, Wisconsin and Michigan, 1833 to 1909. No imprint. 105 p. MiD-B. Farmer and merchant, born in Scotland. [4328]

Oliver, James, 1836-1918. Ancestry, early life and war record of James Oliver... Athol: Athol transcript co., 1916. 151 p. Auto., p. 25-102. WHi. Mass. physician in the Union army. [4329]

Oliver, Mrs. Jennie Harris. Pen alchemy. Oklahoma City: Dunn, 1939. 62 p. OkOk. Writer of magazine stories who lived in Oklahoma in the 20th century. [4330]

Oliver, John Rathbone, b. 1872. Foursquare... N.Y.: Macmillan, 1929. 305 p. WU. Psychiatrist, teacher at Johns Hopkins University, medical officer for the municipal courts of Baltimore. [4331]

Oliver, Simeon, b. 1903. Son of the smoky sea, by Natchuk. N.Y.: Messner, 1941. 245 p. DLC. The author was brought up in Alaska. After earning money by mining and fishing, he came to Chicago to study medicine. [4332]

Olmsted, Frederick Law, 1822-1903. Frederick Law Olmstead, landscape architect...(Volume I): Early years and experiences... N.Y.: Putnam's, 1922. 131 p. WU. Fragmentary and disjointed notes, useful for an account of the experiences which led to his career as a landscape architect. [4333]

O'Malley, Charles J., b. 1867. It was news to me. Boston: Bruce [4334]

Humphries, 1939. 409 p. NN. Journalist and advertising man.

Omwake, John, 1854-1939. J.O., [4335] being the autobiographical notes of John Omwake. Cinc.: Stewart Kidd, 1922. 40 p. OC. Publisher of playing cards, president of printing company in Ohio.

One woman's war... N.Y.: Mac- [4336] aulay, 1930. 295 p. DLC. Hospital worker in France during the first World War.

O'Neale, Margaret. See Eaton, Mrs. Margaret (O'Neil).

Opium eating. An autobiograph- [4337] ical sketch. By an habituate. Phila.: Claxton, Remsen & Haffelfinger, 1876. 150 p. PP. While serving in the Union army, the author was taken prisoner. Later, illness led to the drug habit.

Oppenheim, Mrs. Bertha Els- [4338] berg. Winged seeds. N.Y.: Macmillan, 1923. 242 p. DLC. The author and her husband tell of their attempt to make a summer home of a farm.

Oppenheim, James, 1882-1932. [4339] The mystic warrior. N.Y.: Alfred A. Knopf, 1921. 119 p. NN. The first thirty-one years in the life of a poet and novelist.

Orchard, Harry (pseud.). See Horsley, Albert E.

Orcutt, Hiram. Reminiscences [4340] of school life; an autobiography by Hiram Orcutt, L.L.D. ... Cambridge: pr. by the Univ. press, 1898. 193 p. DLC. Teacher, principal and superintendent of schools in New England.

Orcutt, Philip Dana. The white [4341] road of mystery: the note-book of an American ambulancier... N.Y.: John Lane, 1918. 173 p. DLC. Member of American Ambulance Field Service in France during the first World War.

Orcutt, Reginald, b. 1894. Mer- [4342] chant of alphabets. Garden City, N.Y.: Doubleday, Doran, 1945. 300 p. DLC. Business executive in firm manufacturing linotype.

Orcutt, William Dana, b. 1870. [4343] In quest of the perfect book... Boston: Little, Brown, 1926. 316 p. Auto., p. 3-71. DLC. Type and book designer in Boston.

Orcutt, William Dana, b. 1870. [4344] The magic of the book; more reminiscences and adventures of a bookman. Boston: Little, Brown, 1930. 314 p. Auto., p. 19-34, 65-79, 107-217. DLC. See the description of the previous item.

Ord, James, 1786?-1873. The [4345] memoirs of James Ord... Altoona: Altoona times tribune, 1920. 28 p. WHi. Indian agent in Michigan, holder of minor government positions in Washington, D.C., soldier in the War of 1812.

O'Reilly, Edward S., 1880-1946. [4346] Roving and fighting... N.Y.: Century, 1918. 354 p. WHi. Military adventurer, beginning with service in Spanish-American War, who served in Chinese, Mexican and Venezuelan armies.

O'Reilly, Harrington. See Nelson, John Young.

O'Reilly, William, b. 1823. The [4347] life, adventures and public services of William O'Reilly. From notes prepared by himself. Wilkes-Barre, Pa.: Evening Leader pub. house, 1888. 147 p. DLC. Merchant and then city constable in Pa.

Orgain, Druscilla (Johnston), [4348] b. 1843. From dawn to eventide. N.Y.: Eaton & Gettinger, 1918. 59 p. DLC. Teacher in Tennessee, Mississippi and Texas.

O'Riley, Ora Catherine. Praised [4349] be the name of Jesus. Okla. City: Thomas Benton Williams, 1939. 55 p. OkOk. Choctaw Indian, convert to Catholicism, operatic singer.

Orpen, Adela Elizabeth Richards.[4350] Memories of the old emigrant days in Kansas, 1862-1865. London: W. Blackwood, 1926. 320 p. WHi. A story of childhood in early Kansas.

Orr, Thomas, 1832-1923. Life [4351] history. N.p.: 1930. 52 p. CSmH. The author's parents moved with Mormons from Illinois, to Missouri and then to Utah. In Utah the author was a stager, and then in 1869 he became a farmer.

Osbon, Bradley Sillick, 1827- [4352] 1912. A sailor of fortune...by Albert Bigelow Paine. N.Y.: McClure, Phillips, 1906. 332 p. DLC. During the Civil War, Captain Osbon was a correspondent for New York newspapers. He was with the Mexican Navy during revolution against Maximilian.

Osborn, Chase Salmon, b. 1860. [4353] The iron hunter. N.Y.: Macmillian, 1919. 316 p. DLC. The author came to Michigan in 1887 and developed considerable holdings in the iron mining areas. From 1910 to 1912 he was Governor of Michigan.

Osborn, Elbert, 1800-1881. Passages in the life and ministry of Elbert Osborn... N.Y.: 1847-50. 2 vols. MH. Methodist clergyman in New York and Mass. [4354]

Osborn, Henry Fairfield, 1857-1935. Fifty-two years of research... N.Y.: Scribner, 1930. 160 p. Auto., p. 55-73. DLC. Professor of natural science at Princeton, and of biology at Columbia. Member of the staff of the American Museum of Natural History. [4355]

Osborn, Mrs. Jennie (Stoughton), b. 1848. Memories. Medicine Lodge, Kansas: Press of the Barber county index, 1935. 109 p. DLC. Teacher in Missouri and Kansas who married a Kansas farmer. [4356]

Osborn, Lucy Reed (Drake), b. 1844. Heavenly pearls set in a life... N.Y.: Revell, 1894. 364 p. DLC. The author, the wife of a Congregationalist clergyman, did missionary work in New England, the Midwest, India, and Australia. [4357]

Osborn, Vera (Maynard). There were two of us. N.Y.: McGraw-Hill book co., 1944. 327 p. NN. Recollections of childhood and youth in Charlotte, Mich., and of college days. [4358]

Osbourn, James, 1780-1850. The lawful captive delivered. Baltimore: pr. by John D. Toy, 1835. NcWAtC. "Primitive" Baptist clergyman in Maryland and North Carolina. [4359]

Osgood, Jacob, 1777-1844. The life and Christian experience of Jacob Osgood... Warner, N.H.: 1873. 137 p. NN. Farmer in New Hampshire who founded a sect called Osgoodites. [4360]

Osgood, Samuel, b. 1784. A sermon delivered...on the termination of the fortieth year of his ministry. Springfield: G. W. Wilson, printer, 1849. 33 p. Auto., p. 9-33. MnHi. Congregationalist clergyman in Mass. (1809-49). [4361]

Osherowitch, Mendel, b. 1888. Geschichten fun mein leben. N.Y.: Forward association, 1945. 489 p. OCl. Russian born Jew who was editorial writer for a Yiddish language paper in New York City; historian; and biographer. [4362]

Osland, Birger, b. 1870. A long pull from Stavenger; the reminiscences of a Norwegian immigrant. Northfield: Norwegian-American historical association, 1945. 263 p. WHi. The author operated a steamship line to Norway. During the first World War he was U.S. Military Attache in Norway. [4363]

Oss, Olga Bertine (Osnes), b. 1897. Triumphs of faith; personal experiences in service for the King. South Bend: Review & Herald pub. co., 1935. 159 p. DLC. Mission worker in China for the Seventh Day Adventists. [4364]

Ossoli, Sarah Margaret (Fuller), 1810-1850. Memoirs...Boston: Phillips, Sampson & co., 1852. 2 vols Auto., vol. 1, p. 11-52. WHi. The youthful days in Massachusetts of the later social critic and writer. [4365]

Osten-Sacken, Charles Robert von, 1828-1906. Record of my life work in entomology. Cambridge, England: Univ. press, 1903. 204 p. DLC. The author did important scientific work while in this country, which he left in 1877. From 1856 to 1871 he was a diplomatic officer in the Russian embassy in Washington. [4366]

Ostrander, Alson Bowles, b.1849. An army boy of the sixties; a story of the plains. Yonkers-on-Hudson: World book co., 1924. 272 p. WHi. Indian fighter. [4367]

Oswald, Mrs. Helen K. That book in the attic; the true story of a girl who passed through the fires of affliction and persecution that she might obey God and His Word. Mountain View: Pacific press pub. association, 1939. 160 p. DLC. A spiritual account in which the author explains her conversion to Adventism. [4368]

Otero, Miguel Antonio, b. 1859. [4369]

My life on the frontier. N.Y.:
Press of the pioneers, 1935-39.
2 vols. WHi. Covers 1864-97.
The locale is Kansas, Colorado
and New Mexico. See also the
next item.

Otero, Miguel Antonio, b. 1859. [4370]
My nine years as governor of
the Territory of New Mexico,
1897-1906. Albuquerque: Univ.
of New Mexico press, 1940. 404 p.
WHi. As described by the title.

Otter, William, b. 1789. History [4371]
of my own times; or, the life and
adventures of William Otter.
Emmitsburg: 1835. 357 p. DLC.
The author, born in England,
was later a plasterer, chiefly
in Pennsylvania and Maryland
(1810-1835).

Ouimet, Francis. A game of [4372]
golf; a book of reminiscences...
Boston: Houghton Mifflin, 1932.
273 p. DLC. American amateur
champion.

Overbeck, Mrs. Alicia O'Rear- [4373]
don. Living high; at home in the
Far Andes. N.Y.: Appleton-
Century, 1935. 382 p. DLC. Wife
of geologist tells of her experiences in Bolivia.

Overstreet, Phillip P., b. 1902. [4374]
Miraculous deliverance...Cinc.:
God's Bible school, 1934. 109 p.
DLC. After a life of crime in
the southern and midwestern
states, the author is pardoned,
and he decides to become an
evangelist.

Ovington, Mrs. Adelaide (Alex- [4375]
ander). An aviator's wife. N.Y.:
Dodd, Mead, 1920. 169 p. DLC.
As described by the title.

Owen, Bessie. Aerial vagabond. [4376]
N.Y.: Liveright, 1941. 260 p.
DLC. Aviatrix.

Owen, Dock, b. 1835. Campfire [4377]
stories and reminiscences.
Greenwood: Index pub. co., n.d.
47 p. CSmH. Confederate soldier.

Owen, Mrs. Narcissa (Chisholm)[4378]
b. 1831. Memoir...Washington?:
1907? 126 p. DLC. The granddaughter of an Indian chief, who
taught music and art in Arkansas.

Owen, Robert Dale, 1801-1877. [4379]
Twenty-seven years of autobiography. Threading my way. N.Y.:
Carleton, 1874. 360 p. WHi. Social
reformer, abolitionist, member
of the Indiana state legislature.
The author, born in Scotland, was
the son of Robert Owen.

Owen, T. Grafton. Drippings [4380]
from the eaves. Seattle: pr. by
Lowman & Hanford, 1911. 172 p.
WHi. A 19th century account of
a Methodist clergyman who turns
to the Unitarians.

Owens, James, b. 1827. Recol- [4381]
lections of a runaway boy, 1827-
1903. Pittsburgh: Keystone label
co., 1903. 185 p. WHi. Merchant,
oil prospector, building contractor
in Pa. The author was born in
Ireland.

Owens-Adair, B. A. See Adair,
Bethenia Angelina (Owens).

Oxx, Thomas H. History of a [4382]
whaling voyage in the Pacific
Ocean, 1834-38. Pelham Manor:
1892. 39 p. Nh. By a Rhode Island
sailor.

Oyabe, Jenichiro, b. 1867. A [4383]
Japanese Robinson Crusoe. Boston: Pilgrim press, 1898. 219 p.
DLC. After much travel, the author
came to the U.S. to study. Here
he became an evangelical missionary.

Ozanne, T. D. The South as it [4384]
is... London: Saunders, Otley &
co., 1863. 306 p. Auto., p. 223-
306. DLC. Englishman who spent
21 years in the U.S. as a missionary. He served in New England,
Pennsylvania, Mississippi and
Louisiana. He left for England
in 1862.

# P

Packard, Hezekiah, 1761-1849. [4385]
Memoir of Rev. Hezekiah Packard, D. D.,chiefly autobiographical.
By Alpheus Spring Packard. Brunswick: J. Griffin, 1850. 68 p. Auto.,
p. 2-37. DLC. Congregational
clergyman in Maine.

Packard, Joseph, 1812-1902. [4386]
Recollections of a long life.
Washington: B.S. Adams, 1902.
364 p. WHi. Episcopal clergyman
who was a professor in the Theological Seminary of Virginia.

Packard, Silas Sadler, 1826- [4387]
1898. My recollections of Ohio...
N.Y.: Ohio Society of New York,
1890. 26 p. NN. Pioneer life in Ohio.

Packer, Mrs. Jane B. (Knight), [4388] b. 1824. Life and spiritual experiences of Mrs. Dr. Jane B. Packer, clairvoyant physician...Taunton: Sweet, 1892. 80 p. DLC. Spiritualist doctor, born in Canada, who lived in New England.

Packwood, William Henderson, [4389] b. 1832. Reminiscences, written down by Fred Lockley. No imprint. 54 p. WaU. Indian fighter in forties in the area to the west of the Mississippi. The author was a member of the U.S. Army.

Paddack, William C., b. 1831. [4390] Life on the ocean...Cambridge: Riverside press, 1893. 242 p. DLC. Merchant seaman, whaler.

Paderewski, Ignacy Jan, 1860- [4391] 1941. The Paderewski memoirs. N.Y.: Scribner, 1938. 404 p. DLC. Polish pianist who often played in the U.S.

Pagano, Don Albert. Bluejackets.[4392] Boston: Meador, 1932. 138 p. DLC. U.S. Navy sailor in Nicaragua, 1926-1927.

Page, Harry S. Between the [4393] flags; the recollections of a gentleman rider. Derrydale press, 1929. 313 p. DLC. New York socialite tells of his horsemanship.

Page, Joel C., b. 1832. Recollec- [4394] tions of sixty years in the shoe trade. Ed. by Arthur L. Evans. Boston: A. L. Evans co., 1916. 215 p. Auto. p. 11-61. CU. Salesman and merchant of shoes who lived in New England. Later he travelled extensively as a salesman.

Page, Priscilla Sewall (Webster), [4395] b. 1823. Personal reminiscences ...N.Y.: J. J. Little, 1886. 160 p. DLC. Childhood in Maine; domestic life in Washington, D.C.

Page, Thomas Manning. Bohem- [4396] ian life: the autobiography of a tramp. St. Louis: Sun Pub. co., 1884. 451 p. DLC. Union army soldier. Peddler of patent medicine, cabin crewman, factory laborer.

Paige, Charles C., b. 1838. Story [4397] of the experiences of Lieut. Charles C. Paige in the Civil war of 1861-65, as told by himself. Franklin, N.H.: The Journal-Transcript press, 1916. 146 p. NhD. Union army.

Paine, Margaret Fletcher (Kent) [4398] 1835-1931. My ninety-five milestones. Chicago: Murray, 1932. 136 p. DLC. The wife of a Methodist clergyman in Iowa.

Paine, Ralph Delahaye, 1871- [4399] 1925. Roads of adventure... Boston & N.Y.: Houghton Mifflin, 1922. 452 p. NN. Adventures of a newspaperman and war correspondent in the Cuban Insurrection, the Spanish-American War, the Boxer rebellion, and the first World War.

Paine, Susanna. Roses and [4400] thorns; or, Recollections of an artist...Providence: B. T. Albro, printer, 1854. 204 p. DLC. School teacher and portrait painter in New England.

Painter, J.H., 1841-1921. Remin- [4401] iscences and notes...Des Moines: Christian index pub. co., 1900. 302 p. Auto., p. 17-93. OrEuN. Clergyman of the Christian Church in Iowa, Kansas, Missouri.

Painter, Thomas, 1760-1841. [4402] Autobiography...Washington: 1910. 106 p. DLC. The author served in the Revolutionary army. Later he was a sailor and shipowner.

Palmer, Edward E., b. 1871. [4403] Forty years of rustling. Wooster: 1942. 363 p. DLC. Patent medicine, etc.

Palmer, Eric, b. 1912. Riding the [4404] air waves...N.Y.: Liveright, 1930. 329 p. DLC. Ham radio operator who lived in Brooklyn.

Palmer, Frederick, b. 1873. [4405] With my own eyes...Indianapolis: Bobbs-Merrill, 1933. 396 p. WHi. War correspondent in the Philippines, China at time of Boxer Rebellion, Russo-Japanese war, First World War.

Palmer, George Herbert, 1842- [4406] 1933. The autobiography of a philosopher. Boston: Houghton Mifflin, 1930. 137 p. WU. Professor of philosophy at Harvard.

Palmer, John C. R. Explanation [4407] ...Boston: pr. for the author, 1831. 191 p. DLC. Sailor, imprisoned for attempted robbery. Covers 1825-1830.

Palmer, John McAuley, 1817- [4408] 1900. Personal recollections...

Cinc.: Robert Clarke co., 1901. 631 p. WHi. Lawyer, Illinois politician, member of Union army.

Pancoast, Charles Edward, 1818- [4409] 1906. A Quaker forty-niner: the adventures of Charles Edward Pancoast on the American frontier. Phila.: University of Pennsylvania press, 1930. 402 p. NN. In California to 1854.

Panunzio, Constantine Maria, [4410] b. 1884. The soul of an immigrant. N.Y.: Macmillan, 1921. 329 p. WHi. The Americanization of an Italian who became a community center worker.

Papashvily, George. Anything [4411] can happen, by George and Helen Waite Papashvily. N.Y. & London: Harper, 1945. 202 p. NN. A story of the Americanization of a Russian immigrant. Typical activities: box lunch business, machinist, sculpture.

Papazian, Masasseh Garabed. [4412] Yete Hisoon Dary Yeridasartanayi. Los Angeles: Bozart press, 1938. 43 p. CBPac. In Armenian. The story of a clergyman in New York, Mass., and California.

Paret, William, 1826-1911. [4413-4414] Reminiscences. Phila.: George W. Jacobs, 1911. 209 p. CBCh. Episcopalian clergyman in New York, Michigan (in the sixties), Pennsylvania (1868-76), Washington, D.C. (1876-85), and then Bishop of Maryland.

Parisot, Pierre Fourier. The [4415] reminiscences of a Texas missionary. San Antonio: Johnson bros., 1899. 227 p. WHi. Catholic missionary who went to Texas about 1850.

Park, No-Yong, b. 1899. China- [4416] man's chance...Boston: Meador, 1940. 182 p. WU. College teacher, public lecturer, born in the U.S., tells of his attempts at Americanization and why he gave them up.

Parker, Mrs. C. H. See Parker, Mrs. Cornelia (Stratton).

Parker, Mrs. Cornelia (Stratton) [4417] b. 1885. ...Wanderer's circle. Boston: Houghton Mifflin, 1934. 345 p. WU. Novelist, writer of travel books.

Parker, David Bigelow, 1842- [4418] 1910. A Chautauqua boy in '61 and afterwards... Boston: Small, Maynard, 1912. 388 p. NN. Union army soldier; U.S. Marshal in Virginia; Chief post office inspector, district of Virginia.

Parker, Ezra Knight. Campaign [4419] of Battery D, First Rhode Island light artillery... Providence: R.I. historical soc., 1913. KyU. Union army.

Parker, Francis Wayland, 1837- [4420] 1902. "An autobiographical sketch". (In, William M. Giffin, School days in the fifties. Chicago: Flanagan co., 1906. 137 p.) p. 110-137. DLC. The writer tells of his teaching experiences in New Hampshire, Ohio and Mass.

Parker, George Martin Nathaniel [4421] b. 1861. Footprints from the city to the farm. Newton: Kansas pr. co., 1914. 160 p. DLC. Farm life in Arkansas.

Parker, Henry, b. 1835. Auto- [4422] biography of Henry Parker. No imprint. 8 p. ICU. An escaped slave from West Virginia who became a laborer in Michigan and Ohio.

Parker, James, 1854-1934. The [4423] old army... Phila.: Dorrance, 1929. 454 p. WHi. Army officer tells of Indian fighting in the West, Spanish-American War, and the first World War.

Parker, James W., b. 1793. Nar- [4424] rative... Louisville: Morning courier office, 1844. 95 p. ICN. Texas farmer.

Parker, John Monroe, b. 1852. [4425] An aged wanderer... San Antonio: n.d. TxU. Cowboy, Indian fighter in Kansas and Texas following 1865.

Parker, Mary, b. 1848. Remin- [4426] iscences and letters. Phila.: G. H. Buchanan, 1891. 303 p. Auto., p. 9-74. DLC. The daughter of a Baptist minister in Ohio tells of the misfortunes which befell the family.

Parker, Maude. The social side [4427] of diplomatic life. Indianapolis: Bobbs-Merrill, 1926. 305 p. WHi. Wife of the U.S. Ambassador in Rome.

Parker, Theodore, 1810-1860. [4428] Autobiography, poems and prayers. Boston: American Unitarian association, 1911? 486 p. Auto., p. 3-16, 50-82, 273-413. WHi. Unitarian clergyman in New England.

Parker, Theodore, 1810-1860. [4429] Theodore Parker's experiences as a minister... Boston: Rufus Leighton, 1859. 182 p. WHi. See the preceding entry.

Parker, William Harwar, 1826-1896. [4430] Recollections of a naval officer, 1841-1865. N.Y.: Scribner, 1883. 372 p. WHi. Mexican War and Civil War (Confederate).

Parkhill, John. The life and [4431] opinions of Arthur Sneddon (pseud.). Paisley, Scotland: J. Cook, 1860. 188 p. DLC. The author, born in Scotland, was a farmer in Vermont and a weaver in New Jersey.

Parkhurst, Charles Henry, 1842-1933. [4432] My forty years in New York. N.Y.: Macmillan, 1923. 256 p. WHi. Presbyterian clergyman, political and social reformer. See also his, Our fight with Tammany (1895).

Parkinson, John, b. 1861. Inci- [4433] dents by the way. Los Angeles: 1935. 342 p. WHi. Architect.

Parkinson, Richard, 1748-1815. [4434] A tour in America in 1798, 1799, and 1800 ... London: J. Harding & J. Murray, 1805. 2 vols. Auto., vol. 1, p. 1-248. DLC. English agriculturist who farmed in Maryland.

Parkman, Francis, 1823-1893. A [4435] life of Francis Parkman, by Charles H. Farnham. Boston: Little, Brown & co., 1901. 394 p. Auto., p. 318-332. WHi. Tells of how he began to write history, and of difficulties with his eyesight.

Parley, Peter (pseud.). See Goodrich, Samuel Griswold.

Parmalee, Moses Payson, 1834-1902. [4436] Life scenes among the mountains of Ararat. Boston: Mass. Sabbath school society, 1868. 265 p. DLC. Missionary in Turkey.

Parsons, Edward L., b. 1868. [4437] Autobiography...No imprint. 9 leaves. CBCh. Teacher of philosophy at Stanford, and then Episcopalian clergyman in California.

Parsons, Julia Stoddard, d. 1946. [4438] Scattered memories. Boston: Bruce Humphries, 1938. 169 p. NN. Schooldays in Europe; social life in Washington, D.C., and Italy.

Parsons, Louella Oettinger, [4439] b. 1885. The gay illiterate. Garden City: Doubleday, Doran, 1944. 194 p. WU. Journalist who specialized in the Hollywood movie colony.

Parsons, Samuel, 1844-1923. [4440] Memories of Samuel Parsons, landscape architect of the Department of public parks, New York; ed. by Mabel Parsons. N.Y.: G.P. Putnam's sons, 1926. 150 p. DLC. As described by the title.

Parton, James, 1822-1891. Tri- [4441] umphs of enterprise, ingenuity and public spirit. N.Y.: Virtue & Yorston, 1872. 677 p. Auto., p. 13-21. WHi. Historian tells of his early experiences as a writer.

Partridge, Bellamy. Big family. [4442] N.Y.: McGraw-Hill, 1941. 323 p. WU. Biographer, historian and novelist tells of his youth in this nineteenth century account of New York.

Pasma, Henry Kay, b. 1881. [4443] Close-hauled. N.Y.: Frederick A. Stokes co., 1930. 312 p. NN. Experiences as a sailor; later as a Dutch immigrant in America.

Passebois, Louis Ferdinand, [4444] b. 1874. From infidelity to Christianity... Essex Junction: Roscoe pr. house, 1916. 180 p. Auto., p. 15-154. DLC. Seventh Day Adventist, born in France, who did mission work in New York, New Hampshire, Vermont, Switzerland and Egypt.

Passebois, Louis Ferdinand, [4445] b. 1874. Adventures of a modern Huguenot. Nashville: Southern pub. association, 1940. 160 p. DLC. See the preceding item. In this work, the author tells of his more recent experiences.

Patri, Angelo. A schoolmaster [4446] of a great city. N.Y.: Macmillan, 1917. 221 p. WU. Superintendent of schools in New York City.

Patrick, Joseph M. Civil war [4447] memoirs... Enid, Oklahoma: Drummond & Patrick, n.d. 52 p. Ia-HA. Union army soldier.

Patrick, Mary Mills, 1850-1946. [4448] Under five sultans. N.Y.: Century, 1929. 357 p. DLC. The author taught in a woman's college in Turkey for 50 years.

Patterson, James Howard, [4449] b. 1867. Of me I sing; or, Me and education... Nappanee, Ind.: E. V. publishing house, 1940. 304 p. NN. Memoirs of a country schoolteacher in West Virginia.

Patterson, Lawson B. Twelve [4450] years in the mines of California ...Cambridge: pr. by Miles & Dillingham, 1862. 108 p. Auto., p. 34-74. DLC. From 1849 to 1861.

Patterson, Samuel, b. 1785. A [4451] narrative... 2d ed., enl. Providence: pr. at the Journal office, 1825. 164 p. DLC. Merchant sailor.

Pattie, James Ohio, b. 1804? The [4452] personal narrative of a voyage to the Pacific... ed. by Timothy Flint. Cinc.: E. H. Flint, 1833. 300 p. Auto., p. 13-253. DLC. Covers 1824-1830. Trader, trapper on expedition from St. Louis to the Pacific Coast. The authenticity of this account has been challenged.

Patton, James, 1756-1845. Bi- [4453] ography. Ashville: 1850. 34 p. NcU. North Carolina merchant.

Paul, Mrs. Almira, b. 1790. The [4454] surprising adventures of Almira Paul, a young woman, who, garbed as a male, has... actually served as a common sailor, on board of English and American armed vessels without a discovery of her sex being made... Boston: pr. for N. Coverly, Jr., 1816. 24 p. DLC. War of 1812. The author was born in Nova Scotia.

Pauls, Theodore. Bells at sun- [4455] set; an autobiographical narrative. Boston: Chapman & Grimes, 1942. 84 p. NN. Early life in Germany; coffee business in New York.

Paulson, David, 1868-1916. Foot- [4456] prints of faith. Hinsdale: Life boat pub. co., 1921. 118 p. NbLU. Medical missionary in Illinois.

Paulson, Ole, b. 1832. Erin- [4457] dringer. Minneapolis: Free church book concern, 1907. 245 p. DLC. Lutheran clergyman, born in Norway, who served in Minnesota, Wisconsin and North Dakota.

Paver, John M., b. 1839. What I [4458] saw from 1861 to 1864... Indianapolis: Scott-Miller co., 1906? 100 p. WHi. Union army soldier.

Paxton, John D., 1784-1868. A [4459] memoir of J. D. Paxton, D. D., late of Princeton, Indiana. Phila.: Lippincott, 1870. 358 p. Auto., p. 13-303. DLC. Presbyterian clergyman in the Midwest.

Paxton, Virginia Margaret. [4460] Penthouse in Bogata. N.Y.: Reynal & Hitchcock, 1943. 304 p. DLC. Wife of a newspaperman who lived in Bogata for two years.

Payne, Daniel Alexander, 1811- [4461] 1893. Recollections of seventy years... Nashville: A.M.E. Sunday school union, 1888. 335 p. DLC. Negro Methodist clergyman in New York, Ohio and Pa.

Payne, Dillon H., b. 1847. Recol- [4462] lections. No imprint. 100, 55 p. Ia-HA. Iowa lawyer.

Paynter, John Henry, b. 1862. [4463] Joining the navy; or, abroad with Uncle Sam. Hartford, Conn.: American pub. co., 1895. 298 p. NN. Experiences of a young Negro as cabin boy on the U.S. ships Ossipee and Juniata on a cruise around the world.

Paynter, John Henry, b. 1862. [4464] Horse and buggy days with Uncle Sam. N.Y.: Margent press, 1943. 190 p. NN. A negro's experiences in the Federal service, principally in the Bureau of Internal Revenue.

Payton, William, b. 1870. The [4465] last man over the trail. Kinsley: 1939. 60 p. DLC. Cowboy in Nebraska who rode the Chisholm Trail. Later he was a rancher, after which he operated a drug store in Kansas.

Peabody, Charles. Twenty years [4466] among the colporteurs. N.Y.: Am. tract soc., 1865. 91 p. CBSK. In the Midwest, 1843-63.

Peabody, Frank, b. 1876. The [4467] story of a Kansan. Topeka: Crane, 1904. 120 p. KHi. Hobo, coal miner and carpenter in Kansas and Illinois.

Peacock, John, b. 1804. A [4468] sketch of the Christian experience, call to the ministry, and ministerial labors of the Rev. John Peacock... Concord, N.H.: pr. by Tripp & Osgood, 1851. 127 p. DLC. Baptist in New Hampshire.

Peak, Howard Wallace, b.1856. [4469] A ranger of commerce; or, 52 years on the road. San Antonio: Naylor, 1929. 262 p. NN. Memories of a Texas commercial traveller.

Peak, John, 1761-1842. Memoir [4470] of Elder John Peak, written by himself... Boston: pr. by J. Howe, 1832. 203 p. WHi. Baptist clergyman in Vermont and New Hampshire.

Pearne, Thomas Hall, b. 1820. [4471] Sixty-one years... Cinc.: Curt & Jennings, 1899. 506 p. WHi. Methodist clergyman in New York, Wyoming, Oregon, Ohio. U.S. Consul to Jamaica.

Pearse, James, b. 1786. A nar- [4472] rative... Rutland: pr. by W. Fay, 1825. 144 p. CLU-C. Farmer in pioneer Mississippi and Louisiana.

Pearson, James Larkin, b. 1879. [4473] Autobiographical sketch. No imprint. 20 p. NcU. North Carolina poet.

Pearson, Thomas Gilbert, 1873- [4474] 1943. Adventures in bird protection; an autobiography... N.Y., London: D. Appleton-Century co., 1937. 459 p. NN. The writer was secretary and later president of the National Association of Audubon Societies.

Pearson, Trued Granville, 1827- [4475] 1905. En skånsk banbrytare i Amerika. Oskarshamn: A. B. Axel Melchior, 1937. 135 p. MnHi. The author, a midwestern farmer and politician, came to the U.S. from Sweden in 1851.

Peary, Marie Ahnighito, b.1893. [4476] The snowbaby's own story. N.Y.: Stokes, 1934. 304 p. DLC. Daughter of American explorer tells of her early life in Greenland, where she was born.

Peary, Robert Edwin, 1856-1920. [4477] Nearest the Pole... N.Y.: Doubleday, Page, 1907. 411 p. WU. To the Arctic Circle.

Peary, Robert Edwin, 1856-1920. [4478] Northward over "the great ice". N.Y.: Stokes, 1908. 2 vols. WHi. The record of his Arctic work.

Peary, Robert Edwin, 1856-1920. [4479] The North Pole. N.Y.: Stokes, 1910. 373 p. WHi. The story of his expedition to the North Pole.

Pease, Albert S., 1828-1914. [4480] ...Selections from his poems, with an autobiography... N.Y.: J. T. White, 1915. 117 p. Auto., p. 75-89. WHi. Poet, newspaper publisher and editor in New York.

Peattie, Donald Culross, b.1898. [4481] The road of a naturalist. Boston: Houghton Mifflin, 1941. 315 p. WU. As described by the title.

Peattie, Roderick, b. 1891. The [4482] incurable romantic. N.Y.: Macmillan, 1941. 270 p. WU. Geologist, professor at Ohio State University.

Peck, George, 1797-1876. The [4483] life and times of Rev. George Peck... N.Y.: Nelson & Phillips, 1874. 409 p. WHi. Methodist clergyman who was editor of religious periodicals.

Peck, George Wilbur, 1840-1916. [4484] How private Geo. W. Peck put down the Rebellion... Chicago & N.Y.: Belford, Clarke & co., 1890. 316 p. WHi. A comic account of service in the Union army.

Peck, Minnie Hannah. The view [4485] of roses. San Francisco: 1893. 154 p. C. Lay evangelical worker for the Methodist church in California and Nevada.

Peck, Rufus H., b. 1839? Remin- [4486] iscences of a Confederate soldier ...Fincastle?: 1913. 73 p. DLC. As described by the title.

Peddicord, Kelion Franklin, [4487] 1833-1905. Kelion Franklin Peddicord of Quirk's scouts, Morgan's Kentucky cavalry, C.S.A. By Mrs. India W. P. Logan. N.Y.: Neale, 1908. 170 p. Auto., p. 29-148. DLC. As described by the title.

Peden, Charles. Newsreel man. [4488] Garden City: Doubleday, Doran, 1932. 126 p. DLC. As described by the title.

Pedrick, Howard Ashley, 1863- [4489] 1941. Jungle gold... By Will de Grouchy. Indianapolis: Bobbs-Merrill, 1930. 295 p. DLC. Mining engineer in Dutch Guiana.

Peer, Frank Sherman. The hunt- [4490] ing field with horse and hound in America, the British Isles and France. N.Y.: M. Kennealey, 1910. 319 p. CoHi. As described by the title.

Pegler, George. Autobiography [4491] of the life and times of the Rev. George Pegler... Beaver, Minn.: 1875. 532 p. DLC. Sailor, born in England, becomes Methodist clergyman in Canada, New York, Wisconsin and Minnesota.

Peirce, Augustus Baker, 1840- [4492] 1919. Knocking about. New Haven: Yale univ. press, 1924. 176 p. DLC. Sailor.

Peirce, Henry Augustus, 1808- [4493] 1885. Biography... San Francisco: A. L. Bancroft, 1880. 24 p. CSmH. Based on an ms. autobiography. Boston merchant in the China trade, U.S. Diplomatic officer in the Hawaiian Islands.

Peirce, Parker I., b. 1845. The [4494] adventures of "Antelope Bill" in the Indian war of 1862. Marshall?: 1898. 243 p. DLC. Minnesota pioneer who fought Indians in 1862.

Peixotto, Ernest Clifford, b.1869.[4495] The American front. N.Y.: Scribner, 1919. 230 p. DLC. World War I.

Pell, Stuyvesant Morris, 1905- [4496] 1943. Scribblings of an outdoor boy... Princeton: Princeton univ. press, 1945. 75 p. DLC. Ranger in Maine, naturalist.

Pellet, Elias Porter, b. 1837. [4497] Three generations. Salyar, Colombia: 1896? 14 p. Auto., p. 2-12. DLC. Union army soldier; member of U.S. Diplomatic staff in Colombia.

Pelley, William Dudley, b. 1885. [4498] The door to revelation... Ashville: Pelley publishers, 1939. 481 p. WHi. Leader of the Silvershirts tells how he arrived at his plans to save America from subversives.

Pellum, Daniel Henry, b. 1831. [4499] Scattered thoughts... Alba?: 1904. 32 p. Auto., p. I-IV. DLC. Farmer and justice of the peace in Georgia.

Pelton, John Cotter, b. 1826. [4500] Life's sunbeams and shadows. San Francisco: pr. by the Bancroft co., 1893. 260 p. DLC. Teacher, superintendent of schools in California.

Pember, Phoebe Yates, 1823- [4501] 1913. A southern woman's story. N.Y.: G. W. Carleton & co., 1879. 192 p. WHi. Confederate nurse.

Pendleton, James Madison, [4502] 1811-1891. Reminiscences of a long life. Louisville: Press Baptist book concern, 1891. 203 p.
DLC. Baptist clergyman in Kentucky, Tennessee, Ohio and Pennsylvania.

Penn, W.E., b. 1832. The life and[4503] labors of... the Texas evangelist ... St. Louis: C. B. Woodward, 1896. 352 p. TxH. Baptist clergyman in Texas, and in the Southeast.

Pennell, Joseph, 1857-1926. The [4504] adventures of an illustrator, mostly in following his authors in America and Europe. Boston: Little, Brown, 1925. 372 p. WU. As described by the title.

Penney, James Cash, b. 1875. [4505] J. C. Penney, the man with a thousand partners... N.Y.: Harper, 1931. 222 p. WHi. Merchant.

Pennington, James Emery. Rec-[4506] ollections. Potter? Kansas: 1933. 222 p. KHi. Following 1865 the author was a mule freighter in Utah and Montana, and then a dealer in livestock and farmer in Kansas.

Pennington, James W.C. The [4507] fugitive blacksmith; or, Events in the history of James W. C. Pennington, pastor of a Presbyterian church, New York, formerly a slave in the state of Maryland, United States. 2d ed. London: Charles Gilpin, 1849. 87 p. NN. As described by the title.

Penny, Alexander, b. 1845. Rem-[4508] iniscences... St. Louis: Keymer pr. co., 1923. 182 p. MoHi. A St. Louis merchant, born in Scotland, tells mainly of his youthful days abroad, and a little about his business.

Pennypacker, Samuel Whitaker, [4509] 1843-1916. The autobiography of a Pennsylvanian. Phila.: John C. Winston, 1918. 564 p. WHi. Lawyer, municipal judge, governor (1903-1907), historian.

Pepin, Francois. A narrative [4510] of the life and experience of Francois Pepin... Detroit: George B. Pomeroy, 1854. 76 p. MiD-B. A Canadian Catholic who came to Michigan where he was converted to the Protestant faith.

Pepper, George Wharton, b.1867. [4511] Philadelphia lawyer... N.Y.: Lippincott, 1944. 407 p. WHi. Lawyer and U.S. Senator.

Pepper, George Wharton, b.1867.[4512]

In the Senate. Phila.: Univ. of Pa. press, 1930. 148 p. WHi. U.S. Senator from Pennsylvania, 1922-27.

Pepper, George Whitfield, 1833- [4513] 1899. Under three flags... Cinc.: Pr. by Curts & Jennings, 1899. 542 p. WHi. Methodist clergyman, born in Ireland, who served in Ohio and was then made U.S. Consul in Milan.

Percy, William Alexander, [4514] b. 1885. Lanterns on the levee... N.Y.: Knopf, 1941. 347. WU. A writer tells of his life on a Mississippi cotton plantation.

Perkins, Abraham, 1807-1900. [4515] Autobiography... Concord: Rumford press, 1901. 22 p. Auto., p. 10-22. WHi. Shaker minister in New England.

Perkins, George Douglas, 1840- [4516] 1914. George Douglas Perkins. No imprint. 127 p. Auto., p. 17-22. IaHi. Newspaper editor, publisher and political figure in Iowa.

Perkins, George Gilpin, 1839- [4517] 1933. A Kentucky judge. Washington: Press of W. F. Roberts co., 1931. 315 p. NN. As described by the title.

Perkins, Joseph D., b. 1851. [4518] Autobiography... No imprint, 1932? 124 p. TxU. Missouri judge and lawyer.

Perkins, Justin, 1805-1869. A [4519] residence of eight years in Persia, among the Nestorian Christians; with notices of the Muhammedans ... Andover: Allen, Morrill & Wardwell, 1843. 512 p. NN. Missionary labors in Persia.

Perkins, Nathan E., b. 1824. [4520] Events and travels...1824-87. Camden: 1887. 490 p. PP. Farmer, nurseryman, dealer in real estate in New Jersey.

Perkins, Norah, b. 1879. [4521] "Through the mill..." Brooklyn: Brooklyn Eagle press, 1916. 142 p. NN. Twentieth century evangelist in New York, Minnesota, Illinois, Wisconsin and Nebraska.

Perrine, Henry E., b. 1825. A [4522] true story of some eventful years in grandpa's life... Buffalo: Hutchinson, 1885? 303 p. WHi. A frontier account of mining in California.

Perry, Bliss, b. 1860. And glad- [4523] ly teach. Boston: Houghton Mifflin, 1935. 315 p. WU. Professor of English at Williams, Princeton and Harvard; editor of the Atlantic Monthly.

Perry, David, b. 1741. Recollec- [4524] tions of an old soldier... Windsor: pr. by Republican & Yeoman, 1822. 55 p. DLC. At Ticonderoga and with Wolfe at Quebec.

Perry, Ichabod Jeremiah,1758- [4525] 1839. Reminiscences of the Revolution. Lima, N.Y.: Ska-hase-ga-o Chapter, Daughter of the American Revolution, 1915. 63 p. NN. As described by the title.

Pershing, John J., b. 1860. My [4526] experiences in the world war. N.Y.: F. A. Stokes co., 1931. 2 vols. WHi. By the Commander-in-Chief of the American Expeditionary Forces.

Peters, Charles, b. 1825. The [4527] autobiography of Charles Peters... Sacramento: La Grave, 1915? 231 p. Auto., p. 1-34. WHi. Miner in California in 1849.

Peterson, Daniel H. The look- [4528] ing-glass: being a true report and narrative of the life, travels and labors of the Rev. Daniel H. Peterson, a colored clergyman; embracing a period of time from the year 1812 to 1854, and including his visit to western Africa... N.Y.: Wright, 1854. 150 p. NN. Methodist clergyman in Pa.

Petroff, Peter, 1826-1894. Ante- [4529] mortem depositions... San Francisco: T. J. Davis, 1895. 124 p. DLC. Union army soldier, born in Russia, who loses arm and becomes a watchman in Conn.

Petrova, Olga, b. 1886. Butter [4530] with my bread. Indianapolis: The Bobbs-Merrill co., 1942. 371 p. NN. Stage and screen star, born in England, who also wrote plays and novels.

Pettay, Orange L. Five years in [4531] Hell... Caldwell: Citizens' press print, 1883. 104 p. DLC. Imprisoned five years for robbery in Ohio.

Petter, Rodolphe, b. 1865. Rem- [4532] iniscences of past years in mission service among the Cheyenne... Newton: Herald pub. co., 1936. 79 p. Auto., p. 3-54. CLSM. Swiss

Mennonite missionary, who beginning with 1890 labored among the Indians in Oklahoma for 45 years.

Pettijohn, Jonas, b. 1813. Autobiography... Clay Center: Dispatch pr. house, 1890. 104 p. KHi. Farmer and Presbyterian mission worker among Sioux Indians in Minnesota; farmer and mission worker for United Brethren in Kansas. [4533]

Petty, George W. In camp with L company... N.Y.: W. H. Crawford co., printers, n.d. 142 p. DLC. This company did not reach Cuba during the War with Spain. [4534]

Peyton, John Lewis, 1824-1896. The American crisis; or, pages from the notebook of a state agent during the Civil war. London: Saunders, Otley, 1867. 2 vols. WHi. The author represented the Confederacy in England. [4535]

Phelan, James, 1819-1892. "Brief autobiography of James Phelan, 1819-1892, Pioneer merchant". (In, How many miles from St. Jo?, by Sterling B.F. Clark. San Francisco: 1929.) p. 45-52. WHi. California merchant in the fifties. [4536]

Phelps, Elizabeth Stuart. See Ward, Mrs. Elizabeth Stuart (Phelps).

Phelps, Frank Wesley. Autobiography... Seattle: School of Utilarian Economics, n.d. 30 p. WaU. A leader in the Farmer Alliance Movement on the West coast (1883-1906) tells mainly of how to succeed in life. [4537]

Phelps, Harvey H., b. 1854. Personal recollections... Glendale: 1928. 199 p. MnHi. Minnesota lawyer. [4538]

Phelps, General Lee, b. 1864. Tepee trails... Atlanta: Southern Baptist convention, 1937. 126 p. DLC. Cowhand becomes Baptist mission worker among Oklahoma Indians. [4539]

Phelps, William Dane, 1802-1875. Fore and aft... by "Webfoot". Boston: Nichols & Hall, 1871. 359 p. DLC. Sailing master who came to California in 1840. He tells about the Hudson Bay Company in that state. [4540]

Phelps, William Lyon, b. 1865. ...Autobiography, with letters. [4541] N.Y.: Oxford univ. press, 1939. 986 p. WU. Professor of English at Yale, and literary critic.

Philipson, David, b. 1862. My life as an American Jew... Cinc.: J.G. Kidd, 1941. 526 p. WHi. Rabbi and historian, who served in Maryland and Ohio. [4542]

Phillips, Mrs. Catherine (Payton) 1727-1794. Memoirs... London: pr. by James Phillips, 1797. 382 p. ORNeGF. English Quaker minister who was in New England from 1753-1756 (see p. 56-147). [4543]

Phillips, Charles Henry, b.1858. From the farm to the bishopric... Nashville: pr. by the Parthenon press, 1932. 308 p. DLC. Negro Methodist clergyman in Tennessee, Georgia, District of Columbia, and Ohio. [4544]

Phillips, Philip, 1834-1895. Song pilgrimage round the world... N.Y.: Phillips & Hunt, 1882. 216 p. NN. Song leader in religious revivals. [4545]

Phillips, Rufus, b. 1859. Colorado's first industry. LaJunta?: n.d. 17 p. CoHi. Cowboy, beginning with 1877. [4546]

Phillipson, William M., b. 1840. The life and voyages of Wm. M. Phillipson... Sonora: Banner, 1924. 114 p. DLC. Sailor in U.S. Navy, and merchant sailor. Miner in California. The author was born in England. [4547]

Phillipson, William M., b. 1840. Eleven years before the mast; or, life among the pirates in the Indian ocean. Sonora: Banner, 1923. 91 p. DLC. Sailor. [4548]

Philputt, James McBride, 1860-1932. "That they may all be one;" autobiography and memorial of James M. Philputt, apostle of Christian unity. Ed. by Lillian Reynolds Philputt and Herbert Lockwood Willett. St. Louis, Mo.: Christian board of publication, 1933. 314 p. NN. Clergyman of the Disciples of Christ in New York, Missouri, Virginia and Illinois. [4549]

Pickard, Samuel, b. 1820. Autobiography of a pioneer; or, the nativity, experience, travels, and ministerial labors of Rev. Samuel Pickard, the "converted" Quaker... ed. by O.T. Conger. Chicago: Church & Goodman, 1866. [4550]

403 p. DLC. In the mid-west.

Pickens, William, b. 1881. Burst- [4551] ing bonds... Boston: Jordan & More, 1923. 222 p. DLC. Negro educator in the South. This is an enlarged version of his Heir of Slaves.

Pickett, Charles Edward. [4552] ...Some leaves from the life of a Pacific slope pioneer of 1842. San Francisco: 1877. 15 p. CU-B. Newspaper publisher in Oregon in forties and politician in California in fifties.

Pickett, LaSalle (Corbell),1848- [4553] 1931. What happened to me. N.Y.: Brentano's,1917. 366 p. NN. Family life in the south before, during and after the Civil War by the wife of a Confederate officer.

Pickett, William D., b. 1827. A [4554] sketch...Louisville: John P. Morton, 1904. 26 p. WyU. Railroad engineer in Texas, Kentucky, Arkansas and Tennessee.

Pickford, Arthur. Westward to [4555] Iowa. Mason City: Mason City Globe-Gazette, 1940. 97 p. Auto., p. 1-33. DLC. An English boy tells of being brought to Wisconsin in 1866 where he spent ten years.

Pierce, Robinson. It was not [4556] my own idea. N.Y.: Am. foundation for the blind, 1944. 128 p. WU. Blind farmer.

Pierson, Hamilton Wilcox,1817- [4557] 1888. In the brush. N.Y.: Appleton, 1881. 321 p. WHi. Presbyterian clergyman in Kentucky.

Pigott, Levi Woodbury, b. 1831. [4558] Scenes and incidents in the life of a home missionary...Norfolk: 1901. 160 p. NcU. Missionary in the South Atlantic region.

Pike, James, b. 1834. The scout [4559] and ranger. Cinc.: Hawley, 1865. 394 p. WHi. Scout and spy in the Union army; Texas Ranger who fought against the Indians.

Pilcher, Lewis Stephen, 1845- [4560] 1934. A surgical pilgrim's progress... Phila.: Lippincott, 1925. 451 p. WU. Surgeon and professor in New York.

Pilling, Elmer R. Echoes from [4561] the rail, or eighteen years of railroad life. Columbus: London pr. & pub. co., 1899. 124 p. DLC. Railroad worker (section hand, conductor, etc.)

Pinkerton, Allan, 1819-1884. [4562] Criminal reminiscences and detective sketches. N.Y.: G. W. Carleton & co., 1879. 324 p. NN. Founder of the Pinkerton Detective Agency.

Pinkerton, Kathrene Sutherland [4563] (Gedney), b. 1887. Two ends to our shoestring. N.Y.: Harcourt, Brace, 1941. 362 p. NN. Adventures of a woman writer and her husband who have led a carefree, vagabond life in various parts of the country.

Pinkerton, William John, b.1867. [4564] His personal record... Kansas City: Pinkerton pub. co., 1904. 304 p. DLC. Railroad worker, born in Ireland, who started as a laborer and became an engineer.

Pipes, John. Life work. Nash- [4565] ville: 1888. 222 p. Auto., p. 135-168. LU. Methodist clergyman in Louisiana.

Pitezel, John H., 1814-1906. [4566] Lights and shades of missionary life... Cinc.: pr. at the Western book concern, 1857. 431 p. WHi. Methodist missionary to the Chippewa Indians in the region of Lake Superior.

Pitkin, Walter Boughton, b.1878. [4567] On my own. N.Y.: Scribner, 1944. 526 p. WU. Journalist in New York, foreign correspondent and writer of books on various subjects (mainly inspirational).

Pitou, Augustus, 1843-1915. Mas- [4568] ters of the show. N.Y.: Neale, 1914. 186 p. DLC. A sailor who became an actor.

Pittman, R. H., 1870-1941. Mem- [4569] ories of long ago. Front Royal, Va.: pr. by the Buck press, n.d. NcWAtC. Primitive Baptist preacher, mainly in Virginia.

Pitzer, A.W. Dr. Pitzer's own [4570] story. No imprint, 1902? 15 p. KHi. Presbyterian clergyman in Kansas, beginning in 1868, and terminating about 1900.

Pitzer, Henry Littleton, 1834- [4571] 1903. Three frontiers...Muscatine: Prairie press, 1938. 242 p. WHi. On farm in Illinois and Iowa to age 24. Miner and merchant in Colorado.

Platt, Thomas Collier, 1833- [4572] 1910. The autobiography... N.Y.: B.W. Dodge, 1910. 556 p. WHi.

New York senator and political boss.

Pleasants, Henry, b. 1884. From [4573] kilts to pantaloons. West Chester: H.F. Temple, printers, 1945. 198 p. DLC. Boyhood in New York; surveyor's assistant in New Mexico; college student in Pennsylvania.

Plenty-Coups, b. 1848. American [4574] — the life story of a great Indian. (Told to Frank B. Linderman). N.Y.: John Day, 1930. 309 p. WHi. A Crow Indian tells of fighting the white man on the frontier.

Plumb, Ralph Gordon, b. 1881. [4575] Born in the eighties. Manitowac: Brandt pr. co., 1941. 111 p. WHi. A story of boyhood and youth in the middlewest.

Poe, Sophie (Alberding)...Buck- [4576] board days. Ed. by Eugene Cunningham. Caldwell, Idaho. The Caxton printers, 1936. 292 p. NN: The wife of a buffalo hunter, U.S. Marshal and sheriff tells of their frontier life in New Mexico.

Pokagon, Simon, 1830-1899. [4577] O-Gi-Maw-Kwe... Hartford: C. H. Engle, 1899. 255 p. Auto., p. 49-220. WHi. The story of an Indian in white man's country.

Poling, Alonzo, b. 1854. A little [4578] of all sorts. Oklahoma City: 1939. 64 p. OkOk. Homesteader and U.S. Marshal in Oklahoma.

Polk, J.M., b. 1838. Memories of [4579] the lost cause... Austin: 1907. 47 p. DLC. Confederate soldier who, after the War, was a real estate operator in Texas and a plantation owner in Brazil.

Polk, Jefferson J., b. 1802. [4580] Autobiography... Louisville: pr. by J. P. Morton & co., 1867. 254 p. DLC. Kentucky newspaper publisher, physician, Methodist preacher and temperar worker.

Pollak, Simon, b. 1814. The auto- [4581] biography... ed. by Frank J. Lutz. St. Louis: reprinted from the St. Louis Medical Review, 1904. 331 p. MoSHi. Physician, born in Bohemia, in Tennessee and then after 1845 in Missouri.

Pollard, Henry Robinson. Mem- [4582] oirs...Richmond: Lewis pr. co., 1923. 443 p. WHi. Lawyer and politician in Virginia.

Pollock, Channing, b. 1880. Har- [4583] vest of my years...Indianapolis: Bobbs-Merrill, 1943. 395 p. WU. Playwright, novelist, essayist and screen writer.

Pollock, J.M. The unvarnished [4584] west... London: Simpkin, Marshall, 1911. 252 p. DLC. English army officer becomes a rancher in Texas.

Pomeroy, Jesse Harding, b.1859. [4585] Autobiography... Boston: J.A. Cummings, 1875. 32 p. DLC. Murderer.

Pomeroy, Marcus Mills, 1833- [4586] 1896. Journey of life. Volume one. Reminiscences and recollections of "Brick" Pomeroy. N.Y.: Advance thought co., 1890. 252 p. NN. Newspaper publisher and politician in Wisconsin and New York City.

Pond, Enoch, 1791-1882. Auto- [4587] biography... Boston: Congregational Sunday-school society, 1884. 147 p. DLC. Editor of religious magazine; teacher in theological seminary in Maine; Congregational clergyman in Connecticut.

Pond, William Chauncey, b. 1830. [4588] Gospel pioneering... Oberlin: News pr. co., 1921. 191 p. WHi. Congregational clergyman in California from about 1850 to 1920.

Pontgibaud, Chevalier de. See Moré, Charles Albert.

Ponting, Tom Candy, b. 1824. [4589] The story of my life. No imprint. 102 p. MoHi. Cattle trader, born in England, who drove cattle from Texas to the New York market via the northern states of the midwest.

Ponzi, Charles. The rise of Mr. [4590] Ponzi. N.Y.: 1935. 176 p. DLC. Financier, born in Italy, who ran afoul of the law.

Pool, William Alexander, b. 1847. [4591] A brief autobiography... Mansfield, Texas: The author, 1923. 28 p. TxWB. Baptist clergyman in North Carolina and Texas.

Poole, DeWitt Clinton, b. 1828. [4592] Among the Sioux of Dakota: eighteen months' experiences as an Indian agent (1869-70). N.Y.: D. Van Nostrand, 1881. 235 p. DLC. As described by the title.

Poole, Ernest, b. 1880. The [4593] bridge... N.Y.: Macmillan, 1940. 422 p. WU. Novelist.

Pope, Nancy. We three. Garden [4594] City: Doubleday, Doran, 1936. 272 p. NN. A family account, but containing many memories of youth. The locale is unimportant.

Poppleton, Andrew J., 1830-1896. [4595] Reminiscences. No imprint, 1915? 35 p. NbO. Lawyer and politician in Nebraska.

Porcupine, Peter. See Cobbett, William.

Porter, Alyene. Papa was a [4596] preacher. N.Y.: Abingdon-Cokesbury press, 1944. 167 p. NN. Life in a Texas preacher's family.

Porter, Anthony Toomer, 1828- [4597] 1898. Led on. N.Y.: Putnam, 1898. 462 p. WHi. Episcopalian clergyman in the South, and founder of Porter Military Academy. Confederate soldier.

Porter, Burton B., b. 1832. One [4598] of the people... Colton: 1907. 382 p. NN. California miner; Union army soldier.

Porter, Charles Talbot, b. 1826. [4599] Engineering reminiscences... N.Y.: Wiley, 1908. 335 p. WU. Mechanical engineer, inventor.

Porter, David Dixon, 1813-1891. [4600] Incidents and anecdotes of the Civil war. By Admiral Porter. N.Y.: D. Appleton & co., 1885. 357 p. NN. As described by the title.

Porter, Mrs. Gene (Stratton), [4601] 1863-1924. Homing with the birds; the history of a lifetime of personal experience with the birds. Garden City: Doubleday, Page, 1919. 381 p. Auto., p. 3-195. DLC. Writer, photographer, illustrator.

Porter, George Washington, [4602] b. 1849. Autobiography... Punxsutawney: Spirit pub. co., 1929. 203 p. DLC. Pennsylvania merchant who dealt in agricultural implements.

Porter, Henry Holmes, 1835- [4603] 1910. A short autobiography... Chicago: R. R. Donnelley, 1915. 40 p. WHi. Lumber dealer, banker and railroad director in Illinois.

Porter, Henry Miller, 1838-1932. [4604] Autobiography... Denver: 1932. 86 p. CoD. Merchant, banker, cattle raiser, who also had financial interest in railways and telephones. The author's business interests were located in Colorado, Missouri, Idaho, Nevada, California and New Mexico.

Porter, Martha Byrd (Spruill). [4605] Straight down a crooked lane. Richmond: Dietz, 1945. 233 p. WHi. Wife of physician in Virginia.

Porter, Napoleon Bonaparte, [4606] b. 1853. Thirty-two years on the hurricane deck of a freight train... Des Moines: Welch pr. co., 1906. 191 p. IaHi. Brakeman.

Post, M. M. A retrospect... [4607] Logansport: Bringhurst, 1860. 24 p. MnHi. Presbyterian clergyman in Indiana, 1830-60.

Post, Mrs. Permelia Ann (Dra- [4608] per), b. 1820. Autobiography... 2d. ed. Olean: 1902. 99 p. DLC. Wife of Methodist clergyman in New York writes chiefly of her religious experiences.

Potter, Blanche, b. 1864. Recol- [4609] lections of a little life. N.Y.: 1927. 310 p. DLC. Lay church worker, and social worker in New York.

Potter, David, b. 1874. Sailing [4610] the Sulu Sea. N.Y.: Dutton, 1940. 310 p. WHi. U.S. Naval officer tells of the insurrection of 1899-1901 in the Philippines.

Potter, Elam, 1741-1794. Author's [4611] account of his conversion... Boston: T. Kneeland, 1772. 16 p. RPJCB. Itinerant clergyman in Conn. and Mass.

Potter, Eliza. A hairdresser's [4612] experience in high life. Cinc.: 1859. 294 p. DLC. Mainly in New York.

Potter, Israel Ralph, 1744-1826? [4613] Life and remarkable adventures of Israel R. Potter (a native of Cranston, Rhode-Island) who was a soldier in the American revolution...Providence: pr. by H. Trumbull, 1824. 108 p. WHi. As described by the title.

Potter, Jack Myers, b. 1864. [4614] Cattle trails of the old West. Clayton: 1935. 87 p. NN. Rancher in Texas and New Mexico.

Potter, Jack Myers, b. 1864. [4615] Lead steer and other tales. Clayton: pr. by the Leader press, 1939. 116 p. NmU. Reminiscential stories by the author of the preceding item.

Potter, John. Reminiscences of [4616] the Civil war in the United States. Oskaloosa: Globe presses, 1897.

196 p. WHi. Union army.

Potter, Lemuel, 1841-1897. La- [4617] bors and travels of Elder Lemuel Potter, as an old school Baptist minister... Evansville, Ind.: Keuer pr. co., 1894. 362 p. OClWHi. In Illinois and Indiana.

Potter, Ray, 1795-1858. Memoirs [4618] ... Providence: H. H. Brown, printer, 1829. 286 p. DLC. Universalist clergyman in Rhode Island who became Baptist.

Potter, Theodore Edgar, 1832- [4619] 1910. The autobiography of Theodore Edgar Porter. Concord: Rumford press, 1913. 228 p. WHi. Miner in California; member of Walker's expedition to Nicaragua; Indian fighter on the Plains.

Potts, Edward L., b. 1882. "The [4620] bright side"... Louisville: Pentecostal pub. co., 1922. 63 p. DLC. Writer of verses in Alabama who was crippled when a youth.

Pound, Arthur, b. 1884. Time is [4621] a dream. N.Y.: Atlantic monthly co., 1934-1943. 8 parts. MiD-B. An author tells of his early youth and college education in Michigan.

Powderly, Terence Vincent, [4622] 1849-1924. The path I trod. N.Y.: Columbia univ. press, 1940. 460 p. WHi. Leader of the Knights of Labor.

Powell, Aaron Macy, 1832-1899. [4623] Personal reminiscences of the anti-slavery and other reforms and reformers. Plainfield: Anna Rice Powell, 1899. 279 p. OrNeGF. As described by the title.

Powell, Adam Clayton, b. 1908. [4624] Against the tide... N.Y.: R.R. Smith, 1938. 327 p. WHi. Negro Baptist clergyman in New York.

Powell, Arthur Gray, b. 1873. [4625] I can go home again. Chapel Hill: The univ. of North Carolina press, 1943. 301 p. NN. The author, a Georgia lawyer, tells of his life in Blakely, Georgia, until his election as a member of the State Court of Appeals.

Powell, David, 1805-1854? Auto- [4626] biography of the Rev. David Powell, a minister of the New Church signified by the New Jerusalem in the Apocalypse... ed. by the Rev. Wm. H. Benade. Phila.: Committee of the Darby society of the New Church, 1856. 168 p. OClWHi. As described by the title.

Powell, Edward Alexander, [4627] b. 1879. Vive la France. N.Y.: Scribner, 1915. 254 p. DLC. Foreign correspondent during the First World War.

Powell, Edward Alexander, [4628] b. 1879. Yonder lies adventure. N.Y.: Macmillan, 1932. 452 p. DLC. American journalist tells of his thirty years of adventure on four continents.

Powell, Edward Alexander, [4629] b. 1879. Slanting lines of steel. N.Y.: Macmillan, 1933. 307 p. DLC. Foreign correspondent tells of his experiences while covering the First World War.

Powell, Edward Alexander, [4630] b. 1879. Free lance. N.Y.: Harcourt, Brace, 1937. 514 p. NN. Experiences of a journalist and world traveller.

Powell, John Benjamin, b.1888. [4631] My twenty-five years in China. N.Y.: Macmillan, 1945. 436 p. WU. Journalist, editor of periodical.

Powell, Theophilus Shuck, b.1855. [4632] Five years in South Mississippi. Cinc.: Standard pub. co., 1889. 190 p. LU. Baptist clergyman, 1880-85.

Powell, William J. Black wings. [4633] Los Angeles: Ivan Deach, 1934. 218 p. DLC. Negro aviator.

Power, Frederick Dunglison, [4634] 1851-1911. The story of a twenty-three years' pastorate...Cinc.: Standard pub. co., 1899. 58 p. MoCanD. Clergyman of the Disciples of Christ in the District of Columbia, beginning with 1875.

Powers, Caleb, 1869-1932. My [4635] own story; an account of the conditions in Kentucky leading to the assassination of William Goebel, who was declared governor of the state, and my indictment and conviction on the charge of complicity in his murder... Indianapolis: Bobbs-Merrill, 1905. 490 p. NN. The author was formerly Secretary of State of Kentucky. At the time of writing the author was still in prison.

Powers, James T., 1862-1943. [4636] Twinkle little star; sparkling memories of seventy years. N.Y.: G. P. Putnam's sons, 1939. 379 p. NN. Memories of old New York and of the American theatre by an actor.

Powers, Michael, 1769-1820? [4637] Life of Michael Powers, now under sentence of death, for the murder of Timothy Kennedy. Dictated by himself. Boston: Russell & Gardner, 1820. 24 p. Auto., p. 5-13. DLC. As described by the title.

Powers, Stephen. Afoot and [4638] alone. Hartford: 1872. 327 p. WHi. Written by an ethnologist whose work was done in the southern states (east and west), including California.

Powers, Thomas, 1776?-1796. [4639] The narrative and confession of Thomas Powers... Norwich: pr. by John Trumbull, 1796. 12 p. DLC. The condemned man was a Negro who had committed rape in New Hampshire.

Powers, William Penn, b. 1842. [4640] Some annals of the Powers family. Los Angeles: 1924. 304 p. Auto., p. 29-87. WHi. Union army soldier. Manufacturer in Wisconsin.

Powys, John Cowper, b. 1872. [4641] Autobiography. N.Y.: Simon & Schuster, 1934. 595 p. NN. English writer and lecturer, who spent a number of years in America, tells of his literary friendships.

Pratt, Alice Day. The home- [4642] steader's portfolio. N.Y.: Macmillan, 1922. 181 p. WU. Oregon teacher becomes a farmer.

Pratt, Mrs. Harry Rogers. See Rothery, Agnes Edwards.

Pratt, John Barnes. Personal [4643] recollections, sixty years of book publishing. N.Y.: A.S. Barnes, 1942. 67 p. WHi. As described by the title.

Pratt, Julius Howard, 1821-1909. [4644] Reminiscences... N.p.: priv. pr., 1910. 287 p. WHi. Miner in California; manufacturer in New York; public utility development in New Jersey; mine owner in Colorado.

Pratt, Parley Parker, 1807- [4645] 1857. The autobiography of Parley Parker Pratt, one of the twelve apostles of the Church of Jesus Christ of Latter-Day Saints, embracing his life, ministry and travels... ed. by his son, Parley P. Pratt... Chicago: pub. for Pratt bros. by Law, King & Law, 1888. 502 p. NN. As described by the title.

Preble, Jedidiah, 1765-1847. [4646] Birth, parentage, life and experience of Jedidiah Preble, 3d. Portland: Edwards, 1830. 216 p. DLC. Itinerant Methodist clergyman in Maine, New Jersey and Pa.

Prentis, Caroline E. A Kansas [4647] pioneer. Newton: Kansas pr. co., n.d. 16 p. KHi. The author's family came to Kansas in 1859. She was a stenographer, and then married a Kansas newspaper editor.

Prentis, Noble L., b. 1839. [4648] Sketches... N.p.: 1907. 23 p. KHi. Connecticut printer who, after serving in the Union army, became a newspaper reporter and editor in Kansas.

Prentiss, George Lewis, 1816- [4649] 1903. The bright side of life. Asbury Park: Pennypacker, 1901. 2 vols. DLC. Presbyterian clergyman in Maine and New York. Professor at Union Theological Seminary.

Prescott, Jedediah Brown, 1784-[4650] 1861. Memoir of Jedediah B. Prescott, late pastor of the Christian Church in Monmouth. Monmouth: 1861. 135 p. DLC. In Maine.

Preston, James Crockatt, b.1852.[4651] Memoirs, 1856-1926... Springfield: Farm club news, 1927. 228 p. DLC. Farmer in Iowa and Missouri who came from Scotland about 1870. In Iowa he was Secretary of the Iowa Sunday School Association.

Preus, Herman Amberg, 1825- [4652] 1894. Syv foredrag over de kirkelige forholde blandt de norske i Amerika. Christiania: J. Dybwad, 1867. 144 p. DLC. Lutheran clergyman in Wisconsin, 1850-1890.

Price, James L. The autobio- [4653] graphy of James L. Price, Jungle Jim. N.Y.: Doubleday, Doran & co., 1941. 310 p. NN. Adventures in the jungles of Central America, by an explorer, hunter and anthropologist.

Price, James P. Seven years of [4654]

prairie life. Hereford: Jakeman & Carver, 1891. 88 p. DLC. An Englishman on a Kansas farm.

Price, Phinehas, b. 1789. A nar- [4655] rative... Phila.: 1843. 202 p. DLC. Episcopalian circuit rider and physician in Pa.

Price, T.W., b. 1808. The life of [4656] T. W. Price...Selma: Daily times job pr. office, 1877. 80 p. DLC. Alabama teacher, farmer, lawyer, county judge and Confederate office holder.

Prime, Daniel Noyes, 1790-1880.[4657] The autobiography of an octogenarian... Newburyport: W.H. Huse, printers, 1873. 293 p. WHi. Shoe manufacturer in Mass.

Prime, Samuel Irenaeus, 1812- [4658] 1885. Autobiography and memorials. N.Y.: A.D.F. Randolph, 1888. 385 p. DLC. Presbyterian clergyman in New York, editor of religious periodical.

Prince, Henry Shumway, b. 1854.[4659] Autobiography of a bound boy. Worcester: Simonds, 1913. 69 p. DLC. A captain in the Salvation Army tells of his hard youth in Massachusetts.

Prince, Mrs. Nancy (Gardener), [4660] b. 1799. A narrative...Boston: 1850. 87 p. WHi. An ex-slave tells of her missionary work in the West Indies.

Pringle, Mrs. Henry Fowles. See Alderson, Nannie T.

Pritzker, Nicholas Jacob, 1871- [4661] 1941. Three score after ten. Chicago: 1941. 320 leaves. DLC. Chicago lawyer who had first worked in stockyards upon his arrival from Russia.

Probst, Anton, 1842-1866. Trial,[4662] life and execution of Anton Probst... Phila.: T. B. Peterson, 1866. 120 p. Auto., p. 102-111. DLC. Murderer in Pa.

Proctor, Henry Hugh, 1868-1933.[4663] Between black and white... Boston: Pilgrim press, 1925. 189 p. WHi. Congregational clergyman in Georgia.

Prosser, Anna W., 1846-1902. [4664] From death to life... 2d ed. Chicago: Evangel pub. house, 1911. 222 p. DLC. W.C.T.U. mission worker.

Provol, William Lee, b.1877? [4665] The pack peddler. Greenville: Beaver pr. co., 1933. 314 p. DLC. As described by the title. The author was born in Poland.

Pruiett, Moman, 1872-1945. [4666] Moman Pruiett, criminal lawyer. Oklahoma City: pr. by Harlow pub. corp., 1944. 580 p. OCl. In Oklahoma.

Pryor, Joseph William, b.1856. [4667] Doctor Pryor, an autobiography. Cynthia: Hobson press, 1943. 312 p. DLC. Physician in Missouri and Kentucky; professor of medicine at the University of Kentucky.

Pryor, Mrs. Sara Agnes (Rice), [4668] 1830-1912. My day; reminiscences of a long life. N.Y.: Macmillan, 1909. 454 p. WHi. A domestic account, by the wife of a U.S. Congressman, a confederate officer and a New York lawyer.

Pryor, Mrs. Sara Agnes (Rice), [4669] 1830-1912. Reminiscences of peace and war. N.Y.: Macmillan, 1904. 402 p. WHi. A domestic account of social life in Washington prior to the Civil War, followed by life in the South during the Civil War, by the wife of a Confederate officer.

Puddefoot, William George,1842-[4670] 1925. Leaves from the log of a sky pilot. Boston: Pilgrim press, 1915. 200 p. CBPac. Congregational clergyman in Michigan who was born in England.

Pumpelly, Raphael, 1837-1937. [4671] My reminiscences. N.Y.: Holt, 1918. 2 vols. WHi. Geologist. See also his Across America and Asia.

Pupin, Michael Idvorsky, 1858- [4672] 1935. From immigrant to inventor. N.Y.: Scribner, 1923. 387 p. WHi. Physicist, electrical engineer, professor of electro-magnetics at Columbia University.

Purcell, Mrs. Polly Jane (Clay- [4673] pool), b. 1842. Autobiography and reminiscences of a pioneer. Freewater: n.d. 7 p. CSmH. In Oregon, beginning about 1846. An account of farming and Indian fighting.

Purdy, Will E., b. 1862. Sixteen [4674] years in Oregon. Portland: 1912. 126 p. OrU. Merchant.

Purviance, David, 1766-1847. [4675] The biography of Elder David Purviance. New ed. N.p.: 1940. 278 p. Auto., p. 105-184. WHi.

Clergyman of the Christian Church relates his spiritual progress.

Putnam, Benjamin, b. 1788. A [4676] sketch... Woodstock: pr. by David Watson, 1821. 216 p. DLC. A Baptist clergyman (Free Will) in Vermont who became a member of the Christian Church.

Putnam, Carleton, b. 1901. High [4677] journey; a decade in the pilgrimage of an air line pioneer. N.Y.: Scribner's, 1945. 308 p. NN. Memoirs of an air line operator.

Putnam, George Haven, 1844- [4678] 1930. Memories of my youth, 1844-1865. N.Y.: Putnam, 1914. 447 p. WHi. This account deals mainly with his experiences in the Union army.

Putnam, George Haven, 1844- [4679] 1930. Memories of a publisher, 1865-1915. N.Y.: Putnam, 1915. 492 p. WHi. As described by the title.

Putnam, George Palmer, b.1887. [4680] Wide margins; a publisher's autobiography. N.Y.: Harcourt, Brace & co., 1942. 351 p. NN. As described by the title.

Putnam, George Rockwell, [4681] b. 1865. Sentinel of the coasts; the log of a lighthouse engineer. N.Y.: Norton, 1937. 368 p. DLC. Cartographer employed by the U.S. Government.

Putnam, Israel W., b. 1787. A [4682] fifty-years ministry...Middleboro: pr. by Stillman B. Pratt, 1865. 34 p. Auto., p. 14-34. WHi. Congregational minister in Mass. and New Hampshire.

Putnam, Mrs. Nina Wilcox, [4683] b. 1884. Laughing through... N.Y.: Sears, 1930. 340 p. DLC. Novelist.

Putnam, Rufus, 1738-1824. The [4684] memoirs... Boston: Houghton Mifflin, 1903. 460 p. WHi. Soldier in the Revolutionary army.

## Q

Quick, John Herbert, 1861-1925. [4685] One man's life... Indianapolis: Bobbs-Merrill, 1925. 408 p. WHi. Iowa school teacher and lawyer. The author omits mention of his literary activity.

Quinby, Hosea. The prison [4686] chaplaincy, and its experiences. Concord, N.H.: D. L. Guernsey, 1873. 198 p. DLC. In New Hampshire, 1869-71.

Quinby, Josiah, b. 1693. A short [4687] history of a long journey...N.Y.: pr. by John Zenger, 1740. 61 p. DLC. New York merchant.

Quincy, Eliza Susan (Morton), [4688] 1773-1850. Memoir of the life of Eliza S. M. Quincy. Boston: pr. by J. Wilson & son, 1861. 267 p. NN. Social life at the end of the eighteenth and beginning of the nineteenth century, written in 1821.

Quinn, Germain, b. 1866. Fifty [4689] years backstage... Minneapolis: Stage pub. co., 1926. 204 p. DLC. Stage manager in Minneapolis.

Quintard, Charles Todd, 1824- [4690] 1898. Doctor Quintard, chaplain C.S.A. and second bishop of Tennessee; being his story of the war (1861-1865) ed. and extended by the Rev. Arthur Howard Noll. Sewanee, Tenn.: The univ. press, 1905. 183 p. WHi. As described by the title.

Quinton, Robert, b. 1853. The [4691] strange adventures of Captain Quinton... N.Y.: Christian herald, 1912. 486 p. IU. Merchant sailor in the South Seas.

## R

R., I. See Randall, Isabelle.

Raabe, H.E. Cannibal nights; the [4692] reminiscences of a free-lance trader. N.Y.: Payson & Clarke, 1927. 323 p. DLC. Merchant trader in the South Seas. The author was born in Germany, and later settled in New Jersey.

Rabb, Mrs. Mary (Crownover). [4693] Reminiscences of Mary Crownover Rabb, wife of John Rabb. Meridian: 1931. 15 p. TxU. By the wife of a pioneer Texas farmer (1827-36).

Rabbino, Bernhard, 1860-1933. [4694] Back to the home. N.Y.: pr. by Court press, 1933? 182 p. Auto., p. 1-38. DLC. Rabbi, born in Russia, who served in Georgia, Florida, Iowa and Ohio. Later he became a lawyer in New York.

Raboy, Isaac, 1882-1944. Mein [4695] leben (in Yiddish). N.Y.: Jewish people's fraternal order, 1945. 2 vols. DLC. Yiddish literary figure.

Rachmaninov, Sergei, b. 1873. [4696] Rachmaninoff's recollections. London: George Allen, 1934. 272 p. WU. Russian pianist. Two chapters of this book are related to American experiences.

Racine, J. Polk. Recollections [4697] of a veteran, or four years in Dixie. Elkton: 1894. 200 p. ICU. Union army soldier.

Rackett, Arthur Herbert, b.1864. [4698] Arthur H. Rackett's fifty years a drummer. Elkhorn: 1931. 118 p. Auto., p. 9-11. DLC. The author, born in England, played in vaudeville houses, theatres and in military bands.

Racovita, Elena von Dönniges, [4699] 1845-1911. Princess Helene von Racowitza, an autobiography. N.Y.: Macmillan, 1910. 420 p. CU-B. German actress. See p. 295-388 for her American experiences, mainly in California.

Radford, Benjamin Johnson, [4700] 1838-1933. Autobiography... Eureka: 1928. 48 p. Auto., p. 1-20. MoCanD. A clergyman of the Christian Church tells mainly of growing up on a farm in Illinois.

Radziwill, Ekaterina (Rzewuska), [4701] 1858-1941. It really happened. N.Y.: Dial press, 1932. 278 p. NN. Struggles of an aristocratic refugee to maintain herself in New York.

Rafinesque, Constantine Samuel, [4702] 1783-1840. A life of travels and researches in North America and south Europe, or Outlines of the life, travels and researches of C.S. Rafinesque, A.M. Ph.D... containing his travels in North America and the south of Europe; the Atlantic Ocean, Mediterranean, Sicily, Azores, &c. from 1802 to 1835 — with sketches of his scientific and historical researches, &c...Phila.: pr. for the author, by F. Turner, 1836. 148 p. NN. Naturalist.

Ragué, Louis von, 1838-1910. [4703] Lebensbilder aus der innern mission... Hoyleston, Illinois: Evangelische waisenheimat, 1912. 138 p. DLC. Lutheran clergyman in Wisconsin, Minnesota, Illinois and Louisiana. The author was born in Germany.

Railey, Hilton Howell, b. 1895. [4704] Touch'd with madness. N.Y.: Carrick & Evans, 1938. 347 p. NN. Adventures around the world of a public relations man.

Railey, William E., b. 1852. Rec-[4705] ollections... Frankfort: Roberts pr. co., 1937. 24 p. KyHi. Farmer, postmaster and politician in Kentucky.

Railey, William E., b. 1852. The [4706] last reflections of William E. Railey. Frankfort: Roberts pr. co., 1939. 23 p. KyHi. See the preceding item.

Rainsford, William Stephen, [4707] 1850-1933. The story of a varied life... London: Allen & Unwin, n.d. 481 p. WHi. Born in Ireland. Episcopalian clergyman in England, Canada and New York.

Rak, Mary (Kidder), b. 1879. A [4708] cowman's wife. Boston & N.Y.: Houghton Mifflin, 1934. 292 p. NN. Cattle ranching in Arizona.

Rak, Mary Kidder, b. 1879. [4709] Mountain cattle. Boston & N.Y.: Houghton Mifflin, 1936. 275 p. NN. A continuation of the preceding item.

Ralph, Julian, 1853-1903. The [4710] making of a journalist. N.Y.: Harper, 1903. 199 p. WU. As described by the title.

Ramsay, Robert, b. 1851. Rough [4711] and tumble on old clipper ships. N.Y.: Appleton, 1930. 296 p. DLC. Merchant seaman, born in Scotland, who sailed the Great Lakes and who later was a longshoreman in New York.

Rand, Clayton, b. 1891. Ink on my [4712] hands. N.Y.: Carrick & Evans, 1940. 348 p. WU. Rural newspaper editor in Mississippi.

Rand, Festus G., b. 1821. Auto- [4713] biography... Romeo: J. Russell, printer, 1866. 16 p. MiD-B. Nh. Blacksmith in Vermont and New York. Temperance worker.

Randall, Eugene Wilson, 1859- [4714] 1940. Reminiscences and reflections. No imprint. 54 p. MnHi. President of the Minnesota Mutual Life Insurance Company, and Dean of the School of Agriculture of the University of Minnesota. The author was also a teacher and newspaper editor.

Randall, Isabelle. A lady's [4715] ranch life in Montana. London: W.H. Allen, 1887. 170 p. CLU-C. Englishwoman in Montana.

Randell, Jack, b. 1879. I'm alone.[4716] ...Indianapolis: Bobbs-Merrill, 1930. 317 p. NN. Merchant seaman.

Randolph, Buckner Magill. Ten [4717] years old and under... Boston: Ruth Hill, 1935. 127 p. WHi. A physician tells of his youth in the South following the Civil War.

Randolph, Isham, 1848-1920. [4718] Gleanings from a harvest of memories. Columbia: pr. by E. W. Stephens co., 1937. 84 p. DLC. Chief Engineer of the Chicago Sanitary District.

Randolph, Peter. From slave [4719] cabin to the pulpit... Boston: J. H. Earle, 1893. 220 p. DLC. The author was emancipated prior to the Civil War. He became a Baptist clergyman, serving in Massachusetts, Conn., and New York. After the war he served in Virginia.

Rankin, George Clark. The [4720] story of my life. Nashville: Smith & Lamar, 1912. 356 p. WHi. School teacher who became a Methodist clergyman, serving in Texas and in the South Atlantic region.

Rankin, Mary, b. 1821. The [4721] daughter of affliction... Dayton: Printed at the United Brethren printing establishment, 1858. 253 p. Auto., p. 19-181. DLC. A resident of Pennsylvania tells of her protracted illness.

Rankin, Melinda. Twenty years [4722] among the Mexicans... St. Louis: Christian pub. co., 1875. 214 p. WHi. Mainly in Texas, by a missionary of the Christian Church.

Ranlett, Charles Everett, 1816- [4723] 1917. Master mariner of Maine... Portland, Maine: The Southworth-Anthoensen press, 1942. 145 p. WHi. As described by the title.

Ranlett, Louis Felix. Let's go. [4724] Boston: Houghton Mifflin, 1927. 291 p. DLC. A soldier in France during the First World War.

Ranney, David James, b. 1863. [4725] Dave Ranney; or, thirty years on the Bowery. N.Y.: American tract society, 1910. 205 p. DLC. An habitual drinker is reformed and opens a mission house on the Bowery.

Rantoul, Robert Samuel, b.1832. [4726] Personal recollections. Cambridge: 1916. 162 p. WHi. Mayor of Salem, Mass., and Collector of Customs.

Rascoe, Burton, b. 1892. Before [4727] I forget. Garden City: Doubleday, Doran, 1937. 442 p. WU. Dramatic critic, literary editor, newspaper reporter.

Rasmussen, August. Pioneerlivet[4728] i det store danske settlement, Montcalm County, Michigan... fra aar 1856 til aar 1904. Blair, Nebr.: Danish Lutheran pub. house, 1904. 80 p. MoHi. The author, born in Denmark, came to Michigan in 1856, where he engaged in farming. An abbreviated version of this in English was published in 1902.

Rast, Jeremiah, b. 1828. Life [4729] sketches... Louisville: Pentecostal pub. co., 1913. 168 p. Auto., p. 7-99. DLC. Methodist clergyman in Florida and Georgia.

Rathbun, Jonathan, b. 1765. Nar- [4730] rative of Jonathan Rathbun, by Rufus Avery... New London: 1840. 80 p. Auto., p. 9-16. DLC. Farmer in Connecticut, and soldier in the Revolutionary army.

Ravage, Marcus Eli, b. 1884. An [4731] American in the making... N.Y.: Harper, 1917. 265 p. WHi. An immigrant from Rumania tells of his problems in readjustment.

Ravoux, Augustin, 1815-1906. [4732] Reminiscences... St. Paul: Brown, Treacy & co., 1890. 223 p. DLC. Catholic priest, born in France, who served among the Indians in the upper Mississippi Valley, especially in Minnesota.

Rawlings, Mrs. Marjorie (Kin- [4733] nan). Cross creek. N.Y.: Scribner, 1942. 368 p. WU. A novelist tells of her rural life in Florida.

Rawson, Kennett Longley. A [4734] boy's view of the Arctic... N.Y.: Macmillan, 1926. 142 p. DLC. A young boy tells of his trip with an exploring expedition of 1925.

Ray, Emma S., b. 1859. Twice [4735] sold, twice ransomed... Chicago: Free Methodist pub. house, 1926.

320 p. DLC. An ex-slave who did temperance and hospital work in Washington.

Ray, Lloyd P. See Ray, Emma J.

Ray, William, 1771-1827. Poems [4736] ...to which is added a brief sketch of the author's life... Auburn: pr. by U. F. Doubleday, 1821. 254 p. Auto., p. 199-252. DLC. Merchant of New York who was made a captive off the coast of Africa.

Raymond, Cornelia Morse, [4737] b. 1861. Memories of a child of Vassar. Poughkeepsie, N.Y.: Vassar College, 1940. 73 p. NN. Recollections by the daughter of the second president of the college.

Raymond, William Gould, 1819- [4738] 1893. Life sketches... Boston: G.E. Crosby & co., printers, 1891. 304 p. DLC. Chaplain with the Union army; Baptist clergyman in the states of the Atlantic region.

Read, Francis W. G.I. Parson. [4739] N.Y.: Morehouse-Gorham, 1945. 117 p. DLC. An Episcopalian chaplain who served in the Pacific area during the second World War.

Read, Opie Percival, 1852-1939. [4740] I remember. N.Y.: R. R. Smith, 1930. 335 p. DLC. Southern newspaper editor, who later became a novelist.

Reagan, John Henninger, 1818- [4741] 1905. Memoirs, with special reference to secession and the Civil War. By John H. Reagan, postmaster-general of the Confederacy; sometime United States senator; chairman of the Railroad Commission of Texas; president of the Texas State Historical Association. N.Y. & Washington: The Neale pub. co., 1906. 351 p. NN. As described by the title.

Reavis, D.W. I remember. [4742] Takoma Park, Washington, D.C.: Review & Herald pub. association, n.d. 143 p. NbLU. The author did Sabbath school work in Ohio for the Adventists and distributed religious literature in the South.

Rechow, Theodore G., b. 1846. [4743] Autobiography... Bolivar, Mo.: 1929. 29 p. MoHi. Prior to the Civil War the author was a farm laborer and shoemaker in Wisconsin; after the War he was a lawyer in Missouri.

Reckitt, William, b. 1706. Some [4744] account of the life and gospel labours of William Reckitt...Phila.: Printed and sold by Joseph Krukshank, 1783. p. 13-164. MiU-C. English Quaker who served briefly in America.

Redd, Richard Menefee. Remin- [4745] iscences... Lexington: Clay pr. co., 1929. 64 p. WHi. Presbyterian clergyman in Kentucky; Confederate soldier; holder of minor political offices.

Redfield, John Howard, 1815- [4746] 1895. Recollections of John Howard Redfield... Phila.: Morris press, 1900. 360 p. DLC. The author was in the shipping business in Connecticut and New York.

Redfield, Levi, b. 1745. A suc- [4747] cinct account of some memorable events... Brattleborough: B. Smead, 1798. 12 p. CSmH. School teacher in Connecticut and soldier in the Revolutionary army.

Redmond, Juanita. I served on [4748] Bataan. Phila.: J.B. Lippincott co., 1943. 166 p. DLC. Nurse who served in the Pacific area during the second World War.

Reed, Francis R., b. 1833. Ex- [4749] periences of a New York clerk. N.Y.: F. R. Reed, 1877. 125 p. DLC. The author was employed in manufacturing and merchandising companies.

Reed, J. Harvey. Forty years a [4750] locomotive engineer... Prescott: C. H. O'Neil, 1913. 148 p. DLC. As described by the title.

Reed, Joseph Verner, b. 1902. [4751] The curtain falls. N.Y.: Harcourt, Brace, 1935. 282 p. DLC. New York theatrical producer.

Reed, Nathaniel, b. 1862. The life [4752] of Texas Jack. Tulsa: Tulsa pr. co., 1936? 55 p. TxU. Texas desperado.

Reed, Seth, 1823-1924. The story [4753] of my life. Cinc.: Jennings & Graham, 1914. 94 p. DLC. Methodist clergyman in Michigan and Rhode Island.

Reemelin, Charles, b. 1814. Life [4754] of Charles Reemelin...from 1814-1892. Cinc.: Weier & Daiker, printers, 1892. 369 p. WHi. Born in Germany. Farmer, lawyer and political figure in Ohio.

Reese, Clarence Herbert, b.1882. [4755] Pastoral adventure. N.Y.: Fleming

H. Revell, 1938. 205 p. DLC. Episcopalian clergyman in the District of Columbia, Texas, and Pa. During the first World War he was a chaplain in France.

Reese, Lizette Woodworth, 1856- [4756] 1935. A Victorian village... N.Y.: Farrar & Rinehart, 1929. 285 p. WU. School teacher in Maryland, and poet.

Reese, Lizette Woodworth, 1856- [4757] 1935. The York road. N.Y.: Farrar & Rinehart, 1931. 292 p. WU. Youth in Maryland. See also the preceding item.

Regensteiner, Theodore, b.1868. [4758] My first seventy-five years... Chicago: 1943. 285 p. Auto., p. 11-208. DLC. Printer and engraver in Chicago, born in Germany.

Reichenback, Harry, 1882-1931. [4759] Phantom fame. N.Y.: Simon & Schuster, 1931. 258 p. NN. A theatrical press agent tells of his exploits.

Reid, Dudley, b. 1872. Ups and [4760] downs... Des Moines: Monitor press, 1936. 408 p. DLC. Newspaper editor in Missouri and Iowa, and school teacher in Missouri.

Reid, Mayne, 1818-1883. Mayne [4761] Reid, a memoir of his life, by Elizabeth Reid, his widow. London: Ward & Downey, 1890. 277 p. CLSM. Novelist, and participant in the War with Mexico, born in Ireland. Various sections of this book were written by Reid.

Reinsch, Paul Samuel, 1869- [4762] 1923. An American diplomat in China. Garden City: Doubleday, Page, 1922. 396 p. WHi. During 1913-1919.

Remington, Franklin, b. 1865. [4763] Brawn and brains; the adventures of an international contractor. Boston: Bruce Humphries, 1945. 217 p. WU. Engineering contractor whose work carried him to Turkey, Italy and the Balkan peninsula.

Reminiscences of travel. See Clark, Austin S.

Renick, William, b. 1804. Mem- [4764] oirs, correspondence and reminiscences... Circleville: 1880. 115 p. Auto., p. 3-9. WHi. Ohio cattle raiser who sent his product to the eastern market.

Reno, John, b. 1839? The life of [4765] John Reno, the world's first train robber. Seymour, Indiana: pr. by Robert W. Shields, 1940. 48 p. NN. Robber, outlaw in Missouri, Illinois and Ohio.

Reno, Loren Marion, b. 1872. [4766] Reminiscences: twenty-five years in Victoria Brazil. Richmond, Va.: Educational department, Foreign mission board, 1930. 170 p. DLC. Baptist missionary in Brazil.

Replogle, Charles. Among the [4767] Indians of Alaska. London: Headley bros., 1904. 182 p. OrNeGF. Missionary representing the Society of Friends in Alaska.

Repplier, Agnes. In our convent [4768] days. Boston: Houghton Mifflin, 1905. 257 p. WU. An account of youthful days in a convent school.

Restarick, Henry Bond, 1854- [4769] 1933. My personal recollections; the unfinished memoirs of Henry Bond Restarick, bishop of Honolulu, 1902-1920. Honolulu, H.T.: pr. by Paradise of the Pacific press, 1938. 343 p. NN. English-born Episcopal clergyman. Early life in England and Iowa; church work in California; comparatively little on Hawaii.

Revell, Nellie. Right off the [4770] chest. N.Y.: George H. Doran co., 1923. 337 p. NN. A newspaper woman and press agent tells of her four years as a hospital patient.

Revere, Joseph Warren, 1812- [4771] 1880. Keel and saddle... Boston: James R. Osgood, 1872. 360 p. WHi. Naval officer, who after his resignation from the Navy served in the Union army.

Reynolds, Caeser, 1803-1833. [4772] Confessions of two malefactors, Teller & Reynolds... Hartford: Hammer & Comstock, printers, 1833. p. 50-75. DLC. Thief, murderer in Connecticut.

Reynolds, John, 1788-1865. My [4773] own times embracing also the history of my life... Belleville: pr. by B. H. Perryman, 1855. 600 p. WHi. Lawyer and politician in Illinois, member of the U.S. Congress.

Reynolds, John N. The twin [4774] hells... Atchison: Bee pub. co., 1890. 331 p. DLC. An account of his prison experiences in Kansas. The autobiographical portions are found mainly within pages 13-78, and 223-252. The author was convicted for using the mails to defraud.

Reynolds, Silas E. See Eyland, Seth (pseud.).

Rhea, J. H., b. 1827. Thirty years [4775] in Arkansaw... Cedar Rapids: Republican pr. co., 1896. 84 p. Auto., p. 7-33. IaHi. Covers 1829-59. The author tells of his youth on a pioneer farm and of his teaching career.

Rhodes, James Ford, b. 1848. [4776] James Ford Rhodes, American historian, by M. A. DeWolfe Howe. N.Y.: Appleton, 1929. 376 p. Auto., p. 17-29. WHi. Covers to 1891 and tells mainly of the education which made it possible for him to become an historian.

Rice, Mrs. Alice Caldwell [4777] (Hegan). The inky way. N.Y.: Appleton-Century, 1940. 282 p. WU. Writer of children's books.

Rice, Cale Young, 1872-1943. [4778] Bridging the years. N.Y.: D. Appleton-Century, 1939. 269 p. NN. Literary life and friendships of a poet.

Rice, Edward LeRoy, b. 1871. [4779] Monarchs of minstrelsy... N.Y.: Kenny pub. co., 1911. 366 p. Auto., p. 1-4. DLC. Minstrel.

Rice, Edwin Wilbur, 1831-1929. [4780] After ninety years. Phila.: Am. Sunday-School union, 1924. 167 p. WHi. Congregational clergyman who was employed by the Sunday School Union in Wisconsin and Minnesota. Later he edited the Union's publications and wrote many books on religious subjects.

Rice, John Andrew, b. 1888. I [4781] came out of the eighteenth century. N.Y.: Harper, 1942. 341 p. WU. Professor of literature at Nebraska.

Rice, Justin Robert, b. 1872. An [4782] autobiography... Logan?, Montana: 1901. 44 p. DLC. Evangelist who founded Christ's United Followers.

Rice, Mrs. Marguerette Isabella (Shields). See Rice, Justin Robert.

Rich, Louise (Dickinson). We [4783] took to the woods. Phila.: Lippincott, 1942. 322 p. DLC. A 20th century account of a woman's life with her family in the Maine forest.

Richards, Mrs. Anna Matlock. [4784] Memories of a grandmother, by a Lady of Massachusetts. Boston: Gould & Lincoln, 1854. 141 p. MB. Housewife in Massachusetts in the first half of the 19th century.

Richards, Arthur Wherry, b.1832. [4785] Progress of life and thought... Des Moines: Iowa pr. co., 1892. 363 p. DLC. Cabinet maker in Iowa who then served in the Union army.

Richards, Laura Elizabeth [4786] (Howe), 1850-1943. When I was your age. Boston: Estes & Lauriat, 1894. 210 p. NN. Recollections of a childhood in Boston, by the daughter of Julia Ward Howe.

Richards, Mrs. Laura Elizabeth [4787] (Howe), b. 1850. Stepping westward. N.Y.: Appleton, 1931. 405 p. WHi. Writer of literature for children.

Richards, Linda Ann Judson, [4788] 1841-1930. Reminiscences of... America's first trained nurse. Boston: Whitcomb & Barrows, 1911. 121 p. DLC. Superintendent of a training school for nurses in Massachusetts, who organized a training school in Japan for the American Board of Missions.

Richards, Lucy, 1792-1837. [4789] Memoirs... N.Y.: G. Lane & P. P. Sanford, 1842. 272 p. DLC. School teacher, member of the Methodist mission among the Oneida Indians in New York.

Richards, Robert. The Cali- [4790] fornian Crusoe... N.Y.: Stanford & Swords, 1854. 162 p. DLC. An Englishman who embraced Mormonism. He experienced the events affecting the Mormons in Illinois, and then in Utah.

Richards, Robert Hallowell, [4791] b. 1844. His mark. Boston: Little, Brown, 1936. 329 p. WU. Professor of mining engineering in Massachusetts, 1873-1914.

Richards, William, 1819-1899. [4792] On the road to home, and how two brothers got there. N.Y.: Benziger bros., 1895. 117 p. DLC. A spiritual account in which an Episcopalian tells of his conversion to Catholicism.

Richardson, Albert, 1833-1869. [4793]

The secret service, the field, the dungeon and the escape. Hartford: American pub. co., 1865. 512 p. DLC. A war correspondent assigned to the Union army tells of his adventures, including imprisonment at the hands of the Confederates.

Richardson, Clarence B. Pioneering western trails... No imprint. 9 p. WyU. The author was a printer in Wyoming, after which he was in the oil producing business. [4794]

Richardson, John, 1667-1753. An account... 3d ed. London: pr. by Mary Hinde, 1774. 242 p. WHi. Minister of the Society of Friends, born in England, who served in various states in the region of the Atlantic coast (north and south), and in Pa. [4795]

Richardson, Mrs. Mary (Walsham) Few, b. 1821. Scenes in the eventful life of... Columbus: W. G. Hubbard & co., 1894. 266 p. DLC. The author, born in England, was engaged in the millinery business in New Hampshire, and was active in temperance work. [4796]

Richardson, Merrick Abner, b. 1841. Looking back... Chicago: 1917. 349 p. DLC. Chicago manufacturer and writer of tales. [4797]

Richardson, Norval, b. 1877. My diplomatic education. N.Y.: Dodd, Mead, 1923. 337 p. WHi. The author served as Secretary to the American embassy in a number of foreign countries. [4798]

Richardson, Simon Peter, 1818-1899. The light and shadows of itinerant life... Nashville: Methodist Epis. Church, South, 1901. 288 p. TxDaM. Methodist clergyman in Georgia and Florida. [4799]

Richmond, Allen. The first twenty years of my life. Phila.: American Sunday-school union, 1859. 268 p. DLC. A New England farm boy sows wild oats in New York. Remorseful, he returns to New England and is apprenticed to a carpenter. [4800]

Richter, William. Life of William Richter, ten years with the Chippewa Indians... Lansing: W. S. George & co., printers, 1873. 16 p. MiD-B. Trapper and hunter in Michigan, beginning with 1842. [4801]

Rickard, Thomas Arthur, b. 1864.[4802] Retrospect... N.Y.: Whittlesey house, 1937. 402 p. WU. An engineer, born in England, who had considerable experience in the U.S. The author was an editor of mining journals and an historian of mining.

Rickenbacker, Edward Vernon. [4803] Fighting the flying circus. N.Y.: F. A. Stokes co., 1919. 371 p. WHi. World War I account.

Ricketson, Daniel, 1813-1898. [4804] Daniel Ricketson, autobiographic and miscellaneous. New Bedford, Mass.: E. Anthony & sons, 1910. NN. Historian and poet of New Bedford, Mass. The autobiographic material occupies p. 1-66; the remainder of the volume consists of correspondence.

Ricketts, William Pendleton, [4805] b. 1859. 50 years in the saddle. Sheridan: Star pub. co., 1942. 198 p. TxU. Cowboy and rancher in Wyoming. In 1911 he became a member of the Oklahoma legislature.

Riddick, Isaac Hancock, b. 1846. [4806] Four score and five... N.p.: pr. by Riddick bros., n.d. 40 p. MiD-B. Methodist clergyman in Michigan and Minnesota.

Riddle, George W., b. 1839. [4807] History of early days in Oregon... Riddle: Riddle enterprise, 1920. 74 p. CSmH. Farmer and Indian fighter in pioneer Oregon, beginning with 1851.

Ridenour, Peter D., b. 1831. [4808] Autobiography... Kansas City: Hudson press, 1908. 323 p. WHi. Kansas merchant.

Rideout, Mrs. Jacob Barzilla. [4809] Six years on the border. Phila.: Presbyterian board of publication, 1883. 221 p. WHi. Wife of a clergyman on the "prairie" in the seventies.

Ridgway, Charles. Through the [4810] Golden Gate... Yokohama: 1923. 79 p. CSmH. A carpenter on the West Coast, beginning with 1870.

Ridgway, Robert, 1862-1938. [4811] Robert Ridgway. N.Y.: 1940. 370 p. DLC. Engineer connected with railroads in Montana and Wisconsin, and with street railways, water supply in New York, and with subways in New York and Illinois.

Riegelman, Harold, b. 1892. War [4812]

notes of a casual. N.Y.: 1931. 191 p. DLC. Soldier in France during the first World War, and New York lawyer.

Riehlé, Frederick A. Fifty years [4813] of a business man's life; reminiscences. Phila.: 1916. 50 p. DLC. Manufacturer of testing machinery in Pa.

Riesenberg, Felix, 1879-1939. [4814] Living again; an autobiography. Garden City, N.Y.: Doubleday, Doran, 1937. 339 p. NN. Sailor, engineer, author.

Riesenberg, Felix, 1879-1939. [4815] Under sail. N.Y.: Macmillan, 1919. 424 p. WU. A personal account of a voyage around Cape Horn in a wooden sailing ship which left New York in December, 1897.

Riesenfeld, Janet. Dancer in [4816] Madrid. N.Y.: Funk & Wagnalls, 1938. 298 p. NN. Memories of the Civil War in Madrid.

Riggs, Charles Eugene, 1853- [4817] 1930. Reminiscences of a neurologist. Reprinted from Minnesota Medicine, January, 1928. 11 p. MnHi. In Minnesota, beginning with the eighties.

Riggs, Mrs. Mary Buel (Hatch), [4818] 1839-1927. Early days at Santee... Santee: Santee normal training school, 1928. 70 p. NbHi. Written by the wife of a mission worker in Nebraska, who went out to work with Indians in 1870.

Riggs, Stephen Return, 1812- [4819] 1883. Mary and I. Forty years with the Sioux. Chicago: W. G. Holmes, 1880. 388 p. WHi. Missionary in the upper Midwest, and writer on Indian language.

Rihbany, Abraham Mitre. A far [4820] journey. N.Y.: Houghton Mifflin, 1914. 351 p. WHi. An immigrant from Syria tells of his Americanization. Among his experiences was that of editing an Arabic newspaper.

Riis, Jacob August, 1849-1914. [4821] The making of an American. N.Y.: Macmillan, 1902. 443 p. WHi. New York journalist and political reformer, born in Denmark.

Riis, Sergius Martin, b. 1883. [4822] Yankee komisar, by Commander S. M. Riis, former U.S. naval attache in Russia. N.Y.: Robert Speller, 1935. 236 p. NN. Experiences during the Russian revolution of 1917.

Riker, Frederic H. Riker of the [4823] seven seas. N.Y.: Ray Long & Richard R. Smith, 1933. 279 p. NN. A sailor's adventures in various parts of the world.

Riley, Ralph (pseud.). See Brown, John, b. 1843.

Rinehart, Mary (Roberts), b.1876.[4824] My story. N.Y.: Farrar & Rinehart, 1931. 432 p. NN. The writer tells of her hospital training, her literary career as a novelist, and her experiences as a war correspondent.

Ripley, Eliza Moore (Chinn) [4825] McHatton, 1832-1912. From flag to flag; a woman's adventures and experiences in the South during the war, in Mexico, and in Cuba... N.Y.: D. Appleton & co., 1889. 296 p. NN. The experiences of a civilian in the South during the Civil War.

Ripley, Thomas Emerson. A [4826] Vermont boyhood. N.Y.: Appleton-Century, 1937. 234 p. DLC. As described by the title.

Risley, John E., b. 1802. Some [4827] experiences of a Methodist itinerant. Boston: pr. for the author, 1882. 143 p. NjMD. In New England.

Ritchie, Mrs. Anna Cora (Ogden)[4828] Mowatt, 1819-1870. Autobiography of an actress... Boston: Ticknor, Reed & Fields, 1854. 448 p. WU. As described by the title.

Rittenhouse, Jessie Belle. My [4829] house of life... Boston: Houghton Mifflin, 1934. 335 p. WU. Poetry critic and anthologist.

Rittenhouse, Rufus, b. 1825. Boy-[4830] hood life in Iowa. Dubuque: C.B. Dorr, printer, 1880. 23 p. IaHi. On a farm.

Ritter, Jacob, 1757-1841. Mem- [4831] oirs of Jacob Ritter, a faithful minister in the Society of Friends. By Joseph Foulke. Phila.: T. E. Chapman, 1844. 111 p. Auto., p. 2-42. DLC. In Pennsylvania. The author saw service in the Revolutionary army.

Ritter, Mrs. Mary (Bennett), [4832] b. 1860. More than gold in California, 1849-1933. Berkeley: 1933. 451 p. DLC. California teacher and physician, active in work with citizen health groups.

Rixey, Presley Marion, 1852– [4833] 1928. The life story of Presley Marion Rixey... Strasburg, Va.: Shenandoah pub. house, 1930. 518 p. Auto., p. 179–484. WHi. Surgeon-General of the U.S.Navy.

Rizk, Salom, b. 1909. Syrian [4834] Yankee. Garden City: Doubleday, Doran, 1943. 317 p. WHi. A story of Americanization, written by a lecturer.

Robbins, Harvey, b. 1824. The [4835] adventures and escapes of Harvey Robbins... Baltimore: pr. by Sherwood & co., 1861. 22 p. DLC. The author served in the War against Mexico, and was later a guide in the Union army. Between wars he was a farmer in Virginia.

Robbins, Mrs. Sarah (Stuart), [4836] b. 1817. Old Andover days; memories of a Puritan childhood. Boston: The Pilgrim press, 1908. 188 p. CBPac. The writer's father was a clergyman who came to Andover in 1810.

Robbins, Walter Raleigh, 1843– [4837] 1923. War record and personal experiences... Chicago?: priv. pr., 1923. 220 p. WHi. Union army officer.

Robert, the hermit, b. 1769?Life [4838] and adventures of Robert, the hermit of Massachusetts, who lived 14 years in a cave... Taken from his own mouth, by Henry Trumbull. Providence: pr. for H. Trumbull, 1829. 36 p. CSmH. Born in bondage of a white father and Negro mother. Upon his escape he became a hermit.

Roberts, DeWitt C. Southern [4839] sketches... Jacksonville: D.W. Roberts, 1865. 142 p. LNHT Printer in various southern states. The book is mainly that of a civilian recording his experiences in the time of the Civil War, from the viewpoint of a Union sympathizer.

Roberts, Florence. Fifteen years [4840] with the outcast. Anderson, Ind.: Gospel trumpet co., 1912. 472 p. NN. The author did mission work in California in prisons, dance halls, etc.

Roberts, Isaac Phillips, b. 1833. [4841] Autobiography of a farm boy. Albany: J.B. Lyon, 1916. 331 p. WU. Professor of Agriculture at Cornell and at Iowa State College.

Roberts, J.N. Reminiscences [4842] of the Civil war. No imprint. 56 p. KU. Union army.

Roberts, James, b. 1753. The [4843] narrative of James Roberts, soldier in the Revolutionary war, and at the battle of New Orleans. Hattiesburg: Book farm, 1945. 32 p. CU. Negro slave life, and military service.

Roberts, Lemuel, b. 1751. Mem- [4844] oirs of...a Continental soldier. Bennington: pr. by Anthony Haswell, 1809. 96 p. DLC. As described by the title.

Roberts, Mrs. Lou (Conway). A [4845] woman's reminiscences of six years in camp with the Texas Rangers... Austin: press of von Boeckmann-Jones, n.d. 64 p. TxGR. By the wife of a Texas Ranger. The period covered is 1875–1881.

Roberts, Ralph R. A successful [4846] mail order business on five dollars. Kansas City: Roberts pr. co., 1933. 199 p. MoK. The locale is Missouri, and the time is the 20th century.

Roberts, Thomas, 1783–1865. [4847] Memorial of Thomas Roberts... Newark: Starbuck, Jennings & bros., 1867. 278 p. Auto., p. 13–40. DLC. The author, born in Wales, was a Baptist clergyman who served in New York, New Jersey and Pennsylvania.

Roberts, Thomas D., b. 1849. [4848] Means and ways... Boston: James H. Earle, 1893. 141 p. CBPac. The author was born in England. First a jockey, he became an evangelist and in 1888 was made Superintendent of the Boston Industrial Home.

Robertson, George, 1790–1874. [4849] An outline of the life of George Robertson... Lexington: Transylvania pr. co., 1876. 209 p. WHi. Kentucky political and legal figure.

Robertson, George F., b. 1853. [4850] A small boy's recollections of the Civil War... Clover, S.C.: G. F. Robertson, 1932. 116 p. DLC. In Tennessee.

Robie, Bertha E. (Little), b.1866.[4851] A commonplace life. Baldwinville (!): 1929. 342 p. DLC. A

A domestic account by the wife of a physician. The author, active in civil affairs, lived in Michigan, Vermont and Massachusetts.

Robinson, Arthur J., b. 1845. [4852] Memorandum and anecdotes of the Civil war, 1862-1865... Portland, Ore.: pr. by Glass & Prudhomme, 1910. 38 p. WaU. In the Union army.

Robinson, D.G. The life and ad- [4853] ventures of the reformed inebriate, D.G.Robinson, M.D. Boston: Robinson & Graham, 1846. 142 p. DLC. Upon reforming himself, the author became a writer on the subject of temperance.

Robinson, Elsie, b. 1883. I want- [4854] ed out! N.Y.: Farrar & Rinehart, 1934. 299 p. NN. An unconventional newspaper columnist tells of her struggle with the puritanical conventions of New England and how she finally achieved a career.

Robinson, Ezekiel Gilman, 1815- [4855] 1894. Ezekiel Gilman Robinson, an autobiography... Boston: Silver, Burdett & co., 1896. 381 p. Auto., p. 3-122. NN. Baptist clergyman who became professor of theology and president of Brown University.

Robinson, Frank Bruce, b. 1886. [4856] The strange autobiography of Frank B. Robinson, founder of "Psychiana". Mowcow: 1941. 284 p. DLC. A druggist, born in England, revolts against organized religion and develops "Psychiana".

Robinson, Frank Bruce. Life [4857] story... Moscow: pr. by Review pub. co., 1934. 239 p. WaU. See the preceding item.

Robinson, John Buchanan, [4858] b. 1846. Midshipman to Congress. Media: pub. priv., 1916. 323 p. DLC. After resigning his commission in the Navy, the author became a lawyer and politician in Pennsylvania.

Robinson, Josephine (DeMott), [4859] d. 1948. The circus lady. N.Y.: Thomas Y. Crowell, 1926. 304 p. NN. Memoirs of a bareback rider.

Robinson, V.W., b. 1856. A new [4860] pamphlet...containing an autobiographical sketch... No imprint. 66 p. Auto., p. 1-10. KHi. Baptist clergyman in Kansas.

Robinson, William Coburn, [4861] b. 1847. Footprints. No imprint. 76 p. KHi. Banker in Kansas, beginning with 1870. The autobiographical element in this book is slight.

Robinson, William Joseph, [4862] b. 1893. My fourteen months at the front... Boston: Little, Brown, & co., 1916. 201 p. DLC. With British army in France during first World War.

Robinson, William Josephus, [4863] 1867-1936. Doctor Robinson and St. Peter... N.Y.: Eugenics pub. co., 1931. 60 p. DLC. Proponent of birth control, and pacificism.

Robinson, William L. The diary [4864] of a Samaritan. By a member of the Howard Association of New Orleans... N.Y.: Harper, 1860. 324 p. DLC. The Howard Association provided medical aid to victims of epidemics, etc.

Robson, John S., b. 1844. How a [4865] one-legged rebel lives...Richmond: W.H.Wade & co., printers, 1876. 138 p. DLC. After serving in the Confederate army, the author became a tavern keeper in Virginia.

Robuck, J.E. My own personal [4866] experience... Birmingham: Leslie, 1911. 136 p. TxU. After serving in the Confederate army, the author became a merchant in Mississippi.

Roby, Henry W., 1842-1920. [4867] Henry W. Roby's story of the invention of the typewriter. Menasha: George Banta pub. co., 1925. 119 p. Auto., p. 21-89. DLC. Wisconsin inventor, who assisted Christopher Sholes, inventor of the typewriter.

Rochambeau, Jean Baptiste, [4868] 1725-1807. Memoirs of the Marshall Count de Rochambeau, relative to the War of Independence of the United States... Paris: 1838. 114 p. DLC. This account was extracted and translated from the original in French.

Roche, James Jeffrey, 1847- [4869] 1908. By-ways of war; the story of the filibusters. Boston: Small, Maynard & co., 1901. 251 p. DLC. Member of the Walker expedition which fought in Nicaragua, 1855-69.

Roche, John Alexander, b. 1813. [4870] Autobiography and sermons...

N.p.: pr. by Eaton & Mains, n.d. 333 p. Auto., p. 28-152. TxDaM. Methodist clergyman in Maryland, Virginia, Pennsylvania, Delaware and New York.

Roche, Olin Scott, 1852-1935. [4871] Forty years of parish life and work, 1883-1923; an autobiography ... N.Y.: The Friebele press, 1930. 388 p. NN. Protestant Episcopal clergyman, New York City, 1890-1923.

Rochester, Nathaniel, 1752-1831. [4872] "Autobiography" (Fragments of revolutionary history, ed. by Gaillard Hunt. Brooklyn: Historical pr. club, 1892.) p. 99-105. NcU. Soldier in the War for independence.

Rock, William Marks, b. 1857. [4873] Pioneer days...Lyndon: Rose print shop, 1929. 57 p. DLC. Farmer, painter and paperhanger, undertaker. The locale is Kansas.

Rockefeller, John Davison, 1839- [4874] 1937. Random reminiscences of men and events. N.Y.: Doubleday, Page & co., 1909. 188 p. WHi. Ohio producer and distributor of oil.

Rockefellow, John Alexander, [4875] b. 1858. Log of an Arizona trail blazer. Tucson: Acme pr. co., 1933. 201 p. DLC. Miner and rancher in Arizona.

Rockne, Knute Kenneth, 1888- [4876] 1931. The autobiography of Knute K. Rockne. Indianapolis: The Bobbs-Merrill co., 1931. 296 p. NN. Football coach at Notre Dame University.

Rockwell, Alphonso David, 1840- [4877] 1933. Rambling recollections. N.Y.: Hoeber, 1920. 332 p. WU. Physician and teacher of medicine in New York.

Rockwell, Frederick Kress, [4878] 1871-1898. The life and confession of Frederick Kress Rockwell... Being a verbatim stenographic report of his last words... Ridgeway, Pa.: Elk Democrat, 1898. 36 p. DLC. Murderer in Pa.

Rockwood, Charles Robinson. [4879] Born of the desert. Calexico, Cal.: Calexico chronicle, 1930. 44 p. CSmH. The author, beginning with 1892, was a leader in the irrigation and reclamation of land in California.

Rodgers, James B. Forty years [4880] in the Philippines... N.Y.: Board of foreign missions of the Presbyterian Church, 1940. 205 p. WHi. An account of the Presbyterian mission to the Philippines, 1899-1939, in which the author includes his own contribution.

Rodman, Hugh, b. 1859. Yarns of [4881] a Kentucky admiral. Indianapolis: Bobbs-Merrill, 1928. 320 p. WHi. The author rose to the rank of Rear Admiral in the U.S. Navy.

Rodney, George Brydges, b.1872. [4882] As a cavalryman remembers. Caldwell: Caxton printers, 1944. 297 p. WHi. The author served in the War against Spain, in Hawaii and in the western portion of the U.S. The period covered is 1898-1932.

Rodriguez, Jose Policarpo, [4883] b. 1829. "The old guide"... Nashville: Publishing house of the Methodist Epis. Church, South, n.d. 121 p. TxU. The locale is Texas. Rodriguez was hunter, rancher, and Methodist minister.

Roe, Edward Payson, 1838-1888. [4884] Taken alive, and other stories; with an autobiography. N.Y.: Dodd, Mead & co., 1892. 375 p. Auto., p. 7-34. DLC. Chaplain in the Union army. Protestant clergyman in New York. Novelist.

Roe, Mrs. Elizabeth A., b.1805. [4885] Recollections of frontier life. Rockford?: 1895? 295 p. MoHi. The author was married to a clergyman of the Methodist faith, serving in Illinois and Kentucky. The family was also engaged in farming—in Illinois from about 1830 to 1860, and then in Nebraska.

Rogers, Ammi, 1770-1852. Mem- [4886] oirs... 5th ed. Concord: Fisk & Chase, 1833. 264 p. WHi. Episcopalian clergyman in Connecticut.

Rogers, Mrs. Aurelia (Spencer), [4887] b. 1834. N.p.: pr. by Geo. Q. Cannon, 1898. 333 p. UU. The author left Illinois with her Mormon parents in 1848 for Utah. There she became prominent in the education of the young, and taught school.

Rogers, Mrs. Clara Kathleen [4888] (Barnett), 1849-1931. Memories of a musical career. Norwood: pr. at the Plimpton press, 1932. 503 p. WU. An English singer who performed several times in the U.S.

Rogers, Clara Kathleen (Barnett) [4889] 1844-1931. The story of two lives... Norwood: Plimpton press, 1932. 348 p. WU. An English singer tells mainly of her married life. See also the preceding item.

Rogers, George. Memoranda of [4890] the experience, labors and travels of a Universalist preacher. Cinc.: Gurley, 1845. 400 p. MH. In Pennsylvania and in various states of the South Atlantic region. The period covered is roughly the thirties of the 19th century.

Rogers, Henry Munroe, b.1839. [4891] Memories of ninety years. Boston: Houghton Mifflin, 1928. 409 p. WHi. Boston lawyer.

Rogers, John Almanza Rowley, [4892] 1828-1906. Birth of Berea college... Phila.: 1903. 174 p. Auto., p. 47-65. DLC. Congregational clergyman who was one of the founders of Berea College in Kentucky.

Rogers, Mrs. Martha A.(Knight), [4893] b. 1842. The saga of Grandma Rogers. No imprint. 55 p. TxDaM. An account of frontier life in Texas, especially as it relates to the lay work done by the author for the Methodist church.

Rogers, R. C. My wife and I. [4894] Mementos for our children. San Francisco: 1871. 440 p. C. Lawyer and politician in California in the early fifties.

Rogers, Samuel, 1789-1877. Auto-[4895] biography... Cinc.: Standard pub. co., 1880. 208 p. WHi. Clergyman of the Christian Church in Kentucky, Ohio, Missouri and Virginia.

Rogers, William Allen, 1854- [4896] 1931. A world worth while...N.Y.: Harper & bros., 1922. 305 p. NN. Cartoonist and illustrator.

Rogers, William H. The great [4897] Civil war. Personal experiences ... Boston?: 1884? 14 p. MnHi. Union army.

Rohlf, William Amos, b. 1867. [4898] "Good morning, doctor!" Cedar Rapids, Iowa: The Torch press, 1938. 169 p. NN. Recollections of a country surgeon in Iowa.

Rollinson, John K., b. 1882. [4899] Hoofprints of a cowboy and U.S. ranger; pony trails in Wyoming. Caldwell: Caxton printers, 1941. 410 p. WU. As described by the title.

Roman, Charles, b. 1874. A man [4900] remade... Chicago: Reilly & Britton, 1909. 172 p. DLC. Alcoholic and drug addict. The writer was a journalist in Washington, D.C.

Rombauer, Roderick Emile, [4901] b. 1833. The history of a life. St. Louis?: 1903. 146 p. WHi. The author, born in Hungary, was a lawyer and judge in Missouri.

Romig, Emily Craig. A pioneer [4902] woman in Alaska. Colorado Springs: priv. pr., 1945. 136 p. DLC. The author, born in Denmark, went to Alaska with her husband, who was a miner. Later she became a nurse.

Ronayne, Edmond, b. 1832. [4903] Ronayne's reminiscences... Chicago: Free Methodist pub. house, 1900. 445 p. DLC. An Irish immigrant who renounced Catholicism. Later, he denounced secret societies, lecturing on their evils.

Roney, Frank, 1841-1925. Frank [4904] Roney, Irish rebel and California labor leader; an autobiography. Berkeley, California: Univ. of Cal. press, 1931. 573 p. NN. Fenian movement in Ireland; labor leader in California, particularly 1876-86.

Ronning, Nils Nilsen, b. 1870. [4905] Fifty years in America. Minneapolis: Friend pub. co, 1938. 243 p. WHi. Editor of Friend, an independent Lutheran periodical, and author. Ronning was born in Norway. For an account of his youth, see the next item.

Ronning, Nils Nilsen, b. 1870. [4906] The boy from Telemark. Minneapolis: The Friend pub. co., 1933. 150 p. WU. See the preceding item.

Roosevelt, Mrs. Eleanor, b.1884. [4907] This is my story. N.Y.: Harper, 1937. 365 p. WHi. The wife of F.D.R. tells of her married life and of her political activities.

Roosevelt, Robert Barnwell, [4908] 1829-1906. Five acres too much... N.Y.: Harper, 1869. 296 p. DLC. A New York lawyer tells of his sad experiences in operating a farm.

Roosevelt, Theodore, 1858-1919. [4909]
Theodore Roosevelt, an autobiography. N.Y.: Macmillan, 1913. 647 p. WHi. Spanish American War; Governor of New York, twenty-sixth president of U.S.

Roosevelt, Theodore, b. 1887. [4910]
All in the family. N.Y.: Putnam, 1929. 189 p. WHi. An account of youth at Oyster Bay, by the son of the President.

Root, Frank Albert, 1837-1926. [4911]
The overland stage to California... Topeka: Crane, 1901. 630 p. NN. The author was employed by the U.S. Post Office to supervise the mails on the stage line from the Missouri River to the Pacific coast. Much of this book is autobiographical.

Root, George Frederick, 1820- [4912]
1895. The story of a musical life... Cinc.: The J. Church co., 1891. 256 p. Auto., p. 3-222. DLC. Chicago song writer, music teacher and publisher.

Root, Henry, b. 1845. Henry Root [4913] surveyor, engineer and inventor ... San Francisco: pr. for priv. circ., 1921. 134 p. DLC. The author engineered the San Francisco cable cars.

Roper, Daniel Calhoun, b.1867. [4914]
Fifty years of public life... Durham: Duke univ. press, 1941. 422 p. WHi. Commissioner of Internal Revenue, and Secretary of Commerce.

Roper, Moses. A narrative of the [4915] adventures and escape of Moses Roper from American slavery. 5th ed. London: Harvey & Darton, 1843. 122 p. WHi. As described by the title.

Rose, Isaac P., 1815-1899. Four [4916] years in the Rockies... by James B. Marsh. Newcastle: pr. by W.B. Thomas, 1884. 262 p. WHi. A dictated account, by a hunter, trapper and Indian fighter. The time covered is the 1830's.

Rosenbach, Abraham Simon [4917]
Wolf, b. 1876. A book hunter's holiday... Boston: Houghton Mifflin, 1936. 259 p. WU. Dealer in rare books.

Rosencrantz, Herman, 1716-1770.[4918]
The life and confession of Herman Rosencrantz; executed...for counterfeiting. Phila.: J. Chattin, 1770. 10 p. DLC. In Pennsylvania.

Rosendahl, Charles Emery. Up [4919] ship! N.Y.: Dodd, Mead, 1931. 311 p. Auto., p. 1-6, 39-203. DLC. Aviation officer in the U.S. Navy.

Rosenthal, Albert, 1863-1939. [4920]
Albert Rosenthal, painter, lithographer, etcher... Phila.: 1929. 21 p. Auto., p. 3-6. DLC. As described by the title.

Ross, Alexander, 1783-1856. Ad-[4921]
ventures of the first settlers on the Oregon or Columbia river: being a narrative of the expedition fitted out by John Jacob Astor, to establish the "Pacific Fur Company:" with an account of some Indian tribes on the coast of the Pacific. London: Smith, Elder & co., 1849. 352 p. DLC. Fur trader, born in Scotland.

Ross, Alexander, 1783-1856. The [4922] fur hunters of the far west; a narrative of adventures in the Oregon and Rocky Mountains. London: Smith, Elder & co., 1855. 2 vols. DLC. Agent for a British fur company.

Ross, Alexander Milton, 1832- [4923]
1897. Recollections and experiences of an abolitionist, from 1855 to 1865. Toronto: Rowsell & Hutchinson, 1875. 224 p. WHi. As described by the title.

Ross, Edward Alsworth, b. 1866. [4924]
Seventy years of it... N.Y.: Appleton-Century, 1936. 341 p. WU. Professor of sociology at Stanford and Wisconsin.

Ross, Mrs. Elizabeth (Williams). [4925]
A road of remembrance. Cinc.: Powell & White, 1921. 148 p. MoCanD. Lay church worker for the Christian Woman's Board of Missions, especially in Missouri and Iowa.

Ross, H. E. Experiences of a [4926] frontier preacher in southwest Kansas. Danville: 1941. 66 p. KU. Methodist clergyman, and printer, beginning about 1885.

Ross, Harvey Lee, b. 1817. The [4927] early pioneers and pioneer events of the state of Illinois... Chicago: Eastman bros., 1899. 199 p. DLC. Farmer, hotel keeper, Indian trader, postmaster in Illinois. Later Ross was active in the temperance movement in California.

Ross, Malcolm Harrison, b.1895. [4928] Death of a Yale man. N.Y.: Farrar & Rinehart, 1939. 385 p. NN. Evolution of a Yale graduate into a radical through contact with actual industrial conditions.

Ross, Mrs. Marie (Marchand), [4929] b. 1864. Child of Icaria. N.Y.: City pr. co., 1938. 147 p. DLC. An account of youthful days in a "communitarian" project.

Ross, William Cary, b. 1879. A [4930] scrapbook for my grandchildren. N.Y.: G. P. Putnam's sons, 1941. 350 p. NN. Tennessee merchant.

Rosser, Charles McDaniel, [4931] b. 1862. Doctors and doctors, wise and otherwise; on the firing line fifty years. Dallas: Mathis, Van Nort & co., 1941. 388 p. NN. Texas doctor.

Rotch, William. Memorandum [4932] written by William Rotch in the eightieth year of his age. Boston: Houghton Mifflin, 1916. 88 p. WHi. Merchant whaler. The time covered is 1775-1794.

Roth, Augustine Joseph. Out of [4933] the wilderness... 3d ed. Huntington, Ind.: Our Sunday visitor, 1936. 48 p. DLC. Baptist clergyman in Illinois who was converted to Catholicism.

Roth, Kelly, b. 1873. Experi- [4934] ences and travels of an immigrant boy... Los Angeles: 1944. 267 p. DLC. Merchant and real estate dealer in California, born in Hungary.

Roth, Louis. Louis Roth, forty [4935] years with jungle killers, by Dave Robeson. Caldwell, Idaho: The Caxton printers, 1941. 241 p. DLC. Circus animal trainer, born in Hungary. A dictated account.

Roth, Samuel, b. 1893. Stone [4936] walls do not. N.Y.: W. Fargo, 1930. 2 vols. DLC. Poet, born in Galicia.

Rothery, Agnes Edwards, b.1888. [4937] A fitting habitation. N.Y.: Dodd, Mead & co., 1944. 244 p. NN. The writer, author of travel books, tells of her various homes and travels.

Rothstein, Mrs. Carolyn (Green). [4938] Now I'll tell. N.Y.: Vanguard press, 1934. 255 p. DLC. Dancer who married Arnold Rothstein, an underworld figure in New York.

Rounds, Ona Mahitta, b. 1876. [4939] Buck privates on Parnassus. Boston: Meador, 1933. 217 p. DLC. In France as camp librarian for the American army, 1914-18.

Roundtree, Patrick Henry. Auto- [4940] biography. No imprint. 16 p. OrHi. Hotel keeper, freighter in Oregon; farmer, rancher in Washington. Time: the sixties of the 19th century.

Rounsevell, Nelson, b. 1877? The [4941] life story of "N.R."... Panama City: Panama American pub. co., 1933. 180 p. DLC. After an adventurous life the writer settled in Panama where he published a newspaper.

Rover, Ruth. See Bailey, Margaret Jewett.

Rowan, John. Autobiography of [4942] John Rowan, 1782-1785. (Tales of the dark and bloody ground, by Willard Rouse Jillson. Louisville: Dearing pr. co., 1930.) KyHi. Jurist, lawyer, politician in Kentucky and Pennsylvania. This is a brief account of eleven pages.

Rowe, Addie Frances, 1860-1938. [4943] ...An autobiographical sketch. Cambridge: Harvard univ. press, 1939. 27 p. DLC. Research assistant in the Harvard Library who helped scholars prepare books.

Rowe, Joseph Andrew, 1819-1887. [4944] California's pioneer circus. Joseph Andrew Rowe, founder... San Francisco: pr. by H. S. Crocker, 1926. 98 p. DLC. As described by the title. The period covered is the fifties of the 19th century.

Rowell, George Presbury, 1838- [4945] 1908. Forty years an advertising agent, 1865-1905. N.Y.: Printer's ink, 1906. 517 p. WU. Founder of the advertising journal, Printer's Ink.

Royce, Josiah, 1855-1916. Words [4946] of Professor Royce at the Walton Hotel at Philadelphia, December 29, 1915. (In his: The hope of the great community. N.Y.: 1916.) p. 123-136. NN. Professor of philosophy at Harvard tells mainly of his training as a graduate student in Germany.

Royce, Sarah (Bayliss), b. 1819. [4947] A frontier lady; recollections of the gold rush and early California.

New Haven: Yale univ. press, 1932. 144 p. NN. Experiences in a mining camp in 1849.

Rudolph, Joseph, 1841-1934. [4948] ...Early life and Civil war reminiscences of Captain Joseph Rudolph. Ann Arbor, Mich.: Edwards bros., 1941. 36 p. NN. Union army soldier.

Rue, Larry. I fly for news. N.Y.: [4949] Boni, 1932. 307 p. DLC. Foreign correspondent in Afghanistan, Austria, Turkey, Egypt, Morocco.

Rufus, Maude (Squire), b.1880. [4950] Flying grandma; or, going like sixty. Ypsilanti, Mich.: Univ. lithoprinters, 1942. 168 p. NN. Experiences of an amateur woman flyer.

Ruggles, C. Lorain, b. 1823. [4951] Four years a scout and spy... for the Federal army... Zanesville: Hugh Dunne, 1866. 404 p. DLC. Written down by E.C. Downs. Ruggles was a scout for Grant, Sherman, etc.

Ruh, Martin Pedersen, 1841- [4952] 1923. Erindringer... Eau Claire: Fremad pub. co., 1922. 79 p. MnNS. Lutheran clergyman in Wisconsin, Minnesota and Iowa.

Ruhl, Arthur Brown. Antwerp to [4953] Gallipoli; a year of the war. N.Y.: Scribner, 1916. 304 p. NjP. An account dealing with the first World War.

Rumbaugh, Jacob, b. 1839. Rem- [4954] iniscences. Kansas City: Franklin Hudson pub. co., 1910. 103 p. WHi. Kansas farmer.

Rumberger, Frank H., 1859- [4955] 1882. Life and confession of Frank H. Rumberger... Harrisburg: Rumberger & St. Clair, 1882. 56 p. DLC. Petty criminal who finally commits murder in Pa.

Rümelin, Charles. See Reemelin, Charles.

Runcie, Constance Owen, b. 1836.[4956] Divinely led; or, Robert Owen's granddaughter. N.Y.: James Pott, 1880. 36 p. CBCh. A spiritual account in which the author is converted to the Episcopalian church.

Rush, Benjamin, 1745-1813. A [4957] memorial... ed. by Louis A. Biddle. Phila.: 1905. 262 p. Auto., p. 9-130. WHi. Physician in Pa., and professor of medicine.

Rush, William Marshall, b.1887. [4958] Wild animals of the Rockies; adventures of a forest ranger. N.Y.: Harper, 1942. 296 p. WU. As described by the title.

Russell, Arthur Joseph, b. 1861. [4959] Good-bye newspaper row... Excelsior: Minnetonka record press, 1943. 65 p. MnHi. Minnesota editor and publisher. See also his Fourth Street.

Russell, Mrs. Blanche Nichols, [4960] b. 1871. Memoirs of a pioneer school ma'am. Gering: Courier press, n.d. 143 p. NbHi. Nebraska school teacher, beginning about 1890. More is told of her travels than of her career.

Russell, Charles Edward, b.1860.[4961] Bare hands and stone walls; some recollections of a sideline reformer. N.Y.: Scribner, 1933. 441 p. WHi. Economic and social reformer.

Russell, David, b. 1789. Auto- [4962] biography of David Russell, a Boston boy and true American. An account of his travels, romantic adventures, and hair-breadth escapes, by sea and land, in peace and war, at home and abroad, from the age of sixteen years to sixty-seven... Boston: pr. for the author, 1857. 372 p. NN. Adventures in the War of 1812 and in various parts of the world.

Russell, Henry, 1812-1900. [4963] Cheer! Boys, Cheer! Memories of men and music. London: J. Macqueen, 1895. 276 p. DLC. English pianist and composer who spent several years in the U.S.

Russell, Henry, 1871-1937. The [4964] passing show. Boston: Little, Brown & co., 1926. 295 p. DLC. English musician who was made Director of the Boston Opera House.

Russell, James Earl, b. 1864. [4965] Founding Teachers College... N.Y.: Columbia univ., 1937. 106 p. Auto., p. 3-70. WU. By the man who was its Dean for 30 years.

Russell, Lyman Brightmann, [4966] b. 1850. Granddad's autobiography. Comanche: n.d. 30 p. TxH. Texas merchant, lawyer, banker and politician.

Russell, Osborne. Journal of a [4967] trapper; or, nine years in the

Rocky Mountains, 1834-1843. Boise: 1914. 105 p. WHi. As described by the title.

Ruth, Francis Jacob, b. 1805. [4968] The life and work of... Plymouth, Ohio: Advertiser steam pr. house, 1888. 183 p. Auto., p. 5-94. WHi. Lutheran clergyman in Ohio.

Rutledge, Catherine, b. 1833. [4969] "Experience" (Twenty-five years fighting fate, by Samuel W. Shockey. Boston: 1892.) p. 157-189. TxU. A spiritual account by a Methodist.

Rutzebeck, Hjalmar. Alaska [4970] man's luck... N.Y.: Boni & Liveright, 1920. 260 p. DLC. Born in Denmark, Rutzebeck came to Alaska to farm and mine, and to write.

Rutzebeck, Hjalmar. My Alaskan [4971] idyll. N.Y.: Boni & Liveright, 1922. 296 p. DLC. A supplement to the preceding item.

Rux (pseud.). See Devereux, Hyacinthe Daly.

Ryan, John Augustine, b. 1869. [4972] Social doctrine in action; a personal history. N.Y.: Harper, 1941. 297 p. WU. By the Director of the Social Action Department, National Catholic Welfare Conference, who was also a priest and professor at Catholic University of America.

Ryan, Patrick J., b. 1852. Patrick J. Ryan remembers... [4973] Twin Lakes: priv. pr., 1943. 16 p. CoD. Blacksmith and owner of stage line in Colorado. The account ends with 1909.

Ryan, Thomas, 1827-1903. Recollections of an old musician. N.Y.: [4974] Dutton, 1899. 274 p. DLC. Violinist in Boston, born in Ireland.

Ryan, William Redmond. Personal adventures in upper and [4975] lower California, in 1848-9; with the author's experience at the mines. London: W. Shoberl, 1850. 2 vols. DLC. The author was born in England.

Rydell, Carl, b. 1859. Adventures [4976] of Carl Rydell; the autobiography of a seafaring man. London: Edward Arnold & co., 1924. 308 p. NN. Early experiences as an apprentice in the Swedish navy; later as a sailor in Alaskan waters; with the Coast Guard in the Philippines.

Ryder, James Fitzallan, b. 1826. [4977] Voigtländer and I in pursuit of shadow catching... Cleveland: Cleveland pr. & pub. co., 1902. 251 p. Auto., p. 13-228. DLC. Photographer in Ohio.

Ryder, Richard H., b. 1843. The [4978] village color-bearer. Together with a story of a U.S. life-saving service keeper. Brooklyn: G.S. Patton, 1891. 200 p. DLC. The author served in the Union army and then was a guard at a swimming beach in New York (employed by the U.S. Life-Saving Service).

Ryder, William, b. 1805. The [4979] superannuate... N.Y.: G. Lane & C. B. Tippett, 1845. 160 p. DLC. Methodist clergyman in New York.

Ryer, John, 1759-1793. Narrative of the life, and dying speech, [4980] of John Ryer: who was executed at White-Plains, in the county of Westchester, state of New-York, on the second day of October, 1793, for the murder of Dr. Isaac Smith, deputy-sheriff of that county. Danbury: pr. by Nathan Douglas, for the publisher, 1793. 15 p. NN. As described by the title.

Ryland, Zenophon, b. 1844. Biographical sketch...with an auto- [4981] biography. N.p.: 1920. 80 p. Auto., p. 45-78. MoHi. Missouri lawyer and judge who at age 47 decided to become a Presbyterian minister.

Rynning, Thomas Harbo, b.1866. [4982] Gun notches...N.Y.: F.A. Stokes, 1931. 332 p. WHi. Arizona ranger, and Rough Rider in the War with Spain.

Ryus, William Henry, b. 1839. [4983] The second William Penn; a true account of incidents that happened along the old Santa Fe trail in the sixties. Kansas City, Mo.: Press of Frank T. Riley pub. co., 1913. 176 p. DLC. Stage coach driver.

# S

Sacajawea, 1787?-1812. "Bird [4984] woman's story of her capture". (Bird woman, by James W. Schultz. Boston: Houghton Mifflin, 1916. 235 p.) p. 63-111. WHi. Indian guide for Lewis and Clarke.

Sachs, Julius, 1849-1934. Reminiscences of German University [4985] days. N.Y.: 1917. 14 p. NNC. A university professor tells of his student days.

Sagatoo, Mary A. (Henderson) [4986] Cabay. Wah sash kah moqua; or, thirty-three years among the Indians. Boston: C.A.White co., 1897. 140 p. DLC. A white woman marries an Indian and together they go to the Chippewas in Michigan as missionaries.

Sage, Lee. The last rustler. [4987] Boston: Little, Brown, 1930. 303 p. WHi. Cowboy, rustler, moonshiner, in the Rocky Mountain area and in the Southwest.

Sage, Rufus B., b. 1817. Rocky [4988] Mountain life...during an expedition of three years. Boston: Thayer & Eldridge, 1860. 363 p. WHi. Member of an expedition seeking trade with the Indians in the Rocky Mountain region. Also, his experiences as a soldier on the Mexican border.

St. Clair, Labert. I've met the [4989] folks you read about... N.Y.: Dodd, Mead, 1940. 308 p. WU. Correspondent for the Associated Press.

St. Denis, Ruth, b. 1880. Ruth [4990] St. Denis, an unfinished autobiography. N.Y.: Harper, 1939. 391 p. WU. Dancer.

Saint-Gaudens, Augustus, 1848– [4991] 1907. The reminiscences of August Saint-Gaudens. N.Y.: Century, 1913. 2 vols. WU. Sculptor.

Salisbury, William, b. 1875. The [4992] career of a journalist. N.Y.: B.W. Dodge, 1908. 529 p. WU. In Nebraska, Kansas, Illinois.

Sallada, William Henry, b.1846. [4993] Silver sheaves... 2d ed. Des Moines: The author, 1879. 360 p. Auto., p. 19–202. DLC. Union army soldier who lost his sight. After the War he engaged in various commercial and merchandising ventures.

Salmon, David L. Confessions [4994] of a former customers' man, being the inside story of how Wall Street separates the sucker and his money...as told to Dr. Edwin F. Bowers. N.Y.: The Vanguard press, 1932. 251 p. DLC. The author served in a brokerage house for many years.

Salm-Salm, Agnes(Joy) [4995] prinzessin zu, 1844?–1912. Ten years of my life. London: R. Bentley, 1876. 2 vols. WHi. The writer's husband, a military man, was successively in the Union army; with Maximilian in Mexico, and in the Prussian forces fighting France. In each of these ventures, Princess Salm-Salm played a prominent political role.

Salter, Mrs. Mary (Turner), [4996] 1856–1938. In memoriam, Mary Turner Salter. N.p.: 1939. 60 p. Auto., p. 2–6. DLC. Singer and music teacher in New York.

Salter, William, 1821–1910. Forty [4997] years' ministry...Burlington, Iowa: The Congregational Church, 1886. 16 p. IaCrM. Congregational clergyman in Iowa, 1846–86.

Salter, William, 1821–1910. Six- [4998] ty years...Chicago: Pilgrim press, 1907. 326 p. Auto., p.261– 326. WHi. See the preceding item.

Salvager (pseud.). See Groff, Spencer.

Salvini, Tommaso, 1829–1916. [4999] Leaves from the autobiography of Tommaso Salvini. N.Y.: The Century co., 1893. 240 p. NN. The famous Italian actor tells of his tours in America.

Samaroff-Stokowski, Olga, [5000] b. 1882. An American musician's story. N.Y.: W. W. Norton, 1939. 326 p. DLC. Concert pianist, and teacher of music.

Sampson, Abel, b. 1790. The [5001] wonderful adventures of Abel Sampson...written by Edmund Hale Kendall. Lawrence City: 1847. 91 p. DLC. Merchant sailor who during the war of 1812 served on a privateer.

Sampson, William, 1764–1836. [5002] Memoirs... 2d ed. Leesburg: 1883. 432 p. WHi. The writer came to New York from Ireland in 1806, becoming a prominent lawyer, but there is little about his American career in this book.

Samuels, Samuel, 1823–1908. [5003] From the forecastle to the cabin, being the memoirs of Capt. Samuel Samuels of the famous packet ship "Dreadnought." Boston: Charles E. Lauriat co., 1924. 308 p. NN. As described by the title.

Sanborn, Franklin Benjamin, [5004]

1831-1917. Recollections of seventy years. Boston: R. G. Badger, 1909. 2 vols. WU. In Massachusetts: newspaper editor, abolitionist, biographer. There is little about himself in this volume.

Sanborn, Katherine Abbott, 1839- [5005] 1917. Memories and anecdotes. N.Y.: Putnam, 1915. 219 p. WU. Teacher, lecturer and writer of books. See also her two books on her farm experiences. Miss Sanborn taught in New Hampshire, Missouri and New York.

Sande, Hans Markussen, b. 1837. [5006] Mit levnetsløb. Red Wing: Hauges Synodes Trykkeri, 1893. 23 p. MnSL. Farmer in Wisconsin, Illinois and Minnesota. Covers 1852-87.

Sanders, Sue, b. 1880. Our com- [5007] mon herd. N.Y.: Garden City pub. co., 1939. 261 p. NN. Pioneer life in Texas, New Mexico, and Arizona, and the author's later career in the oil industry.

Sandford, Adam Castle, b. 1824. [5008] My recollections of eighty years. Portland: priv. pr., 1909. 100 p. WHi. English born newspaper printer and publisher in New York and Wisconsin.

Sandford, Adam Castle, b. 1824. [5009] The strenuous life of an independent editor. No imprint. 4 p. OrHi. See the preceding item. This covers 1855-77.

Sandifer, Nicholas. Autobiogra- [5010] phy of Nicholas Sandifer. Cinc.: Ebbert & Richardson, 1910. 31 p. KyU. Merchant and judge in Kentucky.

Sands, Benjamin Franklin, 1811- [5011] 1883. From reefer to rear-admiral ... 1827 to 1874. N.Y.: F.A. Stokes, 1899. 308 p. WHi. As described by the title.

Sands, William Franklin, 1874- [5012] 1946. Undiplomatic memoirs. N.Y.: McGraw-Hill, 1930. 238 p. WU. American diplomatic officer in Korea and Japan, 1896-1904.

Sandvik, Marie. Sermons from [5013] the slums...Minneapolis: Minneapolis revival mission, 1943? 59 p. Auto., p. 9-23. MnHi. Evangelist in Minneapolis.

Sanford, Elias Benjamin, 1843- [5014] 1932. Origin and history of the Federal council of the churches of Christ in America. Hartford: Scranton: 1916. 528 p. WHi. Congregational clergyman who was a leader in interdenominational work. Autobiographical references are to be found throughout this work, but see especially p. 1-33.

Sanford, Maria Louisa, 1836- [5015] 1920. Marie Sanford, by Helen Whitney. Minneapolis: Univ. of Minnesota, 1922. 322 p. Auto., p. 1-43. DLC. Teacher in Minnesota.

Sanger, Margaret (Higgins), [5016] b. 1883. Margaret Sanger, an autobiography. N.Y.: W. W. Norton, 1938. 504 p. WU. A leader in the birth control movement.

Sanger, Margaret (Higgins), [5017] b. 1883. My fight for birth control. N.Y.: Farrar & Rinehart, 1931. 360 p. WU. As described by the title.

Sanger, William Cary, b. 1893. [5018] 1934-1935-1936. Newark: Newark pr. co., 1937. 36 p. DLC. A New York poet who was committed by his family to a mental institution.

Sangster, Margaret Elizabeth [5019] (Munson), 1838-1912. ...From my youth up; personal reminiscences by Margaret E. Sangster ...N.Y.: Fleming H. Revell, 1909. 332 p. NN. Novelist and journalist tells of her early life and of her literary acquaintances.

Sanjek, Louis. In silence. N.Y.: [5020] Fortuny's, 1938. 215 p. DLC. Lutheran minister in Pennsylvania who was born in Croatia. Originally the author had planned to become a member of a Catholic order in Croatia.

Sankey, Ira David, 1840-1908. [5021] My life and the story of gospel hymns... Phila.: P. W. Ziegler, 1907. 410 p. DLC. Singing evangelist who served with Dwight Moody.

Santayana, George, b. 1863. Per- [5022] sons and places. The background of my life. N.Y.: Scribner, 1944. 254 p. WU. A philosopher tells of his early life to the point of his graduation from Harvard. Santayana was born in Spain.

Santayana, George, b. 1863. Mid- [5023] dle span. N.Y.: Scribner's, 1945. 187 p. DLC. Covers his years as a professor of philosophy at Harvard.

Santleben, August, 1845-1911. A [5024] Texas pioneer. N.Y.: Neale, 1910. 321 p. TxU. Freighter and stager, born in Germany.

Sargent, Alice Applegate. Fol- [5025] lowing the flag; diary of a soldier's wife. Kansas City: E.B. Barnett, n.d. 91 p. OrU. This account be- bins with her marriage in 1886. Locale: California, Washington, Arizona, New Mexico, Cuba and the Philippines.

Sargent, Dudley Allen, 1849- [5026] 1924. Dudley Allen Sargent; an autobiography. Phila.: Lea & Febiger, 1927. 221 p. NN. Leader in the movement for physical education in America, and physician.

Sargent, Hollis Samuel, b. 1828? [5027] What an engineer remembered. N.p.: 1902. 164 p. KHi. Railroad engineer. The authenticity of this book has been questioned (see letter in files of KHi by E.T.Fay, dated May 31, 1917). Sargent was born in Canada.

Sargent, Leonard, 1857-1944. [5028] Pictures and persons. Washington: St. Anselm's priory, 1931. 95 p. DLC. New England Episcopalian minister who was converted to Catholicism.

Sargent, Martin Phelps, b. 1832. [5029] Pioneer sketches... Erie: Herald pr. & pub. co., 1891. 512 p. InU. Farmer, lumber supplier in Ohio and Pennsylvania, 1850-90.

Sartain, John, 1808-1897. The [5030] reminiscences of a very old man, 1808-1897. N.Y.: Appleton, 1899. 297 p. WHi. Philadelphia engraver who was born in England.

Satterfield, Matilda (Martin). [5031] Glad did I live. Boston: Bruce Humphries, 1938. 204 p. NN. Social life in the U.S. and Europe.

Sauveur, Albert, b. 1863. Met- [5032] allurgical reminiscences. N.Y.: Pub. for the Seeley W. Mudd fund, by the American institute of min- ing and metallurgical engineers, 1937. 67 p. Auto., p. 1-23. DLC. Metallurgical engineer, professor of engineering at Harvard, and editor of mining journals.

Savage, Minot Judson, 1841-1918. [5033] My creed. Boston: G. H. Ellis, 1901. Auto., p. 9-27. WU. A spiritual account by a Unitarian minister.

Savage, William T. A review of [5034] ten years... Concord: McFarland & Jenks, 1859. 17 p. Nh. Congre- gational clergyman in New Hampshire, 1849-89.

Savidge, Charles Wilbur, b.1850. [5035] Have faith in God... Omaha: Beacon press, 1914. 172 p. MnHi. Methodist clergyman in Minne- sota and Nebraska who in 1891 founded the "People's Church".

Savitsch, Eugene de, b. 1903. In [5036] search of complications... N.Y.: Simon & Schuster, 1940. 396 p. WU. A physician, born in Russia, who specialized in the study of vitamins.

Sawyer, Antonia, b. 1856. Songs [5037] at twilight. N.Y.: Devin-Adair, 1939. 204 p. DLC. Concert singer.

Sawyer, Elbert Henry, b. 1843. [5038] Life and teachings of Sawyer. N.Y.: Brown bros., linotypers, 1942. 220 p. DLC. Baptist clergy- man in Kansas, Oklahoma, Illinois and Missouri; college president in Missouri and Colorado; lecturer.

Sawyer, Horace M., b. 1881. Life [5039] of a hobo barber. Oklahoma City, Okla.: McClain & Woodcock, 1922. 50 p. DLC. In the southwest.

Sawyer, Lemuel, 1777-1852. [5040] Auto-biography of Lemuel Sawyer, formerly member of Congress from North Carolina, author of the biography of John Randolph. N.Y.: pub. for the author, 1844. 48 p. NN. As described by the title.

Saxon, Elizabeth (Lyle). A [5041] Southern woman's war time rem- iniscences. Memphis, Tenn.: Press of the Pilcher pr. co., 1905. 72 p. DLC. A civilian's account of her experiences in the South during the Civil War.

Sayle, Robert G., 1860-1940. [5042] Reminiscences. No imprint. 84 p. WHi. Wisconsin physician.

Scarlett, John, 1803-1889. The [5043] life and experience of a converted infidel. N.Y.: Carlton & Phillips, 1854. 274 p. DLC. A spiritual account, in which the author pro- gresses from deism to Methodism. The author served as a minister in New York and New Jersey. See also his autobiographical poem entitled Almond, pub. 1883.

Schacht, Alexander, b. 1894. [5044]
Clowning through baseball.
Grammar and adjectives by Murray Goodman, foreword by John
Kieran, illustrations by Willard
Mullin. N.Y.: A. S. Barnes, 1941.
189 p. NN. Baseball player who
later turned to entertaining baseball crowds as a clown.

Schaefer, Emilie. Erinnerungen [5045]
einer deutschen pfarrfrau aus 52
jähriger amtzeit in Süd-und Nord-
Amerika. St. Louis: Eden pub.
house, 1927. 159 p. DLC. Wife of
an Evangelical clergyman tells
of their life on two continents.

Schaeffer, Luther Melancthon. [5046]
Sketches of travels in South
America, Mexico and California.
N.Y.: James Egbert, printer,
1860. 247 p. DLC. Includes California mining experiences, 1849–
1852.

Schaff, Philip, 1819–1893. The [5047]
life of Philip Schaff, in part autobiographical. N.Y.: Charles
Scribner's sons, 1897. 526 p. NN.
German Reformed Church clergyman and theologian.

Schauffler, Adolphus Frederick, [5048]
1845–1919. Memories of a happy
boyhood. N.Y.: Revell, 1919. 96 p.
CBPac. The author was born in
Constantinople of an American
mother. The locale of this story
is the Ottoman Empire.

Schauffler, William Gottlieb, [5049]
1798–1883. Autobiography of
William G. Schauffler, for forty-
nine years a missionary in the
Orient. N.Y.: Anson D. F. Randolph, 1887. 258 p. NN. Congregational missionary in Turkey.

Schechter, Abel Alan. I live on [5050]
air. N.Y.: Stokes, 1941. 582 p.
Auto., p. 1–454. DLC. Radio
newscaster.

Scheib, Heinrich, 1808–1897. [5051]
Heinrich Scheib... Baltimore:
Schneidereith & Söhnen, 1907?
27 p. DLC. Lutheran pastor and
school teacher in Baltimore, born
in Germany.

Schenberger, Mrs. S. F. Moody. [5052]
A woman's legacy... Wakefield,
Kan.: pub. by A. W. Schenberger,
n.d. 164 p. Auto., p. 9–37. KHi.
The wife of a clergyman in Kansas
beginning with 1879.

Schenkofsky, Henry, b. 1882. [5053]
Cowboy poet... Oakland: pr. by
Messiah's advocate, 1939. 109 p.
DLC. Farm laborer in California,
Washington and Kansas; miner in
Colorado; poet.

Schlatter, Francis, b. 1856. The [5054]
life of the harp in the hand of the
harper. Denver: Smith-Brooks pr.
co., 1897. 191 p. CoD. Alsatian
faith healer who came to live in
Colorado and New Mexico.

Schlatter, Francis, b. 1856. Mod-[5055]
ern miracles of healing... comp.
by Mrs. Ella F. Woodard. Kalamazoo?: 1903. 122 p. DLC. See
the preceding item.

Schley, Winfield Scott, 1839– [5056]
1909. Forty-five years under the
flag. N.Y.: Appleton, 1904. 439 p.
WHi. Officer of the U.S. Navy
who served in the Civil War, and
in the War with Spain.

Schmid, Albert A. Al Schmid, [5057]
marine. By Roger Butterfield.
N.Y.: Farrar & Rinehart, 1944.
142 p. NN. Story of Schmid's
experiences on Guadalcanal,
where he lost his sight, and of his
fight to attain a normal life again.

Schmitt, Leo Francis, b. 1891. [5058]
Grief. Bellevue: International pr.
& pub. co., Chicago: 1928. 311 p.
DLC. Iowa banker.

Schoen-René, Anna Eugénie. [5059]
America's musical inheritance...
N.Y.: Putnam, 1941. 244 p. DLC.
Voice teacher. See especially
p. 3–71.

Schoffen, Elizabeth, b. 1861. "The[5060]
demands of Rome" by Elizabeth
Schoffen (Sister Lucretia)...
Portland: 1917. 223 p. DLC. Nurse
in Catholic hospital in Oregon who
left the Church.

Schofield, John McAllister, 1831-[5061]
1906. Forty-six years in the army.
N.Y.: Century, 1897. 577 p. NN.
The author served in the Union
army, and was Superintendent at
West Point.

Schönauer, Georg. Tramp and [5062]
farmer in USA; fünf jahre kreuz
und quer durch die staaten. Berlin:
Im Deutschen verlag, 1938. 269 p.
DLC. Itinerant farm laborer,
born in Germany, who was in the
the U.S. for five years.

Schoolcraft, Henry Rowe, 1793– [5063]
1864. "Personal reminiscences".
(Western scenes...Auburn: Derby &

Miller, 1853. 495 p.) p. 5-40. WHi. Executive agent for the U.S. Government among the Indians of the Lake Superior territory.

Schouler, James, 1839-1920. Historical briefs; with a biography. [5064] N.Y.: Dodd, Mead, 1896. 310 p. Auto., p. 169-310. WHi. Historian and lawyer in Massachusetts and the District of Columbia.

Schroeder, Seaton, 1849-1922. A [5065] half century of naval service. N.Y.: Appleton, 1922. 443 p. WHi. The author's experiences included service in the War with Spain.

Schuette, Conrad Herman Louis, [5066] b. 1843. Wiggy... Columbus: F. J. Heer pr. co., 1916. 152 p. DLC. Memories of childhood and education in Germany, Ohio and Pennsylvania.

Schuette, John. The story of [5067] John and Rose... Chicago: Donnelley, 1914. 254 p. DLC. The author was a salesman and then a farmer in Wisconsin.

Schulman, Sammy. "Where's [5068] Sammy?" N.Y.: Random house, 1943. 234 p. NN. Experiences of a news photographer.

Schurz, Carl, 1829-1906. The [5069] reminiscences of Carl Schurz. N.Y.: McClure, 1907-1908. 3 vols. WHi. Journalist, politician in Wisconsin, Senator from Missouri, minister to Spain, Union soldier, secretary of the interior. Schurz was born in Germany.

Schussler, Otto F. Pills. Minneapolis: 1924. 48 p. MnM. A [5070] physician who spent two years (unspecified) in Alaska.

Scollard, Mrs. Clinton. See Rittenhouse, Jessie Belle.

Scott, Angelo C. A boyhood in [5071] old Carlyle. Oklahoma City: 1940. 30 p. KHi. A 19th century account of youth in rural Kansas.

Scott, Evelyn. Background in [5072] Tennessee. N.Y.: R. M. McBride, 1937. 302 p. WHi. A writer tells of her youth in Tennessee.

Scott, Hugh Lenox, 1853-1934. [5073] Some memories of a soldier. N.Y.: Century, 1928. 673 p. WHi. The author was a cavalry officer in the West.

Scott, Joe M. Four years service in the Southern army. Mulberry: Leader office print, 1897. [5074] 74 p. TxU. As described by the title.

Scott, John, b. 1820. Recollections of fifty years in the ministry [5075] ... Pittsburgh: Methodist Protestant board of publication, 1898. 495 p. DLC. Methodist clergyman in Ohio and Pennsylvania.

Scott, John, b. 1912. Behind the [5076] Urals; an American worker in Russia's city of steel. N.Y.: Houghton Mifflin, 1942. 279 p. DLC. The author worked in the Russian steel mills for five years.

Scott, Margaret McAvoy, b. 1866. [5077] Memories... Boston: Meador, 1943. 270 p. WHi. School teacher, and operator of a residence hotel.

Scott, Mrs. Marion (Gallagher). [5078] Chatauqua caravan. N.Y.: Appleton-Century, 1939. 310 p. WHi. Actress.

Scott, Matthew, b. 1834. Autobiography... Bridgeport: Trow's [5079] pr. & bookbinding co., New York, 1885. 96 p. DLC. An Englishman who was keeper of Jumbo, Barnam's elephant.

Scott, Orange, 1800-1847. Autobiography of Orange Scott. (The [5080] life of Rev. Orange Scott, by Lucius C. Matlack. N.Y.: Prindle & Matlack, 1851.) p. 5-46. DLC. Methodist clergyman in New England, known for his abolitionist speeches.

Scott, R. G. Memoirs and poetic [5081] sketches. N.p.: Reveille print, n.d. 30 p. Ia-HA. Union army soldier. Railroad and highway engineer in Iowa.

Scott, Robert Lee, b. 1908. God [5082] is my co-pilot. N.Y.: Scribner, 1943. 277 p. DLC. Army flier in the second World War.

Scott, Robert Lee, b. 1908. Runway to the sun. N.Y.: Scribner, [5083] 1945. 218 p. DLC. See the preceding item.

Scott, S. M., b. 1855. The champion organizer of the Northwest; [5084] or, My first sixty days work as an organizer. McPherson: 1890. 192 p. DLC. The author describes his work for the Farmers Alliance.

Scott, Wellington (pseud.). Seventeen years in the underworld. [5085] N.Y.: Abingdon, 1916. 119 p. WU. Thief is sent to prison. He is pardoned, and "goes straight".

Scott, William Berryman. Some [5086]

memories of a paleontologist. Princeton: Princeton univ. press, 1939. 336 p. WU. The author was a professor at Princeton.

Scott, William Earle Dodge, [5087] 1852-1910. Story of a bird lover. N.Y.: Outlook, 1903. 372 p. DLC. Ornithologist in New Jersey.

Scott, Winfield, 1786-1866. Mem- [5088] oirs... N.Y.: Sheldon, 1864. 2 vols. WHi. Army officer. He served in the war of 1812, and against Mexico, and did notable work in pacifying territories occupied by Indians. Scott ran unsuccessfully for the presidency in 1852.

Scoville, Mrs. Adaline Ballou, [5089] b. 1830. Life... Bingham Canyon: 1906. 45 p. USlGS. Wife of Montana miner. In Utah, the author operated a boarding house while her husband worked in a smelter.

Scribner, Benjamin Franklin, [5090] 1825-1900. How soldiers were made; or, the war as I saw it under Buell, Rosecrans, Thomas, Grant and Sherman. New Albany: 1887. 316 p. NN. Officer in the Union army.

Scrymser, James Alexander, [5091] 1839-1918. Personal reminiscences of James A. Scrymser in times of peace and war. N.p.: 1915. 151 p. NN. The author, president of several submarine cable companies, writes of his Civil War experiences and the Parkhurst campaign against Tammany Hall as well as of his work on the submarine cables to Mexico and South America.

Scudday, H. G. The way. DeSoto: [5092] H. G. Scudday, 1898. 24 p. TxU. Methodist clergyman in Texas.

Scudder, Janet, b. 1873. Modeling [5093] my life. N.Y.: Harcourt, Brace, 1925. 297 p. DLC. Sculptor.

Scudder, Robert A., b. 1894. My [5094] experience in the World war. Dover: 1921. 143 p. DLC. Soldier in the first World War.

Scudder, Vida Dutton, b. 1861. [5095] On journey. N.Y.: E. P. Dutton, 1937. 445 p. WU. Teacher of literature at Wellesley, and writer of books on religious subjects.

Seabrook, William Buehler, [5096] b. 1887. No hiding place... Phila.: Lippincott, 1942. 406 p. WU. Adventurer; writer on immigration and witchcraft; alcoholic who was cured.

Seabrook, William Buehler, [5097] b. 1887. Asylum. N.Y.: Harcourt, Brace, 1935. 263 p. WU. The author's account of how he was cured of alcoholism.

Seagrave, Gordon Stifler, b. 1897. [5098] Tales of a waste-basket surgeon. Phila.: Judson press, 1938. 265 p. DLC. Baptist medical missionary in Burma.

Seagrave, Gordon Stifler, b. 1897. [5099] Burma surgeon. N.Y.: W. W. Norton, 1943. 295 p. WU. A Baptist medical missionary in Burma who became a medical officer in the U.S. army.

Searles, James M. Life and [5100] times of a civil engineer. Cinc.: pr. by R. Clarke & co., 1893. 139 p. DLC. The author's work was mainly in Mississippi and Louisiana. This work includes his experiences in the Confederate army.

Searls, Niles, 1825-1907. Auto- [5101] biography of Niles Searles. (The diary of a pioneer... by Niles Searles. San Francisco: Pernau-Walsh pr. co., 1940. 90 p.) p. 65-70. CHi. Miner, lawyer and judge in California.

Sears, W. H. Notes from a cow- [5102] boy's diary. No imprint. 6 p. CoD. In Colorado in 1876.

Sedgwick, Catharine Maria, 1789- [5103] 1867. "Recollections of childhood". (Life and letters of Catharine M. Sedgwick, ed. by Mary E. Dewey. N.Y.: Harper, 1871. 446 p.) p. 13-78. DLC. A novelist tells of her first 15 years in New England, New York and Pennsylvania.

Sedgwick, Henry Dwight, b. 1861. [5104] Memoirs of an epicurean. N.Y.: The Bobbs-Merrill co., 1942. 349 p. NN. Reminiscences of the historian, biographer and essayist of his early life in New York and Stockbridge, Mass., of Harvard College, and of life and travels in Europe.

See, A. N., b. 1840. Autobiogra- [5105] phy. No imprint. 178 p. KHi. Methodist clergyman in Georgia, Iowa, and Kansas.

Seebohm, Benjamin, 1798-1871. [5106] Private memoirs... London:

Provost, 1873. 443 p. DLC. The author, born in Germany, made England his place of residence. During 1846-51, he lived in the U.S., where he served as a minister of the Society of Friends.

Segale, Rosa Maria (Sister), [5107] 1850-1941. At the end of the Santa Fé trail. Columbus: Columbian press, 1932. 347 p. DLC. The author, born in Italy, was a member of a group of Sisters of charity. Her services were rendered mainly in New Mexico.

Seger, John, 1786-1870. Narra- [5108] tive. N.Y.: Holman, 1863. 204 p. WHi. Baptist clergyman in New Jersey and New York.

Seguin, John N. Personal mem- [5109] oirs... San Antonio: pr. at the Ledger book & job office, 1858. 30 p. TxU. Military and political figure in Texas. The period covered is 1834 to 1842.

Seifert, Shirley. ...American [5110] novelist. N.Y.: M. S. Mill co., 1940. 9 p. MoHi. In Missouri (20th century).

Selby, Clarence J., b. 1872. [5111] Flashes of light from an imprisoned soul. Chicago: A. L. Fyfe, printer, 1901. 43 p. DLC. The author, born in England, lived in Chicago where he wrote articles for schools for the blind. Selby was himself both blind and deaf.

Selfridge, Thomas Oliver, 1836- [5112] 1924. Memoirs... N.Y.: Putnam, 1924. 288 p. WHi. Officer in the U.S. Navy who served during the Civil War.

Seligman, Jesse, 1827-1894. In [5113] memoriam, Jesse Seligman. N.Y.: Philip Cowen, 1894. 229 p. Auto., p. 3-16. DLC. Dry goods merchant in the South and later (1850) in California; banker. The author was born in Germany.

Sellstedt, Lars Gustaf, 1819-1911.[5114] From forecastle to Academy... Buffalo: Matthews-Northrup works, 1904. 353 p. WU. Merchant sailor, and painter. The author was born in Sweden.

Selmon, Bertha Eugenia, b.1877. [5115] They do meet... N.Y.: Froben press, 1942. 254 p. DLC. The author and her husband were medical missionaries in China during the first two decades of the 20th century.

Semmes, Raphael, 1809-1877. [5116] Service afloat and ashore during the Mexican war. Cinc.: W. H. Moore, 1851. 480 p. WHi. Naval officer.

Semmes, Raphael, 1809-1877. [5117] Memoirs of service afloat during the war between the states. Baltimore: Kelly, Piet & co., 1869. 833 p. WHi. Confederate naval officer.

Semple, Emily Virginia, b. 1829. [5118] Reminiscences... Santa Barbara: Independent print, 1904? 43 p. Auto., p. 1-24. AU. A story of youth and social life in Alabama.

Seppala, Leonhard. Seppala, [5119] Alaskan dog driver, by Elizabeth M. Ricker. Boston: Little, Brown, 1930. 205 p. DLC. The author, born in Norway, was a well known Alaskan driver of dog teams, and miner.

Service, John, b. 1839. John [5120] Service, pioneer. Prepared from his own words and records, by Fred F. Goodsell. N.p.:1945. 40 p. C. Freighter, farmer, rancher in California, beginning with 1859.

Service, Robert William, b.1876. [5121] Ploughman of the moon; an adventure into memory. N.Y.: Dodd, Mead & co., 1945. 472 p. NN. Early life in Scotland; adventures in the Pacific States, Canada, and Alaska of the well-known Canadian author of Alaskan poetry and fiction.

Sessions, Mrs. Ruth (Huntington)[5122] b. 1859. Sixty-odd, a personal history. Brattleboro: Stephen Daye press, 1936. 429 p. WHi. The mother of Roger Sessions, the composer, tells of her music study in Germany, and of her various reform interests in the U.S.

Seton, Robert, 1839-1927. Mem- [5123] ories of many years (1839-1922). London: John Long, 1923. 320 p. NN. A Catholic prelate tells of his early life in the United States and of his later career as a Church dignitary in Rome.

Sewall, John Smith, 1830-1911. [5124] The logbook of the captain's clerk; adventures in the China seas. Bangor: pr. by Chas. H.

Glass & co., 1905. 278 p. DLC. With Perry, 1853-54, in Japan. Includes experience in China during the Taiping rebellion.

Seward, Frederick William, [5125] 1830-1915. Reminiscences of a war-time statesman and diplomat, 1830-1915... N.Y.: Putnam, 1916. 489 p. WHi. N. Y. journalist, politician, and diplomatic officer.

Seward, William Henry, 1801- [5126] 1872. William H. Seward; an autobiography from 1801 to 1834... N.Y.: Derby & Miller, 1891. 3 vols. WHi. Governor of New York, U.S. Senator, Secretary of State during Civil War.

Sewell, C. W., b. 1828. The non-[5127] descript described. Louisville: n.d. 305 p. MoCanD. School teacher in Tennessee; clergyman of the Christian Church in Tennessee and Kentucky.

Sexton, Lydia, b. 1799. Auto- [5128] biography... Dayton: United Brethren pub. house, 1885. 655 p. KHi. A widow becomes a minister of the United Brethren, serving in Ohio, Indiana, Kansas and Illinois.

Seyffarth, Gustav, 1796-1885. [5129] The literary life of Gustavus Seyffarth... N.Y.: E. Steiger, 1886. 88 p. WHi. A German born Egyptologist tells of his professional writing.

Seymour, Ralph Fletcher, b. 1876. [5130] Some went this way... Chicago: The author, 1945. 294 p. WHi. Book publisher.

Shadid, Michael Abraham, [5131] b. 1882. A doctor for the people; the autobiography of the founder of America's first co-operative hospital. N.Y.: The Vanguard press, 1939. 277 p. NN. The author, a Syrian by birth, tells of his struggles with the medical profession to save his co-operative hospital at Elk City, Oklahoma.

Shafford, John Conrad, d. 1840. [5132] Narrative... N.Y.: G. L. Carpenter, 1840. 24 p. MWA. New York farmer who became a hermit in Canada.

Shaler, Nathaniel Southgate, [5133] 1841-1906. The autobiography... N.Y.: Houghton Mifflin, 1909. 481 p. Auto., p. 3-212. WU. Covers only to 1862. The author tells of his student days at Harvard.

Shane, James B., b. 1840. Not [5134] guilty... Abilene: Reflector pub. co., 1903. 168 p. KHi. Union army soldier. Later he was holder of a minor political office in Kansas, and photographer.

Sharp, William Graves, 1859- [5135] 1922. The war memoirs of William Graves Sharp, American Ambassador to France, 1914-1919. London: Constable, 1931. 431 p. NN. As described by the title.

Sharpe, Mrs. H. A. (Yokum). [5136] Terwilligar. Reminiscences of a minister's daughter, wife and widow. Seymour: 1911 . 50 p. WHi. Wife of a midwestern Methodist clergyman; temperance worker.

Sharpe, John C., 1853-1942. [5137] Memories of Blair, by John C. Sharpe, headmaster of Blair Academy, 1898-1927. Blairstown, N.J.: priv. pr., 1939. 228 p. NN. As described by the title.

Sharpe, Mrs. May Churchill, [5138] b. 1876. Chicago May, her story. N.Y.: Macaulay, 1928. 336 p. DLC. A life of petty crime; prostitute. The author was born in Ireland.

Sharpless, Isaac, 1848-1920. The [5139] story of a small college, by Isaac Sharpless, president of Haverford College, 1887-1917. Phila.: The John C. Winston co., 1918. 237 p. Auto., p. 65-174. DLC. As described by the title.

Shastid, Thomas Hall, b. 1866. [5140] Tramping to failure. Ann Arbor: George Wahr, 1937. 503 p. WHi. Midwest physician, worker for world peace.

Shastid, Thomas Hall, b. 1866. [5141] My second life. Ann Arbor: George Wahr, 1944. 1174 p. Auto., p. 1108-1174. WU. See the preceding item.

Shaw, Anna Howard, 1847-1919. [5142] The story of a pioneer. N.Y.: Harper, 1915. 338 p. WHi. Methodist minister in Michigan; woman rights worker in Mass.

Shaw, David Augustus, 1826- [5143] 1915. Eldorado or California as seen by a pioneer, 1850-1900. Los Angeles, Cal.: B. R. Baumgardt & co., 1900. NN. Miner and farmer in California.

Shaw, Elijah, b. 1771. A short [5144] sketch of the life of Elijah Shaw, who served for twenty-two years in the Navy of the United States... Rochester: Strong & Dawson, printers, 1843. 87 p. DLC. The author served against France in 1798, against Tripoli in 1802-05, against England in 1812-15, and against Algiers in 1815-16.

Shaw, James. Twelve years in [5145] America...incidents illustrative of ministerial life and labor in Illinois... London: Hamilton, Adams & co., 1867. 440 p. DLC. The author, born in England, was a Methodist clergyman in Illinois prior to and during the Civil War.

Shaw, James, b. 1808. Early [5146] reminiscences of pioneer life in Kansas. Atchison: Haskell pr. co., 1886. 238 p. WHi. The author, born in England, was a Methodist clergyman in Illinois prior to and during the Civil War.

Shaw, John Robert, b. 1861. A [5147] narrative of the life and times of John Robert Shaw, the well digger ...Lexington: pr. by D. Bradford, 1807. 180 p. WHi. Soldier in the Revolutionary army; well digger on the Kentucky frontier.

Shaw, William, b. 1860. The evo- [5148] lution of an Endeavorer... Boston: Christian Endeavor world, 1924. 427 p. DLC. Secretary of the United Society of Christian Endeavor, a lay church organ.

Shawn, Mrs. Ted. See St. Denis, Ruth.

Shea, George, 1826-1895. Recol- [5149] lections of my own times. No imprint. 25 p. DLC. Typesetter in Maryland, the District of Columbia and Pa. Covers his early years.

Sheardown, Thomas Simpson, [5150] b. 1791. Half a century's labors in the gospel... Lewisburg?: O. N. Worden & E. B. Case, 1865. 372 p. WHi. Baptist clergyman in New York and Pa., born in England.

Shedd, Henry, b. 1803. Home [5151] missionary life... Mt. Gilead: Sentinel pr. office, 1872. 22 p. MnHi. Presbyterian clergyman in Ohio.

Sheean, Vincent, b. 1899. Per- [5152] sonal history. N.Y.: Doubleday, Doran, 1935. 403 p. WU. Foreign correspondent in Europe and Asia.

Sheedy, Dennis, 1846-1923. The [5153] autobiography... Denver?: 1922? 61 p. CoHi. Montana miner in 1864. Cattle merchant in the Rockies and Southwest. Banker in Colorado. The author was born in Ireland.

Sheehan, Bryan, d. 1772. The [5154] life of Bryan Sheehan... Salem: Samuel & Ebenezer Hall, 1772. PHi. Rapist in Mass.

Sheffield, Delia B. Reminis- [5155] cences. Seattle: Un. of Washington press, 1924. 16 p. CLU-C. The wife of a soldier in the Oregon territory, beginning with 1852.

Sheldon, Asa Goodell, b. 1788. [5156] The life of Asa G. Sheldon... Woborn: E. T. Moody, printer, 1862. 374 p. DLC. Farmer in Mass.

Sheldon, Charles Monroe. Char- [5157] les M. Sheldon, his life story. N.Y.: Doran, 1925. 309 p. WHi. Congregational clergyman, and writer on religious subjects.

Sheldon, Edward Austin, 1823- [5158] 1897. Autobiography. N.Y.: Ives-Butler, 1911. 252 p. Auto., p. 1-180. WU. Educator in New York.

Sheldon, Herbert F. Reminis- [5159] cences of my dealings with criminals in the early history of Franklin County, Kans. Ottawa: 1916. 151 p. KU. County clerk, about 1863.

Sheldon, Mark, 1829-1902. An [5160] autobiographical sketch. San Francisco: Murdock press, n.d. 120 p. WHi. Ore mining and real estate business in California.

Sheldon, Stewart. Gleanings by [5161] the way from '36 to '89. Topeka: G. W. Crane, 1890. 262 p. WHi. Congregational clergyman in Missouri, Colorado and Dakotas, South America, and Mexico.

Shelhamer, E. E. The ups and [5162] downs of a pioneer preacher... Atlanta: Repairer pub. co., 1915. 272 p. DLC. Holiness preacher (Free Methodist) in the midwest and in the South Atlantic States.

Shellrud, Hans C., b. 1878. [5163] Twenty-eight years of interesting experience. Boston: Gorham press, 1916. 245 p. DLC. Farmer in Minnesota and North Dakota, born in Norway.

Shelton, Albert, 1875-1922. [5164]

Pioneering in Tibet... N.Y.: Revell, 1921. 214 p. DLC. Medical missionary in Tibet.

Shelton, Mason Bradford, b.1838. [5165] Rocky Mountain adventures. Boston: Christopher, 1920. 192 p. DLC. Miner in Colorado.

Shepard, Elihu Hotchkiss, b.1795.[5166] The autobiography of Elihu H. Shepard... St. Louis: George Knapp, 1869. 275 p. WHi. The author was a soldier in the war of 1812 and in the war against Mexico, and was professor of languages at St. Louis College.

Shepard, Thomas, 1605-1649. [5167] The autobiography of Thomas Shepard, the celebrated minister of Cambridge, N.E. ...Boston: Pierce & Parker, 1832. 129 p. WHi. New England Congregational divine.

Sheperd, Grand, 1875-1939. The [5168] silver magnet, fifty years in a Mexican silver mine. N.Y.: Dutton, 1938. 302 p. DLC. Operator of a silver mine.

Sheppard, Isaac Applin, b.1827. [5169] Isaac A. Sheppard: a brief account of his ancestors...together with an autobiographical sketch. Phila.: priv. pr. for the use of his family, 1897. 37 p. PHi. Manufacturer of stoves and owner of foundry in Phila.

Sherburne, Andrew, b. 1765. [5170] Memoirs of Andrew Sherburne, a pensioner of the Navy of the Revolution. Utica: William Williams, 1828. 262 p. WHi. As described by the title.

Sherburne, Jacob, b. 1753. A [5171] narrative of the principal incidents in the life and adventures of Capt. Jacob Sherburne... Castine: pr. by B. F. Bond, 1829. 96 p. MH. New England merchant seaman.

Sheridan, Philip Henry, 1831- [5172] 1888. Personal memoirs of P.H. Sheridan, general, United States Army. N.Y.: C. L. Webster, 1888. 2 vols. WHi. As described by the title.

Sherman, Charles Phineas, [5173] b. 1874. Academic adventures: a law school professor's recollections and observations. New Haven: The Tuttle, Morehouse & Taylor co., 1944. 314 p. NN. The author taught law at Yale University, Boston University, the College of William and Mary, the National University, and the Catholic University of America.

Sherman, Edgar Jay, b. 1834. [5174] Some recollections of a long life. Boston: priv. pr., 1908. 322 p. WHi. Lawyer, jurist and Attorney-General in Mass.

Sherman, Eleazer, b. 1795. The [5175] narrative of Eleazer Sherman, giving an account of his life, experience, call to the ministry of the gospel and travels... Providence: H. H. Brown, printer, 1832. 3 vols. WHi. Baptist in Mass., Rhode Island and Georgia.

Sherman, John, 1823-1900. John [5176] Sherman's recollections of forty years in the House, Senate and cabinet. An autobiography... Chicago: The Werner co., 1895. 949 p. NN. Ohio political figure.

Sherman, Samuel Sterling. Auto-[5177] biography...1815-1910. Chicago: M. A. Donohue, 1910. 117 p. WHi. Alabama educator.

Sherman, Thomas Henry, b.1842.[5178] Twenty years with James G. Blaine; reminiscences by his private secretary... N.Y.: Grafton press, 1928. 194 p. DLC. As described by the title.

Sherman, William Tecumseh,1820-[5179] 1891. Memoirs of General William T. Sherman. N.Y.: Appleton, 1876. 2 vols.in 1. WHi. Covers 1846-1865.

Sherrill, Charles Hitchcock, [5180] 1867-1936. My story book. Brattleboro: priv. pr., 1937. 359 p. DLC. New York lawyer; later a diplomatic officer in Argentina, Turkey, England, and Japan.

Sherrod, Julian, b. 1895. The [5181] autobiography of a bankrupt. N.Y.: Brewer, Warren & Putnam, 1932. 134 p. NN. The tale of a bond salesman in the depression years.

Sherwell, Samuel, b. 1841. Old [5182] recollections of an old boy. N.Y.: Knickerbocker press,1923. 271 p. WHi. Physician who came to the U.S. from England in 1858.

Sherwood, Elisha Barber, 1810- [5183] 1905. Fifty years of the skirmish line. Chicago: Fleming H. Revell, 1893. 264 p. DLC. Presbyterian clergyman in New York, Michigan, Missouri. Teacher at Park College in Missouri.

Sherwood, Mary Elizabeth (Wil- [5184] son), 1830–1903. An epistle to posterity, being rambling recollections of many years of my life. N.Y.: Harper, 1897. 380 p. NN. Social and literary reminiscences of the United States and Europe during the second half of the nineteenth century by a well-known writer.

Sherwood, Mary Elizabeth (Wil- [5185] son), 1830–1903. Here & there & everywhere; reminiscences. Chicago: Herbert S. Stone & co., 1898. 301 p. NN. Reminiscences of European society. See also the preceding entry.

Sherwood, Robert Edmund, [5186] b. 1864. Here we are again; recollections of an old circus clown. Indianapolis: Bobbs-Merrill, 1926. 292 p. DLC. As described by the title.

Shilling, W. N. Ten years on an [5187] Indian reservation as a licensed trader... No imprint. 7 leaves. IdP. In Idaho, 1874–84.

Schindler, Mrs. Mary Dana, [5188] 1810–1883. A Southerner among the spirits. Memphis: Southern Baptist publication society, 1877. 169 p. DLC. In Texas.

Shinn, Jonathan. The memoirs [5189] ... Greeley, Colorado: Weld County Democrat, 1890. 88 p. Co. Ore freighter, stage driver, sheriff in Illinois. Operator of ferryboat and of tavern in Iowa. This account begins about 1825.

Shippen, Edward, 1826–1911. [5190] Thirty years at sea. The story of a sailor's life. Phila.: Lippincott, 1899. 380 p. NjP. As described by the title.

Shirk, David Lawson, b. 1844. [5191] Life and adventures. N.p.: copyright reserved, 1920. 124 leaves. OrU. Cattle rancher in Idaho, Texas, California and Oregon, beginning about 1866.

Shockey, Samuel W., b. 1858. [5192] Twenty-five years of fighting fate. Boston: pr. for the author, 1892. 201 p. Auto., p. 7–156. TxU. Methodist clergyman who served in Texas, Nebraska, Minn., Iowa, Michigan, Alabama and Miss.

Sholes, Charles H., b. 1853. How [5193] I got my education. Cynthiana: Hobson book press, 1944. 35 p. OrHi. In Iowa.

Short, Wallace Mertin, b. 1866. [5194] Let there be light; a study in freedom and faith, being a review of six years ministry in Sioux City, Iowa. Kansas City, Mo.: The Hyde Park press, 1916. 141 p. Auto., p. 1–74. DLC. A Congregationalist minister who differed with his congregation on the issue of prohibition.

Shotwell, John. A victim of re- [5195] venge... San Antonio: E. L. Jackson, 1909. 35 p. TxU. Texas convict, guilty of forgery.

Shotwell, Randolph Abbott, 1844– [5196] 1885. The papers of Randolph A. Shotwell... Raleigh: North Carolina historical comm., 1929. 2 vols. DLC. Confederate soldier; newspaper publisher and political figure in North Carolina.

Shridharani, Krishnalal Jethalal, [5197] b. 1911. My India, my America. N.Y.: Duell, Sloan & Pearce, 1941. 647 p. DLC. In the U.S. the author studied in an American university, lectured and wrote poetry.

Shufelt, S. A letter from a gold [5198] miner. San Marino: Friends of the Huntington library, 1944. 28 p. CLSM. In California, 1850.

Shute, Edward Ashton, b. 1868. [5199] The shearing of the black sheep. Boston: Meador, 1941. 270 p. NN. Reminiscences of a newspaper editor in New Hampshire.

Shute, Henry Augustus, b. 1856. [5200] Farming it. Boston: Houghton Mifflin, 1909. 248 p. DLC. A novelist tries his hand at farming in Massachusetts.

Sibley, Henry Hastings, 1811– [5201] 1891. The unfinished autogiography... Minneapolis: Voyager press, 1932. 75 p. Auto., p. 7–39. WHi. Fur trader in the Michigan, Ohio area. This account closes with 1835.

Sickler, Mrs. Mae (Conrad). [5202] Pioneer years in the Yakima valley. N.p.: 1942. 49 p. WaU. Life on a ranch in Washington, beginning in 1871. From 1890 to 1900 the author taught school.

Siddons, Leonora. The female [5203] warrior... N.Y.: E. E. & G. Barclay, 1843. 23 p. TxU. With Houston

in Mexico.
Sidney. See Blotzman, Sidney.
Sigourney, Mrs. Lydia Howard [5204] (Huntley), 1791–1865. Letters of life. N.Y.: Appleton, 1866. 414 p. WHi. New England poet, novelist and biographer tells of her education, marriage, domestic life and literary efforts.

Sihler, Ernest Gottlieb, b. 1853. [5205] From Maumee to Thames and Tiber... N.Y.: N. Y. univ. press, 1930. 269 p. DLC. Professor of classics in Maryland, Wisconsin and New York.

Sihler, Wilhelm. Lebenslauf... [5206] N.Y.:Lutherischer Verlags-Verein, 1880. 288 p. NN. This, the second volume of his autobiography, covers the American period of his life. A Lutheran clergyman in the Missouri Synod, beginning with 1843.

Sikorsky, Igor Ivan, b. 1889. The [5207] story of the winged-S... N.Y.: Dodd, Mead, 1944. 276 p. DLC. Russian born aeronautical engineer.

Silkwood, Barzillia, b. 1852. [5208] Steps in the Christian life... Cinc.: Jennings & Graham, 1910. 96 p. Auto., p. 9–12. DLC. Clergyman of a Pentacostal sect in California.

Silliman, Benjamin, 1779–1864. [5209] Life of Benjamin Silliman... N.Y.: 1866. 2 vols. WHi. Scientist, professor at Yale.

Silverstein, Abraham. From [5210] Sinai to Calvary. Phila.: 1923. 77 p. DLC. The author was converted to Christianity, and became a missionary.

Simkhovitch, Mrs. Mary Melinda[5211] (Kingsbury), b. 1867. Neighborhood... N.Y.: Norton, 1938. 301 p. WU. Social worker in New York.

Simmons, Edward, 1852–1931. [5212] From seven to seventy... N.Y.: Harper, 1922. 344 p. WU. Mural painter.

Simmons, Furnifold McLendel, [5213] b. 1854. F. M. Simmons, statesman of the new South... Durham: Duke univ. press, 1936. 535 p. Auto., p. 3–69. WHi. U.S. Senator from North Carolina.

Simonian, Mrs. Leonie Bertha [5214] (Bal), b. 1866. Shadow of destiny. Whittier: Western pr. corp., 1933. 216 p. DLC. A singer, born in France, who settled in California.

Simonsen, Severin E. From the [5215] Methodist pulpit into Christian Science... Los Angeles: E. P. Simonsen, 1928. 293 p. DLC. As described by the title.

Simonson, Lee. Part of a life- [5216] time...1919–1940. N.Y.: Duell, Sloan, Pearce, 1943. 100 p. DLC. Stage designer.

Simpson, George Gaylord, b.1902[5217] Attending marvels; a Patagonian journal. N.Y.: The Macmillan co., 1934. 295 p. DLC. Zoologist's adventures during expedition planned by the American museum of Natural History, 1930–31.

Sims, Dorothy (Rice). Curiouser [5218] and curiouser; a book in the jugular vein. N.Y.: Simon & Schuster, 1940. 203 p. NN. A well-known bridge player tells of her career.

Sims, James Marion, 1813–1883. [5219] The story of my life. N.Y.: Appleton, 1884. 471 p. WHi. Gynecologist.

Sims, William Sowden, 1858– [5220] 1936. The victory at sea... N.Y.: Doubleday, Page, 1920. DLC. U.S. naval officer, in the first World War.

Sinclair, Upton Beall, b. 1878. [5221] American outpost... N.Y.: Farrar & Rinehart, 1932. 280 p. WU. Novelist, writer of tracts on social reform.

Sinsabaugh, Christopher George,[5222] b. 1872. Who me?... Detroit: Arnold-Powers, 1940. 377 p. DLC. Editor of automotive trade papers in Chicago and Detroit.

Siple, Paul A., b. 1908. A boy scout[5223] with Byrd. N.Y.: Putnam, 1936. 165 p. WHi. First Byrd expedition, 1928–30.

Siple, Paul A., b. 1908. Scout to [5224] explorer; back with Byrd in the Antarctic. N.Y.: Putnam, 1936. 239 p. DLC. Second Antarctic expedition, 1933–35.

Siringo, Charles A., 1855–1928. [5225] A Texas cowboy; or fifteen years on the hurricane deck of a Spanish pony. Chicago: M. Umbdenstock, 1885. 316 p. DLC. In the Southwest. Covers 1867–83. When this book was out of print it was revised in somewhat different form,as Lone

Star Cowboy (1919). Owned by WHi.

Siringo, Charles A., 1855-1928. [5226] A cowboy detective. Chicago: W. B. Conkey, 1912. 519 p. WHi. Employee of the Pinkertons tells of labor violence, cattle rustlers, moonshiners, etc.

Siringo, Charles A., 1855-1928. [5227] Riata and spurs... Boston & N.Y.: Houghton Mifflin co., 1929. 276 p. DLC. A revision of two earlier books: Lone Star Cowboy, and Cowboy Detective. A 261 page version, published in the same year, is quite different from this version. Owned by DLC.

Sizer, Nelson, 1812-1897. Forty [5228] years in phrenology... N.Y.: Fowler & Wells, 1882. 413 p. WU. A phrenologist tells of his career as a lecturer.

Skarstedt, Ernst Teofil, 1857- [5229] 1929. Vagabond och redaktör... Seattle: Washington pr. co., 1914. 409 p. WaS. Journalist in Chicago with Swedish language newspaper.

Skidelsky, Simon S., b. 1862. The [5230] tales of a traveler...twenty-eight years on the road. N.Y.: A.T. DeLaMare pr. & pub. co., 1916. 108 p. DLC. The writer sold ornamental plants, 1888-1916.

Skiff, Frederick Woodward. Ad-[5231] ventures in Americana. Recollections of forty years collecting books, furniture, china, guns and glass. Portland: Metropolitan press, 1935. 366 p. DLC. A collector of Americana tells of his experiences.

Skinner, Emory Fiske, b. 1833. [5232] Reminiscences. Chicago: Vestal pr. co., 1908. 358 p. WHi. Miner in California; lumber dealer and political figure in Florida.

Skinner, Mrs. Henrietta Channing [5233] (Dana), b. 1857. An echo from Parnassus... N.Y.: Sears, 1928. 275 p. WU. Daughter of Richard H. Dana, tells of her girlhood in New England.

Skinner, James, b. 1828. Sketches [5234] of pioneer life. Quincy, Ill.: John Hall pr. co., 1917. 430 p. MoKU. Methodist clergyman in Missouri, Kansas; minister of the United Brethren in California and Illinois.

Skinner, Otis, b. 1858. Footlights [5235] and spotlights... Indianapolis: Bobbs-Merrill, 1924. 366 p. WU. Actor.

Slade, John, b. 1807. Old Slade; [5236] or, fifteen years adventures of a sailor... Boston: John Putnam, 1844. 108 p. DLC. Sailor.

Sleeper, John Sherburne, 1794- [5237] 1878. Jack in the forecastle... (by Hawser Martingale, pseud.) N.Y.: R. Worthington, 1884. 452 p. DLC. A "faithful account" of his years as a merchant sailor, 1809-1817, by a novelist.

Slettedahl, Erick Berthan. Won- [5238] der experience... (tr. from the Norwegian). Seattle: priv. pr., 1936. 223 p. WaU. Lutheran missionary worker, born in Norway. He served in Minnesota, Wisconsin, Washington and California, beginning with 1884.

Slezak, Leo, 1873-1946. Song of [5239] motley... London: William Hodge & co., 1938. 302 p. DLC. Czech singer who performed in the U.S. with the Metropolitan Opera.

Sloan, Alfred Pritchard, b. 1875. [5240] Adventures of a white-collar worker. N.Y.: Doubleday, Doran, 1941. 208 p. WHi. Executive of General Motors.

Sloan, James Forman, 1874-1933 [5241] Ted Sloan, by himself. N.Y.: Brentano's, 1915. 310 p. NN. Reminiscences of horse racing by a jockey.

Sloan, Richard Elihu, 1857-1933. [5242] Memories of an Arizona judge. Stanford Univ.: Stanford univ. press, 1932. 250 p. WHi. Lawyer, judge of state supreme court, governor of Arizona.

Sloan, William Eyres, 1867-1942.[5243] Recollections of sixty years, 1870 to 1930. Rochester?: 1942. 84 p. DLC. New York merchant.

Sloane, James Renwick Wilson, [5244] 1823-1886. Life and work of J.R.W. Sloane... N.Y.: A. C. Armstrong, 1888. 440 p. Auto., p. 38-85. DLC. School teacher in Kansas and Ohio. Presbyterian minister in New York. Abolitionist.

Slobodkin, Louis, b. 1903. [5245] Fo'castle waltz. N.Y.: The Vanguard press, 352 p. NN. Merchant sailor.

Slocum, Joshua. An authentic [5246] narrative of the life of Joshua

Slocum...comp. by John Slocum Hartford: 1844. 105 p. MiD-B. Soldier of the Revolutionary War, as related to his son.

Slocum, Phebe B. Witnessing. [5247] Brattleboro: E. L. Hildreth, 1899. 99 p. Auto., p. 19-52. DLC. A spiritual account by a Quaker.

Smale, Rudolph. There go the [5248] ships. Caldwell, Idaho: The Caxton printers, 1940. 312 p. NN. Twenty-seven years on American sailing ships.

Small, Abner Ralph, 1836-1910. [5249] The road to Richmond; the Civil war memoirs of Major Abner R. Small of the Sixteenth Maine Volunteers. Berkeley, Calif.: Univ. of California press, 1939. 314 p. NN. Union army.

Small, Floyd B. Autobiography [5250] of a pioneer. Seattle: priv. pr., 1916. 106 p. CSmH. Hunter, Indian fighter, wars with rustlers in Kansas and Wyoming, 1867-1916.

Small, Victor Robert, b. 1888. [5251] I knew 3,000 lunatics. N.Y.: Farrar & Rinehart, 1935. 273 p. DLC. Physician employed in a mental hospital for six years. The locale is not given.

Smallzried, Kathleen Ann, [5252] b. 1909. Press pass; a woman reporter's story. N.Y.: E. P. Dutton & co., 1940. 340 p. NN. In Indiana.

Smith, Adelaide W., b. 1831. [5253] Reminiscences of an army nurse during the Civil war. N.Y.: Greaves pub. co., 1911. 263 p. NN. Union army.

Smith, Alfred Emanuel, b. 1873. [5254] Up to now... N.Y.: Viking press, 1929. 434 p. WHi. New York governor and Democratic candidate for president in 1928.

Smith, Almiron, 1841-1919. Life [5255] among the shadows... Syracuse: Faith tract house, 1899. 217 p. DLC. New York teacher who, after suffering blindness, becomes a revivalist preacher.

Smith, Mrs. Amanda (Berry), [5256] b. 1837. An autobiography; the story of the Lord's dealings with Mrs. Amanda Smith, the colored evangelist; containing an account of her life work of faith...as an independent missionary. Chicago: Meyer & bros., 1893. 506 p. WHi. In the U.S. and abroad.

Smith, Andrew Madsen, 1841- [5257] 1915. Luck of a wandering Dane, by Hans Lykkejaeger (pseud.) Phila.: Matlack & Harvey, 1885. 130 p. DLC. Danish sailor, who after coming to the U.S. became a merchant in California. The original of this, in Danish, is owned by MoHi.

Smith, Art, b. 1894. Art Smith's [5258] story; the autobiography of the boy aviator... San Francisco: Bulletin, 1915. 94 p. C. Stunt flier, racer.

Smith, Benjamin Franklin. A [5259] Maine family. N.p.: priv. pr., 1922. 150 p. WHi. Gold miner in Colorado. One of the founders of the South Omaha Stock Yards Co.

Smith, C. Harold, b. 1860. The [5260] bridge of life. N.Y. & London: D. Appleton & co., 1929. 272 p. NN. Manufacturer of lamp black, born in England, whose business activity extended to New York in the period 1870-1890.

Smith, Calvin, b. 1813. The auto-[5261] biography of Calvin Smith of Smithville. Phila.: Sanford H. Robinson, 1906. 105 p. WHi. The author fought outlaws on the Missouri frontier and served in the Union army.

Smith, Charles Ernest, b. 1855. [5262] Under the northern cross... Milwaukee: Morehouse, 1925. 270 p. WHi. Born in England. Episcopalian clergyman in Maryland and in the District of Columbia.

Smith, Charles Henry, 1826- [5263] 1903. Bill Arp, from the uncivil war to date; 1861-1903. Atlanta: The Byrd pr. co., 1903. 410 p. DLC. Journalist and political figure in Georgia. Member of the Confederate army.

Smith, Charles Henry, 1876- [5264] 1948. The education of a Mennonite country boy. Bluffton: The author, 1943. 169 leaves. InGo. By a teacher of history in Illinois, Indiana and Ohio.

Smith, Mrs. Dama Margaret. I [5265] married a ranger. Stanford Univ: Stanford univ. press, 1930. 179 p. WHi. The author's husband was employed by the National Park Service at Grand Canyon.

Smith, Daniel Elliott Hugen. "A [5266]

plantation boyhood". (California rice plantation of the fifties, by Herbert R. Sass. N.Y.: William Morrow, 1936. 97 p.) p. 59-97. WHi. As described by the title.

Smith, David Burson, b. 1861? [5267] Burson Adair. Bonham: The author, 1925. 371 p. Auto., p. 11-76. TxBea. School teacher in Texas.

Smith, Elias, 1769-1846. The [5268] life, conversion, preaching, travels, and sufferings of Elias Smith. Portsmouth: Beck & Foster, 1816. 406 p. DLC. The author left the Baptist ministry to become one of the founders of the Christian Connection in New England. He was editor of the Herald of Gospel Liberty, a weekly religious newspaper.

Smith, Elizabeth Oakes Prince, [5269] 1806-1893. Selections from the autobiography of Elizabeth Oakes Smith. Lewiston: Lewiston journal, 1924. 161 p. WU. Novelist, contributor to magazines. Advocate of woman's rights.

Smith, Ernest Vernon, b. 1880. [5270] The making of a surgeon; a Midwestern chronicle. Fond du Lac, Wis.: The Berndt pr. co., 1942. 344 p. NN. In Minnesota and Wisconsin.

Smith, Eva Abigail, b. 1879. Eva [5271] Abigail Smith... by Seth Herbert Buell. No imprint. 85 p. Auto., p. 42-52. NbOC. Childhood on a Nebraska farm in the eighties.

Smith, Ferdinand Jacob, b. 1862. [5272] Memoirs... No imprint. 100 p. Ia-HA. Rural physician in Iowa.

Smith, Francis H. My experi- [5273] ence; or, footprints of a Presbyterian to spiritualism. Baltimore: 1860. 232 p. DLC. As described by the title.

Smith, Frank Will, b. 1860. Be- [5274] yond the swivel chair; sixty years of selling in the field. N.Y.: Pacific pub. co., 1940. 45 p. DLC. Travelling salesman (drugs).

Smith, Fred Burton, 1865-1936. [5275] I remember. N.Y.: Fleming H. Revell, 1936. 222 p. WHi. YMCA official, evangelist, proponent of pacifism.

Smith, Fred Burton, 1865-1936. [5276] On the trail of the peacemakers. N.Y.: Macmillan, 1922. 239 p. DLC. See the preceding item.

Smith, Goldwin, 1823-1910. Rem- [5277] iniscences... N.Y.: Macmillan, 1910. 465 p. DLC. English history professor who taught several years at Cornell.

Smith, "Gypsy". See Smith, Rodney.

Smith, Hampton Sidney, Jr. [5278] Tramp reporter. Caldwell, Idaho: The Caxton printers, 1937. 171 p. NN. Tales of a roving reporter who has worked in many parts of the United States.

Smith, Mrs. Hannah (Whitall), [5279] 1832-1911. The unselfishness of God and how I discovered it... N.Y.: Revell, 1903. 312 p. DLC. Spiritual account by a Quaker.

Smith, Harry Bache, 1860-1936. [5280] First nights and first editions... Boston: Little, Brown & co., 1931. 325 p. NN. Dramatic author's reminiscences of the theatre and of his activities as a book-collector.

Smith, Harry Leroy, b. 1887. [5281] Memoirs of an ambulance company officer... Rochester, Minn.: Doomsday press, 1940. 226 p. DLC. Medical officer in France during the first World War.

Smith, Henry Preserved, 1847- [5282] 1927. The heretic's defense; a footnote to history. N.Y.: Charles Scribner's sons, 1926. NN. Presbyterian theologian and teacher tried for heresy.

Smith, Henry W., b. 1844. Rem- [5283] iniscences of a Dakota pioneer. Sioux Falls: M. D. Scott, print, 1929. 11 p. Auto., p. 5-11. DLC. Homesteader from 1872. The author was born in Germany.

Smith, Hosea, b. 1809? The life [5284] of Hosea Smith, a travelling minister, who was left without father or mother or any connexions... Also, his calls into the ministry. Providence: The author, 1833. 60 p. DLC. Itinerant Baptist in Rhode Island and Conn.

Smith, J.R. Universalism as it [5285] is...by a convert from the Universalist ministry, with a sketch of his own experience. Boston: J.D. Flagg, 1861. 204 p. MMeT. In New England.

Smith, James, 1737-1812. An [5286] account... Cinc.: Robert Clarke & co., 1870. 186 p. WHi. After his escape from the Indians in 1759, Smith returned to Pennsylvania where he farmed, fought the Indians and served in the Revolutionary War.

Smith, James Franklin, 1868–1920. A journey across fifty friendly years. N.Y.: Revell, 1920. 128 p. DLC. Presbyterian clergyman in Texas. [5287]

Smith, James L. Autobiography of James L. Smith, including, also, reminiscences of slave life, recollections of the war, education of freedom, causes of the exodus, etc. Norwich: Press of the Bulletin co., 1881. 150 p. NN. The author was a Negro preacher who escaped from Virginia to Connecticut. [5288]

Smith, James M, b. 1819. A work on revivals...2d ed., rev. & enl. St. Joseph, Mo.: pr. for the author, 1885. 304 p. MoHi. Baptist minister in Indiana, Iowa, Missouri. [5289]

Smith, John, 1681–1766. A narrative... Phila.: pr. by Benjamin & Jacob Johnson, 1800. 48 p. Auto., p. 5–18. DLC. New England Quaker who was imprisoned for refusing to bear arms. [5290]

Smith, John, b. 1823. History of the hermit of Erving Castle (written down by George W. Barber). Andover: pr. by W.F. Draper, 1868. 64 p. WHi. In Mass. [5291]

Smith, John, 1851?–1932. Chief John Smith. Walker: Cass county pioneer, 1919? MnHi. Chippewa Chief in Minnesota tells of his hunting, drinking, and relations with whites. [5292]

Smith, John Jay, 1798–1881. Recollections of John Jay Smith, written by himself. Phila.: priv. pr., Press of J.B. Lippincott co., 1892. NN. The author was for many years librarian of the Loganian Library and active in civic affairs of Philadelphia. [5293]

Smith, John Jay, b. 1856. Reminiscences... No imprint. 41 leaves. WaU. Logger, farmer and furniture merchant in state of Washington. [5294]

Smith, John Wesley, b. 1842. Life story... Decatur: Decatur pr. co., 1930. 126 p. KHi. Union army soldier, farmer in Kansas and Iowa. [5295]

Smith, Joseph, 1805–1844. History of Joseph Smith, the Prophet. (History of the church of Jesus Christ of Latter-Day Saints, vol. I. Salt Lake City: Latter-Day Saints, 1902. 493 p.) WHi. Founder of the Mormon church. [5296]

Smith, Joseph Shuter, b. 1893. Over there and back in three uniforms, being the experiences of an American boy in the Canadian, British and American armies... N.Y.: E. P. Dutton, 1918. 244 p. DLC. First World War. [5297]

Smith, Joseph Tate. Eighty years... Phila.: Westminster press, 1899. 279 p. Auto., p. 40–45. DLC. Presbyterian clergyman in Maryland. [5298]

Smith, Mrs. Julia A. The reason why... Boston: The author, 1881. 187 p. DLC. Medium and spiritualist physician in Boston. [5299]

Smith, Julius. Ten years in Burma. Cinc.: Jennings & Rye, 1902. 326 p. DLC. Methodist missionary. Within the main work, autobiographical portions are included. [5300]

Smith, Kate, b. 1910. Living in a great big way. N.Y.: Blue Ribbon books, 1938. 230 p. DLC. Singer of popular songs on radio. [5301]

Smith, Logan Pearsall, b. 1865. Unforgotten years. London: Constable, 1938. 266 p. WU. Essayist and biographer who left America in 1888. Of American interest is his account of student days at Harvard and Haverford. [5302]

Smith, Mrs. Lydia Adeline (Jackson) Button. Behind the scenes; or, life in an insane asylum. Chicago: pr. by Culver, Page, Hoyne, 1879. 257 p. MiU-H. In Michigan. [5303]

Smith, Marian Caroline. I remember. Jacksonville: priv. pr., 1931. 27 p. GEU. A civilian's account of life in Georgia during the Civil War. [5304]

Smith, Mrs. Martha L. Going to God's country. Boston: Christopher pub. house, 1941. 186 p. DLC. A domestic account of pioneer life in the Southwest, especially Oklahoma. [5305]

Smith, Mrs. Mary Ettie V. (Coray). Fifteen years among the Mormons, by Nelson W. Green. N.Y.: Scribner, 1858. 388 p. CSmH. In Illinois, Iowa, Missouri and Utah, beginning with 1843. A domestic account. [5306]

Smith, Matthew Hale, 1810–1879. [5307]

Universalism examined, renounced... Boston: Tappan & Dennet, 1842. 396 p. DLC. A New England Universalist minister tells of the spiritual experiences which led him to a new religious belief.

Smith, Michael. A complete his- [5308] tory of the late American war with Great Britain... 6th ed. rev... to which is added a narrative of the author's sufferings... 2d. ed. Lexington: pr. by F. Bradford, 1816. 287 p. Auto., p. 229-287. DLC. War of 1812.

Smith, Peter, 1802-1880. Me- [5309] morials of Peter Smith...Cambridge: pr. at Riverside press, 1881. 131 p. Auto., p. 3-43. DLC. Operator of spinning mill in Mass., born in Scotland.

Smith, Richard R. Retrospect; [5310] or, sentimental review. Portsmouth: pr. by J. Whitelock, 1806. 24 p. DLC. Spiritual account by a Baptist minister.

Smith, Rodney, 1860-1947. Gipsy [5311] Smith, his life and work, by himself. N.Y.: Fleming H. Revell co., 1906. 330 p. NN. A British evangelist who made many trips to the United States.

Smith, Samuel, 1759-1854. [5312] Memoirs of Samuel Smith, a soldier of the Revolution... N.Y.: 1860. 41 p. WHi. As described by the title.

Smith, Samuel, b. 1792. Inside [5313] out... Hartford: Norton & Russell, 1827. 48 p. CtHT. Thief in New England.

Smith, Samuel Francis, 1808- [5314] 1895. Poems of home and country. N.Y.: Silver, Burdette, 1895. 382 p. DLC. Contains an autobiographic sketch. Poet, New England Baptist clergyman.

Smith, Mrs. Sarah Hathaway [5315] (Bixby), b. 1871. Adobe days... Cedar Rapids: Torch press, 1925. 208 p. WHi. A girl's life on a pioneer sheep ranch in California.

Smith, Seth M., b. 1822. Auto- [5316] biography of your "Uncle Fuller". Elliott, Iowa: 1905. 178 p. CU-B. Miner in California in 1850. Farmer in Wisconsin and Iowa.

Smith, Sidney W., b. 1881. From [5317] the cow camp to the pulpit...a Texas evangelist. Cinc.: Christian leader corp., 1927. 232 p. MoCanD. Minister of the Christian Church, and cowboy.

Smith, Solomon Franklin, 1801- [5318] 1869. Sol Smith's theatrical apprenticeship. Phila.: T.B. Peterson, 1845. 215 p. DLC. Actor, manager.

Smith, Solomon Franklin, 1801- [5319] 1869. The theatrical journeywork of Sol Smith... Phila.: T.B. Peterson, 1854. 254 p. DLC. Continuation of the previous item.

Smith, Solomon Franklin, 1801- [5320] 1869. Theatrical management in the West and South for thirty years ... N.Y.: Harper, 1868. 275 p. WHi. A revised version of the two preceding items.

Smith, Stephen, 1823-1922. Ran- [5321] dom recollections of a long medical life. N.Y.: William Wood, 1911. 27 p. NNNAM. Public health officer, New York.

Smith, Stephen, 1823-1922. Rem- [5322] iniscences of two epochs— anaesthesia and asepsis. Baltimore: 1919. 16 p. NNNAM. See preceding entry.

Smith, Mrs. Susan E.D. The sol- [5323] dier's friend, being a thrilling narrative of Grandma Smith's four years' experience and observation, as matron, in the hospitals of the South... Memphis: pr. by the Bulletin pub. co., 1867. 300 p. ICU. As described by the title.

Smith, Thomas, 1776-1844. Ex- [5324] periences and ministerial labors of Rev. Thomas Smith. N.Y.: Lane & Tippett, 1848. 198 p. DLC. Itinerant Methodist minister in Maryland, Virginia, Delaware and New Jersey.

Smith, Thomas W. A narrative [5325] of the life, travels and sufferings of Thomas W. Smith. Boston: W. C. Hill, 1844. 240 p. DLC. An English sailor who came to the U.S. in the first half of the 19th century in order to enter a religious seminary in Mass.

Smith, Venture, 1729-1805. A [5326] narrative of the life and adventures of Venture, a native of Africa, but resident about sixty years in the United States of America. Middletown: J. S. Stewart, printer, 1897. 41 p. Auto., p. 5-29. DLC. Slave in Connecticut.

Smith, William B. On wheels: [5327] and how I came there. A real story for real boys and girls, giving the personal experiences and observations of a fifteen-year-old Yankee boy as soldier and prisoner in the American Civil war. N.Y.: Hunt & Eaton, 1892. 338 p. NN. As described by the title.

Smith, William Calvin, 1842- [5328] 1921. The private in gray. Dallas: Ford pub. co.,1908. 134 p. TxU. Confederate soldier.

Smith, William Farrar, 1824- [5329] 1903. From Chattanooga to Petersburg under Generals Grant and Butler; a contribution to the history of the war, and a personal vindication. Boston & N.Y.: Houghton Mifflin, 1893. 201 p. NN. As described by the title.

Smith, William Orlando, 1859- [5330] 1932. Fifty years of rhyming and an autobiography. Punxsutawney: Spirit pub. co., 1932. 204 p. Auto., p. 1-18. DLC. Poet and politician in Pennsylvania.

Smith, William Rudolph, 1787- [5331] 1868. Incidents of a journey... to which are added Gen. Smith's autobiography, 1787-1808... Chicago: W. Howes, 1927. 82 p. Auto., p. 9-23. DLC. Covers the first 21 years of his life to the point where he was admitted to the bar in Pennsylvania.

Smithwick, Noah, 1808-1899. [5332] The evolution of a state; or, recollections of old Texas days. Austin: Gammel book co., 1900. 354 p. WHi. His experiences in the war against Mexico, and Indian fighting.

Smock, Mathias, b. 1818. Sketch [5333] of his life. 2d ed. N.p.: 1901. 95 p. Auto., p. 2-17. MoSM. Baptist clergyman in Missouri and member of the Union army.

Smolnikar, Andreas Bernardus, [5334] b. 1795. Denkwürdige ereignisse ... Cambridge: Folsom, Wells und Thurston, 1838. 461 p. DLC. Austrian Catholic in Massachusetts whose dissident ideas led to his dismissal in 1838. The 3 books which follow continue the story of his activities which took place in Pennsylvania.

Smolnikar, Andreas Bernardus, [5335] b. 1795. Denkwürdige ereignisse... Beleuchtung des Beweiss ... Phila.: J. G. Wesselhoeft, 1839. 606 p. Auto., p. 1-515. DLC. See the description above.

Smolnikar, Andreas Bernardus, [5336] b. 1795. Denkwürdige ereignisse im leben des Andreas Bernardus Smolnikar, Dritter band. N.Y.: H. Ludwig, 1840. 856 p. DLC. See the description above.

Smolnikar, Andreas Bernardus, [5337] b. 1795. Eines is noth... Phila.: Julius Bötticher, 1841. 636 p. DLC. This is a continuation of the preceding volume.

Smyth, Mrs. Ellen L. Warren. [5338] Of my times. N.p.: 1936. 77 p. IaHi. Iowa teacher (in the seventies).

Smyth, Joseph Hilton, b. 1901. To [5339] nowhere and return; the autobiography of a Puritan. N.Y.: Carrick & Evans, 1940. 311 p. NN. Literary life in New York, New Orleans, and Paris. Career of a New England-born writer whose drinking habits landed him on the Bowery; story of his eventual rehabilitation.

Smyth, Newman, 1843-1925. [5340] Recollections and reflections... N.Y.: Scribner's, 1926. 244 p. WHi. Congregational minister in Illinois and Connecticut.

Smyth, Thomas, 1808-1873. [5341] Autobiographical notes, letters and reflections. Charleston, S.C.: Walter, Evans & Cogswell co., 1914. 784 p. NN. Presbyterian clergyman and writer, born in Ireland, pastor of the Second Presbyterian Church, Charleston, S.C., 1834-1870.

Sneddon, Arthur (pseud.). See Parkhill, John.

Snelling, Henry Hunt. Memoirs [5342] of a boyhood at Fort Snelling... Minneapolis: priv. pr., 1939. 36 p. DLC. The writer's father was in command of this Minnesota fort. Covers 1820-27.

Snelling, Joseph. Life of Joseph [5343] Snelling, being a sketch of his Christian experience and labors in the ministry. Boston: John M'Leish, 1847. 163 p. NN. Methodist minister in New England.

Snethen, Abraham, 1794-1877. [5344] Autobiography... Dayton: Christian pub. assoc., 1909. 296 p. MoCanD. Farmer and minister in the Christian Church, mainly in Ohio and Indiana.

Snider, Benjamin S., b. 1821. The [5345] life and travels of Benjamin S. Snider...his persecution, fifteen times a prisoner... Washington: The author, 1869. 114 p. DLC. Union army soldier who took up lay preaching after the War in various parts of the country, and was imprisoned on the charge of insanity.

Snider, Denton Jaques, 1841- [5346] 1925. The St. Louis movement in philosophy, literature, education, psychology, with chapters of autobiography. St. Louis, Mo.: Sigma pub. co., 1920. 608 p. DLC. Educator, philosopher, writer.

Snider, Denton Jaques, 1841- [5347] 1925. A writer of books in his genesis... St. Louis: Sigma pub. co., 1910. 668 p. MoS. See the preceding item. Pages 294-446 contain the story of his career in St. Louis.

Snipes, Joseph Franklin. Fifty [5348] years in psychic research. Boston: Chapple pub. co., 1927. 483 p. DLC. Medium in New York.

Snow, David, b. 1799. From [5349] poverty to plenty; or, the life of David Snow... Boston: pr. for the author by J. Bent & co., 1875. 360 p. DLC. Sailor, merchant in Indiana, and banker in Mass.

Snow, William Josiah, b. 1868. [5350] Signposts of experience; world war memoirs of Major General William J. Snow. Washington, D.C.: United States Field Artillery Association, 1941. 317 p. WHi. First World War.

Snyder, Ely, b. 1815. Personal [5351] experiences. Osawatomie: 1897. 12 p. KHi. Blacksmith in frontier Kansas about 1858, and homesteader in Missouri.

Snyder, Gerrit. After fifty [5352] years. By James W. McKean and Gerrit Snyder. Wamego: Reporter pr. & pub. co., n.d. 39 p. Auto., p. 8-24. KHi. Presbyterian clergyman in Kansas and Illinois.

Snyder, William Hawthorn, [5353] b. 1870. The big "I" ... Elmira: Snyder bros., 1940. 203 p. DLC. Job printer in New York.

Sobieski, John, b. 1842. The life [5354] story and personal reminiscences of Col. John Sobieski... Shelbyville: J. L. Douthit, 1900. 384 p. WHi. Prohibitionist; officer in the Union army.

Sojourner Truth. See Truth, Sojourner.

Soldene, Emily. My theatrical [5355] and musical recollections. London: Downey, 1897. 307 p. DLC. English actress and singer who toured the U.S. several times.

Solomon, Jess. From soldier to [5356] preacher... St. Louis: Frederick pr. co., 1924. 40 p. DLC. The author arrived in France just as the first World War was ending. Upon his return to the U.S., he became a preacher in the Methodist church in Kansas.

Sombrero, pseud. Dreizehn [5357] jahre im Westen von Amerika... Nürnberg: H. Ballhorn, 1877. 262 p. DLC. Adventurer and farmer who lived in Texas, New Mexico, Indiana and California.

Son of Old Man Hat. See Left handed, b. 1868.

Sontag, Georg (alias). See Contant, George.

Sorby, H. C., b. 1860. Incidents [5358] of my life... Minneapolis: priv. pr., n.d. 92 p. WHi. Building contractor in Minnesota.

Sorrel, G. Moxley, d. 1901. Rec- [5359] ollections of a Confederate staff officer... N.Y.: Neale pub. co., 1905. 315 p. DLC. As described by the title.

Sothern, Edward Hugh, 1859- [5360] 1933. The melancholy tale of "me"... N.Y.: Scribner's sons, 1916. 409 p. WU. Actor.

Sousa, John Philip, 1854-1932. [5361] Marching along... Boston: Hale, Cushman & Flint, 1928. 384 p. Auto., p. 1-365. DLC. Composer of marching music and bandmaster.

Southack, John, b. 1774. The life [5362] of John Southack... Charlestown? Mass.: pr. for the author, 1809. 119 p. Auto., p. 5-57. DLC. The author was imprisoned for attempted insurance fraud.

Southwick, Sarah H., b. 1821. [5363] Reminiscences of early antislavery days. Cambridge: priv. pr., at the Riverside press, 1893, 39 p. DLC. Abolitionist.

Southworth, George Champlin [5364] Shepard, 1842-1918. Essays and poems ... ed. & pub. by his son George S. Southworth... Indianapolis?: G. S. Southworth, 1929? 288 p. Auto., p. 222-288. DLC. Lawyer, politician in Ohio. Professor of English literature in Ohio. Poet, essayist.

Souza, Ernest (pseud.). See Scott, Evelyn.

Spaeth, Adolph, 1839-1910. Life [5365] of Adolph Spaeth... Phila.: General council pub. house, 1916. 439 p. MnNS. Lutheran clergyman in New York and Pa., born in Germany.

Spalding, Albert, b. 1888. Rise to [5366] follow, an autobiography. N.Y.: Henry Holt, 1943. 328 p. WU. Violinist.

Sparks, S.F. His recollections. [5367] Houston: Union national bank, 1933. 15 p. TxGR. The author tells of his military experiences in Texas in 1835.

Sparks, William. The Apache [5368] kid. Los Angeles: Skelton, 1926. 214 p. DLC. Miner, hunter, peace officer in Arizona.

Sparling, Christopher J. The [5369] Irish-Canuck-Yankee... Chicago: M. A. Donohue, 1910. 360 p. MoHi. The author came to the U.S. from Ireland in 1885. He was a railroad laborer in Minnesota, and operator of a mine in Washington.

Spaulding, John, 1800-1889. [5370] From the plow to pulpit. N.Y.: R. Carter, 1874. 121 p. DLC. Presbyterian minister in New England and Ohio.

Spaulding, Royal Crafts, 1800- [5371] 1880. Autobiographical sketch... Houlton, Maine: Press of William H. Smith, 1891. 53 p. Auto., p. 7-9. WHi. Baptist minister in Maine.

Spear, John M. Twenty years [5372] on the wing. Brief narrative of my travels and labors as a missionary... Boston: W. White, 1873. 47 p. MnHi. A spiritualist. The period covered is 1852-1873.

Spearman, Mrs. Eugenie (Lon- [5373] ergan), b. 1857. Memories. Los Angeles: priv. pr., by Modern printers, 1941. 136 p. DLC. The wife of a banker tells of their life in Illinois, Nebraska, California, and abroad.

Spence, Hartzell, b. 1908. Get [5374] thee behind me; my life as a preacher's son. N.Y.: Whittlesey house, McGraw-Hill book co., 1942. 375 p. NN. Recollections of an Iowa boyhood.

Spencer, Mrs. Clarissa (Young), [5375] b. 1860. One who was valiant. Caldwell: Caxton printers, 1940. 279 p. DLC. A daughter of Brigham Young tells of her childhood in Utah.

Spencer, Jesse Ames, 1816-1898. [5376] Memorabilia of sixty-five years (1820-1886). N.Y.: Thomas Whittaker, 1890. 250 p. NN. Episcopal clergyman, writer, and educator, professor of Greek at the City College of New York, 1869-1881.

Spencer, John W., 1801-1878. [5377] Reminiscences of pioneer life in the Mississippi Valley. Davenport: Griggs, Watson & Day, printers, 1872. 73 p. DLC. Indian fighting and other pioneering experiences in the period prior to 1850. A 1942 reprint is commonly found in research libraries.

Spencer, Thomas J. Civil war [5378] history of Thos. J. Spencer of Detroit, Michigan. N.p.: 1911. 6 p. MiD-B. Union army.

Sperry, Willard Learoyd, b.1882. [5379] Summer yesterdays in Maine; memories of boyhood vacation days. N.Y. & London: Harper, 1941. 263 p. NN. By the Dean of the Divinity School, Harvard University.

Spicer, Tobias, b. 1788. Auto- [5380] biography... Boston: C. H. Peirce, 1851. 312 p. DLC. Methodist minister in New York.

Spies, August Vincent Theodore, [5381] 1855-1887. August Spies' autobiography... Chicago: Nina van Zandt, 1887. 91 p. WHi. Editor of German language newspaper in Chicago, devoted to socialism. Spies was born in Germany.

Spikes, Lottie A. Memories. [5382] Columbus, Georgia: Gilbert pr. co., 1910. 163 p. DLC. A domestic account of life in Georgia, Alabama and Florida.

Spinning, James B., b. 1837. [5383] Autobiography... Rochester: W. G. Spinning, 1900. 108 p. WHi. Printer in New York.

Spivey, Vernon Malone, b. 1902. [5384] A life to share. Chicago: Ed. M. Rowe pr. co., 1944. 305 p. DLC.

Lay preacher in Midwest. Radio broadcaster and editor of religious newspaper in Chicago.

Splan, John, b. 1849. Life with [5385] the trotters. Chicago: H. T. White, 1889. 450, 20 p. Auto., p. 5-271. DLC. Jockey.

Spofford, Jeremiah, 1787-1880. [5386] Reminiscences of seventy years ... Haverhill: E. G. Frothingham, printer, 1867. 40 p. DLC. Physician in Mass.

Sponland, Ingeborg, b. 1860. My [5387] reasonable service. Minneapolis: Augsburg pub. house, 1938. 158 p. NN. Career in Norway and the United States of a Lutheran deaconess nurse.

Spore, William D. A peripatetic [5388] M.D. Mexico: F. P. Hoeck, 1899. 162 p. MoSHi. Physician employed by a steamship line.

Spottswood, Wilson Lee, 1822- [5389] 1892. Brief annals. Harrisburg: M.E. book room, 1888. 351 p. WHi. College president and Methodist clergyman in Virginia, Maryland, and Pennsylvania.

Sprague, Eli Wilmot, b. 1847. [5390] A future life demonstrated; or, twenty-seven years a public medium. Detroit: E. W. Sprague, 1908. 362 p. DLC. In New York, Indiana, Michigan and Pa.

Spring, Gardiner, 1785-1873. [5391] Personal reminiscences... N.Y.: Scribner, 1866. 2 vols. WHi. Presbyterian clergyman in New York.

Springer, John McKenbree, [5392] b. 1873. Pioneering in the Congo. N.Y.: pr. by the Methodist book concern, 1916. 311 p. DLC. Methodist missionary.

Squier, Miles Powell, 1792-1866. [5393] The miscellaneous writings of Miles P. Squier, with an autobiography. Geneva: Press of R. L. Adams, n.d. 408 p. Auto., p. 7-77. WHi. Presbyterian clergyman in New York (home mission worker).

Stacy, Nathaniel, b. 1778? Memoirs... [5394] Columbus: pub. for the author, 1850. 523 p. WHi. Clergyman of the Universalist faith in New York, Ohio, Michigan and Pennsylvania.

Stahl, Ferdinand Anthony, b.1874. [5395] In the land of the Incas. Mountain View: Pacific press, 1920. 301 p. Auto., p. 35-285. DLC. Medical missionary in Peru in the service of the Seventh Day Adventists.

Stahl, Ferdinand Anthony, b. 1874. [5396] In the Amazon jungles. Mountain View: Pacific press, 1932. 116 p. DLC. See the description of the preceding item.

Stahl, John Meloy, b. 1860. Growing up with the West. [5397] N.Y.: Longmans, Green, 1930. 515 p. WHi. Rural newspaper editor in Illinois and Missouri.

Stahler, Enoch, b. 1836. Enoch [5398] Stahler, miller and soldier... Washington: 1909. 30 p. WHi. Union army soldier and miller in Minnesota.

Stancourt, Louis Joseph. A flower [5399] for sign. N.Y.: Macmillan, 1937. 303 p. DLC. A spiritual account by a Catholic.

Standing Bear, Chief Luther, [5400] b. 1868. My people, the Sioux. N.Y.: Houghton Mifflin, 1928. 288 p. WHi. A 20th century account in the main by a graduate of Carlisle who among other occupations tried teaching.

Standing Bear, Chief Luther, [5401] b. 1868. My Indian boyhood. N.Y.: Houghton Mifflin, 1931. 189 p. WHi. See the preceding item. This book was written for young people.

"Stanley". The Jack-Roller; a [5402] delinquent boy's own story. Chicago: Univ. of Chicago press, 1930. 205 p. Auto., p. 47-163. WU. In Chicago.

Stanley, David Sloane, 1828-1902. [5403] Personal memoirs... Cambridge: Harvard univ. press, 1917. 271 p. WHi. Officer in the Union army, who after the War served for many years in the West among the Indians.

Stanley, Henry Morton, 1841- [5404] 1904. The autobiography... N.Y.: Houghton Mifflin, 1909. 551 p. Auto., p. 3-215. WHi. This account closes with 1862 and deals largely with his service in the Confederate army.

Stanley, John. Twelve years of [5405] crime and criminals... Columbus: F. J. Heer pr. co., 1903. 261 p. MoKU. Railroad detective and marshal in Kentucky, Ohio, Indiana and the District of Columbia.

The time: second half of the 19th century.

Stanley, John A. From then until now. No imprint. 64 p. SdHi. Mainly an account of youth in the family of a physician in Wisconsin and Iowa, and then on a homestead in Dakota. Later the author became a newspaper publisher. [5406]

Stanley, M. A mile of gold. Strange adventures on the Yukon. Chicago: Laird & Lee, 1898. 219 p. CSmH. In 1896. [5407]

Stansbury, George Francis, b. 1837. The life of a "lie-out", or the adventures of a rover. Weedsport: G.W. Churchill's press, 1899. 194 p. DLC. Union sailor on an ironclad. [5408]

Stanton, Daniel, 1708-1770. A journal... Phila.: Joseph Crukshank, 1772. 173 p. WHi. Minister of the Society of Friends in Pennsylvania. [5409]

Stanton, Mrs. Elizabeth Cady, 1815-1902. Eighty years and more (1815-1897). N.Y.: European pub. co., 1898. 474 p. WHi. Proponent of woman's rights. [5410]

Stanton, Gerrit Smith, b. 1845. "When the wildwood was in flower"... N.Y.: Ogilvie, 1909. 123 p. DLC. Stock farmer in Iowa. [5411]

Stanton, Henry Brewster, 1805-1887. Random recollections. N.Y.: Harper, 1887. 298 p. DLC. New York political figure and abolitionist. [5412]

Starbuck, Mary Eliza, b. 1856. My house and I; a chronicle of Nantucket. Boston & N.Y.: Houghton Mifflin co., 1929. 293 p. WHi. Mainly an account of youthful days, but includes the later life of a socialite. [5413]

Stark, Mabel. Hold that tiger. Caldwell: Caxton printers, 1938. 248 p. DLC. Tiger trainer, circus performer. [5414]

Starke, Barbara (pseud.). Born in captivity; the story of a girl's escape. Indianapolis: The Bobbs-Merrill co., 1931. 301 p. NN. Adventures hitch-hiking across the United States of a New England-born girl seeking escape from convention. [5415]

Starks, John Jacob, b. 1876. Lo these many years... Columbia: [5416] State co., 1941. 173 p. DLC. Negro educator in South Carolina.

Starnes, Arthur H. Aerial maniac; my experience as a wing walker and a parachute jumper... Hammond, Ind.: pr. by Delaney pr. co., 1938. 137 p. DLC. As described by the title. [5417]

Starr, Eliza Allen, 1824-1901. The life and letters...ed. by James J. McGovern. Chicago: Lakeside press, 1905. 452 p. Auto., p. 21-44. MoSW. An Illinois painter and writer tells of her conversion to Catholicism. [5418]

Starr, Frederick, 1858-1933. In Indian Mexico; a narrative of travel and labor. Chicago: Forbes, 1908. 425 p. DLC. Archeologist. [5419]

Starr, Frederick Ratchford, b. 1821. Farm echoes. N.Y.: Orange Judd co., 1881. 110 p. DLC. A Phila. businessman tries his hand at farming. [5420]

Starr, Henry, b. 1873. Thrilling events... Tulsa, sold by R.D. Gordon, 1914. 51 p. OkHi. Robber, murderer in Oklahoma and Arkansas. [5421]

Starr, Peter, 1744-1829. A half-century sermon, delivered at Warren, March 8, 1822... Norwalk: pr. by S. W. Benedict, 1823. 20 p. NNUT. Clergyman in Connecticut (Congregationalist?). [5422]

Starret, Paul, b. 1866. Changing the skyline... N.Y.: Whittlesey house, 1938. 319 p. DLC. Engineer, builder of sky-scrapers in Chicago and New York. [5423]

Stearns, Harold Edmund, b. 1891. The street I know. N.Y.: Lee Furman, 1935. 411 p. WU. Foreign correspondent. [5424]

Stebbins, Charles M., b. 1829. The new and true religion. Hartsdale: C. M. Stebbins, 1898. 423 p. Auto., p. 311-423. DLC. Owner and builder of telegraph lines in Missouri, Kansas and Nebraska. [5425]

Stebbins, George Cole, b. 1846. Reminiscences and gospel hymn stories. N.Y.: George H. Doran, 1924. 327 p. DLC. Composer of religious hymns. [5426]

Stebbins, Giles Badger, b. 1817. Upward steps of seventy years. N.Y.: United States book co., 1890. 308 p. WHi. Believer in spiritualism, advocate of abolitionism [5427]

Stedwell, Anson, b. 1843. Itiner- [5428] ant footprints. Chicago: pr. by the Free Methodist pub. house, 1915. 339 p. Auto., p. 1-150. DLC. Free Methodist itinerant minister in Illinois, Iowa, Nebraska.

Steed, Thomas, 1826-1910. The [5429] life of Thomas Steed...No imprint. 43 p. CU. The author arrived in Illinois from England in 1844. Later he became a farmer in Utah, and went on missions for the Mormons to England and Australia.

Steedman, Charles, 1811-1890. [5430] Memoir and correspondence of Charles Steedman, Rear Admiral, U.S. Navy, with his autobiography. Cambridge: priv. pr., 1912. 532 p. DLC. His experiences included the siege at Vera Cruz and the war against the Southern states.

Steele, Hiram R., b. 1842. Rem- [5431] iniscences of a long life. N.Y.: priv. pr., 1927. 47 p. GEU. School teacher, cotton planter, lawyer and state judge in Louisiana and Mississippi. This account closes with 1890.

Steele, Joel Dorman, 1836-1886. [5432] Joel Dorman Steele, teacher and author, by Mrs. George Archibald (pseud.). N.Y.: A. S. Barnes & co., 1900. 215 p. Auto., p. xi-xxxiv. WHi. Author of books on chemistry, teacher in New York.

Steele, John Washington, [5433] b. 1843. Coal oil Johnny. Franklin: priv. pr., 1902. 211 p. WHi. An oil operator in Pa. squanders a fortune on drinking, etc.

Steenburgh, Samuel, 1833-1878. [5434] Confession... Albany: Weed, Parsons, 1878. 23 p. DLC. A life of crime (thieving, gambling, murder) in New York.

Steere, Reuben Allen, b. 1838. [5435] Sketch of the life...of Col. R.A. Steere...Danielsonville: pr. by F. U. Scofield, 1883. 20 p. MWA. Midget circus performer.

Stefansson, Vilhjalmur, b.1879. [5436] My life with the Eskimo. N.Y.: Macmillan, 1913. 538 p. Auto., p. 1-435. DLC. The explorer's account of his 1906-07 expedition to northernmost Canada.

Steffan, Martin Robert, b. 1882. [5437] The itinerant horse physician. Chicago: Am. journal of veterinary medicine, 1916. 192 p. DLC. As described by the title.

Steffens, Cornelius Martin, [5438] b. 1866. Adventures in money raising... N.Y.: Macmillan, 1930. 278 p. DLC. By the President of the University of Dubuque.

Steffens, Joseph Lincoln, 1866- [5439] 1936. The autobiography of Lincoln Steffens. N.Y.: Harcourt, Brace, 1931. 873 p. WHi. Journalist and magazine writer, known for his attacks on evil corporate practices.

Steiger, Ernst, 1832-1917. Drei [5440] und fünfzig jahre buchhändler in Deutschland und Amerika. N.Y.: E. Steiger, 1901. 432 p. MoSC. Bookseller in New York City.

Stein, Gertrude, 1874-1946. The [5441] autobiography of Alice B. Toklas ... N.Y.: Harcourt, Brace, 1933. 310 p. WU. This account deals mainly with her life in France, written by the well-known poet and novelist.

Stein, Gertrude, 1874-1946. [5442] Everybody's autobiography. N.Y.: Random house, 1937. 318 p. WU. A sequel to the previous item.

Steiner, Edward Alfred, b. 1866. [5443] From alien to citizen... N.Y.: Fleming H. Revell, 1914. 332 p. WHi. The author was born in the Austro-Hungarian Empire. He came to the U.S. in the latter years of the 19th century, where he was converted from Judaism to Christianity, and became a Congregational clergyman in Ohio and Minnesota and professor of theology at Grinnell College. For his life in Europe, see Against the Current and other works.

Steinert, Morris, 1831-1912. [5444] Reminiscences... N.Y.: G. P. Putnam's sons, 1900. 267 p. DLC. Owner of music store in Connecticut, musician. Steinert was born in Germany.

Steinmeyer, Henry G. A village [5445] childhood. Staten Island: Staten Island historical society, 1941. 31 p. DLC. In New York.

Stelzle, Charles, b. 1869. A son [5446] of the Bowery... N.Y.: George H. Doran, 1926. 335 p. WU. Social worker and minister in New York.

Stempfel, Theodore, 1863-1935. [5447] Ghosts of the past... Indianapolis: priv. pub. 1936. 101 p. DLC.

Indiana banker, born in Germany, who pursued historical research as a hobby.

Stenhouse, Fanny, b. 1829. Expose [5448] of polygamy in Utah. A lady's life among the Mormons...as one of the wives of a Morman elder during a period of more than twnety years. N.Y.: American News co., 1872. 221 p. WHi. The author was born in England.

Stennes, John J., 1865-1950. [5449] Memories. St. Paul: priv. pr., 1935. 160 p. MnS. Teacher, postmaster; insurance and real estate business; county auditor. The author lived in Minnesota.

Stephens, Mrs. Ellen. The cabin [5450] boy wife... N.Y.: C. E. Daniels, 1840. 24 p. WHi. Dressed as a boy, the author worked as a cabin boy on the Mississippi River about 1839, seeking a husband who had deserted her and child.

Stephens, John Vant, b. 1857. [5451] Fourscore, life story (abridged) of John Vant Stephens... Cinc.: 1938. 142 p. DLC. Teacher in Illinois; Presbyterian minister in Tennessee, Kentucky; professor in theological seminary in Pa.

Stephens, Kate, b. 1853. Life at [5452] Laurel Town in Anglo-Saxon Kansas. Lawrence: Alumni ass'n of the Univ. of Kansas, 1920. 251 p. KHi. Student at the University of Kansas in the seventies who spent her youth on a Kansas farm.

Stephens, Lorenzo Dow, b.1827. [5453] Life sketches of a jayhawker of '49...San Jose: 1916. 68 p. DLC. Miner, farmer in California. The author also mined in Nevada, Arizona and Idaho.

Stephenson, Isaac, 1829-1918. [5454] Recollections of a long life, 1829-1915. Chicago: priv. pr., 1915. 265 p. WHi. Lumberman and political figure in Wisconsin.

Sterling, Thomas, b. 1862. Auto- [5455] biography of Tom Sterling; seven years of thrilling adventures of a western peace officer. Santa Monica: Weaver pub. co., 1941. 118 p. DLC. Cowboy in Texas; sheriff, U.S. Marshal in Kansas, Colorado, New Mexico.

Stern, Mrs. Elizabeth Gertrude [5456] (Levin), b. 1890. I am a woman— and a Jew (by Leah Morton, pseud.).
N.Y.: Sears, 1926. 362 p. WHi. A domestic account of marriage between a Jewess and a Christian.

Sternberg, Charles Hazelius, [5457] b. 1850. The life of a fossil hunter... N.Y.: H. Holt, 1909. 286 p. DLC. Paleontologist in the midwest.

Sternberg, Charles Hazelius, [5458] b. 1850. Hunting dinosaurs in the bad lands of the Red Deer River, Alberta, Canada...Lawrence, Kan.: C. H. Sternberg, 1917. 232 p. Auto., p. 1-207. DLC. From 1912-17, the author was employed in collecting specimans.

Sterne, Louis, b. 1835. Seventy [5459] years of active life. London: priv. pr., 1912. 191 p. WHi. Inventor in the fields of transportation and communication.

Stetson, Augusta Emma Simmons [5460] 1842?-1928. Reminiscences... N.Y.: Putnam's, 1913. 1200 p. Auto., p. 1-40. WHi. Prominent Christian Scientist leader.

Stetson, Mrs. Charles Walter. See Gilman, Charlotte Perking.

Stevens, Henry, b. 1818. Sketch [5461] ... Bandera: Enterprise print, n.d. 34 p. TxU. Farmer, lumber miller on Tennessee frontier. Blacksmith in Texas.

Stevens, John Frank, b. 1853. An [5462] engineer's recollections. N.Y.: McGraw-Hill, 1936. 70 p. WU. Civil engineer (railroads and canals).

Stevens, John V. Autobiography [5463] ...Janesville: priv. pr., 1932. WHi. Wisconsin physician.

Stevens, Philander, b. 1819. [5464] Recollections... Brooklyn: 1896. 295 p. CHi. New York merchant in thirties and forties. His business dealings led him to the middlewest in fifties and to the South in the sixties.

Stevenson, Thomas, b. 1874. [5465] Reminiscences... Boston: priv. pr., 1941. 169 p. MH. Boston banker and agriculturalist.

Stevenson, William G. Thirteen [5466] months in the rebel army...by an impressed New Yorker. N.Y.: Barnes & Burr, 1862. 232 p. WHi. As described by the title.

Stevenson, William Yorke, b.1878 [5467] From "Poilu" to "Yank"...Boston & N.Y.: Houghton Mifflin,1918.

209 p. DLC. Soldier in the first World War who served in the French and American armies.

Steward, Austin. Twenty-two [5468] years a slave, and forty years a freeman... Rochester: William Alling, 1857. 360 p. WHi. After obtaining his freedom, the author became a merchant in York York; finally, in 1831, he removed to the Wilberforce Colony in Canada where he was a member of the Board of Managers.

Steward, Theophilus Gould, [5469] b. 1843. From 1864 to 1914... Phila.: pr. by A.M.E., 1921? 520 p. NNC. Professor of history at Wilberforce University, and Methodist clergyman.

Stewart, Charles Samuel, 1795- [5470] 1870. A visit to the South Seas, in the U.S. ship Vincennes... N.Y.: John P. Haven, 1831. 2 vols. DLC. By a chaplain.

Stewart, Mrs. Eliza (Daniel), [5471] 1816-1908. Memories of the crusade... Columbus: W.G. Hubbard, 1888. 535 p. WHi. Temperance worker in Ohio.

Stewart, Mrs. Ellen (Brown). [5472] Life of Mrs. Ellen Stewart... Akron: Beebe & Elkins, printers, 1858. 243 p. NN. Schoolmistress and housewife in New York during the first half of the 19th century.

Stewart, Jane Agnes, b. 1860. I [5473] have recalled. Toledo: Chittenden press, 1938. 190 p. WHi. Social reform worker; prohibitionist, woman's rights, and child welfare.

Stewart, John, b. 1795. Highways [5474] and hedges; or, fifty years of Western Methodism... Cinc.: Hitchcock & Walden, 1870. 396 p. NN. The author labored in Ohio, Virginia, Kentucky, Pennsylvania, Indiana, and Illinois.

Stewart, William Frank. Last of [5475] the fillibusters... Sacramento: Henry Shipley, 1857. 85 p. CSmH. A military account of events in Nicarauga.

Stewart, William Morris, 1827- [5476] 1909. Reminiscences of Senator William Morris Stewart of Nevada... N.Y.: Neale, 1908. 358 p. WHi. Lawyer, frontier miner, U.S. Senator.

Stiles, Robert, b. 1836. Four [5477] years under Marse Robert. N.Y.: Neale, 1903. 368 p. WHi. Confederate officer.

Stilgebouer, Forster George. [5478] Nebraska pioneers... Grand Rapids: Eerdmans, 1944. 414 p. NbO. Covers 1875-1940: Indian raids; school teaching, banking.

Still, Andrew Taylor, 1828-1917. [5479] Autobiography of Andrew T. Still, with a history of the discovery and development of the science of osteopathy... Kirksville, Mo.: pub. by the author, 1897. 460 p. NN. The founder of osteopathy.

Still, James, b. 1812. Early rec- [5480] ollections and life of Dr. James Still. Phila.: pr. for the author by J.B. Lippincott & co., 1877. 274 p. NN. The author was a self-educated Negro physician.

Still, Peter. The kidnapped and [5481] the ransomed. Being the personal recollections of Peter Still and his wife...after forty years of slavery. Syracuse: W. T. Hamilton, 1856. 409 p. ViHaI. Negro teacher in Alaska.

Stillé, Charles Janeway, 1819- [5482] 1899. Reminiscences of a provost. 1866-1880. N.p.: 1880. 58 p. NN. The author relates his experiences as the provost of the University of Pennsylvania.

Stillman, William James, 1828- [5483] 1901. The autobiography of a journalist. Boston: Houghton Mifflin, 1901. 2 vols. WHi. Painter, war correspondent, U.S. Consul in Crete and Rome.

Stillwell, Leander, b. 1843. The [5484] story of a common soldier of army life in the Civil war, 1861-1865. 2d. ed. Erie, Kan.: Franklin Hudson pub. co., 1920. NN. Union army.

Stimson, Frederick Jesup, [5485] b. 1855. My United States. N.Y.: Scribner, 1931. 478 p. WHi. Novelist, lawyer, Ambassador to Argentina.

Stimson, Hiram K., b. 1804. [5486] From the stage coach to the pulpit. St. Louis: R. A. Campbell, 1874. 427 p. WHi. Baptist clergyman in New York.

Stimson, Lewis Atterbury, 1844- [5487] 1917. Civil war memories...N.Y.: Knickerbocker press, 1918. 52 p. NN. Union army.

Stimson, Rodney Metcalf, b.1822. [5488] Autobiography. No imprint. 4 p.

MiD-B. Teacher, newspaper editor, politician, librarian in Ohio. The account closes with 1881.

Stinchfield, Ephraim, 1761-1837. [5489] Some memories of the life, experience, and travels of Elder Ephraim Stinchfield. Portland: pr. by F. Douglas, 1819. 105 p. MH. Baptist clergyman in New England.

Stirling, Yates, b. 1872. Sea duty... N.Y.: Putnam's sons, 1939. 309 p. WHi. Officer in the U.S. Navy. [5490]

Stockell, William. The eventful [5491] narrative of Capt. William Stockell... Cinc.: pr. by S. Ward, 1840. 326 p. DLC. British born sailor who served in the navies of Great Britain, and of the U.S., and who also engaged in whaling.

Stocking, Moses, 1813-1881. A [5492] tribute to the memory of a good man; an autobiography... Wahoo, Nebr.: Independent pr. co., 1882. 11 p. NbHi. Freighter, farmer and sheep raiser in Nebraska.

Stockton, Thomas Hewlings, [5493] 1808-1868. Poems: with autobiographic and other notes. Phila.: W. S. and Alfred Martien, 1862. 321 p. DLC. Poet and Methodist clergyman in Maryland, Ohio and Pennsylvania.

Stockton, Thomas J., b. 1820. [5494] Life sketches... 2d ed. Stanberry: pr. at Advocate book & job office, 1898. 127 p. TxU. Missouri farmer.

Stockton, William Jaspar, [5495] b. 1848. The plains over... Los Banos, Calif.: Los Banos enterprise, 1939. 55 p. CU-B. Miner, farmer in California, beginning with the sixties.

Stoddard, Charles Warren, 1843- [5496] 1909. A troubled heart... Notre Dame, Indiana: Lyons, 1885. 178 p. DLC. The story of a writer's conversion to Catholicism.

Stoddard, John Lawson, 1850- [5497] 1931. Rebuilding a lost faith... N.Y.: F. J. Kennedy, 1923. 222 p. OCX. The story of his conversion to Catholicism by a prominent lecturer.

Stoddard, Richard Henry, 1825- [5498] 1903. Recollections, personal and literary; ed. by Ripley Hitchcock. N.Y.: A. S. Barnes, 1903. 333 p. WU. New England poet and editor of literary magazines.

Stoddart, James Henry, 1827- [5499] 1907. Recollections of a player. N.Y.: Century, 1902. 255 p. WU. English actor who became closely identified with the American stage.

Stokes, Ellwood Haines, 1815- [5500] 1897. The story of fifty years. Ocean Grove: J. B. Rodgers pr. co., 1893. 50 p. DLC. Methodist clergyman in New Jersey.

Stokes, Ellwood Haines, 1815- [5501] 1897. Footprints... Asbury Park: Pennypacker, 1898. 164 p. DLC. An extended version of the preceding item.

Stokes, George W., 1847-1925. [5502] ...Deadwood gold; a story of the Black Hills. Yonkers-on-Hudson, N.Y.: World book co., 1926. 163 p. NN. Union army soldier; pioneer, miner in colorado and Wyoming.

Stoll, William Tecumseh, 1859- [5503] 1931. Silver strike; the true story of silver mining in the Coeur d' Alenes. Boston: Little, Brown & co., 1932. 273 p. CLU-C. In Idaho in the eighties.

Stolworthy, Henry Thomas, [5504] b. 1860. Treasures of truth (written by Lucy S. Burnham). No imprint. 65 p. US1C. Utah cowboy, lay worker for the Mormon church.

Stone, Barton Warren, 1772-1844.[5505] The biography of Elder Barton Warren Stone. Cinc.: James, 1847. 404 p. WHi. Clergyman of the Christian Church in Ohio and Kentucky, editor of Christian messenger. Prior to serving the Christian Church he had been a Presbyterian minister in several Southern states.

Stone, Fred Andrew, b. 1873. [5506] Rolling stone. N.Y.: McGraw-Hill, 1945. 246 p. WU. Star of circus, screen, and vaudeville.

Stone, Goldie (Tuvin), b. 1874. [5507] My caravan of years... N.Y.: Bloch, 1945. 252 p. DLC. Jewish community and social worker in Chicago.

Stone, Melville Elijah, 1848- [5508] 1929. Fifty years a journalist. Garden City, N.Y.: Doubleday, Page, 1921. 371 p. WU. One of the founders of the Associated Press. He was connected in the U.S. with newspapers in Chicago and Washington.

Stone, Richard Cecil, b. 1798. [5509] Life-incidents... St. Louis: Southwestern, 1874. 352 p. MoKU. A New England school teacher leaves for Missouri about 1860 where he is associated with his son's lumber and paper business.

Stone, William Alexis, b. 1846. The [5510] tale of a plain man. 2d ed. Phila.: Winston, 1918. 319 p. WHi. Lawyer, prominent Pennsylvania politician.

Stonebraker, Joseph R. A rebel [5511] of '61. N.Y.: Wynkoop Hallenbeck Crawford co., printers, 1899. 116 p. WHi. Confederate soldier.

Stonebraker, Mrs. Julia [5512] (Peaslee), b. 1833. Twice a pioneer...(written by Charles R. Green). Lyndon: 1897. 12 p. KHi. After spending her youthful years on a farm in Iowa, she was married to a homesteader in Kansas.

Stong, Philip Duffield. If school [5513] keeps. N.Y.: Stokes, 1940. 266 p. WU. Teacher in Minnesota and Kansas; journalist, and novelist.

Story, Joseph, 1779-1845. The [5514] miscellaneous writings of Joseph Story. Boston: Little & Brown, 1852. 828 p. Auto., p. 1-39. DLC. Massachusetts lawyer, judge of state supreme court, justice of U.S. Supreme Court.

Strange, Michael, b. 1890. Who [5515] tells me true. N.Y.: Scribner, 1940. 396 p. WU. Actress, playwright and poet.

Stratton, Joseph Buck, 1815-1903 [5516] Memorial of a quarter-century's pastorate... Phila.: Lippincott, 1869. 69 p. LU. Presbyterian in Mississippi, beginning with 1843.

Straub, Edward Adlum, b. 1845. [5517] Life and civil war services of Edward A. Straub...Milwaukee, Wis.: Press of J. H. Yewdale & sons co., 1909. 246 p. DLC. Union army soldier; merchant and farmer in Illinois.

Straugh, Philip Adam, b. 1858. [5518] The mysterious traveler and his return to the country of his boyhood, by himself. Chicago: M.A. Donohue, 1906. 263 p. DLC. Private detective whose work took him to various regions of the U.S. and abroad.

Straus, Oscar Solomon, 1850- [5519] 1926. Under four administrations. From Cleveland to Taft. Boston: Houghton Mifflin, 1922. 456 p. WHi. German Jewish lawyer, in New York, Ambassador to Turkey, and cabinet member under Roosevelt.

Streeter, F. L. Pastor and peo- [5520] ple. Kansas City, Mo.: Western Baptist pub. co., 1928. 141 p. Auto., p. 50-139. KHi. Baptist clergyman in Kansas, beginning with 1873.

Strickland, Riley. Adventures of [5521] the A.E.F. soldier. Austin: Von Boeckmann-Jones co., 1920. 338 p. TxGR. A military account of the first World War.

Strieter, Johannes, b. 1829. [5522] Lebenslauf des Johannes Strieter ...Cleveland: Leutner, 1904. 183 p. MoSC-H. Lutheran clergyman, born in Germany, who served in Ohio, Wisconsin and Illinois.

Stringfellow, John S. Hell! no! [5523] ... Boston: Meador, 1936. 362 p. DLC. Soldier in the first World War.

Springfield, Thomas, b. 1866. [5524] Life of scout Two Braids... San Antonio: Wood-Brownlee pr. co., n.d. 50 p. CoD. After 40 years with the Indians he becomes a government scout and deputy marshal in Nebraska and Oklahoma.

Stromme, Peer Olsen, 1856- [5525] 1921. Erindringer. Minneapolis: Augsburg, 1923. 429 p. WU. Novelist, literary critic and journalist (in Illinois, Wisconsin and Minnesota).

Strong, Alvah, b. 1809. Auto- [5526] biography of Alvah Strong, July 18, 1809-April 20, 1885. N.p.: priv. pr., 1885? 115 p. NRCR. Newspaper publisher in New York.

Strong, Anna Louise, b. 1885. I [5527] change worlds... N.Y.: Holt, 1935. 422 p. WU. American reporter in Russia, China and Mexico. After her marriage to a Russian she becomes a reporter for the Moscow News.

Strong, George Crockett, 1832- [5528] 1863. Cadet life at West Point. By an officer of the United States army... Boston: Burnham, 1862. 367 p. Auto., p. 7-324. DLC. Member of the class of 1857.

Strong, George W., d. 1866. Five [5529] years of crime in California.

Comp. by Peter A. Forsee. Ukiah City: Forsee, 1867. 46 p. Auto., p. 3-15. CU-B. Thief, murderer (1857-66).

Strong, Henry W. My frontier days. Dallas: 1925? 122 p. WHi. Indian fighter in Texas in sixties and seventies. [5530]

Strong, Isobel. See Field, Mrs. Isobel (Osbourne).

Strong, James Clark, b. 1826. Biographical sketch... Los Gatos: 1910. 106 p. WHi. Union army officer, and political figure in the Territory of Washington. [5531]

Strong, Wallace K. Souvenir... No imprint. 18 p. CSfSP. Court reporter in California, 1876-1906. [5532]

Stroyer, Jacob, b. 1849. My life in the South. New & rev. ed. Salem: Salem Observer book & job print, 1889. 83 p. DLC. Slave in South Carolina, Methodist clergyman in Mass. [5533]

Struve, Gustav, 1805-1870. Disseits und jenseits...Coburg: Streit, 1863, 131 p. WHi. Refuge from Germany who was a journalist in New York, 1851-62. [5534]

Struve, Heinrich von, b. 1812. Ein lebensbild... Leipzig: E. Ungleich, 1895. 145 p. TxU. Texas pioneer farmer, born in Germany. [5535]

Stuart, George Hay, 1816-1890. The life of George H. Stuart, written by himself. Phila.: J.M. Stoddart & co., 1890. 383 p. NN. Philadelphia merchant and philanthropist, active in religious affairs and in the YMCA; president of the United States Christian Commission during the Civil War. [5536]

Stuart, Granville, 1834-1918. Forty years on the frontier as seen in the journals and reminiscences of Granville Stuart, goldminer, trader, merchant, rancher and politician. Cleveland: The Arthur H. Clark co., 1925. 2 vols. NN. As described by the title. [5537]

Stuart, Jesse, b. 1907. Beyond dark hills... N.Y.: Dutton, 1938. 399 p. WU. Poet and short-story writer writes of education in the South and of being a superintendent of schools in Kentucky. [5538]

Stuart, William, b. 1788? Sketches... Bridgeport: The author, 1854. 223 p. DLC. Conn. counterfeiter. [5539]

Stucki, John S., b. 1850. Family history... Salt Lake City: 1932. 164 p. UU. Born in Switzerland, Stucki came with his parents to Utah in 1860 where they lived on a farm. Later, in 1886, he went on a mission to Switzerland for the Mormons. [5540]

Studebaker, J.M. To old Hangtown or bust. Reported by Wells Drury. Placerville: 1912. 48 p. CU-B. The president of the Studebaker corporation tells of the fifties when he was a miner and wheelwright in California. [5541]

Stuel, Samuel Augustus, b. 1849. The sunny road. Memphis: 1925. 160 p. DLC. The son of a southern itinerant clergyman, whose father settles on a farm in Tennessee during the Civil War. [5542]

Stullken, G. My experiences on the plains. Wichita, Kan.: Grit printery, 1913. 36 p. CoD. Soldier in the Union army. [5543]

Sturdevant, Hervey S., b. 1848. Life and adventures...Cornelius: n.d. 127 p. OrU. Laborer in New York and Pennsylvania; farmer in Texas; farmer and Adventist clergyman in Oregon. [5544]

Sturdivant, Cyrus, 1836-1907. Autobiography... N.Y.: Willis McDonald & co., printers, 1879. 96 p. RPB. Steamboat captain, preacher to the poor. The locale is Maine. [5545]

Sturgeon, Isaac Hughes, 1821-1908. Sketch of the incidents in the life of Isaac H. Sturgeon... St. Louis: 1908. 23 p. WHi. Comptroller in St. Louis; Assistant Postmaster under Harrison. [5546]

Sturges, Mary Pemberton (Cady) 1806-1894. Reminiscences of a long life. N.Y.: F. E. Parrish & co., 1894. 245 p. NN. Social life in New York City and Fredericksburg, Va. before the Civil War. [5547]

Sturges-Jones, Marion. Babes in the wood. N.Y.: G. P. Putnam's sons, 1944. 223 p. NN. Experiences of a young woman stenographer in Philadelphia. [5548]

Sturtevant, Julian Monson, 1805-1886. An autobiography... N.Y.: Revell, 1896. 349 p. WHi. President of Illinois College, a school supported by the Congregational [5549]

Church, and clergyman.

Stuyvesant, Moses Sherwood, [5550] d. 1906. Navy record... St. Louis: Perrin & Smith, 1906. 26 p. MoSHi. Officer in the U.S. Navy during the Civil War.

Subaltern in America. See Gleig, George Robert.

Sugimoto, Etsu (Inagaki). A [5551] daughter of the Samurai. Garden City: Doubleday, Page, 1925. 314 p. DLC. Born in Japan; comes to the U.S. for an education where she becomes a university teacher.

Sullins, David, 1827-1918. Recol-[5552] lections of an old man; seventy years in Dixie, 1827-1897. 2d ed. Bristol, Tenn.: The King pr. co., 1910. 426 p. NN. Methodist minister and educator in Virginia and Tennessee; Civil War experiences.

Sullivan, John Lawrence, 1858- [5553] 1918. Life and reminiscences of a 19th century gladiator...Boston: Hearn, 1892. 294 p. DLC. Prize fighter.

Sullivan, Joseph, b. 1864. Be- [5554] coming an American. Boston: Badger, 1929. 124 p. DLC. Episcopalian clergyman, born in Ireland, who served in Wyoming, New York and Massachusetts.

Sullivan, Louis Henry, 1846- [5555] 1924. The autobiography of an idea. N.Y.: American institute of architects, 1924. 329 p. WU. An architect tells of his life to 1900, including his training in Philadelphia, and his work in Chicago.

Sullivan, Mark, b. 1874. The [5556] education of an American. N.Y.: Doubleday, Doran, 1938. 320 p. WHi. Journalist.

Sullivan, Mary. My double life; [5557] the story of a New York policewoman... N.Y.: Farrar & Rinehart, 1938. 302 p. NN. The author was Director of Policewomen.

Sullivan, Thomas. See Fogarty, Tom.

Sullivan, W. John L. Twelve [5558] years in the saddle for law and order on the frontier of Texas... Austin: Von Boeckmann-Jones co., 1909. 284 p. DLC. Peace officer.

Sullivan, William Laurence, [5559] 1872-1935. Under orders... N.Y.: R. R. Smith, 1944. 200 p. WU. A Catholic priest who became a Unitarian clergyman.

Sulzer, Robert Frederick, b.1845.[5560] Planting the outposts... Phila.: The Presbyterian board of publication and Sabbath school work, 1913. 133 p. DLC. By the District Superintendent of Sunday School Missions in Minnesota and North Dakota. The writer was born in Germany.

Summerbell, Carlyle, 1873-1935.[5561] A preacher goes to war... Norwood: Ambrose press, 1936. 106 p. DLC. A clergyman of the Christian church in New England, and chaplain in France during the first World War.

Summerhayes, Martha, 1846- [5562] 1911. Vanished Arizona; recollections of my army life... Phila.: Press of J. B. Lippincott co., 1908. 269 p. NN. By the wife of an army officer. The time described was the sixties and seventies.

Sumner, Francis Bertody, [5563] b. 1874. The life history of an American naturalist. Lancaster: J. Cattell press, 1945. 298 p. DLC. As described by the title.

Sumner, William Graham, 1840- [5564] 1910. "Sketch of William Graham Sumner". (In his, The challenge of facts and other essays. New Haven: Yale univ. press, 1914. 450 p.) p. 3-13. WU. A sociologist tells how he became interested in economic and social problems.

Sumner, William Graham, 1840- [5565] 1910. "Autobiography". (In his, Earth hanger and other essays. New Haven: Yale univ. press, 1913. 377 p.) p. 3-5. DLC. A professor of social sciences at Yale tells of his education in the U.S. and abroad.

Sun Chief. See Talayesva, Don C.

Sunderland, Jabez Thomas, [5566] b. 1842. Ministry of fifteen years in a college town... Ann Arbor: Register pub. co., 1893. 23 p. CBSK. Unitarian in Michigan.

Sunderland, James, b. 1834. [5567] Annals of a life of faith... Kansas City: Lester T. Sunderland, 1923. 281 p. WHi. English born Baptist clergyman in Iowa, Minnesota, and Washington.

Surmelian, Leon Z., b. 1905. I [5568] ask you, ladies and gentlemen. N.Y.: E. P. Dutton & co., 1945. 316 p. NN. Boyhood life in Armenia and early days in the United States.

Sutherland, James Monroe, [5569] b. 1835. From stage to pulpit, by Bob Hart (pseud.). N.Y.: Charles S. Hamilton, 1883. 45 p. DLC. Ballad singer, minstrel, theatre owner who became a Baptist (?) clergyman in New York.

Sutley, Zachary Taylor, 1848- [5570] 1930. The last frontier... N.Y.: Macmillan, 1930. 350 p. WHi. Hunter; Indian fighter; guide; operator of supply train from Texas to Hudson Bay region.

Sutro, Florentine (Scholle), [5571] b. 1864. My first seventy years. N.Y.: Roerich museum press, 1935. 452 p. NN. Social life in San Francisco and New York; reminiscences of travel.

Sutter, John Augustus, 1803- [5572] 1880. Neu-Helvetien; lebens- errinnerungen... Leipzig: Huber, 1934. 122 p. WHi. Gold mining in California, 1834-1864.

Sutter, John Augustus, 1826- [5573] 1897. John A. Sutter, jr. Statement regarding early California experiences. With a biography by Allan R. Ottley. Sacramento: Sacramento book collectors club, 1943. 160 p. Auto., p. 81-129. CHi. Concerning land deals in California in the forties.

Sutton, George Miksch, b. 1898. [5574] Birds in the wilderness; adventures of an ornithologist. N.Y.: Macmillan, 1936. 200 p. WU. As described by the title.

Svobida, Lawrence. An empire [5575] of dust. Caldwell: Caxton, 1940. 203 p. Auto., p. 23-96, 106-185. DLC. Kansas farmer, 1929-39.

Swallow, Silas Comfort, 1839- [5576] 1930. III score & X; or, selections, collections, recollections of seventy busy years... Harrisburg, Pa.: United Evangelical pub. house, 1909. 432 p. NN. Methodist minister and reformer in Pennsylvania; Prohibition candidate for President in 1904.

Swartz, George W., b. 1817. [5577] Autobiography of an American mechanic. Phila.: 1895. 68 p. WHi. Laborer in New York.

Swayze, William, b. 1784. Narrative... Cinc.: R. P. Thompson, printer, 1839. 216 p. TxDaM. Methodist clergyman in N.Y., Mass., Pa. [5578]

Swearingen, George, 1800-1829. [5579] The life and confession of George Swearingen... Hagers-Town: W. D. Bell, 1829. 80 p. CSmH. Murderer in the South.

Sweeney, Michael Francis, [5580] b. 1872. Mike Sweeney of the Hill; the autobiography of Michael F. Sweeney, holder of the world record in the high jump for seventeen years; for forty years physical director of The Hill School. N.Y.: G. P. Putnam's sons, 1940. 333 p. NN. As described by the title.

Swenson, Olaf, b. 1883. North- [5581] west of the world... N.Y.: Dodd, Mead, 1944. 270 p. DLC. Trader, hunter, prospector in Alaska and Siberia.

Swett, John, 1830-1913. Public [5582] education in California... N.Y.: American book co., 1911. 320 p. DLC. In part a personal account by a teacher and Superintendent of Public Schools in San Francisco.

Swett, William B., b. 1824. Adventures of a deaf-mute. Boston: Boston deaf-mutes mission, 1874. 48 p. DLC. Carpenter in New Hampshire. [5583]

Swift, John W. An Iowa boy [5584] around the world in the navy... Des Moines: Kenyon pr. co., 1902. 344 p. DLC. As described by the title.

Swisshelm, Mrs. Jane Grey [5585] (Cannon), 1815-1884. Half a century. 3d ed. Chicago: Jansen, McClurg, 1880. 263 p. WHi. Newspaper editor and fighter for abolition and woman's rights in Pennsylvania.

Sykes, Godfrey Glenton, b. 1861. [5586] A westerly trend... Tucson: Arizona pioneer's historical soc., 1944. 325 p. WHi. An English scientist who sought information about the American West. He was a rancher in Kansas, Arizona and Colorado.

Syllavan, Owen (pseud.), d. 1756. [5587] A short account... Boston: reprinted & sold by Green & Russell, 1756. 12 p. MWA. Counterfeiter.

Symington, Mrs. Elsie Hillen. [5588] By light of sun. N.Y.: Putnam, 1941. 196 p. DLC. Writer on gardening who lived in the Middle Atlantic and Southern states.

Symonds, Henry Clay, d. 1900. [5589] Report of a commissary of subsistence, 1861-65. Sing Sing, N.Y.: 1888. 207 p. WHi. In the Union army.

Sype, Mrs. Marinda, b. 1869. [5590] Life sketches and experience in mission work. Cedar Rapids: 1912. 144 p. NbLU. Teacher, evangelist for the Seventh Day Adventists in Oklahoma, Iowa.

# T

Taft, Mrs. Helen (Herron). [5591] Recollections of full years. N.Y.: Dodd, Mead & co., 1914. 395 p. DLC. A domestic account, closing in 1912, by the wife of William Howard Taft.

Taft, Horace Dutton, b. 1861. [5592] Memories and opinions. N.Y.: Macmillan, 1942. 336 p. WHi. Headmaster of school in Conn.

Taft, Stephen Harris, 1825-1918. [5593] An empire builder...by Fred H. Taft. Los Angeles: Parker, Stone & Baird, 1929. 259 p. Auto., p. 10-16. IaHi. Youth on a pioneer farm in New York.

Taft, Mrs. William Howard. See Taft, Helen (Herron).

Talayesva, Don C., b. 1890. Sun [5594] Chief, the autobiography of a Hopi Indian. New Haven: Yale univ. press, 1942. 460 p. Auto., p. 25-381. WHi. Arizona Indian. A frontier account.

Talbot, Ethelbert, b. 1848. My [5595] people of the plains. N.Y.: Harper, 1906. 265 p. DLC. Episcopalian Bishop of Idaho and Wyoming.

Talbot, Marion, b. 1858. More [5596] than lore. Chicago: Univ. of Chicago, 1936. 222 p. WU. By the Dean of Women at the University of Chicago.

Talbot, Silas. An historical [5597] sketch to the end of the Revolutionary war of the life of Silas Talbot... N.Y.: pr. by G. & R. Waite, for H. Caritat, 1803. 147 p. MiU-C. U. S. Naval officer.

Talcott, James Frederick, [5598] b. 1866. Swift and still waters... N.Y.: pr. by the Alexander press, 1943. 280 p. DLC. The writer, who lived in New York and New Jersey, was engaged in manufacturing and in trust companies.

Tallmadge, Benjamin, 1754-1835.[5599] Memoir... N.Y.: pr. at the Gilliss press, 1904. 167 p. WHi. Soldier in the Revolutionary War.

Talmage, Thomas DeWitt, 1832- [5600] 1902. T. DeWitt Talmage as I knew him. London: J. Murray, 1912. 308 p. WHi. Clergyman of the Dutch Reformed Church in New York and Pa. Lecturer, and editor of Christian Herald.

Tamagawa, Kathleen, b. 1893. [5601] Holy prayers in a horse's ear. N.Y.: Ray Long & Smith, 1932. 264 p. NN. The story of a daughter of a Japanese father and an Irish mother and her reactions to her environment both in the United States and in Japan.

Tamblyn, Jeremiah W., b. 1851. [5602] Sweet memories of a trustful life. Morristown: E. A. Smith & sons, printers, 1924. 85 p. DLC. Free Methodist minister in New York, Maryland, Virginia and Pa.

Taney, Roger Brooke, 1777- [5603] 1864. "Early life and education". (In, Memoir of Roger Brooke Taney, by Samuel Tyler. Baltimore: John Murphy, 1872.) p. 17-95. WHi. This account closes with 1801 and tells of his early law practice and service in state legislature of Maryland, 1799-1800.

Tanner, Annie Clark, b. 1864. A [5604] Mormon mother... Salt Lake City: Deseret news press, 1941. 294 p. US1C. Wife of Mormon in Utah. Upon separation from her husband she became a church worker. During the first World War she farmed in Colorado.

Tanner, John, 1780?-1847. A [5605] narrative of the captivity and adventures of John Tanner during thirty years residence among the Indians. N.Y.: Carvill, 1830. 426 p. WHi. Hunter, trader.

Tapscott, Samuel Wallace, [5606] b. 1877. Backward glances... Booneville: Booneville pr. co., 1943. 218 p. DLC. Farmer, teacher, justice of the peace, newspaper publisher, owner of telephone company. Locale: Mississippi. Time: From 1890.

Tarbeaux, Frank, b. 1852. The [5607] autobiography of Frank Tarbeaux as told to Donald H. Clarke. N.Y.:

Vanguard, 1930. 286 p. WU. Frontier bandit in the Black Hills. Adventurer in the U.S., Egypt and Hawaii.

Tarbell, Daniel, b. 1811. Incidents of real life. Montpelier: 1883. 92 p. MH-BA. Farmer, building contractor, banker in New Hampshire in the thirties. [5608]

Tarbell, Ida Minerva, b. 1857. All in the day's work. N.Y.: Macmillan, 1939. 412 p. WHi. Journalist, writer on social and economic reform. [5609]

Tardy, William Thomas, b.1870? Trial and triumphs... Marshall, Texas: 1919. 116 p. WHi. Baptist clergyman in Arkansas, Texas and Louisiana. [5610]

Tarkington, Joseph, 1800-1891. Autobiography... Cinc.: Curts & Jennings, 1899. 171 p. Auto., p. 65-151. ICU. Methodist clergyman in Tennessee and Indiana. [5611]

Tasker, Robert Joyce, b. 1903. Grimhaven. N.Y.: Knopf, 1928. 241 p. DLC. Robber in California writes from his prison. [5612]

Tate, Charles Spencer, b. 1865. Pickway, a true narrative. Chicago: Golden rule press, 1905. 159 p. DLC. Gambler becomes YMCA worker in Spokane, mission worker in Chicago and Pittsburgh, Methodist clergyman in Illinois. [5613]

Taylor, Albert Reynolds, b.1846. Autobiography... Decatur, Ill.: Review pr. co., 1929. 180 p. KHi. College president in Kansas and Illinois. [5614]

Taylor, Charles Forbes, b.1899. Up to now... N.Y.: Revell, 1938. 140 p. DLC. Singing evangelist who came with father from England, and who eventually settled here. [5615]

Taylor, Mrs. Clementine E' Damie (Edmond)... Record of her family and events of her life. Berkeley: 1931. 15 p. CSmH. Chiefly useful for its account of life in California in the sixties as seen by a young girl. In 1878 she married a school teacher. There is also material on her belief in spiritualism. [5616]

Taylor, Drew Kirksey, b. 1857. Taylor's thrilling tales of Texas ... San Antonio: Guaranty bond pr. co., 1926. 93 p. DLC. Rancher, Indian fighter, Texas Ranger, U. S. Marshal. [5617]

Taylor, Fitch Waterman, 1803-1865. The broad pennant... N.Y.: Leavitt, 1848. 415 p. WHi. U.S. naval officer in the Mexican War. [5618]

Taylor, George W., 1803-1891. Autobiography... Phila.: 1891. 74 p. DLC. Farmer, merchant in Pa. [5619]

Taylor, Graham. Pioneering on social frontiers. Chicago: The Univ. of Chicago press, 1930. 457 p. WU. Teacher of sociology in the Chicago Theological Seminary, and Chicago social worker. [5620]

Taylor, James P., b. 1846. Pioneer life... N.p.: 1931. 19 p. CSfSP. An Australian who was a miner and druggist in British Columbia and who became a coal merchant in California. [5621]

Taylor, Jeremiah H., 1798-1882. Sketches of the religious experience and labors of a layman. Hartford: Press of Case, Lockwood & co., 1867. 236 p. NNG. In New York, to the year 1858. [5622]

Taylor, John, 1752-1833. A history of ten Baptist churches... Frankfort: pr. by J.H. Holeman, 1823. 300 p. WHi. Baptist clergyman in Virginia and Kentucky. [5623]

Taylor, Justus Hurd, b. 1834. Joe Taylor. N.Y.: W. R. Jenkins co., 1913. 248 p. DLC. Actor, minstrel. [5624]

Taylor, Landon, 1813-1885. The battlefield reviewed. Narrow escape from massacre by the Indians of Spirit Lake... Rocky Mountain history and tornado experiences... Chicago: pub. for the author, 1881. 375 p. WHi. Methodist clergyman in Iowa and Ohio. [5625]

Taylor, Mrs. Lydia (Pettengill), b. 1872. From under the lid. Portland: pr. by Glass & Prudhomme, 1913. 125 p. DLC. Prostitute in Minnesota, Montana, Washington and Oregon. [5626]

Taylor, Marie (Hansen), 1829-1925. On two continents... N.Y.: Doubleday, Page & co., 1905. 309 p. NN. Social and literary reminiscences in Europe and America of the wife of Bayard Taylor. [5627]

Taylor, Marion, b. 1845. The life of Christ; also, a brief story or history of my life. Morgantown: Acme pub. co., 1909. 190 p. Auto., [5628]

p. 97-186. DLC. Methodist itinerant clergyman in West Virginia.

Taylor, Marshall William, [5629] b. 1878. The fastest bicycle rider in the world; the story of a Negro boy's indomitable courage... Worcester: Wormley pub. co., 1928. 431 p. DLC. National champion, 1898-1900.

Taylor, Nathaniel William, 1823- [5630] 1875. Life on a whaler...New London: New London county historical soc., 1929. 208 p. Auto., p. 1-189. DLC. Physician. His experiences on the whaler occurred 1851-53.

Taylor, Richard, 1826-1879. Des- [5631] truction and reconstruction: personal experiences of the late war. By Richard Taylor, lieutenant-general in the Confederate army. N.Y.: D. Appleton & co., 1879. 274 p. NN. As described by the title.

Taylor, Mrs. Susie King, b.1848. [5632] Reminiscences of my life in camp with the 33d United States colored troops, late 1st S.C. volunteers. Boston: The author, 1902. 82 p. DLC. Negro laundress.

Taylor, Thomas Ulvan. Fifty [5633] years on forty acres. Austin: 1938. 306 p. Auto., p. 1-123. DLC. Dean of the Engineering School, 1906-1936, at the University of Texas.

Taylor, William, 1821-1902. [5634] Story of my life; an account of what I have thought and said and done in my ministry of more than fifty-three years in Christian lands and among the heathen. By William Taylor, bishop of the Methodist Episcopal Church for Africa. N.Y.: Hunt & Eaton, 1896. 748 p. NN. Early ministry in Virginia and California; experiences in Australia, Africa and India.

Taylor, William, 1821-1902. Sev- [5635] en years street preaching in San Francisco... N.Y.: pub. for the author by Carlton & Porter, 1857. 394 p. WHi. Methodist, beginning with 1849.

Taylor, William, b. 1850. Select [5636] poems and autobiography. Adams, Ind.: J. C. Smith, printer, 1888. 52 p. Auto., p. 3-7. DLC. Indiana blacksmith, poet, who was born in Scotland.

Taylor, William Henry, 1835- [5637] 1917. "Some experiences of a Confederate assistant surgeon". (In his, De Quibus, discourses and essays. Richmond, Va., The Bell book & stationery co., 1908. 308 p.) p. 298-337. DLC. As described by the title.

Teague, Charles Collins, b. 1873. [5638] Fifty years a rancher... Los Angeles: Ward Ritchie, 1944. 199 p. WU. Citrus and walnut rancher in California.

Teale, Edwin Way, b. 1899. Dune [5639] boy; the early years of a naturalist. N.Y.: Dodd, Mead & co., 1943. 255 p. WU. Along Lake Michigan.

Teasdale, Thomas Cox, 1808- [5640] 1891. Reminiscences and incidents of a long life. St. Louis.: National Baptist pub. co., 1887. 385 p. WHi. Baptist clergyman in New England, Ohio and Pa.

Teller, William, 1805-1833. [5641] Confessions of two malefactors... Hartford: Hammer & Comstock, printers, 1833. p. 2-49. DLC. Thief, murderer in Conn.

Temple, Shirley, b. 1928. My [5642] young life. Garden City: Garden City pub. house, 1945. 253 p. DLC. Child movie star.

Tempski, Armine von, b. 1899. [5643] Born in paradise... N.Y.: Duell, Sloan & Pearce, 1940. 342 p. DLC. Hawaiian novelist tells of her girlhood on a stock ranch.

Tennen, Max, b. 1871. Tsvey [5644] veltn. N.Y.: 1937. 166 p. NN. In New York: worker in the clothing industry, peddler, clothing contractor, owner of grocery store. The author, a Jew, was born in Europe.

Terhune, Albert Payson, 1872- [5645] 1942. To the best of my memory. N.Y.: Harper, 1930. 272 p. WHi. Journalist, writer of stories about dogs.

Terhune, Mrs. Mary Virginia [5646] (Hawes), 1830-1922. Marion Harland's autobiography... N.Y.: Harper, 1910. 497 p. WHi. Novelist and writer on home management.

Terrell, Mrs. Mary (Church). A [5647] colored woman in a white world. Washington, D.C.: Ransdell, 1940. 436 p. NN. The author, an educator and lecturer, for eleven years a member of the Washington Board of Education, has been active in public affairs and the advancement of the Negro race.

Tetrazzini, Mme. Luisa, 1874– [5648] 1940. My life of song. London: Cassell, 1921. 328 p. DLC. Includes experiences in America, by an opera singer.

Tevis, John, 1792–1861. Sixty [5649] years in a school room...by Julia Ann Tevis...to which is prefixed an autobiographical sketch of Rev. John Tevis. Cinc.: Western Methodist book concern, 1878. 489 p. Auto., p. 13–35. WU. Methodist clergyman in Kentucky, Ohio and Tennessee.

Tevis, Julia Ann (Hieronymus), [5650] b. 1799. Sixty years in a school room...Cinc.: Western Methodist book concern, 1878. 489 p. Auto., p. 39–489. ICN. Governess in Virginia, and co-founder and principal of the Science Hill Female Academy in Kentucky.

Thacker, Page (pseud.). See Burwell, Letitia M.

Thaden, Mrs. Louise McPhetridge, b. 1906. High, wide and [5651] frightened. N.Y.: Stackpole, 1938. 263 p. DLC. Aviatrix.

Thatcher, Albert Garrett, 1846– [5652] 1928. Albert Garrett Thatcher. No imprint. 87 p. PSC. Manufacturer of machinery in Pa.

Thaw, Evelyn (Nesbit). See Nesbit (Evelyn).

Thayer, John Adams, 1861–1936. [5653] Astir, a publisher's life-story. Boston: Small, Maynard, 1910. 302 p. WHi. Advertising manager and publisher of magazines.

Thayer, William Makepeace, [5654] 1820–1898. Unfinished autobiography... Boston: Barta press, 1898? 108 p. RPB. Congregational clergyman in Mass. Author of moralistic books.

Thébaud, Augustus J., 1807–1885.[5655] Forty years in the United States of America (1839–1885). N.Y.: U.S. Catholic historical society, 1904. 363 p. WHi. Catholic priest born in France, who served in New York, New Jersey, and Kentucky.

Thoburn, James Mills, 1836– [5656] 1922. My missionary apprenticeship. N.Y.: Phillips & Hunt, 1887. 386 p. NcD. In India, 1859–1884.

Thomas, Abel Charles, [5657–5658] 1807–1880. Autobiography... Boston: Usher, 1852. 408 p. WHi. Universalist clergyman in Ohio and Pa.

Thomas, Augustus, 1857–1934. [5659] The print of my remembrance. N.Y.: Scribner's, 1922. 477 p. WU. Dramatist.

Thomas, C. The frontier school-[5660] master, the autobiography of a teacher... Montreal: pr. by John Lovell, 1880. 465 p. TxU. In Vermont, mainly prior to 1860. The author also served in the Union army.

Thomas, Christian Frederick Theodore. See Thomas,

Thomas, David K. Wild life in [5661] the Rocky Mountains... N.p.: C. E. Thomas, 1917. 221 p. CSmH. Mining, Indian fighting, beginning about 1857.

Thomas, Ebenezer Smith, 1775– [5662] 1845. Reminiscences... Hartford: 1840. 101 p. WHi. Newspaper publisher in Ohio and South Carolina. The account closes with 1830.

Thomas, Edward J., b. 1840. [5663] Memoirs of a southerner, 1840–1923. Savannah, Ga.: 1923. 64 p. DLC. Soldier in the Confederate army. Landowner.

Thomas, Hampton Sidney, [5664] b. 1837. Some personal reminiscences of service in the cavalry of the army of the Potomac. Phila.: L. R. Hamersley & co., 1889. 26 p. DLC. Union army.

Thomas, Henry, 1815–1846? The [5665] life and confession of Henry Thomas, alias Thomas Dean, alias James Mitchell, the burglar... as taken from his own lips...by Rev. David Whitcomb. Columbus, Ohio: C. C. & G. R. Hazewell, printers, 1846. 60 p. DLC. Murderer, thief in Ohio.

Thomas, James A. A pioneer [5666] tobacco merchant in the Orient. Durham: Duke univ. press, 1928. 339 p. DLC. The writer was associated with the tobacco industry in India, Europe and the U.S. as salesman and sales manager.

Thomas, Mrs. Jeannette (Bell). [5667] The sun shines bright... N.Y.: Prentice-Hall, 1940. 275 p. WU.

Singer of folk songs.

Thomas, John J., b. 1838. Fifty [5668] years on the rail. N.Y.: Knickerbocker press, 1912. 191 p. DLC. Railroad engineer.

Thomas, Joseph, 1791-1835. The [5669] life of the pilgrim, Joseph Thomas ...Winchester: J. Foster, printer, 1817. 372 p. DLC. Frontier clergyman of the Christian Church in Kentucky, North Carolina, Virginia.

Thomas, Nathan Macy, 1803- [5670] 1887. Birthright member of the Society of Friends, pioneer physician...friend and helper of the fugitive slave... Cassopolis, Mich.: Stanton B. Thomas, 1925. 106 p. MiU-H. In Michigan.

Thomas, Theodore, 1835-1905. [5671] Theodore Thomas, a musical autobiography... Chicago: McClurg, 1905. 2 vols. WU. Conductor of symphony orchestras, born in Germany.

Thomashefsky, Bessie, b. 1873. [5672] Mein lebens geschichte (in Yiddish). N.Y.: 1916. 304 p. DLC. Actress on the Yiddish stage in New York City.

Thomashefsky, Boris, 1866- [5673] 1939. Mein leben geschichte (in Yiddish). N.Y.: Trio press, 1937. 385 p. DLC. Actor on the Yiddish stage in New York City.

Thomasson, Nelson, b. 1839. [5674] Recollections of 12 years I served in the 5th U.S. Infantry. Chicago: 1926. 10 p. DLC. Union army, followed by service in Arizona and New Mexico.

Thompson (pseud.). The story [5675] of a strange career... N.Y.: Appleton, 1902. 362 p. OrMcL. Sailor, including service during the Civil War. The account closes with 1866.

Thompson, Benjamin, 1843-1884.[5676] The life and adventures of...the famous Texan, by William M. Walton. Austin: 1884. 229 p. Auto., p. 5-196. DLC. Texas "bad man". The writer claimed this to be mainly a dictated account.

Thompson, Charles Lemuel, [5677] b. 1839. ...An autobiography. N.Y.: Revell, 1924. 289 p. WHi. General Secretary of the Board of Home Missions of the Presbyterian church.

Thompson, David, 1770-1857. [5678] David Thompson's narrative... Toronto: Champlain society, 1916. 582 p. WHi. Canadian fur trader in Oregon, Washington and Montana. Covers 1784-1812.

Thompson, Dow. A mind that [5679] was different. Oklahoma City: Harlow pub. co., 1931. 117 p. DLC. Professor of Business Administration in a small midwest college.

Thompson, Edward Herbert, [5680] 1860-1935. People of the serpent; life and adventure among the Mayas. Boston: Houghton Mifflin co., 1932. 301 p. DLC. American archaelogist in Yucatan. He also served there as Consul.

Thompson, George. My life... [5681] Boston: Federhen, 1854. 87 p. MWA. "Hack" writer.

Thompson, John, 1784-1868. [5682] Autobiography... Farmington: pr. by the Franklin journal co., 1920. 152 p. WHi. Maine farmer. The account closes with 1819.

Thompson, John, b. 1812. The life [5683] of John Thompson, a fugitive slave. Worcester: J. Thompson, 1856. 143 p. WHi. As described by the title.

Thompson, Nathan. Ten years. [5684] No imprint. 15 p. CoU. Congregational clergyman in Colorado, 1865-75.

Thompson, Slason, 1849-1935. [5685] Way back when; recollections of an octogenarian, 1849-1929. Chicago: A. Kroch, 1931. 364 p. NN. Newspaperman's experiences in San Francisco, New York, Cincinnati, and Chicago.

Thompson, Thomas, b. 1708? An [5686] account of two missionary voyages... London: pr. for B. Dod, 1758. 87 p. DLC. Episcopalian who came to New Jersey from England in 1745. The American portion is found within pages 1-24.

Thompson, William. Reminis- [5687] cences of a pioneer, by Colonel William Thompson, editor Alturas, Cal., Plain-dealer. San Francisco: 1912. 187 p. NN. Early days in Oregon and the Modoc War.

Thompson, Wilson. Autobiogra- [5688] phy... Cinc.: Moore, Wilstach & Baldwin, 1867. 497 p. NNC. Licentiate serving the Baptists in Missouri, Kentucky, Illinois, Ohio and Indiana.

Thomson, Samuel, 1769-1843. A [5689] narrative of the life and medical discoveries of Samuel Thomson... 2d ed. Boston: pr. by E.G. House, 224 p. WHi. Physician in Mass.

Thorburn, Grant, 1773-1863. [5690] Life and writings of Grant Thorburn... N.Y.: E. Walker, 1852. 278 p. WHi. Business: seedsman in New York; author of books of informal history. See also, Grant Thorburn In His Golden Age. Thorburn was born in Scotland.

Thoreau, Henry David, 1817-1862.[5691] Walden... Boston: Ticknor & Fields, 1854. 357 p. DLC. Has been described as follows: "two years spent close to nature," showing the "efforts required to provide the minimum essentials of food and shelter."

Thorek, Max, b. 1880. A sur- [5692] geon's world; an autobiography. Phila.: J. B. Lippincott, 1943. 410 p. NN. Career of an Hungarian-born Chicago doctor.

Thornton, Abel, 1799-1827. The [5693] life of Elder Abel Thornton... Providence: Office of the Investigator, 1828. 132 p. NNC. Itinerant Free-Will Baptist in New England, New York and Pa.

Thornton, Anthony, b. 1814. A [5694] sketch and personal reminiscences of Judge Anthony Thornton of Shelbyville, Illinois. No imprint. 62 p. IHi. Illinois lawyer. The account closes with 1896.

Thorpe, Lars O., b. 1847. [5695] Erindringer fra mit første aar i Amerika. Decorah: Trykt hos B. Anundsen pub. co., 1913. 8 p. MnSL. Minnesota politician tells of his youth.

Throckmorton, George. Remin- [5696] iscences... Burlington: reprinted from the Daily Republican, n.d. 10 p. KHi. The story of a youth who in the sixties and seventies lived on a farm with his parents in Kansas.

Through the mill, by 4342. See Bartlett, George Leighton.

Thurston, Howard, 1869-1936. [5697] My life of magic. Phila.: Dorrance, 1929. 273 p. WU. As described by the title.

Ticknor, George, b. 1791. Life, [5698] letters and journals of George Ticknor. Boston: J. R. Osgood, 1877. 2 vols. Auto., vol. 1, p. 5-16. WHi. Born and educated in New England. After being trained in the law, he went to Europe in 1815 to further his literary interests. Only the first few pages of this work constitute formal autobiography.

Tietjens, Mrs. Eunice (Ham- [5699] mond), b. 1884. The world at my shoulder. N.Y.: Macmillan, 1938. 341 p. WU. Poet.

Tilden, William Phillips, 1811- [5700] 1890. Autobiography...Boston: pr. by G. H. Ellis, 1891. 288 p. CBSK. Unitarian clergyman in New England. The autobiographical portion ends with 1862.

Tilden, William Tatem, b. 1893. [5701] Aces, places and faults. London: R. Hale, 1938. 304 p. DLC. Tennis champion.

Tillman, Mrs. Frances (Nelson) [5702] A little girl goes barnstorming. Baltimore: pr. by the Barton-Gillet co., 1939. 35 p. NN. Memories of the theatre in the western part of the United States.

Tillson, Mrs. Christiana [5703] (Holmes), 1798-1872. Reminiscences of early life in Illinois. Amherst?: 1873. 138 p. MoHi. Life on a pioneer farm, 1822-27.

Tilmon, Levin, b. 1807. A brief [5704] miscellaneous narrative of the more early part of the life of L. Tilmon, pastor of a colored Methodist Congregational church in the city of New York. Jersey City: W. W. & L. A. Pratt, printers, 1853. 97 p. Auto., p. 5-27. MWA. An account of how he came to be a clergyman, in which he attacks the prevailing apprenticeship system.

Tilton, George Fred, b. 1861. [5705] "Cap'n. George Fred" himself. Garden City: Doubleday, Doran, 1928. 295 p. WHi. Whaler.

Timberlake, Henry, d. 1765. The [5706] memoirs of Lieut. Henry Timberlake... London: pr. for the author, 1765. 160 p. DLC. Indian fighter in the French and Indian wars.

Timmins, Arthur Henry, b. 1907.[5707] Coming, sir! the autobiography of a waiter, by Dave Marlowe (pseud.). London: George G. Harrap, 1937. 267 p. NN.

Experiences of an English waiter and ship steward in both England and the United States.

Tinker, Frank Glasgow, b. 1909. [5708] Some still live. N.Y.: Funk & Wagnalls, 1938. 313 p. DLC. Pilot of airplane on the Republican side in the Spanish Civil War.

Tippett, Edward D. The experi- [5709] ences and trials of Edward D. Tippett, preceptor... Washington: pr. by W. Greer, 1833. 120 p. DLC. Teacher in Washington, D.C. who claimed to have discovered the principle of perpetual motion.

Tobey, Warren P. The cabin [5710] boy's log... Boston: Meador, 1932. 173 p. DLC. Whaler out of New Bedford.

Todd, Aaron, 1813-1840. The life [5711] and confession of Aaron Todd... Springfield, Ill.: Walters & Weber, printers, 1840. 15 p. IHi. Illinois criminal.

Todd, Charles Burr. The con- [5712] fessions of a railroad man. N.Y.: N.Y.: S.R.I. Community, 1904. 159 p. DLC. Land agent (Nebraska and Iowa); passenger and freight agent in New England.

Todd, John M., b. 1821. A sketch [5713] of the life of John M. Todd (sixty-two years in a barber shop)... Portland: W. W. Roberts, 1906. 324 p. Auto., p. 3-28, 33-57. DLC. Barber.

Tollemache, Stratford, b. 1864. [5714] Reminiscences of the Yukon. London: E. Arnold, 1912. 316 p. WaU. A Canadian miner and fur trader in Alaska, beginning with 1898.

Tomashefsky, Boris. See Thomashefsky, Boris.

Tome, Philip, b. 1782. [5715-5716] Pioneer life; or, thirty years a hunter. Buffalo: 1854. 238 p. WHi. In New York, Pa., and nearby regions.

Tomes, Robert, 1817-1882. My [5717] college days. N.Y.: Harper, 1880. 211 p. WHi. In Connecticut, in the late thirties.

Tompkins, Daniel Augustus, [5718] 1851-1914. A builder of the new south, by George Tayloe Winston. Garden City, N.Y.: Doubleday, Page, 1920. 403 p. DLC. Builder and promoter of the manufacturing of textile products, mainly in South Carolina and Georgia.

Tom's experience in Dakota... See Miller, A. P.

Toney, Lemuel Gordon, b. 1875. [5719] What a life...(by Eddie Leonard, pseud.). N.Y.: E. Leonard, 1934. 240 p. DLC. Singer, minstrel, stage and screen actor, radio performer.

Toney, Marcus Breckenridge, [5720] b. 1840. The privations of a private...Nashville, Tenn.: pr. for the author, 1905. 133 p. NN. Confederate soldier.

Tonk, William, b. 1848. Memoirs [5721] of a manufacturer. N.Y.: Presto, 1926. 311 p. ICN. Manufacturer of pianos and music merchant in Chicago and New York.

Tooker, Manly, 1799-1860. [5722] Poems, and jottings of itinerary in western New York. Rochester: E. Darrow & brother, 1860. 160 p. RPB. New York clergyman of the Methodist faith.

Toole, Gerald, 1838-1862. An [5723] autobiography of Gerald Toole, the state's prison convict... Hartford: Press of Case, Lockwood & co., 1862. 48 p. DLC. Irish born criminal in Conn.

Toponce, Alexander, 1839-1923. [5724] Reminiscences of Alexander Toponce, pioneer, 1839-1923. Ogden: 1923. 248 p. WHi. Miner and operator of staging business in Utah, Montana, Nevada and Wyoming.

Torrance, Margaret (Gillies), [5725] b. 1887. I like to remember. Minneapolis: 1944. 366 p. MnHi. A domestic account by the wife of a businessman in Minneapolis.

Torrey, George Arnold, 1838- [5726] 1911. A lawyer's recollections in and out of court. Boston: Little, Brown, 1910. 227 p. WHi. In Mass.

Torrey, Reuben Archer, b.1856. [5727] Anecdotes and illustrations. N.Y.: Revell, 1907. 185 p. OrEuN. Revivalist clergyman, and Superintendent of the Moody Bible Institute.

Torrey, William, b. 1814. [5728] Torrey's narrative... Boston: Press of A.J. Wright, 1848. 300 p. DLC. Merchant seaman.

Torry, Alvin, b. 1797. Auto- [5729] biography of Rev. Alvin Torry, first missionary to the Six Nations. Auburn: W. J. Moses, 1861. 358 p.

DLC. Methodist missionary to the Indians in New York and Canada.

Tou, Erik Hansen, 1857-1917. [5730] Den Lutherske frikirkes hedningemission paa Madagaskar. Minneapolis: Frikirkens bokhandels trykkeri, 1898. 38 p. MnMAu. Lutheran clergyman in North Dakota, and missionary to Madagascar.

Towle, Nancy, b. 1796. Vicissitudes... 2d ed. Portsmouth, N.H.: pr. by John Caldwell, 1833. 310 p. DLC. Itinerant minister in many parts of the U.S. and Europe. [5731]

Towne, Charles Hanson, b.1877. [5732] So far, so good. N.Y.: J. Messner, 1945. 245 p. DLC. Newspaperman, and magazine editor in New York.

Towne, Charles Hanson, b.1877. [5733] Adventures in editing. N.Y.: Appleton, 1926. 238 p. DLC. Editor of Cosmopolitan, Smart Set and McClure's.

Townley, Charles Valentine, [5734] b. 1855. Other days. Olathe: Johnson county Democrat press, 1930. 152 p. KHi. Owner of race horses in Kansas, beginning with 1892. The autobiographical portion is contained mainly within pages 5-40.

Townsend, Francis Everett, [5735] b. 1867. New horizons...Chicago: J. L. Stewart, 1943. 246 p. WHi. Originator of the Townsend Plan of pensions for the aged.

Townsend, Francis Torrey, [5736] b. 1829. Autobiography of Francis Torrey Townsend...White River Junction, Vt.: Cummings the printer, 1905. 102 p. DLC. Union soldier; farmer in South Dakota.

Townsend, George Alfred, 1841- [5737] 1914. Campaigns of a noncombatant... N.Y.: Blelock, 1866. 368 p. WHi. By a newspaper correspondent with the Union forces.

Townsend, Thomas C., b. 1799. [5738] Reminiscences... Des Moines: Carter, Hussey & Curl, printers, 1874. 265 p. Auto., p. 7-88. WHi. Baptist clergyman in Indiana, Iowa, Virginia and Kentucky.

Tracht, Stephen. Stephen [5739] Tracht's life and experience. 4th ed. Galion: 1913. 125 p. DLC. Spiritualist, phrenologist.

Tracy, Harry (alias). Tracy the [5740] bandit... by W. B. Hennessy. N.p.: 1902. 336 p. MoKU. A 20th century bank robber, horse thief, cattle rustler and murderer. The locale: the states west of the Mississippi River.

Tracy, Russel Lord, b. 1860. [5741] Some experiences of Russel Lord Tracy. Salt Lake City: Porte pub. co., 1941. 211 p. UU. Merchant in Minneapolis and in Wyoming. Founder of loan and trust company in Wyoming and in Utah.

Trafton, Mark, 1810-1901. Scenes [5742] in my life... N.Y.: Nelson & Phillips, 1878. 349 p. Auto., p. 7-278. DLC. Methodist itinerant preacher in Maine, Mass., Rhode Island and New York. Member of the U.S. Congress from Mass.

Train, Arthur Cheney, 1875- [5743] 1945. My day in court. N.Y.: Scribner, 1939. 520 p. NN. New York lawyer, assistant district attorney, and author of the Mr. Tutt stories.

Train, George Francis, 1829- [5744] 1904. My life in many states and in foreign lands. N.Y.: Appleton, 1902. 348 p. WHi. Promoter of shipping and railroad interests in the U.S. and abroad (especially in England and Australia.)

Trask, Leonard, b. 1805. A brief [5745] historical sketch...Portland: pr. by D. Tucker, 1858. 48 p. DLC. Maine farmer who was made an invalid by calcification of the bones.

Traver, Robert (pseud.). See Voelker, John Donaldson.

Travers, Jerome Dunston, [5746] b. 1887. The fifth estate... N.Y.: Knopf, 1926. 259 p. DLC. Golfing champion.

Travers, Libbie Miller. Sectarian shackles. N.Y.: Macmillan, 1926. 149 p. DLC. Mississippi school teacher tells of her progress from membership in the Christian Church to non-denominationalism. [5747]

Travis, Joseph, 1786-1858. Auto-[5748] biography... Nashville: E. Stevenson & J. E. Evans, 1856. 238 p. WHi. Methodist clergyman in South Carolina, North Carolina and Georgia.

Traylor, Samuel White, 1869- [5749] 1947. Out of the southwest; a Texas boy. Allentown: pr. by Schlicher & son, 1936. 255 p. NN.

Mine operator, engineer, manufacturer of heavy machinery.

Trelawney-Ansell, Edward Clarence. I followed gold. N.Y.: Furman, 1939. 312 p. DLC. English prospector and speculator in Nevada mining companies. [5750]

Trevor, Roland. See Triplett, Robert.

Trimble, Allen, 1783-1870. Autobiography and correspondence. Columbus?: 1909. 240 p. Auto., p. 1-110. WHi. Ohio politician. [5751]

Tripler, Mrs. Eunice (Hunt), 1822-1910. Eunice Tripler... N.Y.: Grafton press, 1910. 184 p. CHi. Wife of army surgeon, and daughter of army officer: Florida during the campaign against the Seminoles; Mexico in the forties; California in the fifties; city of Washington during the Civil War. [5752]

Triplett, Robert, 1796?-1852. Roland Trevor...showing how to make and lose a fortune, and then to make another. Phila.: Lippincott, Grambo & co., 1853. 415 p. DLC. Mine operator and railroad builder in Kentucky. Land speculator in Texas. [5753]

Tris, A. C. Sixty years' reminiscences... Lebanon, Pa.: Report pub. co., 1908. 161 p. Ia-HA. Clergyman from Holland. In America the Synod of the Associate Presbyterian Church sent him to do missionary work in Iowa in 1854. In 1861 he began missionary work among the Jews in New York. [5754]

Trobriand, Philippe Régis Denis de Keredern, comte de, 1816-1897. Quatre ans de campagnes à l'armée du Potomac. Paris: A. Lacroix, Verboeckhoven, 1867-68. 2 v. NN. Civil War recollections of the author, a Frenchman who came to this country before the War, became a naturalized citizen, and after the War entered the regular army. [5755]

Trott, Harold Williams, b. 1900. Campus shadows. Hemlock, N.Y.: Crosset & Williams, 1944. 371 p. DLC. New York physician who was born in Canada. [5756]

Trout, Peter L. My experiences at Cape Nome, Alaska... Seattle, Wash.: Lowman & Hanford stationery & pr. co., 1899. 42 p. DLC. Miner. [5757]

Trowbridge, Charles Christopher, 1800-1883. Personal memoirs... Detroit: 1893. 42 p. MiU-H. Indian agent, later a banker in Michigan. [5758]

Trowbridge, John Townsend, 1827-1916. My own story... Boston: Houghton, Mifflin, 1903. 482 p. WU. Poet. [5759]

Trowbridge, Silas Thompson, b. 1826. Autobiography... Vera Cruz: pr. for the family of the author, 1872. 288 p. MiD-B. Surgeon with the Union army. [5760]

Trudeau, Edward Livingston, 1848-1915. An autobiography. Phila.: Lea & Febiger, 1916. 322 p. WU. Physician who was a pioneer student of tuberculosis. [5761]

Trumbull, Henry Clay, 1830-1903. War memories of an army chaplain... N.Y.: Scribner, 1898. 421 p. NN. In the Union army. [5762]

Trumbull, John, 1756-1843. Autobiography, reminiscences and letters...from 1756 to 1841. N.Y.: Wiley & Putnam, 1841. 439 p. WHi. Painter. [5763]

Truth, Sojourner. Narrative... Boston: 1850. 144 p. WHi. After her emancipation from slavery in 1828, the author lectured against slavery in many states of the North. [5764]

Tryon, Lewis Royer, b. 1872. Poor man's doctor. N.Y.: Prentice-Hall, 1945. 233 p. NN. Doctor in the mining regions of Pennsylvania and an employee of the Veterans Administration. [5765]

Tschetter, Katharina, b. 1880. My life story, 1880-1945. Chicago: 1945. 46 p. InGo. Mennonite missionary in North Carolina, Tennessee and Illinois. [5766]

Tubbee, Okah. A sketch of the life of Okah Tubbee, alias, William Chubbee...By Laah Ceil Manato: Elaah Tubee, his wife. Springfield, Mass.: pr. for O. Tubbee by H. S. Taylor, 1848. 84 p. DLC. A slave in Mississippi and Louisiana who claimed he was Choctaw Indian who was kidnapped. [5767]

Tuck, Amos, 1810-1879. Autobiographical memoir of Amos Tuck. Paris: pr. by Clarke & Bishop, 1902. 92 p. NN. New Hampshire lawyer and anti-slavery congressman. [5768]

Tuck, Henry Carlton, b. 1864. Four years at the University of [5769]

Georgia, 1877–1881. Athens: 1938. 251 p. Auto., p. 1–67. DLC. As described by the title.

Tucker, Joseph Clarence, 1828– [5770] 1891. To the golden goal and other sketches. San Francisco: W. Doxey, 1895. 303 p. Auto., p. 11–157. CSmH. California miner.

Tucker, Louis, b. 1872. Clerical [5771] errors. N.Y.: Harper, 1943. 354 p. WHi. Anglican clergyman in Southeast.

Tucker, Patrick T., b. 1854. [5772] Riding the high country. Caldwell: Caxton printers, 1933. 210 p. NN. Montana cowboy.

Tucker, Sophie, b. 1884. Some [5773] of these days... Garden City: Doubleday, Doran, 1945. 309 p. WU. Singer in night clubs, etc.

Tucker, William Jewett, 1839– [5774] 1926. My generation... Boston: Houghton Mifflin, 1919. 464 p. WU. President of Dartmouth and Andover; Congregational clergyman in New York and New Hampshire.

Tufts, Cynthia Whitaker, 1860– [5775] 1920. Cynthia Whitaker Tufts. Chicago: pr. by the Univ. of Chicago press, 1920. 83 p. ICU. Covers to 1891. Teacher in Mass., Conn., and New Jersey.

Tufts, Henry, b. 1748. A narra- [5776] tive of the life, adventures, travels and sufferings of Henry Tufts... Dover, N.H.: pr. by Samuel Bragg, jun., 1807. 366 p. MWA. New England criminal.

Tufts, Mrs. Lucy (Harris). "The [5777] younger sister." West Palm Beach: L. H. Tufts, 1929. 284 p. DLC. The story of a girl in New York and of her family contacts.

Tuhi, John, 1800–1817. Life and [5778] confession of John Tuhi...who was executed...for the murder of his brother. N.p.: 1817. 12 p. MWA. In New York.

Tullar, Grant Colfax. Written [5779] because...Orange: Tullar studio, 1937. 111 p. Auto., p. 49–75. DLC. Hymn writer and music publisher.

Tulley, Jim. Beggars of life. [5780] N.Y.: Boni, 1924. 336 p. WU. Hobo.

Tully, Samuel, 1771–1812. The [5781] life of Samuel Tully...Boston: Watson & Bangs, 1812. 36 p. CSmH. Pirate.

Tunney, Gene, b. 1898. A man [5782] must fight. Boston: Houghton Mifflin, 1932. 288 p. DLC. His career as a prize fighter.

Tunney, Gene, b. 1898. Arms for [5783] the living. N.Y.: Funk, 1941. 279 p. DLC. Covers same ground as preceding item except that his work for the Navy as athletic director is added.

Turczynowicz, Laura (Black- [5784] well) de Gozdavia. When the Prussians came to Poland, the experiences of an American woman during the German invasion. N.Y. & London: Putnam's, 1916. 281 p. DLC. The author had married a Polish nobleman.

Turner, Bridges Alfred, b.1908. [5785] From a plow to a doctorate... Hampton: 1945. 89 p. LND. Negro teacher in Arkansas, and Virginia, and graduate student in Pennsylvania.

Turner, Cyrus S., b. 1856. Eight [5786] and one-half years in Hell. Des Moines: 1912. 69 p. IaU. The author relates his experiences in mental institutions in Iowa and Colorado.

Turner, James William, b. 1848. [5787] Half a century in the school room...Carrier Mills, Ill.: Turner pub. co., 1920. 412 p. DLC. Teacher in Illinois.

Turner, John. Pioneers of the [5788] West... Cinc.: Jennings & Pye, 1903. 404 p. DLC. Nebraska storekeeper and farmer, born in England.

Turner, Joseph Addison, 1826– [5789] 1868. Autobiography...Atlanta: The library, Emory univ., 1943. 20 p. WHi. Poet, and member of the Georgia Senate.

Turner, Nat, 1800?–1831. Con- [5790] fessions of Nat Turner...Richmond: T. R. Gray, 1832. 24 p. WHi. Negro who led an insurrection of slaves in Virginia.

Turner, Samuel Hurlbeart,1790– [5791] 1861. Autobiography of the Rev. Samuel H. Turner, D.D., late professor of Biblical learning and the interpretation of Scripture in the General Theological Seminary of the Protestant Episcopal church in the United States of America. N.Y.: A.D.F. Randolph, 1864. 292 p. NN. As described by the title.

Turner, William S., b. 1826. [5792]

Story of my life. Cinc.: n.d. 343 p. Auto., p. 11-44. CSmH. Methodist clergyman who served in the middlewest in the forties, then to the Hawaiian Islands, and finally to California and Washington.

Turnley, Parmenas Taylor, [5793] b. 1821. Reminiscences... Chicago: Donohue & Henneberry, printers, 1892. 448 p. WHi. Army officer, on the plains and in the Southwest, including service in the Mexican War.

Turnour, Jules, d. 1931. The [5793A] autobiography of a clown. New ed. N.Y.: Dodd, Mead, 1931. 98 p. WU. As described by the title.

Turpeau, David Dewitt. Up [5794] from the cane-brakes. No imprint, 1942? 43 p. WHi. Negro Methodist clergyman in Ohio, and member of the state legislature.

Tuthill, Mrs. H. N., b. 1814. An [5795] interesting narrative...Lawrence: pr. by Robert Bower, 1874. 29 p. WHi. The author, whose husband failed to support her, was forced to take in washing for a living.

Tuttle, Daniel Sylvester, 1837- [5796] 1923. Reminiscences of a missionary bishop. N.Y.: Whittaker, 1906. 489 p. WHi. Episcopalian clergyman in Missouri, Utah, Montana and Idaho.

Tweed, Mrs. Blanche Marie Louise Oelrichs. See Strange, Michael (pseud.).

Tweed, George Ray. Robinson [5797] Crusoe, U.S.N. ... N.Y.: McGraw Hill, 1945. 267 p. WHi. Sailor on Guam who hid out from the Japanese.

Twichell, Mrs. Agnes (Anderson)[5798] Memories. N.p.: 1938. 16 leaves. MnHi. An account of youthful days on a Minnesota farm in the sixties.

Tyler, Daniel, 1799-1882. Daniel [5799] Tyler: a memorial volume... New Haven: 1883. 186 p. Auto., p. 1-65. WHi. Army officer. Alabama industrialist. This account covers his first 62 years.

Tyler, Frederick Stansbury, [5800] b. 1882. Fifty years of yesterdays (1882-1932). Harrisburg, Pa.: The Evangelical press, 1932. 38 p. DLC. Lawyer in the District of Columbia.

Tyler, George Crouse, 1867- [5801] 1946. Whatever goes up—; the hazardous fortunes of a natural born gambler. Indianapolis: Bobbs-Merrill, 1934. 317 p. NN. Career of a theatrical producer.

Tyler, Joseph Zachary, 1848- [5802] 1926. Recollections of my Richmond pastorate. Richmond: Julian C. Anderson, printer, 1901. 45 p. OClWHi. Clergyman of the Christian Church in Virginia. The author comments briefly on his pastorates in Georgia and Ohio.

Tyler, Mary Hunt (Palmer). [5793] Grandmother Tyler's book... 1775-1866. N.Y.: Putnam, 1925. 366 p. WHi. Wife of the playwright and lawyer tells of their life in Vermont.

Tyler, Mason Whiting, 1840- [5804] 1907. Recollections of the Civil War. N.Y.: Putnam, 1912. 367 p. WHi. Union army.

Tyler, William Seymour, 1810- [5805] 1897. Autobiography...N.p.: 1912. 324 p. Auto., p. 5-145. WHi. Professor of Greek at Amherst.

Tyng, Stephen Higginson, 1800- [5806] 1885. "Autobiography, 1800 to 1845". (Record of the life and work... comp. by Charles R. Tyng. N.Y.: Dutton, 1890. 682 p.). p. 15-145. CBCh. Episcopalian clergyman in the District of Columbia in the twenties; in Pennsylvania, 1829-45.

# U

Ueland, Andreas, b. 1853. Recol-[5807] lections of an immigrant. N.Y.: Minton, Balch, 1929. 262 p. WHi. Lawyer and judge in Minnesota who was born in Norway.

Ueland, Brenda. Me. N.Y.: G.P. [5808] Putnam's sons, 1939. 351 p. NN. Frank account of the efforts of a young woman to break away from the conventions of her Minnesota environment and lead a literary life in New York.

Uncle Dudley (pseud.). See Norwood, John Wall.

Uncle Jeff. See Mayfield, Thomas Jefferson.

Underhill, Charles Edmond, [5809] b. 1859. Sketches...Caldwell: Caxton printers, 1942. 141 p. DLC.

Lawyer and politician in Iowa.

Underwood, Mrs. Lillias (Hor- [5810] ton), b. 1851. Fifteen years among the top-knots...Boston: Am. tract society, 1904. 271 p. DLC. Presbyterian medical missionary in Korea.

Underwood, Marsh. The log of a [5811] logger. Portland: Kilham, 1938. 62 p. DLC. In New England, Wisconsin, Washington and Oregon.

Unonius, Gustaf Elias Marius, [5812] 1810-1902. Minnen... 2 uppl. Upsala: Schultz, 1862. 2 vols. DLC. Pioneer farmer and Episcopalian clergyman in the Wisconsin Territory, born in Sweden. This work was given an English translation in 1950.

Untermeyer, Louis, b. 1885. [5813] From another world... N.Y.: Harcourt, Brace, 1939. 394 p. WU. Writer for Masses, and Seven Acts tells mainly of the persons he knew.

Upchurch, John Jordan, 1822- [5814] 1887. The life, labors and travels of Father J. J. Upchurch, founder of the Ancient order of united workmen. San Francisco: A. T. Dewey, 1887. 264 p. NN. An early founder of mutual aid societies.

Upshur, George Lyttleton, [5815] b. 1856. I recall them... N.Y.: Wilson-Erickson, 1936. 271 p. WHi. The author began his business career in California where he was a banker and dealer in real estate. Later he was an oil broker in Wall Street.

Urban, John W. My experiences [5816] mid shot and shell... Lancaster: for the author, 1882. 633 p. WHi. Union army.

Urbantke, Carl von, 1831-1891. [5817] Aus meinen lebensführungen. Cinc.: Jennings & Pye für den autor, 1902. 169 p. DLC. A Methodist circuit rider in Texas, born in Germany.

Ussher, Clarence Douglas, [5818] b. 1870. An American physician in Turkey. Boston: Houghton Mifflin, 1917. 338 p. WU. Medical missionary.

# V

Vaierio, Eusebio Atanasio. [5819] Sieges and fortunes of a Trinidadian in search of a doctor's diploma. Phila.: Dewey & Eakins, 1909. 48 p. ViHaI. Includes his experiences in Virginia, New York, New Jersey and Pa.

Vail, Enos Ballard, b. 1843. [5820] Reminiscences of a boy in the Civil War. Brooklyn: pr. by the author for priv. distribution, 1915. 159 p. DLC. Union army.

Vail, Israel Everett, b. 1842. [5821] Three years on the blockade. N.Y.: Abbey press, 1902. 171 p. WHi. Experiences in the Union navy.

Vaill, Joseph, 1790-1869. A [5822] memorial sermon... Springfield: Samuel Bowles & co., 1864. 42 p. DLC. Congregational clergyman in Mass.

Vallée, Rudy, b. 1901. Vagabond [5823] dreams come true. N.Y.: Dutton, 1938. 262 p. DLC. Band leader, singer.

Van Alstine, John, 1779-1819. [5824] Life and dying confession of John Van Alstine... Cooperstown: pr. by H. & E. Phinney, 1819. 24 p. DLC. Murderer (New York).

Van Alstyne, Mrs. Frances Jane,[5825] (Crosby), 1820-1915. Memories of eighty years... Boston: Earle, 1906. 253 p. NN. Writer of gospel hymns.

Van Brunt, Mrs. Leonora L. [5826] (Bigelow), b. 1812. Autobiography ... Westmoreland, Kan.: Alliance news plant, 1891. 43 p. KHi. A tale of domestic woe. The writer settled a homestead in Kansas with her husband about 1858.

Vance, Rowland Boyd, b. 1919. [5827] They made me a leatherneck. N.Y.: W. W. Norton, 1943. 175 p. DLC. Life in a "boot" camp in Virginia.

Van Cleve, Benjamin, 1773-1821. [5828] Memoirs... Cinc.: Abingdon press, 1912. 71 p. DLC. Surveyor, farmer in Ohio.

Van Cleve, Mrs. Charlotte [5829] Ouisconsin (Clark), 1819-1907. "Three score years and ten"...

3d ed. Minneapolis: 1888. 176 p. WHi. Daughter of army officer at Fort Snelling, Minnesota; in Michigan the author and her husband taught school; in 1856, to Minnesota where they farmed.

Van Cott, Mrs. Maggie (Newton), [5830] b. 1830. The harvest of the reaper ... N.Y.: N. Tibbals, 1876. 360 p. WHi. A dictated account by an evangelist who served the Methodist Church in New England and the Middle West.

Vandeleuer, John (pseud.). A [5831] history... Montpelier: Wright & Sibley, 1812. 96 p. CSmH. A native of Holland who while engaged in fur trading on the Pacific Coast is left by his ship. Subsequently, he marries an Indian. The period covered is from 1784 to 1791.

Vandenhoff, George, 1820-1884. [5832] Leaves from an actor's notebook... N.Y.: Appleton, 1860. 347 p. WU. An English actor who often performed in the U.S.

Vanderbilt, Cornelius, b. 1898. [5833] ...Farewell to Fifth avenue. N.Y.: Simon & Schuster, 1935. 260 p. DLC. Member of socially prominent family who became a journalist.

Vanderbilt, Cornelius, b. 1898. [5834] Personal experiences of a cub reporter. N.Y.: Sully, 1922. 212 p. WU. As described by the title.

Vanderbilt, Mrs. Gloria (Morgan), b. 1904. Without prejudice. [5835] N.Y.: E. P. Dutton, 1936. 338 p. NN. Social life in the United States and Europe.

Vanderbreggen, Cornelius, [5836] b. 1915. A leatherneck looks at life. Phila.: Westbrook, 1944. 179 p. MH. Officer in the Marines, 1938-40.

Van der Kemp, Francis Adrian, [5837] 1752-1829. Francis Adrian Van der Kemp, 1752-1829: an autobiography... N.Y.: Putnam, 1903. 230 p. WHi. The writer came from the Netherlands in 1788 to New York. In the new world he farmed and translated Dutch colonial records of New York.

Vanderlip, Frank Arthur, b.1864. [5838] From farm boy to financier... N.Y.: Appleton-Century, 1935. 312 p. WHi. Banker.

Vanderlip, Washington Baker, [5839] b. 1867. In search of a Siberian Klondike...set forth by Homer B. Hulbert. N.Y.: Century, 1903. 315 p. DLC. Prospector, employed by American and Russian development companies.

Van der Lippe, Adalbert, b.1827. [5840] Selbstbiographie. Cleveland: Deutsches verlagshaus der Reformierten Kirche, 1894. 246 p. Auto., p. 5-62. MnHi. Clergyman of an evangelistic Presbyterian religious group, in Missouri. The writer was born in Germany.

Van der Smissen, Hillegonda C., [5841] b. 1848. Bilder aus meinem leben. Newton: Bethel deaconess hospital, 1934? 86 p. InGo. Deaconess in a Mennonite hospital in Kansas.

Van der Veer, Judy. The river [5842] pasture. N.Y.: Longmans, Green, 1936. 213 p. DLC. Ranch life in California.

Van der Veer, Judy. Brown hills. [5843] N.Y.: Longmans, Green, 1938. 273 p. DLC. See previous entry.

Van der Veer, Judy. A few [5844] happy ones. N.Y.: Appleton-Century, 1943. 247 p. DLC. See previous entries.

Van de Water, Virginia Belle [5845] (Terhune), b. 1865. The heart of a child; some reminiscences of a reticent childhood. Boston, Mass.: W. A. Wilde co., 1927. 225 p. NN. In New York and Europe while travelling with her parents.

Van Doren, Carl Clinton, b.1885. [5846] Three worlds. N.Y.: Harper, 1936. 317 p. WU. Boyhood in Illinois; professor of literature at Columbia, critic and biographer.

Van Dyke, Henry. Fighting for [5847] peace. N.Y.: Scribner, 1917. 247 p. NjP. Soldier, first World War.

Vansant, Nicholas, b. 1823. Sun- [5848] set memories. N.Y.: Eaton & Mains, 1896. 271 p. ODW. Methodist clergyman in New Jersey.

Van Sickel, S. S., b. 1826. Thril- [5849] ling adventures... Topeka: Blade prntg. est., 1877. 31 p. KHi. Hunter in the Indian Territory tells of his troubles with the Indians, 1874-75.

Van Slyke, D. C., b. 1898. The [5850] wail of a drug addict. Grand

Rapids: Eerdmans pub. co., 1945. 121 p. DLC. After being cured, the author became an evangelist for the Nazarene church in Oregon and Idaho.

Van Vechten, Carl, b. 1880. Sac- [5851] red and profane memories. N.Y.: Knopf, 1932. 230 p. WU. Disjointed essays by a poet.

Van Wagner, Ernest L., d. 1947. [5852] New York detective, by Ernest L. Van Wagner, inspector commanding detectives, New York City Police Department (retired). N.Y.: Dodd, Mead, 1938. 304 p. NN. As described by the title.

Vare, William Scott, 1867-1934. [5853] My forty years in politics. Phila.: Swain, 1933. 225 p. WHi. Pennsylvania politician.

Varns, M. Lucille, b. 1908. Life [5854] sketches of M. Lucille Varns; being a narrative of my life and experience to 1929... Applecreek: Amiet printshop, 1929. 20 p. DLC. Despite serious physical handicaps the author was an active lay church worker in Ohio.

Vassa, Gustavus, b. 1745. The [5855] interesting narrative of the life of Olaudah Equiano, or Gustavus Vassa. Halifax: J. Nicholson, 1813. 514 p. DLC. An African slave who was owned, among others, by a Virginia planter and a Pennsylvania Quaker. Though he lived mainly in England, he contributed to the abolitionist movement in the U.S.

Vassar, Matthew, 1792-1868. [5856] The autobiography and letters of Matthew Vassar. ed. by Elizabeth Hazelton Haight. N.Y.: Oxford univ. press, 1916. p. 19-34. DLC. This account, by the benefactor of Vassar College, tells of the author's career in the brewery business to 1812.

Vauclain, Samuel Matthews, [5857] 1856-1940. Steaming up! N.Y.: Brewer & Warren, 1930. 298 p. NN. Career with the Pennsylvania Railroad and with the Baldwin Locomotive Works.

Vaughan, Victor Clarence, 1851- [5858] 1929. A doctor's memories. Indianapolis: Bobbs-Merrill, 1926. 464 p. WU. Biochemist, professor of medicine at University of Michigan.

Vaughn, Miles Walter. Covering [5859] the Far East. N.Y.: Covici, Friede, 1936. 408 p. DLC. Journalist with the United Press who for many years served in Japan, China, Manchuria.

Vaughn, Robert, b. 1836. Then [5860] and now; or, thirty-six years in the Rockies...1864-1900. Minn.: Tribune pr. co., 1900. 461 p. DLC. The author, born in Wales, was a farmer in the midwest, and miner and rancher in Montana.

Veatch, George Lovett, 1861- [5861] 1936. The sign-post of opportunity. Chicago: priv. print, 1937. 211 p. DLC. Salesman, merchant, manufacturer in Illinois and California.

Vedder, Elihu, 1836-1923. The [5862] digressions of V. Boston: Houghton Mifflin, 1910. 521 p. WU. Painter.

Veenstra, Johanna. Pioneering [5863] for Christ in the Sudan. Grand Rapids: Smitter book co., 1926. 233 p. DLC. Missionary.

Veil, Charles, b. 1896. Adven- [5864] ture's a wench. N.Y.: Morrow, 1934. 340 p. DLC. Soldier adventurer.

Veiller, Bayard, 1869-1943. The [5865] fun I've had. N.Y.: Reynal & Hitchcock, 1941. 373 p. NN. Career of a newspaperman and dramatist in New York and Chicago.

Velazquez, Loreta Janeta, b. 1842. [5866] The woman in battle; a narrative of the exploits, adventures and travels of Madame Loreta Janeta Velazquez, otherwise known as Lieutenant Harry T. Buford, Confederate States Army... Hartford: T. Belknap, 1876. 606 p. NN. Confederate spy, born in Cuba.

Venable, Matthew Walton, b. 1847. [5867] Eighty years after...Charleston: Hood-Hiserman-Brodhag, 1929. 108 p. DLC. Confederate soldier, civil engineer in Kentucky.

Venable, William Henry, 1836- [5868] 1920. A Buckeye boyhood. Cinc.: Robert Clarke, 1911. 190 p. DLC. On a farm in Ohio.

Venth, Carl, b. 1860. My mem- [5869] ories. San Antonio: Alamo pr. co., 1939. 130 p. Auto., p. 5-68. TxGR. Teacher of music in New York, violinist.

Ventresca, Francesco, b. 1872. [5870]

Personal reminiscences of a naturalized American. N.Y.: Ryerson, 1937. 252 p. WHi. An Italian, who taught languages in the schools of Chicago, tells of his Americanization.

Ver Mehr, Jean Leonhard Henri [5871] Corneille. Checkered life. San Francisco: A. L. Bancroft & co., 1877. 476 p. NN. Early life in Europe; career as an Episcopal clergyman in New Jersey and California; educational work in California.

Vestal, Blum, b. 1874. From the [5872] saloon to the pulpit. Greensboro: pr. by Apostolic messenger co., 1911. 61 p. NcWatC. Holiness preacher in North Carolina.

Victor, Mrs. Sarah Maria, [5873] b. 1827. The life story of Sarah M. Victor...convicted of murdering her brother... Cleveland: Williams pub. co., 1887. 431 p. DLC. As described by the title.

Vidrine, Euzebe, 1898-1924. The [5874] life of Euzebe Vidrine. Opelousas: Clarion co., 1924. 36 p. DLC. Murderer in Louisiana.

Vielé, Mrs. Teresa (Griffin), [5875] b. 1832. "Following the drum"... N.Y.: Rudd & Carleton, 1858. 256 p. DLC. The writer's husband was an officer in the U.S. Infantry, on the Texas frontier.

Vilas, Logan Archbold, b. 1891. [5876] My life–to my children. N.p.: 1934. 279 p. DLC. Hunter and trapper, mainly in Wisconsin, who later became a stunt flier.

Villard, Henry Hilgard, 1835– [5877] 1900. Memoirs... Boston: Houghton Mifflin, 1904. 2 vols. WHi. Civil War journalist, and railroad financier.

Villard, Oswald Garrison, [5878] b. 1872. Fighting years... N.Y.: Harcourt, Brace, 1939. 543 p. WU. Journalist, and reforming editor of Nation magazine.

Vincent, Mrs. Elizabeth Kipp. [5879] In the days of Lincoln... Gardena: Spanish American institute press, 1924. 35 p. DLC. The memories of girlhood in Washington during the Civil War.

Vincent, Walter Borodell, b.1845.[5880] Life as I have known it... Boston: Lothrop, Lee & Shepard, 1924. 291 p. DLC. Lawyer and jurist in Rhode Island.

Vincent, William David. My book [5881] life. Spokane: Spokane study club, 1935. 32 p. WaSp. Book collector, historian.

Vinton, John Adams, 1801-1877. [5882] The Symmes memorial...and an autobiography by John Adams Vinton. Boston: 1873. 184 p. Auto., p. I-X. DLC. Congregational clergyman in New England.

A Virginia girl in the Civil war, [5883] 1861-1865; being a record of the actual experiences of the wife of a Confederate officer...ed. by Myrta L. Avary. N.Y.: Appleton, 1903. 384 p. WHi. As described by the title.

Vivian, Mrs. Martha Campbell, [5884] b. 1831. Down the avenue of ninety years. N.p.: 1924. 138 p. MoSHi. The writer's husband was in the cattle business in Texas and Missouri prior to the Civil War. Included is an account of her life in Missouri during the War.

Voelker, John Donaldson, b.1903.[5885] Trouble shooter, the story of a Northwoods prosecutor, by Robert Traver (pseud.). N.Y.: Viking, 1943. DLC. Michigan lawyer.

Voigtländer, O. Drei jahre in [5886] Alaska. (written by L. Sommer). Berlin: Haus, n.d. 30 p. CU-B. German miner, 1902-05.

Volk, Mrs. Almira (Ketchum), [5887] 1810-1906. The autobiography... No imprint. 65 p. WHi. A domestic account: homestead in Illinois; miller in Wisconsin; homestead in Kansas; logger and merchant in Wisconsin.

Volk, Katherine Magdalene, [5888] b. 1883. An American "schwester" ... Cleveland: Schulte pr. co., 1916. 39 p. DLC. Red Cross nurse in Europe during first World War.

Volk, Katherine Magdalene, [5889] b. 1883. Buddies in Budapest. Los Angeles: Kellaway-Ide, 1936. 253 p. DLC. See the preceding item.

Von Borcke, Heros. See Borcke, Heros von.

Von Miklos, Josephine (Brogden)[5890] I took a war job. N.Y.: Simon & Schuster, 1943. 223 p. DLC. An Austrian born commercial designer who worked in a munitions factory and in a shipyard during the second World War.

Vontrees, Ross. A soldier story. [5891] N.p.: 1925. 35 p. IaHi. In France during the first World War.

Voorhees, Luke. Personal rec- [5892] ollections of pioneer life on the mountains and plains of the great west. Cheyenne?: 1920? 76 p. CSmH. Buffalo hunter, and Indian figher; Colorado miner in the fifties; political figure in Wyoming.

Voorhis, Robert, b. 1769? Life [5893] and adventures of Robert, the hermit of Massachusetts... (written down by Henry Trumbull). Providence: 1829. 36 p. WHi. As described by the title.

Voronaeff, Paul. 13 years in [5894] Soviet Russia. Beech Grove: pub. by the author, 1945. 44 p. DLC. Born in America of Russian parents, the author was taken to Russia by his father who was a Baptist missionary.

Vorse, Mrs. Mary Marvin [5895] (Heaton). A footnote to folly: reminiscences of Mary Heaton Vorse. N.Y.: Farrar & Rinehart, 1935. 407 p. NN. Writer and social worker, active in labor affairs.

# W

Waddel, John Newton, 1812-1895. [5896] Memorials of academic life... Richmond: Presbyterian committee of publication, 1891. 583 p. WHi. By the Chancellor of the University of Mississippi.

Waddell, Alfred Moore, 1834- [5897] 1912. Some memories of my life ... Raleigh: Edwards & Broughton pr. co., 1908. 249 p. DLC. Lawyer, member of the U.S. House of Representatives from North Carolina.

Waddell, Hope Masterton, [5898] b. 1804? Twenty-nine years in the West Indies and central Africa: a review of missionary work and adventure, 1829-1858. London: T. Nelson & sons, 1863. 861 p. NcU. By a Presbyterian missionary.

Waddington, Mary King. My [5899] first years as a French woman, 1876-1879. N.Y.: Scribner's, 1914. 278 p. WHi. The wife of a French political figure tells of her social and political life.

Wade, Alexander L., b. 1832. [5900] Life sketch of Alexander L. Wade, teacher and author of Morgantown. Morgantown, W.Va.: 1904. 8 p. Wv-Ar. In West Virginia.

Wadsworth, Peleg, 1748-1829. A [5901] story about a good little boy; how he became a great man and had little good boys of his own. Portland, Maine: 1903. 49 p. NN. Story of the boyhood and Revolutionary War experiences of the author, a Revolutionary general and congressman, written in 1795 in the form of letters to his children.

Wagenseller, George Washington [5902] b. 1868. Personal recollections of half a century. Middleburg, Pa.: press of the Middleburgh post, 1919. 99 p. DLC. Pa. school teacher, principal, owner of country newspaper.

Wagman, Dorothy Godfrey, [5903] b. 1893. An immigrant in Japan, by Theodate Geoffrey (pseud.). Houghton Mifflin, 1926. DLC. The wife of an American business man in Japan.

Wagner, Charles. Seeing stars. [5904] N.Y.: Putnam's, 1940. 403 p. DLC. New York concert agent and producer of theatricals.

Wagner, Friedelind, b. 1918. [5905] Heritage of fire. N.Y.: Harper, 1945. 225 p. DLC. The granddaughter of Wagner tells of her youth in Germany, her schooling in England, Hitler, and how she came to the U.S.

Wagner, Henry Raup, b. 1862. [5906] Bullion to books... Los Angeles: Zamorano club, 1942. 370 p. DLC. Businessman who made fortune in silver and gold mining, and who became well known as a collector of books on America.

Waheenee. See Maxidiwiac (Hidatsa Indian).

Wainright, Samuel Hayman, [5907] b. 1863. Campaigning for Christ in Japan. Nashville: pub. house of the M.E. Church, South, 1915. 170 p. DLC. Episcopal missionary tells of the evangelical campaign conducted in 1913.

Wakeman, Edgar, b. 1818? The [5908]

log of an ancient mariner...San Francisco: A. L. Bancroft, printers, 1878. 378 p. WHi. Merchant sailor, chiefly on the Pacific Coast.

Walcot, James. The new pilgrim's [5909] progress... London: M. Cooper, 1748. 316 p. Auto., p. 9–252. DLC. Episcopal missionary to South Carolina and Jamaica, who tells how he converted the Indian, Gelashmin.

Wald, Lillian D., b. 1867. House [5910] on Henry street. N.Y.: Holt, 1915. 317 p. WU. Social worker in New York.

Wald, Lillian D., b. 1867. Win- [5911] dows on Henry street. Boston: Little, Brown, 1934. 348 p. WU. Continues the preceding title to the year 1934.

Waldeck, Theodore J. On safari. [5912] N.Y.: Viking, 1940. 208 p. DLC. In Africa on hunting, collecting and exploring expeditions.

Walden-Pell, Mrs. Orleana [5913] Ellery, b. 1810. Recollections of a long life. London: W. P. Griffith & sons, 1896. 120 p. RPB. Childhood in New Orleans, social life in Newport and New York.

Waldman, Leibele. Cantor [5914] Leibele Waldman...song divine. N.Y.: Saravan house, 1941. 273 p. DLC. Singer, New York City. Jew.

Waldman, Louis, b. 1892. Labor [5915] lawyer. N.Y.: Dutton, 1944. 394 p. WHi. New York lawyer, socialist, member of the New York legislature, representative of labor interests, Jew.

Walker, Felix Hampton, 1753– [5916] 1828. Memoirs of the late Hon. Felix Walker, of North Carolina ...ed. by Sam'l R. Walker. New Orleans: A. Taylor, printer, 1877. 19 p. DLC. Soldier in the Revolutionary War who later became a member of the North Carolina House of Commons, and member of the U. S. House from North Carolina.

Walker, James Barr, 1805–1887. [5917] Experiences of pioneer life in the early settlements and cities of the West. Chicago: Sumner & co., 1881. 310 p. NN. Presbyterian clergyman, editor, writer on religious topics, who lived in the Ohio Valley.

Walker, W. S. Between the tides [5918] ... Los Gatos, Calif.: W. S. & Glenn Walker, printers, 1885. 250 p. CHi. Laborer and miner in California who became a newspaper publisher.

Walker, William, 1824–1860. The [5919] war in Nicaragua. Mobile: Goetzel, 1860. 431 p. WHi. A military account by an adventurer, covering the years 1855–60.

Walker, William Holmes, b.1820. [5920] The life incidents... N.p.: 1943. 87 p. USlC. Mormon pioneer farmer in Utah who previously was employed as a farm laborer in Illinois by Joseph Smith.

Walkley, Charles Thomas, [5921] b. 1869. ...Reminiscences of a fire chaplain in the city of New York. Hartford, Conn.: Church missions pub. co., 1940. 9 p. DLC. Chaplain assigned to the New York City fire department. The author was an Episcopalian.

Wall, Evander Berry, 1861–1940. [5922] Neither pest nor puritan; the memoirs of E. Berry Wall. N.Y.: The Dial press, 1940. 314 p. WHi. Social life at home and abroad.

Wallace, Addison Alexander, [5923] b. 1862. Memoirs...Nutley, N.J.: 1945. 67 p. MoHi. Presbyterian clergyman in Missouri.

Wallace, Charles, d. 1850. A [5924] confession of the awful and bloody transactions in the life of Charles Wallace, the fiend-like murderer... New Orleans: E.E. Barclay, 1851. 31 p. DLC. As described by the title.

Wallace, Ethel. From scenes [5925] like these; life in a Christian family. Phila.: Hathaway bros., 1945. 223 p. CBB. A 20th century account of a family in Philadelphia who tried to live according to Christian precepts.

Wallace, Henry, 1836–1916. [5926] Uncle Henry's own story of his life... Des Moines: Wallace pub. co., 1917–19. 3 vols. WU. Presbyterian clergyman in Iowa who turned to agricultural journalism and the writing of books on agricultural subjects.

Wallace, Lewis, 1827–1905. Lew [5927] Wallace; an autobiography. N.Y.: Harper, 1906. 2 vols. WHi. Indiana lawyer and political figure who

Wallace, R. C. A few memories [5928] of a long life. No imprint. 67 p. CLU-C. Chiefly an account of his experiences in the Civil War. After the War he was a pioneer farmer and a merchant in Montana.

Wallace, William Alexander Anderson. See Hall, Robert, b. 1814.

Wallace, William H., 1848-1937. [5929] Speeches and writings of Wm. H. Wallace with autobiography. Kansas City, Mo.: The Western Baptist pub. co., 1914. 308 p. Auto., p. 246-308. DLC. Missouri lawyer and judge of local criminal court.

Wallack, John Lester, 1820- [5930] 1888. Memories of fifty years. N.Y.: Scribner's, 1889. 190 p. WHi. Actor, dramatist who was born in the U.S., but educated and trained on the stage in England.

Wallale, Daniel H. Shanghaied [5931] into the European war. Chicago: League of humanity, 1916. 15 p. DLC. An American farm implement salesman in Europe who claims he was illegally signed into the British army, and who deserted after serving in France.

Wallett, William Frederick. The [5932] public life of W. F. Wallett, the queen's jester... London: Bemrose, 1870. 188 p. C. An English account of life in the theatre and circus, including a number of visits to the U. S.

Walling, George Washington, [5933] b. 1823. Recollections of a New York chief of police. N.Y.: Caxton book concern, 1887. 608 p. WHi. As described by the title.

Walmsley, Amasa E., 1806-1832. [5934] Life and confession of Amasa E. Walmsley, who was...convicted... of the murder of John Burke and Hannah Frank...taken from his own mouth, in presence of Stephen Wilmarth,...jailer. Providence, R.I.: 1832. 16 p. DLC. As described by the title.

Walsh, Christy, b. 1891. Adios [5935] to ghosts! N.Y.: 1934. 43 p. NN. Reminiscences of a ghost writer of American sports.

Walsh, Mrs. Richard John. See Buck, Pearl S.

Walsh, Stuart P. Thirteen years [5936] of scout adventure. Seattle: Lowman & Hanford, 1923. 174 p. DLC. Scout master in Illinois who later went to Washington, D.C., as an executive in the scout organization.

Walska, Ganna. Always room at [5937] the top. N.Y.: R. R. Smith, 1943. 504 p. WU. Polish opera singer who performed frequently in the U.S.

Walters, Alexander, 1858-1917. [5938] My life and work, by Alexander Walters, bishop of the African Methodist Episcopal Zion Church. N.Y.: Fleming H. Revell co., 1917. 272 p. NN. Participant in various Negro activities as well as in religious work.

Walther, Anna Hilda Louise, [5939] b. 1878. A pilgrimage with a milliner's needle. N.Y.: Frederick A. Stokes, 1917. 250 p. DLC. A Danish woman who brought her millinery talents to N.Y.

Walton, Frank Emulous, b. 1909. [5940] The sea is my work shop; memoirs of a life guard. N.Y.: E. P. Dutton, 1935. 249 p. NN. Career of a life guard on the Pacific Coast.

Walton, George (alias). See Allen, James, 1809-1837.

Walworth, Clarence Augustus, [5941] 1820-1900. The Oxford movement in America; or, glimpses of life in an Anglican seminary. N.Y.: The Catholic book exchange, 1895. 175 p. NN. The story of the conversion of the author and many of his friends from the Episcopal Church to Catholicism.

Walz, Edgar A., b. 1859. Retro- [5942] spection. N.p.: 1931. 31 p. NN. Ranch owner and life insurance salesman in Minnesota, New Mexico and New York.

Wampler, Ernest M. China suf- [5943] fers. Elgin, Ill.: Brethren pub. house, 1945. 277 p. DLC. Missionary of the Church of Brethren in 20th century China.

Wanless, William, 1865-1933. An [5944] American doctor at work in India. N.Y.: Fleming H. Revell, 1932. 200 p. Auto., p. 13-164. DLC. Presbyterian medical missionary.

Ward, David, 1822-1900. The [5945] autobiography of David Ward.

N.Y.: 1912. 194 p. DLC. Youth on a pioneer homestead in Michigan, beginning 1836. Later the author became a surveyor and lumberer.

Ward, Mrs. Elizabeth Stuart [5946] (Phelps), 1844-1911. Chapters from a life. Boston & N.Y.: Houghton Mifflin, 1897. 278 p. WHi. Mass. writer known mainly for the religious theme of her novels.

Ward, Genevieve, 1837-1922. [5947] Both sides of the curtain. London: Cassell, 1918. 292 p. NN. Recollections of an American actress who spent much of her life abroad.

Ward, Lester Frank, 1841-1913. [5948] Glimpses of the cosmos. N.Y.: Putnam's, 1913-18. 6 vols. WU. The "mental autobiography" of a sociologist.

Ward, Samuel Ringgold, b.1817. [5949] Autobiography of a fugitive Negro: his anti-slavery labours in the United States, Canada & England. London: J. Snow, 1855. 412 p. WHi. His abolitionist activities were mainly in the Middle Atlantic States.

Ward, William Henry. All sides [5950] of life... Des Moines: Iowa pr. co., 1886. 400 p. Auto., p. 5-27. IaHi. A bare recital of minor political positions held in Iowa, by a poet.

Ward, William T. My fifty [5951] years in the active ministry... Tisdale, Kansas: 1942. 16 p. KHi. Methodist in Kansas, beginning with 1892.

Warde, Frederick Barkham, [5952] 1851-1935. Fifty years of make-believe. N.Y.: International press syndicate, 1920. 310 p. WU. Actor.

Warde, James Cook. Jimmy [5953] Warde's experiences as a lunatic ...in the Arkansas lunatic asylum. Little Rock: Tunnah Pittard, printers, 1902. 300 p. DLC. As described by the title.

Wardner, James F., b. 1846. [5954] Jim Wardner, of Wardner, Idaho. N.Y.: Anglo-American pub. co., 1900. 154 p. WHi. Miner on the Northwest frontier.

Ware, Henry, 1794-1843. The [5955] recollections...(by Jotham Anderson, pseud.). Boston: Christian register office, 1824. 118 p. CSmH. Unitarian minister, editor of religious periodical, tells the story of his religious life in New England.

Ware, Thomas, 1758-1842. [5956] Sketches of the life and travels of Rev. Thomas Ware...N.Y.: T. Mason & G. Lane, 1839. 264 p. DLC. Methodist clergyman in Maryland, Delaware and in New England.

Waring, George Edwin, 1838- [5957] 1898. Whip and spur. Boston: James R. Osgood, 1875. 245 p. WHi. Officer in the Union army.

Waring, Guy, b. 1859. My pio- [5958] neer past. Boston: Humphries, 1936. 256 p. WHi. Ranchman in Washington in the eighties.

Warmoth, Henry Clay, 1842- [5959] 1931. War, politics and reconstruction... N.Y.: Macmillan, 1930. 285 p. WHi. Union soldier, lawyer and governor of Louisiana.

Warner, Arthur. A land-lubber's [5960] log... Boston: Little, Brown, 1930. 300 p. DLC. After working his way as a sailor, the author worked in Australia as sheep herder and miner.

Warner, Lucien Calvin, 1841- [5961] 1914. Personal memoirs...N.Y.: Association press, 1915. 190 p. WHi. New York industrialist and philanthropist.

Warner, Matt, 1864-1938. The [5962] last of the bandit riders. Caldwell, Idaho: Caxton printers, 1940. 337 p. NN. Recollections of a bandit, working out of Utah, whose career extended from 1876 to 1896.

Warner, Orson C., b. 1800. The [5963] life of Orson C. Warner...Hartford: pr. for the author, 1829. 161 p. MiD-B. Sailor.

Warren, Mrs. Anna Caspar [5964] (Crowninshield), 1815-1905. Reminiscences of my life for my children. Cambridge: 1910. 66 p. WHi. Domestic life in New England.

Warren, Edward, b. 1828. A [5965] doctor's experiences...Baltimore: Cushings & Bailey, 1885. 613 p. Auto., p. 15-540. DLC. Medical Inspector, Army of Northern Virginia; professor of medicine in Maryland; chief surgeon with the War Department of Egypt.

Warren, Edward Henry, 1873- [5966] 1945. Excerpts from Spartan education... Cambridge: pr. at

the Riverside press, 1943. 36 p.
NN. The author was professor of
law at the Harvard University Law
School

Warren, Mrs. Eliza (Spalding), [5967]
1837-1919. Memoirs of the west
... Portland, Oreg.: Marsh pr.
co., 1916? 153 p. Auto., p. 13-46.
DLC. Youth in Oregon, beginning
about 1837, in family of missionaries to the Indians. Later, she
married a cattle rancher in the
Willamette Valley.

Warren, George Henry. The [5968]
pioneer woodsman as he is related
to lumbering in the Northwest.
Minneapolis: Press of Hahn &
Harmon, 1914. 184 p. MnM. Surveyor and dealer in timberlands
in Wisconsin and Minnesota.

Warren, Henry Watermann, [5969]
b. 1838. Reminiscences of a
Mississippi carpet-bagger.
Holden, Mass.: 1914. 110 p. WHi.
Speaker of the House, Mississippi.

Warren, John Collins, 1778-1856.[5970]
Life of John Collins Warren,
compiled chiefly from his autobiography...by Edward Warren.
Boston: Ticknor & Fields, 1860.
2 vols. WHi. Surgeon in Mass.

Warren, Joseph. A glance back- [5971]
ward at fifteen years of missionary life in North India. Phila.:
Presbyterian board of publication,
1856. 256 p. WHi. As described
by the title.

Warren, Sam. Shirt tail inn, [5972]
history of a pioneer's early life
in the "Far West". (written down
by Mrs. Martha A. (Robinson)
Warren.) Houston: Southwest
pr. plant, 1930. 61 p. MoHi.
Miner in the Rocky Mountains.

Warren, Thomas Robinson,1828-[5973]
1915. Dust and foam... N.Y.:
Scribner, 1859. 397 p. DLC.
Sailor, California miner, adventurer.

Warren, William Wilkins, 1814- [5974]
1890. The autobiography and
genealogy of William Wilkins
Warren. Cambridge: J. Wilson
& son, 1884. 59 p. DLC. Merchandising business in West
Indies and in Mass.

Wartegg, Baroness de. See
Hauk, Minnie.

Wash, W. A. Camp, field and [5975]
prison life...St. Louis: Southwestern book & pub. co., 1870.

382 p. Auto., p. 17-348. MnHi.
Confederate soldier.

Washburn, George, b. 1833. Fifty[5976]
years in Constantinople...Boston:
Houghton Mifflin, 1909. 316 p. WU.
Director of Robert College.

Washburn, Ichabod, 1798-1868. [5977]
Autobiography and memorials...
by Henry T. Cheever. Boston:
Lothrop, 1878. 222 p. Auto., p. 15-
78. WHi. Manufacturer in Mass.,
and philanthropist.

Washburn, John, d. 1837. Life [5978]
and confession... Phila.: 1842.
23 p. MoSM. Murderer, robber
in Tenn., Miss., Louisiana and
Kentucky.

Washburne, Elihu Benjamin, [5979]
1816-1887. Recollections of a
minister to France, 1869-1877.
N.Y.: Scribner's, 1887. 2 vols.
WHi. As described by the title.

Washington, Booker Taliaferro, [5980]
1859?-1915. Up from slavery...
N.Y.: Doubleday, Page, 1909.
330 p. WHi. Negro educator.
This book is a later version of
his Story of My Life.

Washington, Booker Taliaferro, [5981]
1859?-1915. Working with the
hands... N.Y.: Doubleday, Page,
1904. 246 p. WHi. Sequel to the
preceding item.

Washington, Booker Taliaferro, [5982]
1859?-1915. My larger education
... N.Y.: Doubleday, Page, 1911.
313 p. WHi. Includes experiences
not given in the two preceding
works.

Washington, Lawrence Daniel. [5983]
Confessions of a schoolmaster.
San Antonio: Naylor, 1939. 354 p.
DLC. Rural schoolmaster in
North Carolina, Virginia, Kentucky
and Texas.

Waterbury, Luther T., b. 1875. [5984]
Reminiscences of an invalid...
Kirksville, Mo.: Journal pr. co.,
1905. 48 p. DLC. The story of
his life after being paralyzed in
a Missouri coal mine accident.

Waterbury, Maria. Seven years [5985]
among the freedmen. Chicago:
T. B. Arnold, 1890. 198 p. Auto.,
p. 9-61. MoKU. Missionary
worker, teacher among Negroes
in the South.

Waterhouse, Benjamin, 1754- [5986]
1846. A prospect of exterminating
the small pox... Cambridge: pr.

by William Hilliard, 1800-02. 40, 139 p. Auto., p. 3-36, 5-53. WU. A physician's experiments with vaccination, 1799-1802.

Waterworth, J. A. My memories [5987] of the St. Louis board of fire underwriters, its members and its work. St. Louis: Skarr pr. co., 1926. 170 p. MoSHi. By the president of the Board, 1881-99.

Watkins, Oliver, b. 1793. The [5988] trial and a sketch of the life of Oliver Watkins...the facts of his history, obtained in part from his own mouth... Providence: H. H. Brown, printer, 1830. 36 p. PP. Murderer.

Watrous, Charles, b. 1827. Writ- [5989] ten for my grandchildren. N.Y.: press of William R. Jenkins, 1912. 147 p. C. The writer was a dry goods clerk in Connecticut; a whaler for three years; and a merchant in California.

Watry, Francis. From the [5990] Roman Catholic altar to the Protestant pulpit. N.Y.: Fleming H. Revell, 1894. 51 p. CBSK. A 19th century account. The writer became a Congregational clergyman.

Watson, Elkanah, 1758-1842. [5991] Men and times of the Revolution; or, Memoirs of Elkanah Watson, including journals of travel in Europe and America, from 1777 to 1842, with his correspondence with public men and reminiscences and incidents of the Revolution. Ed. by his son, Winslow C. Watson. N.Y.: Dana & co., 1856. 560 p. NN. Merchant, promoter of canals, and of agriculture.

Watson, Henry, b. 1813. Narra- [5992] tive of Henry Watson, a fugitive slave. Boston: B. Marsh, 1848. 48 p. WHi. As described by the title.

Watson, Mrs. Rachel. The life [5993] of my family... N.Y.: The author, 1871. 93 p. DLC. A domestic account of life on a farm in N.Y.

Watson, Samuel Newell, b. 1861. [5994] Those Paris years... N.Y.: Fleming H. Revell co., 1936. 347 p. DLC. Episcopal clergyman in Missouri, Iowa, Ohio, New Jersey and California, who was rector in Paris for seven years preceding and during the first World War.

Watson, Thomas Augustus, 1854- [5995] 1934. Exploring life... N.Y.: Appleton, 1926. 315 p. WHi. Inventor, and manufacturer of marine steam engines in Mass.

Watson, William. The adventures [5996] of a blockade runner... N.Y.: Macmillan, 1892. 324 p. WHi. Civil War account of service to the Confederacy.

Watters, William, 1751-1829. A [5997] short account of the Christian experience, and ministereal labours, of William Watters. Alexandria: pr. by S. Snowden, 1806? 142 p. NN. Methodist minister laboring in Maryland and Virginia.

Watterson, Henry, 1840-1921. [5998] "Marse Henry", an autobiography. N.Y.: Doran, 1919. 2 vols., WHi. Newspaper editor in Tennessee and Kentucky.

Wattles, Gurdon Wallace, b. 1855 [5999] Autobiography... N.Y.: Scribner, 1922. 268 p. WHi. Omaha banker and operator of street railways.

Watts, Richard Cannon, 1853- [6000] 1930. Memoirs... Columbia, S. C.: R. L. Bryan, 1938. 179 p. WHi. Lawyer, politician in South Carolina who became Chief Justice of the State Supreme Court.

Waugh, Bobby. My life in the [6001] prize ring. Rochester, Minn.: 1926. 76 p. DLC. As described by the title.

Waugh, John William Worthing- [6002] ton, b. 1850. The story of my life. No imprint. 16 p. MoHi. The author moved to Missouri in 1871 where he was a teacher, and a clergyman of the Christian Church.

Waugh, Lorenzo, b. 1808. Auto- [6003] biography... 4th. & enl. ed. San Francisco: Francis, Valentine, printers, 1888. 358 p. WHi. Methodist clergyman in Ohio, Missouri and California.

Waugh, Mrs. Lucy F., b. 1826. [6004] Twilight memories, 1826-1903. Rothville: 1903. 65 p. DLC. A domestic account of life in Missouri during the Civil War.

Way, Frederick. Pilotin' comes [6005] natural. N.Y.: Farrar & Rinehart, 1943. 250 p. WHi. On the Mississippi and Ohio Rivers.

Wayland, Francis, 1796-1865. A [6006] memoir...including selections from his personal reminiscences and correspondence, by his sons Francis Wayland and H. L. Wayland. N.Y.: Sheldon, 1867. 2 vols. DLC. Baptist clergyman, President of Brown University, author of popular textbooks. His work was done in New York and Rhode Island.

Waylen, Edward. Ecclesiastical [6007] reminiscences of the United States. London: W. Straker, 1846. 542 p. DLC. English Episcopal missionary who spent 11 years in the U.S., mainly in Maryland.

Wayman, Alexander Walker, [6008] 1821-1895. My recollections... Phila.: A.M.E. book rooms, 1881. 250 p. WHi. Methodist minister who served in many states east of the Mississippi River.

Weaver, Benjamin. The first [6009] settling of Atchison Co., Kansas. St. Joseph: E. B. Weaver, 1898. 41 p. KU. By a homesteader who arrived in 1855.

Weaver, Mrs. John Van Alstyn. See Wood, Peggy.

Webb, Mrs. Eliza (Bowen), [6010] b. 1790. The female marine... 4th ed. N.p.: pr. for the author, 1818. 120 p. MWA. This edition contains material which appeared separately under different titles. The subject is the War of 1812. The author was also known as Lucy Brewer, Louisa Baker, and Mrs. Lucy West.

Webb, James Josiah, 1818-1899. [6011] Adventures in the Santa Fé trade, 1844-1847... Ed. by Ralph P. Bieber... Glendale, Calif.: The Arthur H. Clark co., 1931. 301 p. NN. Pioneer trader.

Webb, John P. Boy of the [6012] Ozarks. Steelville, Mo.: n.d. 72 p. MoHi. An account of his youth on a farm in the thirties in Missouri.

Webb, William. The history of [6013] William Webb... Detroit: E. Hoekstra, 1873. 77 p. DLC. A slave who escaped and became a servant to an officer in the Union army. After the War he was a laborer in Missouri, Indiana and Michigan.

Weber, John B., b. 1842. Auto- [6014] biography. Buffalo: J. W. Clement co., 1924. 286 p. WHi. Member of the House of Representatives from New York, and Commissioner of Immigration, Port of New York.

Webfoot (pseud.). See Phelps, William Dane.

Webster, Daniel, 1782-1852. [6015] "Autobiography". (Private correspondence of Daniel Webster, ed. by Fletcher Webster. Boston: Little, Brown, 1857. Vol. I.). p. 1-27. WHi. Covers to 1816, when he left New Hampshire. Tells of his education and early legal experiences, and of his election to Congress.

Webster, Kimball, 1828-1916. [6016] The gold seekers of '49... Manchester: Standard book co., 1917. 240 p. DLC. The period covered is 1849-54. The writer was a miner in California and a land surveyor in Oregon.

Weed, Thurlow, 1797-1883. Auto- [6017] biography... Ed. by Harriet A. Weed. Boston: Houghton Mifflin, 1883. 657 p. WHi. Newspaper editor and politician in New York.

Weekley, William Marion, 1851- [6018] 1926. Twenty years on horseback; or, itinerating in West Virginia. Dayton: United Brethren pub. house, 1907. 135 p. DLC. Clergyman in the United Brethren Church.

Weeks, Alfred Leonard Edward, [6019] b. 1875. Autobiography of Alfred Leonard Edward Weeks and Annie Elizabeth Cooke Weeks. New Bern: n.d. 27 p. Auto., p. 3-17. NcU. Baptist clergyman and educator in North Carolina. The story of his wife is given on p. 19-27.

Weeks, Mrs. Annie Elizabeth (Cooke). See Weeks, Alfred Leonard Edward.

Weeks, Elbert Wright, 1850- [6020] 1932. A record: history, biography, memory, pioneer times and peoples, Guthrie Center, Iowa. Guthrie Center: The Guthrie press, 1932. 96 p. Autobiographical preface. IaHi. Iowa farm laborer and lawyer.

Weeks, George F., b. 1851. Cali- [6021] fornia copy. Washington: Washington College press, 1928. 346 p. WHi. Newspaper publisher and editor in California who was striken by tuberculosis.

Weenaas, August, 1835-1924. [6022] Livserindringer fra Norge og Amerika. Bergen: A. S. Lunde,

1935. 280 p. MnHi. Norwegian-born professor of theology, affiliated with the Lutheran Church, who taught in Illinois, Wisconsin and Minnesota. The author came to the U.S. in 1868.

Weenaas, August, 1835-1924. [6023] Mindeblade, eller otte aar i Amerika. Volden: R. P. Hjelles forlag, 1890. 136 p. MnU. See the previous item.

Wegener, G. J. A brief story of [6024] my life. New Orleans: 1942. 47 p. Auto., p. 35-47. MoSC-H. Lutheran clergyman in Missouri, Louisiana, Illinois and Ohio. The author came to the U.S. from Germany in 1871.

Wehde, Albert. Since leaving [6025] home. Chicago: Tremonia pub. co., 1923. 575 p. NN. The author, a German immigrant, tells of his early experiences in this country and in Central America; later, of his services to Germany during World War I and of his imprisonment at Leavenworth for the latter activities.

Wehner, George B. A curious [6026] life. N.Y.: Horace Liveright, 1929. 402 p. NN. The author was a spiritualist medium.

Weibel, Johann Eugen, b. 1853. [6027] Vierzig Jahre missionär in Arkansas. Luzern: Raeber, 1927. 320 p. MoSU. The author, a missionary born in Switzerland, came to Arkansas about 1880.

Weinstein, Gregory, b. 1864. [6028] Reminiscences of an interesting decade, the ardent eighties. N.Y.: International press, 1928. 182 p. Auto., p. 7-68. DLC. A Russian who came to the U. S. to escape persecution of the Jews. In New York he became a printer and then a reporter on various socialist newspapers.

Weir, Robert Fulton, 1838-1927. [6029] Personal reminiscences of the New York Hospital from 1856 to 1900. Some Civil War recollections, 1861-1865. No imprint. 67 p. NjP. By a surgeon.

Weis, Julius, b. 1826. Autobio- [6030] graphy... New Orleans: Goldman's pr. office, n.d. 27 p. LNHT. Jewish peddler and merchant in Louisiana. The writer came to the U.S. from Germany.

Welch, John Allen, b. 1834. Per- [6031] sonal memoirs... Hutchinson, Kan.: 1920. 125 p. KHi. After his youthful days on an Iowa farm, in 1854 the writer became a miner in California.

Weldon, S. James. Twenty years [6032] a fakir. Omaha: Gate city book co., 1899. 374 p. DLC. Travelling salesman and promoter of schemes which bordered on racketeering.

Welles, Alonzo Merritt. Remin- [6033] iscent rambles. Denver: W. F. Robinson, 1904. 459 p. WHi. A smoothly written account by a tenderfoot miner in the far West. The period covered is the seventies.

Welles, Edward R. The thirteenth [6034] anniversary sermon...St. Paul: Press pr. co., 1872. 17 p. MnHi. Clergyman of the Christ Church, in Minnesota.

Welles, Henry Titus, 1821-1898. [6035] Autobiography...Minneapolis: M. Robinson, 1899. 2 vols. WHi. Railroad promoter and banker in Minnesota.

Welling, Richard Ward Greene, [6036] b. 1858. As the twig is bent. N.Y.: Putnam, 1942. 295 p. WHi. Political reformer in New York.

Wellman, Francis Lewis, 1854- [6037] 1942. Luck and opportunity. N.Y.: Macmillan, 1938. 214 p. NN. New York lawyer.

Wellman, Frederick Creighton, [6038] b. 1879. Life is too short. Phila.: J. B. Lippincott, 1943. 348 p. NN. A doctor and world traveller who visited Africa, Europe and South America.

Wellman, William Augustus, [6039] b. 1896. Go, get 'em! Boston: The Page co., 1918. 284 p. DLC. The author served with a French flying group during the first World War.

Wells, Carolyn, d. 1942. The rest [6040] of my life... Phila. & N.Y.: J. B. Lippincott, 1937. 295 p. NN. Detective story writer, and anthologist.

Wells, Charles Knox Polk, [6041] b. 1851. Life and adventures of Polk Wells...Halls, Mo.: G. A. Warnica, 1907. 259 p. WHi. A smoothly written account by an outlaw of the far West.

Wells, Charles Wesley, b. 1841. [6042] A frontier life. Cinc.: Jennings &

Pye, 1902. 313 p. WHi. A Methodist clergyman on the Nebraska frontier.

Wells, James Monroe, b.1838. [6043] "With touch of elbow"... Phila.: Winston, 1909. 362 p. NN. By an officer in the Union army.

Wells, Lemuel Henry, 1841-1936.[6044] A pioneer missionary. Seattle: Progressive pr. co., 1932. 167 p. NN. Protestant Episcopal clergyman in the Pacific Northwest.

Wells, Linton. Blood on the [6045] moon...Boston: Houghton Mifflin, 1937. 418 p. WU. The twentieth century adventures of a foreign correspondent in the Far East, Africa and Europe.

Wells, Rolla, 1856-1944. Episodes of my life. St. Louis, Mo.: [6046] William J. McCarthy, 1933. 510 p. NN. Industrialist and mayor of St. Louis; Democratic politician, treasurer of the National Democratic Committee, 1912-16.

Wells, Theodore, b. 1788. Narratives of the life and adventures [6047] of Capt. Theodore Wells, of Wells, Me., giving a minute account of his voyages and the places visited. Biddeford: J. E. Butler, printers, 1874. 204 p. WHi. Merchant sailor.

Wells, William Charles, 1757- [6048] 1817. Two essays...with a memoir of his life... London: pr. for A. Constable (etc.), 1818. 439 p. Auto., p. vii-lx. DLC. Physician and physicist in South Carolina, who left for England in 1784.

Wells, William Morris, b. 1857. [6049] The desert's hidden wealth. Los Angeles: 1934. 232 p. NN. Farmer and real estate dealer in the pioneer days of Kansas.

Welsh, Lilian, b. 1858. Reminiscences of thirty years in Baltimore... [6050] Baltimore: The Norman, Remington co., 1925. 167 p. NN. Physician and member of the Goucher College faculty; active in the struggle for the higher education of women.

Welter, Everhard, b. 1818. Forty-two years of eventful life in two [6051] wars, in the great wild west and in Washington, D.C. ... Washington, D.C.: 1888. 33 p. DLC. U.S. Army officer, born in Germany, who served in Kansas, Nebraska, and in the War with Mexico, 1845-48.

Wemyss, Francis Courtney, [6052] 1797-1859. Twenty-six years of the life of an actor and manager... N.Y.: Burgess, Stringer & co., 1847. 2 vols. WHi. Emigrating from England in 1822, the author was connected mainly with the New York stage.

Wendler, Henry, 1836-1927. [6053] Reminiscences...(written by J. Orin Oliphant). Cheney, Wash.: priv. pr., 1926. 20 p. CSmH. Cabinet maker in Ohio, Michigan and California. In 1886 he went to the Territory of Washington where he was a farmer and merchant.

Wendte, Charles William, 1844- [6054] 1931. The wider fellowship; memories, friendships, and endeavors for religious unity, 1844-1927. Boston, Mass.: The Beacon press, 1927. 2 vols. NN. Unitarian clergyman in Chicago, Cincinnati, Newport, R.I., and the Pacific Coast.

Wenger, Martin Light, b. 1820. [6055] Wenger memoirs, and autobiography of Martin Light Wenger... South Bend: C. B. Hibberd, 1898. 102 p. InU. Farmer in Pennsylvania and Indiana.

Weininger, Franz Xavier, 1805- [6056] 1888. Erinnerungen aus meinem leben in Europa und Amerika... 1805 bis 1885. Columbus: J. J. Jessing, 1886. 682 p. MoSU. A Jesuist missionary who came to the U.S. in 1848 and who visited every region of the country.

Werner, Herman. On the western frontier with the U.S. cavalry. [6057] No imprint. 98 p. MtHi. An account of Indian fighting in the eighties in Oregon.

Werner, Morris Robert, b. 1897. [6058] "Orderly!" N.Y.: J. Cape & H. Smith, 1930. 214 p. DLC. A story of the first World War, during which the author served in France.

Werner, Ralph (pseud.). The [6059] female impersonators...ed. by Alfred W. Herzog. N.Y.: The Medico-Legal journal, 1922. 295 p. Auto., p. 53-169. DLC. Androgyne in New York's underworld.

Wertheimer, Max, b. 1863. [6060] From Rabbinism to Christ... Ada, Ohio: Wertheimer publications, 1934. 91 p. DLC. A German

Jew who left his Ohio Rabbinate to become first a Christian Scientist and then a Baptist minister.

Wesson, William H., b. 1813. [6061] "Calais-morale"; or, fifty years' gleanings in the sea of readings. Richmond, Va.: P. Keenan, 1882. 288 p. DLC. Merchant in Virginia and North Carolina.

West, Benjamin, 1738-1820. The [6062] life and studies of Benjamin West, Esq. ...prior to his arrival in England; compiled from material published by himself. By John Galt. Phila.: pr. by Moses Thomas, 1816. 196 p. MiU-C. Artist in Philadelphia and New York.

West, Leoti L., b. 1851. The [6063] wide northwest...as seen by a pioneer teacher. Spokane: Shaw & Borden, 1927. 286 p. Auto., p. 9-231. DLC. In the Territory and State of Washington.

West, Mrs. Lucy (Brewer)(pseud.). See Webb, Mrs. Eliza (Bowen).

West, Maria Abigail, 1827-1894. [6064] Romance of missions; or, life and labor in the land of Ararat. N.Y.: Randolph, 1875. 710 p. NjP. Missionary in Turkey.

West, Simeon Henry, b. 1827. [6065] Life... Bloomington, Ill.: Pantagraph pr. co., 1908. 298 p. DLC. Miner in California who moved to Illinois where he was a farmer and a member of the state legislature. In his old age he turned to spiritualism.

Weston, Silas. Four months in [6066] the mines of California...2d ed. Providence: Albro, 1854. 46 p. DLC. As described by the title. This is the same as his, Life in the Mountains.

Wetherill, Mrs. Winslow. See Faunce, Hilda.

Wettstein, Bernard, b. 1840. A [6067] true history of three orphans. Dunkirk, N.Y.: Service print shop, 1917. 180 p. DLC. Dutch immigrant who became a merchant sailor.

Weyerhaeuser, Frederick, [6068] b. 1834. Pioneer lumberman, by William B. Hill. Minneapolis: 1940. 62 p. WaU. Owner of lumber mill in Illinois who came to the U.S. from Germany. This account, which closes with 1869, was dictated.

Whalon, Mark. Rural free delivery; recollections of a rural mailman. Brattleboro: Stephen Daye press, 1942. 135 p. WU. In Vermont. [6069]

Wharton, Mrs. Edith Newbold [6070] (Jones), 1862-1937. A backward glance. N.Y.: Appleton-Century, 1934. 385 p. WU. Novelist who spent many of her later years in France.

Wheeler, Mrs. Candace (Thurber), 1827-1923. Yesterdays in a busy life. N.Y.: Harper, 1918. 427 p. DLC. N.Y.: Lecturer and writer on decorative arts. [6071]

Wheeler, Crosby Howard, 1823- [6072] 1896. Ten years on the Euphrates· ... Boston: American tract society, 1868. 330 p. NN. Missionary work in Asiatic Turkey.

Wheeler, Ephraim, 1762-1806. [6073] Narrative... Stockbridge: 1806. 23 p. MH-L. Criminal assault in New England.

Wheeler, Homer Webster, b.1848.[6074] The frontier trail; or, from cowboy to colonel; an authentic narrative of forty-three years in the old west as cattleman, Indian fighter and army officer. Los Angeles: Times-Mirror press, 1923. 334 p. WHi. On the plains.

Wheeler, John Brooks, 1853- [6075] 1942. Memoirs of a small-town surgeon... N.Y.: Frederick A. Stokes, 1935. 336 p. NN. Medical practice in Burlington, Vt., where the author was professor of surgery in the Medical School of the University of Vermont.

Wheeler, Thomas, d. 1686. A [6076] thankefull remembrance of Gods mercy... Cambridge: Samuel Green, 1676. 32 p. Auto., p. 1-10. DLC. An Indian attack during King Philip's War.

Wheelock, Julia S. The boys in [6077] white; the experience of a hospital agent in and around Washington. N.Y.: pr. by Lange & Hillman, 1870. 274 p. CoU. Civil War nurse in Washington, D.C., 1862-65.

Whidden, John D., b. 1832. [6078] Ocean life in the old sailing ship days, from forecastle to quarterdeck. Boston: Little, Brown, 1908. 314 p. DLC. Merchant sailor.

Whiffen, Blanche (Gaston), [6079] 1844-1936. Keeping off the shelf.

N.Y.: E. P. Dutton, 1928. 203 p. NN. Stage experiences in England and the United States.

Whipple, Henry Benjamin, 1822– [6080] 1901. Lights and shadows of a long episcopate; being reminiscences and recollections of the... bishop of Minnesota. N.Y.: Macmillan, 1899. 576 p. WHi. Episcopal clergyman who worked much among the Indians.

Whipple-Haslam, Mrs. Lee. [6081] Early days in California; scenes and events of the '50s as I remember them. Jamestown, Calif.: 1925. 34 p. DLC. Childhood reminiscences of frontier mining towns by the daughter of a forty-niner.

Whitaker, Fess, b. 1880. History [6082] of Corporal Fess Whitaker. Louisville: Standard pr. co., 1918. 152 p. MoSM. After spending his youth in the Kentucky mountains, the author became a fireman and then engineer on the Santa Fe.

Whitaker, Robert, b. 1863. "Why [6083] callest thou me good!" Los Gatos, Calif.: Progressive press pub. co., 1913. 112 p. OrU. Baptist clergyman in Mexico, Oregon and California who criticized Christianity for its failure to cope with social and economic evils.

Whitall, James, b. 1888. English [6084] years. N.Y.: Harcourt, Brace & co., 1935. 335 p. NN. Literary life and friendships of an American expatriate in England.

White, Alma (Bridewell), b.1862. [6085] Looking back from Beulah. Denver: Pentecostal Union, 1902. 307 p. MtHi. Montana teacher goes to Utah in eighties to work for Methodists as missionary. She then renounces Methodism and becomes an evangelical missionary in Wyoming, Montana, Oregon and Washington.

White, Alma (Bridewell), b.1862. [6086] The story of my life. Zarephath, N.J.: Pillar of Fire, 1919-24. 3 vols. WHi. Recapitulates and continues the preceding item.

White, Alma (Bridewell), b.1862. [6087] Truth stranger than fiction. Zarephath, N.J.: Pillar of Fire, 1936. 256 p. Auto., p. 11–186. DLC. See the two preceding items to which this book adds little.

White, Andrew Dickson, 1832– [6088] 1918. Autobiography... N.Y.: Century, 1905. 2 vols. WHi. College professor at Michigan and President of Cornell. Also U.S. Minister to Russia, and State Senator in New York.

White, Edward Lucas, b. 1866. [6089] Matrimony. Baltimore: Norman pub. co., 1932. 356 p. DLC. Teacher novelist, poet tells of his married life in Maryland.

White, Elijah. Ten years in [6090] Oregon... Compiled by Miss A. J. Allen. Ithaca: Mack, Andrus & co., 1848. 399 p. Auto., p. 17–327. DLC. The experiences of a Methodist medical missionary, 1836-46.

White, Elizabeth, d. 1660. The [6091] experiences of God's gracious dealing with Mrs. Elizabeth White ... Boston: S. Kneeland & T. Green, 1741. 21 p. MB. A spiritual account.

White, Ellen Gould (Harmon), [6092] 1827–1915. Life sketches of Ellen G. White, being a narrative of her experience to 1881 as written by herself; with a sketch of her subsequent labors and of her last sickness compiled from original sources. Mountain View, Calif.: Pacific press pub. assoc., 1915. 480 p. NN. The author was a preacher of the Seventh-Day Adventist denomination. In Maine and Michigan.

White, Ellen Gould (Harmon), [6093] 1827–1915. A sketch of the Christian experience... Battle Creek: Review & herald, 1884. Auto., p. 7–67. OrEuN. See the preceding item. This book consists of a series of "evidences" for Christianity.

White, Eugene E. Service on the [6094] Indian reservations, being the experiences of a special Indian agent ... Little Rock: Arkansas democrat co., 1893. 336 p. CSmH. In the West generally.

White, George, b. 1764. A brief [6095] account of the life, experience, travels and gospel labors of George White an African. N.Y.: pr. by John C. Totten, 1810. 60 p. NNC. Methodist in Virginia, Maryland, New York and New Jersey.

White, George Miles. From [6096] boniface to bank burglar; or, the price of persecution; how a successful business man, through the miscarriage of justice, became a notorious bank looter, by George M. White, alias George Bliss. Bellows Falls, Vt.: Truax pr. co., 1905. 495 p. NN. As described by the title.

White, George Starr, b. 1866. My [6097] biografy, compiled from the author's personal diaries and yearly record books since 1876. Los Angeles, Calif.: 1936. 567 p. NN. Physician and surgeon who practiced in New York and California; much on his feuds with the medical profession over his unorthodox methods.

White, James, 1821-1881. Life [6098] sketches... Battle Creek: Press of the Seventh-Day Adventist pub. association, 1880. 416 p. WHi. Clergyman of the Seventh-Day Adventist Church in Michigan and Maine.

White, James, 1821-1881. Life [6099] incidents in connection with the great advent movement... Battle Creek, Mich.: Seventh-Day Adventist pub. association, 1868. 373 p. OrEuN. See the preceding item.

White, James Clarke, 1833-1916. [6100] Sketches from my life, 1833-1913. Cambridge: Riverside press, 1914. 326 p. NN. Physician in Boston and instructor in the Harvard Medical School.

White, James E., b. 1846. A life [6101] span and reminiscences of railway mail service, by James E. White, ex-General Superintendent of Railway Mail Service. Phila.: Deemer & Jaisohn, 1910. 274 p. NN. The author was connected with the service from 1866 to 1907.

White, Josiah, 1781-1850. Josiah [6102] White's story... Phila.: Press of G. H. Buchanan co., 1909? 75 p. WU. Businessman in Pennsylvania, engaged in canal navigation, coal mining.

White, K., b. 1772. A narrative [6103] ... Schenectady: 1809. 127 p. DLC. The author was born in Scotland, and came to New England as a child. This book concerns her matrimonial difficulties, debts, etc.

White, Leslie Turner, b. 1903. [6104] Me, detective. N.Y.: Harcourt, Brace & co., 1936. 302 p. NN. Experiences of a detective on the staff of the Los Angeles district attorney.

White, Owen Payne, 1879-1946. [6105] The autobiography of a durable sinner. N.Y.: G. P. Putnam's sons, 1942. 344 p. NN. Episodes in the career of a Texas-born journalist, both in Texas and New York.

White, Pearl, 1889-1938. Just [6106] me. N.Y.: Doran, 1919. 179 p. DLC. Screen star.

White, William Alanson, 1870- [6107] 1937. William Alanson White, the autobiography of a purpose. Garden City, N.Y.: Doubleday, Doran, 1938. 293 p. WU. Psychiatrist, editor of Psychoanalytic Review.

White Horse Eagle, b. 1822. We [6108] Indians...as told to Edgar von Schmidt-Pauli. London: T. Butterworth, 1931. 255 p. WHi. Osage chief, who claimed to be 107 years old when he dictated this account.

White Mountain, Mrs. See Smith, Dama Margaret.

Whitecar, William B. Four [6109] years aboard the whaleship... Phila.: Lippincott, 1860. 413 p. DLC. During the fifties.

Whitehouse, Mrs. Vira (Boar- [6110] man), b. 1875. A year as a government agent. N.Y. & London: Harper & brothers, 1920. 316 p. DLC. In Switzerland during the first World War where she represented a committee responsible for public information and propaganda.

Whitely, Isaac H., b. 1853. Rural [6111] life in Texas. Atlanta: J. P. Harrison & co., printers, 1891. 82 p. DLC. Veterinarian, peddler of patent medicine.

Whiting, Perey, b. 1868. Auto- [6112] biography of Perry Whiting, pioneer building material merchant of Los Angeles... Los Angeles: pr. by Smith-Barnes, 1930. 334 p. DLC. As described by the title.

Whitlock, Brand, 1869-1934. [6113] Forty years of it. N.Y.: Appleton, 1914. 373 p. WHi. Journalist, lawyer, reform mayor of Toledo.

Whitlock, Brand, 1869-1934. [6114] Belgium: a personal narrative. N.Y.: Appleton, 1919. 2 vols. WU. U.S. Minister to Belgium, 1914-17.

Whitman, Ezekiel Cheever. See Cheever, Ezekiel.

Whitman, Walt, 1819-1892. Notes [6115] on Walt Whitman, as poet and person, by John Burroughs. N.Y.: American news co., 1867. 108 p. ICN. Written in part by Whitman, and in part the result of personal contact with Burroughs. See also the Autobiographia, a "synthetic" autobiography.

Whitmore, Frederic. A Florida [6116] farm. Springfield, Mass.: The Ridgewood press, 1903. 114 p. DLC. A poet who tried truck farming.

Whitney, Barney. Fifty years [6117] a teacher. Syracuse: C. W. Bardeen, 1902. 76 p. OU. Teacher, principal and school commissioner in New York. The period covered is 1852-1902.

Whitney, Caspar, 1862-1929. The [6118] flowing road, adventuring on the great rivers of South America. Phila.: Lippincott, 1912. 319 p. DLC. Explorer.

Whitney, J. J., 1830-1890. Recollections of the War of the [6119] Rebellion. Fort Pierre, S.D.: Fairplay print, 1902. 155 p. SdHi. An assistant surgeon with the Union army.

Whitney, James Parker, 1835- [6120] 1913. Reminiscences of a sportsman. N.Y.: Forest & Stream pub. co., 1906. 467 p. NN. Largely fishing experiences in various parts of North America.

Whitney, Orson Ferguson, [6121] b. 1855. Through memory's halls... Independence, Mo.: Zion's pr. co., 1930. 424 p. UU. Editor of Deseret Evening News, bishop in the Mormon Church, State Senator in Utah, historian and poet.

Whitney, Wilson, b. 1845. Epochs [6122] and phases of Christian experience. Greensburg: Press of the Observer pub. co., 1909. 96 p. DLC. Baptist clergyman in Indiana.

Whitridge, Joshua Barker, [6123] b. 1789. An autobiographical sketch... Charleston, S.C.: Walker & Evans, printers, 1856. 3 p. MHi. Physician in South Carolina, beginning with 1815.

Whittemore, Thomas, 1800-1861. [6124] The early days of Thomas Whittemore, an autobiography...1800 to A.D. 1825. Boston: Usher, 1859. 348 p. Auto., p. 191-348. WHi. Universalist clergyman in Mass.

Whittingham, Harrison. That [6125] farm, recounting the adventures of a dry-goods merchant who went back to the land. Garden City, N.Y.: Doubleday, Page & co., 1914. 229 p. DLC. Commercial farmer in New York.

Wickey, Harry, b. 1892. Thus [6126] far... N.Y.: American artists' group, 1941. 303 p. Auto., p. 1-107. DLC. Painter, sculptor, etcher who lived mainly in New York.

Wickersham, James, b. 1857. [6127] Old Yukon... Washington, D.C.: Washington law book co., 1938. 514 p. WHi. U.S. District Judge in Alaska, delegate to the U.S. Congress from Alaska, lawyer.

Widener, Peter Arrell Brown, [6128] b. 1895. Without drums. N.Y.: Putnam, 1940. 279 p. DLC. Philadelphia social leader.

Wierse, Paul. Eighty-eight [6129] weeks in purgatory... Charleston: McFarlane pr. & pub. co., 1920. 103 p. DLC. South Carolina journalist who was imprisoned for sedition in 1918.

Wiggin, Kate Douglas (Smith), [6130] 1856-1923. My garden of memory ... Boston: Houghton Mifflin, 1923. 465 p. WU. Kindergarten teacher, writer of books for children.

Wiggin, Samuel Adams, b. 1832. [6131] Sprigs of Acacia. Elkton, Md.: pr. by W. K. Wright, 1885. 292 p. DLC. Autobiographical preface tells of service with Union army, and government clerkship in Washington, by a poet.

Wiggington, William R., b. 1819. [6132] Life and labors...No imprint. 40 p. MoSHi. Farmer and Baptist clergyman in Missouri.

Wight, John Green, b. 1842. Auto- [6133] biography and miscellanea. Utica: Press of L. C. Childs, 1912. 235 p. DLC. Principal and teacher in secondary schools of New York, Maine, Mass., and Pa.

Wight, Joseph Kingsbury, 1824- [6134] 1917. Reminiscences of fifty years in the ministry. No imprint, 1898? 10 p. WHi. After study at Princeton the author became a clergyman in N.Y. and then a missionary in China.

Wight, Samuel F. Adventures in [6135] California and Nicaragua in rhyme. Boston: pr. by Alfred Mudge, 1860. 84 p. CU-B. Miner in California who then went to Nicaragua with Walker.

Wightman, Mrs. Elias R. See Helm, Mary (Sherwood) Wightman.

Wikoff, Henry, 1813-1884. The [6136] adventures of a roving diplomatist. N.Y.: Fetridge, 1857. 299 p. WHi. A socialite who served both the U.S. and England in minor diplomatic missions.

Wikoff, Henry, 1813-1884. The [6137] reminiscences of an idler. N.Y.: Fords, Howard & Hulbert, 1880. 596 p. NN. Writer and diplomat, who spent much of his time in Europe. Largely devoted to the story of his contacts with society.

Wikoff, Henry, 1813-1884. My [6138] courtship and its consequences. N.Y.: Derby, 1855. 438 p. WU. A highly personal account of an engagement and an abduction, by an American socialite.

Wilber, Lewis, 1816-1839. Dying [6139] confession of Lewis Wilber, who was executed..., at Morrisville, ...N.Y....for the murder of Robert Barber... . Morrisville: pr. at the office of the Madison observer, 1839. 16 p. MWA. As described by the title.

Wilbur, Lafayette, b. 1834. Life [6140] of Lafayette Wilbur (autobiography) and family genealogy. Jericho, Vt.: Press of K. C. Butler, 1881. 75 p. DLC. Lawyer in Vermont.

Wilcox, Alanson, 1832-1924. [6141] ...Autobiography. Cleveland: Judson pr. co., 1912. 125 p. MoCanD. Clergyman of the Disciples of Christ in Michigan, Mass., Pa., and Ohio.

Wilcox, Ella (Wheeler), 1855- [6142] 1919. The story of a literary career. Holyoke, Mass.: Elizabeth Towne, 1905. 60 p. NN. The author's career as poet and novelist up to 1884.

Wilcox, Ella (Wheeler), 1855- [6143] 1919. The worlds and I. N.Y.: G. H. Doran, 1918. 420 p. WHi. Poet, novelist.

Wilcox, Mrs. Tabitha McSween. [6144] Incidents of a city missionary's life. Louisville: Pentecostal pub. co., 1916. 121 p. TxU. In Austin, Texas. The period covered is the late 19th and early 20th centuries.

Wild, Asa, b. 1794. A short [6145] sketch of the religious experience and spiritual travels of Asa Wild, of Amsterdam, N.Y. ... Amsterdam, N.Y.: pr. for the author by D. Wells, 1824. 96 p. Auto., p. 3-53. MWA. A spiritual autobiography.

Wilder, Fred Calvin. War ex- [6146] periences of F. C. Wilder. Belchertown, Mass.: F. C. Wilder, 1926. 118 p. DLC. Soldier in the first World War.

Wilder, George Albert, b. 1855. [6147] The white African. Bloomfield, N.J.: Morse press, 1933. 192 p. DLC. The author was born in Africa, of American parents. After securing an education in the U.S., he returned to Africa as a missionary among the Zulus.

Wilder, Harris Hawthorne, 1864- [6148] 1928. The early years of a zoölogist; the story of a New England boyhood. Ed. by Inez W. Wilder. N.Y.: Harbor press, 1930. 73 p. WU. As described by the title.

Wilder, Marshall Pinckney, [6149] 1859-1915. The people I've smiled with. N.Y.: Cassell, 1889. 268 p. DLC. A dwarf who became known as a humorist. He travelled much in the eastern states and to England.

Wilding, George Cleaton. Mem- [6150] ories of a mountain circuit. Richwood, W.Va.: Nicholas news co., 1924. 78 p. NjMD. Methodist clergyman in the Ohio, Mississippi and Columbia valleys, in the Puget Sound, and New Jersey.

Wile, Frederic William, b. 1873. [6151] News is where you find it. N.Y.: Bobbs-Merrill, 1939. 505 p. WU. Newspaperman in Chicago to 1900; foreign correspondent in Germany and England to 1919.

Wiley, Harvey Washington, [6152] 1844-1930. An autobiography. Indianapolis: Bobbs-Merrill, 1930. 339 p. WU. Teacher of chemistry, government chemist, lecturer on pure food reform.

Wiley, Henry Ariosto, 1867- [6153] 1943. An admiral from Texas, by Henry A. Wiley, U.S.N. retired, formerly admiral and commander-in-chief, United States Fleet.

Garden City, N.Y.: Doubleday, Doran, 1934. 322 p. NN. Recollections of naval life, 1883-1929.

Wilhelm, Daniel B., b. 1811. Recollections of "Uncle Daniel". Baltimore: J. F. Weishampel, jr., printer, 1883. 22 p. DLC. Baptist lay church worker in Maryland. [6154]

Wilhelm, Fritz. Kampf als wirtschaffs-pionier in übersee im dienste der deutschen industrie. Hamburg: Broschek, 1930. 223 p. DLC. German electrical engineer who was employed in St. Louis, Kansas City and Chicago. The American experiences are found within pages 29-94. [6155]

Wilkerson, James. Wilkerson's history... Columbus: 1861. 43 p. MoSM. A former slave becomes a Methodist clergyman, serving in Ohio and Indiana. [6156]

Wilkie, Franc Bangs, 1832-1892. Pen and powder. Boston: Ticknor, 1888. 383 p. WHi. A journalist's experiences while reporting the Civil War for the New York Times. [6157]

Wilkie, Franc Bangs, 1832-1892. Personal reminiscences of thirty-five years of journalism. Chicago: F. J. Schulte & co., 1891. 324 p. NN. Chicago journalist who worked mostly on W. F. Story's Chicago Times; also Civil War correspondent for the New York Times. [6158]

Wilkins, Benjamin Harrison, b. 1856. "War boy;" a true story of the Civil War and re-construction days. Tullahoma: Wilson bros. pr. co., 1938. 84 leaves. NN. The story of the author's youth in Louisiana. [6159]

Wilkins, Isaac, 1742-1830. My services...during the American revolution. Brooklyn: Historical pr. club, 1890. 23 p. DLC. A Loyalist who fled to England and returned to the colonies as a British soldier. [6160]

Wilkinson, John, 1821-1891. The narrative of a blockade-runner. N.Y.: Sheldon, 1877. 252 p. WHi. Confederate naval officer. [6161]

Willan, John, b. 1852. Preaching Christ for sixty years... Eau Claire: 1933. 38 p. DLC. Evangelist in Wisconsin and Washington. [6162]

Willard, Benjamin J., b. 1828. Captain Ben's book. A record of the things which happened to Capt. Benjamin J. Willard, pilot and stevedore... Portland, Maine: Lakeside press, printers, 1895. 204 p. WHi. Off the coast of Maine. [6163]

Willard, Frances Elizabeth Caroline, 1839-1898. Glimpses of fifty years... Chicago: Woman's temperance pub. association, 1889. 698 p. WHi. Temperance worker. [6164]

Willard, Joseph Augustus, b.1816. Half a century with judges and lawyers. N.Y. & Boston: Houghton Mifflin, 1895. 371 p. DLC. After a decade as a sailor, the author became Clerk of the Supreme Court of Massachusetts. [6165]

Willard, Josiah Flynt, 1869-1907. My life (by Josiah Flynt, pseud.) N.Y.: Outing pub. co.,1908. 365 p. WU. The author was employed by a railway company to study tramps and criminals. [6166]

Willard, Sidney, 1780-1856. Memories of youth and manhood. Cambridge: John Bartlett, 1855. 2 vols. WHi. To the year 1830, by a professor of languages at Harvard. [6167]

Willcox, R. N. Reminiscences of California life... Avery: Willcox print, 1897. 290 p. DLC. Miner in California, miller and farmer in Ohio. [6168]

Willemse, Cornelius William, 1871-1942. Behind the green lights. N.Y. & London: Alfred A. Knopf, 1931. 364 p. NN. Episodes from the career of a Dutch-born New York detective. [6169]

Willemse, Cornelius William, A cop remembers. N.Y.: E. P. Dutton, 1933. 344 p. NN. See preceding entry. [6170]

Willett, Edward, 1701-1794. The matrimonial life of Edward Willett; with a variable style. N.Y.: Thomson, 1812. 35 p. NNQ. New York farmer tells story of his married life for benefit of his children. [6171]

Willey, Mrs. Chloe, b. 1760. A short account of the life and remarkable views of Mrs. Chloe Willey of Goshen, N.H. Written by herself. Amherst: pr. by Joseph Cushing, 1807. 33 p. WHi. A spiritual account. [6172]

Willey, Samuel Hopkins, 1821-1914. Thirty years in California; a contribution to the history of the [6173] state, from 1849 to 1879. San Francisco: A. L. Bancroft, 1879. 76 p. NN. Pioneer Presbyterian clergyman and educator in California.

Willey, Samuel Hopkins, 1821- [6174] 1914. Decade sermons. Two historical discourses occasioned by the close of the first ten years' ministry in California... San Francisco: Towne & Bacon, 1859. 46 p. DLC. Covers 1849-50.

Willey, Samuel Hopkins, 1821- [6175] 1914. The history of the first pastorate of the Howard Presbyterian church, San Francisco, California, 1850-1862... San Francisco: Whitaker & Ray, 1900. 171 p. DLC. Includes much personal history.

Williams, Albert, 1809-1893. A [6176] pioneer pastorate. San Francisco: Wallace & Hassett, printers, 1879. 240 p. WHi. Presbyterian clergyman in California, beginning in 1849.

Williams, Clark, b. 1870. The [6177] story of a grateful citizen. An autobiography. N.Y.: 1934. 2 vols. WHi. Banker, State Controller, New York, civil leader.

Williams, Mrs. Elizabeth (Whit- [6178] ney). A child of the sea; and life among the Mormons. Harbor Springs: E. W. Williams, 1905. 229 p. WHi. An account of youth spent in Michigan, in part in the Mormon colony led by James J. Strang.

Williams, Frederick Benton (pseud.). See Hamblen, Herbert Elliott.

Williams, Henry Horace, b. 1858. [6179] The education of Horace Williams. Chapel Hill, N.C.: The author, 1936. 200 p. DLC. Professor of philosophy in North Carolina.

Williams, Isaac D., b. 1821? [6180] Sunshine and shadow of slave life ...East Saginaw, Mich.: Evening news pr. & binding house, 1885. 91 p. DLC. A Virginia slave who escaped to Canada.

Williams, James, b. 1825. Life [6181] and adventures of James Williams, a fugitive slave... San Francisco: Women's union print, 1873. 108 p. WHi. Services in underground railway. Miner in California. Lay church worker in Sacramento.

Williams, James, b. 1834. [6182] Seventy-five years on the border. Kansas City: Standard pr. co., 1912. 207 p. WHi. Missouri farmer on the frontier.

Williams, James E. Fifty-eight [6183] years in the Pan-Handle of Texas. Austin: Firm foundation pub. house, 1944. 137 p. TxWB. Pioneer rancher. The period covered is roughly the second half of the nineteenth century.

Williams, John A. B., d. 1893. [6184] Leaves from a trooper's diary. Phila.: 1869. 103 p. Auto., p. 7-77. DLC. Union army.

Williams, John G., b. 1824. A [6185] forty-niner's experience in the Klondike... Boston: Pinckham press, 1897. 29 p. DLC. As described by the title.

Williams, Mrs. Marion Moffet. [6186] My life in a Mormon harem. Minneapolis: 1920. 198 p. Auto., 1-103. UHi. A tale of domestic woe within a Mormon family.

Williams, Michael, b. 1878. The [6187] book of the high romance. A spiritual autobiography. New ed. N.Y.: Macmillan, 1926. 406 p. DLC. A journalist, born in Canada, tells of his return to the Catholic faith.

Williams, R. H., b. 1831. With [6188] the border ruffians; memories of the Far West, 1852-1868, by R. H. Williams, sometime lieutenant in the Kansas Rangers and afterward captain in the Texan Rangers. Ed. by E. W. Williams... London: John Murray, 1907. 478 p. NN. The locale is Virginia, Kansas and Texas. The author, born in England, was a rancher, Indian fighter and Confederate ranger.

Williams, Rebecca (Yancey), [6189] b. 1899. Carry me back. N.Y.: E. P. Dutton, 1942. 320 p. NN. Youthful days and social life in Lynchburg, Va., during the first quarter of the twentieth century.

Williams, Robert G., b. 1831. [6190] Thrilling experiences of the Welsh evangelist R. G. Williams, reformed drunkard and gambler; or, forty-eight years in the light and love of Jesus Christ. Chicago: Marks & Williams, 1896. 139 p. NN. The author was a hotel man and gambler before his conversion; his later career took him over much of the United States as an evangelist and mission worker.

Williams, Samuel, b. 1813. Four [6191] years in Liberia. A sketch of the life of the Rev. Samuel Williams... Phila.: King & Baird, printers, 1857. 66 p. DLC. Negro missionary worker in Liberia.

Williams, Mrs. W. L. Golden [6192] years... Dallas: Baptist standard pub. co., 1921. 157 p. TxWB. Lay worker for the Baptist church in Texas.

Williams, Wythe, b. 1881. Passed [6193] by the censor; the experience of an American newspaper man in France. N.Y.: E. P. Dutton, 1916. 270 p. DLC. Correspondent of the New York Times covering the first World War in France.

Williamson, E. M., b. 1835. [6194] Confederate reminiscences, 1861-1865. Danville: McDaniel pr. co., 1935. 39 p. DLC. As described by the title.

Williamson, Passmore. Narra- [6195] tive of the facts in the case of Passmore Williamson. Phila.: Pa. Anti-slavery society, 1855. 24 p. MWA. A story of a southern slave.

Williamson, Peter, 1730-1799. [6196] French and Indian cruelty... N.Y.: J. Jackson, 1758. 104 p. DLC. The writer, born in Scotland, was captured by the Indians during the French and Indian War.

Willis, Mrs. Olympia Brown, [6197] 1835-1926. Acquaintances, old and new among reformers. N.p.: 1911. 115 p. WHi. Feminist.

Williston, Samuel, b. 1861. Life [6198] and law; an autobiography. Boston: Little, Brown, 1941. 347 p. NN. Professor of law at the Harvard Law School.

Wills, Helen, b. 1906. Fifteen- [6199] thirty; the story of a tennis player. N.Y.: Charles Scribner's sons, 1937. 311 p. NN. As described by the title.

Wills, Henry O. Twice born... [6200] Cinc.: Western Methodist book concern, 1890. 223 p. NbLU. Evangelist in Detroit, who had previously been a thief, convict, ward heeler.

Wilmer, James Jones, 1749- [6201] 1814. Memoirs. Baltimore: pr. by Samuel & John Adams, 1792. 16 p. MBAt. Episcopal clergyman in Delaware, Virginia and Maryland. For a short time he was associated with the Church of the New Jerusalem.

Wilmot, Franklin A. Disclosures [6202] and confessions of Frank A. Wilmot, the slave thief and Negro runner, with an accurate account of the under-ground railroad! ... by a late conductor on the same. Also full particulars of the plans adopted for running off slaves from the southern states to the Canadas... Phila.: Barclay & co., 1860. 38 p. NN. Authentic?

Wilson, Benjamin Davis, 1811- [6203] 1878. Benjamin Davis Wilson, 1811-1878. Pasadena: n.d. 40 p. CSmH. Indian fighter who came across the plains to Santa Fe in 1833. In California he was a rancher, coming to that state about 1845.

Wilson, Mrs. Edith (Bolling), [6204] b. 1872. My memoir. Indianapolis: Bobbs-Merrill, 1939. 386 p. WHi. The wife of the President tells of her domestic and political life.

Wilson, Edward. The golden [6205] land... Boston: J.E. Farwell, 1852. 42 p. CSmH. California miner who came in 1849.

Wilson, Elijah Nicholas, 1842- [6206] 1915. Among the Shoshones. Salt Lake City: Skelton, 1910. 222 p. DLC. The author lived with the Indians for two years when a young lad. Later he was a trapper, Indian fighter, stage driver, guide, etc. The locale is Utah and the time is from 1850.

Wilson, Emily, b. 1840. The for- [6207] gotten girl. N.Y.: The Alphabet press, 1937. 28 p. DLC. Family life in a New England village prior to 1865.

Wilson, Francis, b. 1854. Recol- [6208] lections of a player. N.Y.: pr. at the DeVinne press, 1897. 81 p. DLC. Comedy actor, mostly in New York.

Wilson, Francis Mairs Hunting- [6209] ton. Memoirs of an ex-diplomat. Boston: Bruce Humphries, 1945. 373 p. MWA. The period covered is 1897-1913.

Wilson, Henry Lane, 1857-1932. [6210] Diplomatic episodes in Mexico, Belgium and Chile. Garden City, N.Y.: Doubleday, Page, 1927.

399 p. DLC. Ambassador, 1897–1914.

Wilson, Hugh Robert. The edu- [6211] cation of a diplomat. N.Y.: Longmans, Green, 1938. 224 p. WHi. Assistant Secretary of State, and Minister to Switzerland. Covers to 1917.

Wilson, Hugh Robert. Diplomat [6212] between wars. N.Y.: Longmans, Green, 1941. 344 p. WHi. In Switzerland, Japan, Germany and France. The period covered is 1917–1938.

Wilson, James Andrew. ...Life, [6213] travels, and adventures. Austin: Gammel's book store, 1927. 200 p. WHi. Constable and City Marshall in Tennessee in the eighties.

Wilson, James Harrison, 1837– [6214] 1925. Under the old flag; recollections of military operations in the war for the union, the Spanish war, the Boxer rebellion, etc. By James Harrison Wilson, brevet major-general, U.S.A.; late major-general, U.S.V.; engineer and inspector-general on Grant's staff; commander Third Cavalry Division, Army of the Potomac; commander Cavalry Corps M.D.M., etc. N.Y. & London: D. Appleton & co., 1912. 2 vols. NN. As described by the title.

Wilson, John Alfred. Adventures [6215] ... Toledo: Blade pr. & paper co., 1880. 237 p. WHi. Union soldier, member of Andrews raiders.

Wilson, Mrs. Luzena Stanley, [6216] b. 1821. Luzena Stanley Wilson, '49er; memories recalled years later for her daughter Correnah Wilson Wright. Mills College, Calif.: The Eucalyptus press, 1937. 61 p. WHi. California innkeeper during the gold rush days.

Wilson, Margaret Isabel, [6217] b. 1877. Borderland minds. Boston: Meador, 1940. 203 p. Auto., p. 19–157. DLC. Teacher in midwest tells of mental problems, treatment.

Wilson, Obed Gray, b. 1836. My [6218] adventures in the Sierras. Franklin: Editor pub. co., 1902. 215 p. WHi. Gold miner in California.

Wilson, Robert, b. 1747. The [6219] travels of that well-known pedestrian, Robert Wilson... London: pr. for the author, sold by G. Kearsley, 1807. 244 p. DLC. An English adventurer in the U.S., 1779–1781, who fought with the British troops.

Wilson, William Hasell, 1811– [6220] 1902. Reminiscences of a railroad engineer. Philadelphia: Railway world pub. co., 1896. 62 p. NN. Railroad construction engineer, mostly in Pennsylvania.

Wilson, William Hasell, 1811– [6220A] 1902. Reminiscences... Ed. by Elizabeth B. Pharo. Phila.: Patterson & White, 1937. 68 p. NN. Experiences in railroad construction work in Pennsylvania; Civil War experiences with the Pennsylvania Railroad. Less detailed than the preceding title.

Winans, Mrs. Hubert Charles. See Brush, Katharine.

Winans, William H. Reminis- [6221] cences and experiences in the life of an editor. Newark: 1875. 200 p. WHi. In New York and New Jersey, by a newspaper man.

Winant, Cornelius, d. 1928. A [6222] soldier's manuscript. Boston: Merrymount press, 1929. 140 p. DLC. The author served with the French forces in the first World War.

Winchester, Charles Wesley. [6223] Reminiscences... Louisville: Pentecostal pub. co., 1911. 255 p. WHi. Methodist clergyman in New York.

Winchevsky, Morris, 1856–1932. [6224] Erinerungen. (In his: Gesamlte werk. N.Y.: Freiheit pub. association, 1927–28.) Vols. IX-X. NN. Russian born Jew who came to the U.S. in 1894 and who wrote for the Yiddish socialist press. He was also known for his Yiddish poems and essays.

Windom, Mrs. Jane (Hutcheson). [6225] European school days in the eighteen seventies. Princeton, N.J.: pr. at the Princeton univ. press, 1931. 160 p. Auto., p. 21–157. DLC. Born in Ohio, educated in Europe.

Windy Bill (pseud.). See Goodkind, Ben.

Wing, Samuel B. The soldier's [6226] story... Phillips: 1898. 118 p. WHi. In the Union army.

Winn, Matt J., b. 1862. Down the [6227]

stretch... N.Y.: Smith & Durrell, 1945. 292 p. WHi. Manager of race track in Kentucky.

Winnemucca, Sarah. *See* Hopkins, Mrs. Sarah W.

Winship, Mrs. Amy Davis, b.1831. [6228] My life story. Boston: Badger, 1920. 164 p. WHi. Wisconsin reformer.

Winslow, Mrs. Anna J. (Frazer), [6229] b. 1848. Jewels from my casket. Los Angeles: Nazarene pub. co., 1910. 193 p. WHi. Quaker minister in Oregon, California, Iowa, Kansas, Indiana, Nebraska, Oklahoma and North Carolina.

Winslow, Carroll Dana, 1889- [6230] 1932. With the French flying corps. N.Y.: Scribner, 1917. 226 p. DLC. With the French forces in the first World War.

Winslow, Kenelm, b. 1863. A [6231] life against death. Seattle, Wash.: Lowman & Hanford, 1933. 292 p. NN. Physician and surgeon in Massachusetts and Seattle, Wash.; experiences as a medical officer in World War I.

Winston, Robert Watson, [6232-6233] b. 1860. It's a far cry. N.Y.: Holt, 1937. 381 p. WHi. North Carolina lawyer, judge of Superior Court (1889-95) and State Senator (1885).

Winterfield, (Captain). The voy- [6234] ages, distresses and adventures ...New ed. London: pr. for Ann Lemoine, 1800. 48 p. CSmH. The writer, born in Scotland, served in the British army during the American Revolution.

Winters, Erastus. In the 50th [6235] Ohio serving Uncle Sam. No imprint, 1910? 188 p. KyMidF. Civil War account.

Wise, Frederick May. Marine [6236] tells it to you. N.Y.: Sears, 1929. 366 p. WHi. By an officer in the U. S. Marines.

Wise, Henry Augustus, 1819-1869. [6237] Los gringos; or, an inside view of Mexico and California. N.Y.: Baker & Scribner, 1849. 453 p. DLC. By a U.S. Naval officer, the years being 1846-49.

Wise, Isaac Mayer, 1819-1900. [6238] Reminiscences; tr. from the German by David Philipson. Cinc.: L. Wise & co., 1901. 367 p. DLC. Rabbi, born in Bohemia (Austria).

Had congregations in New York City, Ohio, Pa. Publisher of Jewish newspapers, and founder of Hebrew Union College.

Wise, John, 1808-1879. Through [6239] the air: a narrative of forty years' experience as an aëronaut ... Phila.: Today pr. & pub. co., 1873. 606 p. Auto., p. 27-31, 247-606. DLC. Balloonist.

Wise, John Sergeant, 1846-1913. [6240] The end of an era. Boston & N.Y.: Houghton, Mifflin, 1899. 474 p. NN. Officer in the Confederate army.

Wishard, John G., b. 1863. Rem- [6241] iniscences of a doctor; a personal narrative. Wooster, Ohio: The Collier pr. co., 1935. 374 p. DLC. Presbyterian medical missionary in Kudistan, Persia, who later settled in Ohio.

Wishard, John G., b. 1863. Twen- [6242] ty years in Persia. Chicago,etc.: Revell, 1908. 344 p. DLC. See preceding entry.

Wistar, Isaac Jones, 1827-1905. [6243] Autobiography. N.Y.: Harper, 1938. 530 p. WHi. Soldier in the Union army; forty-niner in California; industrialist.

Wister, Jones, 1839-1917. Jones [6244] Wister's reminiscences. Phila.: pr. for priv. circulation by J.B. Lippincott co., 1920. 459 p. DLC. Operator of iron mills in Pa.

Witham, James W., b. 1856? [6245] Fifty years on the firing line. Chicago: 1924. 214 p. DLC. Farmer in Illinois and Iowa who was active in the work of the Farmers' Alliance in Iowa and Minnesota.

Witherbee, Orville O. The be- [6246] ginning of myself. Los Angeles: pr. by the Shepherd press, 1934. 123 p. DLC. The story of boyhood in the family of a Wisconsin country doctor.

Withers, Robert Enoch, b. 1821. [6247] Autobiography... Roanoke, Va.: The Stone pr. & mfg. co. press, 1907. 550 p. Vi. Physician, newspaper editor and Virginia political figure who also served as U.S. Consul at Hong Kong.

Withington, Alfreda Bosworth. [6248] Mine eyes have seen; a woman doctor's saga. N.Y.: E. P. Dutton, 1941. 311 p. WU. During the first World War the writer served in

Mass., Labrador and in Europe. After the War, she served in the rural areas of Kentucky.

Witten, George. Outlaw trails; [6249] a Yankee hobo soldier of the Queen. N.Y.: Minton, Balch & co., 1929. 252 p. DLC. A hobo tells of his leaving for Africa where he fought with the English against the Boers.

Witter, William Clitus, b.1842. [6250] A family record. With a brief biographical sketch of William Clitus Witter. N.Y.: John Polhemus pr. co., 1892. 33 p. DLC. A patent and trademark lawyer who lived in New York.

Witting, Victor. Minnen fråu [6251] mitt lif ... Worcester, Mass.: Trycet & Burbank, 1902. 576 p. MBNew. Swedish immigrant who first was a seaman and then a Methodist clergyman.

The woes of war: a letter of [6252] sorrow. By a southern lady. London: Ridgway, 1862. 25 p. DLC. Presumably written by the wife of a Louisiana plantation owner.

Wolcott, Mrs. Frances (Met- [6253] calfe), b. 1851. Heritage of years ... N.Y.: Minton, Balch & co., 1932. 286 p. WHi. By the wife of a member of the U.S. Congress from New York who tells of their life in Washington, Colorado and abroad. Covers period to 1889.

Wolf, Isadore Julius, b. 1864. A [6254] family doctor's notebook. N.Y.: Fortuny's, 1940. 315 p. Auto., p. 15-61. DLC. A Jewish doctor, born in Germany, who in addition to his private practice taught at the University of Kansas.

Wolfe, Thomas, b. 1900. The [6255] story of a novel. N.Y.: Scribner, 1936. 93 p. DLC. A novelist tells of his becoming a writer, after gaining an education in North Carolina and Mass.

Wolwoff, Israel. I yield to des- [6256] tiny; from shop to synagogue. N.Y.: 1938. 81 p. DLC. A Russian born Jew, who after a life as a merchant in Russia and the U.S., becomes a cantor in New York.

Womack, J.P. Reminiscences. [6257] Jonesboro: Cabeb Watson, 1939. 171 p. MWA. State Superintendent of Public Instruction in Arkansas, president of a teachers college,

1929-38.

Wood, A. B., d. 1945. Fifty years [6258] of yesterdays. Gering: Courier press, 1945. WHi. Newspaper publisher in Nebraska.

Wood, Clement, b. 1888. The [6259] glory road; an autobiography. N.Y.: The Poets press, 1936. 287 p. NN. By a poet.

Wood, Eric Fisher, b. 1889. The [6260] note book of an attache... N.Y.: Century, 1915. 345 p. DLC. Attache in the American embassy in France during the first World War.

Wood, Frank, b. 1850. Life and [6261] travels of Frank Wood, and stories of every day events, written by himself. Muskegon, Mich.: The News & reporter office, 1880. 54 p. DLC. Itinerant peddler and merchant in Hampshire, and laborer in Michigan. The writer was born in Canada.

Wood, James Craven, b. 1858. [6262] An old doctor of the new school. Caldwell, Idaho: The Caxton printers, 1942. 398 p. DLC. Homeopathist who practiced in Ohio and Michigan.

Wood, John Allen, b. 1828. Auto- [6263] biography of Rev. J. A. Wood... Chicago: Christian witness co., 1904. 113 p. DLC. Methodist clergyman in Vermont, New York, Pennsylvania.

Wood, M. D. Fruit from the [6264] jungle. Mountain View, Calif.: Pacific press pub. association: 1919. 331 p. Auto., p. 6-14. DLC. Seventh-Day Adventist, briefly a Methodist, who was a missionary in India.

Wood, Peggy, b. 1892. How young [6265] you look, memoirs of a middle-sized actress. N.Y.,Toronto: Farrar & Rinehart, inc., 1941. 277 p. DLC. As described by the title.

Wood, William Burke, 1779-1861.[6266] Personal recollections of the stage... Phila.: Baird, 1855. 472 p. WHi. Canadian born actor and theatrical manager, chiefly in Philadelphia.

Woodard, Luke, b. 1832. Sketches [6267] of a life at 75... Richmond, Ind.: Nicholson pr. co., 1907. 246 p. Auto., p. 1-100. IaHi. Quaker minister in N.Y. and Indiana who left for England in 1894.

Woodard, Solomon B., b. 1838. [6268] Story of a life... Richmond, Ind.: Nicholson pr. co., 1928. 115 p. OrNeGF. School teacher, farmer, minister of the Society of Friends in Indiana.

Woodbridge, Timothy, 1784- [6269] 1862. The autobiography of a blind minister... Boston: Jewett, 1856. 312 p. NjR. In Mass., Conn., Ohio and New York.

Woodbury, James, b. 1819. Auto- [6270] biography. Bath, Maine: Maine temperance advocate press, 1870. 32 p. Nh. Temperance worker in Maine.

Woodbury, John Hubbard. How I [6271] found it, North and South; together with Mary's statement. Boston: Lee & Shepard, 1880. 295 p. DLC. A husband and wife story of an unsuccessful attempt to farm in Mass. and Florida.

Woodbury, John Taylor, b. 1863. [6272] Vermillion cliffs... St. George? 1933. 88 p. Auto., p. 56-73. DLC. Teacher, farmer, justice of the peace, city councilman in Utah.

Woodbury, Mrs. Josephine [6273] (Curtis). War in heaven. Sixteen year's experience in Christian Science mind healing. 3d ed. Boston: Samuel Usher, 1897. 72 p. CU. Teacher of Christian Science in Boston.

Woodcock, Eldred Nathaniel, [6274] b. 1844. Fifty years a trapper and hunter... Columbus: A. R. Harding, 1913. 318 p. DLC. In many parts of the country.

Wooden Leg, b. 1858. A warrior [6275] who fought Custer. Minneapolis: Midwest co., 1931. 384 p. WHi. As described by the title.

Woodfill, Samuel. Woodfill of [6276] the regulars; a true story of adventure from the Arctic to the Argonne. By Lowell Thomas. Garden City, N.Y.: Doubleday, Doran, 1929. 325 p. NN. Thirty-three years in the U.S. regular army; service in the Philippines, Alaska, the Mexican border and the first World War.

Woodman, Charles T., b. 1802. [6277] Narrative of Charles T. Woodman, a reformed inebriate. Boston: Theodore Abbot, 1843. 208 p. NN. The author, a lecturer for the Washingtonian temperance movement tells of his early career as a drunkard and of his prison experiences in Massachusetts institutions.

Woodruff, Janette. Indian oasis. [6278] (told to Cecil Dryden). Caldwell: Caxten, 1939. 325 p. WHi. A government worker with Indians, 1900-1929, in Montana, Nevada and Arizona.

Woodruff, Wilford. Leaves [6279] from my journal. Salt Lake City: Juvenile instructor office, 1881. 96 p. CU-B. To Missouri in the thirties with the Mormons. Missions to Arkansas, Tennessee, Maine and England.

Woods, James, 1814?-1886. Rec- [6280] ollections... San Francisco: Joseph Winterburn & co., 1878. 260 p. WHi. Presbyterian clergyman in California in the pioneer period.

Woods, John Franklin, b. 1865. [6281] God's marvelous grace to me. Huntington: 1936. 175 p. DLC. A railroad worker becomes a clergyman in the Pilgrim Holiness Church in West Virginia.

Woods, Samuel Davies, b.1845. [6282] Lights and shadows of life on the Pacific Coast. N.Y. & London: Funk & Wagnalls, 1910. 474 p. DLC. Lawyer, member of the U.S. Congress from California; early twentieth century.

Woodson, Marion Marle, 1882- [6283] 1933. Behind the door of delusion ... N.Y.: Macmillan, 1932. 325 p. DLC. Experiences within an asylum for the mentally disturbed.

Woodward, Corodon Roswell, [6284] b. 1831. Recollections... N.p.: 1906. 917 p. WHi. Hardware merchant in Illinois.

Woodward, George, b. 1863. The [6285] memoirs of a mediocre man. Phila.: Harris & Partridge, 1935. 216 p. DLC. Physician in Conn. and Pa. Member of the State Senate in Pa.

Woodward, Helen (Rosen), b.1882.[6286] Through many windows. N.Y.: Harper, 1926. 387 p. WHi. Advertisement copy writer.

Woodward, Helen (Rosen), b.1882.[6287] Three flights up. N.Y.: Dodd, Mead, 1935. 260 p. NN. Memories of the author's childhood in a New York tenement district.

Woodworth, Maria Beulah, b.1844. [6288] The life, work, and experience of Maria Beulah Woodworth, evangelist. St. Louis: pub. for the author by the Commercial pr. co., 1894. 451 p. DLC. Lay evangelical worker for Church of God in many states of the union.

Woolf, Samuel Johnson, 1880- [6289] 1942. Here am I. N.Y.: Random house, 1941. 374 p. NN. An artist's memories of his various sitters.

Woolley, Edward Mott. Free- [6290] lancing for forty magazines. Cambridge: Writer pub. co., 1927. 320 p. DLC. Magazine writer, newspaper reporter in Chicago, San Francisco.

Woolley, Solomon Jackson, [6291] b. 1828. Life, recollections and opinions... Columbus: Cott & Hann, 1881. 325 p. DLC. Adventurer who settled down to farming and agricultural experimentation in Texas.

Woolson, Constance Fenimore, [6292] 1840-1894. The old stone house (by Ann March, pseud.). Boston: Lothrop, 1873. 427 p. OC1W. Novelist tells of her early life in Cleveland.

Woolworth, Solomon. Experi- [6293] ences in the Civil War. Newark, N.Y.: 1904. 79 p. NN. In the Union army.

Wootton, Richens Lacy, 1816- [6294] 1893. "Uncle Dick" Wooten, by Howard L. Conrad. Chicago: Dibble, 1890. 473 p. TxU. A largely autobiographical account by a Rocky Mountain trapper, guide, hunter and Indian fighter.

Worby, John. The other half... [6295] N.Y.: Lee Furman, 1937. 307 p. WU. Tramp.

Worcester, Elwood, 1863-1940. [6296] Life's adventure; the story of a varied career. N.Y.: Scribner's, 1932. 362 p. NN. Episcopal clergyman and educator, best known for his connection with the Emmanuel movement for mental healing, in New York, Pa., Mass.

Wordon, James M., b. 1812. The [6297] life and adventures... New London: Starr & Farnham, printers, 1855. 40 p. DLC. Merchant sailor.

Worrall, James, 1812-1885. [6298] Memoirs of Colonel James Worrall, civil engineer, with an obituary postcript by a friend. Harrisburg: Meyers, 1887. 111 p. Auto., p. 6-99. DLC. From Ireland to Pa.

Worsham, John H. One of Jack- [6299] son's foot cavalry... N.Y.: Neale, 1912. 353 p. WHi. As described by the title.

Worstall, Florence Mabel. A [6300] true life story and a modern miracle of a drug-addict for eight years, who was saved by the grace of God, from an everlasting hell... Wilmington: K. A. Horner co., printers, 1929. 28 p. DLC. In Pa.

Wrench, Mrs. John. See Kimbrough, Emily.

Wright, A. B. Autobiography of [6301] Rev. A. B. Wright. Cinc.: Cranston & Curts, 1896. 447 p. MBNew. Methodist clergyman in Kentucky.

Wright, Eugene. The great horn [6302] spoon. Indianapolis: Bobbs-Merrill, 1928. 320 p. WU. Sailor in Mediterranean and Indian seas.

Wright, Frank Lloyd, b. 1869. [6303] An autobiography... N.Y.: Duell, Sloan & Pearce. 1943. 560 p. WHi. Wisconsin architect.

Wright, Frank Lloyd, b. 1869. [6304] An autobiography. Book six: Broadacre City. N.Y.: 1943. 30 p. WHi. A supplement to the preceding item. See the preceding item.

Wright, George Bert, b. 1881. [6305] Two years experiences as a prisoner (sic) in the United States penitentiary of Leavenworth, Kansas... Leavenworth: Leavenworth bag co., 1915. 70 p. DLC. For wrongful use of mail.

Wright, George Frederick, 1838- [6306] 1921. Story of my life and work. Oberlin: Bibliotheca Sacra, 1916. 459 p. WHi. Geologist, editor of Bibliotheca Sacra, professor of New Testament literature at Oberlin.

Wright, Harold Bell, 1872-1944. [6307] To my sons. N.Y.: Harper & bros., 1934. 261 p. NN. Earlier career of the author until he became well established as a novelist.

Wright, Henry Clarke, b. 1797. [6308] Human life: illustrated in my individual experience as a child, a youth, and a man. Boston: Bela Marsh, 1849. 414 p. MWA. Congregational clergyman in New England.

Wright, Louise (Wigfall). A [6309] southern girl in '61; the war-time

Wright, Richard, b. 1909. Black [6310] boy, a record of childhood and youth. N.Y.: Harper, 1945. 228 p. WU. A Negro writer tells of his youth in Mississippi.

Wright, Samuel, b. 1821. The [6311] story of my life. The experience of...for forty years a class-leader in the Methodist Episcopal church... N.Y.: 1891. 191 p. RPB. Wisconsin gardener.

Wright, Solomon Alexander, [6312] d. 1937. My rambles as East Texas cowboy, hunter, fisherman, tie-cutter... Austin: Texas folklore society. 1942. 159 p. WHi. A 20th century account.

Wright, Virgil M., b. 1859. Ten [6313] years on the road. Indianapolis: F. H. Smith, 1893. 398 p. DLC. Travelling salesman in the South and Midwest.

Wright, William Henry, 1856- [6314] 1934. The Grizzly bear; the narrative of hunter-naturalist... N.Y.: Scribner, 1909. 274 p. Auto., p. 3-12. DLC. As described by the title.

Wurzbach, Emil Frederick, [6315] b. 1838. Life and memoirs... San Antonio: Yanaguana society, 1937. 39 p. WHi. Texas ranger, teamster, miner and Confederate soldier, 1845-65.

Wyatt, Mrs. Sophia Hayes. The [6316] autobiography of a landlady of the old school...Boston: pub. for the author, 1854. 296 p. NN. School teacher, hotel keeper in New England.

Wyatt, William, 1812-1879. The [6317] life and sermons of Rev. William Wyatt of the Wyoming conference ... Albany: Charles Van Benthuysen & sons, 1878. 405 p. NjMD. Methodist clergyman.

Wyckoff, James, b. 1826. Sketch [6318] of the life of James Wyckoff, comprising an account of his lamentable affliction and astonishing cure! Buffalo: Jewett, Thomas & co., printers, 1846. 32 p. DLC. The writer suffered from a stomach ulcer which he claims he cured with sarsparilla.

Wyckoff, Richard Demille, [6319] 1873-1934. Wall Street ventures and adventures through forty years. N.Y. & London; Harper & bros., 1930. 313 p. NN. Experiences in the New York stock market.

Wyeth, John Allan, 1845-1922. [6320] With sabre and scalpel... N.Y.: Harper, 1914. 534 p. WHi. Confederate soldier, surgeon and medical educator in New York.

Wylie, Ida Alena Ross. My life [6321] with George... N.Y.: Random house, 1940. 350 p. WU. English novelist, who devotes a small portion of this book to her experiences in Hollywood where she wrote movie scenarios.

Wyman, Seth, 1784-1843. The [6322] life and adventures of Seth Wyman, ...a life spent in robbery, theft, gambling... Manchester: J. H. Cate, printer, 1843. 310 p. WU. In Massachusetts.

Wynn, W. O., b. 1846. A brief [6323] sketch... No imprint. 16 p. TxWB. Confederate soldier who prior to the War was a cowboy in Texas.

# Y

Yale, Caroline Ardelia, 1848- [6324] 1933. Years of building; memories of a pioneer in a special field of education. N.Y.: L. MacVeagh, The Dial press, 1931. 311 p. DLC. Teacher of the deaf in Mass.

Yan, Phou Lee. See Lee, Yan Phou.

Yancey, Mrs. Dolly Kennedy. [6325] The tramp woman, a book of experiences. St. Louis: Britt pub. co., 1909. 94 p. MoKU. In the South and Middle West.

Yankoff, Peter Demetroff, [6326] b. 1885. Headlights to success; or, the story of a Bulgarian boy. Ft. Smith: The author, 1920. 373 p. ArU. Physician in Arkansas who was born in Bulgaria.

Yankoff, Peter Demetroff, [6327] b. 1885. Peter Menikoff; the story of a Bulgarian boy in the great American melting pot. Nashville: Cokesbury press, 1928. 294 p. DLC. Born in Bulgaria, the author tells in the third person of his medical education in the U.S., and of his social work during summers for the Presbyterian church in Illinois and Missouri.

Yarbrough, George W. Boyhood [6328] and other days in Georgia. Nashville: M. E. Church, South, 1917. 248 p. Auto., p. 13-95. WHi. Methodist clergyman in Georgia.

Yarn of a Yankee privateer. [6329] Ed. by Nathaniel Hawthorne. N.Y.: Funk & Wagnalls, 1926. 308 p. WHi. Includes his imprisonment by the British in 1812.

Yates, Robert L. When I was a [6330] harvester. N.Y.: Macmillan, 1930. 174 p. DLC. A New York youth tells of wheat harvesting in Canada.

Ybarra, Thomas Russell, [6331] b. 1890. Young man of the world. N.Y.: I. Washburn, 1942. 316 p. DLC. Foreign correspondent in Europe, Central and South America. Much of his youth was spent in Venezuela which he describes in Young Man of Caracas.

Yeater, Mrs. Sarah Jeanette [6332] (Ellis), b. 1832. Civil war experiences... Sedalia: 1910. 57 p. MoHi. By the wife of a Missouri merchant.

Yellow Wolf, 1855-1935. ...His [6333] own story, told to Lucullus Virgil McWhorter. Caldwell: Caxton, 1940. 291 p. WHi. A frontier account, telling of the struggle of a Nez Perce Indian against the force of the white man's arms.

York, Alvin Cullum, b. 1887. [6334] Sergeant York... Garden City: Doubleday, Doran, 1928. 309 p. WHi. By a World War I hero.

York, Brantley, 1809-1891. [6335] Autobiography... Durham: Seeman printery, 1910. 139 p. WHi. Professor of logic and rhetoric at Rutherford College, North Carolina.

Yorke, Elenor. My weapon is [6336] love; an autobiography. Chicago: The Oceanic pub. co., 1945. 193 p. NN. Story of a poet and actress, who was a strong believer in American isolationism and advocated the use of love as a means of settling the world's ills.

Youell, George, b. 1868. Lower [6337] class. Seattle: Caxton printers, 1938. 265 p. NN. Experiences of an English immigrant in Michigan and Washington state, together with earlier career as a deep-sea fisherman in the North Sea.

Youff, Ulv (pseud.). Ulven... [6338] London: Chapman & Dodd, 1923. 163 p. C. A Norwegian born pianist, living in New York and California, who fell a victim to tuberculosis.

Youle, W. E., 1847-1926. Sixty- [6339] three years in the oilfields. N.p.: Fuller pr. co., n.d. 61 p. CSmH. In Pennsylvania and California.

Young, Ann Elizabeth. Wife no. [6340] 19...story of a life in bondage... Hartford: Dustin, Gilman, 1876. 605 p. WHi. By one of Brigham Young's wives.

Young, Arthur Henry, b. 1866. [6341] Art Young... N.Y.: Sheridan, 1939. 467 p. WU. Cartoonist known for his contributions to New Masses and Liberator.

Young, Chester Smith. Twenty- [6342] five years a country parson in Missouri. Barnard: Rush pr. co., 1931. 111 p. MoK. United Brethren, and then a Methodist.

Young, Dan, b. 1783. Autobiogra- [6343] phy of Dan Young, a New England preacher of the olden time. N.Y.: Carlton & Porter, 1860. 380 p. NN. Methodist minister in New England and later in Ohio.

Young, Duncan Francis. Behind [6344] the grill; some experiences of a country bank cashier. N.Y.: Abbey press, 1901. 105 p. DLC. In Louisiana.

Young, Ella, b. 1867. Flowering [6345] dusk. N.Y.: Longmans, Green, 1945. 341 p. DLC. Irish born writer and poet.

Young, Harry, b. 1849. Hard [6346] knocks... Portland: Wells, 1915. 242 p. DLC. Railroad worker, buffalo hunter, mule skinner in Arkansas, Kansas, Colorado, the Dakotas, and Wyoming.

Young, Hugh Hampton, b. 1870. [6347] Hugh Young, a surgeon's autobiography. N.Y.: Harcourt, Brace, 1940. 554 p. WU. Urologist.

Young, Jacob, 1776-1859. Auto- [6348] biography of a pioneer... Cinc.: Poe & Hitchcock, 1860. 528 p. WHi. Methodist clergyman in Ohio, Tennessee, Mississippi and Virginia.

Young, John Duncan, b. 1856. [6349] A Vaquero of the brush country... partly from the reminiscences of John Young, by James Frank Dobie. Dallas: Southwest press, 1929. 297 p. WHi. Southwest cowboy.

Young, John R., b. 1837. Memoirs [6350] of John R. Young, Utah pioneer, 1847, written by himself. Salt Lake City, Utah: The Deseret news, 1920. 341 p. DLC. Nephew of Brigham Young who tells the story of the flight from Illinois to Utah, and of his missionary work in the Hawaiian Islands and in the British Isles.

Young, Lot D. Reminiscences [6351] of a soldier of the orphan brigade. Paris, Ky.: n.d. 99 p. WHi. Confederate soldier.

Young, Peter, 1784-1836. A [6352] brief account of the life and experience, call to the ministry, travels and afflictions. Portsmouth, N. H.: pr. by Beck & Foster, 1817. 168 p. NcWatC. Clergyman of the "Christian Connection" church in Maine.

Young, Robert Anderson, 1824- [6353] 1902. Reminiscences. Nashville, Dallas: Methodist Episcopal Church, South, 1900. 154 p. DLC. Episcopal clergyman in Tennessee and North Carolina.

Young, Rosa, b. 1890. Light in [6354] the dark belt... St. Louis: Concordia pub. house, 1929. 148 p. LND. A teacher and lay mission worker for the Evangelical Lutheran Church in Alabama.

Young, Samuel, b. 1821. The [6355] history of my life... Pittsburgh: Herald pr. co., 1890. 147 p. WHi. Newspaper editor and publisher in Pennsylvania.

Young, Samuel Hall, 1847-1927. [6356] Hall Young of Alaska... N.Y.: Revell, 1927. 448 p. WHi. Presbyterian missionary worker in Alaska.

Young, William E. Shark! [6357] Shark! The thirty-year odyssey of a pioneer shark hunter... N.Y.: Gotham house, 1933. 287 p. Auto., p. 15-252. DLC. As described by the title.

Young, William Pennypacker, [6358] b. 1866. A Ford dealer's twenty year ride. Hempstead, N.Y.: Twenty year ride pub. co., 1932. 157 p. DLC. In Pennsylvania.

Youngblood, Charles L., b. 1826. [6359] A mighty hunter... Chicago: Rand, McNally, 1890. 362 p. DLC. Buffalo hunter, trapper and Indian fighter in Kansas; farmer in Iowa.

Younger, Cole, 1844-1916. The [6360] story of Cole Younger, by himself; being an autobiography of the Missouri guerilla captain and outlaw, his capture and prison life... Chicago: press of the Henneberry co., 1903. 123 p. DLC. Confederate who after the War was imprisoned for bank robbery in Minnesota.

Younger, Cole, 1844-1916. Con- [6361] vict life at the Minnesota State Prison... St. Paul: W. C. Heilbron, 1909. 155 p. DLC. An account of the robbery in Minnesota which led to his imprisonment, and a description of his life in prison.

Younger, Thomas Coleman, See Younger, Cole.

Youtsey, Henry E. Short stories. [6362] Frankfort, Ky.: Roberts pr. co., 1919. 58 p. KyRE. Assassin in Kentucky.

Yung Wing, 1828-1912. My life in [6363] China and America, by Yung Wing ...Commissioner of the Chinese Educational Commission, associate Chinese minister in Washington... N.Y.: H. Holt & co., 1909. 286 p. DLC. Chinese businessman and diplomatic officer.

# Z

Zagel, Hermann H. Aus [6364] frühlingstagen: erinnerungen aus dem fröhlichen bubenleben. Peoria: 1923. 231 p. DLC. Story of youth in Illinois in the last quarter of the 19th century.

Zahl, Paul Arthur, b. 1910. To [6365] the lost world. N.Y.: Knopf, 1939. 268 p. DLC. Naturalist on expeditions into South America.

Zakrzewska, Marie Elizabeth, [6366] 1829-1902. A woman's quest... ed. by Agnes C. Vietor, N.Y.: Appleton, 1924. 514 p. Auto., p. 3-287. WU. Physician, woman's rights advocate.

Zausner, Philip, b. 1884. Un- [6367] varnished, the autobiography of a Union leader. N.Y.: Brotherhood publishers, 1941. 381 p. WHi. Jewish leader of union of painters and decorators.

Zeigler, William Abraham, [6368] b. 1862. On this side of Jordan. Benton: 1945. 177 p. DLC. Telegraph operator in South and Southwest who became a lay missionary worker for the Presbyterian church in Texas and Louisiana.

Zhitlowsky, Chaim, 1865-1943. [6369] Zikhroynes fun main lebn. N.Y.: Zhitlowsky farlag committee, 1935-40. 3 vols. NN. Born in Russia. The story of a Jewish writer.

Ziegler, John A. M., b. 1855. [6370] Father and son. Phila.: pub. for the author, 1929. 285 p. Auto., p. 135-226. MoSC. Lutheran clergyman in Kansas, Iowa, Kentucky, Ohio and California.

Zinsser, Hans, 1876-1940. As I [6371] remember him... Boston: Little, Brown, 1940. 443 p. WU. Physician.

Zollers, George DeHaven. [6372] Thrilling incidents on sea and land. 7th ed. Elgin, Illinois: Brethren pub. house, 1909. 411 p. ICN. Civil War experiences in the Union army with Pennsylvania forces. After serving on a whaler following the war he became a clergyman (Brethren) in Illinois.

Zora, Lucia, b. 1877. Sawdust [6373] and solitude...ed. by Courtney Ryley Cooper. Boston: Little, Brown, 1928. 230 p. DLC. Animal trainer in circuses; life on a Colorado ranch.

Zorn, Carl Manthey, b. 1846. [6374] Dies und das aus frühem amtsleben ... St. Louis: Concordia pub. house, 1912. 203 p. MoSC. German born Lutheran clergyman, who after serving as a missionary in the East Indies came to the U.S. in 1876, living in Minnesota and Missouri.

Zorn, Carl Manthey, b. 1846. [6375] Dies und das aus dem leben lines ostindischen missionars. Zweite auflage. St. Louis: Concordia pub. house, 1907. 292 p. MoSC. This book covers the period 1871-73, prior to his coming to the U.S.

Zorn, Carl Manthey, b. 1846. [6376] Grossvaters jugenderinnerungen... Milwaukee: Northwestern pub. house, 1910. 2 vols. MoSC-H. His life in Germany where he was trained for the Lutheran ministry.

Zunser, Eliakum, 1840-1913. A [6377] Jewish bard... N.Y.: Zunser jubilee committee, 1904. 44 p. PU. Russian born writer of Jewish songs who emigrated to the United States.

# A Note on the Subject Index

This index is designed to reveal the following: the occupations of the autobiographers; where they lived; and the important historical events (such as the Civil War) in which they played a part.

Some autobiographies do not lend themselves to identification by occupation, such as accounts of spiritual development, physical infirmity and mental illness. These are entered under appropriate headings, but unlike the occupational entries, are not further identified by place.

For the United States, the geographical divisions employed are those used by the Bureau of the Census. These are: Pacific, Mountain, East North Central, West North Central, South Atlantic, Middle Atlantic, New England, East South Central, and West South Central.

In addition to the designations described above, autobiographies are subdivided by periods (1800-1850, 1850-1900, etc.) No autobiography is entered under more than one of these periods.

To accommodate those interested in the history of immigrant groups, a special entry, Foreigners in the U.S., has been made. This group is further subdivided under the names of the countries from which the immigrants came.

Autobiographies of Americans who lived abroad are entered under the names of the appropriate country. When several countries are involved, the name of the continent is substituted. Thus, for example, readers seeking European accounts, should refer also to the entries under Germany, France, etc.

# Subject Index

Abolitionists, 280, 387, 569, 594, 773, 1025, 1081, 1126, 1130, 1178, 1209, 1248, 1257, 1624, 1625, 1626, 1639, 1648, 1861, 1892, 1940, 2298, 2346, 2543, 2645, 2812, 2940, 3246, 3386, 3423, 3558, 3734, 3771, 3787, 3800, 3978, 4075, 4379, 4623, 4923, 5004, 5080, 5244, 5363, 5412, 5427, 5585, 5670, 5764, 5768, 5855, 5949, 6181, 6202
—See also Social reformers
Abyssinia, (1900-1945), 1162
Actors (1800-1850), 457, 943, 2656, 3621, 4828, 5318, 5319, 5320, 6052, 6266
—(1850-1900), 302, 692, 1312, 1440, 1654, 1855, 2161, 2239, 2551, 2691, 2984, 3453, 3557, 3678, 4037, 4102, 4200, 4212, 4568, 5078, 5235, 5360, 5624, 5930, 5947, 5952, 6079, 6208
—(1900-1945), 183, 325, 1005, 1017, 1137, 1260, 1490, 1651, 1652, 1906, 1916, 2263, 2264, 2520, 2753, 2762, 2879, 2973, 3008, 3119, 3362, 3400, 3440, 3542, 3543, 3915, 3939, 4286, 4530, 4636, 5506, 5515, 5642, 5672, 5673, 5702, 5719, 6106, 6265, 6336
—See also Comedians, Minstrels, Vaudevillians
Aden (1900-1945), 1687
Admirals. See Seamen-U.S.
Adventurers and vagabonds (to 1800), 537
—(1800-1850), 378, 943, 1642, 2314, 2479, 2628, 4838, 4962, 5132, 5893
—(1850-1900), 142, 333, 550, 553, 1616, 2483, 2971, 3209, 3480, 3561, 4113, 4251, 4299, 4352, 4467, 4619, 4869, 5291, 5475, 5607, 5919, 5973, 6032, 6135, 6249, 6291
—(1900-1945), 439, 596, 606, 1303, 1337, 1364, 1488, 1613, 1813, 1814, 1984, 2013, 2057, 2148, 2227, 2301, 2370, 2411, 2521, 2525, 3130, 3177, 3297, 3392, 3449, 3517, 3518, 3541, 3563, 3654, 3684, 3920, 3996, 4346, 4563, 4941, 5096, 5415, 5780, 5864, 6295, 6325
Advertisers and public relations men (1850-1900), 751, 4068, 4945.
—(1900-1945), 166, 210, 491, 770, 1895, 2423, 2531, 2756, 3333, 3385, 3719, 3973, 4334, 4704, 4759, 5653, 6286
Aeronautical engineers. See Engineers
Afghanistan (1900-1945), 4949
Africa (1800-1850), 4528, 5898
—(1850-1900), 600, 601, 984, 1752, 1859, 1959, 2357, 2438, 2442, 2784, 3055, 3111, 4195, 5634, 6147
—(1900-1945), 57, 490, 573, 811, 1002, 1303, 1390, 1481, 1488, 1838, 2542, 2753, 2785, 3050, 3192, 3328, 3329, 3330, 3972, 4008, 4143, 4199, 5392, 5863, 5912, 6038, 6045, 6249
Air Corps. See Aviators—military, and individual wars, e.g., World War I—Air Corps., etc.
Alaska: Adventurers and vagabonds, 3541
—Authors, 4970, 4971
—Doctors, 1536, 3201, 5070
—Domestic relations, 2995, 4902
—Engineers, 3535
—Farmers and farm life, 4970, 4971
—Fishermen, 4332
—Hunters and trappers, 694, 3483, 3660, 5581
—Immigrants. Danish, 4970, 4971 Norwegian, 5119
—Indians, life among, 4767
—Judges, U.S., 6127
—Lawyers, 2404, 6127
—Merchants, 694, 5581
—Miners and mining life, 79, 674, 921, 1271, 1556, 1605, 1944, 2019, 2118, 2325, 2345, 2404, 2437, 2552, 3580, 4332, 4970, 4971, 5119, 5407, 5581, 5757, 6185
—Missionaries. Presbyterian, 6356. Quaker, 4767
—Negroes, 5481
—Nurses, 4902
—Peace officers, 2453
—Pioneers, 811, 2437, 4902, 5407, 5481, 5757, 6185
—Representatives, U.S., 6127

Alaska (cont.): Restaurants and taverns, proprietors and workers, 3383
—Scientists, 2824
—Social workers, 366
—Soldiers, 2400, 6276
—Surveyors, 2437
—Teachers, 808, 1986, 5481
—Teamsters, 5119
—Whalers, 694
Alcoholics (to 1800), 1600
—(1800-1850), 2081, 2117, 2295, 2632, 4853, 6277
—(1850-1900), 366, 442, 1297, 2055, 3102, 4103, 4268, 4725, 6190
—(1900-1945), 1045, 1193, 2368, 3676, 4900, 5096, 5097, 5339
Ambassadors. See Diplomats
American Indians. See Indians, autobiographies by
American Revolution: British—Army, 6160, 6219, 6234; Loyalists, 588, 1201, 1867, 1936, 3060, 4058, 6160; Navy, 2089
—Colonial—Allies, 4080, 4868; Army, 286, 398, 680, 732, 812, 853, 1168, 1345, 1545, 1876, 1953, 2002, 2003, 2290, 2319, 2663, 3018, 3441, 3752, 3797, 4034, 4315, 4402, 4525, 4613, 4684, 4730, 4747, 4831, 4843, 4844, 4872, 5147, 5246, 5286, 5312, 5599, 5901, 5916; Chaplains, 2093; Civilians, 1443, 5991; Government officials, 38, 2985, 3811; Navy, 148, 1869, 3089, 5170, 5597
Amputees. See Physically handicapped
Anarchists (1850-1900), 4134
—(1900-1945), 1364, 2094, 2212
—See also Communists, Socialists, Social reformers
Anarctic (1900-1945), 858, 859, 860, 4302, 5223, 5224
Animal trainers (1850-1900), 1198, 3062, 3682, 3683
—(1900-1945), 770, 4935, 5414, 6373
—See also Circus performers
Announcers, radio. See Communications workers
Anthropologists. See Scientists
Arabia. See Aden, Iran
Archbishops. See Bishops and archbishops
Archeologists. See Professors, Scientists
Architects (1800-1850), 2087, 4017
—(1850-1900), 611, 713, 4333, 4440, 5555
—(1900-1945), 627, 1307, 3250, 4433, 6303, 6304
Arctic (1850-1900), 545, 694, 1220
—(1900-1945), 861, 2929, 3667, 3668, 4255, 4477, 4478, 4479, 4734
Argentina (1800-1850), 3227
—(1900-1945), 2798, 5180, 5217, 5485

Armenia (1850-1900), 46
Army. See Soldiers, and individual wars, e.g., American Revolution: Army; Civil War: Union—Army; etc.
Army Air Corps. See Aviators: Military, and individual wars, e.g., World War I: Air Corps., etc.
Arsonists. See Criminals
Art collectors (1850-1900), 2981
—(1900-1945), 1070, 3961
Art critics. See Critics
Artisans (1800-1850), 221, 816, 3475, 4371, 4431, 4800, 5461
—(1850-1900), 149, 930, 1219, 1860, 2005, 2085, 2228, 2415, 2658, 3178, 3271, 3526, 4467, 4713, 4743, 4785, 4810, 4873, 4973, 5030, 5351, 5398, 5541, 5583, 5636, 6053
—(1900-1945), 1282, 4758, 4920
—See also Factory workers, Laborers
Artists. See Painters
Asia (1850-1900), 994, 1507
—(1900-1945), 403, 573, 2513, 3268, 4131, 5152, 6045
Assassins. See Criminals
Astronomers. See Scientists
Athletes (1800-1850), 1802, 4313
—(1850-1900), 154, 1200, 2624, 2702, 4150, 5553, 5629
—(1900-1945), 1009, 1055, 1246, 1512, 1515, 1721, 1840, 2600, 2620, 2719, 2952, 3040, 3628, 3650, 3831, 3880, 4208, 4372, 5044, 5580, 5701, 5746, 5782, 5783, 5940, 6001, 6199
Athletics: Officials (1850-1900), 4150
—(1900-1945), 3880, 4876
Attachés. See Diplomats
Attorneys. See Lawyers
Attorneys General. See Politicians
Auctioneers (1850-1900), 3062
Australia (1850-1900), 355, 1902, 4089, 4357, 5429, 5634, 5744
—(1900-1945), 2411, 5960
Austria (1850-1900), 3133
—(1900-1945), 2580, 4949
Austro-Hungarian Empire. See Successor states
Authors (to 1800), 4170
—(1800-1850), 637, 665, 872, 2234, 5040, 5129, 5681, 5691, 5698, 6006
—(1850-1900), 66, 131, 138, 189, 233, 239, 430 562, 816, 817, 956, 980, 1001, 1025, 1037, 120 1301, 1784, 1919, 2067, 2106, 2399, 2546, 264 3451, 3665, 3674, 4111, 4187, 4787, 4797, 5004, 5005, 5184, 5185, 5302, 5346, 5347, 5364, 5418, 5432, 5900, 6071, 6137
—(1900-1945), 260, 306, 331, 336, 420, 450, 627, 632, 672, 867, 1122, 1146, 1162, 1189, 1200, 1278, 1450, 1562, 1792, 1797, 1939, 1954 2107, 2108, 2168, 2188, 2324, 2459, 2531, 254 2589, 2611, 2813, 3057, 3109, 3377, 3476, 37

Authors (1900-1945) (cont.), 3807, 3859, 3916, 4094, 4330, 4362, 4417, 4563, 4567, 4583, 4601, 4695, 4777, 4814, 4937, 4970, 4971, 5095, 5096, 5104, 5339, 5538, 5588, 5645, 5743, 5808, 5846, 5895, 5935, 6040, 6084, 6130, 6345, 6369
—See also Critics, Journalists, Novelists, Playwrights, Poets
Authors' wives (1850-1900), 71
Automobile engineers. See Engineers
Aviators: Civilian, 987, 1064, 1167, 1264, 1724, 1725, 1984, 2204, 2263, 2264, 2372, 2550, 3021, 3513, 3540, 4376, 4633, 4950, 5258, 5417, 5651, 5876. Military, 861, 1162, 1532, 1598, 4919
—See also World War I–Air Corps, World War II–Air Corps

# B

Bakers, caterers, cooks (1850-1900), 826
—(1900-1945), 427, 1737, 3333, 3425
Balkens (1900-1945), 573
Ballet dancers. See Dancers
Balloonists, 6239
Ballroom dancers. See Dancers
Band leaders. See Conductors
Bankers (1800-1850), 5608
—(1850-1900), 308, 363, 633, 663, 706, 733, 759, 926, 1097, 1127, 1540, 1657, 1860, 1940, 1983, 2015, 2075, 2282, 2334, 2549, 2618, 2661, 2807, 2853, 2895, 3395, 3495, 3782, 3901, 3932, 4097, 4256, 4603, 4604, 4861, 4966, 5113, 5153, 5349, 5758, 5815, 6035,
—(1900-1945), 466, 683, 828, 1101, 1188, 1494, 1941, 2157, 2373, 2899, 3072, 3147, 4263, 4276, 5058, 5447, 5465, 5478, 5838, 5999, 6177
—See also Financers
Barbers, hairdressers (1800-1850), 2340, 4612
—(1850-1900), 5713
—(1900-1945), 1039, 5039
Bartenders. See Restaurants and taverns, proprietors and workers
Baseball players. See Athletes
Beauticians. See Barbers, hairdressers
Beggars. See Adventurers and vagabonds
Belgian Congo (1900-1945), 2606, 3159
Belgium (1900-1945), 6114, 6210
Bell collectors (1900-1945), 3962
Bermuda (1900-1945), 2854
Bicyclists. See Athletes
Billiards players (1900-1945), 2761
Biographers. See Authors
Biologists. See Scientists

Bishops and archbishops: Catholic (1900-1945), 4304
—Episcopal (1800-1850), 1020. (1850-1900), 1068, 2280, 3245, 4413-4414, 5595, 5796, 6080. (1900-1945), 739, 3240, 3390, 3391, 4239, 4769
—Methodist (1850-1900), 3343, 5634. (1900-1945), 2077
—Mormon (1800-1850), 3994 (1850-1900), 3399, 6121. (1900-1945), 363
—See also Clergymen
Blacksmiths. See Artisans
Blind. See Physically handicapped
Bolivia (1850-1900), 51
—(1900-1945), 4373
—See also South America
Book collectors (1850-1900), 187, 4160
—(1900-1945), 5231, 5280, 5881, 5906,
Book designers (1900-1945), 4343, 4344
Bookkeepers. See Office workers
Booksellers (to 1800), 756, 757
—(1800-1850), 8, 2710
—(1850-1900), 429, 532, 691, 956, 1144, 1991, 4168, 5440
—(1900-1945), 2662, 4917
—See also Printers, Publishers
Borneo (1850-1900), 2770
Botanists. See Scientists
Boxers. See Athletes
Boy Scouts of America: Officials. See Social workers
Brazil (1850-1900), 1859, 4579
—(1900-1945), 2348, 3199, 4039, 4766
Bridge players (1900-1945), 1364, 5218
Brigands. See Criminals
Britain. See England, Ireland, Scotland
British Commonwealth of Nations. See individual nations
Broadcasters. See Radio announcers and operators
Bums. See Adventurers and vagabonds
Burglars. See Criminals
Burma (1850-1900), 940, 3761, 5300
—(1900-1945), 5098, 5099
Bus drivers. See Teamsters
Businessmen. See Bankers, Executives, Financiers, Industrialists, Merchants, Real estate dealers and promoters, Salesmen

# C

Cabinet makers. See Artisans
Cabinet members, U.S. (1850-1900), 594, 2075, 2105, 5069, 5126, 5176
—(1900-1945), 1429, 2792, 2912, 3355, 3356, 3814, 4914, 5519
Canada (to 1800) 3729
—(1800-1850), 3735, 4491, 5132, 5468, 5729

Canada (cont.): (1850-1900), 2922, 3699, 4707, 5570, 5949
— (1900-1945), 512, 899, 1002, 1620, 3449, 3508, 3660, 5436, 5458, 6248, 6330
Cantors. See Singers
Capitalists. See Bankers, Financiers, Industrialists, Real estate dealers and promoters.
Captains, Army. See Soldiers
Captains, Navy. See Seamen-U.S.
Card players. See Bridge players, Gamblers
Carpenters. See Artisans
Cartoonists (1900-1945), 4896, 6341
— See also Illustrators
Caterers. See Bakers, caterers, cooks
Cattlemen. See Ranchers and ranch life
Cellists. See Musicians
Central America (1900-1945), 1117, 1323, 1441, 2598, 3775, 4653, 6331
Ceylon (1850-1900), 2770
— (1900-1945), 3877
Chambermaids. See Hotels and inns, proprietors and workers
Chaplains (1800-1850), 5470
— (1850-1900), 3084, 4686
— (1900-1945), 3686
— See also Civil War-Chaplains, World War I-Chaplains, etc.
Charitable association officials. See Social workers
Chauffeurs. See Teamsters
Chemists. See Scientists
Chessmasters (1900-1945), 3738
Childhood reminiscences: Date undetermined, 2706, 3136, 6246
— (to 1800), 613, 873, 1075, 1641, 3553, 5331, 5603, 5901, 6167
— (1800-1850), 59, 62, 82, 106, 167, 174, 175, 334, 502, 570, 571, 618, 623, 658, 721, 783, 785, 818, 831, 836, 855, 886, 924, 926, 983, 1033, 1104, 1181, 1182, 1288, 1317, 1403, 1414, 1475, 1670, 1686, 1896, 1924, 2155, 2394, 2491, 2507, 2657, 2667, 2685, 2808, 2815, 2819, 2833, 2868, 2894, 2915, 3069, 3122, 3205, 3359, 3416, 3627, 3636, 4029, 4038, 4073, 4117, 4351, 4365, 4395, 4438, 4571, 4700, 4775, 4800, 4830, 4836, 5019, 5103, 5118, 5149, 5204, 5284, 5342, 5512, 5593, 5698, 5752, 5829, 5868, 5913, 5945, 5967, 6012, 6031, 6308
— (1850-1900), 4, 7, 40, 70, 77, 80, 83, 89, 123, 132, 137, 143, 161, 191, 194, 232, 233, 250, 259, 268, 377, 382, 392, 432, 437, 460, 474, 476, 511, 512, 531, 534, 541, 567, 603, 629, 644, 684, 689, 750, 761, 778, 824, 827, 833, 887, 896, 912, 917, 986, 989, 991, 1016, 1018, 1057, 1067, 1079, 1088, 1099, 1101, 1102, 1110, 1128, 1166, 1180, 1245, 1279, 1298, 1329, 1354, 1361, 1378, 1389, 1437, 1477, 1494, 1501, 1521, 1631, 1636, 1640, 1649, 1658, 1718, 1731, 1757, 1875, 1879, 1882, 1921, 1951, 1982, 2049, 2082, 2092, 2101, 2106, 2138, 2165, 2191, 2211, 2231, 2300, 2329, 2344, 2408, 2429, 2431, 2489, 2539, 2553, 2554, 2582, 2610, 2659, 2676, 2678, 2679, 2726, 2754, 2760, 2777, 2816, 2852, 2861, 2870, 2871, 2906, 2959, 2960, 2972, 2991, 3031, 3036, 3068, 3091, 3096, 3097, 3098, 3113, 3133, 3156, 3168, 3192, 3236, 3243, 3258, 3260, 3290, 3294, 3315, 3361, 3429, 3459, 3562, 3584, 3607, 3630, 3632, 3635, 3673, 3679, 3714, 3817, 3854, 3936, 3991, 3999, 4001, 4015, 4041, 4051, 4068, 4079, 4084, 4100, 4118, 4136, 4147, 4175, 4186, 4188, 4247, 4265, 4276, 4285, 4350, 4442, 4508, 4573, 4575, 4621, 4659, 4678, 4717, 4737, 4757, 4768, 4786, 4850, 4887, 4906, 4910, 4929, 5022, 5048, 5066, 5071, 5104, 5136, 5233, 5266, 5271, 5315, 5375, 5379, 5401, 5406, 5413, 5452, 5542, 5616, 5695, 5696, 5798, 5838, 5845, 5846, 5879, 6081, 6082, 6148, 6159, 6178, 6206, 6207, 6225, 6292, 6328, 6364, 6376
— (1900-1945), 29, 388, 899, 918, 944, 1133, 1352, 1372, 1515, 1724, 1831, 1904, 1958, 2209, 2250, 2339, 2383, 2416, 2729, 2907, 2967, 3217, 3232, 3319, 3469, 3589, 3702, 3802, 3808, 3822, 3834, 3890, 3897, 4002, 4040, 4155, 4217, 4358, 4476, 4594, 4596, 4826, 5072, 5374, 5445, 5568, 5639, 5642, 5643, 5777, 5894, 6189, 6287, 6310
Children, autobiographies by (1850-1900), 4119
— (1900-1945), 4734
— See also Juvenile Delinquents
Chile (1900-1945), 5217, 6210
China (1800-1850), 3610
— (1850-1900), 3429, 3827, 4163, 4216, 5124, 6134, 6214
— (1900-1945), 50, 102, 339, 1064, 1085, 1118, 1337, 1813, 1831, 1857, 1890, 1984, 2013, 2388, 2477, 2903, 3306, 3521, 3564, 3905, 4157, 4346, 4364, 4399, 4405, 4631, 4762, 5115, 5527, 5859, 5943
Chiropractors (1900-1945), 384
Christian Scientist practitioners (1850-1900), 399
Church workers: Date undetermined, 4742
— (to 1800), 315, 1826
— (1800-1850), 997, 1206, 1843, 3419, 5622

Church workers (cont.): (1850-1900), 132, 253, 379, 429, 568, 648, 717, 738, 786, 804, 834, 945-955, 1131, 1261, 1293, 1589, 2382, 2415, 2532, 2921, 3117, 3365, 3420, 3421, 3590, 3708, 3809, 3948, 4042, 4044, 4466, 4485, 4651, 4893, 5460, 5504, 5536, 5560, 5841, 6154, 6181, 6273, 6311
— (1900-1945), 129, 779, 1486, 2110, 2215, 2235, 2902, 2938, 3231, 3314, 3394, 3930, 4051, 4609, 4925, 5148, 5384, 5387, 5590, 5604, 5854, 6192, 6354, 6368
—See also Social reformers, Social workers, Temperance workers
Circus performers (1850-1900), 1913, 2195, 2527, 2551, 2597, 3976, 4944, 5435
— (1900-1945), 305, 1458, 4859, 5186, 5414, 5506, 5793A
—See also Animal trainers
Civil engineers. See Engineers
Civil servants: Local (1800-1850), 821, 2751. (1850-1900), 149, 2461, 3873, 4718, 4848, 5159, 5321, 5322. (1900-1945), 4331, 5449
—State (1850-1900), 3389, 4741, 6165. (1900-1945), 138, 1786, 1796, 2538, 2834, 2945, 3114, 3128, 3547, 3824, 4635, 6177
—U.S. (to 1800), 286. (1800-1850), 381, 3626, 3891, 4345, 4927. (1850-1900), 77, 416, 585, 677, 685, 749, 780, 1028, 1043, 1997, 2005, 2031, 2805, 3118, 3225, 3951, 4018, 4418, 4726, 4911, 4978, 5546, 6014, 6101, 6131, 6152. (1900-1945), 14, 111, 1172, 1199, 1267, 1299, 1381, 1768, 1877, 2088, 2360, 2413, 2486, 2574, 2585, 2885, 3037, 3061, 3107, 3396, 3401, 4263, 4464, 4681, 4705, 4706, 4914, 4958, 5449, 5765, 6069, 6211, 6278
—See also Indian agents
Civil War: Confederate-Army, 121, 137, 190, 298, 301, 332, 374, 400, 419, 461, 462, 467, 517, 550, 551, 579, 580, 604, 649, 660, 729, 884, 971, 972, 976, 1058, 1069, 1153, 1205, 1235, 1342, 1357, 1358, 1375, 1398, 1411, 1413, 1484, 1565, 1621, 1674, 1680, 1704, 1717, 1729, 1956, 1966, 1974, 1989, 1994, 2039, 2124, 2146, 2153, 2170, 2180, 2229, 2247, 2262, 2309, 2338, 2385, 2409, 2440, 2441, 2449, 2461, 2479, 2612, 2701, 2743, 2789, 2795, 2803, 2806, 2832, 2835, 2843, 2845, 2853, 2877, 2887, 2891, 2947, 2964, 3022, 3059, 3065, 3120, 3228, 3347, 3502, 3576, 3613, 3700, 3730, 3790, 3798, 3850, 3900, 4035, 4049, 4090, 4129, 4132,
4202, 4241, 4253, 4311, 4377, 4486, 4487, 4553, 4579, 4597, 4745, 4865, 4866, 5074, 5100, 5196, 5263, 5328, 5359, 5404, 5466, 5477, 5511, 5631, 5663, 5720, 5867, 5975, 6188, 6194, 6240, 6299, 6315, 6320, 6323, 6351, 6360
—Chaplains, 1347, 4690
—Civilians, 80, 186, 364, 391, 636, 761, 799, 826, 833, 910, 1034, 1076, 1082, 1142, 1528, 1822, 2127, 2386, 2510, 2956, 3194, 3428, 3555, 3673, 3842, 3866, 4074, 4188, 4668, 4669, 4825, 4839, 4850, 5041, 5304, 5542, 5552, 5883, 6159, 6252, 6309
—Doctors, 1041, 1424, 4047, 5637
—Government officials, 1507, 4535, 4656, 4741
—Navy, 3152, 4089, 4430, 5117, 5996, 6161
—Nurses, 407, 1370, 4501, 5323
—Spies, 2313, 2464, 5866
Civil War: Union-Army, 12, 30, 95, 116, 134, 181, 182, 256, 335, 397, 416, 431, 496, 499, 513, 518, 525, 563, 569, 584, 635, 644, 794, 840, 842, 856, 879, 882, 898, 903, 931, 959, 984, 1028, 1051, 1071, 1121, 1152, 1194, 1203, 1204, 1242, 1266, 1291, 1317, 1332, 1335, 1371, 1379, 1391, 1412, 1455, 1593, 1597, 1607, 1611, 1612, 1647, 1672, 1692, 1741, 1744, 1765, 1773, 1790, 1832, 1854, 1860, 1870, 1871, 1873, 1915, 1923, 1937, 1952, 1979, 1980, 1988, 2012, 2059, 2115, 2123, 2130, 2132, 2143, 2145, 2244, 2245, 2249, 2276, 2278, 2302, 2337, 2432, 2485, 2506, 2522, 2570, 2578, 2619, 2670, 2692, 2700, 2701, 2799, 2805, 2839, 2962, 2972, 3014, 3027, 3028, 3052, 3081, 3118, 3146, 3148, 3166, 3168, 3200, 3208, 3238, 3252, 3292, 3308, 3313, 3366, 3415, 3539, 3549, 3570, 3585, 3586, 3597, 3690, 3699, 3705, 3713, 3736, 3758, 3776, 3813, 3837, 3865, 3871, 3892, 3903, 3912, 3913, 3957, 3968, 3982, 3983, 4011, 4018, 4070, 4121, 4163, 4167, 4168, 4178, 4194, 4226, 4238, 4242, 4277, 4301, 4337, 4396, 4397, 4408, 4418, 4419, 4447, 4458, 4484, 4497, 4529, 4559, 4598, 4616, 4640, 4648, 4678, 4697, 4771, 4785, 4835, 4837, 4842, 4852, 4897, 4948, 4951, 4978, 4993, 5061, 5069, 5081, 5090, 5091, 5112, 5134, 5172, 5179, 5249, 5261, 5295, 5327, 5329, 5333, 5345, 5354, 5378, 5398, 5403, 5484, 5487, 5502, 5517, 5531, 5543, 5589, 5632, 5660, 5664, 5674, 5736, 5755, 5804, 5816, 5820, 5927, 5928, 5957, 5959, 6013, 6043, 6131, 6184, 6214, 6215, 6226, 6235,

Civil War: Union—Army (cont.), 6243, 6293, 6372
—Chaplains, 385, 560, 755, 851, 1247, 1740, 1938, 2320, 2448, 2860, 3219, 4738, 4884, 5762
—Civilians, 218, 474, 776, 1175, 1251, 1973, 1975, 2820, 2901, 3546, 5536, 5752, 5879, 5884, 6004, 6220A, 6332
—Doctors, 356, 664, 864, 1096, 1410, 1794, 1924, 2006, 3034, 3470, 3656, 4064, 4329, 5760, 5965, 6029, 6119
—Government officials, 1420, 5126
—Navy, 115, 294, 526, 1004, 1059, 1333, 1546, 1846, 2655, 3174, 3186, 4600, 5056, 5408, 5430, 5550, 5675, 5821
—Nurses, 253, 469, 1753, 2732, 3386, 3537, 3538, 4218, 5253, 6077
—Spies, 438, 733, 4220
—War correspondents, 741, 4352, 4793, 5737, 5877, 6157, 6158
Civil War. See also Reconstruction
Clergymen: Denomination undetermined (to 1800), 1349, 1844, 3729, 4611
—(1800-1850), 519, 2218, 2748, 2814, 2881, 3150, 3242, 4233, 4313, 5731
—(1850-1900), 518, 698, 1078, 1487, 1816, 1892, 1901, 2147, 2229, 2318, 2666, 2768, 3002, 3079, 3680, 4550, 4686, 4884, 5289, 5545, 5727, 6134
—(1900-1945), 366, 725, 1265, 1708, 1993, 2150, 2796, 4068, 4412, 5446
—See also Clergymen: minor sects
Clergymen: Adventist. See Clergymen: Seventh Day Adventist
—Anglican. See Clergymen: Episcopal
Clergymen: Baptist (to 1800), 2093, 2714, 2842, 2924, 3371, 5268, 5310, 5623
—(1800-1850), 195, 196, 730, 888, 1024, 1192, 1257, 1328, 1399, 1473, 1743, 2490, 2942, 2948, 3011, 3185, 3262, 3452, 3581, 3725, 3836, 3946, 4269, 4284, 4359, 4468, 4470, 4618, 4676, 4847, 5108, 5150, 5175, 5284, 5371, 5486, 5489, 5693, 5738, 6006, 6132
—(1850-1900), 67, 84, 110, 125, 140, 230, 266, 369, 396, 640, 702, 731, 813, 916, 1060, 1077, 1091, 1104, 1218, 1251, 1296, 1358, 1382, 1431, 1480, 1679, 1684, 1706, 1891, 2064, 2281, 2299, 2359, 2387, 2533, 2534, 2943, 3010, 3084, 3111, 3134, 3384, 3428, 3642, 3695, 3730, 3766, 3771, 3908, 4096, 4325, 4327, 4502, 4503, 4591, 4617, 4632, 4719, 4738, 4855, 4860, 5038, 5289, 5314, 5333, 5520, 5567, 5569, 5640, 5688, 6083, 6122
—(1900-1945), 359, 1287, 1305, 1314, 1314A, 2120, 2269, 2867, 3230, 3907, 3933, 4067, 4125, 4569, 4624, 4933, 5610, 6019, 6060

Clergymen: Brethren (1850-1900), 4065, 4172, 6372
—See also Clergymen: United Brethren
Clergymen: Catholic priests—Date undetermined, 4306
—(to 1800), 4043
—(1800-1850), 5334
—(1850-1900), 409, 778, 1031, 1365, 2703, 2704, 3304, 4732, 5123, 5655
—(1900-1945), 317, 504, 592, 771, 2392, 3160, 3303, 3442, 4972, 5559
—See also Bishops and archbishops: Catholic. Monks. Nuns.
Clergymen: Christian Church (to 1800), 2193
—(1800-1850), 1905, 2103, 2536, 3073, 3536, 4650, 4675, 4676, 4895, 5268, 5344, 5505, 5669, 6352
—(1850-1900), 319, 501, 2174, 2237, 2730, 2782, 3792, 4032, 4401, 4700, 5127, 5802, 6002
—(1900-1945), 662, 1125, 2905, 5317, 5561
—See also Clergymen: Disciples of Christ
Clergymen: Church of Christ (1850-1900), 1466
—(1900-1945), 1668, 3655
Clergymen: Church of God (1800-1850), 1948, 2724, 3625
Clergymen: Church of Jesus Christ of Latter-day Saints. See Clergymen: Mormon
Clergymen: Congregational (to 1800), 1811, 2759, 5167, 5422
—(1800-1850), 85, 174, 593, 634, 1143, 1547, 1630, 1864, 2037, 2298, 2652, 2680, 4361, 4385, 4587, 4682, 5822, 5882, 6308
—(1850-1900), 11, 229, 370, 405, 530, 638, 666, 781, 782, 891, 1056, 1135, 1209, 1240, 1249, 1262, 1590, 1734, 1735, 1930, 2076, 2186, 2243, 2333, 2346, 2615, 2708-2709, 2710, 2788, 2913, 3647, 3685, 3862, 3919, 4289, 4588, 4670, 4780, 4892, 4997, 4998, 5014, 5034, 5161, 5340, 5549, 5654, 5684, 5774, 5990
—(1900-1945), 336, 682, 704, 1438, 2456, 2925, 2926, 2927, 3524, 3594, 3888, 4663, 5157, 5194, 5443
Clergymen: Disciples of Christ (1800-1850), 238, 574, 844, 971, 1360, 1791, 1856, 2763, 2766, 3325, 3418, 3768, 4634, 6141
—(1900-1945), 53, 54, 890, 1185, 2990, 4549
—See also Clergymen: Christian Church
Clergymen: Dutch Reformed. See Clergymen: Reformed Church in America
Clergymen: Episcopal (to 1800), 588, 2980, 5686, 6201

Clergymen: Episcopal (cont.), (1800–1850), 289, 742, 2758, 2937, 4021, 4655, 4886, 5791, 5806, 5812
— (1850–1900), 625, 643, 1316, 1435, 1715, 2156, 2267, 2268, 2518, 2883, 4231, 4239, 4386, 4413–4414, 4597, 4707, 4769, 5028, 5376, 5871, 6044, 6353
— (1900–1945), 214, 323, 591, 922, 1505, 1610, 1698, 2163, 3221, 3274, 3303, 3852, 4437, 4755, 4871, 5262, 5554, 5771, 5921, 5994, 6296
—See also Bishops and archbishops: Episcopal
Clergymen: Friends. See Clergymen: Quaker
Clergymen: German Reformed. See Clergymen: Reformed Church in U.S.
Clergymen: Jewish (1850–1900), 4694, 6060, 6238
— (1900–1945), 426, 3803, 4542
Clergymen: Latter-day Saints. See Clergymen: Mormon
Clergymen: Lutheran (to 1800), 4145
— (1800–1850), 1554, 1740, 4107, 4968
— (1850–1900), 202, 546, 646, 1555, 1606, 1910, 2141, 2454, 2693, 2694, 3126, 3612, 3980, 4022, 4258, 4457, 4652, 4703, 4952, 5051, 5206, 5365, 5522, 5730, 6370, 6374
— (1900–1945), 220, 1405, 2054, 3310, 3504, 3515, 5020, 5238, 6024
Clergymen: Mennonite (1800–1850), 2616, 4298
— (1900–1945), 424, 3256
Clergymen: Methodist—Date undetermined, 1238
— (to 1800), 2051, 2111, 5997, 6095
— (1800–1850), 37, 94, 141, 282, 283, 341, 408, 417, 547, 548, 610, 686, 711, 747, 755, 773, 911, 936, 963, 964, 971, 1014, 1158, 1159, 1160, 1274, 1275, 1313, 1539, 1927, 1928, 2072, 2166, 2295, 2602, 2603, 2634, 2842, 2948, 2992, 3339, 3340, 3423, 3478, 3500A, 3588, 3805, 3806, 3981, 4016, 4223, 4354, 4483, 4491, 4528, 4580, 4646, 4827, 4979, 5043, 5080, 5324, 5343, 5380, 5474, 5493, 5578, 5611, 5649, 5704, 5722, 5742, 5748, 5956, 6343
— (1850–1900), 96, 98, 119, 133, 157, 184, 199, 365, 385, 440, 514, 561, 595, 744, 745, 746, 796, 797, 802, 850, 854, 917, 919, 973, 982, 1008, 1120, 1207, 1209, 1243, 1272, 1284, 1347, 1355, 1369, 1418, 1457, 1463, 1495, 1537, 1557, 1709, 1716, 1740, 1829, 1861, 1893, 1938, 1945, 1968, 2055, 2074, 2102, 2112, 2126, 2198, 2283, 2289, 2302, 2304, 2320, 2331, 2341, 2384, 2391, 2448, 2517, 2540, 2557, 2565, 2569, 2686, 2731, 2998, 3077, 3102, 3105, 3120, 3181, 3184, 3189, 3211, 3212, 3286, 3318, 3343, 3558, 3694, 3716, 3758, 3772, 3852, 3874, 3884, 3896, 3904, 3918, 3992, 4009, 4028, 4052, 4054, 4057, 4082, 4088, 4153, 4192, 4229, 4238, 4240, 4256, 4380, 4461, 4471, 4513, 4565, 4720, 4729, 4753, 4799, 4806, 4870, 4883, 4926, 5035, 5075, 5092, 5105, 5142, 5146, 5162, 5192, 5234, 5389, 5428, 5469, 5500, 5501, 5533, 5552, 5576, 5602, 5625, 5628, 5634, 5635, 5792, 5817, 5830, 5848, 6003, 6008, 6042, 6156, 6223, 6251, 6263, 6301, 6317
— (1900–1945), 139, 198, 208, 621, 701, 1195, 1599, 1663, 1712, 1955, 2224, 2593, 2625, 2779, 2847, 2849, 2900, 3524, 4023, 4114, 4115, 4245, 4544, 5215, 5356, 5613, 5794, 5938, 5951, 6150, 6328, 6342
—See also Bishops and archbishops: Methodist
Clergymen: Millennial Church. See Clergymen: Shaker
Clergymen: Minor sects (to 1800), 6201
— (1800–1850), 234, 2121, 3534, 3756, 3993, 4273, 4360, 4626
— (1850–1900), 316, 916, 1154, 1918, 1931, 3279, 5208, 6034
— (1900–1945), 1767, 2207, 3493, 5035, 5872, 6281
Clergymen: Moravian. See Clergymen: United Brethren
Clergymen: Mormon (1800–1850), 700, 4645
— (1850–1900), 2979, 3522, 3622, 3943, 4209
—See also Bishops and archbishops: Mormon
Clergymen: Nazarene (1900–1945), 412, 5850
Clergymen: Presbyterian (to 1800), 5505
— (1800–1850), 255, 820, 1046, 1089, 1277, 1930, 1931, 2084, 2272, 2297, 2396, 2869, 3064, 3220, 3525, 3689, 4021, 4205, 4206, 4326, 4459, 4507, 4607, 5151, 5370, 5391, 5393, 5917, 6174
— (1850–1900), 46, 695, 724, 889, 1027, 1029, 1031, 1262, 1320, 1397, 1690, 1780, 1935, 1999, 2670, 3066, 3265, 3409, 3520, 3685, 3707, 3826, 3883, 3919, 4110, 4432, 4557, 4570, 4649, 4658, 4745, 5183, 5244, 5282, 5298, 5341, 5352, 5516, 5677, 5840, 5926, 6173, 6175, 6176, 6280
— (1900–1945), 60, 2673, 3594, 3929, 4165, 4981, 5287, 5451, 5923
Clergymen: Priests. See Clergymen: Catholic priests
Clergymen: Protestant Episcopal. See

Clergymen: Episcopal
Clergymen: Quaker (to 1800), 193, 1038, 1165, 1907, 2335, 3121, 3751, 4031, 4204, 4795, 5409
—(1800-1850), 2640, 2641, 2974, 3204, 3787, 4831
—(1850-1900), 1259, 2009, 2831, 2982, 6229, 6267, 6268
—(1900-1945), 2595, 4137
Clergymen: Rabbis; See Clergymen: Jewish
Clergymen: Reformed Church in America (1800-1850), 1908
—(1850-1900), 5600
—(1900-1945), 444
Clergymen: Reformed Church in U.S. (1850-1900), 5047
Clergymen: Reformed Dutch. See Clergymen: Reformed Church in America
Clergymen: Reformed German. See Clergymen: Reformed Church in U.S.
Clergymen: Reorganized Church of Jesus Christ of Latter-day Saints. See Clergymen: Mormon
Clergymen: River Brethren. See Clergymen: Brethren
Clergymen: Seventh Day Adventist (1800-1850), 344
—(1850-1900), 2664, 3034, 5544, 6092, 6093, 6098, 6099
—(1900-1945), 3293
Clergymen: Shaker (1850-1900), 226, 4515
Clergymen: Society of Friends. See Clergymen: Quaker
Clergymen: Unitarian (1800-1850), 1073, 1547, 3591, 3800, 4428, 4429, 5700, 5955
—(1850-1900), 110, 230, 498, 620, 775, 1176, 1209, 1262, 1627, 2050, 2076, 3263, 3647, 4380, 5033, 5566, 6054
—(1900-1945), 2456, 5559
Clergymen: United Brethren (1800-1850), 1911, 2837, 4222
—(1850-1900), 2172, 3146, 3326, 4312, 5128, 5234, 6018
—(1900-1945), 6342
—See also Clergymen: Brethren
Clergymen: United Society of Believers in Christ's Second Appearing. See Clergymen: Shaker
Clergymen: Universalist (to 1800), 436, 4169
—(1800-1850), 1115, 3263, 3706, 3934, 4273, 4618, 4890, 5307, 5394, 5658, 6124
—(1850-1900), 248, 280, 465, 1084, 1496, 2369, 5285
Clergymen: See also Chaplains, Evangelists, Missionaries, Monks, Nuns, Theologians
Clergymen as authors (to 1800), 2759
—(1800-1850), 1115, 5917
—(1850-1900), 11, 316, 4780, 5341, 5376, 5654
—(1900-1945), 336, 370, 5157
—See also Religious journalists
Clergymen's wives (1800-1850), 1633, 4885
—(1850-1900), 42, 1090, 1396, 2791, 3737, 4060, 4216, 4357, 4398, 4608, 4809, 5045, 5052, 5136
—(1900-1945), 2494, 3024, 6019
Clerks. See Office workers
Clubwomen (1850-1900), 1433, 2783
—(1900-1945), 2323, 3408
—See also Social reformers, Social workers, Socialites
Coaches, sports. See Athletic officials
—Voice. See Music teachers
College administrators (1850-1900), 809, 5482
—(1900-1945), 704, 3583, 4124, 4714, 4965, 5596, 5633
—See also College presidents, Educators, Professors
College presidents (to 1800), 3054
—(1800-1850), 1669, 2297, 2680, 4205, 6006
—(1850-1900), 151, 338, 361, 364, 372, 693, 1153, 1399, 1495, 1710, 1935, 1965, 2178, 2401, 2414, 2434, 2435, 2540, 2763, 3681, 3689, 3855, 3856, 3883, 4054, 4855, 5038, 5389, 5549, 5774, 5896, 6088
—(1900-1945), 48, 257, 370, 424, 524, 843, 1302, 1599, 1734, 2048, 2054, 2119, 2471, 2501, 2955, 3108, 3256, 3577, 4157, 5139, 5438, 5614, 6257
—See also College administrators, Educators, Professors
College professors (to 1800), 4957
—(1800-1850), 742, 820, 872, 1143, 2353, 2680, 3282, 3423, 4587, 5166, 5209, 6167
—(1850-1900), 131, 151, 338, 524, 693, 798, 825, 830, 1077, 1153, 1254, 1495, 1664, 1710, 1764, 1897, 1965, 2004, 2036, 2284, 2401, 2465, 3067, 3234, 3321, 3414, 3510, 3681, 4028, 4271, 4386, 4406, 4416, 4437, 4560, 4649, 4791, 4841, 4855, 4877, 4946, 5183, 5282, 5364, 5376, 5469, 5564, 5565, 5791, 5805, 5948, 5965, 6022, 6023, 6075, 6088, 6100, 6306, 6335
—(1900-1945), 17, 235, 269, 299, 331, 388, 736, 897, 1019, 1189, 1327, 1330, 1348, 1751, 1804, 1863, 2054, 2088, 2336, 2457, 2484, 2496, 2516, 2596, 2681, 3026,

College professors (1900-1945)(cont.), 3032, 3036, 3462, 3491, 3493, 3562, 3577, 3583, 3774, 3778, 3779, 3921, 4109, 4331, 4355, 4448, 4482, 4523, 4541, 4667, 4672, 4781, 4924, 4972, 5023, 5032, 5086, 5095, 5173, 5205, 5443, 5451, 5551, 5620, 5679, 5846, 5858, 5966, 6050, 6179, 6198, 6254

College students (to 1800), 873, 5603
— (1800-1850), 855, 5698, 5717
— (1850-1900), 40, 250, 587, 750, 897, 989, 1033, 1034, 1197, 1873, 1961, 2309, 2498, 2519, 2554, 2726, 2820, 2960, 3036, 3099, 3156, 3192, 3562, 4051, 4124, 4147, 4266, 4776, 4946, 4985, 5022, 5104, 5133, 5193, 5302, 5452, 5528, 5565, 5769, 6376
— (1900-1945), 209, 388, 476, 1018, 1193, 1367, 1696, 1799, 2214, 2484, 2850, 3367, 3496, 4332, 4358, 4573, 4621, 5511, 5785, 5819, 6255, 6327

College teachers. See College professors
Colombia (1850-1900), 2739, 3083, 3790, 4497
— (1900-1945), 3652, 4460
Columnists. See Journalists
Comedians (1800-1850), 2656
— (1850-1900), 2007, 6208
— (1900-1945), 2753, 3543
—See also Humorists
Communications workers. See Aviators-civilian, Radio announcers and operators, Railroad workers, Seamen-merchant, Teamsters, Telegraphers, Telephone operators
Communists (1900-1945), 373, 539, 1996, 2185
—See also Anarchists, Socialists, Social reformers
Composers (1800-1850), 82
— (1850-1900), 188, 1866, 2018, 2071, 2812, 3110, 4912, 5426, 5825, 6377
— (1900-1945), 155, 564, 1241, 1559, 2032, 2057, 2058, 2446, 2493, 3599, 3760, 4179, 5361, 5779,
—See also Composers, Musicians
Concert agents. See Showmen
Concert singers. See Singers
Conductors (1850-1900), 188, 1072, 2605, 3110, 5671
— (1900-1945), 180, 1419, 3712, 5361, 5823
—See also Composers, Musicians
Conductors, railroad. See Railroad workers
Congressmen. See Representatives-U.S., Senators-U.S.
Conscientous objectors. See Social reformers
Constables. See Peace officers
Consuls. See Diplomats

Contractors. See Industrialists
Conversions: Date undetermined, 975
— (to 1800),1683, 2430, 3659, 5268
— (1800-1850),289, 748, 1139, 1191, 2043, 2218, 2421, 2937, 3035, 3117, 3267, 3507, 4792, 5043, 5307, 5941
— (1850-1900), 96, 390, 707, 771, 787, 1031, 1174, 1386, 1516, 1551, 1848, 2222, 2366, 3195, 3215, 3570, 3818, 3965, 4268, 4380, 4510, 4903, 4956, 5028, 5060, 5418, 5443, 5496, 5497, 5990, 6060, 6190
— (1900-1945), 426, 454, 932, 1269, 1380, 1416, 1460, 1485, 1505, 1610, 1949, 2162, 2215, 2368, 2590, 2697, 3012, 3206, 3231, 3240, 3253, 3303, 3407, 3442, 3476, 3807, 4349, 4368, 4933, 5210, 5215, 5872
—See also Religious experiences
Convicts. See Prisoners
Cooks. See Bakers, caterers, cooks
Counterfeiters. See Criminals
Cowboys: Date undetermined, 507
— (1850-1900), 6, 56, 185, 192, 303, 307, 425, 446, 683, 880, 1066, 1203, 1215, 1216, 1217, 1447, 1523, 1697, 2153, 2417, 2431, 2458, 2476, 2498, 2499, 2674, 2823, 2908, 3006, 3225, 3300, 3333, 3372, 3376, 3586, 3596, 3876, 3885, 3910, 3985, 3990, 4234, 4319, 4425, 4465, 4539, 4546, 4805, 5102, 5225, 5227, 5455, 5504, 5772, 6323, 6349
— (1900-1945),14, 823, 1283, 2969, 3061, 3378, 3660, 3835, 3954, 4010, 4066, 4899, 4987, 5317, 6312
—See also Ranchers and ranch life
Crete (1850-1900), 5483
Criminals (to 1800), 112, 819, 1409, 2023, 2587, 3070, 3484, 4639, 4918, 4980, 5154, 5587, 5776
— (1800-1850), 88, 162, 241, 246, 389, 1227, 1600, 1615, 1946, 2149, 2190, 2202, 2308, 2314, 2354, 2467, 2586, 2588, 2672, 2793, 2794, 2841, 3044, 3145, 3342, 3370, 3479, 3566, 3754, 4020, 4116, 4407, 4637, 4772, 5313, 5362, 5539, 5579, 5641, 5665, 5711, 5778, 5781, 5824, 5934, 5978, 5988, 6073, 6139, 6322
— (1850-1900), 477, 479, 505, 928, 931, 1015, 1106, 1123, 1239, 1306, 1350, 1375, 1407, 1411, 1453, 1527, 1699, 1827, 1947, 1963, 1999, 2152, 2175, 2222, 2330, 2361, 2447, 2462, 2548, 2557, 2637, 2648, 2649, 2958, 2965, 2994, 2996, 3078, 3086, 3295, 3341, 3498, 3727, 3728, **3758**, 3769, 4069, 4126, 4531, 4585, 4662, 4752, 4765, 4878, 4955, 5434, 5529, 5607, 5676, 5723, 5873,

Criminals (1850-1900)(cont.), 5924, 5962, 6041, 6096, 6200, 6360, 6361
—(1900-1945), 200, 330, 447, 509, 510, 577, 606, 849, 878, 1003, 1208, 1491, 1682, 1949, 2288, 3095, 3380, 3417, 3574, 4010, 4191, 4374, 4635, 4987, 5085, 5138, 5195, 5421, 5612, 5740, 5874, 6362
—See also Juvenile delinquents
Cripples. See Physically handicapped
Critics (1900-1945), 1290, 1660, 1925, 2459, 2862, 3491, 3492, 4083, 4108, 4541, 4727, 4829, 5525, 5813, 5846
—See also Authors, Journalists
Croatia. See Jugoslavia
Cuba (1850-1900), 206, 550, 4320, 4399, 4825
—(1900-1945), 219, 1446, 3103, 5025
Curators. See Museum keepers
Customs officials. See Civil servants, U.S.
Czechslovakia (1900-1945), 1162

# D

Dancers (1850-1900), 2007, 2161, 4212
—(1900-1945), 1458, 1681, 1819, 1820, 2062, 2575, 4816, 4938, 4990
Deaf. See Physically handicapped
Deans, college. See College administrators
Deep sea divers. See Divers
Delinquent women. See Prostitutes and fallen women
Delinquents. See Juvenile delinquents
Denmark (1850-1900), 4906
—(1900-1945), 1764
Dentists (1850-1900), 913, 3167
—(1900-1945), 2008, 2735
Designers (1900-1945), 460, 627, 2544, 5216
Detectives (1850-1900), 433, 2551, 2767, 4221, 4562, 5226, 5227, 5405, 5518, 6166
—(1900-1945), 1769, 2889, 5852, 6104, 6169, 6170
—See also Peace officers, Policemen
Deviates, sexual. See Sexual deviates
Dietitians, 47
Diplomats (to 1800), 2985
—(1800-1850), 6136
—(1850-1900), 131, 138, 151, 430, 483, 677, 816, 984, 1028, 1081, 1344, 1383, 1507, 1647, 1733, 1995, 2151, 2700, 3043, 3083, 3281, 3351, 3785, 3790, 3893, 3951, 4089, 4471, 4493, 4497, 4513, 5012, 5069, 5125, 5483, 5519, 5979, 6088, 6137, 6247
—(1900-1945), 102, 598, 1687, 1764, 2140, 2348, 2465, 2487, 2618, 2778, 2885, 2888, 3053, 3199, 3671, 3672, 3942, 4091, 4092, 4105, 4271, 4762, 4798, 4822, 5135, 5180, 5485, 5680, 6114, 6209, 6210, 6211, 6212, 6260
Diplomats' wives (1850-1900), 2020, 2021
—(1900-1945), 2439, 4427
Dipsomaniacs. See Alcoholics
District Attorneys. See Lawyers, Politicians
Divers (1900-1945), 1303, 1720
Doctors: Date undetermined, 2875
—(to 1800), 1157, 4957, 6048
—(1800-1850), 64, 555, 872, 957, 1112, 1190, 2418, 3763a, 3974, 4033, 4580, 4581, 4655, 4853, 5386, 5670, 5689, 5970, 5986, 6123
—(1850-1900), 20, 73, 335, 356, 520, 529, 656, 661, 795, 825, 830, 835, 863, 864, 1041, 1096, 1254, 1273, 1309, 1314, 1314A, 1343, 1453, 1483, 1534, 1666, 1732, 1808, 1889, 1897, 1924, 2004, 2144, 2577, 2715, 2720, 2722, 2738, 2823, 2921, 2944, 3027, 3277, 3565, 3887, 4053, 4160, 4201, 4560, 4877, 5026, 5182, 5219, 5321, 5322, 5388, 5479, 5480, 5630, 5761, 5858, 5965, 6029, 6075, 6100, 6247, 6320, 6366
—(1900-1945), 17, 50, 58, 197, 219, 225, 262, 299, 331, 339, 367, 395, 779, 837, 904, 920, 1124, 1163, 1378, 1446, 1536, 1543, 1552, 1575, 1591, 1617, 1640, 1742, 1877, 1890, 1932, 1957, 2096, 2287, 2360, 2367, 2424, 2561, 2579, 2584, 2623, 2683, 2745, 2755, 2826, 2919, 2928, 2941, 3004, 3201, 3293, 3301, 3327, 3464, 3481, 3579, 3580, 3646, 3743, 3747, 3748, 3843, 3844, 3972, 4109, 4131, 4157, 4189, 4247, 4667, 4817, 4832, 4833, 4863, 4898, 4931, 5036, 5042, 5070, 5098, 5099, 5131, 5140, 5141, 5251, 5270, 5272, 5463, 5692, 5756, 5765, 6038, 6050, 6097, 6231, 6241, 6248, 6254, 6262, 6285, 6326, 6347, 6371
Doctors. See also subdivisions under wars, e.g., Civil War: Confederate-Doctors, Spanish-American War-Doctors, etc.
Doctors' wives (1850-1900), 2109
—(1900-1945), 622, 4605, 4851
Domestic relations (to 1800), 245, 6103, 6171
—(1800-1850), 10, 251, 602, 726, 807, 938, 1136, 1779, 1865, 2455, 2653, 2836, 3223, 3237, 3241, 3251, 3740, 4693, 4784, 5204, 5450, 5472, 5803, 5887, 5993
—(1850-1900), 19, 69, 107, 132, 170, 176,

SUBJECT INDEX — Domestic relations–Clergymen

Domestic relations (1850-1900) (cont.),
207, 274, 343, 383, 394, 511, 523, 531,
762, 988, 1092, 1184, 1270, 1393, 1444,
1510, 1583, 1628, 1757, 1793, 2033, 2092,
2158, 2184, 2187, 2206, 2253, 2273,
2286, 2300, 2382, 2507, 2654, 2660,
2669, 2833, 2852, 2933, 2995, 3017,
3045, 3116, 3258, 3260, 3345, 3446,
3545, 3548, 3631, 3783, 3854, 4007,
4044, 4051, 4071, 4077, 4111, 4119,
4305, 4356, 4395, 4426, 4553, 4576,
4647, 4668, 4669, 4818, 4845, 4902,
5306, 5382, 5448, 5604, 5616, 5627,
5795, 5826, 5884, 5964, 6004, 6138,
6186, 6340
— (1900-1945), 506, 669, 670, 808, 887,
1102, 1498, 1783, 1817, 1838, 1857, 1888,
2038, 2118, 2698, 2705, 2752, 2844,
2902, 3119, 3133, 3283, 3289, 3309,
3552, 3569, 3710, 3773, 3775, 3940,
4292, 4338, 4373, 4375, 4460, 4708,
4709, 4783, 4937, 4938, 5265, 5305,
5373, 5456, 5527, 5725, 6089
— See also Authors' wives, Clergymen's
wives, Diplomats' wives, Doctors'
wives, Politicians' wives, Soldiers'
wives
Domestic workers. See Servants
Dominican Republic (1900-1945), 806
Drama critics. See Critics
Dramatists. See Playwrights
Dressmakers. See Tailors
Drug addicts. See Narcotics addicts
Drunkards. See Alcoholics
Dumb. See Physically handicapped
Dutch Guiana (1900-1945), 4489

# E

East Indies (1850-1900), 6374, 6375
East North Central: Abolitionists, 773
1130, 2298, 3423, 3771, 3787, 4075,
5670
— Actors, 5673
— Adventurers and vagabonds, 553, 606,
4467
— Advertisers and public relations men,
751, 770, 3333
— Alcoholics, 442, 1297
— Animal trainers, 3062
— Architects, 5555, 6303, 6304
— Art Collectors, 3961
— Artisans, 1860, 4467, 4743, 4758, 5636,
6053
— Athletes, 154
— Athletic officials, 4876
— Auctioneers, 3062
— Authors, 131, 336, 562, 867, 1189, 2107,
3057, 4094, 4797, 5364, 5418

— Bankers, 466, 663, 706, 759, 828, 1127,
1941, 1983, 2075, 2618, 2895, 4603,
5447, 5758
— Bishops and archbishops: Episcopal,
1020
— Booksellers, 4168
— Cabinet members, U.S., 2075, 5176
— Childhood reminiscences, 259, 268,
382, 512, 541, 618, 644, 783, 855, 926,
989, 1101, 1102, 1245, 1288, 1317, 1649,
1924, 2082, 2106, 2300, 2329, 2431,
2489, 2491, 2706, 2777, 2815, 2816,
2819, 2852, 2861, 2868, 2870, 2907,
2991, 3168, 3205, 3217, 3459, 3627,
3630, 3632, 3808, 3834, 3854, 4038,
4073, 4100, 4147, 4351, 4571, 4575,
4621, 4700, 4887, 5066, 5406, 5639,
5846, 5868, 5945, 6178, 6225, 6246,
6292, 6364
— Church workers, 132, 834, 997, 3117,
3314, 4742, 5384, 5854, 6311
— Civil servants: Local, 2751, 4718. State,
2538. U.S., 1028, 1172, 1299, 1997, 4927
— Clergymen: Denomination undetermined,
518, 1078, 1262, 2150, 2318, 2666, 2768,
3002, 3680, 4550, 6269. Baptist, 702,
1104, 1257, 1328, 2359, 3262, 3642,
3695, 3771, 3836, 4067, 4284, 4325,
4502, 4617, 4933, 5038, 5289, 5640,
5688, 5738, 6060, 6122. Brethren,
4172, 6372. Catholic priests, 504,
3303. Christian Church, 319, 2103,
2174, 2237, 2782, 4895, 5344, 5505,
5802. Congregational, 336, 638, 666,
891, 1240, 1734, 1930, 2186, 2298, 2708–
2709, 2788, 3524, 3685, 4670, 4780,
5340, 5443, 5549. Disciples of Christ,
238, 4549, 6141. Episcopal, 214, 323,
643, 1505, 2267, 2268, 3303, 4413–4414,
5812, 5994. Jewish, 4542, 4694, 6060,
6238. Lutheran, 1405, 1554, 2454,
2693, 3126, 3310, 3504, 3612, 3980,
4022, 4652, 4703, 4952, 4968, 5238,
5522, 6024, 6370. Mennonite, 424.
Methodist, 184, 385, 408, 711, 755, 773,
796, 797, 919, 936, 963, 1008, 1120,
1195, 1274, 1275, 1313, 1355, 1539, 1557,
1599, 1716, 1740, 1893, 1927, 1928, 2126,
2295, 2448, 2517, 2565, 2686, 2847,
3077, 3212, 3286, 3423, 3478, 3588,
3805, 3806, 3884, 4009, 4057, 4461,
4471, 4491, 4513, 4544, 4753, 4806,
5075, 5142, 5192, 5428, 5469, 5474,
5493, 5611, 5613, 5625, 5649, 5792,
5794, 5830, 6003, 6150, 6156, 6343,
6348. Minor sects, 1767, 1918, 3279,
3493, 3756. Mormon, 700. Presbyterian, 60, 820, 1029, 1031, 1780, 1930,
1931, 1935, 2084, 2396, 2670, 3685,
3689, 3826, 4459, 4607, 5151, 5183,

East North Central: Clergymen–Presbyterian (cont.), 5352, 5370, 5917. Quaker, 2009, 2595, 2982, 3787, 4137, 6229, 6267, 6268. Seventh Day Adventist, 2664, 3034, 3293, 6092, 6093, 6098, 6099. Unitarian, 110, 1176, 3647, 5566, 6054. United Brethren, 3146, 5128, 5234. Universalist, 248, 1496, 3706, 3934, 5394, 5658.
—Clergymen as authors, 336, 5917
—Clergymen's wives, 3024, 4885
—Clubwomen, 2323
—College administrators, 5596
—College presidents 151, 338, 524, 1734, 1935, 2471, 2540, 3689, 5549, 5614
—College professors, 17, 131, 338, 388, 524, 820, 830, 1189, 1254, 1764, 1804, 1897, 2036, 2088, 2336, 2353, 2484, 2681, 3321, 3423, 3462, 3774, 4271, 4482, 4924, 5205, 5469, 5620, 5858, 6022, 6023, 6088, 6306
—College students, 989, 1197, 4332, 4621
—Composers, 1866, 3599, 4912
—Criminals, 505, 606, 931, 1615, 1949, 1963, 2361, 2447, 2586, 2841, 3095, 3295, 3380, 4531, 4765, 5138, 5665, 5711
—Critics, 5525
—Dentists, 913
—Detectives, 5405
—Diplomats, 131, 1028, 2618, 3351, 4513, 6114
—Doctors, 17, 299, 395, 656, 830, 1096, 1254, 1343, 1617, 1666, 1897, 2424, 2715, 2722, 2944, 3004, 3027, 3201, 3293, 3743, 3748, 3763a, 5042, 5270, 5463, 5670, 5692, 5858, 6241, 6262
—Doctors' wives, 4851
—Domestic relations, 132, 176, 523, 807, 988, 1184, 1757, 2184, 2253, 2507, 2833, 2852, 2995, 3116, 3241, 3251, 3631, 4426, 5306, 5373, 5887
—Educators, 111, 404, 616, 1225, 2298, 2396, 2511, 2707, 2782, 2982, 3351, 3435, 3488, 3612, 5177
—Engineers, 55, 961, 2160, 2681, 3397, 4718, 4811, 5423
—Evangelists, 1374, 1416, 1836, 2535, 4521, 5830, 6162
—Executives, 925, 2573, 3664
—Farmers and farm life, 518, 544, 575, 618, 676, 687, 706, 783, 852, 1101, 1126, 1184, 1317, 1646, 1726, 1853, 1924, 2106, 2190, 2197, 2233, 2300, 2343, 2410, 2431, 2489, 2491, 2537, 2841, 2991, 3168, 3261, 3358, 3432, 3559, 3763a, 3969, 3989, 4073, 4147, 4258, 4328, 4571, 4728, 4743, 4754, 4885, 4927, 5006, 5029, 5067, 5316, 5344, 5517, 5703, 5812, 5828, 5860, 5868, 5887, 5920, 5945, 6055, 6065, 6168, 6245, 6268
—Gardeners, 6311
—Financiers, 2066, 3353
—Governors, 1923, 2618, 3742, 4353
—Historians, 1363, 1997, 4542, 5447, 5469
—Hotels and inns, proprietors and workers, 3062, 4927
—Hunters and trappers, 310, 962, 1759, 3432, 4801, 5876
—Immigrants: Austrian, 395, 3288. Canadian, 4510. Danish, 4728. Dutch, 1497. English, 2361, 3599, 4790, 5111, 5429, 6337. German, 1860, 2537, 2651, 3454, 3455, 4754, 5381, 5447, 5522, 6068. Irish, 4513. Italian, 5870. Lithuanian, 2781. Norwegian, 1554, 2599. Polish, 3218. Russian, 4661. Scottish, 4328, 5636. Swedish, 5812. Welsh, 5860.
—Indian agents, 4345, 5063, 5758
—Indian fighters, 789, 1224, 2723, 2915
—Indians, 1244
—Indians, life among, 2861, 3241, 3432, 4566, 4801, 4986
—Industrialists, 263, 264, 272, 759, 841, 926, 1036, 1311, 1343, 1362, 1744, 1971, 1972, 1976, 1977, 2060, 2066, 2183, 2599, 2754, 2956, 3056, 3083, 3670, 3732, 3950, 4073, 4123, 4190, 4353, 4603, 4640, 4797, 4874, 5423, 5454, 5721, 5861, 6068, 6168
—Inventors, 478, 2060, 3732, 4867
—Jews, 76, 549, 2781, 3257, 3288, 5507
—Journalists, 3, 127, 259, 435, 470, 751, 1095, 1295, 1297, 1353, 1650, 1755, 2201, 2379, 2515, 2815, 2912, 3170, 3218, 3454, 3455, 3620, 4992, 5222, 5229, 5252, 5381, 5397, 5488, 5508, 5685, 5865, 6113, 6151, 6158, 6290
—Judges: State, 3076, 3741. U.S., 535, 714, 1172, 3410
—Labor leaders, 3093
—Laborers, 23, 452, 754, 2851, 4258, 4422, 4661, 4743, 5920, 6013, 6261
—Lawyers, 442, 478, 535, 663, 714, 764, 877, 1172, 1274, 1275, 1363, 1368, 1434, 1436, 1801, 1903, 2001, 2194, 2305, 2618, 3076, 3619, 3670, 3755, 4408, 4661, 4754, 4773, 5364, 5694, 5885, 5927, 6113
—Librarians, 5488
—Lumbermen, 16, 452, 2922, 4207, 5811, 5945
—Mayors, 1462, 2508, 2509, 3056, 3346, 6113
—Medical journalists, 656
—Merchants, 178, 222, 773, 829, 1127, 1252, 1646, 1667, 2601, 2647, 2829,

SUBJECT INDEX

East North Central: Merchants (cont.), 2915, 3062, 3063, 3087, 3257, 3346, 3432, 3763a, 3899, 4262, 4328, 4603, 4927, 5029, 5201, 5349, 5517, 5861, 6284
—Militiamen and National guardsmen, 3820
—Miners and mining life, 961, 2723, 2848, 4467
—Missionaries—Catholic, 3812. Denomination undetermined, 3863, 4986. Medical, 4456. Mennonite, 5766. Methodist, 1782, 4566.
—Music teachers, 41, 1866, 3975, 4912
—Musicians, 1866, 3975
—Negroes, 521, 754, 830, 1094, 1195, 2305, 2851, 2874, 3351, 4422, 4461, 4544, 5794, 6013, 6156
—Novelists, 1353, 1363, 2106, 5525, 6113
—Office workers, 3257, 4230
—Painters, 2568, 5418
—Peace officers, 1274, 1275, 5189, 5405, 6213
—Philanthropists, 272, 1801, 2647
—Photographers, 76, 1156, 4977
—Pioneers, 273, 310, 408, 687, 706, 755, 789, 807, 1004, 1377, 1554, 1924, 1927, 1928, 2106, 2190, 2197, 2233, 2334, 2396, 2491, 2723, 2751, 2815, 2816, 2829, 2868, 3002, 3205, 3241, 3251, 3432, 3559, 3631, 3706, 3899, 4236, 4280, 4328, 4387, 4571, 4801, 4885, 4927, 5201, 5670, 5703, 5812, 5828, 5829, 5887, 5917, 5945, 6348
—Playwrights, 1353, 5865
—Poets, 1363, 3462, 3514, 3599, 4094, 5364, 5493, 5636
—Policemen, 1094
—Politicians, 264, 273, 521, 706, 751, 759, 764, 1436, 1622, 2194, 2305, 3281, 3288, 3755, 3950, 4408, 4586, 4754, 5069, 5364, 5454, 5488, 5751, 5927,
—Politicians' wives, 1970, 3030
—Presidents, U.S., 3509
—Printers, 1297, 4335, 4758, 5008, 5009
—Prisoners, 1053, 1949, 1963, 3095, 4531
—Prostitutes and fallen women, 606
—Publishers, 127, 435, 1297, 2271, 2809, 3346, 4013, 4014, 4586, 4912, 5008, 5009, 5662
—Radio announcers and operators, 5384
—Railroad workers, 834, 925, 2035, 3025, 4291
—Ranchers and ranch life, 4180, 4764
—Real estate dealers and promoters, 23, 273, 5968
—Religious journalists, 184, 336, 424, 707, 865, 866, 867, 2237, 3423, 5384, 5505, 5917, 6238, 6306
—Representatives: State, 535, 1172,

339   East North Central—East South Central

3763a, 4379, 5794, 6065. U.S., 902, 1295, 2025, 2538, 3056, 3076, 3351, 3410, 4773, 5176
—Restaurants and taverns, proprietors and workers, 1299
—Salesmen, 23, 328, 1333, 1619, 2746, 3062, 3139, 4123, 5067, 5861
—Scientists, 1548, 2651, 3165, 4271, 4482, 5858, 6306
—Senators: State, 1728, 1903, 1997, 2001. U.S., 1368, 1969, 3320, 5176
—Showmen, 5673
—Singers, 9
—Social reformers, 44, 45, 562, 688, 1997, 2186, 2424, 3093, 3101, 6228
—Social workers, 111, 549, 599, 663, 673, 1154, 1677, 2874, 5507, 5613, 5620, 5936, 6327
—Socialists, 5381
—Socialites, 2323
—Spiritualists, 852, 3164
—Suffragists, 599
—Surveyors, 5828, 5945, 5968
—Teachers, 616, 784, 997, 1929, 2036, 2643, 2830, 2935, 3058, 3398, 3632, 3664, 4420, 5244, 5264, 5451, 5488, 5787, 5829, 5870, 6268
—Teamsters, 1094, 3261, 5189
—Telegraphers, 2481, 3062
—Temperance workers, 2295, 3262, 3787, 4075, 5471
—Theologians, 3321, 3774, 6022, 6023, 6306
—Vice-Presidents, U.S., 3742
East South Central: Abolitionists, 1081, 1892
—Authors, 872, 3057, 5538
—Bakers, caterers, cooks, 427
—Bishops and archbishops: Methodist, 2077. Mormon, 363
—Childhood reminiscences, 89, 382, 785, 1641, 2894, 2915, 3031, 3714, 4850, 5072, 5118, 5542, 6082, 6310
—Church workers, 1206, 2235, 3708, 6354
—Civil servants: State, 4635. U.S., 3118, 4705, 4706
—Clergymen; Baptist, 84, 359, 916, 1287, 1296, 1328, 1358, 1743, 2064, 2093, 2299, 2867, 2942, 3730, 4502, 4632, 5623, 5688, 5738. Catholic priests, 1365, 5655. Christian Church, 662, 2103, 2730, 3792, 4895, 5127, 5505, 5669. Church of Christ, 1466. Congregational, 4892. Denomination undetermined, 1892. Disciples of Christ, 1185, 1360, 2766, 3418, 3768. Episcopal, 922, 6353. Lutheran, 6370. Methodist, 157, 208, 514, 686, 747, 911, 963, 964, 971, 1272, 1712, 1893, 2849, 3102, 3181, 3211,

East South Central: Clergymen—Methodist (cont.), 3340, 3343, 3524, 3772, 3918, 4115, 4544, 4580, 5192, 5474, 5552, 5611, 5649, 6301, 6348. Minor sects, 916. Nazarene, 412. Presbyterian, 255, 1089, 2670, 3409, 4557, 4745, 5451, 5516. Unitarian, 1073, 1627.
—Clergymen's wives, 4060, 4885.
—College presidents, 693, 2048, 4157, 5896
—College professors, 693, 872, 1664, 2353, 4667
—College students, 3192
—Criminals, 389, 849, 1239, 2447, 2467, 2548, 3145, 4635, 5978, 6362
—Detectives, 5405
—Diplomats, 1081
—Doctors, 555, 957, 1309, 4053, 4580, 4581, 4667, 6248
—Doctors' wives, 2109
—Domestic relations, 132, 1444, 2660, 5382
—Educators, 1761, 1892, 2048, 2064, 2077, 2299, 2849, 3090, 3532, 3765, 4115, 4892, 5538, 5552
—Engineers, 2806, 4554, 5100, 5867
—Evangelists, 495, 2199
—Farmers and farm life, 89, 247, 785, 1168, 1342, 1605, 2190, 2730, 2894, 2915, 3798, 4072, 4472, 4656, 4705, 4706, 5431, 5461, 5542, 5606
—Hunters and trappers, 75, 500, 576, 1340, 4295
—Immigrants: English, 3071. German, 459
—Indian fighters, 500, 576, 1340, 1402
—Indians, 5767
—Industrialists, 264, 3780, 5606, 5753, 5799
—Jews, 459
—Journalists, 427, 1113, 1114, 1462, 1858, 3071, 4130, 4712, 5998
—Judges: Branch undetermined, 4517, 4942, 5010. Local, 4656, 5606. State, 5431. U.S., 4049
—Laborers, 5147
—Lawyers, 1476, 2397, 2661, 2894, 3489, 3700, 3814, 4656, 4849, 4942, 5431
—Librarians, 1341
—Mayors, 4294
—Medical journalists, 872
—Merchants, 3960, 4072, 4249, 4866, 4930, 5010
—Missionaries: Mennonite, 5766. Mormon, 6279
—Negroes, 359, 1065, 1761, 2026, 2064, 2299, 2303, 2940, 3037A, 3343, 3730, 4544, 6310
—Office workers, 2957, 3231
—Peace officers, 5405
—Philanthropists, 459
—Pioneers, 500, 576, 957, 1168, 1340, 1641, 2190, 2894, 2978, 4472, 5461, 5669, 6348
—Poets, 3181, 4620, 5538
—Politicians, 976, 1081, 1341, 1402, 1476, 2299, 2397, 3118, 3210, 3714, 4705, 4706, 4745, 4849, 4942
—Prisoners, 849, 4062
—Publishers, 101, 4580, 5606
—Radio announcers and operators, 2495
—Real estate dealers and promoters, 3914
—Religious journalists, 5505
—Representatives: State, 4049, 5969. U.S., 1339, 3350
—Salesmen, 484, 2545
—Scientists, 3532
—Socialites, 708, 5118
—Sportsmen, 6227
—Tailors, 1168
—Teachers, 208, 384, 484, 926, 1050, 2730, 2978, 4176, 4348, 4656, 5127, 5431, 5606, 5650, 5983, 6354
—Temperance workers, 1360, 4580
—Theologians, 1664
—Woodsmen and guides, 4295
Economists. See Professors
Editors. See Journalists
Educators. Here are entered school administrators and theorists of education. See also College administrators, College professors, College presidents, Teachers. (1800–1850), 63, 64, 404, 2298, 2347, 2396, 2414
—(1850–1900), 25, 372, 616, 690, 885, 1210, 1679, 1892, 2064, 2299, 2402, 2488, 2534, 2567, 2707, 2740, 2749, 2782, 2880, 2982, 3066, 3090, 3212, 3351, 3374, 3389, 3435, 3532, 3612, 3765, 4144, 4340, 4500, 4597, 4887, 4892, 5026, 5158, 5177, 5346, 5347, 5376, 5552, 5582, 5871, 5976, 5980, 5981, 5982, 6117, 6173, 6238, 6320
—(1900–1945), 111, 231, 257, 843, 935, 1155, 1183, 1225, 1302, 1305, 1442, 1468, 1585, 1671, 1761, 1957, 2048, 2077, 2457, 2511, 2596, 2849, 2990, 3335, 3488, 3726, 4115, 4135, 4446, 4551, 5137, 5416, 5538, 5592, 5647, 6019, 6050, 6257, 6296
Egypt (1850–1900), 1507, 1855, 3587, 5607, 5965
—(1900–1945), 4444, 4949
Electrical engineers. See Engineers
Embalmers. See Morticians
Engineers: Date undetermined, 716
—(1850–1900), 51, 55, 355, 758, 1231, 2160, 2713, 2806, 3833, 4554, 4599, 4718, 4791,

Engineers (1850-1900)(cont.), 4913, 5081,
  5100, 5462, 5867, 6220, 6220A, 6298
—(1900-1945), 228, 961, 1070, 1392, 1809,
  2342, 2629, 2681, 2924, 3332, 3397,
  3531, 3535, 3551, 4112, 4489, 4672,
  4811, 4814, 5032, 5207, 5423, 5749
—See also Inventors
England (to 1800), 5855
—(1800-1850), 1771, 2043, 3204, 3468,
  5930, 6136, 6279
—(1850-1900), 479, 980, 1092, 1209, 1507,
  1733, 2555, 2710, 2891, 2961, 3055,
  3298, 3689, 3716, 3795, 3801, 3854,
  3951, 4200, 4251, 4261, 4707, 5429,
  5744, 5949, 6079, 6149, 6267, 6350
—(1900-1945), 541, 1102, 1598, 1823, 2013,
  2348, 2622, 2753, 3807, 3905, 4112,
  4138, 4490, 5180, 5905, 5931, 6084,
  6151
Engravers. See Artisans
Entomologists. See Scientists
Envoys. See Diplomats
Essayists. See Authors
Europe (1800-1850), 998, 1633, 4438,
  5731
—(1850-1900), 994, 1389, 2128, 2882,
  2960, 3662, 3749, 5184, 5185, 5627,
  5666, 5845, 6137, 6225
—(1900-1945), 471, 472, 1002, 1290, 1609,
  2044, 2062, 2885, 2888, 3268, 3400,
  3464, 3492, 3852, 3939, 3942, 3947,
  4008, 4131, 4143, 4271, 5031, 5104, 5152,
  5835, 6038, 6045, 6248, 6331
Evangelists (1800-1850), 3179
—(1850-1900), 140, 495, 740, 787, 1727,
  1836, 1964, 1968, 2199, 2535, 3038,
  3055, 3215, 3634, 4000, 4056, 4087,
  4153, 4503, 4782, 4848, 5021, 5054,
  5055, 5255, 5256, 5727, 5830, 6162,
  6190, 6200, 6288
—(1900-1945), 60, 932, 1374, 1416, 1460,
  1550, 2022, 2162, 3006, 3442, 3524,
  3629, 3905, 3906, 4048, 4165, 4228,
  4374, 4521, 5013, 5275, 5276, 5317,
  5615, 5850
—See also Clergymen
Executives (1850-1900), 25, 733, 924,
  925, 2011, 2189, 2853, 3664, 3871, 4272
—(1900-1945), 165, 166, 231, 466, 491,
  839, 2181, 2573, 2633, 2638-2639,
  3143, 3398, 4309, 4342, 4714, 5240
Explorers (to 1800), 3239, 3456, 4288
—(1800-1850), 1868, 2034, 2116, 2954
—(1850-1900), 2293, 2374
—(1900-1945), 858, 859, 860, 861, 1373,
  1620, 1798, 1799, 1862, 2030, 2608,
  2929, 3667, 3668, 3669, 4255, 4302,
  4477, 4478, 4479, 4653, 4734, 5223,
  5224, 5436, 5912, 6118

# F

Factory workers (1850-1900), 709, 710,
  924, 4396
—(1900-1945), 2070, 2167, 3278, 3287,
  4411, 5076, 5644
—See also Artisans, Laborers
Family life. See Domestic relations
Farmers and farm life (to 1800), 315,
  697, 821, 1168, 1422, 1443, 1876, 3797,
  4730, 5286
—(1800-1850), 130, 145, 570, 618, 727,
  783, 785, 810, 816, 817, 852, 992, 1007,
  1127, 1414, 1670, 1779, 1924, 2190, 2491,
  2528, 2616, 2772, 2808, 2841, 2894,
  2915, 2978, 3249, 3432, 3763a, 4073,
  4360, 4424, 4431, 4472, 4571, 4656,
  4693, 4754, 4775, 4800, 4830, 4885, 4927,
  5132, 5156, 5344, 5461, 5535, 5593,
  5608, 5619, 5682, 5703, 5745, 5812,
  5828, 5837, 5868, 5887, 5993, 6012,
  6031, 6132,
—(1850-1900), 89, 93, 105, 107, 123, 126,
  128, 134, 170, 205, 237, 247, 379, 437,
  451, 487, 492, 518, 531, 534, 544, 561,
  569, 575, 585, 605, 631, 633, 652, 660,
  687, 696, 706, 728, 761, 771, 778, 780,
  804, 815, 827, 869, 917, 937, 1010, 1016,
  1042, 1062, 1067, 1076, 1088, 1090, 1091,
  1099, 1101, 1110, 1126, 1149, 1180, 1184,
  1214, 1231, 1234, 1256, 1279, 1317, 1342,
  1346, 1354, 1465, 1494, 1519, 1520, 1540,
  1544, 1636, 1639, 1640, 1646, 1658, 1685,
  1688, 1718, 1726, 1772, 1793, 1853, 1874,
  1885, 1921, 1979, 1987, 1989, 2005, 2010,
  2028, 2053, 2065, 2083, 2106, 2112,
  2115, 2157, 2172, 2187, 2191, 2197, 2205,
  2206, 2211, 2220, 2233, 2255, 2281,
  2294, 2300, 2302, 2306, 2343, 2373,
  2410, 2415, 2431, 2444, 2489, 2500,
  2537, 2539, 2552, 2553, 2558, 2564,
  2604, 2609, 2621, 2643, 2654, 2676,
  2692, 2726, 2730, 2765, 2776, 2838,
  2848, 2857, 2864, 2920, 2933, 2975,
  2991, 3025, 3033, 3035, 3086, 3091,
  3113, 3123, 3136, 3168, 3183, 3189, 3192,
  3261, 3313, 3315, 3326, 3358, 3361,
  3365, 3368, 3375, 3415, 3457, 3559,
  3571, 3575, 3635, 3679, 3690, 3693,
  3788, 3798, 3809, 3848, 3849, 3925,
  3926, 3948, 3969, 3987, 3989, 4024,
  4071, 4072, 4084, 4128, 4136, 4147,
  4209, 4247, 4258, 4262, 4276, 4328,
  4351, 4356, 4421, 4475, 4499, 4506,
  4520, 4533, 4578, 4651, 4673, 4705,
  4706, 4728, 4743, 4807, 4835, 4873,
  4908, 4940, 4954, 5006, 5029, 5120,
  5143, 5271, 5283, 5294, 5295, 5316,

Farmers and farm life (1850-1900)
(cont.), 5351, 5406, 5411, 5420, 5429,
5431, 5452, 5453, 5492, 5494, 5495,
5512, 5517, 5540, 5542, 5544, 5606,
5696, 5736, 5788, 5798, 5826, 5829,
5860, 5920, 5928, 5945, 6009, 6020,
6049, 6053, 6055, 6065, 6168, 6182,
6245, 6268, 6271, 6291, 6359
—(1900-1945), 261, 312, 676, 803, 808,
912, 1133, 1352, 1417, 1472, 1605, 2257,
2291, 2316, 2317, 2351, 2497, 3135, 3149,
3296, 3460, 3501, 3640, 3641, 3649,
3770, 3971, 4040, 4556, 4642, 4733,
4970, 4971, 5053, 5067, 5163, 5200,
5465, 5575, 5604, 5638, 6116, 6125,
6272, 6330
Farm journalists (1850-1900), 212, 5926
—(1900-1945), 1456, 3135
Farm leaders (1850-1900), 205, 4537,
5084
—(1900-1945), 1456, 6245
Fascists, 4112
Fashion designers. See Designers
Fashion models. See Models
Felons. See Criminals, Prisoners
Ferryboat men. See Seamen-merchant
Feudists (1850-1900), 3085
—(1900-1945), 4030
Financiers (to 1800), 1748
—(1800-1850), 297, 3353
—(1850-1900), 5, 293, 416, 1097, 1653,
1839, 2066, 3395, 3782, 4267, 5877,
5987, 6035
—(1900-1945), 1150, 1494, 1562, 3222,
3474, 4091, 4263, 4276, 4590, 4994,
5181, 5598, 5741, 5815, 6319
—See also Bankers
Firemen (1900-1945), 2583
First World War. See World War I
Fishermen (1800-1850), 752
—(1900-1945), 3954, 4332, 6312, 6357
Folk singers. See Singers
Football players. See Athletes
Foreign correspondents (1850-1900),
485, 486, 784, 994, 3298, 3299, 3308,
4320
—(1900-1945), 304, 375, 376, 541, 573,
1162, 1289, 1459, 1884, 1990, 2388, 2513,
2863, 3020, 3268, 3270, 3305, 4008,
4143, 4399, 4405, 4567, 4628, 4630,
4949, 5152, 5424, 5527, 5859, 6045,
6151, 6331
Foreigners in U.S.: Australian (1850-
1900), 1634. (1900-1945), 3191, 3928
—Austrian (1900-1945), 3005, 3444
—Canadian (to 1800), 5678. (1850-1900),
2734. (1900-1945), 5121, 5714
—Chinese (1850-1900), 6363
—Cuban (1800-1850), 1834. (1850-1900),
1040. (1900-1945), 909
—Czechoslovakian (1900-1945), 4198,
5239
—Danish (1850-1900), 3125
—Dutch (1900-1945), 1530
—English (to 1800), 915, 1116, 1469, 1470,
4434, 4543, 4744. (1800-1850), 279,
457, 734, 1080, 1177, 1285, 1898, 3175,
3176, 3337, 4975, 5106, 6007. (1850-
1900), 324, 391, 453, 650, 668, 1655,
1739, 1845, 2040, 2041, 2328, 2688,
2696, 2977, 3173, 3352, 3718, 3724,
3953, 4104, 4133, 4225, 4384, 4555,
4654, 4715, 4888, 4889, 4963, 5079,
5145, 5277, 5311, 5355, 5499, 5586,
5932. (1900-1945), 172, 173, 463, 893,
894, 941, 1105, 1119, 1161, 1449, 1506,
1563, 1673, 2159, 2474, 3387, 3388,
3786, 3829, 4584, 4641, 4802, 4964,
5707, 5750, 6321
—French (to 1800), 1023. (1800-1850),
1595, 3379. (1850-1900), 458, 881,
3357, 3977. (1900-1945), 590, 1561,
2364, 3124
—German (1800-1850), 278, 1665. (1850-
1900), 243, 393, 580, 1140, 2581, 3154,
3443, 3458, 4699, 5357. (1900-1945),
2626, 3349, 3445, 3465, 4146, 5062,
5886, 6155
—Greek (1800-1850), 974
—Indian (1900-1945), 3307, 4149, 5197
—Iranian (1850-1900), 33
—Irish (1800-1850), 1294. (1850-1900),
1535. (1900-1945), 4156, 4314
—Italian (to 1800), 3811.
(1850-1900), 171, 2086, 4999. (1900-
1945), 1268, 5648
—Japanese (1850-1900), 4321, 4383
—Korean (1900-1945), 3131
—Mexican (1900-1945), 2203
—Norwegian (1850-1900), 2976, 3001
—Polish (1900-1945), 4391, 5937
—Rumanian (1900-1945), 2422
—Russian (1850-1900), 4366. (1900-
1945), 13, 985, 1800, 4696
—Scottish (to 1800), 630. (1850-1900),
1448
—Swedish (1900-1945), 3717
—Venezuelan (1900-1945), 4254
—Welsh (1900-1945), 4279
Foresters. See Woodsmen and guides
Forgers. See Criminals
Formosa (1800-1850), 3610
Forty-niners, 5, 278, 324, 1147, 1219,
1237, 1357, 1415, 1508, 1608, 1902, 2469,
2711, 3244, 3273, 3375, 3431, 3709,
3873, 3882, 3964, 4409, 4450, 4527,
4947, 5046, 6016, 6205, 6243
—See also Pioneers—Miners and mining
life, Pacific—Miners and mining life,
Pacific—Pioneers.

France (to 1800), 2985
— (1800–1850), 5899
— (1850–1900), 483, 784, 1092, 2049, 2483, 2568, 2700, 3259, 5979
— (1900–1945), 258, 304, 464, 476, 493, 504, 578, 996, 1618, 2013, 2307, 2372, 2406, 2618, 2716, 2825, 2826, 2827, 2850, 2939, 3020, 3305, 3473, 3497, 3598, 3624, 3858, 3927, 3959, 3997, 4019, 4127, 4138, 4148, 4250, 4261, 4294, 4336, 4341, 4490, 4526, 4627, 4724, 4755, 4812, 4862, 4939, 5135, 5281, 5297, 5339, 5356, 5441, 5442, 5467, 5561, 5891, 5994, 6058, 6070, 6193, 6212, 6222, 6230, 6260
French Foreign Legion. See Adventurers and vagabonds
Frontier accounts. See Pioneers
Fur traders. See Merchants

## G

Gamblers (1800–1850), 252, 2311, 2312, 6322
— (1850–1900), 675, 1541, 1581, 1629, 2055, 2095, 2462, 3570, 3965, 5613, 6190
— (1900–1945), 1193, 1364, 3676
— See also Adventurers and vagabonds, Criminals
Gardeners (1850–1900), 3935, 6311
Genealogists (1850–1900), 223
Geologists. See Scientists
Germany (1850–1900), 485, 486, 2519, 3859, 4946, 4985, 4995, 5066, 5122, 6376
— (1900–1945), 1102, 1576, 1687, 1906, 2140, 2513, 2778, 3959, 6151, 6212
Girl Scout officials. See Social workers
Golfers. See Athletes
Government employees and officials. See Cabinet members, U.S., Civil servants, Governors, Indian agents, Judges, Mayors, Representatives, Senators, Presidents–U.S., Vice-Presidents–U.S. See also Politicians
Governors (to 1800), 2985
— (1800–1850), 995, 2179, 3626, 4315, 5126
— (1850–1900), 461, 810, 840, 1324, 1335, 1564, 1923, 2105, 2356, 2570, 2717, 3613, 3849, 4311, 4909, 5959
— (1900–1945), 683, 1263, 1348, 1596, 2505, 2618, 3567, 3648, 3742, 4174, 4353, 4370, 4509, 5242, 5254
— See also Politicians
Great Britain. See England, Ireland, Scotland
Greece (1900–1945), 1687, 2778
Greenland (1900–1945), 3669, 4476

Guatemala (1850–1900), 1344
Guiana. See Dutch Guiana
Guides. See Woodsmen and guides

## H

Hairdressers. See Barbers, hairdressers
Haiti (1850–1900), 3351
— (1900–1945), 1162
Hawaii: Adventurers and vagabonds, 1337, 5607
— Artisans, 1219
— Bishops and archbishops: Episcopal, 4769
— Childhood reminiscences, 502, 3636, 5643
— Clergymen: Methodist, 1284. Mormon, 901
— Diplomats, 4493
— Doctors, 661
— Industrialists, 2772, 3825
— Journalists, 3299
— Merchants, 653
— Missionaries: Denomination unstated, 1109. Congregational, 565. Methodist, 5792. Mormon, 6350.
— Politicians, 3503
— Printers, 2522
— Ranchers and ranch life, 5643
— Soldiers, 4882
— Surveyors, 3636
Herders. See Ranchers and ranch life
Highwaymen. See Criminals
Historians (1800–1850), 31, 5690, 5837
— (1850–1900), 25, 32, 281, 483, 593, 1363, 1965, 1997, 2129, 2645, 3550, 4224, 4435, 4441, 4509, 4741, 4776, 4804, 5064, 5469
— (1900–1945), 1662, 1770, 3003, 3226, 3402, 4108, 4362, 4542, 5104, 5447, 5881, 6121
— See also College professors
Hoboes. See Adventurers and vagabonds
Homesteaders. See Pioners, Farmers and farm life
Homosexuals. See Sexual deviates
Hoodlums. See Criminals, Juvenile delinquents
Honduras (1850–1900), 1709
Hong Kong (1850–1900), 6247
— (1900–1945), 1687, 3745
Hotels and inns, proprietors and workers (1800–1850), 145, 618, 4927, 6316
— (1850–1900), 170, 469, 1408, 2228, 2472, 3062, 3322, 4142, 4940, 5089, 6190, 6216
— (1900–1945), 966, 967, 5077
— Humorists (1850–1900), 1093, 4290, 6149
— (1900–1945), 309, 420, 1113, 1114

Humorists. See also Comedians
Hunters and trappers (to 1800), 576, 3432
—(1800–1850), 35, 36, 273, 310, 402, 500, 743, 939, 962, 1107, 1340, 1759, 1909, 2614, 2689, 2876, 2968, 3463, 4243, 4452, 4801, 4916, 4967, 5605, 5715–5716
—(1850–1900), 90, 92, 97, 239, 287, 301, 683, 694, 905, 1121, 1203, 1215, 1216, 1221, 1523, 1644, 1763, 2028, 2226, 2431, 2433, 2466, 2619, 2746, 2873, 2932, 2964, 2970, 3048, 3189, 3505, 3545, 3848, 3924, 3952, 4015, 4078, 4210, 4213, 4883, 5250, 5368, 5570, 5849, 5892, 6206, 6274, 6294, 6314, 6346, 6359
—(1900–1945), 14, 75, 118, 3188, 3483, 3660, 3954, 4295, 4653, 5581, 5876, 5912, 6312
—See also Pioneers, Sportsmen

# I

Ice skaters. See Athletes
Illnesses, accounts of (1800–1850), 3617, 4721, 6318
—(1850–1900), 2068
—(1900–1945), 1703, 1789, 2080, 2169, 2213, 3839, 4770, 6021, 6338
—See also Mentally ill, Physically handicapped
Illustrators (1850–1900), 382
—(1900–1945), 4504, 4601, 4896
—See also Painters
Immigrants: Armenian (1850–1900), 552. (1900–1945), 5568
—Australian (1850–1900), 5621
—Austrian (1800–1850), 5334, 5335, 5336, 5337, 6238. (1850–1900), 395, 3288, 5443. (1900–1945), 420, 2052, 3523
—Austro-Hungarian Empire. See Successor states
—Belgian (1900–1945), 3324, 4179
—British. See Immigrants: English, Immigrants: Irish, Immigrants: Scottish, Immigrants: Welsh
—Bulgarian (1850–1900), 6326, 6327. (1900–1945), 1035
—Canadian (to 1800), 6266. (1800–1850), 3585, 4388, 4454, 4510, 5027. (1850–1900), 192, 487, 585, 1164, 1251, 1592, 1752, 3139, 3467, 3732, 3948, 6187, 6261. (1900–1945), 5756
—Chinese (1850–1900), 3429
—Croatian. See Immigrants: Jugoslavian
—Cuban (1850–1900), 5866
—Czechoslovakian (1800–1850), 3722, 3723, 4581
—Danish (1850–1900), 546, 3002, 4208, 4245 4728, 4821, 4902, 5257. (1900–1945), 3000, 4970, 4971, 5939
—Dutch (to 1800), 5831, 5837. (1850–1900), 556, 557, 558, 5754, 6067, 6169, 6170. (1900–1945), 1497, 3745, 4443
—English (to 1800), 4169. (1800–1850), 494, 883, 1158, 1159, 1325, 1347, 1841, 2948, 3500a, 3737, 3956, 4371, 4491, 4790, 4796, 5008, 5009, 5030, 5150, 5325, 5429, 5448, 5491, 6052. (1850–1900), 366, 498, 605, 608, 631, 709, 710, 1231, 1255, 1351, 1440, 2361, 2444, 2456, 2518, 2741, 2765, 2771, 2979, 3017, 3071, 3079, 3248, 3271, 3522, 3526, 3599, 4119, 4141, 4547, 4670, 4698, 4769, 4848, 5111, 5182, 5260, 5262, 5567, 5788, 5832, 6188, 6337. (1900–1945), 24, 682, 1366, 3403, 3733, 3872, 4193, 4530, 4856, 4857, 5615
—Finnish (1850–1900), 3512
—French (to 1800), 436, 2327, 4043. (1800–1850), 3935, 4732, 5655. (1850–1900), 2643, 3972, 4444, 4445, 5214, 5755. (1900–1945), 1013, 1526
—German (to 1800), 769, 853, 2430, 4145, 4310. (1800–1850), 1250, 1860, 2043, 2053, 2206, 2651, 2857, 3282, 4754, 5051, 5113, 5129, 5206, 6030, 6051, 6056. (1850–1900), 109, 220, 329, 459, 1256, 1912, 1985, 2074, 2375, 2454, 2537, 2605, 2609, 2627, 2956, 3295, 3310, 3316, 3454, 3455, 3457, 3491, 4091, 4134, 4703, 5024, 5054, 5055, 5069, 5283, 5365, 5381, 5440, 5444, 5447, 5522, 5534, 5535, 5560, 5671, 5817, 5840, 6024, 6060, 6068, 6254, 6374. (1900–1945), 326, 2367, 3449, 3528, 4455, 4692, 5905, 6024
—Greek (1900–1945), 2131
—Hungarian (1800–1850), 4901. (1850–1900), 3285, 3303, 3308. (1900–1945), 581, 4934, 4935, 5692
—Irish (to 1800), 4204. (1800–1850), 128, 692, 2117, 2635, 2704, 3044, 4381, 4513, 4761, 4903, 4974, 5002, 5341, 6298. (1850–1900), 1074, 1386, 1542, 2498, 2925, 2926, 2927, 3171, 3348, 3665, 3682, 3683, 3759, 3830, 3863, 4052, 4300, 4564, 4707, 4904, 5133, 5369, 5554, 5723, 6345. (1900–1945), 3385, 3442, 3851
—Italian (1800–1850), 3812, 4257. (1850–1900), 572, 5107, 5870. (1900–1945), 1423, 4410, 4590
—Japanese (1900–1945), 5551, 5601
—Jugoslavian (1900–1945), 22, 5020
—Latvian (1900–1945), 3923
—Lithuanian (1850–1900), 2781. (1900–1945), 3135
—Norwegian (1800–1850), 1554, 2931. (1850–1900), 152, 451, 452, 648, 2599,

Immigrants—Industrialists

Immigrants: Norwegian (1850-1900)
(cont.), 2934, 3365, 3367, 3677, 4213,
4308, 4363, 4457, 4905, 5163, 5238,
5387, 5807, 6022, 6023. (1900-1945),
2600, 3021, 4259, 5119, 6338
—Polish (1850-1900), 4665. (1900-1945),
3218. See also Immigrants: Russian
Jewish
—Rumanian (1850-1900), 450. (1900-
1945), 2585, 4731
—Russian (1800-1850), 2911, 4529. (1850-
1900), 970, 2975, 4661, 4672. (1900-
1945), 1550, 1852, 2252, 2671, 4411,
4701, 5036, 5207
—Russian Jewish (1850-1900), 159, 160,
161, 549, 1138, 1278, 1543, 1570, 3287,
4694, 5673, 6028, 6224, 6369, 6377.
(1900-1945), 158, 2524, 4362, 6256
—Scottish (to 1800), 2924, 6103, 6196.
(1800-1850), 924, 1637, 3058, 4316,
4328, 4379, 4431, 4921, 4922, 5309,
5690. (1850-1900), 891, 2101, 2274,
3516, 3856, 3867, 3929, 4508, 4651,
4711, 5636
—Serbian. See Immigrants: Jugoslavian
—Slovakian. See Immigrants: Czechoslovakian
—Spanish (1800-1850), 2218. (1850-1900),
5022
—Swedish (1800-1850), 3785, 5114, 5812.
(1850-1900), 1756, 3025, 3047,3051,3321,
3394, 3515, 4260, 4262, 4475, 4976,
6251. (1900-1945), 1584
—Swiss (1800-1850), 3302. (1850-1900),
2365, 2933, 5540, 6027. (1900-1945),
1605, 3158
—Syrian (1900-1945), 2376, 2545, 4820,
4834
—Turkish (1900-1945), 4189
—Welsh (1800-1850), 4847, 6190. (1850-
1900), 2848, 5860. (1900-1945), 117
Impresarios. See Showmen
India (1800-1850), 5971
—(1850-1900), 847, 1103,1676, 2241, 2712,
2770, 2858, 3785, 4251, 4357, 5634,
5657, 5666
—(1900-1945), 219, 1222, 1303, 1337, 1746,
1813, 2727, 3143, 3397, 3807, 3845,
3877, 3995, 4115, 4161, 5944, 6264
Indian agents (1800-1850), 939, 4345,
5063, 5758
—(1850-1900), 1169, 4592, 6094
—(1900-1945), 1310
—See also Civil servants: U.S.
Indian fighters (to 1800), 576, 789, 2098,
5286, 5706, 6076, 6196
—(1800-1850), 500, 719, 939, 1224, 1340,
1402, 1824, 2285, 2650, 2723, 2915,
3606, 4389, 4916, 5088, 5332, 5377,
6203

—(1850-1900), 90, 97, 135, 239, 287, 301,
307, 332, 362, 379, 499, 550, 615, 737,
905, 928, 942, 958, 959, 1012, 1150,
1208, 1235, 1331, 1359, 1395, 1492, 1580,
1644, 1656, 1730, 1763, 1773, 1778, 1926,
1988, 2355, 2403, 2409, 2427, 2433,
2444, 2466, 2570, 2580, 2642, 2721,
2797, 2804, 2805, 2840, 2910, 3048,
3052, 3172, 3238, 3292, 3347, 3365,
3372, 3482, 3505, 3575, 3677, 3790,
3848, 3970, 3982, 3983, 4151, 4181, 4226,
4367, 4423, 4425, 4494, 4559, 4619,
4673, 4807, 5250, 5403, 5478, 5530,
5570, 5617, 5661, 5687, 5892, 6057,
6074, 6188, 6206, 6294, 6359
—See also Pioneers, Scouts; U.S. Army,
Soldiers
Indians (to 1800), 162
—(1800-1850), 516, 1244, 4984, 5767
—(1850-1900), 77, 163, 515, 1731, 1732,
1818, 1962, 2142, 2220, 2344, 2646,
2760, 3117, 3438, 3793, 4574, 4577,
5292, 5401, 6108, 6275, 6333
—(1900-1945), 1318, 3433, 3439, 4349,
5400, 5594
Indians, life among (to 1800), 2987, 3432,
5286, 5831, 6196
—(1800-1850), 68, 164, 402, 978, 2876,
3241, 3857, 3891, 4566, 4789, 4801, 5605,
5729
—(1850-1900), 290, 410, 977, 979, 1387,
1513, 1567, 2332, 2831, 2861, 2966,
3080, 3437, 3998, 4533, 4732, 4767,
4818, 4819, 4986, 4988, 5187, 5524,
6206
—(1900-1945), 1321, 1322, 1888, 2377,
4228, 4532
Industrialists (1800-1850), 617, 628, 1236,
1760, 2099, 2675, 2898, 3007, 4159,
4492, 4657, 5608, 5753, 5799, 5856,
5977, 5991, 6102
—(1850-1900), 18, 43, 206, 213, 227, 264,
270, 292, 368, 422, 445, 759, 822, 827,
841, 883, 923, 926, 980, 1011, 1047,
1253, 1310, 1334, 1343, 1362, 1482, 1507,
1522, 1592, 1596, 1647, 1719, 1744, 1749,
1830, 1860, 1878, 1960, 1971, 1972, 2045,
2061, 2066, 2438, 2523, 2549, 2599,
2627, 2737, 2754, 2772, 2807, 3056,
3083, 3186, 3313, 3375, 3711, 3732,
3780, 3782, 3825, 3864, 3867, 3950,
3960, 4013, 4014, 4073, 4232, 4353,
4381, 4603, 4640, 4644, 4746, 4797,
4813, 4874, 5091, 5160, 5169, 5260,
5309, 5358, 5425, 5433, 5454, 5509,
5652, 5718, 5721, 5744, 5877, 5961,
6068, 6168, 6243, 6244
—(1900-1945), 14, 263, 272, 581, 683, 838,
1036, 1070, 1188, 1392, 1570, 1762, 1795,
1825, 1842, 1933, 1976, 1977, 2060, 2079,

Industrialists (1900-1945)(cont.), 2157, 2183, 2322, 2363, 2552, 2553, 2629, 2735, 2774, 2872, 2899, 2956, 3037, 3147, 3171, 3250, 3300, 3338, 3412, 3531, 3619, 3670, 3745, 4123, 4190, 4272, 4363, 4677, 4763, 4794, 5007, 5259, 5423, 5598, 5606, 5749, 5861, 5906, 5995, 5999, 6046
Innkeepers. See Hotels and inns, proprietors and workers
Insane. See Mentally ill
Insurance agents. See Salesmen
Interior decorators (1900-1945), 3939
Inventors (to 1800), 4034
—(1800-1850), 1236, 2240
—(1850-1900), 18, 478, 1181, 3732, 3794, 3795, 4001, 4599, 4867, 4913, 5459
—(1900-1945), 2060, 2629, 2936, 2991, 3021, 3323, 3332, 3796, 5995
—See also Engineers
Iran (1800-1850), 4519
—(1850-1900), 430, 1108, 2465, 3016, 6241, 6242
—(1900-1945), 598, 2348, 4271
Iraq (1900-1945), 2698, 2699
Ireland (1800-1850), 3204
—(1850-1900), 1517, 3716
—(1900-1945), 2227
Israel (1900-1945), 549
Italy (1850-1900), 276, 1000, 2049, 2568, 5123, 5483
—(1900-1945), 2348, 3020, 3671, 3672, 4427, 4438, 4763

## J

Japan (1850-1900), 1995, 2248, 3827, 4788, 5012, 5124
—(1900-1945), 1337, 1602, 2013, 2348, 3647, 3823, 5180, 5859, 5903, 5907, 6212
Jazz musicians. See Musicians
Jews (1800-1850), 2043
—(1850-1900), 49, 460, 569, 870, 1286, 2217, 2590, 3257, 3288, 4091, 4227, 5443, 5519
—(1900-1945), 49, 76, 158, 426, 459, 581, 970, 1957, 2029, 2094, 2162, 2209, 2215, 2230, 2560, 2773, 2781, 3072, 3255, 3285, 3404, 3474, 3476, 3757, 3923, 4695, 5210, 5456, 5507, 5644, 5672, 5673, 5914, 5915, 6254, 6367
Jockeys (1850-1900), 4848, 5385
—(1900-1945), 4307, 5241
Journalists: Date undetermined, 1858
—(1800-1850), 483, 494, 774, 1112, 2815, 2897, 4203, 6017
—(1850-1900), 189, 194, 228, 244, 259, 284, 329, 414, 419, 435, 470, 482, 543, 607, 612, 657, 671, 751, 993, 994, 1074, 1093, 1196, 1295, 1297, 1427, 1445, 1455, 1462, 1572, 1588, 1659, 1766, 1785, 1854, 1926, 2164, 2255, 2271, 2292, 2412, 2488, 2515, 2554, 2555, 2570, 2594, 2617, 2786 2810, 2921, 3053, 3209, 3222, 3401, 3451, 3454, 3455, 3550, 3871, 3922, 3967, 3979, 4152, 4224, 4290, 4516, 4648, 4710, 4740, 4821, 5004, 5019, 5069, 5125, 5229, 5263, 5381, 5483, 5488, 5498, 5508, 5525, 5532, 5534, 5585, 5685, 5998, 6028, 6121, 6151, 6158, 6221, 6247, 6355
—(1900-1945), 3, 127, 166, 240, 260, 285, 427, 497, 508, 541, 556, 557, 558, 582, 586, 632, 870, 969, 990, 1003, 1095, 1113, 1114, 1148, 1187, 1200, 1228, 1353, 1367, 1385, 1428, 1429, 1478, 1479, 1538, 1553, 1586, 1587, 1609, 1614, 1650, 1660, 1662, 1750, 1755, 1900, 1978, 1998, 2000, 2029, 2125, 2201, 2315, 2379, 2458, 2459, 2460, 2541, 2571, 2682, 2771, 2787, 2912, 2930, 2990, 3020, 3026, 3029, 3071, 3109, 3170, 3218, 3225, 3278, 3280, 3284, 3287, 3305, 3377, 3413, 3477, 3615, 3620, 3701, 3715, 3720, 3721, 3788, 3808, 3868, 3923, 3937, 3938, 3973, 4003, 4025, 4083, 4130, 4252, 4281, 4294, 4323, 4324, 4334, 4362, 4439, 4480, 4523, 4567, 4631, 4712, 4714, 4727, 4760, 4820, 4854, 4900, 4959, 4989, 4992, 5199, 5222, 5252, 5278, 5397, 5439, 5513, 5556, 5609, 5645, 5732, 5733, 5833, 4834, 5865, 5878, 6021, 6105, 6113, 6129, 6224, 6290
—See also Foreign correspondents and War correspondents under names of wars, e.g., World War I-War correspondents. See also Farm journalists, Labor journalists, Medical journalists, Religious journalists
Judges: Branch undetermined (to 1800), 4942. (1850-1900), 379, 2151, 2677, 2843, 4517, 4901, 4981, 5101, 5174, 5694, 5880. (1900-1945), 3516, 4518, 5010, 5807
—Local (1850-1900), 1011, 1891, 2114, 2576, 3878, 4311, 4499, 4509, 4656. (1900-1945), 2277, 3519, 5606, 5929, 6272
—State (to 1800), 554. (1800-1850), 680, 5514. (1850-1900), 810, 1171, 1921, 1922, 2953, 3076, 3932, 5431, 6232-6233. (1900-1945), 1404, 1921, 2100, 3741, 4303, 5242, 6000
U.S. (1800-1850), 3489, 3739, 5514. (1850-1900), 488, 535, 714, 1172, 3213, 3410, 4049. (1900-1945), 215, 1230, 3276, 3521, 6127

SUBJECT INDEX

Juvenile delinquents (1900-1945), 540, 2148, 5402
—See also Criminals

## K

Kidnappers. See Criminals
Korea (1850-1900), 984, 5012, 5810
—(1900-1945), 1032, 2013

## L

Labor journalists (1850-1900), 767
Labor leaders (1850-1900), 767, 1351, 3093, 4622, 4904
—(1900-1945), 22, 109, 373, 539, 845, 1468, 1886, 2217, 2524, 2562, 2613, 3789, 5895, 5915, 6367
Laborers (to 1800), 3070, 5147
—(1800-1850), 3731, 5920
—(1850-1900), 39, 451, 452, 487, 575, 754, 815, 1094, 1326, 1551, 2083, 2444, 2609, 2851, 3033, 3248, 4213, 4258, 4260, 4422, 4529, 4661, 4711, 4743, 5544, 5577, 5918, 6013, 6020, 6261
—(1900-1945), 23, 803, 1423, 5053
—See also Artisans, Factory workers, Servants
Lame. See Physically handicapped
Larcenists. See Criminals
Lawyers (to 1800), 3739, 3753, 3763, 4170, 4315, 4942, 5603
—(1800-1850), 386, 448, 488, 613, 680, 766, 1112, 1274, 1275, 1623, 1843, 1967, 2828, 3489, 3755, 4203, 4773, 4849, 5002, 5331, 5514, 5768, 6015
—(1850-1900), 12, 138, 361, 414, 415, 418, 442, 461, 478, 535, 598, 649, 663, 714, 750, 764, 840, 848, 877, 1033, 1043, 1050, 1063, 1100, 1171, 1172, 1319, 1324, 1335, 1344, 1363, 1368, 1379, 1415, 1436, 1454, 1462, 1476, 1564, 1588, 1714, 1785, 1837, 1839, 1903, 1912, 1921, 2001, 2063, 2100, 2151, 2194, 2221, 2282, 2305, 2358, 2378, 2397, 2498, 2505, 2576, 2618, 2661, 2676, 2677, 2684, 2713, 2744, 2834, 2843, 2887, 2894, 3076, 3102, 3213, 3487, 3527, 3572, 3604, 3637, 3648, 3670, 3679, 3700, 3830, 3840, 3893, 3932, 4061, 4091, 4256, 4267, 4270, 4278, 4303, 4311, 4408, 4462, 4509, 4518, 4538, 4595, 4656, 4743, 4754, 4858, 4891, 4894, 4901, 4966, 4981, 5064, 5101, 5174, 5242, 4364, 5431, 5476, 5485, 5510, 5519, 5694, 5726, 5807, 5880, 5897, 5927, 5929, 5959, 6000, 6020, 6037, 6140, 6232-6233, 6250, 6282

347  Juvenile delinquents—Mathematicians

—(1900-1945), 102, 166, 168, 340, 624, 1122, 1150, 1229, 1230, 1263, 1404, 1434, 1801, 1885, 2083, 2404, 2560, 2665, 2780, 2811, 2909, 2945, 2996, 3112, 3255, 3276, 3393, 3402, 3516, 3521, 3605, 3619, 3704, 3726, 3814, 3828, 3942, 4081, 4154, 4173, 4193, 4263, 4274, 4511, 4582, 4625, 4661, 4666, 4685, 4694, 4812, 5173, 5180, 5743, 5800, 5809, 5885, 5915, 5966, 6113, 6127, 6198
Lecturers (1800-1850), 665, 3500A, 4316, 6277
—(1850-1900), 1001, 1021, 1022, 1210, 2061, 2256, 2527, 2577, 3538, 3707, 3840, 4139, 4140, 4416, 5005, 5038, 5228, 5600, 6071
—(1900-1945), 1228, 2074, 2725, 3663, 3781, 5647, 6152
Lesbians. See Sexual deviates
Liberia (1850-1900), 3815, 6191
Librarians (1800-1850), 5293
—(1850-1900), 277, 5488
—(1900-1945), 586, 589, 1341, 4943
Lieutenant-governors. See Politicians
Literary critics. See Critics
Local government employees and officials. See Governors and local subdivisions under Civil servants, Judges, Representatives, Senators. See also Politicians
Lumbermen (1800-1850), 3033
—(1850-1900), 16, 105, 152, 295, 452, 683, 815, 1101, 1520, 2325, 2922, 3375, 3431, 4207, 4213, 5294, 5945
—(1900-1945), 2735, 3467, 4259, 5811

## M

Madagascar (1850-1900), 2151, 5730
Magazine writers. See Journalists
Magicians (1800-1850), 533
—(1850-1900), 3153
—(1900-1945), 2622, 5697
Magistrates. See Judges
Malaya (1850-1900), 2770
—(1900-1945), 839
Manchuria (1900-1945), 5859
Manufacturers. See Industrialists
Marine engineers. See Engineers
Marines, U.S. (1900-1945), 806, 846, 5836, 6236
—See also Seamen-U.S., Soldiers, and under specific wars, e.g., World War I-Marine Corps
Married life. See Domestic relations
Marshals. See Peace officers
Mathematicians. See Professors, Scientists

Mayors (1850-1900), 1462, 1839, 3346, 4726
—(1900-1945), 2508, 2509, 3056, 4294, 6046, 6113
—See also Politicians
Mechanical engineers. See Engineers
Mechanics. See Artisans
Medical doctors. See Doctors
Medical journalists (1800-1850), 872
—(1850-1900), 656
—(1900-1945), 17
Medical missionaries. See Missionaries: medical
Mediums. See Spiritualists
Mentally ill (1800-1850), 2866
—(1850-1900), 52, 1950, 2065, 2592, 3291, 3369, 3955, 5303, 5345, 5786, 5953
—(1900-1945), 1, 76, 225, 406, 715, 1795, 1934, 2279, 2478, 2668, 2983, 3232, 3422, 5018, 6217, 6283
—See also Illnesses, accounts of
Merchants (to 1800), 2200, 2601, 3137, 3427, 3432, 4034, 4170, 4687, 5831, 5991
—(1800-1850), 62, 178, 617, 628, 645, 653, 769, 1127, 1280, 1281, 1578, 1914, 2321, 2829, 2915, 2968, 3463, 3763a, 3902, 4235, 4257, 4310, 4452, 4453, 4736, 4921, 4922, 4927, 5201, 5349, 5464, 5468, 5605, 5619, 5690, 6011
—(1850-1900), 222, 270, 363, 456, 552, 608, 647, 694, 696, 712, 749, 773, 780, 783, 829, 1042, 1169, 1252, 1301, 1304, 1336, 1447, 1454, 1482, 1608, 1611, 1646, 1667, 1675, 1718, 1815, 1950, 1973, 2014, 2085, 2151, 2262, 2296, 2334, 2410, 2433, 2441, 2443, 2444, 2445, 2472, 2564, 2578, 2647, 2746, 2747, 2821, 2857, 3047, 3062, 3063, 3082, 3139, 3142, 3346, 3363, 3364, 3368, 3448, 3554, 3690, 3799, 3861, 3899, 3924, 3935, 3960, 3966, 4018, 4072, 4128, 4163, 4227, 4232, 4249, 4262, 4308, 4328, 4347, 4381, 4394, 4493, 4506, 4508, 4536, 4571, 4602, 4603, 4604, 4674, 4692, 4796, 4808, 4866, 4966, 4988, 4993, 5010, 5029, 5113, 5153, 5187, 5232, 5257, 5444, 5517, 5536, 5537, 5621, 5788, 5928, 5974, 5989, 6030, 6053, 6061, 6111, 6261, 6284
—(1900-1945), 87, 538, 832, 1110, 1486, 1762, 1796, 1803, 1851, 2376, 2504, 2781, 2938, 3087, 3257, 3333, 4411, 4455, 4465, 4505, 4846, 4856, 4857, 4930, 4934, 5243, 5294, 5581, 5644, 5741, 5861, 5939, 6112, 6256, 6358
—See also Book sellers, Real estate dealers and promoters, Salesmen
Meteorologists. See Scientists
Mexican War: Army, 279, 550, 614, 719, 927, 1048, 1773, 2039, 2409, 2472, 2689, 2878, 3052, 3347, 3790, 3873, 4163, 4270, 4761, 4835, 5088, 5166, 5332, 5793, 6051
—Navy, 752, 4430, 5116, 5430, 5618, 6237
Mexico: Date undetermined, 2875
—(1800-1850), 378, 5752, 6237
—(1850-1900), 965, 1709, 1735, 1995, 2403, 3080, 4086, 4352, 4825, 4995, 5046, 5161, 6083
—(1900-1945), 375, 376, 837, 1064, 1102, 1364, 1697, 2846, 2889, 2923, 3037, 3197, 3378, 3541, 3568, 3944, 4040, 4099, 4346, 5168, 5203, 5419, 5527, 6216
Middle Atlantic States: Abolitionists, 1178, 1257, 2298, 2940, 3423, 3787, 3978, 4075, 5244, 5412, 5585, 5949
—Actors, 692, 1137, 4286, 4636, 5672, 5673, 6052, 6208, 6266
—Adventurers and vagabonds, 2227, 3209, 3518
—Advertisers and public relations men, 491, 2423
—Architects, 627, 4017, 4440, 5555
—Art collectors, 1070
—Artisans, 2005, 3271, 3475, 4371, 4431, 4713, 5030
—Athletes, 1009, 2620, 3880, 4150
—Athletic officials, 3880, 4150
—Authors, 189, 233, 260, 420, 627, 632, 637, 665, 817, 956, 1122, 1146, 1301, 1562, 2108, 2459, 3451, 4170, 4362, 5339, 5432, 5588, 5743, 5808, 5846, 6006, 6071, 6369
—Bankers, 368, 1097, 1941, 2899, 3072, 3932, 4263, 4276, 6177
—Barbers, hairdressers, 4612
—Booksellers, 691, 956, 5440
—Cabinet members, U.S., 5126, 5519
—Childhood reminiscences, 40, 232, 233, 392, 460, 476, 511, 613, 818, 824, 873, 887, 899, 924, 1033, 1128, 1757, 1951, 1982, 2155, 2209, 2231, 2610, 2657, 2667, 2678, 2906, 3068, 3069, 3122, 3168, 3243, 3260, 3290, 3315, 3319, 3553, 3991, 4001, 4155, 4285, 4442, 4573, 4737, 4910, 4929, 5066, 5103, 5104, 5331, 5445, 5593, 5777, 5845, 6287
—Church workers, 253, 717, 779, 804, 955, 1131, 1261, 1589, 2110, 2532, 2921, 3419, 3590, 3930, 4609, 5536, 5622
—Civil servants: Local, 821, 5321, 5322. State: 2834, 3128, 6177. U.S., 1199, 1267, 1381, 1768, 2005, 3951, 4978
—Clergymen: Denomination undetermined, 698, 725, 1262, 1844, 2218, 3079, 3150, 3242, 4412, 4884, 5446, 6134, 6269. Baptist, 140, 195, 196, 266, 396, 730, 888, 1024, 1060, 1104, 1257, 1480, 1706,

Middle Atlantic States: Clergymen, Baptist (cont.), 2093, 2387, 2714, 2842, 2948, 3084, 3581, 3581, 3907, 4284, 4502, 4624, 4719, 4738, 4847, 5108, 5150, 5486, 5569, 5640, 5693, 6006. Catholic priests, 4306, 5655. Christian Church, 501, 2193, 2536, 3536, 4032. Church of Christ, 1668. Church of God, 1948, 2724. Congregational, 11, 405, 1547, 1735, 2186, 2298, 2333, 2925, 2927, 4289, 5774. Disciples of Christ, 4549, 6141. Episcopal, 323, 1505, 2156, 2268, 3274, 4021, 4231, 4239, 4413-4414, 4655, 4707, 4755, 4871, 5376, 5554, 5686, 5806, 5871, 5921, 5994, 6296. Jewish, 426, 6238. Lutheran, 1405, 1555, 1740, 3126, 3504, 3515, 4145, 5020, 5365. Mennonite, 424, 2616, 4298. Methodist, 94, 96, 282, 283, 341, 547, 548, 610, 621, 701, 711, 744, 745, 746, 919, 1008, 1014, 1158, 1159, 1160, 1207, 1313, 1457, 1539, 1829, 2102, 2166, 2224, 2320, 2331, 2341, 2540, 2569, 2602, 2603, 2625, 2634, 2779, 2842, 3077, 3212, 3339, 3423, 3478, 3500A, 3558, 3716, 3758, 3806, 3884, 4016, 4082, 4088, 4229, 4354, 4461, 4471, 4491, 4528, 4646, 4870, 4979, 5043, 5075, 5324, 5380, 5389, 5474, 5493, 5500, 5501, 5576, 5578, 5602, 5704, 5722, 5742, 5848, 6095, 6150, 6223, 6263. Minor sects, 316, 1911, 1931, 2121, 3279, 3493, 3534, 3993. Presbyterian, 695, 1397, 1690, 2272, 2297, 2869, 3064, 3220, 3409, 3525, 3689, 4165, 4205, 4206, 4326, 4432, 4507, 4649, 4658, 5183, 5244, 5391, 5393. Quaker, 193, 1038, 1165, 1259, 2335, 2640, 2641, 3121, 3204, 3751, 3787, 4031, 4204, 4795, 4831, 5409, 6267. Reformed Church in America, 444, 1908, 5600. Unitarian, 110, 1547, 2050, 3647. United Brethren, 2837, 4222. Universalist, 248, 465, 1496, 3934, 4890, 5394, 5658
—Clergymen as authors, 11, 316, 5376
—Clergymen's wives, 4608
—College administrators, 4965, 5482
—College presidents, 48, 843, 1669, 2297, 2501, 3054, 3681, 3855, 3856, 4205, 5139, 5389, 6088
—College professors, 269, 736, 742, 798, 825, 1327, 2004, 2516, 3026, 3032, 3036, 3282, 3423, 3562, 3681, 3778, 4355, 4523, 4560, 4649, 4672, 4841, 4877, 4957, 5086, 5205, 5376, 5451, 5805, 5846
—College students, 40, 1033, 1367, 1873, 4266, 4573, 5302, 5528, 5785, 5819
—Comedians, 6208
—Composers, 188, 1241, 2493
—Conductors, 188, 3712
—Criminals, 162, 1003, 1015, 1453, 1527, 1699, 1827, 1947, 1949, 2152, 2222, 2354, 2793, 3044, 3070, 3086, 3342, 3479, 3484, 3566, 4662, 4878, 4918, 4955, 4980, 5434, 5778, 5824, 6139
—Critics, 1290, 2459, 2862, 4083, 5813, 5846
—Dancers, 4938
—Designers, 627, 2544
—Detectives, 4221, 5852, 6169, 6170
—Diplomats, 3951, 4091, 4092, 5125, 5180, 5519
—Doctors, 58, 335, 356, 529, 779, 795, 825, 872, 920, 1190, 1309, 1453, 1483, 1543, 1617, 1666, 1808, 1924, 1957, 2004, 2144, 2561, 2738, 2921, 3646, 3974, 4033, 4560, 4655, 4877, 4957, 5321, 5322, 5480, 5756, 5765, 6029, 6097, 6285, 6320
—Domestic relations, 10, 511, 726, 887, 988, 1136, 1779, 2653, 2669, 3260, 3545, 4119, 4305, 4668, 4938, 5472, 5993, 6171
—Educators, 843, 1210, 1957, 2298, 2347, 2567, 2740, 2749, 2880, 3066, 4446, 5137, 5158, 5376, 6117, 6238, 6296, 6320
—Engineers, 55, 1070, 1392, 3397, 3551, 4672, 4811, 5423, 6220, 6220A, 6298
—Evangelists, 932, 1416, 3006, 3215, 4048, 4165, 4521, 5255
—Executives, 165, 166, 466, 491, 924, 4309
—Factory workers, 924, 3278, 3287, 5644
—Farm journalists, 212
—Farmers and farm life, 697, 727, 804, 817, 821, 1465, 1779, 2005, 2616, 3086, 3135, 3168, 3249, 3315, 3368, 3432, 4024, 4520, 4908, 5029, 5132, 5286, 5420, 5593, 5619, 5837, 5993, 6055, 6125
—Financiers, 293, 1097, 1562, 1653, 1748, 4091, 4263, 4267, 4276, 4994, 5598, 5815, 6319
—Governors, 4315, 4509, 4909, 5126, 5254
—Historians, 4362, 4509, 5690, 5837
—Hotels and inns, proprietors and workers, 966, 967, 4142
—Humorists, 420
—Hunters and trappers, 3545, 5715-5716
—Immigrants: Austrian, 420, 5335, 5336, 5337. Canadian, 5756. Danish, 4821, 5939. Dutch, 556, 557, 558, 5837, 6169, 6170. English, 494, 1158, 1159, 1351, 1841, 2741, 3079, 4119, 5030, 5150, 5260, 6052. French, 1013 German, 329, 769, 2375, 3282, 4091, 4145, 4692, 5365, 5440, 5534. Irish, 692, 1074, 1386, 1542, 2117, 3044, 4381, 4707, 5002, 6298. Italian,

Middle Atlantic States: Immigrants, Italian, 1423. Jugoslavian, 5029. Latvian, 3923. Norwegian, 2931. Rumanian, 450. Russian, 970, 2252, 2671, 2911, 4701. Russian Jewish, 158, 1138, 1543, 1570, 2524, 3287, 4362, 5673, 6028, 6256, 6369. Scottish, 924, 5690. Swiss, 2365. Welsh, 117, 4847.
—Indian fighters, 5286
—Indians, life among, 68, 977, 5729
—Industrialists, 43, 272, 292, 368, 617, 838, 923, 1070, 1236, 1253, 1392, 1570, 1760, 1762, 1878, 2045, 2060, 2061, 2774, 2899, 3711, 4123, 4381, 4644, 4746, 4813, 5091, 5169, 5260, 5423, 5433, 5598, 5652, 5721, 5856, 5961, 6102, 6244
—Inventors, 1236, 2060, 4034
—Jews, 49, 426, 460, 870, 970, 1286, 1957, 2029, 2209, 2560, 3072, 3255, 3285, 3923, 4091, 5519, 5644, 5672, 5673, 5914, 5915
—Journalists, 3, 189, 244, 260, 284, 329, 494, 508, 541, 556, 557, 558, 582, 586, 607, 657, 671, 870, 993, 994, 1003, 1074, 1113, 1114, 1196, 1353, 1478, 1479, 1538, 1586, 1609, 1650, 1755, 1900, 2029, 2125, 2164, 2271, 2292, 2379, 2459, 2460, 2571, 2617, 2682, 2921, 2930, 3020, 3026, 3170, 3209, 3278, 3284, 3287, 3305, 3451, 3923, 4025, 4083, 4294, 4362, 4480, 4567, 4821, 5125, 5534, 5585, 5685, 5732, 5733, 5833, 5834, 5865, 5878, 6017, 6028, 6105, 6221, 6355
—Judges, 2677, 4942. Local, 2576, 4509. State, 3932. U.S., 3276
—Labor leaders, 845, 1351, 2524, 5915
—Laborers, 23, 39, 1094, 1423, 3033, 3070, 4260, 4711, 5544, 5577
—Lawyers, 340, 386, 418, 766, 848, 1033, 1100, 1122, 1379, 1839, 1967, 2358, 2560, 2576, 2665, 2677, 2834, 2909, 3255, 3276, 3393, 3604, 3814, 3828, 3840, 3932, 4091, 4170, 4263, 4267, 4315, 4509, 4511, 4694, 4812, 4858, 4942, 5002, 5180, 5331, 5510, 5519, 5603, 5743, 5915, 6037, 6250
—Lecturers, 665, 1210, 2061, 3840, 5600, 6071
—Librarians, 5293
—Lumbermen, 2922, 4207
—Merchants, 456, 617, 647, 696, 712, 769, 829, 1280, 1301, 1336, 1578, 1762, 1803, 2445, 3082, 3137, 3368, 3427, 3935, 3966, 4034, 4170, 4347, 4381, 4602, 4687, 4736, 5029, 5243, 5464, 5468, 5536, 5619, 5644, 5690, 5939, 6256, 6358
—Miners and mining life, 4085
—Minstrels, 5569

—Missionaries: Denomination undetermined, 68, 1141, 1737. Methodist, 1771, 4789, 5729. Mormon, 4040. Presbyterian, 5754. Seventh Day Adventist, 4444
—Monks: Catholic, 3045
—Music teachers, 41, 489, 3712, 4996, 5869
—Musicians, 489, 3712, 4026, 5869, 6338
—Negroes, 39, 94, 195, 196, 698, 1094, 2341, 2569, 2740, 2940, 3419, 3558, 4229, 4461, 4507, 4528, 4624, 4719, 5468, 5480, 5704, 5785, 5949, 6095
—Novelists, 313, 314, 508, 760, 1353, 1475, 2850, 4884
—Nuns, Catholic, 1386, 1881
—Nurses, 2365, 2986, 3306
—Office workers, 4749, 5548
—Oil well drillers, 6339
—Painters, 179, 476, 654, 1070, 3196, 4183, 6062, 6126
—Peace officers, 4347
—Philanthropists, 272, 923, 1070, 1261, 1748, 3072, 5536, 5856, 5961
—Photographers, 1156, 2137, 4289
—Physical culturists, 4150
—Pioneers, 613, 2166, 5286, 5593, 5715-5716
—Playwrights, 692, 1074, 1137, 1353, 3278, 3778, 4286, 5865
—Poets, 484, 1423, 2850, 3451, 4480, 5018, 5330, 5493, 6115
—Policemen, 4164, 5933
—Politicians, 386, 473, 494, 845, 1351, 1379, 1381, 1872, 2016, 2290, 2292, 2358, 2375, 2428, 2576, 2665, 2899, 2909, 3137, 3255, 3828, 3951, 3966, 4091, 4185, 4572, 4586, 4942, 5125, 5254, 5330, 5412, 5510, 5576, 5743, 5853, 6017
—Politicians' wives, 527, 1146, 6253
—Printers, 2016, 2176, 2271, 2757, 5008, 5009, 5149, 5353, 5383, 6028
—Prison officials, 3382, 3618
—Prisoners, 1699, 1936, 1949, 3086, 3879, 4287
—Publishers, 320, 637, 956, 960, 1030, 1196, 1286, 1603, 1693, 2016, 2482, 2493, 2736, 3354, 3841, 4480, 4586, 4679, 4680, 5008, 5009, 5526, 5902, 6355
—Railroad workers, 717, 924, 2117, 4291, 5857
—Real estate dealers and promoters, 249, 3042, 3966, 4520
—Religious journalists, 11, 110, 804, 1397, 2156, 2387, 3423, 4658, 5600, 6238
—Representatives: State, 607, 5915. U.S., 340, 418, 766, 1295, 4858, 6014
—Restaurants and taverns, proprietors and workers, 420, 1013, 3158, 3653, 3675

# SUBJECT INDEX

Middle Atlantic States: Salesmen, 647, 659, 1619, 2545, 3593, 4123, 5942
—Scientists, 91, 146, 147, 817, 1568, 1781, 2104, 2347, 2516, 3581, 3974, 4177, 4355, 4672, 5086, 5087
—Sculptors, 6126
—Senators: State, 158, 6088, 6285. U.S., 4315, 4511, 4512, 4572, 5126
—Servants, 2252
—Showmen, 542, 626, 2046, 2122, 3411, 4751, 5673, 5904, 6052, 6266
—Singers, 65, 1723, 1805, 1879, 1880, 2539, 4996, 5569, 5914, 6256
—Social reformers, 665, 1748, 1841, 2029, 2186, 2347, 2460, 2917, 2921, 3196, 4283, 4432, 4821, 5091, 5576, 5878, 6036, 6296
—Social workers, 21, 673, 928, 1336, 1538, 1708, 2254, 2381, 3285, 3592, 3784, 3818, 4306, 4609, 4725, 5211, 5446, 5536, 5613, 5910, 5911,
—Socialists, 870, 2665, 5915, 6028
—Socialites, 527, 874, 999, 1000, 2171, 2242, 2265, 2349, 2350, 2532, 3092, 3749, 3816, 3984, 4393, 5547, 5571, 5833, 5835, 5913, 6128
—Spiritualists, 627, 1451, 1452, 2741, 3506, 5348
—Sportsmen, 3508
—Suffragists, 1178, 1609, 2567, 5585
—Teachers, 586, 1223, 1234, 1807, 2036, 2347, 2395, 2564, 3135, 3229, 3233, 3302, 3840, 4157, 4177, 4298, 4789, 5005, 5255, 5432, 5472, 5775, 5902, 6117, 6133
—Temperance workers, 1397, 2869, 2917, 3758, 3787, 3978, 4075, 4725
—Theologians, 49, 3750, 4649, 5451
Military. See Aviators—military, Marines, Scouts, U.S.Army, Seamen—U.S., Soldiers, and under specific wars, e.g., World War I—Army
Military engineers. See Engineers
Militiamen. See Soldiers
Milliners. See Merchants
Mineralogists. See Scientists
Miners and mining life (1800-1850), 275, 718, 719, 1219, 1503, 1508, 1608, 2418, 2469, 2711, 2723, 3244, 3273, 3494, 3709, 3873, 3902, 4243, 4527, 4947, 5572, 6016, 6205
—(1850-1900), 5, 79, 92, 181, 228, 254, 377, 422, 432, 583, 585, 608, 644, 753, 880, 883, 921, 929, 930, 942, 1011, 1049, 1093, 1120, 1203, 1271, 1357, 1499, 1513, 1531, 1549, 1551, 1556, 1594, 1638, 1657, 1773, 1874, 1902, 1952, 2010, 2028, 2031, 2114, 2151, 2153, 2251, 2259, 2294, 2325, 2345, 2403, 2410, 2420, 2431, 2437, 2443, 2479, 2529, 2551, 2552, 2572, 2621, 2670, 2689, 2848, 2873, 2932, 3105, 3165, 3180, 3189, 3235, 3326, 3431, 3485, 3559, 3804, 3849, 3861, 3882, 3889, 3910, 3911, 3964, 4128, 4152, 4230, 4450, 4467, 4522, 4547, 4571, 4598, 4619, 4644, 4875, 5046, 5089, 5101, 5143, 5153, 5165, 5198, 5232, 5259, 5316, 5368, 5407, 5453, 5476, 5495, 5502, 5503, 5537, 5541, 5661, 5724, 5757, 5770, 5839, 5860, 5892, 5918, 5954, 5972, 5973, 6031, 6033, 6065, 6066, 6081, 6135, 6168, 6181, 6185, 6218, 6315
—(1900-1945), 23, 99, 490, 674, 961, 1605, 1787, 1944, 2019, 2118, 2168, 2362, 2404, 2411, 2450, 2846, 3381, 3383, 3568, 3580, 3759, 3949, 4010, 4085, 4332, 4489, 4970, 4971, 5053, 5119, 5168, 5369, 5581, 5960
—See also Forty-niners
Mining engineers. See Engineers
Ministers, diplomatic. See Diplomats
Ministers, religious. See Clergymen
Minstrels (1850-1900), 765, 3141, 5569, 5624
—(1900-1945), 4779, 5719
—See also Vaudevillians
Mission workers. See Social workers
Missionaries: Adventist. See Missionaries: Minor Sects, Missionaries: Seventh Day Adventist
—Denomination undetermined (1800-1850), 68, 164, 1737, 3610, 4519, 4660. (1850-1900), 290, 1109, 1173, 1356, 1567, 1676, 1981, 3016, 3055, 3863, 4195, 4436, 4558, 4819, 4986, 5256, 5656-5657, 5985, 6027, 6064, 6072, 6134, 6147, 6191. (1900-1945), 1085, 1141, 1233, 2598, 3159, 3192, 3823, 3870, 4039, 5210, 5863
—Anglican. See Missionaries: Episcopal
—Baptist (1800-1850), 3857. (1850-1900), 600, 601, 940, 1061, 1103, 1637, 2733, 3111, 3761, 6083. (1900-1945), 1117, 1321, 2044, 2727, 4539, 4766, 5098, 5099
—Brethren (1900-1945), 5943. See also Missionaries: United Brethren
—Catholic (1800-1850), 3812. (1850-1900), 409, 572, 4415, 6056. (1900-1945), 3877
—Christian Church (1850-1900), 4722. See also Missionaries: Disciples of Christ
—Church of Jesus Christ of Latter-Day Saints. See Missionaries: Mormon
—Congregational (1800-1850), 2225, 5049. (1850-1900), 530, 565, 965, 977, 1248, 1735, 2357, 2434, 2435, 2442, 4357, 5161. (1900-1945), 2119
—Disciples of Christ (1900-1945), 2606. See also Missionaries: Christian Church
—Episcopal (to 1800), 5909. (1850-1900), 2468, 5796. (1900-1945), 5907

Missionaries: Friends. See Missionaries: Quaker
—Interdenominational (1900-1945), 1584
—Lutheran (1850-1900), 5730, 6374, 6375. (1900-1945), 4199
—Medical (1800-1850), 6090. (1850-1900), 1635, 1752, 2248, 2858, 3827, 4788, 5810, 6241, 6242. (1900-1945), 50, 1032, 1390, 1481, 2514, 3306, 3328, 3329, 3330, 3995, 4157, 4161, 4456, 5098, 5099, 5115, 5164, 5395, 5396, 5818, 5944
—Mennonite (1900-1945), 4532, 5766
—Methodist (1800-1850), 1160, 1244, 1771, 1782, 4566, 4789, 5729, 6090. (1850-1900), 847, 982, 1212, 2223, 3461, 3716, 3815, 5300, 5634, 5792, 6085, 6086, 6087. (1900-1945), 1602, 2542, 4115, 5392
—Minor sects (1850-1900), 6085. (1900-1945), 1323, 1441, 2923, 3810, 6087, 6144
—Mormons (1800-1850), 3994, 6279. (1850-1900), 719, 723, 901, 3080, 5429, 5540, 6350. (1900-1945), 4040
—Presbyterian (1800-1850), 4533, 5898, 5971. (1850-1900), 46, 1029, 1108, 1432, 2241, 2332, 2712, 3009, 3875, 5754, 5810, 6241, 6242, 6356. (1900-1945), 1322, 4880, 5944
—Protestant Episcopal. See Missionaries: Episcopal
—Quaker (1800-1850), 2327. (1850-1900), 2784, 4767. (1900-1945), 2785, 3103.
—Reorganized Church of Jesus Christ of Latter-day Saints. See Missionaries: Mormon
—River Brethren. See Missionaries: Brethren
—Seventh Day Adventist (1900-1945), 4364, 4444, 4445, 5395, 5396, 6264
—Society of Friends. See Missionaries: Quaker
—Unitarian (1900-1945), 3647
—United Brethren (1850-1900), 1959, 4533. See also Missionaries: Brethren
Models (1850-1900), 4212
Monks: Catholic (1800-1850), 3405
Morocco (1900-1945), 996, 4949
Morticians (1850-1900), 4873
Motion picture actors. See Actors
Motion picture producers. See Showmen
Mountain: Actors, 3362
—Adventurers and vagabonds, 2227
—Artisans, 2085, 2415, 4973
—Authors, 1037, 1797
—Bakers, caterers, cooks, 1787, 3383
—Bankers, 683, 2807, 4604, 5153
—Bishops and archbishops: Episcopal, 5595. Mormon, 3399, 6121

—Childhood reminiscences, 377, 567, 1515, 1904, 2092, 2191, 2250, 2760, 4002, 4015, 4040, 4351, 4887, 5375, 6206
—Church workers, 379, 2382, 2415, 3231, 3365, 3420, 3421, 3948, 4042, 4485, 5504, 5604
—Civil servants: State, 3547. U.S., 3225, 3396, 4958, 6278
—Clergymen: Baptist, 3384, 3907. Congregational, 666, 5161, 5684. Denomination undetermined, 1894, 1993, 2147. Episcopal, 625, 2518, 5554, 5796. Methodist, 385, 1716, 1938, 4471, 6317. Mormon, 700, 3522, 3943, 4209, 4645. Nazarene, 5850. Presbyterian, 724. United Brethren, 2172, 3326
—College presidents, 257, 5038
—Cowboys, 6, 307, 446, 683, 823, 1066, 1215, 1216, 1283, 1523, 2431, 2476, 2674, 2969, 3225, 3333, 3372, 3378, 3660, 3876, 3910, 4546, 4899, 4987, 5102, 5504, 5772
—Criminals, 3095, 4987, 5962
—Dentists, 2008
—Detectives, 433, 2767
—Doctors, 2096, 2683
—Domestic relations, 69, 1817, 1888, 2033, 2092, 2382, 2654, 2995, 3017, 3345, 3631, 4576, 4708, 4709, 5265, 5306, 5448, 5604, 6186, 6340
—Educators, 257, 2488, 3726, 5887
—Engineers, 55, 716, 758, 1231, 4811
—Evangelists, 1416, 2535, 5054, 5055, 5850
—Farmers and farm life, 312, 379, 605, 1062, 1231, 1472, 1987, 2010, 2172, 2191, 2294, 2317, 2415, 2552, 2604, 2654, 3035, 3326, 3457, 3948, 4209, 4351, 5429, 5540, 5604, 5920, 5928, 6272
—Financiers, 5741
—Gamblers, 2095
—Governors, 683, 2570, 3849, 4370, 5242
—Historians, 6121
—Hotels and inns, proprietors and workers, 1408, 5089
—Hunters and trappers, 36, 90, 92, 97, 239, 402, 683, 939, 1523, 1644, 1763, 1909, 2226, 2431, 2614, 2689, 2746, 2932, 2968, 3463, 3660, 3924, 4015, 4078, 4210, 4452, 4916, 4967, 5368, 5892, 6206, 6294
—Immigrants: Canadian, 3467, 3948. English, 605, 608, 1231, 1255, 1366, 2518, 3017, 3248, 3522, 5448. Norwegian, 2934, 3365. Swiss, 5540
—Indian agents, 939, 1310
—Indian fighters, 90, 97, 239, 307, 379, 499, 737, 928, 939, 1235, 1331, 1359, 1644, 1763, 1926, 1988, 2403, 2650, 2804, 2840, 2721, 3365, 3372, 4226,

SUBJECT INDEX

Mountain: Indian fighters (cont.), 4916, 5661, 5892, 6203, 6206, 6294
—Indians, 1962, 2142, 2760, 5594
—Indians, life among, 402, 978, 1322, 1387, 1567, 1888, 3080, 3437, 4988, 5187, 6206
—Industrialists, 980, 1744, 2737, 2807, 4232, 4644, 4794
—Journalists, 632, 1455, 1659, 2379, 2458, 2488, 2570, 2594, 3225, 3413, 6121
—Judges, 379, 3516. Local, 3519, 6272. State, 5242
—Labor journalists, 767
—Labor leaders, 767
—Laborers, 1551, 3248
—Lawyers, 3516, 3726, 4061, 5242, 5476
—Lumbermen, 683, 1101, 2325, 3467
—Merchants, 363, 608, 1304, 1851, 2085, 2321, 2746, 2747, 2968, 3463, 4128, 4232, 4452, 4571, 4604, 4988, 5153, 5187, 5741, 6011
—Miners and mining life, 92, 99, 254, 377, 608, 644, 753, 1120, 1551, 1594, 1787, 2010, 2257, 2259, 2294, 2362, 2403, 2420, 2431, 2437, 2450, 2846, 2932, 3105, 3235, 3326, 3381, 3383, 3889, 3910, 3949, 4128, 4571, 4875, 5053, 5089, 5153, 5165, 5259, 5368, 5453, 5476, 5502, 5503, 5661, 5724, 5860, 5892, 5972, 6033
—Missionaries: Denomination undetermined, 1567. Methodist, 6085, 6086, 6087. Minor sects, 6085, 6086, 6087. Mormon, 1851, 3080. Presbyterian, 1322, 1432
—Novelists, 224
—Nuns: Catholic, 5107
—Peace officers, 56, 644, 892, 907, 1213, 2552, 3225, 4982, 5368, 5455
—Pioneers, 69, 90, 92, 97, 307, 379, 446, 567, 655, 800, 869, 939, 1062, 1121, 1215, 1216, 1594, 1659, 1763, 1909, 2010, 2033, 2172, 2226, 2257, 2259, 2321, 2403, 2420, 2421, 2437, 2654, 2747, 2840, 2918, 2932, 2968, 3235, 3311, 3360, 3372, 3463, 3533, 3631, 3889, 3910, 3924, 3948, 4078, 4244, 4282, 4351, 4369, 4452, 4571, 4576, 4916, 4967, 4973, 4983, 5007, 5250, 5429, 5453, 5476, 5502, 5562, 5661, 5724, 5860, 5892, 5920, 5928, 5972, 6011, 6033, 6203, 6206, 6294, 6350
—Poets, 6121
—Policemen, 2797
—Politicians, 99, 307, 379, 1304, 1788, 2488, 3413, 5892, 6272
—Printers, 1037, 4794
—Prisoners, 3095, 4209
—Prostitutes and fallen women, 5626
—Publishers, 1455, 2271, 3413
—Railroad workers, 254, 644, 3467, 4291
—Ranchers and ranch life, 72, 81, 118, 312, 321, 363, 377, 631, 679, 683, 869, 876, 914, 968, 1066, 1083, 1086, 1101, 1170, 1215, 1216, 1366, 1579, 1797, 1821, 2065, 2294, 2362, 2476, 2840, 2846, 2934, 3311, 3381, 4282, 4604, 4614, 4615, 4708, 4709, 4875, 5191, 5250, 5860, 5942, 6373
—Real estate dealers and promoters, 2085, 4209
—Representatives: State, 723, 2259, 2636. U.S., 3849
—Salesmen, 5942
—Scouts, U.S. Army, 1121, 1215, 1216, 2476, 2767, 4210
—Senators: State, 2362, 2807, 6121. U.S., 900, 5476
—Social reformers, 2797, 3519,
—Social workers, 366
—Soldiers, 307, 869, 939, 1235, 1308, 1359, 2721, 5674
—Soldiers' wives, 265, 5025, 5562
—Spiritualists, 722
—Sportsmen, 2988, 3197
—Suffragists, 1037
—Surveyors, 2437, 2918, 4055
—Tailors, 1787
—Teachers, 1851, 2415, 2457, 4887, 6085, 6086, 6087, 6272
—Teamsters, 794, 2797, 3372, 3533, 4351, 4506, 4973, 4983, 5724, 6206
—Telegraphers, 1304
—Woodsmen and guides, 939, 1215, 1216, 4015, 4958, 6206, 6294
Murderers. See Criminals
Museum keepers (1900-1945), 801, 1006
Music, patrons of. See Philanthropists
Music critics. See Critics
Music teachers: Date undetermined, 3958
—(1850-1900), 41, 108, 296, 597, 1866, 2018, 3110, 3214, 3712, 3764, 4098, 4912, 4996
—(1900-1945), 489, 2742, 3975, 5000, 5059, 5869
Musical comedy stars. See Actors, Singers, Vaudevillians
Musicians (1850-1900), 2, 109, 1072, 1689, 1866, 2018, 3764, 4098, 4974, 5122, 5444
—(1900-1945), 217, 489, 1439, 1707, 2230, 2446, 2492, 3019, 3629, 3712, 3975, 3996, 4026, 4179, 4698, 5000, 5366, 5869, 6338
—See also Composers, Conductors, Minstrels, Music teachers, Singers

# N

Narcotics addicts (1800-1850), 938
— (1850-1900), 1151, 1837, 4103, 4337
— (1900-1950), 3232, 3666, 3895, 4900, 5850, 6300
National Guardsmen. See Soldiers
Naturalists. See Scientists
Naval Air Corps. See Aviators-Military, and individual wars, e.g., World War I - Air Corps, etc.
Navy. See Seamen-U.S., and individual wars, e.g., American Revolution-Navy, Civil War: Union-Navy, etc.
Negroes (to 1800), 94, 3729, 4639, 4843, 6095
— (1800-1850), 136, 195, 196, 1473, 1489, 1625, 1626, 1771, 1775, 1776, 2340, 3011, 3115, 3419, 3731, 4313, 4507, 4528, 5468, 5481, 5704
— (1850-1900), 39, 133, 134, 521, 561, 698, 738, 754, 826, 830, 1094, 1243, 1251, 1293, 1901, 1961, 1968, 2064, 2151, 2299, 2305, 2306, 2341, 2569, 2731, 2740, 2851, 3010, 3111, 3140, 3343, 3351, 3428, 3487, 3558, 3596, 3730, 4229, 4422, 4461, 4463, 4719, 5256, 5288, 5480, 5533, 5629, 5632, 5938, 5980, 5981, 5982, 6156, 6191
— (1900-1945), 29, 122, 359, 549, 1195, 1265, 1442, 1488, 1761, 1850, 2250, 2492, 2512, 2608, 2613, 2874, 2886, 2890, 3040, 3041, 3886, 4135, 4191, 4464, 4544, 4551, 4624, 4633, 4735, 5416, 5647, 5785, 5794, 6310
— See also Slaves
Neurologists. See Doctors
Neurotics. See Mentally ill
New England States: Abolitionists, 280, 387, 594, 1025, 1257, 1624, 1625, 1626, 1940, 2645, 2812, 3800, 5004, 5080, 5363, 5768
— Actors, 302
— Adventurers and vagabonds, 5291, 5893
— Artisans, 149, 221, 816, 2658, 3178, 4713, 4800, 5583
— Athletes, 1055
— Authors, 816, 1001, 1025, 1784, 2645, 2813, 5004, 5095, 5691, 5698, 6006
— Authors' wives, 71
— Bakers, caterers, cooks, 826
— Bankers, 1188, 1940, 1941, 5349, 5465, 5608
— Barbers, hairdressers, 2340
— Bishops and archbishops: Episcopal, 1068, 3390, 3391
— Booksellers, 429, 1144
— Cabinet Members, U.S., 594
— Childhood reminiscences, 7, 59, 62, 82, 106, 161, 174, 250, 334, 689, 831, 886, 944, 983, 1016, 1018, 1057,1075, 1133, 1181, 1182, 1317, 1361, 1372, 1378, 1403, 1631, 1686, 1757, 1875, 2049, 2394, 2507, 2554, 2678, 2679, 2685, 2754, 2808, 2833, 3096, 3097, 3098, 3136, 3236, 3359, 3416, 3630, 4029, 4155, 4365, 4395, 4659, 4786, 4800, 4826, 4836, 5103, 5104, 5204, 5233, 5284, 5379, 5413, 5698, 5901, 6148, 6207, 6308
— Church workers, 429, 738, 955, 4044, 6273
— Civil servants: Local, 149, 4848. State, 2945, 3114, 6165. U.S., 780, 4726, 6069
— Clergymen: Denomination undetermined, 1262, 1349, 1487, 1708, 1844, 2218, 2748, 2881, 3729, 4233, 4313, 4412, 4611, 4686, 5289, 5545, 6269. Baptist, 67, 110, 140, 195, 196, 230, 888, 1024, 1192,1382, 2387, 2490, 2942, 2948, 3010, 3084, 3185, 3371, 3452, 3642, 3725, 3946, 4125, 4269, 4468, 4470, 4618, 4676, 4719, 4855, 5175, 5284, 5314, 5371, 5489, 5640, 5693, 6006. Catholic priests, 5334. Christian Church, 1905, 2536, 3073, 3536, 4650, 4676, 5268, 5561, 6352. Church of God, 3625. Congregational, 85, 174, 229, 370, 593, 634, 704, 781, 782, 1056, 1135, 1143, 1438, 1547, 1590, 1630, 1811, 1864, 2037, 2076, 2186, 2243, 2333, 2652, 2680, 2759, 2913, 3862, 3919, 4361, 4385, 4587, 4682, 5034, 5167, 5340, 5422, 5654, 5774, 5822, 5882, 6308. Disciples of Christ, 6141. Episcopal, 289, 742, 1505, 2267, 2758, 2883, 4231, 4239, 4886, 5028, 5554, 6296. Lutheran, 2454, 3504. Methodist, 37, 141, 282, 701, 1160, 1369, 1457, 1861, 2224, 2331, 2341, 2593, 2634, 2847, 3212, 3478, 3500A, 4028, 4052, 4088, 4223, 4354, 4646, 4753, 4827, 5080, 5343, 5533, 5578, 5742, 5830, 5956, 6263, 6343. Minor sects, 234, 316, 4273, 4360. Presbyterian, 2869, 3066, 3265, 3409, 3919, 4649, 5370. Quaker, 1907, 2982, 4031, 4204. Seventh Day Adventist, 6092, 6093, 6098, 6099. Shaker, 226, 4515. Unitarian, 110, 230, 498, 620, 1547, 2050, 2076, 2456, 3263, 3591, 3647, 3800, 4428, 4429, 5700, 5955, 6054. Universalist, 280, 465, 1115, 1496, 2369, 3263, 4169, 4273, 4618, 5285, 6124
— Clergymen as authors, 316, 370, 1115, 2759, 5654
— College administrators, 704, 4124

New England (cont.): College presidents, 151, 370, 1710, 2401, 2434, 2680, 4855, 5774, 6006
— College professors, 151, 897, 1143, 1330, 1348, 1710, 2457, 2465, 2680, 3510, 3921, 4028, 4406, 4523, 4541, 4587, 4791, 4855, 4946, 5023, 5032, 5095, 5173, 5209, 5565, 5966, 6075, 6100, 6167, 6198
— College students, 897, 2554, 2960, 3156, 4051, 4124, 5022, 5104, 5133, 5302, 5698, 5717, 6255
— Composers, 82, 2812, 3110
— Conductors, 2605, 3110
— Criminals, 88, 112, 241, 2023, 2202, 2308, 2794, 3078, 3754, 4020, 4637, 4639, 4772, 5154, 5313, 5539, 5587, 5641, 5723, 5776, 5934, 6073, 6322
— Critics, 4541
— Dentists, 2735
— Detectives, 4221
— Diplomats, 816, 1647
— Doctors, 64, 1112, 1157, 1273, 1378, 1591, 1932, 2755, 2928, 4201, 5386, 5689, 5970, 6075, 6100, 6231, 6248, 6285
— Doctors' wives, 4851
— Domestic relations, 245, 602, 1628, 2455, 2836, 3223, 3740, 4044, 4783, 4784, 5204, 5803, 5964, 6103
— Educators, 25, 63, 64, 404, 885, 1585, 2402, 2457, 2982, 4144, 4340, 5592, 6296
— Engineers, 4791, 5032
— Evangelists, 1964, 2162, 3038, 3179, 3215, 5830
— Executives, 25
— Factory workers, 709, 710
— Farmers and farm life, 697, 780, 1007, 1016, 1133, 1317, 1417, 1422, 1443, 1876, 2257, 2291, 2808, 2978, 3033, 3135, 3136, 3460, 3797, 4360, 4431, 4730, 4800, 5156, 5200, 5465, 5608, 5682, 5745, 6271
— Financiers, 3222
— Fishermen, 752
— Gamblers, 6322
— Governors, 840, 1348, 1564, 2356
— Historians, 25, 31, 32, 593, 2645, 3550, 4224, 4435, 4804, 5064
— Hotels and inns, proprietors and workers, 3322, 6316
— Immigrants: Armenian, 552. Austrian, 5334. Canadian, 4388. English, 498, 709, 710, 1325, 2741, 3500A, 4796, 5325. Irish, 3171, 3830, 4052, 4974, 5723. Russian Jewish, 159, 160, 161. Scotch, 5309, 6103. Syrian, 2376
— Indian fighters, 2098, 6076
— Indians, life among, 164, 4789
— Industrialists, 43, 213, 227, 628, 1188, 1522, 1647, 1760, 1971, 1972, 2099, 2675, 2735, 2898, 3007, 3171, 3186, 4159, 4657, 4746, 5309, 5608, 5977, 5995
— Inventors, 3794, 5995
— Jews, 2162
— Journalists, 612, 774, 1112, 1196, 1297, 1750, 1854, 1998, 2554, 2555, 2571, 2787, 3170, 3222, 3550, 3871, 4203, 4224, 4523, 5004, 5199, 5498
— Judges, 5174, 5880. Local, 2277. State, 1404, 5514. U.S., 5514
— Labor leaders, 373
— Laborers, 3731, 4529
— Lawyers, 840, 1112, 1229, 1404, 1564, 2063, 2684, 2744, 2828, 2945, 3637, 3763, 3830, 4203, 4891, 5064, 5173, 5174, 5514, 5726, 5768, 5880, 5966, 6015, 6140, 6198
— Lecturers, 1001, 3500A, 6277
— Librarians, 277, 4943
— Lumbermen, 295, 3033, 4207, 5811
— Mayors, 4726
— Merchants, 62, 552, 628, 645, 653, 696, 780, 1252, 1280, 1281, 1578, 1815, 1914, 1973, 2200, 2376, 2564, 2821, 3142, 3448, 4235, 4394, 4493, 4796, 5974, 5989, 6261
— Missionaries: Denomination undetermined, 164. Congregational, 4357. Mormon, 4040, 6279. Seventh Day Adventist, 4444
— Music teachers, 296, 597, 3110
— Musicians, 1689, 4974
— Negroes, 195, 196, 738, 826, 1625, 1626, 1775, 1776, 2340, 2341, 2436, 3010, 3729, 3731, 4313, 4639, 4719, 5288, 5326, 5533
— Novelists, 2106, 2277, 2554, 2555, 4203, 5204, 5946
— Nurses, 4788
— Painters, 2568, 4490
— Philanthropists, 566, 5977
— Philosophers, 4406, 4946, 5022, 5023
— Pioneers, 1422, 1443, 1518, 2098, 2978
— Poets, 1007, 1087, 1134, 2554, 2555, 4203, 4804, 5204, 5314, 5498
— Policemen, 296
— Politicians, 1188, 1229, 3448, 3830
— Printers, 1144, 1297, 1361, 2427, 3733, 4224, 4269, 4648
— Prison officials, 2208
— Prisoners, 5723, 6277
— Publishers, 213, 1196, 1297, 1338, 1564, 2182, 2236, 3222, 3354, 3869
— Railroad workers, 925, 1859, 5712
— Real estate dealers and promoters, 149, 1940, 2099, 4203
— Religious journalists, 2387, 4587, 5268, 5955

New England States (cont.): Representatives-State, 2356, 2526, 2658, 2828. U.S., 594, 840, 1404, 1647, 5742, 5768, 5901, 6015
—Restaurants and taverns, proprietors and workers, 812, 826
—Salesmen, 780, 989, 1619, 4394
—Scientists, 91, 291, 1330, 2526, 2680, 5209
—Sculptors, 276
—Senators: State, 3186. U.S., 2684
—Servants, 1775, 1776, 2340, 2455
—Showmen, 311, 1774, 3178, 3411
—Singers, 302, 3110
—Social reformers, 150, 221, 230, 816, 2186, 5290, 6296
—Social workers, 1585, 1964
—Socialites, 236, 566, 3749, 3816, 5413, 5913
—Soldiers, 563, 1518, 1569
—Spiritualists, 1522, 2741, 4388, 5299
—Sportsmen, 3182, 4086, 4393
—Suffragists, 78, 2812, 5142
—Surveyors, 3797
—Tailors, 1422
—Teachers, 63, 67, 619, 1075, 1223, 1325, 1573, 1806, 1833, 2395, 3935, 3135, 3275, 3302, 3448, 3917, 4106, 4340, 4420, 4490, 4747, 5005, 5509, 5660, 5775, 6133, 6316, 6324
—Temperance workers, 429, 1564, 1632, 2869, 3354, 4052, 4796, 6270, 6277
—Theologians, 2759, 4028
—Woodsmen and guides, 295
Newspapermen. See Journalists
Nicaragua (1850-1900), 1616, 2971, 4619, 4869, 5475, 5919, 6135
—(1900-1945), 4392
Norway (1900-1945), 2487, 3306, 4363
Novelists (1800-1850), 4203, 5204
—(1850-1900), 313, 1093, 1363, 1475, 1766, 1917, 2465, 2554, 2555, 2786, 2810, 2817, 2818, 2961, 3067, 4761, 4884, 5269, 5485, 5646, 5946, 6142, 6143
—(1900-1945), 204, 224, 314, 371, 508, 667, 760, 772, 868, 1187, 1353, 1385, 1500, 1509, 1662, 1899, 2196, 2277, 2307, 2494, 2850, 2916, 3041, 3170, 3226, 3296, 3312, 3317, 3491, 3492, 3886, 3997, 4045, 4265, 4339, 4417, 4530, 4583, 4593, 4683, 4740, 4824, 5110, 5221, 5441, 5442, 5513, 5525, 6070, 6089, 6113, 6255, 6307
—See also Authors
Nudists. See Physical culturists
Nuns: Catholic (1850-1900), 1386, 3746, 4317, 5060, 5107
—(1900-1945), 1881, 3611, 4005
Nurses (1850-1900), 253, 1183, 3972, 4788, 4824, 5060, 5841
—(1900-1945), 2365, 2377, 2874, 2986, 3202, 3203, 3306, 3881, 4735, 4902, 5387
—See also Civil War: Confederate-Nurses, Civil War: Union-Nurses, World War I-Nurses, etc.

## O

Office workers (1850-1900), 3257, 4230, 4647, 4749, 5178, 6344
—(1900-1945), 2957, 3231, 5548
—See also Executives
Oil well drillers (1850-1900), 6339
—(1900-1945), 2764, 3088
Oilmen. See Industrialists
Orchestra leaders. See Conductors
Organists. See Musicians
Ornithologists. See Scientists
Ottoman Empire. See Successor states
Outlaws. See Criminals

## P

Pacific states: Actors, 3362, 3453
—Adventurers and vagabonds, 2227, 3480
—Artisans, 930, 3271, 4810, 5541, 6053
—Athletes, 5940
—Bankers, 633, 1101, 1941, 2282, 2334, 2549, 3147, 3495, 5113, 5815
—Bishops and archbishops: Episcopal, 3245, 4239
—Book collectors, 5881
—Childhood reminiscences, 4, 29, 167, 571, 684, 991, 1437, 1477, 1521, 1636, 2553, 3584, 3817, 3897, 4002, 4186, 4265, 5266, 5315, 5616, 5967, 6081
—Church workers, 3314, 4042, 4485, 6181
—Civil servants: State, 1796, 3389. U.S., 416, 585, 677, 2031
—Clergymen: Denomination undetermined, 2666, 4412. Baptist, 5567, 6083. Catholic priests, 771. Christian Church, 2905. Congregational, 666, 704, 891, 4588. Episcopal, 591, 4021, 4437, 4769, 5871, 5994, 6044. Lutheran, 3310, 5238, 6370. Methodist, 119, 1557, 2112, 2565, 2847, 3105, 3189, 3212, 3904, 4471, 5634, 5635, 5792, 6003, 6150. Minor sects, 5208. Mormon, 3943. Nazarene, 5850. Presbyterian, 1320, 3520, 6173, 6174, 6175, 6176, 6280. Quaker, 4137, 6229. Seventh Day Adventist, 5544. Unitarian, 110, 6054. United Brethren, 5234. Universalist, 1496
—Clubwomen, 3408
—College presidents, 1599, 3108

SUBJECT INDEX 357 Pacific States

Pacific States (cont.): College professors, 235, 1863, 2336, 3414, 3779, 4437, 4924
—Composers, 564
—Cowboys, 1447
—Criminals, 509, 510, 1208, 1306, 1407, 4126, 5529, 5612
—Dentists, 913
—Detectives, 6104
—Diplomats, 677, 1344
—Doctors, 20, 1124, 1163, 1309, 1640, 2418, 2579, 2683, 3579, 3580, 4832, 6097, 6231
—Domestic relations, 19, 132, 251, 274, 343, 726, 1783, 2033, 2300, 2752, 2995, 3548, 5373, 5616
—Educators, 1155, 3212, 3389, 4500, 5582, 5871, 6173
—Engineers, 716, 4913
—Evangelists, 4048, 5850, 6162
—Farm leaders, 4537
—Farmers and farm life, 585, 618, 633, 696, 771, 808, 810, 992, 1076, 1149, 1234, 1520, 1636, 1688, 1874, 2112, 2300, 2444, 2553, 2558, 2564, 2609, 2643, 2772, 2864, 3025, 3033, 3123, 3183, 3189, 3415, 3575, 3649, 3788, 3849, 3925, 3926, 4642, 4673, 4807, 4940, 5053, 5120, 5143, 5294, 5453, 5495, 5544, 5638, 6053
—Financiers, 5, 416, 3474
—Firemen, 2583
—Governors, 810
—Historians, 281, 5881
—Hotels and inns, proprietors and workers, 618, 2472, 4940, 6216
—Hunters and trappers, 35, 75, 92, 273, 939, 962, 1107, 2873, 2932, 3189, 4078, 4210, 4243, 4452
—Immigrants: Australian, 5621. Danish, 5257. English, 24, 4193, 6337. French, 5214. German, 1250, 1985, 2609. Hungarian, 4934. Norwegian, 4259. Swedish, 1584
—Indian agents, 939
—Indian fighters, 135, 719, 737, 939, 942, 2403, 2444, 2642, 2804, 4673, 4807, 5687, 6057
—Indians, 2760
—Indians, life among, 979, 3998, 5831
—Industrialists, 883, 1334, 1482, 1592, 1749, 2523, 2549, 2552, 2553, 2772, 3147, 4232, 5160, 5861
—Inventors, 4913
—Jews, 3474, 4227
—Journalists, 228, 414, 2271, 2594, 3170, 3218, 3305, 3401, 3788, 3979, 4003, 4152, 4323, 4324, 4439, 5532, 5685, 6021, 6290
—Judges: Branch undetermined, 5101. Local, 3878. State, 810, 1922, 2953

—Labor leaders, 22, 4904
—Laborers, 2444, 2609, 5053, 5918
—Lawyers, 414, 649, 1319, 1344, 1415, 2282, 2780, 3527, 3679, 4061, 4193, 4270, 4894, 5101, 6282
—Lecturers, 2527, 4140
—Librarians, 589
—Lumbermen, 152, 1520, 3431, 4259, 5294, 5811
—Merchants, 608, 696, 832, 1447, 1482, 1608, 1611, 1796, 2014, 2151, 2296, 2334, 2410, 2441, 2443, 2444, 2472, 3861, 3902, 3924, 4163, 4227, 4452, 4536, 4674, 4921, 4922, 4934, 5113, 5257, 5294, 5621, 5831, 5861, 5989, 6053, 6112
—Miners and mining life, 5, 92, 228, 275, 422, 583, 585, 718, 719, 883, 929, 930, 942, 1011, 1049, 1357, 1499, 1503, 1508, 1513, 1531, 1549, 1605, 1608, 1638, 1657, 1773, 1874, 1902, 1952, 2031, 2114, 2151, 2153, 2403, 2410, 2418, 2437, 2443, 2469, 2479, 2529, 2621, 2670, 2689, 2711, 2873, 2932, 3165, 3180, 3189, 3235, 3244, 3273, 3431, 3485, 3494, 3559, 3709, 3804, 3849, 3861, 3873, 3882, 3902, 3911, 3964, 4152, 4230, 4243, 4450, 4522, 4527, 4547, 4598, 4619, 4644, 4947, 5046, 5101, 5143, 5198, 5232, 5316, 5369, 5453, 5495, 5541, 5572, 5770, 5918, 5954, 5973, 6016, 6031, 6065, 6066, 6081, 6135, 6168, 6181, 6205, 6218
—See also Forty-niners
—Missionaries: Methodist, 6090. Minor sects, 6085, 6086, 6087
—Music teachers, 108
—Musicians, 6338
—Negroes, 29, 122, 2151, 6181
—Novelists, 204, 3312
—Nuns: Catholic, 5060
—Nurses, 3202, 3203, 3881, 5060
—Oil well drillers, 6339
—Painters, 3259
—Peace officers, 2325, 4030
—Philanthropists, 177
—Photographers, 1156, 2137
—Pioneers, 4, 19, 20, 92, 135, 167, 251, 273, 337, 343, 413, 414, 480, 481, 571, 583, 585, 633, 684, 719, 810, 883, 929, 939, 991, 992, 1049, 1107, 1147, 1149, 1234, 1237, 1250, 1320, 1357, 1377, 1415, 1482, 1503, 1508, 1520, 1521, 1549, 1608, 1874, 1902, 1922, 1952, 2033, 2112, 2133, 2153, 2259, 2326, 2403, 2410, 2429, 2437, 2443, 2451, 2472, 2479, 2553, 2558, 2642, 2711, 2864, 2873, 2914, 2932, 3123, 3189, 3235, 3244, 3273, 3375, 3415, 3431, 3485, 3494, 3548, 3559, 3575, 3584, 3709, 3817, 3849,

Pacific states: Pioneers (cont.), 3873, 3878, 3882, 3902, 3911, 3924, 3925, 3926, 3964, 4078, 4152, 4186, 4226, 4243, 4409, 4450, 4452, 4522, 4527, 4536, 4552, 4673, 4807, 4921, 4922, 4940, 4947, 5046, 5101, 5120, 5143, 5155, 5198, 5202, 5315, 5316, 5453, 5531, 5541, 5572, 5573, 5621, 5687, 5752, 5831, 5954, 5958, 5967, 6016, 6031, 6044, 6063, 6066, 6081, 6090, 6135, 6173, 6174, 6175, 6176, 6203, 6205, 6216, 6218, 6243, 6280
—Playwrights, 122
—Poets, 235, 484
—Politicians, 5, 416, 480, 929, 1149, 1237, 1319, 1344, 1447, 2132, 2441, 2479, 4030, 4552, 4894, 5531
—Printers, 228, 2271, 2523, 3733, 4162
—Prisoners, 509, 510, 3334, 3608, 4095, 5612
—Prostitutes and fallen women, 5626
—Publishers, 228, 281, 674, 1691, 4323, 4324, 4552, 5918, 6021
—Railroad workers, 2031, 2035, 2479
—Ranchers and ranch life, 254, 696, 1234, 1250, 1415, 1426, 1447, 1520, 1579, 1646, 1657, 2300, 2326, 2451, 2553, 3638, 3788, 3804, 4180, 4186, 4940, 5120, 5191, 5202, 5315, 5842, 5843, 5844, 5958, 5967, 6203
—Real estate dealers and promoters, 585, 607, 618, 2472, 2479, 2549, 2579, 3147, 3494, 3644, 4879, 4934, 5160, 5573, 5815
—Representatives: State, 649, 1922, 2953. U.S., 6282
—Restaurants and taverns, proprietors and workers, 1608
—Salesmen, 26, 3331, 3644, 4030, 5861
—Scientists, 793, 1781, 3414, 3692
—Scouts, U.S. Army, 2873, 4210
—Senators: U.S., 1147, 3814
—Showmen, 2216, 3411
—Singers, 108, 1985, 5214
—Social reformers, 4095, 4323, 6083
—Social-workers, 585, 2390, 4840, 5613
—Socialites, 4215, 5571
—Soldiers, 939, 6057
—Soldiers' wives, 5025, 5155, 5752
—Spiritualists, 5616
—Sportsmen, 3197, 3508
—Suffragists, 1691, 2473
—Surveyors, 2437, 6016
—Tailors, 1526
—Teachers, 337, 411, 633, 1155, 1319, 1636, 2643, 3189, 3917, 4500, 4642, 4832, 5202, 5582, 6063
—Teamsters, 3861, 4940, 5120
—Temperance workers, 480, 2527, 4927
—Woodsmen and guides, 939

Painters (to 1800), 6062
—(1800–1850), 1694, 2463, 3468, 4490, 5763
—(1850–1900), 109, 179, 430, 792, 998, 1054, 2128, 2568, 3259, 3573, 3602, 3603, 5114, 5212, 5418, 5483, 5862
—(1900–1945), 118, 144, 392, 449, 476, 654, 1070, 1450, 1819, 1820, 2052, 3129, 3196, 4066, 4141, 4183, 4920, 6126, 6289
—See also Illustrators
Paleontologists. See Scientists
Palestine. See Israel
Panama (1800–1850), 2418
—(1900–1945), 1172, 1233, 3107, 4941
Paralytics. See Physically handicapped
Pathologists. See Doctors
Peace officers (1800–1850), 1274, 1275, 5189
—(1850–1900), 56, 203, 322, 644, 892, 907, 1213, 1511, 1697, 2028, 2173, 2325, 2552, 2999, 3113, 3225, 3616, 3677, 3703, 3885, 4347, 4418, 4559, 4578, 4982, 5368, 5405, 5455, 5558, 5617, 6188, 6213, 6315
—(1900–1945), 2453, 3106, 4030, 4249, 5524
—See also Detectives, Policemen
Peddlers. See Merchants
Penologists. See Social reformers
Perjurers. See Criminals
Persia. See Aden, Iran
Peru (1850–1900), 51
—(1900–1945), 5395, 5396
Philanthropists (to 1800), 1748
—(1800–1850), 5856
—(1850–1900), 566, 923, 1261, 2647, 4864, 5536, 5961, 5977
—(1900–1945), 177, 272, 459, 1070, 1801, 2363, 3072, 3623
—See also Social reformers, Social workers
Philippines (1850–1900), 4405, 4976
—(1900–1945), 499, 578, 1102, 1118, 1446, 2069, 2580, 2823, 3130, 3469, 3564, 4275, 4610, 4748, 4880, 5025, 6276
Philosophers (1850–1900), 3856, 4406, 4946, 5022, 5346, 5347
—(1900–1945), 5023, 6179
—See also Professors, Theologians
Photographers (1850–1900), 1534, 2028, 2949, 2950, 3300, 4977, 5134
—(1900–1945), 76, 100, 1064, 1156, 1303, 1604, 2137, 3049, 3050, 4289, 4488, 4601, 5068
Physical culturists (1850–1900), 211, 4150
—(1900–1945), 3947
Physically handicapped (1800–1850), 175, 597, 997, 1280, 1281, 2602, 2603, 2800, 5745, 6269

SUBJECT INDEX 359 Physically handicapped–Pioneers

Physically handicapped (cont.): (1850–1900), 176, 604, 875, 2061, 2286, 2546, 2599, 3013, 3156, 3266, 4246, 4435, 4993, 5111, 5255, 5583
—(1900–1945), 538, 651, 1400, 2057, 2058, 2450, 2547, 2575, 2750, 3157, 3404, 3595, 4318, 4556, 4620, 5057, 5854, 5984
—See also Illnesses, accounts of
Physicians. See Doctors
Physicists. See Scientists
Pianists. See Musicians
Pilots, aircraft. See Aviators
Pioneers, 15, 413, 414, 480, 481, 655, 800, 811, 981, 1406, 1571, 1611, 1657, 1922, 2133, 2179, 2266, 2334, 2421, 2751, 2815, 2859, 2914, 2918, 3360, 3597, 3691, 3697, 3703, 3791, 3878, 3898, 3990, 4171, 4226, 4236, 4244, 4280, 4369, 4387, 4409, 4552, 4893, 5007, 5109, 5261, 5351, 5531, 5573, 6216, 6243, 6350
—Artisans, 4973, 5461, 5541
—Childhood reminiscences, 4, 167, 432, 567, 570, 571, 613, 629, 684, 827, 991, 1067, 1521, 1641, 1658, 1670, 1924, 2106, 2211, 2429, 2491, 2553, 2816, 2868, 2894, 2972, 3205, 3584, 3635, 3817, 3999, 4136, 4186, 4350, 4351, 4571, 5315, 5342, 5593, 5829, 5945, 5967, 6012, 6081, 6206
—Clergymen, 408, 666, 755, 1248, 1320, 1554, 1927, 1928, 2112, 2166, 2172, 2396, 2664, 2733, 3002, 3706, 4926, 5146, 5234, 5625, 5669, 5812, 5917, 6042, 6044, 6090, 6173, 6174, 6175, 6176, 6280, 6348
—Cowboys, 446, 1215, 1216, 2153, 3372, 3586, 3885, 3910, 4425
—Doctors, 20, 957, 2418, 5670
—Domestic relations, 19, 69, 251, 343, 394, 807, 933, 934, 1377, 2154, 2933, 3241, 3251, 3548, 3631, 3783, 4007, 4071, 4576, 4693, 4902, 5155, 5305, 5562, 5752, 5826, 5875, 5887
—Farmers and farm life, 105, 379, 451, 570, 585, 687, 706, 810, 815, 827, 869, 937, 992, 1010, 1062, 1067, 1149, 1168, 1214, 1234, 1422, 1443, 1520, 1540, 1658, 1670, 1685, 1772, 1874, 1924, 2010, 2028, 2053, 2106, 2112, 2172, 2187, 2190, 2197, 2205, 2206, 2211, 2233, 2302, 2343, 2444, 2491, 2500, 2528, 2553, 2558, 2654, 2864, 2894, 2920, 2933, 2978, 3113, 3123, 3189, 3313, 3358, 3375, 3415, 3432, 3559, 3575, 3635, 3693, 3809, 3848, 3849, 3925, 3926, 3948, 4071, 4128, 4136, 4258, 4262, 4328, 4424, 4472, 4571, 4578, 4673, 4693, 4807, 4885, 4927, 4940, 5120, 5143, 5283, 5286, 5351, 5406, 5429, 5453, 5461, 5512, 5535, 5593, 5703, 5788, 5812, 5826, 5828, 5829, 5887, 5920, 5928, 5945, 6009, 6012, 6049, 6182
—Hunters and trappers, 90, 92, 97, 273, 301, 310, 402, 500, 576, 939, 1107, 1121, 1215, 1216, 1340, 1759, 1763, 1909, 2028, 2226, 2433, 2466, 2873, 2876, 2932, 2964, 2968, 2970, 3048, 3189, 3432, 3463, 3848, 3924, 4078, 4213, 4243, 4452, 4801, 4883, 4916, 4967, 5250, 5570, 5605, 5715–5716, 5849, 5892, 6206, 6294, 6359
—Indian fighters, 90, 97, 135, 301, 307, 332, 362, 379, 500, 576, 789, 958, 1340, 1763, 1778, 2098, 2285, 2355, 2403, 2433, 2444, 2466, 2642, 2723, 2840, 3048, 3372, 3575, 3606, 3848, 4425, 4494, 4673, 4807, 4916, 5250, 5286, 5332, 5377, 5478, 5530, 5570, 5617, 5661, 5687, 5892, 6203, 6206, 6294, 6359
—Indians, life among, 5605, 5831, 6206
—Journalists, 1659, 4152
—Laborers, 4213
—Lawyers, 138
—Lumbermen, 1520, 3375, 3431, 4213
—Merchants, 178, 1169, 1482, 2321, 2433, 2443, 2444, 2472, 2601, 2747, 2829, 2968, 3364, 3432, 3463, 3899, 3902, 3924, 4018, 4328, 4452, 4536, 4571, 4921, 4922, 4927, 4988, 5201, 5537, 5605, 5621, 5788, 5831, 5928, 6011
—Miners and mining life, 5, 92, 432, 583, 585, 719, 883, 929, 1049, 1503, 1508, 1549, 1594, 1608, 1874, 1902, 1952, 2028, 2153, 2257, 2259, 2403, 2410, 2420, 2437, 2443, 2479, 2711, 2723, 2873, 2932, 3180, 3189, 3235, 3244, 3273, 3431, 3485, 3494, 3559, 3709, 3849, 3873, 3882, 3889, 3902, 3910, 3911, 3964, 4152, 4243, 4450, 4522, 4527, 4571, 4947, 5046, 5101, 5143, 5198, 5407, 5453, 5476, 5502, 5537, 5541, 5572, 5661, 5724, 5757, 5860, 5892, 5954, 5972, 6016, 6031, 6033, 6066, 6081, 6135, 6185, 6205, 6218, 6315
—See also Forty-niners
—Peace officers, 14, 56, 203, 322, 644, 892, 907, 1213, 1511, 2028, 2173, 2325, 2552, 2999, 3113, 3225, 3677, 3885, 4578, 5189, 5368, 5455, 5558, 5617, 6315
—Politicians, 273, 810, 995, 3075
—Ranchers and ranch life, 642, 869, 1169, 1215, 1216, 1234, 1250, 1415, 1520, 2124, 2326, 2451, 2840, 2934, 2970, 3048, 3311, 3586, 3638, 4282, 5120, 5202, 5250, 5315, 5537, 5617, 5860, 5958, 5967, 6183, 6203
—Real estate dealers and promoters,

Pioneers: Real estate dealers and promoters, 2114, 3494
—Teachers, 337, 1171, 2591, 2978, 3466, 5481, 5829, 6063
—Teamsters, 3372, 3533, 4973, 4983, 5024, 5120, 5570, 5724, 6206, 6315
—Woodsmen and guides, 939, 1215, 5570, 6206, 6294
Pirates. See Criminals
Plantation life, 833, 1528, 2582, 3427, 3447, 3944, 4117, 4514, 4579, 5266, 6252
—See also Slaves
Playwrights (to 1800), 1695
—(1850-1900), 692, 1074, 5930
—(1900-1945), 122, 1137, 1353, 1474, 1509, 2187, 2210, 3278, 3294, 3778, 3802, 4286, 4530, 4583, 5280, 5515, 5659, 5865
Poets: Date undetermined, 1700
—(1800-1850), 1007, 1134, 1430, 4203, 5204, 5493
—(1850-1900), 484, 1326, 1363, 2554, 2555, 3181, 3451, 3514, 3526, 4480, 4756, 4804, 5314, 5330, 5364, 5498, 5636, 5759, 5789, 6115, 6131, 6142, 6143
—(1900-1945), 235, 1087, 1265, 1423, 2057, 2058, 2177, 2850, 2916, 3041, 3177, 3294, 3462, 3517, 3518, 3595, 3599, 3767, 3807, 3859, 3886, 4046, 4094, 4339, 4473, 4620, 4778, 4936, 5018, 5053, 5441, 5442, 5515, 5538, 5699, 5851, 6089, 6121, 6259, 6336, 6345
Prisoners. See Criminals
Poland (1900-1945), 27, 549, 5784
Police magistrates. See Judges
Policemen: Date undetermined, 4164
—(1850-1900), 296, 1094, 2502, 2797, 5933
—(1900-1945), 5557
—See also Detectives, Peace officers
Politicians (to 1800), 286, 473, 2016, 2290, 3137, 3753, 4942
—(1800-1850), 273, 381, 386, 494, 1402, 1569, 1622, 1623, 2428, 3075, 4185, 4552, 4849, 5109, 5751, 6017
—(1850-1900), 5, 138, 264, 361, 379, 416, 480, 521, 604, 706, 751, 759, 929, 976, 1058, 1081, 1149, 1171, 1237, 1266, 1304, 1319, 1344, 1351, 1379, 1436, 1447, 1476, 1588, 1592, 1714, 1745, 1912, 2133, 2151, 2194, 2292, 2299, 2305, 2358, 2397, 2441, 2479, 2488, 2576, 3118, 3281, 3288, 3311, 3448, 3714, 3755, 3766, 3785, 3830, 3893, 3950, 3951, 4158, 4253, 4408, 4475, 4516, 4572, 4586, 4595, 4745, 4754, 4894, 4966, 5069, 5088, 5125, 5134, 5178, 5196, 5232,
5263, 5330, 5364, 5412, 5454, 5488, 5531, 5537, 5892, 5927, 5950, 6200, 6247
—(1900-1945), 12, 215, 307, 764, 845, 1110, 1183, 1188, 1229, 1230, 1341, 1381, 1428, 1788, 1872, 2375, 2438, 2665, 2899, 2909, 3149, 3210, 3255, 3335, 3402, 3413, 3704, 3828, 3942, 3966, 4027, 4030, 4081, 4091, 4154, 4274, 4582, 4705, 4706, 5254, 5576, 5743, 5809, 5853, 6000, 6046, 6272
—See also Cabinet Members, U.S., Governors, Mayors, Presidents—U.S., Representatives, Senators, Vice-Presidents—U.S.
Politicians' wives (1800-1850), 1738
—(1850-1900), 1713, 2687, 3030, 3556, 4668, 6253
—(1900-1945), 512, 527, 1146, 1425, 1970, 3207, 3578, 4907, 5591, 6204
Pony express riders. See Pioneers
Porto Rico. See Puerto Rico
Preachers. See Clergymen
Presidents (1850-1900), 3509
—(1900-1945), 4909
—See also Cabinet Members: U.S., Vice-Presidents: U.S.
Priests. See Clergymen: Catholic Priests
Principals, school. See Educators
Printers (to 1800), 2016
—(1800-1850), 4269
—(1850-1900), 228, 244, 1037, 1144, 1297, 1361, 1849, 2176, 2211, 2271, 2427, 2522, 2523, 2893, 3418, 3526, 4013, 4014, 4162, 4224, 4324, 4648, 4794, 4839, 4926, 5008, 5009, 5149, 5383, 6028
—(1900-1945), 2757, 3733, 4335, 4758, 5353
—See also Booksellers, Publishers
Prison officials (1800-1850), 2208
—(1850-1900), 3618
—(1900-1945), 3382
Prisoners (to 1800), 1936
—(1800-1850), 3735, 5362, 6277
—(1850-1900), 928, 1211, 1384, 1699, 1963, 2175, 2462, 2648, 2997, 3039, 3086, 3341, 3758, 3801, 4062, 4095, 4209, 4287, 4531, 4774, 5723, 6200, 6360, 6361
—(1900-1945), 330, 455, 509, 510, 577, 814, 849, 1053, 1401, 1491, 1493, 1682, 1949, 2094, 2219, 2613, 3012, 3095, 3334, 3608, 3879, 4012, 4166, 4191, 4211, 5085, 5195, 5612, 6025, 6129, 6305
Privateers (to 1800), 148
—(1800-1850), 6329
Producers, motion picture and theatrical. See Showmen
Professors. See College Professors

SUBJECT INDEX 361 Prohibitionists—Religious journalists

Prohibitionists. See Temperance workers.
Prostitutes and fallen women: Date undetermined, 1558
— (to 1800), 61
— (1800-1850), 153
— (1900-1945), 606, 3404, 3676, 5138, 5626
Psychiatrists. See Doctors
Psychologists. See Scientists
Psychotics. See Mentally ill
Public relations men. See Advertisers and public relations men
Publishers (to 1800), 2016
— (1800-1850), 637, 960, 1338, 2234, 2710, 2809, 4552, 4580, 5662
— (1850-1900), 104, 213, 228, 281, 435, 532, 956, 1030, 1196, 1297, 1455, 1564, 1691, 2113, 2182, 2238, 2271, 2482, 2736, 2893, 3222, 3346, 3354, 3713, 3785, 3869, 4013, 4014, 4516, 4586, 4679, 4912, 5008, 5009, 5130, 5196, 5406, 5526, 5918, 6355
— (1900-1945), 101, 103, 127, 320, 674, 1179, 1286, 1603, 1693, 1718, 1719, 2236, 2270, 2393, 2493, 2503, 3335, 3413, 3841, 3909, 4237, 4294, 4323, 4324, 4480, 4643, 4680, 4941, 4959, 5606, 5653, 5779, 5902, 6021, 6258
—See also Booksellers, Printers
Puerto Rico, 197
Pugilists. See Athletes
Pullman porters. See Railroad workers

# R

Rabbis. See Clergymen: Jewish
Racketeers. See Criminals
Radicals. See Anarchists, Communists, Socialists, Social reformers
Radio announcers and operators, 2495, 2892, 3821, 4404, 5050, 5384
Railroad engineers. See Engineers. For locomotive engineers see Railroad workers
Railroad workers (1800-1850), 2117
— (1850-1900), 254, 575, 644, 717, 834, 924, 925, 1398, 1859, 2031, 2067, 2139, 2479, 2574, 2897, 3025, 3596, 4291, 4561, 4564, 4606, 4750, 5027, 5369, 5668, 5712, 5857, 6281, 6346
— (1900-1945), 678, 703, 2035, 2250, 3127, 3467, 3568, 3894, 3971, 6082
Ranchers and ranch life (1800-1850), 1250, 2326, 3638
— (1850-1900), 56, 72, 93, 254, 321, 363, 377, 585, 604, 607, 631, 642, 679, 683, 696, 699, 791, 869, 912, 1066, 1083, 1101, 1164, 1166, 1169, 1170, 1204, 1215, 1216,
1234, 1346, 1415, 1447, 1520, 1574, 1641, 1657, 2065, 2124, 2128, 2255, 2294, 2300, 2451, 2476, 2553, 2771, 2840, 2908, 2934, 2963, 2970, 3048, 3300, 3311, 3338, 3348, 3376, 3586, 3613, 3788, 3804, 3882, 3988, 4086, 4180, 4186, 4282, 4319, 4589, 4604, 4614, 4615, 4764, 4875, 4883, 4940, 5120, 5191, 5202, 5250, 5315, 5492, 5537, 5617, 5860, 5958, 5967, 6074, 6183, 6188, 6203
— (1900-1945), 81, 118, 312, 876, 914, 968, 1086, 1366, 1426, 1579, 1797, 1821, 2362, 2417, 2530, 2846, 3230, 3381, 3643, 4465, 4708, 4709, 4805, 5643, 5842, 5843, 5844, 5942, 5960, 6373
—See also Cowboys
Rapists. See Criminals
Real estate dealers and promoters (1800-1850), 273, 2099, 3161, 3494, 4203, 5573, 5753
— (1850-1900), 149, 618, 926, 1011, 1534, 1940, 1991, 2085, 2114, 2472, 2479, 2549, 2578, 3042, 3047, 3052, 3914, 4209, 4520, 4579, 5160, 5712, 5815, 5968, 6049
— (1900-1945), 23, 249, 2579, 2908, 3147, 3644, 3860, 3966, 4879, 4934, 5449
—See also Salesmen
Reconstruction, 80, 1058, 1183, 1207, 2039, 2305, 2306, 2717, 2963, 4553, 4717, 5959, 6159
—See also Civil War
Red Cross officials. See Social workers
Reformers. See Social reformers
Religious conversions. See Conversions
Religious experiences (to 1800), 1044, 1758, 2856, 3426, 3750, 5310, 6091, 6172
— (1800-1850), 28, 156, 623, 700, 788, 857, 1376, 1601, 1777, 1841, 2602, 2603, 2790, 2884, 2911, 3472, 3536, 3617, 4159, 4675, 4790, 5325, 5334, 5335, 5336, 5337, 5622, 5955, 6145
— (1850-1900), 49, 110, 191, 242, 405, 643, 740, 804, 906, 1077, 1178, 1255, 1365, 1514, 1747, 1849, 3097, 3098, 3184, 3216, 3248, 3391, 3544, 3634, 3694, 3698, 3809, 3956, 4062, 4075, 4322, 4608, 4969, 5033, 5247, 5273, 5279, 6093, 6178
— (1900-1945), 49, 117, 120, 198, 317, 559, 592, 1223, 1587, 1605, 1722, 1958, 2090, 2110, 2773, 3100, 3155, 3221, 3531, 3744, 3846, 3921, 4059, 4166, 5399, 5747, 5925, 6187
—See also Conversions
Religious journalists (1800-1850), 3423, 4483, 4587, 5268, 5505, 5917, 5955
— (1850-1900), 11, 110, 184, 319, 707, 1284, 1397, 2113, 2156, 2198, 2237, 2387, 3066, 3318, 4065, 4658, 4780, 5600, 6238, 6306
— (1900-1945), 336, 424, 865, 866, 867,

Religious journalists (1900-1945)(cont.), 1314, 1314A, 1663, 2054, 3651, 4905, 5384
—See also Clergymen as authors
Reporters. See Journalists
Representatives: State (to 1800), 5603, 5916. (1800-1850), 995, 2828, 3763a, 4379. (1850-1900), 372, 535, 550, 607, 649, 723, 1153, 1172, 1824, 1922, 2259, 2356, 2526, 2570, 2636, 2658, 2953, 2975, 3313, 4049, 5969, 6065. (1900-1945), 2373, 2676, 3657, 5794, 5915
—U.S. (to 1800), 5901, 5916. (1800-1850), 766, 1339, 2179, 3410, 4773, 5040, 6015. (1850-1900), 418, 488, 594, 840, 902, 1295, 1335, 1464, 1467, 1647, 1714, 2221, 2309, 2346, 2538, 2887, 3056, 3076, 3351, 3849, 4311, 4858, 5176, 5742, 5768, 5897, 6014. (1900-1945), 329, 340, 415, 1050, 1148, 1404, 2025, 3350, 4805, 6127, 6282
—See also Politicians
Restaurants and taverns, proprietors and workers: Date undetermined, 1558, 3383
—(to 1800), 812
—(1850-1900), 826, 1608, 2131, 2702, 2823, 4865, 5189
—(1900-1945), 420, 1013, 1299, 3158, 3653, 3675, 3831
Revolutionary War. See American Revolution
Riverboat men. See Seamen: Merchant
Robbers. See Criminals
Rogues. See Adventurers and vagabonds
Rumania (1900-1945), 367
Russia (1800-1850), 1711
—(1850-1900), 1383, 1995, 2398, 5839, 6088
—(1900-1945), 376, 486, 549, 1364, 1550, 1906, 2439, 2484, 2513, 3132, 3133, 3535, 4822, 5076, 5527, 5581, 5894
Rustlers. See Criminals

# S

Sailors. See Seamen
Salesmen (1800-1850), 2314
—(1850-1900), 26, 360, 484, 647, 659, 780, 1333, 1619, 1678, 2426, 2563, 2746, 2956, 3047, 3062, 3094, 3139, 3331, 3960, 4248, 4272, 4394, 4396, 5067, 5666, 6032, 6313
—(1900-1945), 23, 318, 328, 803, 989, 1063, 2270, 2545, 2903, 3593, 3644, 3860, 4030, 4123, 4403, 4469, 4665, 5230, 5274, 5449, 5861, 5931, 5942
—See also Merchants, Real estate dealers and promoters

Salvation Army Officials. See Social workers
Samoa (1900-1945), 2042, 3469
Santo Domingo. See Dominican Republic
Saudi Arabia (1900-1945), 2514
Scientists (to 1800), 6048
—(1800-1850), 216, 2347, 2651, 2680, 3581, 3974, 4638, 4702, 5209
—(1850-1900), 91, 641, 817, 1383, 1387, 1548, 2104, 2284, 2401, 2425, 2526, 2739, 2770, 3108, 3165, 3172, 3414, 3436, 3532, 3614, 3692, 4219, 4271, 4297, 4671, 5087, 5457, 5858, 6152, 6306, 6314
—(1900-1945), 48, 57, 146, 147, 269, 291, 403, 793, 1006, 1026, 1098, 1330, 1552, 1568, 1770, 1781, 1862, 2047, 2516, 2802, 2824, 2890, 3317, 3523, 3796, 3824, 4099, 4177, 4331, 4355, 4474, 4481, 4482, 4496, 4653, 4672, 5086, 5217, 5419, 5458, 5563, 5574, 5680, 6107, 6365
—See also College professors
School administrators. See Educators
School teachers. See College professors, Teachers
Scotland (1900-1945), 2227
Scouts: U.S. Army (1850-1900), 90, 362, 800, 1121, 1203, 1215, 1216, 1644, 1645, 2355, 2476, 2551, 2767, 2873, 3482, 4055, 4210, 5524
—See also Indian fighters, Soldiers
Sculptors (1850-1900), 276, 4991
—(1900-1945), 1756, 1823, 2052, 2695, 4411, 5093, 6126
Seamen: Merchant—Date undetermined, 4293
—(to 1800), 113, 114, 201, 286, 441, 473, 1471, 4492, 5171
—(1800-1850), 34, 106, 275, 310, 344, 653, 943, 1111, 1227, 1280, 1388, 1421, 1489, 1642, 1711, 1754, 1868, 2455, 2658, 2821, 2931, 2993, 3079, 3169, 3336, 3342, 3588, 3601, 4036, 4214, 4235, 4236, 4269, 4407, 4451, 4491, 4540, 5001, 5114, 5236, 5237, 5349, 5728, 5963, 6047, 6165, 6297
—(1850-1900), 342, 522, 536, 705, 880, 1129, 1132, 1202, 1315, 1461, 1560, 1736, 2097, 2136, 2419, 2454, 2475, 2523, 2624, 3187, 3269, 3406, 3418, 3434, 3486, 3600, 3867, 3945, 4140, 4300, 4390, 4396, 4492, 4547, 4548, 4568, 4691, 4711, 4723, 4814, 4815, 4976, 5003, 5189, 5190, 5248, 5545, 5908, 5973, 6067, 6078, 6163, 6251
—(1900-1945), 443, 1186, 1226, 1300, 1367, 1488, 1529, 2521, 3051, 3759, 3872, 4443, 4716, 4823, 5245, 5960, 6005, 6302
—See also Privateers, Slavers, Whalers
Seamen: U.S. (to 1800), 113, 114, 2822
—(1800-1850), 790, 1828, 2258, 2566, 2711,

Seamen: U.S. (1800-1850)(cont.), 2896,
  3639, 3941, 4101, 4771, 5144, 5491, 6237
—(1850-1900), 115, 294, 434, 536, 777,
  1052, 1315, 1546, 1846, 1943, 2017, 2232,
  2374, 3688, 3865, 4430, 4463, 4547,
  4858, 4976, 5011, 5056, 5065, 5112,
  5124, 5430, 5675
—(1900-1945), 1232, 1300, 1720, 1842,
  1847, 2042, 2073, 2078, 3425, 3686,
  4392, 4610, 4822, 4833, 4881, 5490,
  5584, 6153
—See also specific wars, e.g., Civil War:
  Union-Navy, World War I-Navy, etc.
Seamstresses. See Tailors
Second World War. See World War II
Secretaries. See Office workers
Senators: State (1850-1900), 415, 1903,
  1997, 2001, 2346, 2807, 3186, 5789,
  6088, 6232-6233
—(1900-1945), 158, 1179, 1719, 1728, 2362,
  3860, 6121, 6285
Senators: U.S. (1800-1850), 448, 3626,
  4315
—(1850-1900), 461, 488, 750, 900, 1147,
  1368, 2064, 2105, 2684, 3083, 4572,
  4741, 5069, 5126, 5176, 5476
—(1900-1945), 1969, 3320, 3567, 3814,
  4264, 4511, 4512, 5213
—See also Politicians
Serbia. See Jugoslavia
Servants (to 1800), 853
—(1800-1850), 1775, 1776, 2340, 2455
—(1850-1900), 2135, 3428
—(1900-1945), 2252, 2512
—See also Laborers
Sexual deviates (1900-1945), 2027, 3511,
  6059
Sheepmen. See Ranchers and ranch life
Sheriffs. See Peace officers
Shoe makers. See Artisans
Showmen (1800-1850), 3621, 5318, 5319,
  5320, 6052, 6266
—(1850-1900), 26, 311, 1121, 1774, 3178,
  3411, 3722, 3723, 4944
—(1900-1945), 542, 626, 2046, 2122, 2210,
  2216, 4689, 4751, 5673, 5801, 5904
Siam. See Thailand
Singers (1850-1900), 9, 108, 302, 503,
  895, 1326, 1985, 2539, 3110, 3163, 3678,
  4098, 4545, 4996, 5021, 5037, 5569
—(1900-1945), 65, 258, 908, 1723, 1805,
  1879, 1880, 2250, 2370, 2801, 3512, 3851,
  3931, 4063, 4349, 5214, 5301, 5615, 5667,
  5719, 5773, 5823, 5914, 6256
Skaters. See Athletes
Slavers, 1643
Slaves, 39, 94, 134, 136, 271, 468, 561,
  720, 749, 754, 826, 1065, 1094, 1502,
  1624, 1625, 1626, 1661, 1901, 2026, 2275,
  2299, 2303, 2310, 2340, 2352, 2436,
  2559, 2569, 2607, 2851, 2940, 2946,
  2951, 3037A, 3055, 3070, 3104, 3111,
  3115, 3140, 3344, 3487, 3558, 3699,
  3731, 3762, 4422, 4507, 4660, 4719,
  4735, 4838, 4843, 4915, 5288, 5326,
  5468, 5481, 5533, 5683, 5764, 5767,
  5790, 5855, 5949, 5992, 6013, 6156,
  6180, 6181, 6195
—See also Negroes, Plantation life
Social reformers: Date undetermined,
  4182
—(to 1800), 1748, 3978, 5290
—(1800-1850), 221, 665, 816, 2311, 2312,
  2347, 2865, 4379
—(1850-1900), 32, 44, 150, 358, 455, 562,
  1707, 1841, 1997, 2186, 2797, 2917, 2921,
  3093, 3101, 3246, 4283, 4432, 4623,
  4821, 5091, 5122, 5473, 5576, 6083,
  6228
—(1900-1945), 44, 45, 688, 1614, 1746,
  2029, 2177, 2322, 2424, 2460, 2769,
  2811, 2925, 2927, 3196, 3519, 3609,
  3803, 4095, 4196, 4323, 4474, 4498,
  4863, 4928, 4961, 4972, 5016, 5017,
  5131, 5140, 5141, 5221, 5275, 5276, 5439,
  5609, 5647, 5735, 5878, 6036, 6152,
  6296, 6336
—See also Abolitionists, Anarchists,
  Church workers, Communists, Philanthropists, Socialists, Suffragists,
  Temperance workers
Social workers: Date undetermined, 4306
—(1850-1900), 42, 366, 428, 469, 495,
  585, 663, 673, 928, 1154, 1336, 1964,
  2274, 2381, 2390, 2690, 2694, 3023,
  3424, 3818, 5536, 5613, 5814
—(1900-1945), 21, 111, 124, 129, 262, 382,
  470, 471, 472, 549, 599, 1538, 1585,
  1677, 1708, 1746, 1863, 2254, 2366,
  2874, 2886, 3000, 3264, 3285, 3592,
  3598, 3701, 3784, 3831, 3832, 3845,
  4122, 4173, 4296, 4410, 4609, 4725,
  4840, 5211, 5275, 5276, 5446, 5507,
  5620, 5895, 5910, 5911, 5936, 6327
Socialists (1850-1900), 3560, 5381, 6028
—(1900-1945), 109, 870, 1493, 1746, 2665,
  2925, 2927, 3594, 3789, 5915, 6224
—See also Anarchists, Communists,
  Social reformers
Socialites (1800-1850), 4688, 5547, 6136
—(1850-1900), 80, 236, 566, 999, 1000,
  2171, 2215, 2260-2261, 2349, 2350, 2510,
  2532, 2882, 3092, 3446, 3662, 3749,
  3816, 3854, 4074, 4111, 4215, 5118, 5413,
  5571, 5913, 6137, 6138
—(1900-1945), 527, 708, 874, 1002, 2091,
  2242, 2265, 2323, 2854, 3984, 4393,
  4438, 5031, 5833, 5835, 5922, 6128,
  6189
—See also Clubwomen, Sportsmen

Soldiers—South Atlantic

Sociologists. See Professors
Soldiers (to 1800), 1518, 3198, 4524
—(1800-1850), 378, 939, 1224, 1569, 1920, 3227, 4389, 5088, 5109, 5203, 5367, 5799, 6051
—(1850-1900), 192, 307, 499, 550, 563, 737, 763, 805, 869, 958, 959, 1012, 1150, 1204, 1235, 1292, 1308, 1359, 1395, 1580, 1582, 1961, 2278, 2293, 2427, 2570, 2580, 2721, 2743, 2910, 3052, 3224, 3277, 3366, 3549, 3587, 3790, 3847, 3887, 3970, 3982, 3983, 4004, 4011, 4151, 4181, 4367, 4423, 4988, 5061, 5073, 5172, 5179, 5403, 5674, 5793, 6057, 6074, 6214
—(1900-1945), 74, 169, 197, 578, 768, 2823, 3037, 3820, 4138, 4275, 4346, 4526, 4882, 6276
—See also Indian fighters, Scouts: U.S. Army, and under specific wars, e.g., World War I—Army, etc.
Soldiers' wives (1850-1900), 265, 474, 475, 609, 933, 934, 1394, 3556, 4995, 5025, 5155, 5562, 5752, 5875
—(1900-1945), 3254, 4050
Song writers. See Composers
South America (1800-1850), 2657
—(1850-1900), 4251, 4299, 5045, 5046, 5161
—(1900-1945), 1373, 1441, 1550, 1552, 2598, 2888, 3483, 3775, 6038, 6118, 6331, 6365
South Atlantic: Abolitionists, 1126
—Adventurers and vagabonds, 142, 252, 550
—Architects, 713, 4017
—Artisans, 4371
—Athletes, 4313
—Authors, 189, 1122, 3916, 4187, 5040, 5900
—Bankers, 2015, 4256
—Bishops and archbishops: Episcopal, 4413-4414
—Cabinet members: U.S., 1429
—Childhood reminiscences, 80, 132, 137, 143, 175, 750, 761, 833, 836, 986, 1099, 1298, 1475, 1882, 1896, 1958, 2582, 2870, 2871, 3562, 3589, 3673, 3936, 4079, 4118, 4175, 4757, 5603, 5752, 5879, 6189, 6328
—Church workers, 129, 315, 568, 786, 1826, 1843, 2938, 6154
—Civil servants: Local, 2461, 4331. State, 3824. U.S., 286, 749, 1877, 3626, 4345, 4418, 6131
—Clergymen: Baptist, 359, 369, 1251, 1257, 1287, 1305, 1399, 1431, 1473, 1480, 1679, 1743, 2064, 2093, 2269, 2534, 2714, 2924, 3011, 3428, 3452, 3766, 4327, 4359, 4569, 4591, 4719, 5175,

364

SUBJECT INDEX

5623, 5738, 6019. Catholic priests, 4043, 4972. Christian Church, 319, 1125, 2193, 2905, 4895, 5669, 5802. Church of Christ, 1668. Congregational, 4663. Denomination undetermined, 1816, 1844, 1901, 2318, 2814. Disciples of Christ, 53, 54, 574, 2763, 3325, 3418, 3768, 4549, 4634. Episcopal, 1435, 1698, 2267, 2268, 2937, 2980, 3852, 4386, 4413-4414, 4755, 5262, 5771, 5806, 6201, 6353. Jewish, 4542, 4694. Lutheran, 1405, 1910, 4107, 5051. Methodist, 133, 157, 365, 417, 547, 548, 711, 802, 854, 1207, 1272, 1284, 1495, 1709, 1893, 2102, 2289, 2320, 2731, 2847, 2992, 3102, 3211, 3318, 3716, 3852, 3874, 4054, 4192, 4229, 4238, 4256, 4544, 4720, 4729, 4799, 4870, 5105, 5162, 5324, 5389, 5474, 5493, 5552, 5602, 5628, 5634, 5748, 5956, 5997, 6095, 6328, 6348. Minor sects, 916, 2121, 2207, 5872, 6281. Presbyterian, 46, 60, 255, 1027, 1089, 1999, 3066, 3883, 4110, 5298, 5341. Quaker, 1259, 1907, 2974, 2982, 3751, 4204, 4795, 6229. United Brethren, 4222, 6018. Universalist, 1084, 3934, 4890.
—Clergymen as authors, 5341
—Clergymen's wives, 6019
—College administrators, 3583
—College presidents, 361, 1399, 1495, 1599, 2178, 2414, 2763, 2955, 3883, 5389
—College professors, 269, 299, 1495, 1764, 1804, 2401, 3067, 3414, 3583, 4331, 4386, 4972, 5173, 5205, 5965, 6050, 6179, 6335
—College students, 1034, 2309, 3562, 5769, 5819, 6255
—Criminals, 200, 931, 1106, 1600, 1999, 2467, 2587
—Detectives, 5405
—Diplomats, 3893, 6247
—Doctors, 73, 299, 367, 835, 1041, 1877, 1932, 5965, 6048, 6050, 6123, 6247
—Doctors' wives, 622, 4605
—Domestic relations, 383, 762, 988, 3045, 3289, 4305, 4395, 4668, 4669, 5382, 6089
—Educators, 1305, 1679, 2064, 2414, 2534, 2982, 3374, 3532, 5416, 5552, 5647, 6019, 6050
—Engineers, 961
—Evangelists, 2199
—Executives, 2189
—Farmers and farm life, 130, 145, 205, 315, 761, 912, 1099, 1127, 1168, 1544, 1989, 2306, 2497, 3149, 4499, 4733, 4835, 6116, 6271
—Governors, 1263, 2179, 2505, 2717, 2985,

SUBJECT INDEX

South Atlantic: Governors (cont.), 3626, 3648, 4311
—Historians, 4542, 5064
—Hotels and inns, proprietors and workers, 145
—Hunters and trappers, 905
—Immigrants: English, 5262. French, 4043. German, 2430, 2627, 5051. Irish, 5341. Scottish, 2924, 4316
—Indian fighters, 550, 905, 1773, 2285, 2804
—Industrialists, 270, 1795, 2627, 5718
—Journalists, 189, 284, 1196, 1427, 1428, 1429, 1858, 3222, 3620, 3937, 3938, 4900, 5263, 5508, 6129, 6247
—Judges: Branch undetermined, 2843. Local, 4311, 4499. State, 554, 680, 6000, 6232-6233. U.S., 488, 3213, 3739
—Labor leaders, 373
—Laborers, 1094
—Lawyers, 361, 415, 488, 613, 680, 750, 1122, 1263, 1623, 1843, 2221, 2505, 2843, 2887, 3112, 3213, 3648, 3739, 3753, 3893, 4256, 4311, 4582, 4625, 5064, 5173, 5800, 5897, 6000, 6232-6233
—Lecturers, 4316, 5647
—Lumbermen, 5232
—Merchants, 62, 87, 270, 749, 1280, 2938, 3427, 4310, 4453, 6061
—Miners and mining life, 23, 961
—Missionaries: Baptist, 2733. Denomination undetermined, 4558. Episcopal, 5909. Mennonite, 5766. Methodist, 1711. Mormon, 1851
—Negroes, 39, 133, 359, 1094, 1251, 1473, 1624, 1625, 1626, 1901, 2026, 2064, 2305, 2306, 2310, 2340, 2569, 2731, 3011, 3115, 3140, 3428, 4229, 4313, 4422, 4507, 4544, 4719, 4735, 5288, 5533, 5647, 5785, 5790, 6095, 6180
—Novelists, 868, 3067
—Nurses, 1183, 4735
—Painters, 144, 1054
—Peace officers, 4418, 5405
—Philanthropists, 566
—Philosophers, 6179
—Physical culturists, 211
—Physically handicapped, 175
—Pioneers, 1168, 2179, 2266, 2285, 5669
—Poets, 3595, 4473, 4756, 5493, 5789, 6131
—Politicians, 286, 361, 1428, 1623, 2305, 3149, 3753, 3766, 4158, 4582, 5196, 5232, 5263, 6000, 6247
—Politicians' wives, 1425, 4668
—Printers, 3733, 5149
—Prisoners, 814, 1493, 2613, 4012, 6129
—Publishers, 1196, 2503, 5196, 5662
—Real estate dealers and promoters,

South Atlantic: Governors-Statesmen

1991, 3860, 3914
—Religious journalists, 1284, 3318
—Representatives: State, 550, 3657, 5603, 5916. U.S., 415, 488, 1464, 2179, 2221, 2309, 2887, 4311, 5040, 5897, 5916
—Restaurants and taverns, proprietors and workers, 4865
—Salesmen, 3860
—Scientists, 48, 3414, 3532, 3824, 4331, 6048
—Senators: State, 415, 3860, 5789, 6232-6233. U.S., 488, 750, 2064, 3626, 3860, 5213
—Social reformers, 5647
—Social workers, 129, 5936
—Socialites, 80, 566, 874, 2242, 4074, 5547, 6189
—Tailors, 1168, 3140, 4310
—Teachers, 401, 681, 786, 912, 1127, 1263, 2567, 2763, 3582, 4120, 4316, 4449, 4756, 5051, 5650, 5709, 5785, 5900, 5983
—Temperance workers, 568, 4735
—Theologians, 4386
Soviet Union. See Russia
Spain (1850-1900), 3281, 5069
—(1900-1945), 376, 598, 1364, 1459, 2465, 3270, 3469, 4816, 5708
Spanish-American War: Army, 169, 499, 578, 737, 763, 768, 970, 976, 1200, 1308, 2069, 2574, 3130, 3292, 3983, 4138, 4346, 4423, 4534, 4882, 4909, 4982, 6214
—Doctors, 1446
—Marine Corps, 3450
—Navy, 294, 1232, 1546, 1846, 5056, 5065
—Nurses, 1752
—War correspondents, 1187, 4399, 4405
Spiritualists (1800-1850), 852
—(1850-1900), 722, 1021, 1022, 1451, 1452, 1522, 2246, 2741, 3074, 3164, 3506, 3530, 4322, 4388, 5188, 5273, 5299, 5372, 5390, 5427, 5616, 5739, 6065
—(1900-1945), 627, 3433, 3629, 4856, 4857, 5348, 6026
Sports coaches, managers, officials. See Athletics officials
Sportsmen (1850-1900), 1883, 2134, 2412, 2718, 3182, 4086, 6120
—(1900-1945), 1524, 2389, 2630, 2631, 2644, 2988, 3144, 3197, 3272, 3508, 4393, 4490, 5734, 6227
—See also Socialites
Stage coach drivers. See Teamsters
Stage designers. See Designers
State government employees and officials. See Governors, and state subdivisions under Civil Servants, Judges, Representatives, Senators. See also Politicians
Statesmen. See Politicians

Stenographers. See Office workers
Streetwalkers. See Prostitutes and fallen women
Strongmen. See Physical culturists
Structural engineers. See Engineers
Students. See Childhood reminiscences, Children, autobiographies by, College students
Suffragists (1850-1900), 528, 1037, 1178, 1691, 2473, 2567, 2812, 3538, 5142, 5269, 5410, 5473, 5585, 6197, 6366
— (1900-1945), 78, 599, 1183, 1609, 2486, 4196
—See also Social reformers
Surgeons. See Doctors
Surveyors (to 1800), 3797
— (1800-1850), 5828
— (1850-1900), 2437, 2918, 3636, 4055, 5945, 5968, 6016
— (1900-1945), 4084
Sweden (1850-1900), 982, 3785
— (1900-1945), 4105
Swimmers. See Athletes
Swindlers. See Criminals
Switzerland (1850-1900), 5540
— (1900-1945), 2465, 4444, 6110, 6211, 6212
Syria (1850-1900), 530, 3009, 3043
— (1900-1945), 918

# T

Tahiti (1900-1945), 476
Tailors (to 1800), 1168, 1422
— (1800-1850), 4310
— (1850-1900), 3140
— (1900-1945), 1526, 1787
Taiwan. See Formosa
Tap dancers. See Dancers
Tavern keepers. See Restaurants and taverns, proprietors and workers
Taxidermists (1900-1945), 57
Teachers: Date undetermined, 411
— (to 1800), 4106, 4747
— (1800-1850), 8, 63, 67, 1075, 1127, 1223, 1325, 2347, 2395, 2591, 2978, 4298, 4316, 4400, 4656, 4789, 5244, 5472, 5488, 5509, 5650, 5660, 5709, 5829, 6316
— (1850-1900), 42, 77, 208, 337, 401, 451, 484, 586, 604, 616, 619, 633, 639, 681, 771, 784, 786, 926, 997, 1042, 1050, 1145, 1171, 1234, 1263, 1319, 1540, 1573, 1577, 1636, 1806, 1807, 1885, 1894, 1966, 2036, 2083, 2281, 2378, 2415, 2452, 2457, 2564, 2567, 2643, 2730, 2763, 2783, 2830, 2935, 2966, 3047, 3058, 3099, 3138, 3151, 3189, 3193, 3229, 3233, 3275, 3302, 3398, 3448, 3466, 3571, 3582, 3633, 3664, 3674, 3737, 3840, 3873, 3900, 3917, 4176, 4340, 4348, 4356, 4378, 4420, 4500, 4685, 4714, 4720, 4756, 4760, 4775, 4832, 4887, 4960, 5005, 5015, 5051, 5127, 5202, 5255, 5338, 5431, 5432, 5449, 5451, 5478, 5481, 5582, 5606, 5775, 5787, 5900, 5902, 5985, 6002, 6063, 6085, 6086, 6087, 6117, 6130, 6133, 6152, 6268, 6324
— (1900-1945), 384, 808, 912, 1019, 1118, 1155, 1833, 1850, 1851, 1929, 1986, 2377, 2556, 2798, 3100, 3135, 3190, 3296, 3367, 3373, 3696, 3940, 4040, 4120, 4157, 4177, 4449, 4642, 5077, 5264, 5267, 5400, 5513, 5590, 5785, 5870, 5983, 6089, 6272, 6354
—See also College professors
Teachers, voice. See Music teachers
Teamsters (1800-1850), 145, 5189
— (1850-1900), 794, 815, 1094, 2797, 3261, 3372, 3533, 3861, 4128, 4351, 4506, 4940, 4973, 4983, 5024, 5120, 5492, 5570, 5724, 6206, 6315, 6346
— (1900-1945), 862, 2250, 5119
Telegraphers (1850-1900), 1304, 3062, 4123
— (1900-1945), 2481, 6368
Temperance workers (to 1800), 3978
— (1800-1850), 2295, 2869, 3015, 3262, 3734, 3787, 4580, 4853, 6277
— (1850-1900), 429, 442, 480, 568, 871, 917, 1360, 1397, 1564, 1629, 1632, 2256, 2380, 2527, 2624, 2632, 2917, 3138, 3354, 3386, 3538, 3758, 3777, 4052, 4075, 4197, 4664, 4713, 4796, 4927, 5136, 5354, 5471, 5473, 6164, 6270
— (1900-1945), 1314, 1314A, 4725, 4735
—See also Social reformers
Tennis players. See Athletes
Texas Rangers. See Peace officers
Thailand (1850-1900), 3875
— (1900-1945), 3870
Theatrical designers. See Designers
Theatrical managers and producers. See Showmen
Theologians (to 1800), 2759, 3750
— (1800-1850), 5296
— (1850-1900), 49, 1664, 3321, 4028, 4386, 4649, 5047, 5282, 5791, 6022, 6023, 6306
— (1900-1945), 49, 2054, 3774, 5443, 5451
—See also Philosophers
Thieves. See Criminals
Tibet (1900-1945), 1814, 5164
Track and field athletes. See Athletes
Traders. See Merchants; Pioneers—Merchants
Trades union officials. See Labor leaders

SUBJECT INDEX 367

Tramps. See Adventurers and vagabonds
Traveling salesmen. See Salesmen
Truck drivers. See Teamsters
Turkey (1800-1850), 2225, 5049
—(1850-1900), 1108, 2434, 2435, 2791, 4436, 5048, 5519, 5976, 6064, 6072
—(1900-1945), 1102, 2119, 2348, 2778, 4091, 4092, 4138, 4271, 4448, 4763, 4949, 5180, 5818

## U

Undertakers. See Morticians
Union of Soviet Socialist Republics. See Russia
Union officials. See Labor leaders
U.S. armed forces. See Aviators—Military, Marines, Scouts, U.S.Army, Seamen—U.S., Soldiers, and under specific wars, e.g., World War I—Army
U.S. government officials. See Cabinet members—U.S., Diplomats, Indian agents, Presidents—U.S., Vice-Presidents—U.S., and the subdivision U.S. under Civil servants, Judges, Representatives, Senators. See also Politicians
University administrators, professors, presidents, students. See College administrators, Professors, Presidents, Students

## V

Vagabonds. See Adventurers and vagabonds
Vaudevillians (1850-1900), 1913, 2007
—(1900-1945), 1559, 3162, 3915, 5506
—See also Minstrels
Venezuela (1900-1945), 219, 598, 1233, 3652, 4346
Veterinarians (1850-1900), 6111
—(1900-1945), 1566, 3272, 5437
Vice-Presidents: U.S. (1900-1945), 3742
—See also Cabinet members—U.S., Presidents—U.S.
Violinists. See Musicians
Voice teachers. See Music teachers

## W

War correspondents. See Foreign correspondents and under specific wars, e.g., Civil War: Union—War correspondents
Wardens. See Prison officials
War of 1812: Army, 1545, 2116, 2809,

Tramps—West North Central

2855, 3247, 3410, 3558, 4185, 4345, 4843, 5088, 5166, 5308
—British Army, 2192
—Civilians, 2931
—Navy, 34, 790, 1134, 1705, 1754, 3430, 4454, 4962, 5001, 5144, 6010, 6329
Wars. See American Revolution, War of 1812, Mexican War, Civil War, Spanish-American War, World War I, World War II
Weight lifters. See Athletes, Physical culturists
West Indies (1800-1850), 4660
—(1850-1900), 4297, 4471, 5974
—(1900-1945), 1233, 2013
West North Central States: Abolitionists, 569, 1248, 1639, 2346
—Adventurers and vagabonds, 3517, 4467
—Advertisers and public relations men, 210
—Architects, 3250
—Artisans, 2228, 4467, 4785, 4873, 5351, 5398
—Authors, 138, 331, 1792, 2187, 3674, 4111, 5346, 5347
—Bankers, 308, 733, 926, 1494, 1540, 1860, 1983, 2373, 3147, 3782, 4097, 4861, 5058, 5478, 5999, 6035
—Bishops and archbishops: Episcopal, 2280, 6080
—Booksellers, 4168
—Cabinet members: U.S., 5069
—Childhood reminiscences, 83, 123, 191, 194, 432, 437, 531, 534, 570, 603, 613, 778, 827, 917, 1067, 1079, 1088, 1102, 1110, 1180, 1279, 1354, 1414, 1494, 1640, 1658, 1670, 1718, 1724, 1731, 1921, 2092, 2106, 2138, 2191, 2211, 2300, 2329, 2339, 2383, 2416, 2429, 2539, 2659, 2676, 2726, 2972, 3036, 3091, 3113, 3192, 3607, 3635, 3679, 3702, 3822, 4084, 4117, 4136, 4188, 4217, 4247, 4276, 4350, 4351, 4571, 4775, 4830, 5071, 5271, 5342, 5374, 5406, 5452, 5512, 5695, 5696, 5798, 5829, 6012, 6031
—Church workers, 648, 1486, 3117, 3314, 3809, 4042, 4651, 4925, 5560, 5590, 5841
—Civil servants: Local, 3873, 5159, 5449. State, 138. U.S., 749, 3061, 5449, 5546
—Clergymen: Denomination undetermined, 3002. Baptist, 110, 640, 702, 731, 813, 1104, 1218, 1328, 1684, 2281, 2533, 3134, 3384, 3908, 4860, 5038, 5289, 5333, 5520, 5567, 5688, 5738, 6132. Catholic priests, 409, 778, 2703, 2704, 3304, 4732. Christian Church, 501, 662, 4491, 4895, 6002. Congregational, 1240, 1249, 2346, 2615, 2708-2709, 3888, 4780, 4997, 4998, 5161, 5194, 5443. Disciples of Christ, 844, 890, 1185, 1856, 2990,

West North Central States: Clergymen-
Disciples of Christ (cont.), 4549.
Episcopal, 625, 922, 2268, 5994. Jewish, 4694. Lutheran, 202, 220, 546,
646, 1606, 2054, 2141, 2454, 3310, 3504,
4022, 4258, 4457, 4703, 4952, 5206,
5238, 5730, 6024, 6370, 6374. Mennonite, 424, 3256. Methodist, 139, 198,199,
408, 561, 917, 1238, 1355, 1418, 1463,
1716, 1740, 1938, 1955, 2198, 2302, 2384,
2391, 2998, 3772, 3992, 4009, 4238,
4245, 4491, 4806, 4926, 5035, 5105,
5146, 5192, 5234, 5356, 5428, 5625,
5951, 6003, 6042, 6342. Minor sects,
1154, 3493, 5035, 6034. Mormon, 3943.
Presbyterian, 889, 1277, 2084, 2670,
2673, 3066, 4570, 4981, 5183,, 5352,
5840, 5923, 5926. Quaker, 6229.
Seventh Day Adventist, 2664. Unitarian,
3647. United Brethren, 2172, 3326, 5128,
6342. Universalist, 3706, 3934
—Clergymen's wives, 3024, 4398, 5052
—Clubwomen, 2783
—College administrators, 4714
—College presidents, 372, 424, 1302,
1965, 2054, 3256, 3577, 5038, 5438,
5614
—College professors, 331, 1965, 2054,
2088, 2496, 3234, 3321, 3493, 3577,
4781, 4841, 5166, 5183, 5443, 6022,
6023, 6254
—College students, 2214, 2498, 2726,
5193, 5452
—Cowboys, 1523, 2458, 2476, 2499, 2908,
2969, 3061, 3372, 3660, 3910, 4425,
4465
—Criminals, 1350, 1375, 1411, 2175, 2649,
2965, 3095, 3566, 4765, 5607, 6360,
6361
—Critics, 5525
—Diplomats, 138, 3785, 3942, 5069
—Doctors, 331, 1534, 1889, 2287, 2623,
2823, 2919, 3004, 3301, 3481, 3564,
3747, 3844, 4053, 4247, 4581, 4667,
4817, 4898, 5070, 5270, 5272, 5479,
6254
—Domestic relations, 170, 207, 531, 1092,
1393, 1793, 2187, 2833, 2844, 2933,
3283, 3569, 3631, 3940, 4071, 4111,
4356, 4647, 4818, 4845, 5306, 5373,
5725, 5826, 5884, 5887, 6004
—Educators, 372, 935, 1183, 1302, 3335,
5346, 5347
—Engineers, 55, 2342, 3833, 5081
—Evangelists, 787, 1460, 1836, 2535,
2664, 4087, 4521, 5013
—Executives, 733, 4714
—Farm journalists, 5926
—Farm leaders, 6245
—Farmers and farm life, 105, 123, 126,
128, 134, 170, 237, 437, 451, 487, 492,
531, 534, 561, 569, 570, 575, 631, 652,
660, 728, 778, 803, 827, 937, 1010, 1016,
1042, 1067, 1088, 1110, 1180, 1214, 1279,
1317, 1342, 1354, 1414, 1494, 1540, 1639,
1640, 1658, 1670, 1685, 1718, 1726, 1772,
1793, 1885, 1921, 1979, 1987, 2028, 2065,
2083, 2106, 2172, 2187, 2191, 2205, 2211,
2220, 2281, 2300, 2302, 2316, 2343, 2351,
2373, 2500, 2528, 2539, 2604, 2621,
2676, 2692, 2726, 2765, 2776, 2848,
2857, 2920, 2933, 2975, 3091, 3113,
3192, 3313, 3326, 3358, 3375, 3415, 3571,
3635, 3640, 3679, 3690, 3693, 3770,
3788, 3809, 3848, 3971, 3987, 4071,
4084, 4128, 4136, 4247, 4258, 4276,
4356, 4506, 4533, 4571, 4651, 4775, 4830,
4873, 4885, 4954, 5006, 5053, 5163,
5271, 5283, 5295, 5316, 5351, 5406,
5411, 5452, 5492, 5494, 5512, 5575,
5696, 5736, 5788, 5798, 5826, 5829,
5887, 6009, 6012, 6020, 6031, 6049,
6132, 6182, 6245, 6359
—Financiers, 1150, 1494, 1839, 2066,
3782, 5987, 6035
—Governors, 995, 1324, 1335
—Historians, 1363, 1965
—Hotels and inns, proprietors and
workers, 170, 469, 618, 2228
—Hunters and trappers, 90, 1121, 1523,
1644, 2028, 2466, 2619, 3660, 3848,
4452, 5250, 5849, 6359
—Immigrants: Canadian, 487. Danish,
546, 3002. English, 2765, 4769, 5788.
French, 4732. German, 220, 1912, 5206,
5283, 5560, 5840, 6374. Hungarian,
4901. Irish, 128, 3348. Italian, 572,
Norwegian, 152, 451, 452, 648, 4457,
4905, 5163, 5807. Russian, 2975.
Scottish, 4508, 4651. Swedish, 3047.
Swiss, 2933
—Indian agents, 1169, 4592
—Indian fighters, 90, 499, 615, 1150, 1235,
1395, 1644, 1656, 1730, 2466, 2570, 2721,
2910, 3238, 3372, 3606, 3848, 4181,
4425, 4494, 5250, 5377, 5478, 6359
—Indians, 1731, 1732, 1818, 2220, 3793,
5292
—Indians, life among, 290, 2377, 4533,
4732, 4818
—Industrialists, 422, 822, 827, 926, 1011,
1744, 1825, 1830, 1860, 2322, 3250,
3313, 3375, 3412, 3782, 3864, 3867,
4013, 4014, 5259, 5358, 5425, 5509,
5999, 6046
—Jews, 76, 569, 6254
—Journalists, 194, 329, 586, 969, 1148,
1445, 1455, 1572, 1586, 1650, 1785, 2201,
2379, 2458, 2810, 3020, 3170, 3922, 4516,
4648, 4714, 4760, 4959, 4992, 5397, 5525

SUBJECT INDEX 369 West North Central

West North Central States (cont.),
 Judges–Branch undetermined, 4518,
 4901, 4981, 5807. Local: 1011, 2114,
 5929. State: 1171, 1921, 4303
—Laborers, 451, 452, 487, 803, 1326,
 1551, 2083, 4260, 5053, 6013, 6020
—Lawyers, 12, 138, 168, 448, 613, 624,
 764, 1050, 1063, 1150, 1171, 1324, 1335,
 1363, 1454, 1714, 1785, 1837, 1839, 1885,
 1912, 1921, 2083, 2194, 2378, 2498, 2676,
 2713, 3572, 3605, 3704, 3942, 4081,
 4154, 4278, 4303, 4462, 4518, 4538,
 4595, 4685, 4743, 4901, 4981, 5807,
 5809, 5929, 6020
—Librarians, 586
—Lumbermen, 105, 3375
—Mayors, 1839, 6046
—Merchants, 178, 749, 773, 783, 1042,
 1110, 1169, 1454, 1486, 1675, 1718, 2441,
 2504, 2578, 2857, 3047, 3087, 3333,
 3363, 3364, 3554, 3690, 3799, 3899,
 4452, 4465, 4506, 4508, 4808, 4846,
 5741, 5788, 6011
—Miners and mining life, 181, 432, 2028,
 2437, 2572, 3326, 3910, 4467
—Missionaries: Denomination undetermined, 290, 1894. Catholic, 409, 572,
 3812. Congregational, 1248. Episcopal,
 2468, 5796. Methodist, 2223. Minor
 sects, 3810. Presbyterian, 4533, 5754.
 United Brethren, 4533
—Musicians, 2
—Negroes, 134, 561, 1502, 1350, 6013
—Novelists, 1363, 2810, 5525
—Nurses, 5841
—Office workers, 4647
—Painters, 448, 654
—Peace officers, 2028, 2502, 3113, 5455,
 5524
—Philosophers, 5346, 5347
—Photographers, 76, 1534, 2028, 5134
—Pioneers, 90, 178, 408, 432, 451, 570,
 613, 642, 655, 800, 827, 933, 934, 937,
 995, 1010, 1067, 1121, 1169, 1171, 1248,
 1377, 1406, 1540, 1658, 1670, 1685, 1772,
 2028, 2106, 2114, 2154, 2172, 2187, 2205,
 2211, 2302, 2334, 2343, 2429, 2437,
 2466, 2500, 2528, 2859, 2920, 2933,
 2972, 3002, 3113, 3311, 3313, 3358,
 3360, 3364, 3372, 3375, 3466, 3533,
 3597, 3606, 3631, 3635, 3693, 3706,
 3809, 3848, 3898, 3899, 3910, 4071,
 4128, 4136, 4171, 4236, 4258, 4350,
 4369, 4425, 4452, 4494, 4571, 4885,
 4926, 4983, 5146, 5234, 5250, 5261,
 5283, 5342, 5351, 5377, 5406, 5478,
 5512, 5570, 5625, 5788, 5826, 5829,
 5849, 5887, 6009, 6011, 6012, 6042,
 6049, 6182, 6359
—Playwrights, 2187

—Poets, 1326, 1363
—Politicians, 12, 138, 764, 1110, 1171,
 1183, 1266, 1592, 1714, 1745, 1912, 2194,
 2441, 3311, 3335, 3704, 3785, 3942,
 4027, 4081, 4154, 4516, 4595, 5134, 5809,
 5950, 6046
—Printers, 244, 2211, 2893, 3733, 4013,
 4014, 4324, 4926
—Prisoners, 1211, 1384, 2175, 3039, 3095,
 4774, 6025, 6305, 6360, 6361
—Prostitutes and fallen women, 5626
—Publishers, 1718, 2113, 2238, 2893,
 3335, 3713, 3785, 4237, 4516, 4959,
 6258
—Railroad workers, 3025, 5369
—Ranchers and ranch life, 72, 642, 968,
 1164, 1169, 2128, 2530, 2908, 3311, 3348,
 3788, 3882, 3988, 4465, 5250, 5492
—Real estate dealers and promoters,
 926, 1011, 1534, 2114, 2578, 2908, 3047,
 3052, 5449, 5712, 5968, 6049
—Religious journalists, 2054, 2113, 2198,
 4905
—Representatives: State, 372, 995, 2373,
 2570, 2676, 2975, 3313. U.S., 329, 1050,
 1148, 1335, 1714, 2346
—Restaurants and taverns, proprietors
 and workers, 2131, 5189
—Salesmen, 803, 1063, 1333, 3047, 3094,
 5449, 5942
—Scientists, 5457, 5458
—Scouts, U.S. Army, 1121, 2476, 4055,
 5524
—Senators: State, 2346. U.S., 448, 3083,
 4264, 5069
—Showmen, 4689
—Singers, 258, 1326
—Social reformers, 2322
—Social workers, 42, 428, 469, 495,
 3424, 6327
—Socialites, 3984, 4111
—Soldiers, 563, 1150, 1235, 1292, 1395,
 2721, 2910, 4181, 5793, 6051
—Soldiers' wives, 265, 933, 934, 1394
—Sportsmen, 3197, 5734
—Suffragists, 1183
—Surveyors, 2437, 4084, 5968
—Teachers, 42, 451, 639, 771, 1042, 1145,
 1171, 1540, 1577, 1850, 1885, 1894, 1929,
 2083, 2281, 2377, 2378, 2452, 2830,
 3047, 3151, 3398, 3466, 3571, 3674,
 3696, 3873, 3900, 3940, 4356, 4685,
 4714, 4760, 4775, 4960, 5005, 5015,
 5244, 5338, 5449, 5478, 5513, 5590,
 6002
—Teamsters, 3372, 3533, 4128, 4983,
 5492
—Telegraphers, 4123, 6368
—Temperance workers, 917
—Theologians, 2054, 3321, 5443, 6022, 6023

West South Central States: Adventurers and vagabonds, 142, 378, 2148, 2314
—Architects, 2087
—Authors, 4330, 5339
—Bankers, 2157, 2661, 2853, 4966
—Barbers and hairdressers, 5039
—Bishops and archbishops: Episcopal, 739. Methodist, 3343
—Cabinet members, 2105
—Childhood reminiscences, 70, 77, 388, 629, 912, 1166, 1352, 2967, 3361, 4188, 4596, 5913, 6159
—Church workers, 2902, 3314, 4042, 4893, 5590, 6192, 6368
—Civil servants: U.S., 77, 4018
—Clergymen: Denomination unstated, 2796. Baptist, 125, 1091, 1314, 1314A, 1891, 2120, 2943, 3111, 3230, 3933, 4096, 4503, 4591, 5038, 5610. Catholic priests, 3160. Christian Church, 5317. Congregational, 2456. Disciples of Christ, 971, 1856, 2766, 3418. Episcopal, 4755. Lutheran, 1405, 2694, 4703, 6024. Methodist, 98, 139, 198, 199, 440, 595, 973, 1537, 1539, 1955, 2055, 2198, 2283, 2304, 2900, 3120, 3524, 3588, 3772, 3896, 4023, 4153, 4240, 4565, 4720, 4883, 5092, 5192, 5817. Minor sects, 916. Presbyterian, 60, 255, 724, 1046, 3409, 4110, 5287. Quaker, 2831, 6229. United Brethren, 2172. Universalist, 1496, 3934
—Clergymen's wives, 1090, 3737
—College administrators, 5633
—College presidents, 364, 1153, 4054
—College professors, 1153, 2596
—Cowboys, 14, 56, 185, 192, 303, 425, 446, 507, 880, 1066, 1215, 1216, 1217, 1523, 1697, 2417, 2458, 2476, 2498, 2823, 2969, 3225, 3300, 3376, 3596, 3835, 3876, 3885, 3910, 3954, 3985, 4234, 4319, 4425, 4539, 4805, 4987, 5225, 5227, 5317, 5455, 6312, 6323, 6349
—Criminals, 1123, 1239, 1375, 1491, 1946, 2175, 2314, 2462, 2996, 3095, 3370, 3566, 3574, 3727, 4191, 4752, 4987, 5195, 5421, 5676, 5874, 5924, 5978
—Dentists, 3167
—Diplomats, 2151
—Doctors, 837, 1314, 1314A, 1742, 2715, 2875, 3843, 4931, 5131, 6326
—Domestic relations, 107, 394, 506, 2206, 2902, 2995, 3345, 3773, 3783, 4007, 4305, 4693, 5305, 5884
—Educators, 2596, 6257
—Engineers, 2713, 4554, 5100, 5749
—Evangelists, 495, 2535, 3006, 4153, 4228, 4503, 5317
—Executives, 2853

—Farmers and farm life, 93, 107, 917, 1090, 1091, 1256, 1342, 1346, 1352, 1519, 1987, 2053, 2115, 2157, 2172, 2206, 3361, 3501, 3641, 4040, 4262, 4421, 4424, 4472, 4578, 4693, 5431, 5535, 5544, 6291
—Financiers, 297
—Gamblers, 2462
—Governors, 461, 1596, 2105, 3567, 3613, 4174, 5959
—Historians, 2129, 3226, 4741
—Hunters and trappers, 14, 75, 287, 301, 1215, 1216, 1221, 1523, 2689, 2968, 2970, 3048, 4213, 4883, 6312
—Immigrants: English, 883, 2771, 3737. German, 1256, 2053, 2206, 5024, 5535, 5817, 6030. Italian, 4257. Swiss, 6027
—Indian fighters, 287, 301, 332, 362, 499, 958, 959, 1492, 1778, 1824, 3048, 3347, 4425, 4559, 5332, 5530, 5617
—Indians, 5767
—Indians, life among, 1321, 2332, 2831, 2966, 4228, 4532
—Industrialists, 14, 1596, 1719, 1744, 2157, 3300, 3338, 3619, 5749
—Journalists, 419, 1588, 2458, 2771, 2897, 3029, 3615, 6105
—Judges: Branch undetermined, 2151. Local, 1891. State, 2100, 5431. U.S., 215, 1230
—Juvenile delinquents, 2148
—Laborers, 1326, 4213
—Lawyers, 461, 649, 1230, 1588, 2100, 2151, 2996, 3487, 3489, 4274, 4666, 4966, 5431, 5959
—Lumbermen, 4213
—Mentally ill, 1950
—Merchants, 1950, 2262, 2968, 3139, 4018, 4257, 4310, 4966, 5153, 6030, 6111
—Miners and mining life, 880, 3910, 6315
—Missionaries: Baptist, 1321, 2733, 4539. Catholic, 4415. Christian Church, 4722. Denomination undetermined, 6027. Mennonite, 4532. Minor sects, 6144. Mormon, 6279. Presbyterian, 2332
—Music teachers, 3975
—Musicians, 3975
—Negroes, 1850, 2151, 3111, 3343, 3487, 3596, 4191, 4843, 5785
—Novelists, 3226, 5110
—Office workers, 6344
—Oil well drillers, 2764, 3088
—Peace officers, 14, 203, 322, 1511, 1697, 2173, 2999, 3106, 3616, 3677, 3703, 3885, 4249, 4559, 4578, 5524, 5558, 5617, 6188, 6315
—Philanthropists, 4864
—Photographers, 3300
—Pioneers, 14, 301, 332, 362, 394, 446, 629, 958, 981, 1214, 1215, 1216, 1571, 1778, 2053, 2124, 2172, 2206, 2591, 2733, 2968,

SUBJECT INDEX 371 West North Central

West South Central States: Pioneers (cont.), 2970, 3048, 3075, 3691, 3703, 3783, 3791, 3885, 3910, 4007, 4018, 4213, 4262, 4424, 4425, 4472, 4578, 4693, 4883, 4893, 5007, 5024, 5109, 5305, 5332, 5367, 5461, 5530, 5535, 5558, 5570, 5875, 6183, 6315
—Poets, 1326, 1700
—Politicians, 215, 604, 1058, 1230, 1588, 2151, 3075, 4253, 4274, 4966, 5109
—Politicians' wives, 1713
—Prisoners, 1491, 2175, 2219, 2462, 2997, 3095, 4012, 4191, 5195
—Publishers, 103, 104, 1179, 1719
—Railroad workers, 1398, 2897
—Ranchers and ranch life, 56, 72, 93, 604, 699, 791, 912, 1066, 1164, 1166, 1204, 1215, 1216, 1346, 1574, 2124, 2417, 2771, 2963, 2970, 3048, 3230, 3300, 3338, 3376, 3613, 3643, 3988, 4319, 4589, 4614, 4615, 4805, 4883, 5191, 5617, 6183
—Real estate dealers and promoters, 4579, 5753
—Religious journalists, 1314, 1314A, 2198
—Representatives: State, 1153, 1824. U.S., 1467, 4805
—Restaurants and taverns, proprietors and workers, 2823
—Salesmen, 26, 2314, 4469
—Scientists, 1098
—Scouts: U.S. Army, 1215, 1216, 2476, 5524
—Senators: State, 1179, 1719. U.S., 461, 2105, 3567, 4741
—Showmen, 26
—Singers, 1326
—Social reformers, 5131
—Social workers, 2694
—Socialites, 3984
—Soldiers, 192, 958, 1204, 1308, 3847, 5109, 5367, 5793
—Soldiers' wives, 1394, 5875
—Spiritualists, 5188
—Tailors, 4310
—Teachers, 77, 604, 1118, 1850, 1966, 2591, 2830, 2966, 3193, 3696, 3737, 3900, 4348, 4378, 5267, 5431, 5590, 5785, 5983
—Teamsters, 5024
—Temperance workers, 1314, 1314A
—Veterinarians, 6111
—Woodsmen and guides, 1215, 1216
Whalers (to 1800), 4932
—(1800-1850), 886, 1504, 1522, 2566, 3499, 4382, 4390, 5491
—(1850-1900), 296, 380, 545, 694, 1202, 1219, 1220, 1887, 1942, 2136, 2398, 2522, 5630, 5705, 5710, 5989, 6109
—See also Seamen: Merchant

White collar workers. See Office workers
Women's rights advocates. See Suffragists
Woodsmen and guides (1800-1850), 939
—(1850-1900), 295, 1215, 1216, 2551, 5570, 6206, 6294
—(1900-1945), 4015, 4295, 4958
—See also Lumbermen
Workers. See Factory workers, Office workers, Laborers, and Servants
World War I: Air Corps, 493, 2371, 2407, 2408, 4803
—Allies, service with, 464, 596, 1812, 1813, 2405, 2406, 2408, 2904, 3658, 3838, 3853, 3858, 4093, 4261, 4862, 5297, 5467, 5931, 6039, 6222, 6230
—Army, 74, 86, 169, 267, 300, 421, 476, 578, 735, 768, 1150, 1392, 1525, 1533, 1701, 1702, 1810, 2545, 2716, 2728, 2729, 2939, 3037, 3497, 3529, 3645, 3819, 3927, 3959, 4019, 4138, 4250, 4363, 4423, 4495, 4526, 4724, 4812, 4939, 4953, 5094, 5297, 5350, 5356, 5467, 5521, 5523, 5847, 5891, 6058, 6146, 6276, 6334
—Chaplains, 444, 504, 3473, 5561
—Civilians, 124, 471, 549, 996, 1618, 1863, 2486, 2825, 2826, 2827, 2886, 2926, 2927, 3403, 3598, 3832, 3852, 3923, 3963, 4341, 5784, 5994, 6025, 6129
—Doctors, 367, 1258, 1446, 1877, 5281, 6231, 6248
—Government officials, 2912, 5135, 6110, 6260
—Marine Corps, 3450, 4085
—Navy, 357, 3471, 5220
—Nurses, 124, 3490, 3986, 4127, 4336, 5888, 5889
—War correspondents, 306, 632, 2989, 4399, 4405, 4627, 4629, 4824, 6151, 6193
World War II: Air Corps, 327, 2477, 4006, 5082, 5083
—Allies, service with, 1598, 2525, 3820, 4148
—Army, 1276, 2400, 2470, 3624
—Chaplains, 3687, 4739, 4755
—Civilians, 1835, 2167, 2753, 3564, 3701, 3745, 5890
—Doctors, 5099
—Marine Corps, 1992, 3615, 4076, 4184, 5057, 5827
—Merchant Marine, 2148, 3661
—Navy, 5797
—Nurses, 4748
—War correspondents, 240, 1162, 1289, 3615
Wrestlers. See Athletes
Writers. See Authors, Critics, Journalists, Novelists, Playwrights, Poets

## Y

Y.M.C.A. officials. See Social workers
Yucatan (1850–1900), 550
— (1900–1945), 5680
Yugoslavia. See Jugoslavia

## Z

Zoo directors (1900–1945), 423
Zoologists. See Scientists